The Road to Disunion

Secessionists at Bay
1776–1854

By William W. Freehling

THE ROAD TO DISUNION

Volume I Secessionists at Bay, 1776–1854
Volume II Secessionists Triumphant, 1854–1861

The Road to Disunion

VOLUME I

Secessionists at Bay
1776–1854

WILLIAM W. FREEHLING

New York   Oxford
OXFORD UNIVERSITY PRESS
1990

Oxford University Press

Oxford   New York   Toronto
Delhi   Bombay   Calcutta   Madras   Karachi
Petaling Jaya   Singapore   Hong Kong   Tokyo
Nairobi   Dar es Salaam   Cape Town
Melbourne   Auckland

and associated companies in
Berlin   Ibadan

Published by Oxford University Press, Inc.,
200 Madison Avenue, New York, New York 10016

Oxford is a registered trademark of Oxford University Press

Library of Congress Cataloging-in-Publication Data
Freehling, William W., 1935–
The road to disunion / William W. Freehling.
p.   cm.
Contents: v. 1. Secessionists at bay, 1776–1854
ISBN 0-19-505814-3 (v. 1)
1. United States—History—Civil War, 1861–1865—Causes.
2. Secession.   3. Southern States—Politics and
government—1775–1865.   4. United States—Politics and
government—1815–1861.   I. Title
E468.9.F84   1990
973.7'11—dc20   89-26511   CIP

2 4 6 8 9 7 5 3 1

Printed in the United States of America
on acid-free paper

For Alison

Preface

Two decades ago, I envisioned a quick solution to an important mystery. I would research the few months of the southern secession crisis, 1860–1. My findings would reveal short-run causes of disunion. My chronicle would illuminate long-run reasons why the South strode down the road to disunion.

Those simplistic beginnings failed to anticipate secession's complicated climax. Manuscripts on disunion particularly exuded such a variety of Southerners as to shatter my imagined South. Seeking more perspective than a culminating crisis could provide, I reluctantly took one step, then another back down the road to disunion. Had I known that I would ultimately arrive in Thomas Jefferson's era, I might never have left Abraham Lincoln's. But at this culminating moment, I rejoice at the extended odyssey backwards. No shorter journey could have yielded this rich story.

My chief objection to previous accounts of the antebellum South, including my own, is that portraits tend to flatten out the rich varieties of southern types. The South is sometimes interpreted as this, sometimes as that. But whatever the interpretation, the image is usually of a monolith, frozen in its thisness or thatness. The southern world supposedly thawed only once, in the so-called Great Reaction of the 1830s. Then Thomas Jefferson's South, which considered slavery a terminable curse, supposedly turned into John C. Calhoun's South, which considered enslavement a perpetual blessing. Thereafter, little supposedly changed, little varied, little remained undecided. Gone from this timeless flatland is the American nineteenth century's exuberant essence: growth, movement, profusion of pilgrims, a chaotic kaleidoscope of regions, classes, religions, and ethnic groups.

The truth—the fresh understanding that makes a new epic of the antebellum South possible—is that before and after the mid-1830s in the South, as well as the North, change was omnipresent, varieties abounded, visions multiplied. Antebellum Southerners constantly acted on their knowledge that their world was not set in stone, that many destinies beckoned, that clashes of sections and classes, of ossified cultures and raw frontiers divided South as well as nation. Whenever someone declaims on *a* South, premodern or egalitarian republican or whatever, ask them which South is meant, and when? The answers begin a more informative analysis of a world so lushly various as to be a storyteller's dream.[1]

Secessionists are the desperadoes in the Old South's story. They sought to forge a culture most historians assume had long since been consolidated—a region standing monolithically for slavery's permanent glory. They winced at fellow Southerners who clung to the Jeffersonian dream that slavery would slowly drain away, assuming the right conditions could be secured. Between Calhoun's unconditional desire to perpetuate slavery and Jefferson's conditional hope to end the institution, so many Southerners fought for so many visions that secessionists lost and lost and lost, losing finally all confidence in winning. After Abraham Lincoln was elected in 1860, this minority of the southern minority conspired to bring off a last gamble. In 1861, to extremists' amazement, disunion triumphed. This is the tale of how and why vanquished secessionists became victors—and of a South which remained too divided for the victors to win their gamble with the sword.

While Yankees frequently people and lend perspective to this story of the southern road to disunion, my focus rarely deviates from the slaveholders' domain. The value of the regional concentration transcends the South, for in national *mainstream* politics an aggressively defensive slavocracy so often seized the offensive. Outside the mainstream, northern extremists attacked first. But antislavery Yankees began to capture the northern majority's sympathy only after Southerners demanded national proslavery laws. Both the Slavepower's demands for legislative protection and the way the minority pushed demands through majoritarian processes violated northern senses of democratic government. When issues changed from black slavery to white republicanism, from an unfortunate institution on the other section's turf to unacceptable ultimatums about a common democratic government, Yankees stiffened into anti-southern postures.[2]

These southern drives for minority protection flowed partly out of fears that the South could not stand solid against the northern extreme. The most committed slaveholders particularly worried about their less committed, less enslaved hinterlands lying close to the free North. Concern about whether a free and open republican milieu could weaken despotism in lightly enslaved areas helps explain why a slaveholder minority, when facing a smaller abolitionist minority, continually offended Northerners' majoritarian sensibilities with attempts to shutter off democratic challenges.

The irony was that the enslaved South was itself deeply into democratic cults. As inegalitarian as slavery was, it also impelled southern variations on American nineteenth-century egalitarianism. I here follow debates between southern-style and northern-style egalitarian republicans, as well as between Southerners and each other, that go beyond "mere" political history narrowly defined. I hope to show that two antithetical abstract systems, democracy and despotism, when forced to rub against each other in close southern quarters, intriguingly intermeshed to shape not just a politics but a world. I also seek to show that the narrative literary form, sadly maligned among professional historians these days, remains invaluable to humanize how a collision of abstractions helped produce the crisis of a people.

My narrative of the various Souths' encounter with despotism and democracy remains unfinished at the end of this volume. A subsequent volume will carry the story from the mid-1850s to the outbreak of war. Much information in Volume II may add credibility to Volume I. The main discussion of proslavery ideology, for example, had to be in Volume II because most of the South's greatest proslavery writers published not during some fancied Great Reaction in the mid-1830s but twenty years later, uncomfortably close to the time of southern rebellion.[3] That last-minute effort to forge a world, a world view, and a nation—the major theme in Volume II—reveals much about earlier clashes over the kind of world Southerners wanted. So, too, Volume II's discussion of Caribbean expansion, which South Carolina Disunionists rather opposed and southwestern Unionists usually favored, will illuminate earlier divisions between older and newer Deep Souths. Still another important theme in my subsequent volume, the most secessionist South's fear that Abraham Lincoln would build a Republican Party in the least secessionist South, will re-emphasize a key theme in this volume, the difference between the more southern and the more northern sections of the South over whether slavery should be terminated, always on the assumption that proper conditions could be obtained.

While Volumes I and II may someday reinforce each other, Volume I will least need reinforcement. Early in American national history, earlier than historians' conventional periodization indicates, clashing Souths wove patterns insidious to perpetual Union. The resulting demand that the nation shore up the not-so-democratic institution of slavery came so to infest the southern-dominated Jackson movement as to define much of so-called Jacksonian "Democracy"—this years before the so-called Era of Sectional Controversy.

Subsequent events in the post-Jackson era more or less repeated, as human affairs will, patterns more or less repeated earlier. The Kansas-Nebraska Act of 1854 was something of a repeat of Texas Annexation in 1845, just as annexation was something of a repeat of the Gag Rule Controversy of 1835–6. More repetitions of similar patterns brought on the secession crisis of 1860–1. The final crisis bore resemblances to and is easier to understand in the perspective of nullification/secession crises in 1850–2 and 1832–3. I look forward to recounting the climactic secession epic, the saga my younger shade found so elusive. But the final acts, as I at last came to understand, become explicable only with their 85 years of antecedents. This earlier story, on the other hand, will always stand on its own, as the tale of various Souths' defining steps down the road to disunion.

I am grateful to institutions who helped me craft this volume. The Guggenheim Foundation, the National Humanities Foundation, and the Horace Rackham

School of the University of Michigan helped finance three years of research in southern archives. A liberal teaching load at The Johns Hopkins University helped lighten more years of writing.

The greatest lighteners kept reassuring me that all would work when much was frustrating. I am thinking of Jack and other colleagues at the Hopkins, of Anne and Craig and Joel—and especially of Alison. These volumes are a pittance of what I dedicate to her.

The Johns Hopkins University   William W. Freehling
July 4, 1989
   Liberty's birthday in the republic
   slaveholders helped to make

Contents

Illustrations

Maps

The Road to Disunion

Secessionists at Bay
1776–1854

Prologue:
The Spirit of Montgomery

Rhett wore a black suit as he waited to surrender the revolution. The date: February 18, 1861, inauguration day for President-elect Jefferson Davis. The place: Montgomery, Alabama, provisional capital of the provisional Southern Confederacy. Rhett's uncomfortable task: to greet the President-elect when the inaugural parade reached the white capitol and to present him to the lily-white Confederate Congress. White is beautiful, so the infant republic proclaimed, in its manifestos, its buildings, its taste in skin. But Robert Barnwell Rhett, like Southerners everywhere, usually donned black when the occasion called for dress.

Rhett, South Carolina's most notorious Disunionist, had less trifling confusions in mind as he glared down Montgomery's main street. The parade crept up the hill, matching hesitations Rhett discerned throughout the South. After thirty years of frustration, he stood so near, yet so far from his ambition. Three months earlier, Abraham Lincoln's election had handed Disunionists an opportunity. In December of 1860, Rhett's South Carolina had seceded from the Union. Five Lower South states had quickly followed. Texas would allegedly soon join in.

Now, here in Montgomery, Rhett had helped mold a new republic, dedicated to the proposition that Virginia's Thomas Jefferson had been a fool. Natural rights were unnatural. Men were created unequal. Black bondage was blessed. On and on went the litany that turned Jefferson on his head. How sweet to exclaim eternal truths and to be free of hypocritical Yankee sneers.

Free at last, if the revolution did not slide backwards. That spector soured Rhett's celebrations. So often, South Carolina had tremulously pushed revolution. So often, nervous precipitators had then retreated. In 1832–3, Rhett had helped bring off the first confrontation crisis, the Nullification Controversy. Even though the South's favorite politician, President Andrew Jackson, had trouble rallying other Southerners to coerce Carolina hotheads, Nullifiers had lost their nerve. In 1850–2, Rhett had helped secretly plot another confronta-

3

tion crisis. That time, Southerners had so ignored Carolina that few even knew about the abortive plotting. In 1860, extremists beyond Carolina had at last conspired to encourage Carolinians to begin.

But how long would revolutionary nerves hold out? Most slave states remained in the Union two months after South Carolina had seceded. The last nonseceding state in the deepest South, Texas, would supposedly soon join the new slaveholding republic. Only fifteen years earlier, however, the then-independent and then-not-so-enslaved republic of Texas had made ambiguous gestures towards antislavery England. Worried Southerners had demanded that Texas be instantly annexed. The most important gesturer, then-Texas president Sam Houston, was now governor of the state. Houston had recently called slavery evil and disunion an abomination. With that foot-dragger as leader, had the Deep South's western hinterland been sufficiently consolidated?

Robert Barnwell Rhett worried more about northern hinterlands. The eight Upper South states had lately voted against immediate secession, when they bothered to vote. One anti-secessionist state, Delaware, possessed fewer than 2000 slaves. Another, Maryland, had almost as many free blacks as slaves. Others, especially Virginia and Kentucky, had sporadically debated schemes to remove slaves. If war came, would such Southerners desert to the North?

Rhett also spied potential desertions in Montgomery. Some worried slaveholders from black-belt southern Alabama hinted that compromise might be preferable to war. Some irritated nonslaveholders from white-belt northern Alabama hinted that if rich men refused to compromise, poor men might refuse to fight.

And the slaves? They heard everything. They affected to know nothing. They cheered proslavery speeches. They burned Lincoln in effigy. Slave behavior was always hard to read. Did this behavior hint at pretense? Might something other than straw Lincolns someday light neighborhoods? Masters—mistresses too—denied thinking such thoughts.[1]

No wonder Robert Barnwell Rhett stood in the shadows, awaiting someone else's parade. The times hardly called for notorious revolutionaries. Rhett's cause demanded a legitimacy only conservative opponents could supply. The cause needed the frigid respectability of Mississippi's Jefferson Davis.[2]

Two days earlier, William Lowndes Yancey had summed up the need in a phrase. Yancey, Montgomery's favorite Disunionist and fire-eaters' shrewdest tactician, had stood on the balcony of the Exchange Hotel, Davis by his side and hundreds below. He had gazed into the dark night, past the crowd and up the hill to the shadowy capitol, America's newest City on the Hill. Long since he had learned, amongst Alabama's coarse politicos, the lesson Rhett would never learn amidst South Carolina's haughty patricians. An elitist who would command commoners must stay but a half-inch ahead. So, as the crowd hushed, Yancey had introduced the President-elect with a prayer dressed up as praise: "The man and the hour have met."[3]

How Rhett must have winced as citizens screamed approval. For Jefferson Davis had long cooperated with Disunionists' foe, the Southern National Democratic Party. Whether manipulating presidential cabinets or maneuvering the United States Senate, Davis had usually advocated the National Democrats' main line—that disunion was folly because the South could rule the Union through the party. In 1858, when Davis came close to breathing northern territorial heresies, Mississippi's legislature had demanded explanations. In November 1860, he had warned Rhett against disunion. Would he now lead a retreat back into the Union?

Rhett nursed one consolation. Things could be worse. At least Davis had opposed the Compromise of 1850. The presidency might have gone to Howell Cobb of Georgia, now Presiding Officer of the Confederate Congress. Cobb, an even more notorious National Democrat than Davis, had lauded the Compromise of 1850 and had helped poison the subsequent Davis-led resistance movement. A decade later, in December 1860, Fatty Cobb had wished to remain comfortably clubby in Washington.

The presidency might also have been bestowed on Alexander Stephens, now Vice President-elect of the Confederacy. Stephens, a bitter man with an emaciated body, had spoken in Georgia two months earlier, arguing that secession was insanity. In 1850 he had helped Cobb stop resistance in Georgia. In 1845 Stephens had urged that slavery was too evil to spread. With this previously softhearted advocate but a heartbeat from power, Rhett might be reduced to praying for Davis's health!

At last the joy of the inaugural parade broke through, pushing morbid prayers out of mind. Bands blared. Dust swirled. Boys raced for the best positions. Marching out front, with sky blue pants and bright red coats, were Captain Semnes's Columbus Guards. They proudly displayed Georgia's coat of arms while performing Zoave tactics. Along came Herman Arnold's band, playing a catchy tune. Before long, a nation would be humming "I wish I were in Dixie Land." Then more troops. Then the imminent commander-in-chief. Prancing white horses drew Davis's silk-lined carriage. The entourage stopped at Rhett's feet. When Davis clambered down, white belles in white dresses surrounded the President-elect. They hung a wreath around his arm as whites shouted and blacks danced along the avenue. With Rhett on one side and Stephens on the other, Davis stepped into the white capitol.

The trio approached the spiral staircase, each step so perfectly balanced that the whole curved up without support. Brown tobacco stains marred snow-white stone. Too much spittle had missed too many spittoons. As they ascended, these rather polished aristocrats caught the scent of not-so-polished frontiersmen. Here elegant gentlemen and seedy boors mixed uneasily. At the second landing, the congressional chamber loomed ahead. Here southeastern elitists and southwestern egalitarians would have to get together.

Rhett introduced Davis to the Congress with cold formality—"Allow me to present to you the Honorable Jefferson Davis, who in obedience to your choice has come to assume the important trust you have confided to his care." Davis, seeking to melt the ice, briefly begged support. Then all proceeded out to the warm sunlight and supporters warmer still.[4]

When the clock struck one, Jefferson Davis laid his hand on the Bible and took the oath of office from Howell Cobb. Then Davis stood alone on the decaying portico, between towering white pillars. As he swung around for his inaugural address, he stretched straight and lean, aggressively maximizing middling height. His square, tough chin anchored an aesthetic, rectangular face. His long forehead hinted at intelligence. His neatly brushed gray hair seemed that of a prophet.

But it was his eyes, his blue-gray eyes, which gave him away. They were sunk into high cheekbones. One eye, nearly blind and covered with film, was the site of excruciating pain. The other eye saw through men with painful clarity. Jefferson Davis, waiting for applause to end so that he could define a culture's destiny, looked like a man who had seen and suffered.

Today he suffered over a southern destiny he saw was obscure. War, he suspected, was imminent. The South, he knew, was ill-prepared. As United States Secretary of War a few years earlier, he had worried about the South's poor military state. As President-elect in the past few days, he had jolted along the section's primitive railroads. Could so industrially underdeveloped a society defeat northern industrial might?

Not, Davis knew, unless the South pulled together. The President was an expert on southern divisions. He had cooperated, at arm's length, with Disunionists in opposing the Compromise of 1850. He had then learned how devoutly men such as Rhett believed that those an arm's length apart were disguised traitors. During the ensuing decade, Davis had watched fellow Southern National Democrats feud endlessly. Some hoped to reopen the African slave trade. Others denounced that as kidnaping. Some dreamed of seizing South America. Their opponents decried that as piracy. Here in Montgomery, advocates of reunion battled proponents of war. Louisiana delegates, exuding the aggressive commercialism of New Orleans, sought a republic encompassing the entire Ohio-Missouri-Mississippi river system. South Carolina delegates, reflecting Charleston's hidebound conservatism, wished to exclude nonslaveholding members.

More distressing still, half the South missed today's festivities. The lawn below Davis contained no representatives of more northern, more populated, more industrialized, more militarily strategic Upper South slave states. Here again, Davis's personal experience prevented illusions. He had resided more often in the Upper South than on his Deep South plantation. He had been educated in Kentucky, had served military apprenticeships in Missouri and Arkansas, and had often vacationed in Virginia while helping to govern from Washington. He thus understood why the Lower South came to Montgomery while the Upper South anchored in Washington. He knew that the more northern the location of a slave state, the less cotton was grown, the fewer plantations existed, and the more land was dotted with primarily nonslaveholders harvesting primarily grains. Despite less of a stake in slavery, the Upper South would likely become prime Civil War battleground. Another South's revolution, these Southerners shuddered, might annihilate their South first.

Davis's inaugural address sought to ease these problems. The address, men discovered with relief, was sprinkled with reassurances. War, Davis reassured moderates, would come only if the North began it. Reunion, he reassured extremists, was not likely. True, northern states might join the Southern Confederacy. But unless he mistook "the judgment and will of the people, a reunion with the States from which we have separated is neither practicable nor desirable."

So much for reassuring secessionists. Davis's more critical task was to attract nonseceding Southerners. To do this, he reached into his heritage, past recent struggles between National Democrats and Disunionists, past his Mississippi plantation, past his Missouri soldiering and Kentucky education to bedrock, to the Southerner whose name was part of his own. Southerners everywhere, Jefferson Davis declared, cherished Thomas Jefferson's right of revolution. The southern republic "merely asserted the right which the Declaration of Independence" declared "inalienable." Davis applauded the American idea that "governments rest on the consent of the governed, and that it is the right of the people to alter or abolish them."[5]

The crowd enjoyed Davis's effort. Congressmen especially voiced approval. If Virginians would not fight for black slavery, they might fight for Thomas Jefferson. With fresh hope, lawmakers returned to troubling tasks.[6]

One legislator, however, viewed Davis's departing figure with troubled distaste. Robert Barnwell Rhett, ears attuned to every syllable, heard old ambiguities in the new address. Davis had merely claimed that the people rejected reunion. He had not promised to reject a popular change of heart. Nor had he barred nonslaveholding states from entering the Southern Confederacy. If Davis could not lead Southerners back to Washington, he might attract Northerners down to Montgomery!

And why did Davis have to mouth St. Thomas's idiocies? Inalienable rights! Rights of revolution! The principles of 1776! The South had revolted to escape those ideas. What a foundation for a great slaveholding republic![7]

The ensuing Civil War would mock Rhett's doubts about Davis. South Carolinians would soon be wishing their President was less inflexible. Still, the spirit Rhett thought Davis personified was abroad in the land on this Inauguration Day. It was the very divisive spirit Davis had tried his best to master. But would Davis's best—could anyone's best— pull this land together? Could any man or idea make one people out of jealous yeomen and arrogant planters, Union-loving Marylanders and Union-smashing Alabamians, pretending slaves and wary masters, post-seventeenth-century South Carolinians and pre-twentieth-century Louisianians? As they brooded over the past and stewed about the future, the suspicious South Carolinian and the tortured Mississippian knew that one question of the half-century had become the question of the hour: Would there ever, ever, ever, be *a* South?

PART I

A SWING AROUND THE
SOUTHERN CIRCLE

In the mid-1850s, a tourist circling the various Souths could informatively guess about whether *a* South might emerge. The trip was popular. Published travel accounts about it sold well, especially Frederick Law Olmsted's. A historian, lacking Olmsted's opportunity to interview the then-living, must rely largely on written records such as Olmsted's.

More vivid remains also help reanimate bygone times. A latter-day sojourner can experience southern climates and topographies now exactly as Southerners felt geographic forces then. Many buildings on plantations and in cities have been restored to antebellum appearances. One can still ride old steamboats down the Mississippi, still stay overnight in plantation Big Houses, still stroll through old Charleston, old Natchez, old Savannah. If a historian spends a day, for example, moving from the exquisite gardens of the Louisiana plantation restoration, Rosedown, to the rich manuscripts at the Louisiana State University Library at Baton Rouge, to the haunting church graveyard at St. Francisville, physical and literary artifacts breathe life into each other. After many such days in many parts of the South, the lost world almost seems palpably to loom, daring a traveler from another century to find that South.

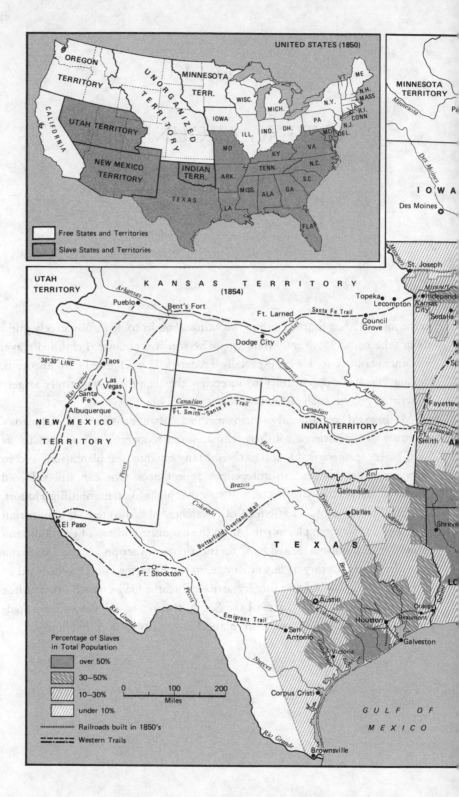

UNITED STATES (1850)

OREGON TERRITORY

MINNESOTA TERR.

CALIFORNIA

UTAH TERRITORY

NEW MEXICO TERRITORY

UNORGANIZED TERRITORY

WISC.

IOWA

MICH.

ILL.

IND.

OH.

MO

KY

TENN.

ARK.

INDIAN TERR.

MISS.

ALA

GA

LA

TEXAS

FLA

VT ME

N.H. MASS

N.Y.

R.I. CONN

PA

N.J.

MD DEL.

VA

N.C.

S.C.

Free States and Territories

Slave States and Territories

MINNESOTA TERRITORY

IOWA

Des Moines

UTAH TERRITORY

KANSAS TERRITORY
(1854)

Arkansas

Pueblo

Bent's Fort

Ft. Larned

Santa Fe Trail

Topeka
Lecompton

Kansas
City

Sedalia

St. Joseph

Independ

Council
Grove

Dodge City

Arkansas

36°30' LINE

Taos

Las
Vegas

Santa
Fe

Albuquerque

NEW MEXICO
TERRITORY

Cimarron

Canadian

Ft. Smith-Santa Fe Trail

Canadian

Arkansas

Fayettev

INDIAN TERRITORY

Ft.
Smith

Rio Grande

Pecos

Red

Red

Brazos

Gainsville

Colorado

Dallas

Shreve

El Paso

Butterfield Overland Mail

TEXAS

Trinity

Sabine

Ft. Stockton

Pecos

Rio Grande

Emigrant Trail

San
Antonio

Colorado

Austin

Brazos

Guadalupe

Houston

Orange

Beaumont

Galveston

Victoria

LC

Nueces

Percentage of Slaves
in Total Population

over 50%

30–50%

10–30%

under 10%

Railroads built in 1850's

Western Trails

0   100   200
Miles

Corpus Cristi

GULF OF
MEXICO

Rio Grande

Brownsville

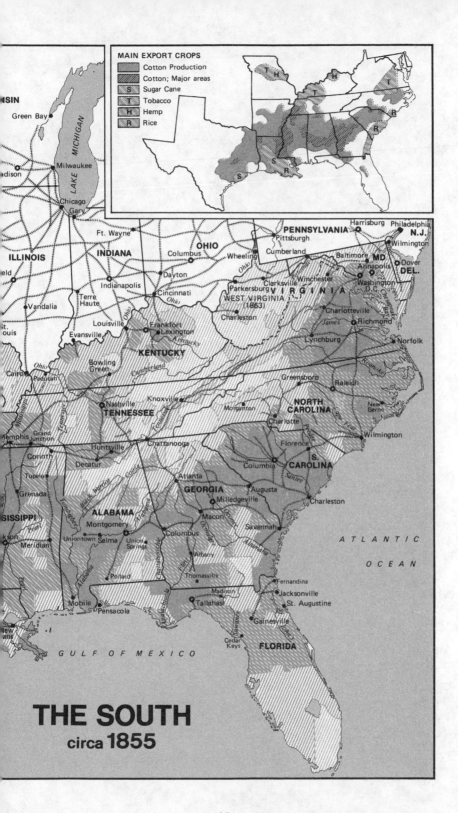

MAIN EXPORT CROPS

- Cotton Production
- Cotton; Major areas
- S Sugar Cane
- T Tobacco
- H Hemp
- R Rice

THE SOUTH
circa 1855

CHAPTER 1

St. Louis to New Orleans

Exotic cultures, like flamboyant lovers, may appear simple at first. Travelers, senses altered and assaulted, see only the obvious. For a fleeting moment, cultural identity seems clear. Only later do subtleties and confusions intrude.[1]

– 1 –

First impressions of the South in the mid-1850s were sharpest on a summer day in the most tropical South's most enslaved, so-called black-belt regions. The very air there made southernness distinctive. Humidity pressed down, warning the speedy that they rushed toward exhaustion. Quiet strolls produced drenching sweat. In the fields, laborers moved indolently, glistening as they toiled. More fortunate citizens wandered about, listlessly hunting a breeze. Even omnipresent, oversized insects seemed to prefer a squashing underfoot to energetic hustle.

In early springtime first impressions were more delightful. Fugitives from packed-down slush on northern streets found a seeming blanket of snow on Deep South trees. The white blossoms of the dogwood created the illusion. Beneath the trees, blossoms of a dozen hues covered azalea bushes. That pungent scent came from purple wisteria, fragrant with the promise of seduction. Majestic live oaks presided, green even when shedding, dripping with mournful moss, as if both exalting and grieving over the persistence of the South.

Southerners lacked such fantasies. They were too rural a folk, too close to the earth. They were too afflicted by tropical caprice: by searing droughts, flooding rains, murderous epidemics. But in the glory of the spring, southern thoughts turned romantic amidst the buds and blossoms.

Or did slaves, more than tropical profusions, make southernness instantly distinctive? To a Yankee freshly arrived in a plantation area, the numbers of blacks seemed a fantasy. Slaves, appearing to outnumber white superiors, moved gracefully, as if to some internal beat. They also shuffled about, as if will-less

13

puppets. They seemed at once cowed by and somehow free of those they called Massa.

Tinges of freedom seeped out in blacks' churches. Nothing here smacked of prim upper-class white services. Nor did truly black religion resemble the charades at plantation churches, where white missionaries catechized drowsing slaves on Christ's command that servants obey masters. A very different black evangelical service struck travelers as a "real African tornado." Here black preachers conjured up a black Moses who would, in a life beyond life, lead his people to the promised land. As preachers offered freedom, not now but soon, shouts of "Hallelujah" erupted. All around pandemonium reigned: worshipers weeping, bodies twisted, men writhing on the floor, women raising their hands, wails louder, louder, louder.[2]

Slave religion, with its hint of spirits untamed, contrasted with slave auctions, a taming process no observer dared miss. At a sale, travelers found black males lining one wall, females the other, all faces shining as if newly polished. One young slave, when approached, pointed to "a new wife here in de lot. I wishy you buy her, master, if you gwine to buy me." A mother with three children, one an infant at breast, had just been sold away from her husband. "My heart was a'most broke," she sighed.

A dog stood on hind legs. He wolfed a scrap. Slaves, including the mother, laughed. The slave-dealer's voice, smothering hilarity, put the woman and her three children up for sale. An assistant took "the baby from the woman's breast," holding it "aloft . . . to shew that it was a veritable sucking-baby." The auctioneer talked up the "capital woman," hard worker, "still young, and three children" too. He reluctantly accepted an opening $850 bid. He begged "an advance, if you please gentlemen. . . . Thank you, sir—$860. . . ."[3]

The tourist knew such smashing of human ties was but part of slavery's story. Intimacy between owners and slaves also captured attention. In the North, whites shrank from scarce blacks. In the black-belt South, white babies sucked black breasts. White and black lads raced across fields, hugging when they sprawled. On trains, black servants sat by white ladies. All munched candy from the same paper bag. Brown-skinned mulattoes indicated that blacks and whites sometimes more intimately connected. Those proud of being white, dressed curiously in black, enmeshed with slaves in an intoxicating land— might they furtively crave a sensuality they called stained?[4]

The best way to answer such questions and sort out first impressions was to visit a plantation. A major establishment had at least fifty slaves and a thousand acres. The lovely entrance avenue, lined with perfectly spaced live oak trees, ran past enough buildings to make up a respectable village. Church, school, blacksmith shop, stable, cotton gin, and corn mill created the air of a self-sufficient community. At the head of the avenue stood the patriarch's white-columned house. The life-style within seemed as far from modernity as the Greek architecture without. "The planter," exclaimed one traveler, "is a denomadized Arab;—he has fixed himself with horses and slaves in a fertile spot, where he guards his woman with Oriental care, exercises patriarchal sway, and is at once fierce, tender, and hospitable."[5]

The hospitality pressed on an outsider could be more fierce than tender. The patriarch might ask his visitor for a first impression. An obvious response, that the place seemed a refuge from modernity, could set off a verbal explosion. One's host's words came in a torrent, almost too fast for the slurring drawl, while one slave led away the horse and another brought drinks.* *Modernity,* ran the diatribe, *alias savage competition alias every man an enemy. Modernity—alias money-grubbing alias hustle-bustle alias no time for anything. Modernity—alias Anarchism alias Abolitionism alias unsexed female fanatics—Mark my words, Sir, if we leave this Union, your modern North will erupt in class war. The South, sir, stands for conservatism, hierarchy, and order.*[6]

The scene, viewed from the verandah, looked orderly enough. Slaves labored in small gangs of fewer than twenty workers. A black slave foreman called a driver directed each gang. A white man called an overseer lolled in the shadows, ostensibly driving the drivers. All occasionally glanced up to see if Massa was watching.

The butler, deftly balancing drinks, stepped lively in a uniform a general might envy: clean livery, black boots, white ruffles. The planter signaled him over. *Have you ever had a servant like this?* the host asked. *His father served my father. His son serves my son. He knows we'll take care of him. We know he'll serve us. Reciprocal duties. That's the secret of cooperative community. You Northerners worship mammon alias selfishness alias individualism run amuck. Industrialists starve their "wage slaves." We treasure our family servants.*

The tirade brought to mind proslavery books read before coming to Dixie. Southern defenses swiftly turned into inflamed offenses—assaults on all aspects of free labor society. Polemics for slave labor, when perused back home, had been easy to dismiss. On a planter's verandah the plantation mystique seemed more compelling.

The planter, marshaling evidence, nodded towards slave cabins, with vegetable gardens out front. *Over there,* boasted the squire, *my fellows grow crops after hours and sell products to buy extras.* The planter turned towards his butler, whom he called Pompey. *Northerners think all men hate to be slaves. Would you prefer to be free?* The answer, shot back as from a robot, had the air of echoing through the South under circumstances like these. *O no Massa, me no want to be free, have good Massa, you never abuse niggers; no, me no want to be free.*

How, one wondered, did Pompey's statement square with slave sales, broken families, yonder lash? Once again, words drawled out, another speech bearing the sound of rote. *Never sell 'em if I can help it. Hate to see families broken up. When black wives are sold away from husbands or children, we scorn the fiend who does it. We ostracize the monster, Sir. Does wonders. No man can stand condemnation from his peers.*

The whip? Does slaves good to cuff 'em when they're sassy. Does children good too to spank 'em when they're nasty. Sure, occasionally some bullying over-

---

*Quotes printed in italics connote conversations closely based on, but not always identical to, those in surviving sources. See note 6.

seer lays on too many licks. But some parents spank too hard too. Some husbands beat wives. Who would dream of abolishing spanking or marriage? Who besides unsexed fanatics?!

Fact is, we don't need to whip often. Our people respond to kindness. Just last week, a free black asked to be re-enslaved. Northerners can't fathom that. Yanks can't comprehend why our wives stay alone with darkies either.

The reference to wives led the mind back to mulattoes. A discreet inquiry produced a suspicious glare and another answer which seemed repeated for the hundredth time. *More of that than we like. I hate seein' white blood polluted by black. But it's them poor whites and overseers and Yankees come south that done it. Slavery keeps away more disgustin' mixin'. Keeps white women pure. Free slaves and we'd have riot and amalgamation. Would be disgustin', Sir, disgustin'. We'd have to flee.*

Moving inside for dinner, one gasped at the affluence—dark polished furniture, marble mantles, intricately wrought chandeliers. The feast was abundant—quail from the woods, fish from the river, fragrant French wine. Was slavery, then, a profitable system?

Sometimes. Depends on the weather and market. I manage. I feed my people and help fill the world with cotton. Slavery solves the labor problem for us, Sir. Whites can't stand our tropical sun. No white man shines my boots or works my fields. All whites are equal. All blacks are slaves. Everything here is in its place.

Is that, one speculated aloud, why nonslaveholders supported the system? *Reckon. Black slavery perfects white equality. No white, no matter how depraved, wants black marrin' white. No white, no matter how poor, wants to complete with poor blacks. All whites, no matter how wealthy, share with each other. I gin my neighbors' cotton for them free. Can't be no fussin' where all blacks are slaves and all whites are equals.*

Saying farewell, no Southerner could resist a final peroration. *We're a proud people, Sir. Can't stand insults. Ain't going to tolerate abolitionizing fanatics. Tell people up North to hush, Sir, hush. Mind their own business. Cause if they keep up their cant, going be blood, Sir, blood, blood flowing all across the land.*

Riding away, thinking about a black-belt neighborhood, certain images predominated: a romantic land, agrarian, tropical, conservative, sensual yet repressed, cruel yet humane. Above all, dominated by masters possessed by a vision: of racial control, of benevolent hierarchy, of scrupulous order. They were provincial, suspicious, aggressively defensive. They would lay down their lives to ward off meddling outsiders. After a day in their neighborhood, how could anyone, ever, fail to see the South?

– 2 –

First impressions usually retain saving truth. If compelled to choose between a South massed behind a consolidated ruling class and a region where nonslaveholders verged on revolt against divided rulers, informed observers would have gone for the monolith. But slaveholders were too wise to settle for that simplicity. They wove their history around an understanding that theirs was a class and a section uncomfortably unperfected.

Travelers who journeyed most widely in the antebellum South best understood that apprehension. Cracks in the slaveholding class separated not planters from neighboring magnates but Alabama cotton nabobs from South Carolina rice squires, from Virginia tobacco barons, and from Missouri hemp titans. The deepest antagonisms between rich and poor occurred not between a black-belt aristocrat and a neighboring redneck but between planters living way south in areas black with slaves and nonslaveholders living close to the North in all-white neighborhoods. The largest southern question was whether the ruling class could overcome geographic barriers fracturing the class and isolating masters from the most disaffected nonmasters.

Such geographic obstacles hardly created "proslavery" versus "antislavery" Souths. Southerners differed over whether bondage should last decades or forever, over whether perpetuating slavery should be the highest or a somewhat lesser priority, over whether slavery could be terminated under the right conditions or whether no conditions could be right. A geographic formula summed up these differences. The further north the southern state, the cooler the clime, the fewer the slaves, and the lower the relative commitment to perpetuating bondage. Or to put it the other way, the further towards the tropics, the more torrid the weather, the more omnipresent the serviles, and the higher the likelihood that permanent slavery would seem more important than anything. Southern states' northern and southern boundaries divided Dixie into three rough zones, three layers of states running from the Atlantic Ocean on the east past the Mississippi River to the west, piled atop each other like a crooked three-step ladder, and growing less fiery about perpetuating slavery with each step up.

The most southern layer of slave states, the so-called Deep or Lower South, usually bordered on the Gulf of Mexico. The Lower South ran from South Carolina, Florida, and Georgia on the east through Alabama, Mississippi, and Louisiana to Texas on the west. Here, plantations were prevalent and cotton was often king. In the Lower South, Disunionists would triumph after Abraham Lincoln won the presidential election of 1860.

The most northern layer of slave states, the so-called Border South, bordered on northern, free labor states. The Border South ran from Delaware and Maryland on the east through Kentucky to Missouri on the west. Here, plantations were scarcer and cotton cultivation almost nonexistent. In the Border South, Unionists would overcome Disunionists even after Civil War began.

The middle layer of slave states, cutting between Border South and Lower South, was usually called, appropriately, the Middle South. This tier stretched from Virginia and North Carolina on the east through Tennessee to Arkansas on the west. Each Middle South state contained one part resembling more the Lower South, another part resembling more the Border South. Eastern Virginia and western Tennessee had many plantations. Western Virginia and eastern

Tennessee had few. In the Middle South, Unionists would triumph after Lincoln was elected and Disunionists would prevail after Civil War began. Then western Virginia would secede from eastern Virginia, and eastern Tennessee's Andrew Johnson would refuse to secede from the United States Senate. The Middle South was truly a land between.

Statistics in the federal census formed a guidebook to the various Souths.[7] In 1850, more than 21% of Border South blacks but less than 2% of Lower South blacks were free. Forty-six percent of southern free blacks lived in the Border South, compared with 15% in the Lower South. On the other hand, but 12% of southern enslaved blacks lived in the Border South, compared with 55% in the Lower South. In 1850, slaves comprised 17% of the Border South's population, compared with 30% in the Middle South and 47% in the Lower South. The average slaveholder in the Border South held 5 slaves, compared with 8 in the Middle South and 12 in the Lower South. Of the Border South's white families, 22% held slaves, compared with 36% in the Middle South and 43% in the Lower South. Among slaveholders who owned 20 or more slaves in 1850, 6% lived in the Border South, 62% in the Lower South. Among ultra-wealthy titans with over 100 slaves, 1% lived in the Border South, 85% in the Lower South.

These discrepancies seemed permanent and growing. The less tropical the locale, the poorer the yield of cotton; and the cotton boom of the 1850s made raising the fleece seem the most profitable use of slaves. A more northern location in the South also meant closer proximity to Yankees; and increasing Yankee resentments in the 1850s made the fugitive slave problem seem more threatening.

While the geographic position of the most northern South often made slavery seem riskier and less profitable, the Appalachian Mountains, dominating much of the Border and Middle Souths, usually made plantations unthinkable. Mountains occupy some of northeastern Kentucky, most of western Virginia, and almost all of eastern Tennessee before curving and rising gently in the Deep South. Some Appalachian foothills blanket a fraction of western South Carolina; and here, significantly, nonslaveholder hostility to slaveholders sometimes surfaced. More and higher foothills dominate a larger fraction of northern Georgia and Alabama; and here, even more significant disloyalty to the Confederacy would be prevalent. The Deep South also contained extensive piney woods and wiregrass regions, forbidding to plantation agriculture, congenial to hard-scrabble yeomen. Nevertheless, a Lower South locale without extensive mountains and far from the North offered planters widespread opportunities.

Planters in the South's most tropical areas did grasp their opportunities. In 1850 the Lower South grew 95 percent of Dixie's cotton and almost all its sugar and rice. Tobacco, the most significant Middle and Border South slave-grown export crop, was raised primarily in a fraction of eastern Virginia, Eastern and Western Shore Maryland, and Bluegrass Kentucky. Everywhere else, Middle and Border South farmers demonstrated why their states were commonly lumped together as Upper South grain states to distinguish them from Lower

South cotton states. The Lower South, with over two-thirds of the South's most fertile lands and over half its slaves, produced less than a third of the section's corn, less than a fourth of its oats, less than a tenth of its wheat.

Urban and manufacturing figures round out the mid-century statistical portrait. The Border South produced over half of Dixie's industrial products. The Lower South produced less than a fifth. In 1850 the Border South's Baltimore, St. Louis, and Louisville ranked first, third, and fourth in order of size among southern cities, with a combined population of almost 300,000. The Lower South's three largest cities, New Orleans, Charleston, and Mobile, ranked second, fifth, and seventh in Dixie, with a combined population well short of 200,000. The three leading Border South cities, despite twice as many whites as Gulf counterparts, possessed only a fourth as many slaves. In cities and in the countryside, the Border South melted into a North-South twilight zone, more like Chicago than Charleston, more akin to midwestern grain farms than to southwestern cotton plantations.

– 3 –

In the mid-1850s, nothing more swiftly or more colorfully established an image of the various Souths than a steamboat trip down the Mississippi. The most revealing time to travel was in late winter. The best place to catch the steamer for New Orleans was in St. Louis. The best way to reach this mercantile center of the slaveholding Midwest was via train from the nonslaveholding Midwest's hub, Chicago.

The initial view from the train was of a world hurrying after progress. Illinois prairies were thick with farms. Many farmers drove up-to-speed tractors. Only many miles from Chicago were poor farmers equipped with only mules to be seen. Many more miles passed before undeveloped land was evident.

Crossing the Mississippi into slaveholding Missouri, development looked slower still, until one entered fast-growing, barely enslaved St. Louis.[8] This urban mecca for white migrants contained twenty times as many whites as blacks. A leading newspaper, the *St. Louis Democrat,* lashed out at the so-called Slavepower. St. Louis conversations betrayed Chicago-style desires for more whites, more factories, more free soil, free labor, free men.

The opinion omnipresent in St. Louis was that a little slavery was giving Missouri too little democracy. Undemocratic attempts to consolidate black slavery, urged the *St. Louis Democrat,* had gone farthest in neighboring Kansas territory. A tiny minority of slaveholders from Missouri had allegedly seized the Kansas territorial legislature, passed tyrannical sedition laws, and turned "Bleeding Kansas" into a mecca of mobs. Missouri slaveholding roughnecks used such undemocratic tactics, so one heard in St. Louis, because in a fair democratic fight the minority would be routed. Nonslaveholders outnumbered slaveholding voters 6–1 in Missouri, 60–1 in Kansas. Nonslaveholding states already surrounded Missouri on two sides. Make Kansas territory the third nonslaveholding side and the Missouri minority would be cornered.

Missouri's slaveholders, so the *St. Louis Democrat* maintained, hindered economic no less than democratic development. Missouri had too few black laborers because slaves could be more productively exploited in the more tropical Lower South. Yet the too few blacks repelled too many whites. Frontiersmen preferred midwestern states untainted by "niggers" and "nigger tyrants." To attain as much democratic and capitalistic progress as neighboring Illinois, concluded the *Democrat,* Missouri nonslaveholders must pressure slaveholders to sell all slaves down river, where blacks belonged.

The view at the "levee," heart of the St. Louis scene, illustrated the city's largely nonslaveholding situation. For six and a half miles, the levee sprawled along the Mississippi, lapping up Missouri-Ohio-Illinois river traffic. This new entrepôt of the New West had been built in nonslaveholding Yankee haste. Old residences had been torn down. Shoddy warehouses had been thrown up. Wagons, drawn almost onto boats, were packed with tobacco, corn, wheat; groaning mules then dragged them up the towering limestone bluff. White laborers supplied most of the manpower. Blacks were manacled near the New Orleans steamboat, destined to labor further south.

While dealers prodded slaves onto the steamboat, more fortunate voyagers had time to examine the floating palace. The ship rested on a flat keel, with only the rear paddlewheel sunk into the current. Steamboats, so it was said, could run on heavy dew. Up front, the sooty chimney, towering twice as high as the three decks, puffed out pollution. Inside, saloons were gaudily handsome, with Brussels carpets, mirrors, intricate candelabras. It was as if a daft king had built his castle in a steel factory.[9]

In mid-February, when the steamboat glided away from St. Louis, few believed they were in a king's domain. Foliage was shorn from trees. Grass was a stunted brown. The stream was awash with yellow topsoil, destined to enrich terrain down river.

Yet if the Mississippi was carrying Missouri slaves and Missouri topsoil naturally towards the tropics, Missouri slaveholders hardly seemed unnatural Southerners. Out west, according to planters aboard ship, along both Missouri and Kansas shores of the Missouri River, river-enriched terrain invited slaveholding. True, they were off to explore possibilities of higher profits further to the south. True, river bottom lands occupied a thin area of Missouri and Kansas. True, the nonslaveholding majority outside the Border South's thin black belts might prefer all blacks diffused to tropical slave belts.

But for now, Missouri was their home, emphasized these slaveholders. They would live where they wanted, own what they wanted, do what they wanted without officious moralists, from Chicago or St. Louis or Boston, giving them instructions. They would move to the tropics or sell slaves in New Orleans or stay in Missouri, according to what *they* thought best. And they would fight to the death, in Kansas or Missouri or elsewhere, to keep busybodies north or south from running off with their property.

Such utterances indicated that St. Louis hardly spoke for Missouri. The word on board was that slaveholders usually won Missouri statewide elections.

What remained unclear, not least to shipboard orators, was whether planters off to explore prospects further south would always come back up river. The further question was how many slaves might drain away and how many non-plantation regions become angry about minority domination before majorities would revoke the slaveholders' mastery of Kansas—and of Missouri.

Still, as St. Louis, then Missouri, faded from view along the Mississippi, the Kansas battlefield had a way of seeming a far-off abstraction. Missourians on board, with their obsession with the subject, had a way of being single-minded bores. Outsiders saw that Kansas talk quickly bored other Southerners too. Was Kansas, then, of life-and-death importance only in the immediate geographic area? And if Southerners put life-and-death importance on only their local problems, how could different locales come together on a sustained crusade?

– 4 –

River amusements interested the steamboat crowd more than such abstract questions. The greatest entertainment was to race another steamboat down the Mississippi. The sport was unnerving, for river legends featured tales of steamboats swishing too fast and exploding apart. But rejecting yonder steamboat's challenge meant unnaturally repressing the excitement of this fabled river. Adventure triumphed. Black hands jammed fat-pine into flaming furnaces. Swearing firemen tied down safety valves. Passengers scrambled onto barrels, cheering as ships shook and shot ahead.

In three days, the ship steamed into dingy Memphis, river outpost of western Tennessee, a prime Middle South plantation area. Here cotton was hauled aboard. Here more planters stepped down the gang-plank. Conversation swirled around bottomland and timberland, black-land and red-land, slaves and acres and cotton, cotton, cotton.

By breakfast time, two days out of Memphis, steaming beyond Mississippi's Vicksburg, weather and terrain changed as dramatically as passengers. One shot past early spring into early summer. On the banks, forests were full of plum, peach, apple blossoms, untouched trees evidence of untouched soil. Only an occasional slave gang was to be seen. Lush river bottoms seemed to be daring men to come, risk, conquer.

At Natchez, jewel of Mississippi planters, rewards and costs of that challenge seemed beyond control. The town was a planter paradise. Elegant white-columned plantation houses were everywhere. Out of sight, the inelegant Natchez slave auction rang with bids. The Mississippi, having carried and deposited border soil, had yet to carry enough slaves down river.[10]

Steaming on, on past secret bayous and alligator-haunted swamps, one reached a lusher tropical region. In Baton Rouge, the steamboat stopped to pick up sugar. New passengers bragged about making 50% annually growing the sweet cane. They boasted they could make 100% with more bondsmen. They were off to New Orleans slave auctions to make their sweet business sweeter still.[11]

In New Orleans, the hunger for slaves became ever more apparent. Almost the entire lobby of the ironically named St. Louis Hotel was given over to Dixie's most frenzied slave auction. Almost an entire page of New Orleans's favorite newspaper was given over to legislative effort to reopen the African slave trade. The effort had lately failed by a single vote. An editorial assured readers that the vote would yet be overturned. The Border South, went the argument, did not have enough expendable slaves. Only Africa could supply enough labor to mine North America's tropics.[12]

Interest in reopening the African slave trade paralleled enthusiasm for capturing South America. New Orleans banking and mercantile tycoons urged annexing the Caribbean, maybe the Amazon too. Here, at the confluence of the Mississippi and the Gulf, merchant capitalists envisioned New Orleans as commercial center of a republic stretching from Minnesota to Brazil. Today New Orleans imperialists would seize Cuba. Tomorrow they would snatch Nicaragua. Some year they would conquer Mexico. In New Orleans, Manifest Destiny was as southern as hominy and grits.

To the northern notion that Manifest Destiny, southern style, meant spreading despotism rather than democracy, Louisianians countered that black slavery spread white egalitarianism. Democracy and despotism were hardly incompatible, so Southwesterners claimed, where a color line separated white citizens from black serviles. Black inferiors actually increased whites' feelings of equality, equality in the critical way: the possession of the better skin.

New Orleans imperialists scoffed at St. Louis notions that consolidating black slavery required constricting white republicanism. John C. Calhoun to the contrary, the South was in no permanent national minority. Southerners had triumphed through national majorities, as in opening Kansas for slaveholding, and would pile on future victories, as in Caribbean expansion. Locally, boasted Southwesterners, masters, together with would-be masters, were the Lower South majority. Lynch mobs? Don't need them. Sedition laws? Down with the anachronism. We are the future of white men's republicanism.

How different everything in this steaming, optimistic land seemed from the mood in wintry Missouri. St. Louis wished to deport slaves, to cure limping capitalism. New Orleans wished to import slaves, to expand runaway entrepreneurship. New Orleans dreamed of dominating the hemisphere. St. Louis would settle for becoming New Orleans's northern middleman. Missouri River planters tried for 10% profits. Louisiana sugar growers would not settle for 50%. St. Louis citizens, mindful of the Border South's thin black belts and 22% proportion of slaveholders, called slavery an invitation to minority rule. New Orleans leaders, thinking of the Lower South's thick black belt and 43% proportion of slaveholders, called minority rule unnecessary. Missouri slaveholders, fearing free-soil encirclement, were attempting minority despotism in Kansas. Louisiana slaveholders, at the center of a hemispheric slaveholding circle, were confident about wielding local and national majorities.

Such contrasts, dismal to border slavery, overlooked border slaveholders' determination to decide for themselves whether to move down river. But would human determination forever offset inhuman forces? Standing at New Orleans, facing upriver towards St. Louis, northern gales easing tropical heat, a steamboat passenger could almost feel wind, water, cash, cotton, ships, slaves drifting inexorably towards the tropics.

– 5 –

An outsider who wished to share Southerners' sense of the world was wise to savor that moment. He was experiencing a master metaphor of the southern mind. The flow of slavery downward seemed as irreversible to a late antebellum slaveholder as sand in the hourglass. Eventually, it was widely feared in some quarters (and hoped in others), time would run out on slavery and plantations north of the Lower South.

Such predictions fed on the fact that a slave drain had recently moved the plantation South toward the tropics. Before the nineteenth century, North American plantations had been a Western Hemisphere anomaly in being based in relatively untropical spheres. New World colonists established scarce and expensive slaves where yield promised to be greatest; a more tropical location usually meant a more extravagant yield.

But North America's tropics were too far north to yield South America's tropical treasures. Coffee, later-day gem of steaming Brazil, failed to grow anywhere in cooler North America. Rice, the most important product grown in eighteenth-century North America's most tropical areas, thrived only in confined South Carolina and Georgia coastal swamps. Sugar, jewel of most South American slavocracies, seemed to seventeenth- and eighteenth-century North American colonists impossible to raise so far from the equator. Intensive sugar cultivation occurred in southernmost North America largely in the nineteenth century, almost entirely in southern Louisiana and Texas, and only with constant lobbying of the national government for tariff protection against more numerous and more southerly South American plantations.

North American plantation efforts had thus settled most extensively on tobacco, a foul but profitable weed easiest to raise northward, where tropical heat eased off. In 1790, some 60% of southern slaves lived in the Chesapeake Bay regions of Maryland and Virginia. Maryland had almost three times as many slaves as barely settled Georgia. Virginia had more than twice as many slaves as highly developed but rigidly confined coastal South Carolina. West of the South Carolina and Georgia coast, a black face was rare in the most tropical United States.

An invention and a law served to make slave location more tropical. At the turn of the eighteenth into the nineteenth century, Eli Whitney's new cotton gin helped give Deep South settlers better profits in steamier habitats. In 1807, the American Congress banned the African slave trade, forcing new cotton planters to draw serviles from old slave regions.

The Chesapeake Bay world was glad to sell some slaves. The great cotton boom of the early nineteenth century followed on the heels of the great tobacco bust of the late eighteenth century. Low prices and low yields afflicting tobacco growers contrasted with higher prices and higher yields encouraging cotton growers. The resulting forced migration of black folk drove slavery's base down where it apparently belonged: towards most tropical areas, away from Yankee hostility, far from mountaineers who cared little about the institution.

Between 1790 and 1860, Border and Middle Souths lost close to 750,000 slaves, almost the area's entire natural increase. Maryland and Virginia's share of southern slaves sank from 60% to 18%. The Lower South's proportion shot from 21% to 55%. While 27.5% of Border South residents were slaves in 1790, only 16.7% were bondsmen in 1850.

If the southward sale of slaves continued—and in the 1850s the slave drain increased—the plantation South could shrivel over many decades into a handful of Deep South states. As the Upper South's slaves drained away, the region's inhabitants would be freer to suspect that slavery and democracy were alien, freer to feel a greater commitment to permanent Union than to permanent slavery, freer to side with Illinoisans rather than with South Carolinians. If half the South gradually became more than half-northern in commitment, an ever demographically blacker, ever geograpically shrinking North American slave empire was bound to feel holed up, hemmed in, at the northern majority's mercy. With that image, the Mississippi River traveler had reached not the end of a journey but the beginning of doubt that *a* South existed.

CHAPTER 2

New Orleans to Charleston to Baltimore to St. Louis

The slave drain carried slaves southwards except—except for the usual southern exception. South Carolina was especially exceptional in being a Deep South state hemorrhaging slaves. Differences between slave-exporting South Carolina and the slave-importing rest of the Deep South, while less important than dissimilarities between the less enslaved Upper South and the more enslaved Lower South, also threatened the unity and hegemony of the master class. Such east/west differences were omnipresent in a tour across the Lower South, from the Mississippi River to the Atlantic Coast.

– 1 –

In the 1850s, a journey from New Orleans, king of the Mississippi, to Charleston, southern queen city on the Atlantic, was as difficult, appropriately, as moving between two suspicious European principalities. True, a steamboat sailed swiftly and easily from New Orleans through the Gulf, around Florida and up the Atlantic Coast to Charleston. But that sweep outside the Lower South precluded discovery of Souths between Louisiana and South Carolina. Seagoers especially failed to observe that most of the Lower South more resembled expansive New Orleans than contracting Charleston. Indeed, Charleston served so narrowly its contained coastal hinterlands, and New Orleans served so widely the expansive Mississippi River basin, that steamers between them were infrequent.

A mid-nineteenth-century inland traveler thought first of railroads.[1] The thought led to unpleasant travel. Across the Lower South, the iron horse, symbol of a speeding new industrial age, dawdled at the pace of the largely preindustrial communities it connected. A modern jet races over the approximately 650 miles between New Orleans and Charleston in a single easy hour. A modern automobile speeds over the approximately 750 miles of superhighway between the two cities in a single hard day. Mid-nineteenth-century trains could mean-der over the approximately 1000 miles of tracks between the two centers in a long, unforgettable week—if one made connections.

Connections alone made the week unforgettable. No railroad connected New Orleans and Mobile, Alabama, or Mobile and Montgomery, Alabama's capital. One had to take a steamer from New Orleans to Mobile, then transfer to a horse-drawn carriage at Mobile to traverse the 75-mile dirt road to Pollard, Alabama. Fairly direct train tracks to Montgomery and on to Atlanta, Georgia, and Charleston were then available. But one had to transfer successfully between *six* different railroad companies.

If one-third fewer connections seemed desirable, one could take a train from New Orleans to Jackson, Mississippi, then transfer to another railroad between Jackson and Meridian. Since Alabama and Mississippi lacked interest in con-nections, one then had to board a carriage to travel the 75 miles to Uniontown, Alabama. There one's third railroad set off for Selma. No tracks connected Selma and Montgomery. So it was over to a steamboat for the 80-mile journey to the Confederacy's future capital. There, it was hoped, one's fourth train would be ready to meander towards Charleston.

A traveler who disliked interludes in horse-drawn carriages could go all the way, circuitously, by rail. One would then jolt from New Orleans hundreds of miles too far north to Grand Junction, Tennessee, then east to Chattanooga, then back down south to Atlanta, then east again to Charleston—provided one successfully juggled time schedules of *nine* different companies.

The 15- to 30-mile-per-hour pace, with stops at least once an hour, made meeting the next train nerve-wracking. Schedules warned of changes without notice. When schedules were unchanged, only a mathematician could make them jibe. The Deep South was so localized that each city was on its own time. One o'clock in Charleston was two o'clock in Augusta and three o'clock in Atlanta, although the sun rose and set at close to the same time throughout the 200-mile stretch. The Georgia Railroad, serving Atlanta and Augusta, was on Atlanta time; the Augusta and Savannah, uniting those two cities, was on Augusta time; the South Carolina Railroad, connecting Augusta and Charles-ton, was on Charleston time. Standing in Augusta, puzzling over three different time schedules setting forth departures at three successive hours, the brainstorm might strike that all three were leaving at the same moment.

Despite simultaneous arrivals or departures, no collisions need occur. Vari-ous companies' tracks rarely touched or fitted each other's. In Augusta, trav-elers had to drag suitcases a third of a mile from one company's tracks to anoth-er's. In Montgomery, those who had endured the 75-mile carriage ride from Mobile to catch the Pollard-Montgomery train found that the Montgomery-Charleston train required another carriage ride through muddy bottomlands. Anyone stuck in the Montgomery mud while the last train for the week crept off towards Charleston understood particularly well that the Lower South was no consolidated empire.

– 2 –

The happiest Lower South travelers ceased fighting nature. Plantations were erected wherever rivers enriched soil and eased transportation, and southwestern rivers flowed north-south, towards the Gulf. The best way to travel east-west, "unnaturally" between north-south rivers, was to ride on horseback.

High points of slow trips through a spottily settled agrarian civilization occurred along rushing streams. Here population was denser, prosperity more evident. In areas of Mississippi near the Pearl and the Mississippi, in areas of Alabama near the Tombigbee and Alabama river systems, in areas of Georgia near the Chattahoochee and Flint river basins, the words "black belt" seemed appropriate. Population in river counties tended to be around 50% slaves.

But black belts came to seem as thin as river lines on the map. Between rivers, one rode through virgin territory, searching out isolated nonslaveholders or small slaveholders who could supply shelter. Farmers would share rundown cabins and bitter coffee, if enough pennies were offered. But they seemed suspicious of outsiders and determined to talk as little as possible.[2]

Nearer rivers, that mood of sullen struggle remained omnipresent. Tight-lipped nonslaveholders were far more numerous here than expansive planters, and many wealthier planters lived like and sounded like nonslaveholders. Ostentatious planters and fancy houses proved to be exceptions, even on lush river bottoms.

The talk within cramped cabins, if strangers could stimulate talk, was of hurricanes and floods, price of cotton and of slaves, cost of land and yield per acre, making a killing before cotton killed the soil. These agriculturalists' enterprises were more contracted than the New Orleans variety. Although they too were of Gulf rivers, they paid little heed to Gulf imperialism. They had no interest in joining Louisianians in capturing Nicaragua. Nor would they join Missourians in marching on Kansas.

Their South, the Deep South where slaveholders were most frequent, cared most about its immediate neighborhood. The issue was whether to buy a neighbor's extra acre. The enemy was some local tax collector or mortgage holder. The oppressor was unrelenting rains or searing droughts. The indignity was plunging markets. These Southerners sought slight leverage to raise tiny prospects. They could not bear the thought that outsiders might abolish their prospects altogether.

Hospitality toward strangers was more gracious in those infrequent Greek Revival mansions. But even Big House residents, though sometimes affecting to be English country gentlemen, were provincial American strivers. Pages in lovely leather-bound volumes appeared to be uncut. Issues of local newspapers looked well-thumbed. Idle chatter about yesterday's fox hunt would quickly veer off into intense speculation about tomorrow's cotton prices. Indifferent musing about New Orleans's latest foray to capture Cuba would digress into involved discussion of next week's slave auction. Their success in the New

Orleans cotton and slave markets, not New Orleans's success in capturing a Gulf empire or Missouri's success in seizing Kansas, was the true interest of these parochial lords of Gulf rivers.

– 3 –

After tourists moving east had reached Georgia's Flint River, they could cease fighting geography. In eastern Georgia, rivers at last flowed east-west, towards the Atlantic. Little else changed. Again, population between rivers was sparse. Again, many struggling farmers and few ostentatious planters occupied river bottoms. Again, river boats transported largely cotton, this time towards the Atlantic. One passed the Ogmulgee-Oconee-Altamaha river system, then the Ogeechee River basin, then rode alongside the Savannah River.

Across the Savannah and inside upcountry South Carolina, much seemed different. The Carolina upcountry, meaning the hilly piedmont territory up and away from the lowcountry coastal plain, looked to be suffering from a hangover after a spree. Unlike virgin lands between southwestern rivers, upcountry South Carolina soil looked overused. Broomsedge and briar as well as deserted houses and tumbling fences littered the countryside. It was as if an army had ravaged, then roamed off in search of richer pickings.

An entrepreneurial army had indeed lately roamed away from South Carolina. Upcountry Carolina, the Lower South cotton land nearest to the Atlantic, was the first early nineteenth-century area to enjoy the cotton boom. It consequently became the first Lower South region to suffer cotton soil debilitation. Rather than continuing to till earth drained of nutrients, many slaveholders pushed slaves west, to farm the next Lower South frontier.

Those who stayed preferred declining soil to endless unsettlement. Their profits might be less. Their lives would be richer. They would prove that cotton and slaves could generate more than more cotton and more slaves. They aimed not at reckless gambling but at restrained greatness.

Listening to great magnates in great upcountry houses, houses more elegant and talk more polished than anything this side of Natchez, one realized how much this gentry loathed Southerners infatuated with mere dollars. According to ubiquitous Carolina snobbery, crude southwest cotton snobs, concerned only with crass profits, deserted not so much South Carolina as a worthwhile southland. The southern way involved perfecting a family rather than filling a wallet, treating servants mildly rather than exploiting laborers tyrannically, writing a literature rather than gutting a wilderness.[3]

Such talk could sound a little hypocritical. Library shelves revealed uncut pages here too. Gentlemen's desks again displayed well-thumbed plantation accounts. Paintings on walls revealed much spending, little taste. This was a second-generation aristocracy, a little removed from obsessions with cash, a little advanced towards elegant taste, yet still too nouveau-riche to be comfortably aristocratic and too financially unsure to be carelessly forgetful of money-grubbing.

Talk of South Carolina superiority also sounded forced. Braggarts failed to mask their fear that too many dollars and people had ebbed away for those left behind to command those marching ahead. The tone hinted not at a culture proudly in the vanguard but at a civilization edgy about losing its way.

The note of aging, of outliving one's time, became more noticeable on the Carolina coast, amidst lowcountry squires. Sojourners who traveled towards those most famous Disunionists encountered additional geographical barriers to a single South. A dense pine barren separated upcountry and lowcountry Carolina.[4] Beyond the almost uninhabited forest lay lightly inhabited lowcountry swamps. Coastal wetlands looked fertile in a way pine barrens were not. Dank swamps were also forbidding in a way no pine forest could be. Huge trees blocked out the sun. Spanish moss hung low and eerie. Pools of water were blackest black, suggestive of death and dissolution.

Then one suddenly discovered a clearing with living folk, largely black folk. No other southern black belt was remotely as black as this. Skins were blacker, suggesting how relatively few whites had been around. Dialects seemed more African, also suggesting relatively little interracial contact. Population ratios were incredible, not one black for one white, as in southwestern black belts, but ten blacks for one white, assuming a white could be found.

In the summer, whites were especially scarce. Planters, fleeing omnipresent malaria, often left black drivers in charge of the exceptional crops this exceptional land yielded. Inland, expensive gangs of slaves labored over expensive rice fields. On sea islands along the coast, armies of slaves grew the world's most luxurious strand of cotton. Nowhere in the South did the investment seem so huge. Nowhere in the South were investors so far away from investments.

Lowcountry planters could often be found in Charleston.[5] Absentees were relieved to be removed from malaria, proud to be away from being an entrepreneur. Here they entertained in rarified English-style drawing rooms and exchanged latest London gossip.

Here, bragging about being English gentlemen rather than American go-getters rang a little truer. Newspaper writers warned absentee anti-entrepreneurs about their economic risks. Other articles spoke of younger sons, who preferred dissolute idleness to disgusting careerism. The economic question here was whether big spenders and nonmanagerial managers could glean lush enough profits from rice and luxury cotton planting.

As befitted an aristocracy contemptuous of the go-getting nineteenth century, these Anglophiles were as disdainful of galloping egalitarianism as of gauche expansionism. The intolerable error of slavery, southwestern style, they urged, was not so much that slaveholders were money machines as that slavery was considered safe inside a mobocracy. Jealous masses would demolish so aristocratic an institution unless slaveholders insisted on aristocratic republicanism. King Cotton's republic must contain bulwarks against King Numbers.

These gentlemen were contemptuous of other southern solutions. Annex Caribbean commercial culture? The South already was disgustingly Yankee. Seek new southwestern lands? The New South already was forgetful of old

traditions. Move and expand? Better to stay put and conserve. How to eliminate nineteenth-century evils? Adopt state constitutions that gave the rich a
veto against the numbers. Amend the national constitution to allow the minority to nullify the majority. Otherwise secede, secede, secede. Secede from the
Union. Secede from the century. Secede from the scummy herd. Re-establish an
aristocratic republic that would make England envious.

The contrast with other drawing rooms in other Lower Souths was striking.
Charleston's finest scorned new pretensions that rich and poor whites were
equal. Southwesterners scuttled old presumptions that poor whites needed guidance from above. South Carolina wanted out of everything modern, not least
the Union. Louisiana wanted more of all things contemporary, not excluding
possibilities emanating from Washington. South Carolina wished expansion to
give way to consolidation, copying English models in the Old World across the
Atlantic. Louisiana wished conservatism laced with imperialism, seeking new
additions in the New World across the Gulf. South Carolina had the hopeless-
ness of the reactionary so desperate as to be revolutionary. Louisiana had the
hopefulness of the tycoon so confident as to be progressive. These colliding gentries agreed that slavery must be perpetual. But they were as far apart as the
Atlantic is from the Mississippi on how to bring off *a* South.

- 4 -

Charleston's gentlemen, while a century removed from Lower South slavocracies to their west, were even more distinct from Atlantic Coast squires to their
north. Disconnected railroads again underlined the gentry's isolation. Traveling
northward, meandering iron tracks stretched the slightly more than 300 miles
between Charleston and Richmond into well over 400 miles. This time, one had
to juggle schedules of five different companies. This time no single iron horse
could make the trip. Tracks switched from being 4'8" wide to being 5' wide.
Richmond, soon to be meeting ground of the Southern Confederacy's government, displayed the ultimate symbol of a divided South. Six different railroad
lines left Richmond, fanning out in a 360-degree wheel, heading for Souths to
the north, south, east, and west. Nowhere in Richmond did any line touch
another.

The discontinuity in transportation mirrored the discontinuity in terrain
between Charleston and the Upper South. North of Charleston lay more
swamps. Again the sun rarely penetrated overgrown foliage. Again, almost all
residents were blackest black. Again dark pools seemed more like oil than water.
Again the humid air seemed heavy with the danger that sent whites to
Charleston.

Across the North Carolina border loomed a jungle ranker still. No cleared
plantations relieved North Carolina's alligator-infested Dismal Swamp. The few
visitors occasionally glimpsed the most desperate Southerners: fugitive slaves
hiding in this dank wetland.[6]

On the Virginia side of the Dismal Swamp, the world lightened and brightened. Glaring sun scorched cleared terrain. The coastal plain had a wearying, comforting sameness. Many white nonslaveholders worked the flat land. Much now suggested a yeoman's midwestern frontier.[7]

But large plantations, interspersed among more numerous small farms, created a more proper image of a diluted aristocratic culture. Nothing was frontier-like or midwestern about occasional eighteenth-century plantation mansions. These elegantly balanced Georgian brick edifices denoted an older, more settled gentry than did southwestern wooden palaces. Inhabitants' viewpoints recalled Charlestonian hauteur. Southwestern upstarts, scoffed eastern Virginia patricians, tended to be crude, materialistic nigger-drivers. Southwestern plans to expand by reopening the African slave trade were loathsome. Gulf crusades to grow by pirating the Caribbean were criminal. Southerners, Tidewater Virginians rather agreed with coastal South Carolinians, should move less and perfect more.

Yet tobacco patriarchs were hardly to be confused with Charleston's absentee dandies. Virginia magnates actively managed their decaying estates. They used profits from selling slaves to set other slaves to work fertilizing worn soil. While these survivors were not reaping southwestern-style profits, the worst of a long economic depression seemed behind them.

Eastern Virginia squires' political talk, like their economic enterprises, had the feel of an old order painfully adjusting to a new century. Gentlemen proud of eighteenth-century ancestors, in Virginia as in South Carolina, often expressed contempt for the new mobocracy. Virginia's First Families, like Carolina's, often bragged about ancient state constitutional restraints on herd rule. But Virginia's elite, with few exceptions, loathed South Carolina disunionism no less than New Orleans imperialism. A little compromising, gentlemen urged, could save Union and slavery. Virginia's eastern gentry also talked more about lessening state constitutional restraints on Virginia's masses. South Carolina oligarchs scorned Virginia gentlemen for considering giving an inch.

South Carolinians also disliked Virginia gentlemen's tone on slavery. Vague approval of ending bondage, assuming proper conditions, could be heard under proper circumstances in proper Virginia drawing rooms. Proper circumstances meant no "outside agitators" present. Right conditions meant removal of free blacks. But Virginia squires occasionally speculated that their blacks might someday be diffused to Africa or drained to the south, with whites streaming to Virginia to take slaves' place. Lowcountry South Carolinians, in contrast, could not conceive that whites would stream toward malarial swamps.

The distance from South Carolina seemed to grow greater when one approached Richmond.[8] The state capitol could be seen from afar, towering above the industrial smog, apparently an up-to-date seat of power in an up-to-date metropolis. Illusions disappeared upon entering the city. Richmond's streets were unpaved, half her shops uninhabited. The capitol, atop Shockloe Hill, needed repair. The most extensive bands of slaves were at the slave auction, destined to be dispatched to New Orleans. Despite attempts at becoming a wide-awake metropolis, Richmond, like the Virginia countryside, remained

half aging and half asleep. The trip from Carolina to Virginia resulted in a sense
not of passing through a consolidated Old South empire but of moving halfway
towards the North.

– 5 –

While Richmond was less southern than Charleston, points further north
became not very southern at all. At Delaware, the coastal South's northeastern
edge, southernness almost evaporated. By 1850, Delaware's proportion of slaves
had sunk well under 3%, down from 15% in 1790. Wilmington, Delaware's
largest city and best tourist attraction, had all of four slaves. In Wilmington
and along the Delaware countryside, few cared whether quartets of bondsmen
were free.[9]

Maryland, just west from Delaware in the Chesapeake Bay region, was also
debatably southern.[10] The debate was relatively new. In 1790, the state's over
100,000 slaves had comprised a third of the population. Maryland's Eastern and
Western Shore residents had been among the richest, most sophisticated Chesapeake Bay tobacco planters. The state's metropolitan center, Baltimore, had
been in the take-off phase of urban development, economically and artistically.
In ensuing years, no southern and few northern cities would grow so fast.

In the entire antebellum period, no southern craftsman would produce anything as glorious as Baltimore's late eighteenth-century Hepplewhite furniture.
The style, closer to English conceptions than to colonial cabinetry to the north,
was refined with an exquisiteness of line and an intricacy of inlaying foreign to
plain New England. The sophistication of Baltimore's nonslaveholding artisans
meshed with tastes of their delighted customers, the slightly Anglicized, ultra-
elegant gentlemen who kept 10% of the urban population enchained.

By the 1850s, Maryland's creativity was flowing into different endeavors.
An important social experiment involved ending slavery without removing
blacks. On the eve of the Civil War, Maryland's absolute number of slaves was
under 100,000, down 14% from 1790. Her relative percentage of slaves was
under 13%, down almost 300% from 1790. Her free blacks almost outnumbered her slaves.

The slave labor system was especially waning in booming Baltimore, the
South's largest and the nation's third largest city. Baltimore's 25,000 free blacks
contrasted with the city's 2000 slaves. Artistry, like the changed black population, now served a crude new industrialism. No more solitary eighteenth-century cabinetmakers could be found, crafting a little gem of a Hepplewhite sofa.
Instead artistic creativity exuded from huge shipbuilding factories. Here the
world-famed China clipper was built to serve an increasingly nonslaveholding
world economy. No city in the South and few in the nation milled so much
flour, finished so much tobacco, distilled so much liquor. Every other southern
city whined about colonial dependence on "vulgar" northern capitalists. Baltimore, thanks to the mighty banking firm of Alexander Brown and Sons, loaned
excess capital to Yankee vulgarians.[11]

Mid-nineteenth-century conversations in the city's lavishly furnished Victorian drawing rooms sounded hardly different from Victorianism, free-state style. Baltimoreans pointed out proudly that while some of Maryland's slaves had been sold south and a few had been sent to Africa, more had been freed to remain in Maryland. Freedmen had proved that slavery was counterproductive. Capitalists preferred "the well-trained free black, subject to dismissal for misconduct," to "the slothful slave, who has no fear of loss of place."[12]

Entrepreneurs with these attitudes allowed slaves some freedom. The most fortunate bondsmen hired themselves out, splitting wages with masters and slowly saving to buy freedom. Why was Baltimore the most flourishing southern metropolis? Because, to hear Baltimore's titans tell it, only Baltimore had cast off slavery's restrictions on capitalism. If that view of capitalism sounded more like New York's than New Orleans's—well, which southern city was most successfully chasing New York?

More rural portions of elderly Maryland sounded more southern than Baltimore. Among large tobacco planters lining the Chesapeake Bay's Western and Eastern Shores, percentages of slaves and attitudes about bondage were less changed from the eighteenth century. These titans enjoyed superb eighteenth-century Georgian architecture and elegantly appointed Hepplewhite drawing rooms little different from those still to be found in Tidewater Virginia—and once found in Tidewater Baltimore.

Eastern and Western Shore magnates, like planters everywhere in more northern portions of the older South, occasionally pleased a sympathetic visitor with talk about freeing slaves, under right conditions. For now, they found conditions wrong. They talked of residing in an exposed outpost of slavery, of living too close to Yankees who aided fugitive slaves. How was border slavery to last, they wondered, if blacks only half enslaved had to dash but a mile to freedom? A few planters, enraged about runaways, sought re-enslavement of free blacks. That proposition, like Missouri slaveholders' resolve to capture Kansas, indicated that *if* slavery was doomed in Border South not-so-black belts, its demise could come only after a terrific struggle.

– 6 –

Travel northward from Baltimore to the free states was simple, too simple from a southern diehard's perspective. But the better trip, for those who wished to grasp southern complexity, was to complete the southern circle by journeying back to the Border West. Just as traveling between New Orleans and Charleston illuminated east-west differences within the Deep South, so traveling between Baltimore and St. Louis clarified east-west differences within the Border South.

The westerly route out of Baltimore, like the northern, was easy, almost too easy to be southern. Instead of antiquated Deep South modes of journeying, railroad transportation in the most northern South was modern, efficient, a Yankeefied dream.

Southern Yankees in Baltimore had realized the dream. Baltimoreans, anxious to cash in on America's westward thrust, had been determined to rival New York, with its fine canal system, and New Orleans, with its splendid Mississippi River system, as entrepôt of the new West. The only way, for a city commanding the constricted Patapsco River, was an avenue of iron out to western waters.

Not even the title of the railroad—the Baltimore and Ohio—quite caught the imperial dream. Baltimoreans indeed deployed tracks to the Ohio River: to Wheeling and to Clarksburg in western Virginia, then again to Cincinnati. But from Cincinnati, tracks were also constructed out to St. Louis, collecting port of the upper Mississippi Valley. From the banks of the Patapsco, dreamed audacious Baltimoreans, they could dominate the Mississippi.

Construction of the Baltimore and Ohio commenced in 1830. The railroad, 1500 miles long with the same gauge throughout, was completed in 1857. Customers could speed from the Atlantic to the Mississippi in slightly over two days. Down in the Deep South, meandering from the Mississippi to the Atlantic via many railroad companies had taken a long week.[13]

The terrain and people along the Baltimore and Ohio did not seem overly southern. Less than 100 miles out of Baltimore, the iron horse sliced inside the rugged green Allegheny Mountains. This vast mountainous locale segregated western Virginia, eastern Kentucky, and eastern Tennessee from planters who thought themselves the South.

Isolated mountaineers regarded strangers with a suspicion recalling slaveholders'. They also often looked upon slaveholders with a distaste rivaling Yankees'. They sometimes threatened to attack slavery, if slaveholders perpetuated white men's political inequality in state governments. They continually promised to seize arms, if slaveholders tore down *their* beloved Union.[14]

Up at the Wheeling, Virginia, terminus of the Baltimore and Ohio railroad spur, this least southern argument was most omnipresent. Wheelingites, at the geographic latitude of Pittsburgh, warned that if despots wanted tyranny over blacks, they must stop tyrannizing whites. Slaveholders in eastern Virginia, so it was angrily claimed, contrived to restrict white democracy in the state out of fear of the nonslaveholding majority. Slaveholders down South, so it was more angrily claimed, continued to manipulate the Union out of fear of the national nonslaveholding majority. Tyrants, so far as Wheelingites were concerned, could keep their "niggers," if whites could keep Union abroad and gain freedom in Virginia. Or, in other words, Wheeling was neutral about slavery *if*—if slaveholders did nothing to protect minority power, state and national, against that great god: white egalitarian republicanism. Or, to sum up the conclusion Virginia slaveholders came to: if the large minority of black-belt counties dared lift a finger for slavery, the large minority of mountain counties might slap on northern handcuffs.

– 7 –

The few border slaveholders in the mountains, sharing with nonslaveholders a region where slavery was waning and considered dispensable, cared more about other matters. Their occasional talk about slavery always began with affirmations that the subject was no outsider's business—and sometimes ended with whispers that insiders might terminate bondage, under the right conditions. Those whispers indicated yet another time that, in a section-wide perspective, slaveholders' problem was within as well as without their class—that different geographic regions led to different upper classes with different views of upper-class futures.

The difference between squires in the most northern South as opposed to titans in the more southern South concerned whether bondage was temporary or permanent in *their* area. Few in the South's most northern reaches believed that slavery in the most southern South would ever end. But even fewer borderites could conceive that their locale would remain enslaved forever.

Strategies for ending enslavement changed as one went west in the Border South. The ideology no less than the terrain shifted when the train left the mountains and invaded the midwestern plains. Border Southwesterners had little use for the Maryland-Delaware conception that blacks could be freed without removal, and not much more enthusiasm for the idea of removing blacks to Africa.

In Kentucky and Missouri, heretics urged a legislative decreee of future emancipation. Slaveholders, sensible fellows, would beat the deadline by selling or moving slaves southwards. On the appointed day, neither slaves nor blacks would remain. Free whites would pour into a lily-white midwestern mecca.

The western border establishment favored a less heretical way to drain slaves elsewhere. A governmental declaration of future emancipation, so the Kentucky-Missouri "proslavery" crowd believed, would impose on nature. The Upper South should instead continue to sell slaves slowly, naturally, down river. Then over many decades, the Lower South would be the only slave South—and the only South with blacks.

Whether border Southerners preferred to sell slaves southwards or to enact future emancipation or to dispatch blacks to Africa or to control blacks without slavery, almost all whites agreed on slow termination, without outside acceleration. This consensus left no room for William Lloyd Garrison's notion of immediate abolitionism. But the border consensus had no space for Robert Barnwell Rhett's notion of immediate disunion either. In its slaveholder ideology, as in its geographic position, the Border South was a world between.

– 8 –

After travelling around the many Souths, what survived of first impressions that *a* master class dominated *a* South? Plenty. Even where bondage was waning, slaveholders endured. Masters still lashed serviles in barely-enslaved Delaware and in half-free Maryland. Beyond this manumitting corner of the South, slavery's termination was called conditional on blacks' removal. Few hustled to hasten removal. African colonization was a dribble. Slave sales southwards still left many enslaved northward. Decrees of future emancipation floundered in state legislatures. When outside agitators proposed speedier terminations, borderites objected. The South was *a* South in the most crucial consensus, an agreement that Southerners must unhurriedly decide the South's fate for themselves.

Southerners divided, however, on goals and tactics. In Upper South relatively slaveless areas, few hoped to perpetuate bondage forever. In Lower South black belts, few agreed about how to perpetuate the Peculiar Institution. South Carolinians and Southwesterners were like those Deep South railroads running towards nary a connection. Even if the South's feuding tropical domains could permanently unite in the same uncompromising campaign for slavery, ideological, political, or military, their less tropical outposts might compromise in Congress or desert on battlefields.

Despots have a classic response to insufficient unity and commitment. Where consent softens, coercion hardens. Many travel memories suggested that slaveholders could coerce fellow citizens. Whites were sometimes lynched. White legislatures were sometimes gerrymandered. South Carolinians and eastern Virginians urged that perpetuating black slavery required constricting white republicanism. Missouri ruffians turned Kansas democracy into a half-dictatorial fortress.

Another stream of travel recollections, however, indicated that dictatorial imposition on whites had limits. Virginia squires were not successfully stonewalling against a more democratic legislature. Virginia mountain folks were threatening to attack dictatorship over blacks unless slaveholders surrendered aristocratic control over whites. Lower South dictators had no dictatorial power—little power of any sort—over far-off Border South regions with different priorities than perpetuating slavery. The big question was whether authoritarians' modes of social control, half-democratic, half-despotic, could consolidate an ill-connected and sprawling realm, in some spots passionately for slavery—and in some spots content, in a passionless way, to watch slaves dribble away.

PART II

SOCIAL CONTROL

IN A DESPOTS' DEMOCRACY

Let us keep the focus on relationships between despotism and democracy, for that oddity made the late antebellum South especially peculiar. Collision between one of the nineteenth century's most advanced private despotisms and one of its most advanced public democracies defined much of the national debate between northern Republicans and the southern Slavepower. Partially democratic, partially despotic modes of social control also established the Slavepower's power—and lack of power—over its own section.

According to the myth, an impassable racial line separated undemocratic control of blacks from democratic control of whites. New South, New West slaveholders loved that myth. In the spirit of Tennessee's Andrew Jackson, racist egalitarians argued that authoritarian domination, when restricted to other races, intensified equality among whites. Blacks had to be coercively mastered. No white needed a master.

Old South, Old East aristocrats had less use for the color line. In the spirit of South Carolina's John C. Calhoun, these dominators urged that "mere negro slavery" could never sufficiently consolidate ruling-class reign. Rather, independent men of wealth must master all sexes and ages and classes—and races too.

Despite these clear-cut theories, Southern rulers confusingly mixed their regimes. Dictatorial coercions, supposedly reserved for black slaves, corroded democratic persuasion among whites. Egalitarian persuasiveness, supposedly reserved for white citizens, conditioned authoritarian impositions on blacks. Control from above ultimately was neither altogether democratic nor altogether despotic on either side of a blurred color line.

Mongrelized modes of domination sometimes yielded invincible sway over both races. That was so particularly in the Deep South. Compromises between dictatorial remorselessness and democratic permissiveness also sometimes yielded more vulnerable control over slaves and citizens than slaveholders thought safe. That was so particularly in the Border South.

Some edgy Border South leaders eventually demanded that the national republic bolster anti-republican control over blacks—and sometimes over whites too. The resulting national impositions on both races arguably violated color lines between democracy and despotism in the nation no less than in the Slave-power's section. Out of that provoking argument, Abraham Lincoln's Republican Party—and a nation's Civil War—would grow.

CHAPTER 3

Mastering Consenting White Folk

Frictions between democracy and slavery, inescapable in the nineteenth-century South, have proved more escapable elsewhere. The Old South's acute form of the conflict occurred at a unique time and in a peculiar place. In the American nineteenth century, not republicanism per se but an increasingly egalitarian form of republicanism had to be reconciled with slavery, that most unequal of human institutions.[1]

Masters found the reconciliation difficult in the most personal sense, for their two regimes demanded opposite ruling personalities. Egalitarian republics required leaders to play unassuming convincer. Enslaved plantations required elitists to exert overbearing coercion. The egalitarian and elitist inside the same skin often popped out in the wrong realm. Elitists who trespassed onto egalitarians' turf were especially resented among white folk inside black-belt neighborhoods.

– 1 –

Behind the schizophrenia of the elitist as egalitarian lay a shift in human thought about the source of virtue and thus the personality of right leaders. Eighteenth-century Anglo-American Enlightenment theory, like centuries of pre-Enlightenment Western ideology, presumed that the best men should govern and that the governed, whether citizens or slaves, should defer. All humans were assumed to be born equal, including equally emotionally unsteady. Control of passions required long training in enlightened abstractions. Only a few "natural aristocrats" were up to the training.

Republics were thus precarious affairs. Conspiracies to seize power and patronage abounded. Checks and balances between governmental branches helped forestall civic vice. Civic virtue helped more.

Virtuous leadership required financial independence. Dependent poor folk naturally sunk into selfishness and conspiracy. Lesser sorts should thus be selectively barred from voting and altogether barred from holding office. Independent gentlemen armed with civic virtue could alone elevate dependents and save republics.[2]

These elitist assumptions made rule over both slaves and citizens compatible acts of the same eighteenth-century persona. The few natural aristocrats must rationally guide those lesser. The many natural non-aristocrats must willingly defer to those better. Both civic virtue and virtuous plantations depended on wisdom from above and deference from below.

The nineteenth-century Age of Romanticism was founded on a countervailing wisdom: that all humans were born with innately wise instincts. Virtuous insight now was presumed to come not from academic training but from instinctive feelings. Common men with common sense were republican noblemen. Overeducated elitists were civic enemies.

These changed assumptions menaced black slavery. Blacks, even if allegedly inferior intellectually, arguably shared the greater human gifts: right hearts, right intuitions. Harriet Beecher Stowe and the romantic abolitionists of her age seized just this proposition.[3] Worse, egalitarian assumptions sanctioned the sway of ever larger nineteenth-century nonslaveholder numerical majorities, nationally and in the South too. How could imperious slaveholders command a nation and section eager for unpresuming rulers?

The color line provided a freshly consolidated answer. The nineteenth century's newly rampart racism read blacks out of the new biological equality. Civic virtue now required superior racial genes. The slaveholder must now defer to virtuous white citizens but dictate to degraded black noncitizens.

The South's more intractable elitists, continuing to see black slavery as only part of patricians' rightful dictation to all lessers, scorned this partial surrender to egalitarianism. The lie that humans were created wise and wonderful and equal, they believed, promoted the nonsense that slavery must be abolished, that independent men of property must court dependent men impoverished, that nothing in law or constitution should preserve hierarchy from the mob. These old-fashioned commanders, especially powerful in coastal South Carolina and eastern Virginia, stood for saving civic virtue the eighteenth-century way: through the reign of those with the financial independence to be virtuous.

But beyond the oldest South, poorer whites found such elitist republicanism jarring. Their annoyance usually led rulers over blacks to stress the equality of all whites. Race-based slavery, like class-based slavery, nonetheless remained unperfected until well into the 1850s. Even then, neither the great racial proslavery writers, Nott and Cartwright, nor the great class proslavery writers, Fitzhugh, Hughes, and Trescot could altogether keep the realms of the elitist and the egalitarian quite straight. In the Age of Romantic Egalitarianism, the natural outcome of slaveholding democrats' peculiar position was contradiction and confusion over many aspects of right rule, including whether to strut before white folk lesser.

The slaveholding strut was at once natural and counterproductive among white folk in black-belt neighborhoods. Masters' personal intimates, whether wives or children or nonslaveholding neighbors, saw for themselves the source of imperial attitudes: slaveholders' awesome power over slaves. Usually, Massa was all-powerful judge, jury, and jailer on his property. The state rarely intervened, and only when slaves were unconscionably brutalized.[4]

If the state had little coercive authority over masters, the church had none. In Latin America, European kings often empowered Catholic clerics to govern irresponsible slaveholders. Latin American clergymen used that power but rarely. Still, North American clergymen possessed only the classic democratic weapon over despots: to convince.[5]

Private despots' sweeping force lent credibility to their cherished title: MASTER. Few humans, however, master life. Forces beyond our control usually overwhelm us all. To master oneself, to master others, to be master of all one surveys is so unlikely as to make the very concept suspect.

Southern masters' self-esteem, their self-respect, their very survival swung on legitimacy of title. They would *master* infuriating slaves, *master* neighbors and wives, *master* the mistaken North, *master* a Western world moving against mastery. They would be the word. The world would be theirs.

But in their egalitarian republic, they could only master slaves if *their* master, the white majority, concurred; and the majority of nonslaveholding males, however much in awe of the great man of the neighborhood, wished him to treat them as equals. Slaveholders could have more instinctively fulfilled that wish if all slaveless white males had been independent yeomen. Some desperately poor whites, however, ate mud to ease vicious intestinal pains from pellagra. More than 20 percent of white farmers in black belts, owning nary a slave or an acre, were tenants on slaveholders' estates.[6] Other nonslaveholders were on Massa's payroll, or objects of Massa's charity, or users of Massa's cotton gin. Such dependency easily led to patronization.

Even slight condescension could hurt, for southern folk neighborhoods were tight little worlds. A Southerner, if asked to describe his primary allegiance to others, would not likely have said that he was above all an American or a Southerner or a South Carolinian or even a resident of Colleton County. Rather, he was proud to be from Whippy Swamp. A scale of community so tiny maximized cults of personality. Planters intimate with folks, black and white, could epitomize Max Weber's classic category of those who gain right to rule through personal charisma.[7]

Commoners relished the master as charismatic egalitarian. It felt ever so good to be treated as The Man's equal; and in a black-belt neighborhood, nonslaveholders had little economic reason to attack slavery. Rich and poor grew the same crops for the same market. They utilized the same merchant, whether they shipped little or much. Nonslaveholders sold slaveholders extra grain.

Slaveholders ginned nonslaveholders' cotton. Landowners rented landless tenants a few acres. Planters advanced poorer folk a few dollars. Folks were so materialistically intermeshed as to make, at least economically, for one folk neighborhood.[8]

The term "folk," denoting blood relations, was accurate. Nonrelatives in tiny clusters of folk not only cared about each other in the manner of relatives but were often somehow related. Marriage between cousins was ubiquitous. When mothers survived almost yearly childbirths, families were huge. When mothers succumbed, fathers selected a new bride—who produced huge families or succumbed in turn. Between first cousins and second cousins and stepcousins and cousins of stepcousins, a planter had hundreds of relations. Family interconnections so extensive, inside locales of rural intimates so small, created a norm of treating neighbors as if they were, well, folks.[9]

Scholars have a useful label for (white) folks' political ideal: herren*volk* democracy. Neighborhoods of white folk, committed to treating each other as equals, were equally committed to keeping black folks unequal.[10] The herrenvolk southern neighborhood may have been more passionate about white egalitarianism than the northern. Black-belt whites had before their eyes the essence of deviation from independent equality: black slaves.

Unequal dependency also seemed more degraded here because equality looked more achievable. The ruling class, as Southerners sometimes defined the concept, was composed not merely of large planters but of all slaveholders. A poor man with one slave was as much a slaveholder as a rich man with twenty; and twice as many Southerners owned one as owned twenty or more. Equally important, many nonslaveholders expected to own a black someday. A slave characteristically cost less, usually very much less, than a thousand dollars. It was as if every twentieth-century American who owned or expected to own 20 shares of AT & T considered himself a member of the ruling class.[11]

The apparent ease of entrance into the upper crust made failure to do so more galling. The uncomfortable fact remained that most nonslaveholders never became slaveholders, indeed that many tenants and wage earners never became land owners. Amidst minuscule clusters of folk who considered dependency "nigger" and slaveholding achievable, independent slaveholders did have to be careful not to patronize lessers.

Conditions of class encounter often highlighted dependency. Upper and lower classes most often came together not at egalitarian political barbeques but through unequal economic transactions. Neighborly acts such as sharing cotton gins or lending a few dollars could strengthen white brotherhood. But sometimes the lordly said no. Then, lessers never forgot the degradation. Alexander Stephens, when young and poor, was turned down after one little request. He was "fill[ed] with mortification and a due sense of my humble dependence. There is nothing worse than to ask and be refused." Even planters who handed over several charitable dollars, after spending all day taking care of black dependents, easily slipped into feeling they were taking care of white unfortunates.[12]

Paternalistic feelings bred patronizing behavior. Poor farmers who enjoyed economic favors did not enjoy feeling like objects of lordly charity. A Scottish traveler could tell that rich and poor were not "upon an equality—far from it; —for if a man is poor, there are a hundred and fifty ways in which he will feel it." Poorer guests wandering stiffly and ill-at-ease through James Hammond's parlors, while the South Carolina squire silently cursed at their poor appreciation of his paintings, exemplified the point.[13]

Race as a bond between white classes was both a promising and a precarious way to reconcile not-so-equal whites. Racial emphases widened the ruling class to include not merely all slaveholders, whether they owned one black or many, but all males with white skin, whether they owned any. All white men were equally responsible for keeping all blacks unequal.

That racist stance yielded psychological boons. In a system where all whites were supposedly equal, white failures could always glory in being better than "niggers." Furthermore, all whites, whether worse or better on an economic scale, were equal on society's most important scale: skin color. Elitism and egalitarianism could indeed co-exist when racial bases of elitism eased wounds from economic inequality.

Still, racially as well as economically, discrepancies between ideal and fact intruded. Just as some whites had inferior possessions, so some blacks had superior positions. To nonslaveholders, the most galling so-called inferior blacks were black slaveholders. William Ellison of upcountry South Carolina, for example, a master of mechanical engineering, owned his neighborhood's largest, most complicated cotton gin. This free black also owned 63 slaves and 800 acres in 1860. His slaveholdings put him in the top 1 percent of Carolina planters. Six free blacks in Louisiana owned more bondsmen than Ellison did. One owned 152. Another was worth $250,000. These absurdities, as the color line defined the absurd, were exceptions to free blacks' usual hand-to-mouth existence.[14]

Free blacks themselves, an anomaly according to the color line, were not so exceptional. A quarter-million of them, 6 percent of the southern black population in 1860, lived in this land where freedom was supposedly reserved for whites. Free blacks in many black-belt neighborhoods were economically better off than some (supposedly superior) whites, especially than "poor white trash" eating mud to ease pellagra.[15]

Masters more than winked at these ruptures of the color line. They bored other holes. Slaveholders often let (supposedly inferior) black drivers command slaves instead of hiring (supposedly superior) whites to oversee. Yet a master who considered dirt-eating whites trashier than slaves and white overseers worse rulers than black drivers had to proclaim all these white fellows equal members of the ruling class.

Slaveholders' contorted ideology showed difficulties in maintaining the egalitarian pretense. Masters defending mastery kept implying that slaveholders were better than nonslaveholders. Slavery, they often bragged, beneficently prepared masters of blacks to command whites. Then weren't slaveholders better rulers than nonslaveholders?

Slavery, they often reiterated, beneficently created a leisure class, with time for the more worthwhile pursuits of life. Only blacks could bear the tropical heat; only whites could create art and literature. Then weren't slaveholders living more worthwhile lives than tenants and yeomen out slaving in the sun?

Our slaves, they often claimed, permanently work for paternalistic masters, while wage slaves temporarily work for selfish capitalists. Wage slaves could be laid off. Chattel slaves would be forever indulged. Then weren't (supposedly superior) southern whites who worked for wages worse off than (supposedly inferior) black slaves? Indeed, shouldn't (supposedly equal) white wage earners become slaves of (supposedly equal) white employers?

That natural outcome of class-based proslavery ideology was scarcely out the mouth before slaveholders had to make the words unnatural. Planters who congratulated themselves on leisure for finer things of life had to squander leisure and finery on barbecues for plebeians. Patricians proud of being a polished leadership class had to lead huzzahs for the "unpolished". Paternalists, having called wage earners wage slaves, had to tell wage-earning Southerners that slavery had nothing to do with class and everything to do with race. And nonmasters, sensing they were considered inferior, had to overlook times when masters flaunted superiority.

Contradictory cultures love scapegoats. To counter the strain of haughty elites at home, Southerners had the benefit of haughty moralists abroad. Abolitionists called slavery wrong because *all* men, black and white, were created equal. That version of egalitarianism assaulted poor southern whites' one basis of superiority. Abolitionists also declared all southern whites ethically inferior. Moral lightweights, as these Yankees weighed the commodity, included every soul who allowed slavery to continue.

Such attacks united the attacked. When sneering at outside meddlers, masters, confused by being more-than-equal egalitarians, at last could legitimately act every inch the magnate. When storming against northern moralists, tenants and employees and tiny farmers and dirt-eating wanderers, uncomfortable about being less-than-equal egalitarians, could at last act every inch the equal. The resulting defensive defiance, at least in black-belt districts, customarily gave proslavery zealots bountiful support. The further result, at least when Yankees were particularly holier-than-thou, was that even white-belt residents damned outsiders enough to create illusions that *a* South flourished.

– 3 –

A portrait of the scene when rich man met poor would make abstractions about class relationships more vivid. Descriptions of such encounters in the sources are frustratingly few and incomplete. The most tantalizing bit of a portrait occurs in that source so often the best, Mary Chesnut's South Carolina diary. On October 1, 1861, the wealthy belle reported attending "one of Uncle Hamilton's splendid dinners—plate glass, Sèvres china, and everything that was nice to eat." After dinner the gentlemen, while out smoking on the piazza, chatted with one McDonald, a well-digger who had been scratching for water while Uncle Hamilton's guests feasted. "Apparently," reported Mrs. Chesnut, "Squire McDonald," as she contemptuously called the mechanic, "was most at his ease of all. He had his clay pipe in his mouth. He was cooler than the rest, being in his shirtsleeves, and leaned back luxuriously in his chair tilted on its two hind legs, with his naked feet up on the bannister."

Chesnut and her cousin, Louisa, observing at a distance, sniffed that "the mud from the well is sticking through his toes." Was their elegant host "court-ing the country" nonslaveholder a little "*strong*?" After all, as "a free white man," the mechanic had power to deny patriarchs' political office and to dam-age slaveholders' Civil War. More likely, the women speculated, the muddy fellow was present on the mudless piazza because "he is a near-relation."

Relation or not, remarked Cousin Louisa, "see how solemnly polite and attentive Mr. Chesnut is to him."

"Oh! that's his way," responded Mr. Chesnut's wife. "The raggeder and more squalid the creature, the more polite and the softer Mr. Chesnut grows."[16]

There the curtain comes prematurely down on Mrs. Chesnut's scene. Impor-tant questions remain unanswered. Have we seen acted out the drama of ten-sionless egalitarians, where those lesser on the social scale are not "apparently" but truly the most comfortable, having commanded the attention of those higher? Or have we seen staged a faintly strained scene, where slightly resentful lessers wiggle toes a trifle much at slightly condescending aristocrats?

Everything depends on whether the lower-class star of the charade shared the female diarist's view that not all was serenely comfortable in this perfor-mance. Could the well-digger have missed the ladies' scorn? Could the employee have been unaware that Mr. Chesnut insultingly (to an egalitarian) changed his tone when addressing a fellow with muddy toes? If "Squire" McDonald caught undercurrents of condescension emanating from gentlemen dressed to the heels, was the shoeless pipesmoker who was "apparently" utterly at ease actually playing the egalitarian charade a little "*strong*"?[17]

The sources cannot definitively answer for the usual reason: articulate lead-ers leave behind many words, while inarticulate masses largely can be seen only in wordless gestures. We know that the articulate suspected the inarticulate's loyalties. We know that suspicions climactically escalated into worry that Abra-ham Lincoln might organize a lower-class Republican Party in black-belt neigh-borhoods, unless the upper class secured secession. We know that poor men mocked such distrust by enthusiastically fighting the rich men's Civil War for a couple of years. Only in the war's grim last two years did massive lower-class desertion somewhat justify longstanding upper-class distrust. We know too that long after the Civil War, some nonslaveholders bitterly remembered that "all who owned as much as one negro seemed to feel that they were in a separate and higher class" and that "Negroes and poor white men did the work" while slaveholders enjoyed "hunting and fishing and riding around" and that planters "didn't treat white men any better than slaves."[18] Many aspects of upper-class, prewar articulations seem capable of nourishing such latter-day class resentments. But had resentment always been an undercurrent, even when the classes met most harmoniously?

The question of how masters and nonmasters really interacted and really felt about the interaction is so important that historians, despite qualms about guessing, have livened the literature with speculative images. Historians' standard guess features poor farmer, dressed in shabby best, off to celebrate nuptials of some wealthy cousin fifth-removed. That imagined scene feeds on awareness that in a world infatuated with familial domesticity, thin family connections overcame thick class barriers. That is why cousins Louisa and Mary speculated that the well-digger had familial right to occupy his betters' porch.

But this historian found another scene more often hinted at in the sources. Nonslaveholders seem to have most often prepared for rendezvous with those richer not by dressing for weddings or digging for wells but by piling wagons with unbaled cotton and unhusked corn. A rough road usually wandered through such a worker's few acres. A tumbling fence sometimes lined the muddy yard. The single-room cabin was usually weathered and crude, mud chinking logs, windows absent, everything gray in this land of black and white. Inside, drab belongings looked packed in—fireplace roaring for cooking despite the heat, jagged pots and pans, children's quarters in the loft, adults' mattresses on the floor, spinning wheel for wife, breakfast table laden with cornbread, fat bacon, strong black coffee. A torn poster sometimes splashed color on a wall. Revival tracts often were heaped on the packing case.[19] *Like dem ribbons wife has in her hair,* I fancy the owner of such grim premises thinking as he bid his lady farewell.

The route to the plantation passed several slaveless little farms. Down the road, a redneck worked alongside several slaves on a cramped spread. As the land turned richer, river plantations loomed. In the field, slave women, supposedly picking cotton, seemed to stand still. Bright bandanas, more colorful than whites' hair ribbons, shielded their heads from the sun. *Monstrous lazy niggers,* rednecks instinctively reacted. *Puttin' on shows. Do hev to dress purty.*[20]

The plantation's driveway occupied more acres than most yeomen's cornfields. Slave cabins lined a side street. Each cabin, with adjoining garden, resembled rednecks' rude comforts. The Big House ahead was capital of another world.

The plantation owner came out, waving howdy. For almost an hour the two neighbors drawled on, comparing views on politics, weather, cotton. Once they had wasted too much time to be Yankees, they proceeded to a little business. The slaveowner agreed to gin the yeoman's cotton and to buy his corn. *Glad to help,* affirmed the squire. *No way all folks can buy Yankees' durn gins. Folks gotta share. Otherwise Yanks gonna bust us all.*

The yeoman, preparing to depart, thanked his benefactor a bit profusely. Regretting the tone, he struggled for another. *What you gwine do this afternoon?* he asked.

Oh, reckon this day will be like most days, the planter answered. *Be directin' blacks and greetin' neighbors. In between, guess I'll read up yonder where it's cooler. Way nature meant it. Whites readin' and conversin' and directin' and blacks laborin' and sweatin' and servin'. Couldn't pay a white man to tolerate that blazin' sun. Nor could I pay a white man's daughter to suffer my boilin' kitchen.*

The yeoman choked back rage. He stood the sun. Laboring fueled his dreams. *Ain't nothing nigger about sweatin',* he thought. *And ain't nothing nigger about my darlin' cookin'.*

The planter's voice drawled on, slicing through such angry thoughts. *Gonna be readin' one of them fanatic's books today. Full of isms up north— anarchism and free-love ism. Crazy meddlers, think they're better than other folks. Think they can tell us how we should live. Think they can make niggers as wonderful as themselves.*

The yeoman nodded, resentments swerving. *Glad you gwine read it,* he said. *Don't know which I hate worse, a fanatic or a nigger. How'd you like to hev a nigger steppin' up to your darter?* [21]

The slaveholder, relieved, smiled and waved farewell. *Wonder why he gave me that dark look,* the planter mused while watching the yeoman drive off. *Had a funny look when he first came too. Thank heavens these fellas are usually friendly. With a whole world invading, white folk can't be fussing. Gotta move mountains to be brothers.*

– 4 –

And brothers they were in a black-belt neighborhood, even if the brotherhood had elements of strain. Both the brotherhood and the strain were also apparent in rural villages, most Lower South neighborhoods' only excuse for an urban locale.

Every southern county contained at least one village. Each village featured courthouse, church, and country store. Usually a jail, a newspaper, and a tippling house added to the scene. Down Main Street, doctors, lawyers, and merchants offered professional services, while white laborers and black mechanics hustled after customers. On the outskirts, politicians harangued at barbecues. Nearby, revivalists warned of Jehovah's wrath and cocks gouged each other amidst cheering gamblers. At Court House Square, men gathered to chaw and gossip.

Sometimes, villages had permanent populations in the dozens. Occasionally they contained numbers in the hundreds. A few burgeoned to become state capitals or fall-line towns. Always they offered an escape from rural loneliness amidst rural surroundings. Town houses, usually white, columned, and Greek in style, looked like plantation mansions. Cow pastures usually fringed on Main Street. Main Street sometimes contained more chickens than people. Here bucolic country and urbanized cluster merged to form an archetypal southern folk community.[22]

Middle-class village leaders—lawyers, physicians, editors, merchants, bank-

ers, preachers—usually enthusiastically supported the rural regime. Some
owned slaves. Some planned to buy a few. All had everything to lose by espousing antislavery.

Lawyers, for example, ascended by praising the plantation. More lawyers
than planters achieved political prominence in the Old South. Nothing would
have changed if planters had held every office. In black-belt areas, anti-abolitionist speeches paved the road to political success. Political prominence paved
the road to legal success. Oratory, that southern art, gave a fellow notoriety
and assured potential clients that he was a persuasive pleader. Business came
most often from slaveholders—a dreary, profitable round of land titles, wills,
estates, and slave sales. No third estate existed, as in eighteenth-century France,
whereby groups of laborers or farmers hired lawyers to fight seigneurs. Everything dictated that lawyers help unravel slaveholders' tangles and help bolster
the planters' regime.[23]

So it was with other members of the village bourgeoisie. Doctors treated
plantation slaves. Merchants marketed plantation staples. Editors sold proslavery newspapers. Bankers financed slave purchases. Proslavery clerics
preached at slaves and slaveholders. The village bourgeoisie stood resolutely
behind rural seigneurs.

Alas for a planter's peace of mind, village white laborers were not so resolute. White blacksmiths, drayers, bricklayers, carpenters, stone masons, and factory laborers were wage slaves, in a society which declared wage slaves worse
off than chattel slaves. Like yeoman farmers, white employees worked with
their hands, in a world which assumed whites worked with their heads. Unlike
yeoman farmers, wage laborers had to compete with two classes of black men
who, according to proslavery theory, should not have existed. Free blacks often
were village craftsmen. Nominally enslaved black mechanics, allowed to hire
themselves out, lived like freedmen after paying off owners.

Both black groups benefited when white laborers charged high prices, lest
white work be thought "nigger" work. Some blacks prospered so much that
they bought slaves. Other resourceful blacks, as Governor William Gist of South
Carolina noted, hired "white men to work under their direction."[24] Such she-
nanigans turned the southern world topsy-turvy. If all whites were superior and
all blacks needed a master, how could blacks best whites?

Protests were predictable. Petitions bombarded legislatures. Some constituents urged enslaving free blacks. Others demanded that "hiring out" be banned.
All petitioners sought to bolster white psyches by ending black triumphs. "It
must be distinctly and universally understood," Governor Gist answered, "that
the white is the governing race"—even when blacks display superiority "of
intellect." Only drastic action, argued a group of Virginians in 1851, would
"destroy the great cause of jealousy which existed between the nonslaveholders
and slaveholders." If the legislature failed to act, the Virginians warned, "the
day is not far distant when the mechanics and nonslaveholders, generally, will
demand the total expulsion of the negroes from our State."[25]

Legislatures did fail to act, partly because free black labor was valued, partly because white mechanics hardly verged on revolution. Few saw a way to toss millions of slaves out of the United States. None saw benefits from allowing more free blacks to compete. So planters' prime antagonists in nearby villages agreed that blacks, if present, must be enchained.

That was small comfort to nabobs sensing white laborers' resentments. The slavocracy knew that village wage slaves in plantation areas, like yeoman farmers and landless tenants and dirt-eating vagrants, showed scarce tendency to opt for abolition. In a black-belt neighborhood, too many racial, economic, and emotional factors held back class resentments.

Still, the ruling class realistically wondered whether those who had little would always risk everything for those who had much. When the going got roughest, would nonslaveholders' loyalty to slavery measure up to slaveholders'? Would the poor always prefer massive confrontations to mild compromises? Or would danger, disease, deprivation, death cause nascent class resentments to fester? Not heresy, not even disloyalty, but rather unmeasurable degrees of commitment made masters a little uneasy about black-belt neighborhoods as they moved towards encounter with remoter, more lily-white neighborhoods.

- 5 -

Because dominance over whites in black-belt neighborhoods depended on personal contact, masters feared inability to command far-away white-belt neighborhoods. Large planters possessed no charismatic influence over distant nonslaveholders. Rich squires could not gin far-off folks' cotton or lend them nickels or buy their kernels or offer them tenancy. The wealthy could not join remote rednecks in controlling blacks; most residents outside black belts rarely saw blacks. Overweening masters possessed none of their customary controlling techniques over those whom it was most necessary to control.

White-belt neighborhoods were folk communities too. But here white folks were more equal, black folks more absent, and the sale of staples less omnipresent. These more self-sufficient whites, when they thought about that other South, mostly prayed that "niggers" and "nigger tyrants" and debt and banks and cotton, cotton, cotton would not overwhelm their communities. They further hoped that zealots north and south would not cause a civil war. If combat came, alien southern and northern armies might invade, destroying nonslaveholder neighborhoods in battle over far-off slaves.[26]

Very occasionally, relatively slaveless areas assaulted those far-away planters. In thickly populated Upper South cities, white "wage slaves" loathed having to compete for jobs with even a few black chattel slaves. On largely unpopulated Border South frontiers, slaves were too few to develop much of the land, yet plentiful enough to repel many potential white immigrants. Thus white-belt majorities, unlike most black-belt nonslaveholders, sometimes saw compelling economic reasons to drive slaves and blacks out. Equally important, white-belt poorer folk, unlike their black-belt counterparts, possessed neither huge black populations to control, nor dreams of becoming slaveholders, nor a large planter class compellingly resident. Most important of all, since even class differences compounded by geographical separation seldom led to all-out class warfare, remote white-belt areas simply did not care much about black-belt compulsions.

Such neutrality did not make for mastery. The Slave South's chances could be grim if half the South was indifferent about perpetual slavery. Influence over distant folk was a first necessity and a remote prospect for masters who needed to see fellows to control them.

The result of mastery contained—of Massa's very tactics of mastering geographically limited—was the classic bully. The slaveholding democrat, when locked in political contests, local or national, often imperiously demanded that other democrats yield. The tenor of the demand felt like dictatorship rampant on the wrong side of the color line. Masters' imperial attitudes had stirred up slight nonslaveholder resentments inside the black belt. When such masters sought to control white areas geographically far removed, haughty approaches really stirred up the folk. But what was a despot to do but bully when no master or "nigger" or color line was available to establish good old herrenvolk control?

– 6 –

The patriarch, having forced a little condescension on close-by neighbors and a lot of insistence on far-off whites, exerted his haughtier side still more often within his white family. Inside the familial circle as outside it, the color line did not distinguish equals from dependents. A wife was physically weaker and knew less about the world beyond the home. Children were physically smaller and mentally untrained. All were dependents, as dependent as slaves, more dependent than tenants. Such dependency beckoned the elitist rather than the egalitarian side of Massa's persona, even if the dependent was white and therefore "equal."

Yet elitism in white homes defied the same revolution in biological assumption which forced Massa to play egalitarian to poorer whites. Romantic feeling, when triumphant over rational abstraction, undermined the biological basis for domestic no less than political haughtiness. (White) women and children were born with right hearts too. In fact, the American mid-nineteenth-century romantic sensibility assumed that women were born with better Christian intuition than men.

South as well as north, female uses of that liberating assumption took two forms. A tiny minority of women, minuscule in the South, demanded equality everywhere, in political no less than in domestic government. If (white) male equality depended on equal intuitions, and if (white) females had the same or better intuitions, women should vote and should help abolish male mastery.

That alternative left slavemasters cold. They made the tropical South such an icy spot for political feminists that the most advanced ladies, South Carolina's Angelina and Sara Grimké, sought their unsouthern sort of equality up north. Not surprisingly for girls domesticated in the South, the Grimké sisters became exceptions proving the rule. For a time, the Grimkés "unsexed" themselves by giving public antislavery lectures. But upon Angelina's marriage, both ladies largely retired from politics. Their fights for equality became a long battle for control of the same domicile. When Angelina belatedly resumed her quest for nondomestic emancipation, she became a schoolteacher.[27]

The huge majority nationally and an almost unanimous South preferred female power, when exerted, restricted to home and school. Domestic feminists, whose leader was the New Englander Catharine Beecher, called women not inferiors in need of patriarchal guidance but rather superiors who must mold civilized youngsters. Beecher employed a version of separate but superior to urge matriarchal domestic dominance. Boys and girls, she believed, were born different. Females had deeper affections and better intuitions into the human heart. Still, the innately superior should not run for political office. Women should use their superiority to teach males. Home and school, once controlled, could command everything else. Women, ethical arbitrators of the domicile, could moralize boys and men and thus indirectly determine male decisions beyond the house.[28]

A later American generation would condemn this position as feminine surrender. The Old South sometimes savored it as female hegemony, in the right sphere. The southern cult of the lady raised wives, at least in theory, to moral rulership over the Big House. New romantic assumptions about children further crimped patriarchal domineering. Tots, now assumed to be born with right intuitions, presumably needed mother's tender nurture more than father's overbearing dictation.

Such deflation of slaveholders' domestic imperiousness partly reflected familial changes transcending the South. As the eighteenth turned into the nineteenth century and the Industrial Revolution proceeded everywhere in the West, larger and more impersonal factories and farms made the tiny household ever less important economically. But the economy's emerging cold impersonality made warm domestic firesides ever more important emotionally. Husbands and wives, parents and children hardly cherished each other any more than formerly. Familial affection, however, was now more the reason for the family's very existence, and that affection, in an Age of Romanticism, was expressed in more romantically effusive ways.[29]

The American twist on western familial change was to equate sentimental romanticism with parental permissiveness. Male parents especially found a softer domestic rule compatible with less overbearing egalitarian republican command. In past, elitist republican times, patriarchs had more often insisted that children obey. In less egalitarian nineteenth-century England, parents stuck to old insistences. English visitors to Jacksonian America found American children to be rude, bratty, defiant, disobedient, willful, indulged, spoiled, disrespectful—in sum the natural product of permissive disciplinarians. "Imagine a child of three years old in England behaving thus," wrote Captain Frederick Marryat in 1839, when reporting "one instance of a thousand which I witnessed:

'Johnny, my dear, come here,' cried his mamma.

'I won't,' cries Johnny.

'You must, my love, you are all wet, and you'll catch cold.'

'I won't,' replies Johnny.

'Come, my sweet, and I've something for you.'

'I won't.' . . .

'A sturdy republican, sir,' says his father to me, smiling at the boy's resolute disobedience."[30]

Slaveholders smiled at such scenes partly because permissive parenting could yield properly prepared masters. Slaveholders' need for willful heirs with the right convictions placed high premium on correct education. Cuffing boys into orthodoxy might produce little *white* slaves. Permitting lads to think anything might produce William Lloyd Garrisons. Warmly, affectionately, with as many soft words and as few harsh spankings as possible, slaveholding parents taught heirs to consent to orthodoxy. Here, Catharine Beecher's cult of gently persuasive matriarchs combined with America's cult of adorably aggressive children to mesh weirdly with patriarchs' desire for imperial little successors, assuming the lord thought the lady was raising the sons properly.[31]

Still, while changing intellectual, familial, and republican assumptions made patriarchal domestic dictatorship a little unnatural, specifically slaveholding patriarchs also found Beecher-style matriarchal domestic dominance very unnatural, especially when fathers thought mothers were raising heirs improperly.[32] New England, lacking slaves, also lacked the ideal of all-powerful patriarchs, especially awesome in the capital of slaveholder dominance, the Big House itself. The family lay at the heart of slaveholders' class-ridden theory of bondage as a model for male mastery of all races and sexes and ages. To planters who wished to defend more than "mere negro" slavery, the Big House exemplified patriarchs and dependents, superiors and inferiors, a hierarchical world with everyone in his or her place. Husbands as all-powerful and wives and tiny tots as all-powerless proved the perfect model against that supreme example of Yankee egalitarianism-run-amok: female antislavery lecturers "unsexing" themselves by telling males how to rule.

On the other hand, to racist egalitarians happy to base slavery on superior skin color alone, *white* females powerful in the Big House were altogether natural. From their domestic pedestals, upper-class women could influence familial governance in ways Catharine Beecher described, including criticizing how patriarchs raised sons. The fascination of southern upper-class family life is that women, like their men, were of two worlds and fluctuated between two personae.

Not everyone fluctuated. The class-infested side of southern gentry existence embodied in that word "master" led many women towards obedient docility. Even southern women inwardly harboring slightly feminist attitudes characteristically saw outward passivity as their duty. Gertrude Thomas of Georgia, for example, who presciently saw male chauvinism's cruelties, shunned talk about what she saw. One day, she "made use of some remark jesting," and her fiancé, Jeff Thomas, "looked up with *such* a look of sternness! It startled me! and for a *moment* my old feeling of pride overcame me." Feeling "the blood gush to my cheek," she "almost said too much." But "Thank Heaven! I did refrain, and now I love him more." Several years later, Mrs. Thomas was thanking "thee oh Heavenly Father" above all else for *"my husband,"* who possessed "just such a master will as suits my woman's nature, for true to my sex, I delight *in looking up."*[33]

Yet if class-based patriarchal elitism demanded that females look docilely up, race-based white egalitarianism invited moral matrons to speak up, particularly on child raising, whether His Majesty the patriarch liked it or not. When lordly elitists resentfully fought back against mothers' mastery, sparks could fly. Nowhere were marital sparks hotter than in lowcountry South Carolina, center of the most overweening male oligarchs, the very place where cowed wives should have most abounded.

Spats between Thomas Chaplin and his wife Mary provide a rich example. One day son Manny, aged two, "got into a very bad screaming & fretting" fit, including "trying" to throw "dishes & glasses off the table." The patriarch spanked the youngster. The matriarch "attempted" to "interfere & get him off," as was "generally the case." Thomas Chaplin, provoked, continued laying into Manny. Master would teach his boy to "obey me, . . . even if Mrs. C. gets vexed."[34]

Mary Chaplin, fluctuating herself between demanding that the patriarch rule and demanding her equal share of (domestic) ruling power, ultimately reduced the exasperated sometimes-master of the Big House to feeling like "*a very great fool . . .* in the management of children." Chaplin's wife constantly told him to *do* something about urchins. Then when he caught and punished a child, "very often . . . after some wrangling I am told (perhaps in the presence of the child) that I punished him unjustly." The patriarch, supposed to be absolutist judge and jury, considered himself judged "not fit to judge whether or no a child deserves punishment."[35]

Chaplin's overbearing exasperation was not singular in Carolina coastal Big Houses. You admit "I can be kind according to my notion of things, if you submit to the imposition of my will," stormed R. F. W. Allston to his wife. "When you suppose therefore that I am . . . subjecting you to my arbitrary will, you prepare at once to resist the imagined tyranny." The truth is, trumpeted this master accused of mastery, that "in respect of our domestic affairs and those things pertaining to your department particularly, I have for years past exercised no 'will.'" Whenever "I did offer an opinion, it was met too often by a ready counter opinion on your part." Now he "preferred" having "no will."

Allston, who condescendingly addressed his allegedly mastering wife as "my dear child," was hardly will-less. This patriarch here displayed that nervous fluctuation between imperial willfulness and affected will-lessness that occurred everywhere when The Man commanded dependents, alias equals. Allston displayed the same inconsistent dictatorial approach towards his children. "My son," wrote Allston with arrogant pride at being nondictatorial, "you speak of my commanding you to come home and you will obey." But "it is long since," bragged the patriarch, that "I have commanded you." See the world, ordered this allegedly noncommanding lord. When you grow tired of "its emptiness and unprofitableness, then come home and help us."[36]

Allston's words to his son, like the words to his wife, smacked of willfulness swallowed as distastefully as one swallows bile. Why, then, did the "master of all he surveyed" brag about not commanding? Partly because his sensibility was democratic as well as dictatorial—and democratic in a romantically egalitarian style. Partly because home was on the white side of the color line.

Mostly because Massa learned amidst his most intimate folk that egalitarian-style social control could be as effective and more popular than the elitist strut. Most sons came home again. Tiny tots might be slightly riotous, a little rude, a touch silly. But slight indulgences, a little warmth, a dollop of permissiveness produced sober, loyal, effective young heirs. The reward for years of thwarted authoritarianism was the successful transfer of authority itself. But domestic tension had abounded along the way when Massa had carried patriarchal presumption beyond the color line.

– 7 –

Family tensions that occurred when elitists defied racial limits were nothing compared with consequences of destroying racial purity inside the home. One domestic problem provoked such horror as to cause everyone to pretend that the horrible never visited their domicile. The charade, often played, rarely acknowledged, revolved around interracial liaisons productive of mulatto slaves.

The first commandment of racial slavery was that white commanders must not father bondsmen's children. Consequences of breaking that commandment swept beyond the plantation. The southern world abhorred a mulatto as nature abhors a vacuum. Life in Dixie was supposed to be black and white, despot and democrat, elitist and egalitarian, nothing in between. Mulattoes, the ultimate in-between, made a dubiously natural distinction altogether unnatural.

According to southern law, children inherited their mother's legal status. When mother was a free white and father a black slave, their child was free, no matter the color. When mother was a free black and father an enslaved black, their offspring was free, no matter the blackness. When mother was a slave octoroon (had one black great-grandparent in eight) and father a white, the offspring was a slave, although legally and physically white.

Such cases mocked color lines. Practical consequences were almost comic. Charlestonians, unable to distinguish between sun-tanned whites and fair-skinned blacks, required mulattoes to wear black veils. With this substitution of man-made cloth for self-evident traits, Charlestonians announced their natural order was hopelessly unnatural.[37]

The unnatural was all too natural. Ending miscegenation required separating the races. Slavery threw the races together. Master and slave lived together, worked together, walked together across sun-drenched fields. They bathed, clothed, nursed each other. Even cultural differences drew them sexually together. Black songs, dances, and prayers, creations of a folk relatively free of Anglo-Saxon puritanical repressions, set off geysers of white libidinal myth. For centuries, whites had whispered about blacks' allegedly inordinate passions.

Now, in this land of honeysuckle and heat, defenseless blacks were available. No need for lonely lustings or paying prostitutes. White teenagers—older planters too—could pluck forbidden fruit.

A nest of serpents marred this chauvinistic paradise. A young aristocrat's wild oats, unlike those sowed with more difficulty elsewhere, matured on the family estate and sometimes in the family house. Out of sight, out of mind was not possible where the proof resided in the home.

Such close quarters were not so uncomfortable elsewhere. In Latin American Big Houses, where the "stain" more frequently occurred, the phenomenon seemed more natural. Less strait-laced Latin codes of sexual behavior help explain the difference.

North America's greater sense of taboo also came from the greater incongruity of slavery within egalitarianism. Latin American regimes, lacking principles of democratic equality, had no need for color lines to justify coercive inequality. Democracy for whites, despotism for blacks—such inhumanly rigid formulas were irrelevant in Iberian worlds that considered equality to be unnatural and coercion the human norm. Only the North American despot as egalitarian needed to pretend that tan was black and that the natural was unnatural.

No one knew then—no one will ever know—how often blacks and whites sexually interacted. Even in an age almost innocent of birth control, most sexual liaisons produced no children. Even at a time when census figures were growing more precise, statistics on mulattoes were especially inaccurate. Even when census-takers counted mulattoes correctly, they had no idea who fathered slaveholders' slaves.

No matter. Numbers had nothing to do with the felt horrendousness of this "problem." Because the taboo was more loaded, fewer mulattoes served in North America's white parlors. Because each mulatto seemed more unnatural, North American obsession exceeded anything troubling Latin American homes. Some North American planters spent a lifetime praying that their wives did not correctly suspect them of fathering black children. Others forever suffered from mates' mistaken suspicions. With miscegenation a forbidden subject, wives could not accuse. They could but peer. Only in her diary could Mary Boykin Chesnut of South Carolina protest that "*Rachel* and her brood make this place a horrid nightmare to me. I believe in nothing, with this before me."[38]

The worst of slavery, continued Mrs. Chesnut's protest, is to "live surrounded by prostitutes." Husbands "live all in one house with their wives and their concubines, and the mulattoes one sees in every family exactly resemble the white children—and every lady tells you who is the father of all the mulatto children in everybody's household but" her own. These "she seems to think drop from the clouds. . . . My disgust sometimes is boiling over."[39]

The myth of the plantation lady was partly designed to keep resentments from boiling over. Whatever slavery did to male morals, so the argument went, enslaving blacks kept white women pure. Slavery protected fair-skinned damsels from defilement by rape, from degradation by seduction, from despoilment by interracial marriage. With purity guaranteed, plantation mistresses could be moral queen of the home.

Some ladies reveled in their triumphant position. Others disliked the empty triumph. Despite hosannas to family and womanhood, they could merely protest when black families were separated, when pregnant black matrons were ordered to work, when their own children grew up amidst moral contaminations.

The *man*-made myth, thoughtful ladies knew, made women's victory insulting as well as empty. By proclaiming that slavery guaranteed female virtue, chauvinists announced that female virtue, supposedly superior to men's, actually needed male guarantees. Southern men in fact doubted that ladies elevated on moral pedestals were moral enough. Stock white male libidinous fantasies starred enormous black male organs. Masters knew, from underground whispering, about "free-issue" children born to white belles and about white husbands stumbling upon wives abed with blacks. Without slavery to elevate white ladies and shackle black men, how many more pedestals would blacks kick down?

That question led to lynchings. A black supposedly looking with lust upon white ladies risked castration or decapitation. As for a black who tampered "with a white lady," bragged Southrons, "we shoot him down like a dog."[40]

Southern belles, when swept up in occasional hysteria about rape, sometimes appreciated lynchings. But white ladies resented males' constant quaking about female virtue. Mrs. Chesnut ridiculed "a magnate who runs a hideous black harem and its consequences under the same roof with his lovely white wife." The hypocrite "poses as the model of all human virtues. . . . Fancy such a man finding his daughter reading *Don Juan.* 'You with that unmoral book!' And he orders her out of his sight."[41]

This double standard could mar any lady's life. That not-so-feminist protofeminist, Gertrude Thomas of Georgia, like Mary Boykin Chesnut of South Carolina, was raised to be a belle. She picnicked on cake, ham, and biscuit. She skipped off to town for kid gloves and velvet. Her head spun over social punctilio. Should she dress in morning or aft? Who would hand her down from the carriage? Whom would she adore, defer to, marry, join in recommencing the cycle?

Jeff Thomas. There was the perfect catch. Jeff was rich and strong, poised and prominent. His and Gertrude's was a fairybook marriage.

The fairy tale ended quickly. After a miscarriage, Gertrude Thomas winced over pregnant black women slaving under the inhuman sun. If I had "the sole management of a plantation," she wrote, "pregnant women should be highly favored. A woman myself, I can sympathize with my sex, whether white or black."[42]

Mrs. Thomas particularly sympathized with white women damned for interracial sexual intercourse, an offense "which in a man, *very* slightly lowers, and in the estimation of some of his *own sex* rather elevates him." She was "the greatest possible advocate for woman's purity." But if some "harangues directed to *women* were directed" to males who needed haranguing more, "the standard of morality might be elevated."[43]

"A singular little circumstance" indicated whose moral declension bothered her most. One day a darkish stranger knocked. Mrs. Thomas, uncertain whether the stranger was a mulatto, asked him in. Mr. Thomas, equally uncertain, discreetly asked the stranger where he voted. The fellow whispered that blacks could not vote. Gertrude inquired which parent was black. His father, replied the mulatto, was black. His mother was white. "Had he replied the other way," Mrs. Thomas wrote, "*I* should have been tempted to have insulted him." To Gertrude Thomas, white sisterhood took precedence over white men's hypocrisy.[44]

Mrs. Thomas writhed under male hypocrisy. Her house servants included Lurany, a light-skinned unmarried mulatto, and Lulah and Amanda, Lurany's children and "as white as any white child." They knew "little more of the Negroes than I do." They could be sold at any time to any "brute." Who had sired these white slaves? Her father? Her husband? "Between a husband and wife," she wrote, "this is (or should be) a forbidden subject." She had perhaps "rashly ... staked my own reputation upon" her husband's. Should *"actual experience"* prove his reputation unreputable, "then would be dissolved" all dreams "of happiness upon earth."[45]

And so, exploded Mary Chesnut, "wives and daughters," affecting "purity and innocence," pretend "never to dream of what is as plain before their eyes as the sunlight. And they play their part of unsuspecting angels to the letter."[46] In this duplicitous area of southern life, Gertrude Thomas and Mary Chesnut might have added, husbands and wives, mothers and fathers, prayed that somehow, some way, the color line was not as fictitious as it seemed.

– 8 –

Domestic distress such as Mary Chesnut's and Gertrude Thomas's illuminates an emotionally loaded color line inside a schizophrenic regime. Democrats and despots had such different personae and modes of social control that without the color line to separate Dr. Jekyll, elitist coercer, from Mr. Hyde, egalitarian persuader, regimes became uncomfortably confused. Mulattoes did not so much breach the line as smash it, causing everyone to pretend that nothing so catastrophic had happened.

The unusual catastrophe highlighted more usual, less catastrophic tensions. The color line nowhere impassably held back human instincts unnaturally bifurcated. Whether planters were informing rednecks that white necks could not stand the sun, or patriarchs were ordering ladies to coerce unconsenting children, the confusion of the authoritarian with the egalitarian bothered white folk.

But the dictator as egalitarian concealed the haughty manner and honored interracial taboos often enough so that white folks in black belts were almost mastered. Wives' and neighbors' resentments, until deep in the Civil War, were no worse than signs that whites' consent to slavery might someday soften, most likely first in white-belt neighborhoods. Worry about that possibility, one might imagine, should have caused slaveholding democrats to step with relief over the color line, where nothing of democracy, consent, or equality should theoretically have confused elitists' coercion of blacks.

CHAPTER 4

The Domestic Charade, I:
Massa's Act

Slaveholders' very title for North American slavery raised still more questions about whether the color line could segregate the democratic from the despotic. Democratic despots called their form of enslavement both the Peculiar Institution and the Domestic Institution. The despotism was allegedly peculiar because domestic. Unlike all-powerful authoritarians elsewhere, these autocrats supposedly governed all dependents as family folk.

That color-blind formula dissolved color lines. White and black dependents lived in the same domicile under the same patriarch. Slavery was right rule because patriarchs treated impersonal black property as personal white intimates.

Historians, dismissing slaveholders' claim that white families and black slaves were ruled in comparable ways, have proposed just about every other comparison to explain the Peculiar Institution. North American slavery has been measured against Latin American bondage, Russian serfdom, Nazi concentration camps, medieval manors, and American prisons.[1] Southern slaveholders would have protested that all those supposedly comparable dictatorial institutions have nothing faintly domestic about them. To understand our peculiar regime, they would have insisted, one must take the domestic nature of our Peculiar Institution seriously.

The strength of that insistence tells us much about this regime. With dictators throughout history available to them as models, these titans were drawn to their own homes as exemplar of proper dictatorial sway. Yet their homes were precisely the realm where the nineteenth century's more romantic, more permissive, more egalitarian sensibilities worked to soften coercive imperiousness and summon consenting obedience.

Could coerced slaves be even remotely likened to assenting dependents in the Age of Romanticism's newly permissive home? These patriarchs' favorite domestic charade was meant to demonstrate an affirmative answer. Paternalists sought to make their own performance as benevolent fathers, their wives' performance as moral matriarchs, and their slaves' performance as consenting children achieve the total verisimilitude that is possible only when actors are one with their act.

Parallels in ways of controlling white homes and black slaves turned out to be close enough so that charade as reality was sometimes possible. Because control over white family members and black slaves was also so different, the cast's performance more often violated the script. The largest reason why this charade about the benevolent father, the moral matriarch, and the consenting black "boys" swung erratically between credibility and absurdity was that the paternalist swerved between nurturing and coercive versions of paternalistic control.

– 1 –

Masters' softer paternalism was exemplified in that ubiquitous Massa-slave charade. The charade, more omnipresent here than in any other Western Hemisphere slavery system, was performed with particular insistence when strangers visited a plantation. The charade was also often staged, significantly, when visitors were not present, when only Massa clapped for the cast.

According to the script, Massa was no jailer or guard or brutalizing tyrant. He was a paternalist—a nineteenth-century American paternalist. Familial control in the American Age of Romanticism meant an emphasis on education, on affection, on maintaining order through a minimum of punishment and a maximum of persuasion. The patriarch, whether with slaves or children, would not haul out the lash at every transgression. He preferred to teach wards to obey next time.

Blacks were scripted as consenting children. Serviles could occasionally be so silly or stupid or slovenly as to require a cuffing. But because slaves understood that the order imposed from above was benevolent and caring, cowering before violence was not necessary to secure domestic tranquility.

The charade was like a long-run play. As years passed, performances improved, for the star of the show increasingly rejoiced in the plot. As the South moved towards the Civil War, benevolent patriarchy became a partially self-fulfilling prophecy. The more romantic egalitarianism took over in the Big House, the easier slavery was to defend as an extension of domestic consent. The more proslavery theory was raised into self-conscious awareness, the more a planter's self-esteem depended on treating his people like family members. With slave prices soaring and the African market forbidden, only fools risked their slaves' life and health. With plantations rather isolated and slaves living in Massa's house, only masochists would provoke slaves' revengeful fury. Seldom have men had so many reasons to transform grinding tyranny into genial control.

The Man's stake in transforming coerced slaves into consenting dependents helps explain why in the American South black population increased far faster than occurred under slavery elsewhere.[2] Masters and mistresses lavished hours nursing sick slaves, cultivating black friendships, plotting nice holidays, buying pretty trifles. Overseers received instructions never to whip in a passion, always to serve nourishing meals, ever to tend to slave health, never to violate black women. When planters returned from vacation, they relished slaves' homecoming celebrations. When blacks dropped postures of loving "boys" after emancipation, patriarchs were genuinely shocked.[3] Their incredulity measured the depth of their long-standing wish that caring paternalists and grateful servants were more genuine than actors in a phony charade.

– 2 –

But the difficulty of attaining slaves' consent had always been obvious in masters' contrasting heavy-handed punishments. Their brutality subjected slaves to waves of horror never laid on white children. Their racially selective violence was neither peculiar tyranny nor a recognizably domestic deterrent, not at least according to their own conception of nineteenth-century domesticity.

Manuals of instructions, published and unpublished, on southern plantation management constantly prescribed relentless punishment to secure black servility.[4] Masters were instructed to separate the innocent from the guilty scrupulously. They were then instructed to punish the guilty automatically. Patriarchs were told to issue a word, then a blow. When orders were evaded, punishment must follow. When disobedience persisted, punishment must escalate. When contrariness continued, the contrary must be sold. Systematic whippings and chainings and selling bad actors down river were not acts of cruelty but of kindness. Blacks, realizing the slightest misstep automatically yielded brutality, would willingly obey.

Concentrated authority, continued coercive instructions, was as crucial as systematized punishment. Only Massa's will must sway will-less slaves. Dependents must know no other morality or commandments. Slaves must never leave plantations. Blacks must never learn to read or write. Serviles must never hear black preachers. Easily confused slaves must learn only one man's unconfusing commandments.

White communities, continued the tyrannical scenario, must keep slaves' world closed and bondsmen's eyes focused on Massa. Runaways must be hunted down, then whipped into awareness that Massa was inescapable. Nightly patrols must jail slaves who were strolling the countryside or buying from Yankee peddlers. Discussion of antislavery must never occur in the hearing of slaves. Guns and books must never reach slave hands. The community must tar and feather anyone doubting slaveholders' legitimacy.

This coercive model, unlike the domestic model, invites comparisons with totalitarian regimes in every place and century. Tyrants know that if power from above appears limited, those below will test the system. By emphasizing a closed regime, relentless punishment, an all-powerful coercer, the *theory* of plantation management became a little Bible on tyrannical social control.

The southern theory of systematic coercion, even when practiced unsystematically—especially when carried out uncertainly—meant that slaves intimately experienced terror. Slaveholders' domestic analogy must never hide that simplest truth about the so-called Domestic Institution. Slavery, to the slave, partly meant DON'T!, lest one suffer beyond endurance.

Slaves could resist violent deterrence, assuming the risks looked tolerable. They could run away, should they wish to chance snarling dogs and racist rednecks anxious to reduce them to "nigger." They could drink with Yankee peddlers, if they wished to brave the drunken rage of nonslaveholding patrols. They could praise the Lord, black style, should they wish to risk whites busting in, determined to teach "niggers" that no "nigger" God existed. They could break tools and burn barns and slit throats, *if* thoughts of retaliation were endurable.

Slaves contemplating defiance, for example, had to rise above fear of confinement in ball and chain. They had to overcome images of squeezing iron causing flesh to swell, while preventing skin from stretching. Expanding fluids could only press against nerves that were already screaming. A day in irons, in solitary confinement, no food, water, or companion to offer solace—that image did often deter slaves from saying No! to Massa.

Images of beatings, more than memories of irons, deterred blacks from provoking that frightful will. Being whipped, compared with being ironed, might be less horrid because more quickly over. But beatings were more frequent and more instantly agonizing.

A white's slashing blow seldom relied on unaided muscle. Paddles supplied the most dreaded leverage. These long rough wooden clubs, with screws stabbing out one end, cut many times with each administration. Equally notorious were "cow hides." These leather straps were hammer-thick at the striking end, elastic-thin at the swinging end. The thinness whipsawed the thickness into a stinging sledgehammer.

Most often employed was some version of the lash. When most stinging, the lash was a cat-o'-nine-tails: a small handle attached to "a large rope of many strands—the strands unraveled, and a knot tied to the extremity of each." One blow from this "cat" ripped open nine wounds. More merciful and mercifully more common were ropes with fewer strands, all woven together to concentrate leverage on the hard knot at the end.

Whatever the whip, offending slaves were stretched on the ground or up on toes. The lash then sliced open naked skin pulled taut. A customary dose was 39 strikes, "well laid on," crisscrossing the back and snarling at the face with a hiss accentuating the blow.

As Frederick Law Olmsted described "the severest corporeal punishment I witnessed at the South," a slave girl named Sall was ordered to pull up her clothes and lie on her back, private parts exposed. The overseer flogged her "with the rawhide, across her naked loins and thighs." Sall "shrunk away from him, not rising, but writhing, groveling, and screaming, 'Oh don't sir! Oh please stop, master! please sir! please sir! oh, that's enough master! oh Lord! oh master, master, of God, master, do stop! oh God, master, oh God, master!'"

After "strokes had ceased" and "choking, sobbing, spasmodic groans only were heard," Olmsted asked if it was "'necessary to punish her so severely.' . . .

'O yes sir,' answered the lasher, laughing at the Yankee's innocence. Northerners 'have no idea how lazy these niggers are . . . They'd never do any work at all if they were not afraid of being whipped.'"[5]

Sall escaped easily, compared with a perennially disobedient slave. The most dreaded deterrent was neither squeezing irons nor slitting lashes but sundered marriages. Systematic coercion demanded that the systematically disobedient be systematically sold away. My gang, bragged a disciplinarian, has "the reputation of being very orderly," for "I always make it a rule to sell every runaway—and they are fully aware of this."[6]

The threat of selling blacks to the *nouveau* Southwest was slaveholders' new nineteenth-century weapon. Here as in so many ways, an institution growing "better" because less physically horrid was growing worse because more psychologically brutal. Earlier, when already settled Atlantic Coast regions comprised almost the whole South, eighteenth-century masters quite regularly strung up, decapitated, or otherwise mutilated disobedient slaves. That unfamilial deterrence not only seemed unfamily-like but unnecessary in the nineteenth century, when threats of sales to brutal lashers half a continent away could terrify blacks.[7] The threat of being sold down river meant the prospect of separation from wives, offspring, friends—from cherished personal ties that made a slave's lot more endurable. Rumors that frontier slavemasters were the most unendurable brutes increased the deterrent's horror.

Fear, so critical to smashing black resistance, had little to do with how often the frightful was deployed. Slicing open backs with 39 lashes occurred "only" two or three times per plantation per week. Ball and chains were "merely" employed two or three times a month. Selling blacks down river, away from relatives and friends in the quarters, was "seldom" used more than two times a year per plantation. Creditable horror, however, does not require incessant repetitions.[8] The brutalized Sall must be frozen at the center of historical consciousness because every slave every week witnessed a compatriot's lacerations. Slaves performed primarily because terror was an unending image. Their world was in part a dismal dungeon.

– 3 –

But The Man no less than his "boys" shuddered at slavery as a form of jail. Revulsion against despotic violence, instinctive to despots who were egalitarian republicans too, mitigated against constantly terrorizing the willful into willlessness. A Nazi concentration camp guard visiting a plantation would have been outraged that his sort of tyranny lacked his sort of tyrant.

His scorn would have delighted paternalists, whose version of domesticity did not invite members of caring homes to lock doors and windows against each other or to beat each other into wimpering zombies or to sell each other from each other. Because slaveholder violence gave way often enough to inconsistent permissiveness, observers could almost—almost—believe they were watching a version of mid-nineteenth-century parental control.[9]

Thus, instead of the expected patrol out every night, a puzzled visitor usually found none. A South Carolina patrolman who complained that "for two years past" he had never been called up "for an hour's duty" had performed the usual service.[10] Normally, patrols combed forests and plains only during insurrection panics. Once hysteria subsided, patrolmen retired and let blacks roam.

Slaveholders often winked at widespread roaming. Instead of forcing blacks to marry on the plantation, Massas often allowed blacks to travel many miles to see mates living in other Massas' quarters. Some slaves married free blacks. A few free blacks owned slaves.

Slaves were no more sealed off from northern free whites than from southern free blacks. Instead of barring slave rendezvous with Yankee peddlers, masters customarily paid scant attention to such meetings. In fact, by allowing slaves to sell backyard crops and by failing to monitor the cash flow, masters helped provide slaves with some heady ideas. Freedom-loving Yankees, glad to sell cheap whiskey, and free blacks, glad to expand black connections, provided opportunities for a clandestinely open experience no properly closed system could tolerate.

A more common open experience involved black religious meetings. Most slaves had some contact, and many slaves had massive contact, with supposedly outlawed black congregations. Blacks often could celebrate their gospel with their leader preaching their version of the Word. Nat Turner, for one, freely preached his insurrectionary version of Christianity.

Many blacks had access to Turner's other weapons. Bondsmen who spent evenings cleaning guns for hunting with Massa in the morning were not unusual. More unusual was the scene in Austin, Texas, in the summer of 1854, where blacks strolled streets at all hours, "without license from their masters, and sometimes carrying . . . loaded firearms." Strollers were even seen "in daytime, near our corporate limits, with their pistols testing their skill—at targets." "At this moment," warned Franklin Elmore of Charleston, South Carolina, on May 30, 1849, the U.S. Arsenal, with its "cannon muskets, rifles, swords & ammunition is here, *in this City,* without a Sergeants guard, in reach of our negroes."[11]

Charleston's careless approach typified a sloppy regime. Masters and mistresses left doors unlocked, windows open, guns unguarded. Discussions of abolitionism continued in slaves' presence. Everyone pretended not to notice blacks, who pretended not to notice the conversation. Newspapers containing antislavery were strewn around the house. Everyone pretended that domestics could not read a syllable. Whites also usually pretended not to know that literate slaves presided over black religious meetings at night.

The greatest deviance from a closed system occurred not in the occasional freedom whites permitted blacks at night but in the inconsistent discipline masters imposed by day. Planters no more punished blacks after every transgression than patrols imposed curfews every night. If a black planted cotton crookedly, he might be whipped. Then again, he might be warned to try harder. If a black claimed not to hear orders, he might be cuffed. Then again, orders might be repeated. If a worker slowed down, he might be kicked. Then again, he might be given a rest. If a black filched cotton or briefly vacationed or broke hoes, he might be sold down river. Then again, he might be scolded. It all vaguely resembled permissive white parents, clamping down on offspring one moment, letting up the next.

"I had quite an explosion yesterday with my negroes," Linton Stephens wrote to his brother when describing a typical plantation scenario. One favorite slave accused another "of cutting and hauling off my wood for sale." The accused confessed and accused another, who also confessed. What do you suppose I did? Linton asked. "I felt very much like knocking the whole deceitful set in the head." According to his instructions, he should have lashed. Instead, he scolded. After all, culprits were family servants, and "they all pretend great regard for me."[12]

Linton Stephens's most cherished slave, like most slaveholders' pet bondsmen, lived in the Big House and daily ministered to personal whims. The loss of such a servant was like a death in the family. "My house servant Mary is about to die," Linton wrote his brother in 1861. "Never, never did the death of so humble and lowly a personage affect me so profoundly." Mary, "one of the very few truly *grateful* people," was always "humble and lowly." She paid "kindly and careful attention to all the wants and comforts of me and my children." Her "gentle, sorrowing, sympathizing pity" for me revealed a "refinement . . . you would scarcely think a negro capable of. . . . I feel her loss," Stephens concluded, "all the more on account of the very humility of her nature and the lowliness of her station."[13]

A paternalist such as Stephens was not going to beat family servants every time wood was filched. With blacks as with whites inside the familial Big House, he preferred to scold and nurture and teach. He would mold grateful dependents with a minimum of terror and a maximum of guidance.

That governing wish for a social control akin to a parent's created a cruel kindness. Slaveholders demanding obedience but uneasy about systematic terrorizing deployed a psychological tyranny perhaps more terrible than physical brutality. They taught black "boys" that black was ugly. The dominant cultural orthodoxy, that inferior blacks forever needed white masters, was not reserved for white classrooms. Racism was also employed to make blacks grovel before whites.

A powerless slave cannot escape a degree of self-contempt. Whites ever sought to increase black self-revulsion by claiming that "niggers" were "black-assed," as the revealing phrase went. The "black-assed" were stupid and slovenly, innately needing parental guidance.

White churches taught the same unholy lesson. In the mid-nineteenth-century years, masters erected ever more chapels for their slaves and hired ever more local clerics to give special sermons. Resulting clerical performances often emphasized that Christ commanded the ruled to obey.

Much of the way masters deployed secular power, like the way they deployed religious power, was aimed at securing "boys'" willing consent. Ceremonies at patriarchal homecomings, where planters returned home bearing gifts for all "childish" dependents, black and white, in exchange for cheers and protestations of how sorely "father" had been missed, were calculated to be seen as a vote of confidence in familial government. Ceremonies at Christmas time, where gifts were ostentatiously given and thanks for being such generous masters ostentatiously received, could easily be viewed as annual paternalistic re-elections. Granting of small garden plots and wandering privileges were little bribes by masters aimed, in part, at gaining recognition as good "fathers." Permissiveness when "darkies" misbehaved, or firings of unpopular overseers, or sympathy for ailing slaves, or willingness to suspend incredulity when slaves might be pretending to be too sick to work—such benevolent conduct pleased the democrat in the dictator.[14]

Insofar as consent rather than coercion could secure tolerable work and loyalty, permissive paternalism amounted to brilliant slave management. But black "boys," like white lads, needed a tap now and then. "If Cuffee won't work," ran the standard line, "you must make him work. . . . Of course we are to treat the slave as a human being, thoughtfully, wisely, humanely, even tenderly, but that very treatment implies an occasional flogging."[15]

"Cuffee," the name here given the recipient of "occasional flogging," was another revealing southern code word. Like "master," "the people," "boy," "black-assed," and "Domestic Institution," "Cuffee" pointed to the psychology behind the language. "Sambo," posterity's conventional name for master's most desired domestic, was a term less commonly employed in the Old South. "Cuffee" better conveyed the desired meaning. Cuffings, as opposed to whippings or beatings or lashings or smashings, bore connotations of "softer" physical reminders. One had to cuff naughty Cuffee now and then. But social control was more genial when Cuffee could be educated into needing no more cuffings.

With that giveaway word Cuffee, Southerners again broadcast distaste for social control through violent deterrence. At the same time, with their sometime deployment of violence beyond cuffing, these patriarchs broadcast their inability to live up to the preferred domestic system. The essence of their "parenting" could only be inconsistency: disobedience only sometimes met with brutal lashing, patrols only sometimes sent out, a paternalism, in short, based on erratic employment of coerciveness.

– 4 –

Even if control over white children and black slaves had been as similar as pretended, up-to-date paternalists would have had to be inconsistent disciplinarians. Modern parents know that permissive child-raising does not produce docile dependents. Test, test, test is the central theme in an inconsistent parent/child relationship. When children are not sure what punishment will ensue, they experiment. A quasi-permissive domestic authority responds with erratic swings between indulging cute misbehavior and smacking bratty bottoms. Slaveholders who were hauling out balls and chains one moment and enduring feigned ill-nesses the next were, in part, akin to modern parents.

But slavery could no more precisely resemble nineteenth-century familial control than could domestic servitude be comparable to despotic prisons or Nazi concentration camps or medieval manors. The racist base of slavery itself under-cut a color-blind domestic analogy. Patriarchs could not, did not, love members of a despised race remotely in the way they adored their own white children. Democratic parents' ability to teach consent rests in large part on mixing love with persuasion. But men treated like inferior souls will not consent as volun-tarily as children treated like prized treasures.

That matter of color led to a second difference between child-raising and slave-managing. Young Massa was raised to be a mature adult. Cuffee was trained to be an eternal child. The reward of growing up to be masters gave sons incentive to consent, eventually, to norms of indulgent masters. The horror of never growing up gave slaves only the disincentive of succumbing to eternal hard labor.

Still another difference between fathering and mastering was the matter of numbers. An intimacy akin to paternal rule requires tiny numbers of depen-dents. A teacher sometimes gains intimacy with a class of five. A lecturer has a nodding acquaintance with an audience of hundreds. So, too, slaveowners could be intimate with omnipresent house servants. But planters could hardly love as their children seldom-seen field hands. Samuel Hairston of Virginia controlled over a dozen plantations and almost 3000 slaves. Stephen Duncan of Natchez possessed eight plantations and over 1000 slaves. Wade Hampton of South Carolina owned six plantations in several states and over 900 slaves.[16]

Such masters often personally mastered nary a slave. The most important taskmaster in many a house servant's life was not his owner, who added up accounts in the background, but the planter's wife, who administered the house-hold cuffs. The most important boss in many a field hand's life was not his master, whom he rarely saw, but his driver, a fellow slave. The most important superior in many a driver's life was not Massa, who was often off vacation-ing at the Springs, but a hired white overseer, who made no claim to benevo-lent ownership. Such impersonal bureaucracy mocked pretenses of familial intimacy.

The plantation bureaucracy operated unlike a family in that the "boys" helped dictate their own disciplinarian. When selecting drivers, masters had to select natural black leaders. A slavish drone without his peers' respect could not make The Man's orders inescapable. Once selected, drivers wielded power nat-ural to natural leaders but unnatural to innate dependents. Some planters allowed drivers to run entire plantations. No white, patriarchs thought, could manage so well. But they also supposedly thought that no black "boy" could manage anything. Some planters put drivers in charge of intricate sugar and rice machinery. No white, they thought, understood the sophisticated appara-tus. Yet they also claimed to think that no black could understand anything sophisticated. Some planters gave blacks license to transport crops miles down river to commercial depots. No whites, they thought, were such efficient and trustworthy agents. But they also allegedly believed that blacks were inefficient and untrustworthy. All those thoughts added up to uncomfortable realizations that independent patriarchs depended on their "boys" to shuck dependency and assume power.[17]

The case of William Pettigrew illustrates how much father-power could slip to mastered "boys." When Pettigrew was absent on frequent holidays, two black drivers, Moses and Henry, controlled his two North Carolina plantations. "What a blessing it is to have two such men [not boys!]," Massa exclaimed. Their "chief desire I think is to relieve me of as much burden as possible," and "to add to their own character as men of honesty, industry, faithfulness, & success."[18]

Although handing to Moses and Henry father's power to direct, William Pettigrew retained father's power to approve. "Remember me very kindly to the people," he wrote his drivers. "Their good conduct will be very gratifying to me." Those who misbehaved would "be disgraced in my estimation." They would betray "the good name of their home."[19]

When betrayal came, Pettigrew responded not by seizing the power he had abdicated but by slipping in permissive advice. At Christmas time in 1857, Pettigrew was bedeviled by Jack and Frank and Venus and Patience, who allegedly helped themselves to Massa's money and molasses. The thieving, Pettigrew believed, came partly because slaves frolicked at neighboring plantations. During his absence, he wrote to Moses and Henry, "it is my wish [not his command] that the people go from home as little as possible. If I were they," scolded the disappointed patriarch, "I would be ashamed." He was loath to "give a positive order [!], but . . . I wish yourself & the people at Dr. Hardison's & Mr. Murphy's to keep apart." With mixing and mingling, "there must ever be trouble. My idea [but not his order] is, stay at home." Two years later, Pettigrew was still handing a driver written "permission to allow such person or persons, as he may think proper, to go" anywhere from the plantation.[20]

Pettigrew's abdications might appear to be a textbook example of how not to master. Still, his bureaucratic system succeeded. It succeeded because it violated the South's textbook distinction between the "natural" superiority of white men and the "natural" inferiority of black "boys." White supremacists could cling to the "natural" by hiring white overseers to drive black drivers. But overseers, when a rung from the top of the plantation bureaucracy, undercut domesticity from another direction. They made paternalism dependent on the very sort of wage slave that domestic patriarchy had allegedly obliterated.

The South claimed superiority over the North in part because those who owned laborers supervised more familially than did directors interested only in payoff. Overseers sought the highest payoff. They usually owned nary a laborer. They were paid wages for a season. Cuffee was hardly *their* "boy." Serviles would be cuffed paternalistically only if Massa could make adoptive parents paternal.

Massa revealingly tried. Upon being hired, overseers were charged with mixing force and affection in the manner of the new paternalism. "Be *firm,* and at the same time *gentle,*" instructed the South's patriarchal Thomas Afflecks. On the "firm" side, remember that "the only way to keep a negro honest is not to trust him." Punish every dishonest disobedience "without listening to a word of excuse." On the "gentle" side, remember that "occasional rewards have a better effect than frequent punishments." Recall the desirability of dispensing with lashes entirely. Find exquisite balances between the times lashes are necessary and the times indulgence is preferable.[21]

Having tried to transmit their teetering sense of balance, owners had to depend on hirelings to keep teetering to a minimum. Just as William Pettigrew could not withhold power and still give drivers command, so patriarchs had to give paternalistic instructions and hope hirelings would patronize accordingly. Intricacies of overseers' everyday management—discovering whether a complaining slave was really ill, ascertaining who, if anyone, had stolen master's chickens, discerning whether the cowhide or a tongue lashing best fit the latest slave carelessness—all these decisions were difficult. Overseers, judges on the spot, could make master's benevolent instructions deceitful rhetoric or living truth.[22]

Or more accurately, overseers could not altogether master shamming blacks. Slaves, experts at tricking whites who supposedly knew them intimately, mystified supervisors who knew them not at all. Each overseer mystified by a "disobedience"—or was it a "childishness"?—had to decide whether to "be firm" or "gentle."

To make the domesticity analogy more doubtful still, the overseer as substitute parent had to satisfy not only "father" but also the head "boy." Overseers always had theoretical power to compel drivers. But drivers often had actual capacity to oversee overseers. Permanent drivers knew their gangs better than did transitory overseers; and masters cherished long-term head blacks more than short-term white supervisors. So long as drivers balanced the tightrope between loyalty to the Big House and sensitivity to the quarters, these "boys" could maintain more credibility with The Man than could a wage-earning overseer charged with making slavery unlike wage slavery.

Common field hands could also summon masters' power against overseers' power. Just as slaves indirectly helped choose black drivers, so they indirectly helped fire white managers. If slaves considered an overseer brutal or a previous overseer preferable, they could escalate pretended illnesses, intentional accidents, calculated carelessness. If the overseer merely begged and cajoled, crop production declined, and he was in trouble. If the wage slave whipped and whipped, slaves, led by drivers, sometimes complained to Massa.[23]

Some masters demanded that the people speed complaints to the Big House. An Alabama planter instructed his overseer that "each and every slave shall communicate to the master . . . his punishment, the quantity and cause thereof, the existence of any known immorality and the parties engaged in it." Big Daddy was not going to let outsiders abuse his "boys."[24]

When abuse occurred, patriarchs had a dismal choice. They could buy more lashes in the interests of more obedience. Or the owner might emulate James P. Tarry of Alabama in telling his overseer during the long hot summer of 1854 "to withhold your rushing whipping & lashing—for I will not stand it any longer."[25] Whichever side master backed momentarily, he could not tolerate crossfire constantly. To work another season, overseers had to be master psychologists, superb disciplinarians, superior agriculturalists.

Overseers were more often considered ordinary. Chattel slavery, while requiring wage-earning directors, damned wage slaves as degraded. The best men owned bondsmen. The best Southerners scorned a lifetime of being a hireling.

So the best overseers moved up to their own Big Houses, the ordinary plodded from job to job, and planters wailed: Overseers whipped too much. They whipped too little. They were too intimate in the quarters. They took too few pains to be likable. "Of all 'the curses of slavery,'" said South Carolina's James Hammond, "incomparably the greatest is the infernal necessity of having agents." His "stupid, perverse, heedless and thoughtless . . . prime ministers" were "lineal descendants I doubt not of Adam's first overseer—Cain." Black "scamps," added Linton Stephens, "will poach upon you if you allow them one inch of a chance—and then to crown it all they are eternally begging me for little favors and gifts . . . and all for the want of somebody to govern them."[26]

Massa governed too little. Overseers were as capable as the bureaucratic system allowed. Overseers' cursed presence illuminated the impossibility of huge plantations becoming intimate families. Their unending problems personified difficulties inherent in coercing adult "boys" into permanent childhood. Those paid wages to oversee a system supposedly antithetical to wage slavery were perfect scapegoats for a bureaucracy grown uncomfortably unlike a family.

– 5 –

Even if an impersonal bureaucracy could have been like a personal family, sales of "family friends" would have mocked the domestic analogy. "The people" were property as well as folks. Sometimes folks had to be marketed. Sometimes higher prices for individual slaves were so enticing that husband was sold away from wife, wife away from children, brother away from sister. Slave dealers were even better scapegoats than overseers for a partially anti-domestic Domestic Institution.

The Peculiar Institution was assuredly peculiar in that its property owners usually loathed those who transferred property. Agents, such as merchants and stockbrokers who help buy and sell prized property, are usually themselves prized. A handful of Old South slavedealers, such as Thomas Gadsden and Nathaniel Bedford Forrest, were cherished. But most slavetraders were loathed.[27]

Nothing was cheaper than contempt for agents who rewarded hypocrisies. No one was more hypocritical than a "father" selling his "boy." Nothing could be more anti-familial than breaking up slave marriages. Nothing could be more understandable than heaping blame on merchants who coldheartedly offered top dollar for separated people.[28]

Top dollar aside, domestic discipline sometimes mandated broken homes. By threatening to sell enslaved mates away from each other, masters meant to create such a fearful deterrent that slaves would obey and domestic relations would be genial. A single smashed slave family, while unfortunate, might create beneficent harmony on the rest of the plantation.[29]

But destroying families for financial reasons was not true-blue patriarchy. Planters, like most investors, often borrowed. Borrowers, when pressed, had to sell property at least disadvantage. Selling one prime fellow or "wench" was often more advantageous than marketing a group of mixed value. Furthermore, slaveholders, like most American heads of families, wished offspring to inherit the family fortune equally. Equal white division sometimes required dividing black families.[30]

Only a system with powerful personal codes could have so often overcome such powerful impersonal propulsions. Masters went to heroic pains (and they did think, significantly, their pains heroic) to avoid destruction of slave families. Many an heir accepted less so that an estate could be divided without dividing families. Louisiana barred the separation of small children from mothers. Late antebellum Alabama somewhat limited the iniquity. No abolitionist would have believed the number of times, in these two states and elsewhere, slaveholders avoided this ultimate monstrosity.[31]

Still, the monstrous did happen. No self-respecting culprit could avoid squirming over it. Documents illustrating slaveholders' discomfiture were strewn around the South. Whenever such letters are found, the finder becomes almost an unholy voyeur, intruding on a black victim's anguish that is almost unbearable. But undeserved empathy for the white victimizer is a prerequisite for understanding this regime. When black families were split, more than at any moment, the Old South's "domestic" form of slavery revealed its arrogance and hypocrisy.

Witness, for example, South Carolina's Thomas Chaplin in 1845. Chaplin, thrown heavily in debt by high living, saw that he must sell "ten prime negroes. . . . Nothing can be more mortifying and grieving to a man, than to select out some of his negroes to be sold—You know not to whom, or how they will be treated by their new owners, and negroes that you find no fault with— to separate families, mothers & daughters—brothers & sisters—All to pay for your own extravagances."

Two days later, Chaplin was "glad" to be finished with this "most unpleasant thing I have ever had to do. . . . The Negroes at home are quite disconsolate, but this will soon blow over. They may see their children again in time." For the next few months Chaplin spent many hours threatening to duel those who questioned his honor. The acutest questioning came from within. The wider torment was the South's.[32]

The most excruciating expression of that torment, and one of the most priceless of the southern documents this wanderer has stumbled upon, was written far from slave-obsessed South Carolina, up in half-enslaved Maryland.[33] T. D. Jones of Princess Anne County, having sold his slave woman, Eliza, away from her daughter, Jenny, received from the mother a request for the child. The mother's request, with its implicit moral indictment, struck the patriarch as insufferably presumptuous. "I profess to be a christian," Massa Jones wrote back to Eliza, "& have the happy and comforting assurance that I am, by the grace of God, what I profess to be." Still, he would not indulge in arrogant refusal to answer impertinence. "Christian principle" requires one "to have mercy, deal justly, and walk humbly." Mercy mandates "a listening ear to your request." Justice prompts "me to do what is right, and humility constrains me to condescend to answer."

As he condescended to consider his possible inhumanity, the patriarch seemed momentarily to judge himself beneath contempt. "I knew how to estimate the claims of a Mother and to appreciate the affection of a Mother for her child," he winced. "I greatly regret the occasion that resulted in the separation of you from your child."

Then he found a way to regain patriarchal hauteur. The child, he reported, loves Massa more than Momma. Jenny "says she does not want to go away from her master." With amused "annoyance," he reported his inability "to keep her off my heels in the street." With bemused condescension, he wrote that she is as "petted" and as "watchful" a "little spy as you used to be." With affectionate patronization, he recounted his inability to "spurn" his "little orphan's" "caresses." Jenny is so "very fond of me, and I should miss her so very much," concluded the domestic arbiter, that "I have not yet come to a decision" about competing patriarchal and matriarchal claims.

The confused judge at last located the culprit. "If *you* had conducted yourself faithfully," he wrote to Eliza, "no offer could have tempted me." *Your* letter, he charged, continued "*your* ingratitude and faithlessness." Only "indignation or malice" could explain *your* insufferable failure "to inquire after *my* welfare."

Father forgave the snub with patriarchal majesty. He implored Eliza "as one who takes an interest in your wellbeing in this world, and still greater interest for the wellbeing in the eternal world, & above [all] as the one who stood sponsor to you in baptism, to repent of your misdeeds—to cease to do evil & learn to do well," and to pray daily "to God, thro' Jesus Christ ... to help *your* infirmities." Choosing climactic words posterity must try to read without a smirk, he closed "with unfeigned benevolence & charity." (Emphasis throughout these two paragraphs mine.)

"Benevolent charity"? Incredibly, just possibly. All Massa Jones's self-serving presumption must not hide the terrible although remote possibility that the child caught between two sorts of "parenting" was not feigning preference to stay with Big Daddy up river. Terror about what lay with Momma down river could have sadly afflicted the child. So too, the patriarch just might have honestly presumed that his love exceeded an "erring" mother's. But Massa Jones's

letter indicates also guilt behind confidence and doubt behind bluster. In its vac-
illations, its squirming, its totterings, this marvelous, horrid document tells the
tale of the lordly arrogance, the outrageous sincerity, and the painful awareness
of falseness in this "peculiar" "domestic" regime.

– 6 –

Even if slaveholders' impersonal bureaucracy could have personified loving
fathers, and even if slave property could have been sold without devastating
families, slavery's domestic balances would have been precarious. The way the
scales tipped, like most things southern, was geographically predictable. Where
slavery was relatively weak and growing relatively weaker, especially northwards in the South, masters feared that too permissive an approach made mastery a little precarious. Where slavery was relatively strong and growing relatively stronger, especially southwards in the South, masters feared that arbitrary
violence made mastery more than a little anti-paternal.

Benevolent tyranny depends on benevolent tyrants. While southern family
norms beckoned masters towards benevolence, norms alone never bar sadism.
Southern slaveholding neighborhoods, particularly in newer and lower parts of
the South, tended to have their own horror stories—whispered tales of blacks
murdered or crippled or raped or mangled.

Thomas Chaplin again provides an unforgettable example. One day in 1849,
Chaplin served on a jury of inquest at James Sandiford's neighboring lowcountry South Carolina plantation. Roger, one of Sandiford's slaves, "a complete
cripple, being hardly able to walk," had just been found "in the most shocking
situation." Roger had returned from an oyster catch, allegedly late, allegedly
bearing insufficient baskets of oysters. After "30 cuts" with the cowhide, Roger
was allegedly sassy. "For these *crimes*," Massa Sandiford, a "demon in human
shape, . . . had this poor cripple Negro placed in an open outhouse, the wind
blowing through a hundred cracks, his clothes wet to the waist, without a single
blanket & in freezing weather, with shackles on his wrist, & chained to a bolt
in the floor and a chain around *his neck*." At daylight, Roger was found
"choked, strangled, frozen to death." The jury ruled that Roger accidently
"slipped from the position in which he was placed." Chaplin's *"individual* verdict" was *"murdered* by his master."[34]

Roger's murder was hardly the rule. The Linton Stephenses massively outnumbered the James Sandifords. Some murderers of slaves were jailed. More
were ostracized. Still no Southerner could escape the question raised by his own
knowledge of a Roger. Could a peculiarly domestic system give men leeway to
be anti-familial demons?

That question was most relevant in the nouveau Southwest. Everything
about the rawest cotton and sugar belts—relatively uncivilized conditions, owners with relatively new and huge slave gangs, a relatively reckless materialistic
spirit—mitigated against that semi-permissive paternalism found most often on
smaller or older estates. Not infrequently on a crude frontier, overseers whipped

more, permitted less, and won more rewards for hard driving. Much more often in a raw and virgin land, no charade of familial affection existed. Precisely for these reasons, that nineteenth-century threat of selling slaves down river was a terrible new deterrent in this supposedly less terrible era.[35]

Witness James A. Hamilton, a Louisiana sugar planter, who regarded house servants not as pets to pamper but as niggers "turned out to annoy us. I have whipped them until there is no place to whip, and yet they seem to do as usual." He regarded field hands not as erring children but as "awful lazy" devils. They had "to be licked like blazes."[36]

Hamilton possessed no "hope" of making hands "honest and obedient." He had accordingly "punished all the negroes very severely." If they all ran away, which "would not surprise me, . . . I will take it as a godsend—for I am nearly worried to death with them.—If I had a jail—I should lock them up every night."

When the beaten absconded, the would-be jailer took it as no "godsend." "Last night," Hamilton related with savage humor, "my negroes gave a supper party at my place above. Just about the time they were to set down to tea, I waked them up with the contents of my *Gun.* Such scampering you never did see . . . I saved only one of the flock." The survivor was "very badly wounded and may in all probability be disabled for life. This same boy has been shot twice this year, and once before by me."[37]

Hamilton viewed such warfare not with a sadist's contentment but with the brawler's exhaustion. "Next year I must hire someone to whip my negroes," he wrote. Harried nerves and a skipping heart left him feeling "almost dead. One little excitement uses me up, and to fight negroes nearly kills me—damn their hides, I wish they were all in Africa."[38]

Benevolent paternalism? No wonder abolitionists laughed. No wonder patriarchal paternalists regarded even a few John Hamiltons as contemptible betrayers. A master class mocked in its highest aspirations by so dismal, even if uncharacteristic, an example could hardly feel comfortable about a Domestic Institution. The South's paternalistic leaders were rather left to feel that theirs was a ruling class with domestic pretenses as yet uncomfortably underachieved.[39]

– 7 –

While the harsher southwestern disciplinarians mocked the domestic charade, the Upper South's more permissive regime came closer to following the script. Residents of areas further from the tropics, less sure slavery was permanent, more often tipped the balance of coercion and consent towards leniency. The tip left foreign travelers feeling that, compared with black Louisianians, black Marylanders were "less civil, less obliging," less "servile, . . . less cringing," in short "far more independent than" blacks further south.[40]

Border slaves had greater chance to observe and practice freer conditions.

The nonslaveholding North was closer. Border cities, with unusually large free black populations and expanded opportunities for slaves to earn wages, were much more open than cities further south. Even in the more rural northern South, free blacks were much more prevalent than in the more southern South.

This larger atmosphere of freedom often led tyrants not to clamp down more viciously but to allow slaves more liberties. In its more extreme form, the expansion of permissiveness allowed bondsmen to contract their own jobs, pay their own way, and move about as they pleased provided their master was paid a fee. This "hiring out" system, especially prevalent in border cities, came naturally to a world where free blacks demonstrated skills as good as free whites' and where black "wage slaves" demonstrated that race control hardly required chattel slavery.

The "hiring out" system was only the most notorious example of border slavery's tendency to expand freedom within slavery. Another startling example, particularly prevalent in Maryland and Delaware, was to bribe slaves to be good servants by promising freedom in the master's last will and testament. In the late 1850s, when Marylanders debated saving slavery by re-enslaving free blacks, opponents of re-enslavement urged that, without prospects of freedom, border slaves would not work.[41] The novel notion scuttled slaveholders' commonplace belief that Cuffee needed to be cuffed into being an eternal "boy."

Again, some border masters, particularly near free states, forgot instructions that Cuffee must stay home. Some permissive masters gave slaves unrestricted license to wander, hoping to avoid the ultimate wandering. Others, particularly in cities, let slaves marry free blacks, sire free children, worship at free black churches. Others let slaves have money and buy freedom. More taught slaves to read and write. Always the object was the same. Adjust to the northern South's exposed openness by making slavery less provoking for slaves.[42]

Deep South proslavery perpetualists called it all madness—an invitation to razor-slashed jugulars. Twentieth-century social theorists, with their conventional wisdom that a sip of freedom provokes thirst for more, say amen. Which only goes to show that in both centuries theorists have missed tyranny's complexities. Border slaves always sipped freedom. They usually did not run away. They rarely slit master's throat. They almost never revolted. Slaveholders' nonclosed society was a theoretical mess.

It was also working. Masters aware of theoretical danger made theory fail. The border slave establishment handed out privileges with one hand, threatened reprisals with the other, and convinced slaves that a tinge of freedom was preferable to testing out whose throat would be slit. Even in its most lenient forms, the system obeyed the true iron law of tyranny's survival: Always make sure that the balance of privilege and force keeps a subject believing that rebellion would violate his interest.

Border slavery, while obeying that law, balanced coercion and consent at an uneasy level in an uncomfortable spot. Border masters feared that a little outside pressure could upset the balance. Let antislavery Northerners mass too close and too hard and runaways could escalate, white heresy grow, nervous masters sell blacks down river faster. Then a despotic system infused with some democratic modes of social control would come to its ultimate test.

– 8 –

The Domestic Institution would be most tested in the northern South precisely because the domestic analogy was there most apt. Peculiarly in the Border South, the notion that patriarchs could control blacks while going light on brutality and heavy on persuasiveness faintly resembled control over white children. But further southward, slavery could less easily seem truly domestic. Down river, the multiple troubles with the domestic analogy: the contempt for dependents with black skin, the expectation that black but not white "boys" would be eternal children, the impersonal bureaucracy governing many blacks but nary a white dependent, the merchandising of black but not white folk, the brutalizing of slaves alone—all of these factors made governing slaves too dissimilar to governing families. The resulting swings between brutality and permissiveness raised the largest question about Cuffee's constancy. Could so strained a domestic analogy—and so inconstant a terrorizing—sufficiently control that implausible fellow, the grown-up will-less "boy"?

CHAPTER 5

The Domestic Charade, II: Cuffee's Act

Blacks never came close to overturning whites in the prewar period. Still, slave resistance persistently annoyed and sometimes panicked masters. The trouble was that Massa's partially false postures in domestic charades invited Cuffee to dissimulate in distressing—sometimes dangerous—ways.

– 1 –

While most slaves resisted or dissimulated to some degree, a minority capitulated to masters' power. Combinations of brutal lashings and fatherly affection, of savage jailings and fertile garden plots, of wrenching destruction of slave marriages and permissive encouragement to wander and marry sometimes produced true-blue Cuffees. One of North American slavery's horrors—slavemasters called it the glory—was that docile dependents sometimes became grateful worshipers of overbearing paternalists. That is why some enslaved blacks and enslaving whites achieved transracial bonds of affection and sympathy which developed more rarely in the South after emancipation.[1] That is why, during the Civil War, some Cuffees devotedly served soldier-Massas and scorned fake Cuffees fleeing "home."[2]

That is why some slaveholders and slaves shared memories of escapades enjoyed, of adventures accomplished, of camaraderie perfected. In a rural culture, the best times were out of doors, hunting and fishing. At such moments, slave could be teacher, master pupil, and the two allies against the elements. Remember the time that squalls hit the fishermen, the boat turned over twenty times, and Cuffee helped save Massa's life? Remember the time . . . as if anyone could forget.[3]

All those times spent hunting, fishing, crying, and dying together were not, from a modern egalitarian's perspective, paradise lost. Friendship between consenting equals this was never meant to be. Fanny Kemble, an unsympathetic outsider who temporarily was a plantation mistress, derided this paternalism as "that maudlin tenderness of a fine lady for her lapdog."[4] But even she conceded that tenderness existed. Overbearing paternalism could soften and humanize a relationship perhaps most psychologically damaging when most kind.

A *Domestic* Institution also mitigated against slave revolt. The domestic in domestic servitude was so powerful that when chances came to join slave revolts, some solitary Cuffee almost always thought first of protecting his white family against his black brothers. One betrayer usually sufficed to ruin the shrewdest domestic plot.

More than this domestic scenario made North American slave revolts scarce. Underclasses are always aware of the difficulties and dangers in uprisings from below. While a few successful lower class revolutions and a handful of successful slave revolutions dot the historical record, great revolutions have usually been started by powerful groups—by armies, by upper classes, by middle classes, by a stray professor. To a *lumpenproletariat,* to borrow Marx's phrase for the lowest classes, revolution usually seems farfetched.

Still, slaves brought off insurrection less often in North than in South America, despite possessing many similar preconditions for revolution. Some southern terrain, particularly North Carolina's Dismal Swamp, included dense jungles inviting to runaway slave settlements, called maroon colonies in Brazil. Other southern areas, particularly South Carolina's rice swamps, had the same ratio of massive black to tiny white populations that invited a coup d'état in Saint Domingue. At moments of southern history, especially the final Civil War year, southern black belts were especially vulnerable.[5]

Because of such opportunities, North American slaves *plotted* revolution no less often than did Latin American slaves. The North American record teems with planned conspiracies.[6] The difference was that in North America some black domestic almost always alerted some white patriarch in time. Domestic slavery in North America gave patriarchs expanded ways of hearing about revolution. The many slaves who self-consciously played Cuffee had learned all too well how to get along. The few slaves who *became* Cuffee had been all too well rendered gratefully loyal.

Furthermore, just as domestic servitude peculiarly expanded some slaves' loyalty to the Big House, so domestic patriarchs turned peculiarly savage upon hearing of "their peoples'" alleged plotting. The slaveholder wavered between normally pretending he had nothing to fear from "domestic friends" and occasionally acting as if he had everything to fear. Wavering came naturally to The Man who would be both permissive parent and remorseless terrorist. Savage deterrence came equally readily to a semi-open system nervously concerned about the need to be altogether closed. That is why North Americans surpassed more closed slave regimes in reacting with panicky reigns of terror when slave plots were suspected. Thus, because of the very domestication of the system, potential slave insurrectionists faced relatively greater chances both of domestic betrayal and violent counteraction.

Some might think that a system full of half-privileged domestics should have experienced many wide-scale revolts, especially since those half-privileged are supposedly particularly prone to rise against the altogether privileged. But in looser forms of despotism, conservatives anxious to save what they possess are as inevitable as rebels who seek to seize what they lack. North American slave revolts illustrated that two-sided tendency. Somewhat privileged blacks, frustrated by their limited privilege, usually initiated revolutionary plots. But recruitment of the privileged usually produced a slave who was either cynically determined to protect privilege or who honestly appreciated his benefactor. The pet slave turned informer. The counter-revolution was a horror. The informer became a more lionized Cuffee or was given *his* freedom. The surest way to free oneself, under domestic servitude, was not to join a revolution but to betray one to the patriarch.

The Denmark Vesey Conspiracy superbly illustrates domestic slavery's dual tendency. The Vesey Conspiracy, the most widespread and cogent insurrection plot uncovered in the nineteenth-century South, occurred in the right place to compel attention: Charleston, South Carolina, the southern city in the blackest black belt. It transpired at the right moment: 1822, a period when Charlestonians experimented with the loosest paternalistic control they would ever deploy. The conspiracy was based on the shrewdest strategy: keep initial rebels few to avoid betrayal, have the tight knot of ill-armed conspirators seize the city's arsenals in a midnight ambush, then and only then urge the masses to kill for freedom.[7]

Denmark Vesey epitomized openings in the semi-closed society. He was a mulatto in a world supposedly either white or black. He was a free brown in a world allegedly enslaving all non-whites. He was married to several slaves in a world allegedly governed by Massa's monogamous Christianity and by whites' determination to separate black slaves and black freedmen. Vesey also epitomized dangers of half-freedom. Proud of his freedom, he resented his children's enslavement.

Another opening in enslavers' theoretically closed regime gave Vesey liberty to preach freedom. The African Church, a supposedly barred black congregation in Charleston's suburbs, had connections with a Philadelphia free black congregation and a black minister espousing black Christianity. In addition to freedom to marry and freedom to roam and freedom to preach that all God's children—especially his own—should be free, Vesey had access to newspaper stories about northern congressmen urging abolition during the 1820 Missouri Controversy. An early recruit gave Vesey access to a stable, where horses for a potential rebel cavalry paced in their stalls. Another early convert handed the general a key to a store, where guns for Vesey's troops lay ready for seizure. Charleston's main arsenal stood barely guarded on a mid-city street, also vulnerable to surprise attack.

Unfortunately, the wrong semi-enslaved black could take the surprise out of an ambush. Vesey wrestled with the betrayal problem more shrewdly than any other North American black revolutionary. Knowing that slaves were frightened of reprisals if masters heard of plots, Vesey would deploy a reign of terror more terrifying still.[8]

The Charleston establishment at this vulnerable moment was not deploying much terrorizing. "By far the greater number of our citizens," white Charlestonians reported, exulted "in what they termed the progress of liberal ideas." Softhearts hoped that a "mild and generous" system would secure serviles' "affection and gratitude."[9] A control system momentarily depending too much on consent to slavery invited Denmark Vesey to offer slaves something better: consent to freedom. A system relying too little on severe coercion invited the rebel leader to threaten slaves with something worse: more heavyhanded terrorizing. For once an insurgent might both promise more carrots and frighten with more sticks than could The Man.

Until he could ambush The Man's arsenals, Vesey's great obstacle remained his ill-armed recruits' fears of Massas who still possessed the rifles. Vesey's physical presence counterbalanced some apprehensions. A giant of a man, he swore he would mash any betrayer. Gullah Jack, although the tiniest rebel, also helped offset black uneasiness. The wizened former African witch doctor offered voodoo tokens to guard rebels against white violence. Vesey's appeal shrewdly combined African tribal religion with Afro-American Christianity, just as Vesey himself resourcefully combined a tribal tyrant's coercive threats with a democratic chieftain's charismatic persuasion.[10]

Vesey's cleverest way of out-intimidating Massa was to schedule the revolt for a Saturday night, the time many country slaves descended on the city, bearing master's produce for Sunday market. Vesey claimed to have recruited thousands of these visitors. He probably lied. Allowing so many in on the secret when The Man still had the guns would have courted betrayal. But no slave confined to the city could check. Charleston recruits only knew that Vesey swore that his country army had pledged to slaughter his betrayer.

Still concerned that neither his promises of freedom nor his threats of violence might be as compelling as slaveholders' intimidations, Vesey warned recruiters not to approach "waiting men who receive *presents of old coats*, etc., *from their masters*."[11] Indulged slaves were the most likely betrayers. But indulged blacks were also the most likely rebels. Some of Vesey's prime lieutenants were free blacks. More were trusted house slaves.

Ned and Rolla Bennett, for example, favorite retainers of South Carolina's governor, Thomas Bennett, ostentatiously took visitors' coats and praised slavery when the governor entertained the gentry. Bennett's domestic servants, feigning Cuffees in front of whites, at least pretended in front of blacks to be anti-Cuffees. Rolla Bennett told blacks he lusted for the choicest privilege. "*When we have done with the fellows,*" winked this "family friend," "*we know what to do with the wenches.*"[12] Rolla pointed to Massa Thomas's daughter as his future "wench." The slave playing "boy" would then indeed bring his manhood to The Man's attention.

Denmark Vesey, whatever his concern about loyalties of pampered "boys," needed their rage at the pampering they had received. When he mistakenly approached a body servant grateful to Massa, he could only try to terrify the potential betrayer. The strategy proved not quite good enough. At the very moment Rolla Bennett was speaking about his anticipated delight, Vesey's lieutenants recruited one slave too many. A domestic servant, when approached, pretended to agree to rebel. The domestic then scurried to inform Massa about plans for rebellion. Whites investigated. One privileged slave after another put investigators off the trail. Ned Bennett especially laughed off charges that he plotted to murder Massa Thomas. Beloved masters, especially Thomas Bennett, relaxed.

Vesey's lieutenants tensely moved the rebellion up a month. But 72 hours before Cuffees were to become anti-Cuffee, the problem struck again. A black informer told whites about the revised plot.

A no-longer-smiling Governor Bennett, no longer doubting insurrection loomed, sought to crush rebellion without over-reacting. The no-longer-relaxed community, no longer trusting Massa Bennett's under-reactions, brushed him aside. On July 26, 1822, on a long gallows erected for the occasion, Charleston patriarchs executed almost two dozen of "their people." They trampled another "domestic" to death while fighting for the best view. They strung up a dozen more "family friends" in the next few days.

As always in a slaveholder democracy, anti-familial bloodletting could not long be sustained. White republicans soon retreated from unrepublican slaughtering. In August, judges published most of their trial proceedings, purporting to show that the slain had had a "democratic" trial.[13] The judges also urged that executions had deterred blacks quite enough. Blacks, having been forced to watch mass slayings on the gallows, had indeed been compelled to play the faithful domestic.

Two black turncoats who had betrayed Vesey's domestic ambush, having been freed and enriched by grateful whites, chose revealing different domestic paths. One loyal savior of white patriarchs, exemplifying the usual black response to freedom, protected his black family by buying and freeing his wife. The other informer on black brothers, exemplifying a highly unusual black use of opportunity, devastated a black family he purchased. This black slaveholder filled his purse by selling a slave child away from its mother, then maximized his heirs' coffers by ordering them to sell the slave wife away from her husband. His betrayals of one black after another illuminate the way this so-called Domestic Institution could warp homes black and white, even as it perfected its domestic defenses.[14]

– 2 –

Still, if a few genuine Cuffees betrayed revolutions, most slaves were neither utterly dominated nor malignant people who preyed on each other. Instead, pretend Cuffees found and exploited the inconsistent paternalist's weaknesses.

The deadliest weakness was the possibility of murder by an individual slave. The Domestic Institution was as likely to produce the lone assassin as it was unlikely to produce collective insurrection. Cuffee, Massa's informer about plots, slept right next to the bedroom. "Consenting" servants cooked Massa's supper, drove Massa's coach, served Massa's daughter. A little poison slipped into the pot or a harness not fastened properly to the horse and Massa, "accidentally," would be master of nothing. "The negroes as domestics," Jefferson Davis told the Senate in December 1859, "have access at all hours through the unlocked doors of their masters' houses." If "their weak minds should be instigated to arson, murder, and rapine," their "first act of crime" would be dismayingly "easy."[15]

Two months after Davis spoke, a "boy" publicized the ease of domestic murder. The Hon. William Keitt, a state legislator and brother of South Carolina Congressman Lawrence Keitt, lived on a Florida plantation. William Keitt was ailing. One night, his slave crept into the sickroom and slit Massa's throat. Keitt's blood spurted like a geyser. The news swirled around the South like a hurricane.[16]

Southerners more feared individual bloodletting than mass murder, even on rare occasions when the masses struck. During the Vesey Conspiracy, the initial fear was that thousands would rise. With the conspiracy smashed, one creditable fear remained. When the court trying Vesey conspirators published its trial record, one aspect of the plot was not publicized. Gullah Jack, confessed a conspirator, "was going to give me *a bottle with poison to put into my master's pump.*" The italicized words, the forbidden words, were censored for publication.[17]

There it was, the peculiar domestic nightmare of these peculiar masters. Slaveholders sensible enough to guard arsenals could stop collective revolts. Nothing could stop a solitary domestic from poisoning the slumbering household. The only antidote to the individual domestic assassin was the characteristic human response to the horrible: it could never happen to us.

The facts, however, could not make anyone sure. During the Vesey scare, Elias Horry, a revered rice planter, protested when constables arrested his beloved coachman. The patriarch assured authorities "they were mistaken." After hearing troubling evidence, Horry turned to his slave. "Are you guilty?" Horry asked incredulously. "What were your intentions?" The coachman whirled on the paternalist. I desired, screamed the slave, to "kill you, rip open your belly, and throw your guts in your face."[18]

We will watch slaveholders plead that abolitionists be silenced lest southern firesides witness guts-in-your-face. Firesides were precisely the danger spot. Twentieth-century urban dwellers can avoid a ghetto corner on a dark night. Slaveholders could not avoid anti-Cuffee in the house unless the Domestic Institution was shorn of domestic servants. One could not even talk about the danger, think about the unthinkable, for the slightest hint of fear could give domestics ideas. Under these circumstances, abolitionists became superb scapegoats for the way a few domestic assassins exploited the weakness in the domestic script and thereby turned Massa's charade into a dangerous sham.

– 3 –

The more usual way Cuffee violated the domestic script was by exploring Massa's inconsistency. Historians have dubbed slaves' constant probing "day to day resistance."[19] Slaves were indeed daily testing how far resistance could go.

The slave's weapon was deceit. Power was achieved by playing childish parts maladroitly. Missed cues and missing lines were so subtle that masters veered from one exasperated extreme to another. Slaves, masters said, were docile and loving. Slaves, masters also said, were deceptive and lying. Cuffee was usually not anti-Cuffee. But was he Cuffee? Or to rephrase the constant question, who were these "boys" anyway?[20]

Who, indeed? Blacks were at pains to keep whites from knowing. Slaves constantly misunderstood orders, broke tools, abused mules, missed weeds. Was all of this deliberate? Or were "boys" too infantile to labor satisfactorily?[21]

Then, too, so many things were mysteriously missing. That "nice fat rump pork" had been locked in the smoke house. Four little pieces survived. One could have sworn those jewel trinkets had been placed in the drawer. They were gone. Cuffee suddenly had $8 to spend on perfume and silk cravats. Any connection to the $100 missing from the desk?[22]

Equivalent mysteries surrounded slave illnesses. Females periodically claimed awful cramps and bleeding. Male complaints were also heartrending. But were professed illnesses excuses for a vacation? Or was slave health menaced and likely to be made worse by working?[23]

Less petty mysteries surrounded fires and food poisonings. During a drought, fires could spontaneously start. Or a slave could provide a "spontaneous" spark. Again, steaming temperatures and poor refrigeration could easily have spoiled the food Massa and Missus had unfortunately eaten. Alternatively, some resentful cook might have slipped something into the pot.[24]

Everything wrong might be a slave's fault. That easy explanation for life's mysteries menaced serviles. Fortunately for slaves, white families found that easy explanation uncomfortable. More comfortable, if more mystifying, was the conclusion that nothing ugly was Cuffee's fault. Who could say? The only certainty was that mysterious fires and mysterious nausea made the comfortable Big House a domain of queasy discomfort.

At least when slaves ran away, exasperated whites knew who did what. Yet most often "lazy devils" returned voluntarily after a few days. They claimed contriteness. They promised never again to wander. They swore they had disappeared only to have days with mates and children.[25]

Such contrary behavior shrewdly took advantage of the democrat in the slaveholder. A republican could not automatically deploy savage punishment when he had to act as judge and jury and was not sure who, if anyone, was guilty. Nor could a paternalist drawn toward permissiveness automatically lay 39 lashes on poor devils who might not have heard his orders or might be ill or might be tuckered or might be trying their hardest. Nor could patriarchs who assumed darkies were irreversibly stupid and slothful govern as if childish stupidity and sloth were avoidable. In fact, some degree of childlike contrariness was pleasurable. Infantilism proved that the "boys" needed a paternalist.

Still, a child with a match can ruin everything. A youngster who runs away produces a father without children. Children who get away with tiny defiance start wondering if defiance need be tiny. And even if countervailing wills were expressed in ways not so much alarming as annoying, little annoyances could add up to alarming problems. A slothful gang could bring Massa to ruin with labor so poor as to produce crops hardly worth marketing. No wonder that ten times a day The Man was tempted to whip and at the same time tempted to stay his hand. No wonder "boys'" daily assignment was to walk the exquisite line between being so bothersome as to bring the lash to mind and yet not quite bothersome enough to bring the whip on down.

Cuffee's act, Massa's treasure, thus became Massa's exasperation. Cuffee supposedly had to be carried from the field, leg allegedly swollen like a balloon. Massa could discern no puffiness in the leg. Cuffee never touched a watermelon. Hollow melons abounded on the vine. Negroes, it seemed, simply "cannot tell a straight story." One could "have no idea how the scamps will poach upon you if you allow them one inch," whimpered Linton Stephens.[26]

Then, occasionally, violence, seemingly appearing out of nowhere, tore deceit to shreds. Unpremeditated violence did not really come out of nowhere but predictably out of erratic punishment. Inconsistent discipline left definitions of fair discipline hazy. A lashing that seemed right to the lasher could seem undeserved to the lashed. Put the brutal paddle in the hand of the disciplinarian who usually just waved it threateningly. Then tempers could explode when the lasher smashed and smashed.

Masters' inconstant brutality plus slaves' nonviolent dissimulation particularly led to unplanned violence. The man who could play Cuffee perfectly and still think himself not to be Cuffee was an unusually fine human actor. The more usual sort did not quite march to Massa's order and did not quite know if he was as "black-assed" as Massa said.

Events brought clarity. Slaves based what they could get away with on past experience with Massa's temper. But past experience was hardly reliable when provocations deliberately brought Massa to the point of irrational exasperation. When Cuffee miscalculated a shade and went a little too far, Massa sometimes went a lot too far. When a slave expecting a duped father suddenly confronted a lashing zealot, temper tantrum could be met by temper tantrum. An instant later, someone would lie dying.

Sometimes a slave murderer would be a life-long troublemaker. Many plantations contained at least one black full of dark looks and surly manners.[27] More often, the assassin would be an apparent Cuffee. He would be whipped unexpectedly hard. He would strike back instantly, instinctively, stunning even himself, slashing and smashing in retaliatory fury before lighting off for the woods.[28]

More occasionally still, a few hours would elapse between provocation and murder. On an October day in 1856, Lewis B. Norwood's mourning slaves routed North Carolina neighbors from bed. Massa, they wailed, had fallen in the fire and burned to a crisp. While Norwood's corpse was indeed horribly scalded, not a hair was singed. A black confessed. Norwood had locked two bondsmen in outhouses for days after they had allegedly harbored slave runaways. One night they ambushed him, slugged him, crammed a funnel in his mouth, and poured scalding water down his throat.[29]

Southern communities handled such matters with precision. In black-belt Alabama in 1850, an overseer "attempted to flog a boy. Four of the ploughmen stopped their mules and . . . advanced upon him in battle-array." The overseer retreated to the Big House. Owner and agent, armed with double barrel guns, "returned to the field." The black "militia presented a phalanx. The white men aimed their guns, and slaughtered four incontinently. While these victims were weltering in their gore like stuck hogs," the two whites tied up "the original offender, and with a cowhide administered two hundred lashes upon his bare back."[30]

Such coercions sufficed to turn the bravest slave towards careful dissimulation. But such violence was child's play compared with the counter-reaction when whites panicked about insurrections. Some mysterious incident—a rash of house burnings, a series of runaways, a slave's perhaps unseemly look at a white lady—would turn undercurrents of vague fear into moments of intense suspicion. Then a slave would profess to have overheard compatriots plotting revolution.

At that terrible moment, slavery maximized human panic. Slaves were lashed and lashed, lashed some more until they "confessed." "Confessions" implicated others. Others "confessed." Hangings increased. Patrols lynched. The "democratic" South became a dictator's armed camp.

Then, as swiftly as it had come, the terror overran its climax and swelled into absurdity. The community regained its nerve. Democrats scuttled dictatorial courts. Doors were unlocked. Patrols vanished. Master and bondsmen shot deer together in the woods. A favorite handkerchief disappeared. Poker-faced Cuffees displayed exquisite compassion in helping their distraught mistress conduct the futile search. Once again the cast had hit its stride. Once again slaves' dissembling seemed more irritating than dangerous.[31]

– 4 –

Duping Whitey, the essence of slaves' day-to-day pretenses, continued back at the quarters, when night fell and Massas were absent. Blacks then created an Afro-American counterculture which mirrored their duplicity in the face of The Man. Here, like in any true counterculture, slaves raised resistance to higher levels of insight, beauty, and awareness.

Historians have lately recaptured Afro-American slave culture.[32] But disguises helping to define that culture have not been sufficiently emphasized. The centrality of creative pretense in slave culture no less than in slave behavior is most obvious in slaves' dominant fictional tradition. This tradition, originally oral, was later published under the famous label of Brer Rabbit.[33] Brer Rabbit was the supreme con man. "De rabbit is de slickest o' all de animals de Lawd ever made. He ain't de biggest, an' he ain't de loudest but he sho' am de slickest."[34]

Brer Fox was slick too. In Uncle Remus's thinly disguised vocabulary, Massa alias Fox could be as brutally calculating as Cuffee alias Rabbit. Uncle Remus's sagas continually warned the hapless not to overreach themselves. For example, the Monkey who thought he would imitate his owner had lost the sense of reality necessary to be trickier. The owner, when shaving, used the razor's blunt side. He then stealthfully turned the instrument. Monkey, when imitating, slit his own throat. Such sagas warned that resistances grounded in illusions, alias slave insurrections, were a guileless way to be killed.[35]

But when the weaker understood the stronger better than the stronger understood the weaker, illusion could be the trick to power. In one tale, de Fox bore a string of fish de Rabbit envied. The situation was a version of Massa possessing delicacies bondsmen loved to pilfer. De Rabbit lay down in de Fox's path. The conniver, moaning about being deathly ill, beseeched the fisherman to race for a doctor. The situation was a version of slaves feigning illness and masters not knowing what to believe.

De Fox believed. He lay down the fish. He scurried for help. De Rabbit dined and absconded. "Brer Rabbit got de fish," Uncle Remus drolly concluded, "an' got better."[36]

Such fictional celebration of slave manipulation would not necessarily have enraged white manipulators. Sagas of black duplicity were not meant for white ears. Whites did not become really aware of Brer Rabbit until long after slavery perished. Still, tales, like all slave resistances, may have been made ambiguous partially because ubiquitous whites might for once *see*.

What The Man could see, as always, could be looked at two ways. Tales of the powerful confronting the powerless, however loaded with double meaning, were, after all, only about foxes and rabbits. Furthermore, sagas of lessers aggravating superiors were, after all, only fictions and celebrated no more than aggravations.

These aggravations seemed particularly harmless because in many Brer Rabbit tales, rabbits aggravated only rabbits. In one brutal black fantasy, Man has strung de Rabbit up in a tree until the pot is ready. De Squirrel comes along and asks de Rabbit why he is hanging. De Rabbit, claiming to be enjoying a fresh air swing, kindly offers de Squirrel a turn. De Squirrel unties de Rabbit and de Rabbit fastens de Squirrel. So Man feasts on duped squirrel instead of wily rabbit.[37]

Such a con job would have struck a listening paternalist as apt. Just as loyal domestics sometimes betrayed black rebels, so loyal servants sometimes told master who stole his ham—and sometimes complained to Massa about blacks stealing from them. Degrading conditions invite the degraded to prey upon each other as well as upon the degrader. The difference under slavery was that a "father" was self-appointed to stop "boys" from harming other "boys." The more serviles conned each other, the more the paternalist felt needed.

Tales of de Rabbit outfoxing de Squirrel, then, could be heard by de Fox as no danger to the establishment. Even tales of rabbits outwitting foxes, while based on aggravating truth, could be heard as safety valves, as tales of limited triumphs keeping the underclass from thinking about larger triumphs. In such tale-telling, as in slave behavior, "boys" were usually too clever to be seen as out to slay The Man.

– 5 –

Anti-Cuffees masquerading as Cuffees are critical in a place historians have tended to overlook them, at the centerpiece of slave counterculture. Slave religion, correctly celebrated in late twentieth-century revisions as a hallmark of black creativity, has been described as if unrelated to de Rabbit. But slave religion, like slave tales, brought to high consciousness the essential lesson of resistance to this regime. Resisters had to be "de slickest o' all."

Black theologians, like black tale-spinners and work-shirkers, had to lie to thrive. Spreading African theology full of undisguised revolutionary conditioning was a courageous way to die. In Latin America, where the African slave trade lasted longer, where whites' drive to acculturate Africans was pressed less vigorously, where armed revolution once triumphed and maroon runaway colonies often thrived, slave religion was sometimes heavily African in an ominously revolutionary sense.[38] In comparison, the Afro in Afro-American religion was more attenuated. Religious resistance tended to be nonviolent. Black preachers tended to take care that black religion could be heard as a nonrevolutionary version of white Christianity.

Whites tended to see any Afro-American religion as un-American. Whites' favorite black religion was blacks worshipping under a white who preached Christian obedience. Slaves caught cheering while black preachers thundered about freedom could be lashed. Bondsmen caught participating in African celebrations could be lynched.

The resulting black religion had a secretive aspect. To worship, forbidden black style, blacks sometimes had to steal away in the dark night, bound for places called, revealingly, "Hush Harbors." Souls then huddled around a black iron kettle turned upside down. Suppliants prayed into the vessel, beseeching the kettle to hush the sound.

Slave preachers seldom wholly depended on such crude silencing devices. Whites, blacks knew, might eventually hear. Illegitimate messages had to have the sound of legitimate servility. That need, like much else in slaves' condition, yielded an Old Testament-inspired, Moses-oriented theology. White preachers to slaves emphasized St. Paul's injunction that "servants obey in all things your Masters." Slave ministers preferred the Book of Exodus, especially tales of the Red Sea opening to allow Hebrew slaves to escape. Slave sermons dwelled on pitiful David slaying pretentious Goliath, on ridiculed Noah sailing from his scoffers, above all on mighty Moses freeing his people.

"Moses," complained a white Christ-worshipper, "is their ideal of all that is high, and noble, and perfect, in man." Christ became not so much "a *spiritual* Deliverer" as "a second Moses, who would eventually lead *them* out of bondage." Slaves tended to sing not of Jesus the meek but of Jesus as warrior: "Ride on King Jesus, No man can hinder thee."[39]

Spirituals carried slaves back to their favorite river. "Roll, Jordan, roll," they chanted, "Roll, Jordan, roll . . . O my soul a-rise in Heaven, Lord, For to hear when Jordan roll." The black "Looked over Jordan, and what did I see,"

> Comin' for to carry me home,
> A band of angels comin' after me,
> Comin' for to carry me home . . .
> Swing low, sweet chariot,
> Comin' for to carry me home,
> Swing low, sweet chariot,
> Comin' for to carry me home.

The Jordan's sweet chariots would visit them, too. The hero down in Egypt would come to them soon.

> Go down, Moses,
> 'Way down in Egypt land,
> Tell ole Pharoah
> To let my people go.[40]

Such celebrations of freedom ostensibly prayed for release after life. Still, such injunctions could be heard as preparations for freedom on earth. "Run to Jesus," went the spiritual, "shun the danger, I don't expect to stay much longer here." A plea for slaves to run away? Possibly. A joy that stay on earth would soon be over? Possibly. "We'll soon be free," ran another spiritual, "We'll soon be free, We'll soon be free, When de Lord will call us home." Freedom now? Perhaps. Freedom hereafter? Perhaps.

Confused whites could be thankful (and most were shakily thankful) that black theology was somewhat "white." After all, while the ideology went a little heavy on Moses the warrior and light on Jesus the meek, the Old Testament too was white man's tradition. The cultural borrowing, whatever the twist, showed Africans had become at least partially acculturated Westerners. Again, while black preachers came down hard on "freedom" and softly on "obedience," freedom from earthly travail was Christian expectation. Indeed, since prayers for freedom were ostensibly centered on the next world—and black prayers were always ostensibly so centered—eternal hope could become another earthly safety valve, a way to channel instincts in safe directions.

The physical activism in black evangelical counterculture was as rich in double meaning as the theology. Black congregations never sat. Bodies twisted. Drums boomed. Voices chanted. At its climax, the jerking syncopation led to the "ring shout," a circle of worshippers shrieking for freedom soon.

Africanism reborn? Perhaps. African antecedents for ring shouting abounded.[41] Still, black revival culture could also be taken as another twist on white acculturation. White revivals, especially at lower-class, Baptist-Methodist, holy roller extremes, were also activist, emotional, sensual. White celebrants too joined hands and sang in circles. Upper-class whites were prone to hold noses—and check wallets—about as often when contemplating lower-class whites' revivals.[42] The Afro-American style, if somewhat un-American, also somewhat fit an American tradition. Here was why many whites winked at black services and some worshipped under black preachers—worshipped, and wondered, and pretended not to worry.

– 6 –

One notorious anti-Cuffee epitomized doubts, dissimulations, and unsteadinesses on both sides of the Massa-Cuffee charade. In the mid-1830s, Frederick Douglass, then in his early twenties, successfully ran away from slavery in Baltimore. He soon became the most famous northern black abolitionist. Douglass's *Life and Times,* one of the great American autobiographies, ranked with Theodore Dwight Weld's *American Slavery as It Is* and Harriet Beecher Stowe's *Uncle Tom's Cabin* as widely disseminated volumes having incalculable impact on northern public opinion.[43] Because his life and writings sum up much about the Domestic Institution, this runaway's tale demands fresh retelling.

Frederick Douglass was born the wrong half white. From his mother, a black slave, the Marylander inherited thralldom. From his father, an unknown white and perhaps a slaveholder, the future runaway received the contempt of a patriarch running away from responsibility for a child enslaved. Douglass despised his anti-father father, worshipped his caring mother, and adored his mother's mother, who tenderly raised him.

Such attitudes would seem to encourage finding black beautiful and white loathsome. But Douglass disliked much of slaves' cultural blackness. He had no use for conjuring or voodoo or any other traces of African "primitiveness" (so *he* considered it). He carefully scrubbed his voice of slave dialect. He liked to credit the linguistic transformation to a white playmate he barely knew after he was nine.[44]

This transparent excuse for his own efforts to whiten himself showed Douglass's uneasiness about black styles. He was less uneasy about his dislike for some slaves' "black-assed" behavior—fawning, cringing, eyes downcast, worshipful of whites as some superior beings. He "quite lost [his] patience" upon finding "a colored man weak enough to believe" in submission. He found plantation slaves "in point of ignorance and indolence" and "stupid indifference" to be sinking with the worn-out soil into "general dilapidation."[45]

In contrast, Douglass shared enslavers' vision of the ideal personality type: independent, fearless, egalitarian, individualistic, the reverse of everything servile. In this slave's utopian world, whites would repudiate slavery as antithetical to white culture. Blacks would then live up to cultural whiteness better than had whites. Douglass's anguish was that whites, repeating his despised father's act, usually put him down as "nigger," despite his attempt to whiten the very sound of his blackness. Even this black liberator could not liberate himself from scars of slaveholders' black-is-ugly dogmas.

Douglass looked like a man trapped between races. His skin was neither black nor white, but in the phrase he loathed, "yeller." He inherited light eyes and lean lips from his father. His thick black curly hair came from his mother. Right in the middle of his square, tough, yet ethereal face was his most eerie physical characteristic. A thick bony protuberance erupted under his eyebrows and abruptly stopped, before it had fairly begun, at the bridge of his nose. It was as if his jumble of genes had the whole puzzle worked out until one thick piece, fitting nowhere, had to be jammed in.

As a child, Douglass fit in nowhere, in no family, black or white, after being torn from his enslaved grandmother at age six. The tearing was itself a comment on the Domestic Institution. Douglass's grandmother had been assigned to raise him while his mother labored in far-off fields. The baby possessed in his grandmother's crude cabin critical childish belongings: nourishment, continuity, caring. Then, one day, at Massa's command, grandmother and grandson tramped many miles to the home plantation. Douglass knew not why they had been summoned. The grandmother lovingly carried the weary lad part of the way. The grandson uncomplainingly dragged himself part of the way, so as to relieve his beloved of her burden.

They arrived. Frederick could not understand why "Grandmamma" looked so "sad." Grandmamma pointed out to Frederick two sisters and a brother. "Brothers and sisters we were by blood, but slavery had made us strangers." Grandmamma, "affectionately patting me on the head," told Frederick "to go out and play play with them."

The lad, sensing something, reluctantly went. Outside he remained aloof, watching these strangers, his "family," play. Then someone told him Grandmamma was gone. He rushed in. She was nowhere. Frederick "fell upon the ground and wept a boy's bitter tears."[46]

Grandmother's place was taken by black Aunt Katy, no blood aunt to Frederick, who presided over the plantation's anti-family nursery. The tyrannical Katy gave extra food to her own offspring, starved other black children of nourishment and affection, and taught them the meaning of the lash. One day, when Frederick had to steal to eat, his mother paid him the last of her infrequent visits. She gave him a large ginger cake. With "deep and tender pity," she took Frederick into her "strong protecting arms." Douglass learned that night "as I had never learned before, that I was not only a child, but somebody's child. I was grander upon my mother's knee than a king upon his throne."

He went to sleep. When he awoke, his mother had left. He would never see her again. "I knew my mother so little," regretted Douglass decades later, "and have so few of her words treasured in my remembrance."[47]

Three years later, this motherless and grandmotherless boy was transferred to an almost-home. Douglass's owner, who resided on the Eastern Shore of Maryland, lent Frederick to kin living in Baltimore. Douglass's new surrogate owners, Sophia and Hugh Auld, true to the Massa-Cuffee charade, welcomed him as big brother to their child, Tommy. Little white Tommy and little black Freddy romped together, fighting each other's battles in the streets. Sophia Auld, grateful to little Freddy for keeping little Tommy "out of harm's way," taught the black orphan "to regard her as something more akin to a mother than a slaveholding mistress." While little Tommy was clearly "her most dearly loved child, she made me something like his half-brother in her affections. If dear Tommy was exalted to a place on his mother's knee, 'Freddy' was honored by a place at the mother's side."[48]

Then the usual anti-familial time bomb exploded in Douglass's almost family. His master died. He had to be sent back to the Eastern Shore for division of the inheritance. Sophia and little Tommy and little Freddy "wept bitterly, for we were parting," perhaps "forever."[49]

Douglass won a reprieve. His new owner lent him back to Hugh and Sophia Auld. Frederick returned to Baltimore, to a joyous family reunion. But the family charade was growing strained. Before Douglass's departure and reprieve, Mistress Sophia had taught Little Freddy and Little Tommy to read. Massa Hugh, horrified, had ordered the matriarch to halt. The slave, said the patriarch, must know only Massa's word. Sophia, guilty about what horrible thing she had begun, hounded Frederick thereafter to see what reading material he possessed. He grew angry. She grew cold. And little Tommy, now larger, began to lord it over the formerly equal playmate.[50]

The rift in Douglass's latest family led the lad seeking caring kin to black folk. He disliked blacks who acquiesced in servility. He relished helping blacks advance towards literacy and freedom. His new black "family," like all those to follow, consisted of non-kin raising each other to make whites' aspirations black reality too. Hugh Auld, contradictory paternalist, having refused to allow little Freddy to learn letters inside the white household, now allowed hulking Frederick to share lessons inside a black brotherhood.[51]

Soon, another anti-familial time bomb threatened the fraying Auld family charade. Hugh Auld, Frederick's sort-of-patriarchal nonowner, had a disagreement with Frederick's nonpatriarchal owner. Douglass, at age 16, was again dedomesticized. He was ordered out of his Baltimore "home," away from his black brotherhood, back to the Eastern Shore. There he was assigned to the ultimate anti-domestic experience, a year with Edward Covey.

Covey was slave breaker of the Eastern Shore. Lease the man your slave, went the understanding, and you will receive back a modest rent payment and a slave immodestly more docile. Covey's tactic was to order slaves to labor, then ostensibly to leave. He often hid nearby, behind stumps or in high grass or under bushes. If he spied the slightest let up in hard work, he would leap out of hiding and lay into the slave. He whipped Frederick Douglass every week for six months. This regime, unlike Hugh Auld's, was remorseless, 100% slavery in the midst of border looseness.

One hot, humid day, Douglass became dizzy. He lay down. Edward Covey booted Douglass in the side. That not sufficing to rouse the slave, Covey smashed a hickory slab into Douglass's face.

The bleeding slave picked himself up and fled. He ran not towards freedom but to report Massa's damaged property to master. Douglass's owner, at first disconcerted by the damage, ultimately felt compelled to side with the damager. He ordered Douglass back to Covey.

This order showed how loose the most northern South's slavery could become. This desperate slave was not chained and marched back. Instead, he was asked to take himself voluntarily back to the lasher. Frederick showed the power of the system at its loosest by going right on back. But he determined to test the looseness. If Covey came at him again, Douglass resolved to resist.

A fight between Covey and Douglass ensued. The powerful slave bloodied the brutalizer. Covey finally retreated, saving face by saying he would assault again if Douglass misbehaved. No further assaults transpired. The slave had stepped an inch towards freedom.[52]

Six months later, when Douglass's year with Covey was up, Massa assigned his "boy" to a plantation with a milder regime. The better treatment included no whipping, more food, less demands to slave in dizzying heat. Douglass now had to endure neither Auld's emotionally brutal charade nor Covey's physically brutal lashings. He was now just a decently treated field hand, with no pretenses about little Freddy being as dear as little Tommy.

Richer family-like ties to blacks accompanied better treatment from whites. Douglass formed another tiny group of slaves who wished to rise above being "black-assed" through literacy and Christianity. Once, whites, reflecting the need to smash countercultures, broke up Douglass's congregation. More usually, reflecting Hugh Auld's wavering permissiveness, they winked at black education sessions. Douglass enjoyed the shared learning. Then he scheduled a graduation. He conspired to effect a group runaway.

Alas, one conspirator in Frederick's caring brotherhood turned out to value his semi-liberty more than a brothers' gamble on full freedom. He confessed. The Domestic Institution had done its usual twisting work on yet another of Frederick's families.

Conspirators were rounded up. Other masters got their "boys" off scot free by blaming Frederick, the "yeller," for infecting blacks' "childish" imaginations. Frederick's master threatened to sell the instigator down river to Alabama. Then Massa instead decided to send his non-Cuffee back "home," to Hugh Auld's in Baltimore.[53]

"Home" had now lost almost all pretense of domesticity. Little Tommy was now Big Thomas, determined to distance himself from the bad black "boy." But Hugh Auld remained a sort-of-patriarch, trying to do best by not-so-little Freddy. He hired Frederick out to a large shipbuilding concern.

There Douglass learned firsthand what a morass the border slave regime had become. Some fellow workers were enslaved blacks, promised freedom if they worked well. Other slaves hired out their own time, paid masters most of their wages, and saved to buy their freedom. Some workers were free blacks, still others free *whites,* wage slaves doing "nigger work."

That collapse of black/white and slave/free distinctions infuriated white laborers. Douglass fell victim to their wrath. A gang of whites jumped him and almost gouged out his eye. Frederick ran "home."

He found the Aulds to be more sympathetic than his master had been about Edward Covey's assault. "The heart of my once kind mistress Sophia was again melted in pity towards me." In "tears," she washed away the blood, covered the torn eye with "fresh beef," all the while full of "friendly and consoling words." The lad yearning for a home found her attitude "almost compensation" for the brutal beating. "No mother's hand could have been more tender." The Auld familial charade was fleetingly again no act.[54]

Hugh, acting as if his own son had been savaged, went to the police. He found that officials could not touch a white suspect without white witnesses. The frustrated paternalist soon agreed to allow Frederick to hire out his own time and to save towards his purchase price. Douglass had to pay Auld $3 a week. Otherwise, Frederick was now feeling freer, especially since he had found a new black "family" in free blacks' East Baltimore Improvement Society.

Suddenly, the growth toward manhood ended. Douglass was two days late paying Hugh Auld. Auld, again the wavering disciplinarian, responded by taking away Douglass's privileges. No longer able to save towards freedom, Douglass now would have to flee towards liberty.

Formidable deterrents blocked his way. Only Canada, hundreds of miles north of slaveholders' border, would be altogether safe. Even the few dozen miles to the Pennsylvania line looked formidable, what with slave nappers eager to pounce on fugitives and collect bounties. Meanwhile, the alternative journey, if the flight for freedom failed, looked atrocious. The captured runaway might be sold down to sugar lands thick with Edward Coveys.

One new familial circumstance raised the stakes of Douglass's possible gamble. He had fallen in love with a free black. If he successfully escaped, she could join him. They could then marry as free man and free wife. But if he was captured, he would likely be sold away from her.

Encouraged by his fiancée and furious about having his partial privilege taken away, Douglass struck for full privilege. He boarded a train heading north towards freedom. He was dressed as a sailor and carried papers belonging to a seaman. The train conductor asked to see the documents. Douglass's heart pounded. The fellow barely looked.

A train passed by. It carried someone who knew Douglass. Frederick flinched. The man did not spot him. A familiar German blacksmith eyed Douglass suspiciously. The runaway quavered. The man remained silent. A black, perhaps after a runaway bounty, asked leading questions. Douglass moved away. The train crossed the crucial bridge. America's soon-to-be most famous fugitive was home, so he thought, home at last.[55]

– 7 –

I escaped, Frederick Douglass concluded in his autobiography, because a loose form of slavery could not work. As Douglass looked back over his enslavement, he believed that harsh masters had enslaved his spirit, good masters had generated his liberation. At Covey's, he had sought to endure. At Auld's, he had sought to escape. Give the slave "a bad master," concluded Douglass, "and he aspires to a good master; give him a good master, and he wishes to become his own master."[56]

The theory that the man with half a loaf will inevitably revolt has never been put so well or acted out so bravely. But Douglass's tale of border slavery illuminated the reverse of his thesis. His two key acts of liberation, the fight with Covey and flight from Auld, had occurred at the classic moment of slave resistance, not when treatment grew milder but when punishment became arbitrary. Moreover, Douglass's compatriots, experiencing the same loose bonds, did not usually flee. Douglass escaped not because all slaves smash every rusty chain but because rust on chains emboldens the exceptional spirit. The question remains, why was Frederick Douglass the exceptional bondsman willing to gamble half of everything dear?

Perhaps because the Domestic Institution had warped Douglass's domestic situations unusually severely. This institution characteristically raised hopes for familial relationships between blacks and whites, as well as between blacks and blacks, and then twisted and dashed those hopes to one degree or another. But Douglass's hopes were raised higher and savaged more totally than most. Few slaves experienced so strong an emotional inclusion in a white family as did little Freddy or so pure a resentment at not being able to grow up like little Tommy. Few slaves endured so utter a smashing of black kinship ties as did this black, abandoned by his father, ripped from his mother and grandmamma, then bounced in and out of homes from the Eastern Shore to Baltimore.

While Douglass's unusually destructive domestic experiences generated special rebelliousness, his unusual lack of domestic ties left him less to lose than other would-be rebels. As Douglass correctly described his exceptional position, "thousands more would have escaped from slavery but for the strong affection which bound them to their families. . . . The daughter was hindered by the love she bore her mother and the father by the love he bore his wife and children." Douglass had "no relations in Baltimore, and I saw no probability of ever living in the neighborhood of sisters and brothers."[57]

The fugitive would leave behind friends in the East Baltimore Improvement Society. But he had found, in his forced marches from one "home" to the next, that the pain of breaking nonblood ties could be eased by new brotherhoods at the next waystation. He would also leave his fiancee. But they had no children, and she, unlike most blacks who were run away *from*, could freely follow.

Douglass still wavered. Then he left. His friends also wavered. They usually stayed. The wavering was the point. A little shove backward, such as Hugh Auld delivered to Frederick Douglass, or a larger shove forward, such as abolitionists tried to give to runaways, might incline wavering Cuffees towards the daring dash. The border's slightly more vulnerable masters, not any inevitable collapse of all mastery, was the true lesson of Frederick Douglass's passage out of the borderland in between.

– 8 –

Douglass's story also illuminated the way master and man shaped each other. Not even Douglass could flee exploiters' power to make blackness seem black-assed. The one redeeming feature of this "paternalistic" system, physically horrible when most violent, psychologically wrenching when most kind, was that loose control gave slaves some space to form a countervailing culture and personality—and to mold their masters' politics and personality.

Frederick Douglass supremely illustrated slaves' partial control over the Slavepower. Slaves' most potent countervailing weapon, deception, forged one of Southerners' most important characteristics, extreme suspiciousness. Nowhere were slaveholders' suspicions more rooted in plantation reality or more disruptive in national politics than with the fugitive slave problem.

Douglass's form of protest, the individual deceiver as opposed to the group confrontationist, has been called a nihilistic, isolated response that could not dent The Man's sway. The truth is the reverse. When collective resistance was bravely organized, as in the case of Denmark Vesey, resisters were inevitably betrayed. So too, when Douglass sought to organize a collective runaway, he fell victim to the usual collaborator.

But when Douglass and others fled individually, their escapes had far-reaching effect. North American slavery everywhere pitted a controlling system not as total as it pretended to be against Cuffees rarely as loyal as they pretended to be. Because borderlands were the more exposed and least tyrannical slaveholder areas, a few border slaves could maximize concern about whether domestic slavery might be too vulnerable a charade.

That apprehension eventually yielded demands that Congress seal off the Slavepower's northern hinterlands. The two most important mid-nineteenth-century slavery edicts, the Fugitive Slave and Kansas-Nebraska acts, originated in border slaveholders' concern about runaways. Northern determination to circumvent these Slavepower laws increased Southerners' suspicions of Northerners, which increased Northerners' suspicions of Southerners.

Easy enough to see is how such snowballing distrusts, north and south, led to disunion, war, and an army of liberation. Less easy to see but crucial to keep in view is the way supposedly "apolitical" runaways initiated this political process. Even harder to visualize but even more vital to appreciate is the way the charade of Massa and Cuffee, with its strained characterizations, gave the lowly opportunities to shape slaveholders' very way of perceiving. No one made slaveholders more prone to suspect that Yankee "friends" were unfriendly than the individual slave schemer, who trained Massa to see con men everywhere, in the mirror, inside the quarters, beyond the plantation, wherever a democratic world pretended to love a tyrant.

– 9 –

These critical slave contributions to the process leading to Civil War and liberation have been curiously omitted from accounts of enslaved Afro-Americans' accomplishments. Recent historical works have stressed the positive aspects of slave counterculture, the strength of black marriages, the ability to reduce white dominance. Emphasis rests not on the victimization of the enslaved but on the vitality of the victim. An emphasis on blacks' political contribution, when added to accounts of their cultural contribution, risks transforming the history of slavery into even more a celebration of black creativity. If slaves mastered masters' way of seeing, and if that mastery ultimately helped unseat the master class, slaves not only endured. They triumphed.

May nothing here lead to that interpretive extreme. Posterity must keep in mind two truths about slaves: the new truth that blacks partially controlled their own as well as whites' history and the old truth that whites massively controlled blacks in debasing ways. Slavery would not have been so horrendous an institution if it largely caused that productive human suffering which leads to growth, accomplishment, fulfillment, triumph. This institution stifled growth, limited accomplishment, restricted fulfillment.[58]

While the supposedly utterly dependent slave reduced the supposedly utterly independent master to psychologically important dependencies, black dependency remained a heavy burden. Precarious slave marriages were dependent on Big House whims and profits. Slave religion often involved white preachers droning on about obedience. Little trinkets and fatty beef scraps and ability to rest during illness were sometimes dependent on striking the right note of fawning obsequiousness.

Nor was there anything romantic about the only successful counterinsurgency available to the man playing "boy." Slaves trifling with the script did not know they were helping cancel the performance. Cuffees did not foresee that little evasions might goad enslavers into a rabid defensiveness productive of a liberating army. In the tradition of the lowly, Cuffee did only what little he could. Serviles were aware only that they knocked the mighty a little off stride.

To those customarily kicked around the earth, a little counter-push feels very much like heaven. But this taste of earthly heaven was frustratingly limited. Slave culture, with its disguises of freedom now, taught a people to be furtive in their pride. Slave day-to-day resistance, with its indirect twitting of the tyrant, taught serviles to camouflage their rage. Slave tradition of triumph through trickery taught the beaten, in part, how to trick each other. The history of North American abortive slave insurrections records black traitors betraying black liberators. The lore of Brer Rabbit illuminates the degradation of life in quarters where slaves stole from each other as well as from headquarters. A "shame culture," one celebrator of slave culture has called it.[59] Cuffee was indeed ashamed of some consequences of inescapable shams.

Still, all the conning and conniving, the celebration of slick rabbits and the worship under sly preachers, the stealing and lying and tricking and absconding did more than give blacks some saving self-respect. Vaguely, victims hoped they might be ending their victimization. Less vaguely, slaves knew that individual resistance was making the Domestic Institution something other than the master of the charade desired. Slaveholders' deployment of power was too inconsistent, the mix of permissive democratic parent and remorseless impersonal dictator too loose to produce enough consenting serviles. Just as little women chipped back the chauvinism of domestic despots and nonslaveholding majorities gave pause to imperious aristocrats, so resourceful slaves clipped back the sway and presumption of the tyrant. In a hybrid world where the democratic infiltrated the dictatorial, masters could rarely make mastery come out just right.

Those who could not be cocky about altogether mastering slaves were more anxious about mastering freemen. Despite the almost unlimited coercion their world allowed when dictating to blacks, command over lowly "niggers" never quite fit their domestic design. How, then, could slaveholders master a democracy which left despots largely unable to coerce insincerely loyal whites—and convinced that the insincere peopled the earth?

CHAPTER 6

Democrats as Lynchers

According to one partially true myth, lynch mobs operated on the white side of the antebellum southern color line. Another such myth maintains that social control over white folk required their consent. The colliding half-truths show again that the color line was no impassable boundary.

The very word *southern* calls to mind Ku Klux Klans and tarrings and featherings, southern abolitionists fleeing north and northern abolitionists not daring to tiptoe south, bookburnings in front of schools and bonfires in front of post offices. The Ku Klux Klan was a postwar horror. But the Klan inherited a prewar tradition. Could an egalitarian republic remain democratic when lynchers flourished?

That question helped limit lynchers' sway. The slaveholder as democrat could not endlessly terrorize white neighbors. Nor could neighborhood gangs terrorize other Southerners' neighborhoods.

Still, sporadic physical violence did help restrain heretical opinion. Terroristic violence was also the natural extreme of a system which often used verbal intimidation to inhibit dissenters. On the white side of the color line, issues were debated, majorities were rallied, republicans did consent—but this was done within a shadow of coercive proscription supposedly reserved for the control of blacks.

– 1 –

Toleration of dissent draws another classic line between democracy and despotism. Democrats cherish a choice between options. Despots relish dictation of one option. Democrats protect the loyal opposition. Dictators jail dissenters.

This clear line becomes fuzzy when freedom seems threatened by external danger, as in national wars. Then, democrats legitimize repression. So too, legitimate liberty seems illegitimate license when used to foment murder or riot or insurrection. Democrats concede that freedom does not allow people to cry "fire" in a crowded theater. Free government institutionalizes not Anything Goes but freedoms voluntarily surrendered so that the community can endure.

No democratic proposition is simpler in theory. None becomes so tortured in practice. Lines between civil and uncivil freedom, liberty and license, patriotic and unpatriotic dissent, necessary and unnecessary repression are never easy to draw. Distinctions are hardest to formulate in hysterical crises, when dissent is most rampant and unity most vital. At such moments, the question becomes whether freedom under constraint is liberty at all.

The question is easier to answer when courts must sanction coercion. Totalitarian regimes are free to decide what procedures, if any, by what court, if any, must precede punishment. Democrats usually insist that courts try accused traitors. Writs of habeas corpus, rights to trial by jury, power to face and cross-examine accusers—such legal procedures customarily long survive edicts that disagreement is treason. When free speech is abridged without democratic justice, democracy and dictatorship become indistinguishable.

The Old South, as befit a regime both democratic and despotic, had built-in ways to blur but never to obliterate that saving line. The blurring came from slaveholders' ability to call dissenting opinion incendiary. A dictatorship anxious to be a family could not cage blacks off from whites' discussions. In parlors, at rallies, in churches, omnipresent "family friends" heard whites debate. Blacks also saw newspapers they allegedly could not read. This Peculiar Institution peculiarly could not separate the races.

A white dissenter thus could reasonably be heard not as disagreeing with white citizens but as provoking black insurrection. Dissenters could answer that debate was meant for whites. But they could not deny that blacks heard too. Where the unfree heard much said about freedom, talk about abolition became as insurrectionary as screaming "fire" in the proverbial theater.

Democratic courts still had to try accused white insurrectionists. The formula of slavery for blacks, democracy for whites demanded judicial process for white citizens. But a color-obsessed regime also required that only whites could testify against whites. Democratic courts were thus helpless if only blacks had heard whites foment insurrection.

In answer, slaveholders established quasi-despotic courts. Neighborhood patrols could legally maraude anywhere, including inside slave cabins, to investigate insurrection. The legal patrol, alias illegal lynch mob, stood "legally" organized to hear blacks' illegal testimony against whites.

The accused still had to have a "legal" way of answering. Lynch mobs provided the solution: so-called kangaroo courts. Disreputable mobs customarily appointed reputable community leaders to judge those accused outside the courtroom. Democrats here struggled to combine justice and despotism.

Kangaroo courts twice bolstered the master's mastery. Semi-open debate, potentially dangerous to a semi-closed system, could be stifled. Nonslaveholder jealousy, potentially disastrous to slaveholding minorities, could be deflected. Nothing excelled a lynching bee as high point of a dull rural week. Nothing better solidified a folk neighborhood than rich and poor united to tar and feather some alien threat to the public safety. Wealthy citizens, as kangaroo court officials, could point the poor towards purifying their betters' domain. With that reconciliation of a divided neighborhood, a divided regime, and a divided mode of social control, the lynch mob brought horrors usually reserved for blacks down upon shuddering whites.

– 2 –

The shudder must be appreciated. Whites contemplating saying nay to Massa often had to weigh consequences not unlike the fears deterring Cuffee. While blacks suffered brutalization exceedingly more often, whites could also face horrifying brutality. At least The Man lashing his "boy" was sometimes responsible to paternalistic codes. At least when mobs hunted down blacks, white patriarchs remained responsible for protecting their dependents. White dissenters, however, risked the wrath of hundreds of rednecks, responsible only to a hysterical view of conformity. Mercy could come only from squires whose interest often lay with feeding the mob's hysteria.

Responsible planters, judge and jury for the mob, felt least responsible for the most vulnerable whites: outsiders. Northerners or Europeans, recently come to the community and outside the folk nexus of commerce and blood, were particularly suspect. Lacking a protector, facing insiders' fear of strangers, an accused outsider could be more hapless than Cuffee.

The best Cuffee-like role to assume, for non-Southerners under southern guns, was to be more southern than Southerners. Outsiders often passionately declared undying love for slavery and hatred for Yankee fanatics. Like genuine Cuffees and like genuine religious converts, these newly-fanatical new Southerners sometimes became their part. Like fake Cuffees, white superpatriots sometimes dissimulated superbly. Such deceptiveness could raise as exasperating questions about pretense as did black versions.

Dissenting insiders, because related by blood to the community, were less often forced to feign conformity. But they too sometimes shuddered at the mob's definition of loyalty. They too could emulate Cuffee by keeping their disloyalty to themselves.

Some examples illuminate the fear that was responsible for much concealment of dissension. In late 1859, James Powers, an Irish stonecutter, was helping build South Carolina's new capitol in Columbia. Blacks had only the "nigger work" of sweeping up the artisan's rubble. Carolinians, when stopping to admire the rising symbol of whites' republic, seemed a little overeager to find the Irishman's brogue quaint. But they also seemed willing to make this stranger feel part of their racist civilization.

Then another stranger, the Yankee would-be emancipator John Brown, raided Harper's Ferry in Virginia, seeking to rally slave resistance. Carolina patrolmen, some unemployed, some drunk, all up for gang sport, descended on James Powers. These defenders of community values now heard his brogue as a traitor's. Someone urged that hands be laid on the fanatic.

Powers fled. He put nine miles between himself and his tormenters. Then he heard their voices. Nine miles had become a hundred yards. He ran. They attacked. They hauled him back to Columbia, then thrust him in a nine-foot jail cell.

Nine feet of safety were not enough. Rednecks returned. They dragged Powers to the city square. Whites packed the place. Patrolmen called their victim worse than "nigger." They handed lashes to two blacks. Lashers, indistinguishable from slaves lately whipped into sweeping up his debris, now stripped *him*. Revengeful slaves sent cords singing 29 savage times. Powers's blood ran from wounds too painful to count.

Whites lit a bonfire, heated a kettle, and splattered boiling black tar in his cuts. They smeared his uncut skin with burning sludge. They made him do a drunken dance of pain. They exulted that his reeling black face was now "nigger" outside as well as in.

On second thought, they wanted him worse than "nigger." They stuck chicken feathers in the steaming tar. They hooted at their "chicken nigger." They shouted to his bloodied, blackened face that his supposedly white head would roll if he returned.

Returned! He prayed for the mercy of leaving. They mercifully pitched him on the night train to Charleston. Every click of the wheels carried him away from the white state capital. Every tick of the clock found him closer to the rice tyrant's center.

The train arrived. A Charleston mob flung him into jail. For several days they came to hoot, jeer, threaten. Then they came to cart him off. They marched him past taunting crowds. They shoved. He stumbled. He was on the train to New York.[1]

– 3 –

Months later, amidst secession rather than Harper's Ferry hysteria, Levi H. Harris came to know the same helpless fear. Harris, a Marylander representing a Philadelphia patent medicine house, had stopped in New Orleans to peddle drugs. This typical borderite would tolerate sectional differences in hopes of enjoying national commerce. Up north, the Marylander urged sympathy for the South. Down south, Harris urged understanding of the North. Everywhere the neutral sought to make dollars rather than speeches.

In November of 1860, with Abraham Lincoln elected President, New Orleans vigilantes demanded statements from foreign peddlers. It was necessary to root out incendiaries "unsafe for a community to have in its midst." Whites who secretly supported Black Republicanism must reveal their secrets. Outsiders must prove their right to be inside the South.

Rumors flew up and down Canal Street about the Black Republican from Philadelphia. A self-appointed mob selected a committee of "the most respectable" to investigate. "Respectables" visited Harris. They demanded proof he was respectably southern.

A frightened Harris knew not how to answer. If he fulminated like a pro-slavery zealot, those who viewed him "as a northern man would very naturally suspect me of dissimulation." If he soothed in the manner of a non-political Union-saver, he would be suspected of appeasing Black Republicans. He was damned, in this secessionist inquisition, whichever role he played.

He saw a pose to strike. He approved, he said, of a Black Republican's election. Now the South would secede! After secession, Northerners, seeing the South was in earnest, would grant every concession. Secessionists would return. In a reconstructed Union, Levi Harris said, two sections would at last become one nation.

A member of the committee dashed out. He announced that Harris welcomed Lincoln's election. The mob rushed at the traitor. The committee of respectables haplessly conceded inability "to convince the excited mob of the facts." Insiders urged the outsider to flee on the next train.

How? A ticket was expensive. His accounts were unpaid. A customer, perhaps to escape his bill, had first sicked the mob on him. Now all who owed him money knew he could not chase them down. He lacked enough pennies to run away from debtors running away from him.

A customer, taking mercy, shoved a $100 loan into his hand. The mob, showing no mercy, threw him into a carriage. The carriage sped away. He knew not whither he was racing. The carriage stopped. He was at the railroad depot. They were allowing him a "coward's" exile.[2]

– 4 –

The process of exile worked less violently but maybe more painfully on those rarer occasions when the victims were insiders. In the tiny eastern Virginia hamlet of Falmouth, for example, the man bearing the name Moncure Daniel Conway possessed triple proof of belonging. Moncures, Daniels, and Conways had long been First Families of Virginia. Walker Conway, Moncure Daniel Conway's father, embodied patriarchal paternalism. Lordly and despotic, protector of his own and proud to be proslavery, he personified the master who would command the world.

He could not master his son. Moncure Daniel Conway, who loved the patriarch, followed a torturous path towards repudiation of patriarchy. The journey outside southern orthodoxy had many orthodox stopping places: orations on slavery's genius, articles on blacks' inferiority, blasts at Yankee abolitionists.

But he never felt comfortable with his father's hard bluster. Ultimately he felt more comfortable with his mother's gentle qualms. She privately deplored the institution which her husband publicly defended. In the early 1850s, while preaching in Washington, D.C., Moncure Conway went public with his doubts. Then the new heretic contemplated journeying back to Falmouth for a visit.

The head of the family was apprehensive, not least about the family. "If you are willing to expose your own person recklessly," wrote Walker Conway, "I am not willing to subject myself and family to the hazards of such a visit."

Moncure Conway came home anyway. He "was affectionately received by my parents, and all seemed about to go smoothly."

Then the son caught hint of a hazard not even the father suspected. Twice blacks stopped Moncure. They whispered that they were aware that he was antislavery. They inquired if he would lead an insurrection.

The next morning, Moncure Conway reported, "a number of young men, including former schoolmates," surrounded him. They called him "an abolitionist." They demanded he leave. Rougher sorts crowded in. They threatened expulsion. Moncure shuddered, but not because of the "little danger of violence to myself." His numerous, highly placed blood relations, "whatever their disagreements from me, would have seriously resented any injury." When the folk community coerced one of its own, a war between families might ensue.

Walker Conway wanted no part of that bloodletting. Neither did his son. A man who loved parents, brothers, cousins, Moncure Conway declared, "had no right to entangle them in quarrels." A dissenting son also had no right, however inadvertently, to give blacks ideas about slaying a beloved, if misguided, father. The next day, "humiliated and weeping," he exiled himself. For all their more physically awful humiliations, James Powers and Levi Harris shed no more frustrated tears about a republic made partially unrepublican by the mob.[3]

– 5 –

Quantity of whites lynched, like number of blacks whipped, was irrelevant to quality of terror produced. One white tarred and feathered, like one black bleeding from 39 lashes, could cow multitudes into at least pretenses of submission. Many a Yankee migrant to the South, who in a more relaxed regime might have become leader of white resistance, concealed dissension or returned North. Many a southern wanderer from orthodox truth, who in a more tolerant atmosphere might have sought to rally his fellows, exiled himself or shrilly proclaimed pro-southern dogma or feigned indifference to such questions.

Still, the right to dissent, while distorted almost beyond a pure republican's recognition, was rarely totally destroyed. In some areas under some conditions, dissenters dared to challenge the system. Then social control sometimes had to be consolidated the democratic way, often in very tense public discussion.

Twentieth-century totalitarians help put nineteenth-century lynchers in perspective. No southern horror visited upon whites compares with latter-day terrors such as concentration camps or pogroms or secret police. Late nineteenth-century southern ugliness supplies another perspective on mid-nineteenth-century violence. Although the antebellum South's slavery was more dictatorial than the postbellum South's sharecropping, prewar lynchings were pale precursors of the postwar Ku Klux Klan's more frequent, more murderous ceremonies.

Some 300 lynchings of whites transpired between 1830 and 1860. Many years, no lynching occurred. Lynchings abounded only in moments of hysteria, either during insurrection or secession scares. Such moments passed so swiftly—

and with such shamed faces—that "only" one white was usually lynched. "Only" once did a community lynch as many as seven. Victims were almost always Northerners or newcomers or other outsiders. Almost all "outside agitators" violated were exiled rather than hanged. Inside agitators sometimes had to be defeated at the polls. Why, then, did lynch mobs not terrorize more systematically?

One revealing answer is that the Old South's exaltation of the local neighborhood severely limited mob violence. The modern totalitarian nation seeks to coerce various people and vast areas into one totality. In the Old South, tiny clusters of white folk presumed they alone could spill their neighbors' blood.

That cherished conception left no room for coercing many localities into *a* South. Lynching could not ease the South's gravest internal problem, geographic divisions. No bureaucracy, country-wide or state-wide or region-wide, governmental or extra-governmental, existed to fuse many folk neighborhoods into one. No local patrol could terrorize someone else's locality. No patrol of slaveholders could shed a drop of blood in nonslaveholder communities. All the lynching imaginable could yield no greater unity than each neighborhood unified to be different from each other.

The central despotic institution inside black-belt neighborhoods, the plantation, limited purification of even minuscule locales. A tyrannical lynch mob invading a plantation could destroy the tyrant's control within his gates. Rednecks, often resenting squires and detesting "niggers," could gain revenge by kicking and lashing "truths" out of patriarchs' blacks.[4]

A patrol, once arrived upon a plantation to help govern slaves, itself insulted a planter's government. If slaves were out of control, the slaveholder must be overly permissive. Masters, stung by that judgment and anxious to protect dependents, could turn the pack aside with slander about some allegedly still more permissive neighbor. Nonslaveholders then ended up deciding whose "boys" most needed a lynching. No wonder that coercive slaveholders often moved to dissolve rather than deploy mob coerciveness.

During the Christmas season of 1852, for example, 17 North Carolina slaves allegedly conspired to murder Massa Josiah Collins's overseer.[5] Collins either believed the allegation or felt compelled to sell off "villains." Collins's enchained slaves alarmed local townsmen while passing through. Serviles sang and danced a Christmas frolic. They mouthed "great detestation and contempt" for Massa's "half-hearted" punishments. Collins, known for "good management" and "religious ministrations" to slaves, stood accused of sickly leniency.

A mob came to see if Collins had healthily clamped down. He informed vigilantes that his neighbor, Charles Pettigrew, was the real softheart. Collins reported he had inquired if his "people" knew of insurrections. Collins had been told, "without," he maintained, "leading questions being asked," that two Pettigrew slaves had killed Pettigrew's father. He urged folks to investigate.

Upper-class acquaintances of both slaveholders scoffed at the charge. "We all know," wrote a prominent doctor, that slaves constantly employ "false accusation" to avert master's violent displeasure. Collins believes, diagnosed the doctor, because "of his own displeasure . . . for selling or otherwise punishing his slaves."

Collins's lower-class listeners suspected otherwise. They wanted at Charles Pettigrew's "niggers." Pettigrew let it be known they were not welcome. Whether *his* "boys" had killed *his* father was *his* business and *his* patriarchal responsibility.

Another large planter congratulated Pettigrew on his paternalism. You must be "there," wrote James C. Johnston, "to protect your own." Without Pettigrew's presence, gloomed Johnston, "an army" could have driven "negroes into the lake." The incident, continued Johnston, showed that the propertyless would "believe any tale, however absurd," and murder any black suspect, however helpless. Mobs rose "for two reasons: to destroy the property of the master and from hatred to the slaves."

Pettigrew answered that masters must indeed protect slaves from "wicked white people." He ridiculed charges that his father had been murdered. "If I would listen to Collins," wrote the patriarch, "I would probably hang one half my negroes and sell the other half, and be the laughing stock of the whole community." Still, Pettigrew sold one accused black down river. He was too jealous of his reputation to be out-Collinsed by Collins—or to let mobs master his dependents.

Eight years later, during the 1860–1 secession crisis, Pettigrew again pitted paternalism against hysteria. Rumors again abounded. Slaves supposedly believed Abraham Lincoln would emancipate them. Whites allegedly infected blacks with hopes. One Cuffee supposedly told his female owner that 300 slaves massed in the swamp and would soon be marching near her house. Another "poor lady and her family" fled "to the hotel to spend the night, being afraid to remain in her own house." Still another lady, Charles Pettigrew's wife's aunt, dared not journey home. Aunt Mary considered her "people . . . the most innocent." But she feared an "old miscreant" nonslaveholder. The fellow had "prowled around the country since last January," inciting blacks to rise.

Pettigrew's wife waxed hysterical about the white Cuffee. He fooled everyone by "pretending to be a fool." The wise fool had "every intercourse with . . . negroes, and now his plan is nearly ripe for execution." Mrs. Pettigrew begged her husband to buy revolvers.[6]

Charles Pettigrew begged his wife to remember the real difficulty. We must "keep the miserable and low whites from shooting the innocent negro, who is only anxious to keep his lazy bones from labor." Our blacks, he affirmed, are "in infinitely more danger than you are." A nearby community, Pettigrew lamented, put 17 negroes in jail "to keep them from being killed by the negroless."[7]

That danger led blacks to beg another patriarchal Pettigrew to come home. When William Pettigrew answered the summons, his "obedient and industrious" people were relieved to see him. They consider "their master," trumpeted

Massa, "their best protector." Rednecks had "much alarmed" them. Their alarm convinced this Pettigrew too that "negroes are in much more danger from the nonslaveholding whites than the whites are from the negroes."[8] Even with Lincoln's army looming, even with females demanding revolvers, even with white incendiaries allegedly prowling, even with nonslaveholders resenting the wealthy, private patriarchs stood ready to abort the lynch mob, their only instrument for imposing coercive conformity.

– 6 –

The very nature of localistic community and private despotism, then, always stopped section-wide violence and sometimes aborted neighborhood-wide lynchings. But the color line between democracy and despotism limited terrorizing on the local level still more. While white pressures on blacks could legitimately be despotic, white relationships with other whites were illegitimate unless democratic. Democratic law demands democratic courts. Kangaroo courts are not democratic courts. Extralegal violence made law-abiding democrats squirm.

Such squirming could be seen in revealing places at revealing times. Fire-eaters, even when anxious to foment popular hysteria, had doubts about employing hysterical mobs. Thus in late 1859, the *Charleston Mercury,* for 30 years leader of secessionist zealotry, was squeamish about zealous vigilanteeism. "In our indignation at ... the North," warned the editor, Robert Barnwell Rhett, "we are in danger of" declaring men "guilty without proof." Rhett approved of extralegal repression when "necessary to security" and when responsibly administered by "older and discreet men." But "illegal violence on mere suspicion" would "not stand the test of reason and justice."[9]

Private dismay about kangaroo courts matched public pleas for caution. Thomas T. Gantt of St. Louis, for example, when "quite assured" that some "monster" had instigated "negroes to massacre and rapine," was "very little disturbed" to see a white arbitrarily tortured. But Gantt found it "shocking to think of an innocent man being scourged out of his life." Brutalizing "a suspected person in order to make him confess, until he dies under the torture, is really *horrible.*"[10]

Linton Stephens provides a second example of a man trying to reconcile the unreconcilable. Stephens cherished extralegal savaging of troublesome outsiders. He rejoiced to see Northerners "shot across Mason and Dixon's Line blazing in a coat of tar and feathers." He loved to see fanatics "hop like popcorn." Still, Linton Stephens would not administer extralegal violence himself.

A proslavery friend called Linton's refusal to lynch incompatible with approval of lynching. Linton, stung, struggled to justify himself to his famous brother, Alec. "I might be unwilling to clean out a gentleman's privy," Linton wrote, "because the disagreeable work is ungentlemanly. But I might still be glad the disgusting work was done, because he would have a much more comfortable time of it."[11]

Republicans who considered violating whites analogous to cleaning out-houses preferred to cleanse the regime inside democratic courthouses. Southern laws endlessly sought to wrench jurisdiction over white sedition from lynch mobs. State after state declared antislavery seditious because productive of slave insurrection. The Virginia legislature in 1832, for example, outlawed "advis-ing" blacks "to commit insurrection or rebellion." Maryland in 1836 outlawed declarations "having a tendency" to arouse blacks. South Carolina in 1859 found seditious "tendency" in anything "calculated to disaffect any slave." By widening regular courts' license over advice, tendencies, calculations, lawmak-ers sought to make kangaroo courts unnecessary.[12]

By narrowing the range of sedition laws, however, southern judges sought to protect freedom of speech. In 1839, the Virginia Supreme Court limited the potentially seditious to actual members or agents of abolitionist societies. In 1848, the same court liberated a prisoner convicted of calling slavery "merely" *morally* wrong. Repression of moral judgment violated freedom of religion. Only preaching against a *legal* right to slaves could be seditious.[13] Two years later, Samuel Janney, a Virginia heretic, escaped courts altogether by proving he had explicitly upheld the *legal* existence of slavery. He had "merely" attacked southern morals. Judges haplessly could only give the fanatic a moral lecture.[14]

Even when sedition laws were more broadly construed, inciting *blacks* remained the sole seditious act. Even if white discussion had incited black lis-teners, the accused incendiary could urge he never had any "intention" or "ten-dency" to influence blacks. His sedition consisted of trying to win the next election. No republican court could call *that* "tendency" unrepublican.

In mid-January 1861, some South Carolina legislators climactically tried to give republican courts power to coerce heretical citizens. Representative John Harleston Read would outlaw the poisoning of "the minds of those who do not hold slaves against those who do." *That* sedition, declared Read, was "well cal-culated to raise in arms an enemy who might be the most injurious." In upper Carolina, said Read, "a large portion" of whites had "no negroes and no interest in them." South Carolina needed "a law on our Statute Books" against inciting nonslaveholders.

Read's proposal could appear only in South Carolina. No other state had such strong tendencies for dictatorial proclivities to combat democratic sensi-bilities. Yet South Carolina also had a powerful republican impulse. Represen-tative Plowden Weston answered Read by scorning this "most extraordinary Bill that has ever come before" an elected legislature. The bill would jail "the very men who govern at the ballot box, the very men who put us here to govern the country." Weston "had always" put "great faith in free discussions." A republic, concluded this democrat, could not "keep one class down by the strong arm of the law."[15]

Weston's scruples prevailed. Read's bill was tabled. Read's exasperation was not so easily tabled. Dictators hamstrung before republican judges would have to deploy lynch mobs—if they could tolerate the unrepublican stench.

– 7 –

The irony was that the very white courts losing jurisdiction over white citizens were capturing a bit of jurisdiction over black noncitizens.[16] Not that the tale of criminal justice for slaves is any savory story. Republican trials for slaves violated the great divide between private dictatorship over blacks and republican government for whites. Masters thus "tried" 99.9% of slave "criminals." Republican courts usually only heard extreme cases involving black threats to the public safety.

Nor was justice inside courtrooms any joy for the enslaved. Blacks in Mississippi courts were told, on taking the witness stand, that perjury would result in an ear nailed to the wall for an hour and then sliced off. Continued perjury would bring nail and sword upon the other ear. Mississippi did not have to invent all aspects of Reconstruction's brutal "Mississippi Plan" after blacks were free.

Still, while blacks were enslaved, Mississippi led in giving accused slave criminals a little white justice. This southwestern stronghold of rough cotton tycoons guaranteed some indicted slaves jury trials and defense attorneys. This so-called closed society also stripped squires of acquitted slaves, unless the owner paid his slaves' lawyer. The Mississippi High Court of Errors and Appeals several times squashed convictions based on guilty pleas because a defendant was not told of his rights before the pleas.

White judges throughout most of the South sometimes similarly protected black defendants. Such protection extended from right to be informed of indictment through right to appeal to the highest court. State supreme courts took appeals from blacks seriously. Between 1834 and 1861, 31 cases involving blacks allegedly murdering whites came to the highest courts of Mississippi, Alabama, and Louisiana. Sixteen—over 50%—of the convictions were overturned.[17] As the Tennessee Supreme Court summed up the world view yielding such statistics, democratic courts must take "the slave out of the hands of his master," then give him every legal protection "which jealousy of power and love of liberty have induced the freeman to throw around himself."[18]

To which one can almost hear James Powers, Levi Harris, and Moncure Daniel Conway screaming, what about whites?

– 8 –

Judges heard. Courts, having stopped some violations of slaves, could hardly ignore all violations of citizens. Judge Lynch's victims could sue for damages. Such suits, although academic while mobs closed courts, could later become embarrassingly expensive. Vulnerable pocketbooks joined vulnerable consciences to check neighborhood violence.

A memorable incident in Dyersburg, Tennessee, illustrates the deterrent effect.[19] In May 1852, a white allegedly heaved clods of dirt at a slave named

Ned. The black allegedly heaved his hoe in retaliation. The weapon found its target. The white died from a broken neck.

The white community, significantly, did not instantly hang the black by *his* neck. Instead, white democrats placed Ned in prison, pending court trial. A month later, Ned escaped, allegedly with someone's help.

A patrol hunted Ned down. Patrolmen strung him from a tree. They asked Ned who had aided his escape. The terrified black at length nodded to their suggestion that a white man named "Hook, a grocer of low character," was the culprit. Ned, barely breathing, was cut down and returned to jail.

Hook proved harder to jail. Ned, being black, could not testify against a white in white court. Citizens found this paralysis insufferable. Hook had long been detested as a marginal member of white society and an intimate of blacks. He had long been suspected of supplying slaves with liquor and heaven knows what else. Now he stood suspected of freeing a black who had slain a white. Yet whites could not legally touch the "outside troublemaker."

Whites instead instituted lynch law. Governmental officials, fearing extra-governmental injustice, put Hook in jail "to shield him from popular violence." The mob resolved to attack the jail. The government, to protect Hook, would have to shoot its own constituents.

Instead, officials reluctantly surrendered the outsider. The mob, after being given the go-ahead by the kangaroo court's "respectable" leaders, drove 60 lashes into Hook's back. They ordered him to leave in 60 hours.

Vigilantes then raced back to the state jail. They demanded that Ned reveal who else had helped him escape. Ned named a highly respectable insider, J. M. Ridens.

Ridens! Incredulous vigilantes dragged Ned from jail and strung him up on a tree again. Who had helped him escape? *Ridens*. Who? *Ridens*. Who? *Ridens*. They sliced down Ned's barely breathing body. He was returned for trial.

Magistrates sought to try Ridens. But they could not legally listen to Ned's testimony. The mob would again have to supply so-called justice. Many wanted to slash Ridens. But the respectable feared a second shredding of respectable law. Ridens, although supposedly known to be guilty, remained free from legal or illegal justice.

A few months later the community had double reason to thank its leaders for returning to rule under law. Ned, after court trial, received a court-sanctioned deterrence. In the public square, huge irons shaped M and S (for man-slaughter) were rendered red hot and seared into Ned's cheek. The smoking victim then staggered off to 30 years in prison.

Thrills of savagery legally administered contrasted with consequences of savagery illegally deployed. Hook returned. He sued for damages. The court had to listen. Judges ruled that the community had to bestow a cash settlement on its victim.

So the black, Ned, who all assumed had murdered a white, had not lost his life. The outsider, Hook, who all assumed had let the "nigger" loose, had moved back inside the community and had made insiders pay for defying democracy. The insider, Ridens, who most "knew" had violated the color line, had been rendered untouchable by democracy's line against despotism. Even in moments of terrifying arbitrariness, those wielding violence had eventually remembered—and had paid for momentarily forgetting—that they were accountable citizens too.

– 9 –

Restraints on violence also conditioned the white South's two worst sprees of lynch mobs. The Mississippi slave insurrection scare of 1835 set a never-to-be-broken antebellum record for lynching whites. The alleged expulsion of James Birney from Kentucky in the same year offered the most famous illustration of supposedly violent purification. But checks on lynching, emanating as usual from both democratic and dictatorial sides of southern sensibility, left Mississippi and Kentucky, even at these two coercively closed moments, somewhere in the middle on closed/open and consent/coercion spectrums. Equally significant, Cotton and Border Souths, even during a shared hysterical moment, occupied different spots on a totalitarian spectrum. During its purest reigns of terror, as during everything else, the geographically divided South was no purely closed society—nor a single society of any sort.

The year 1835 was the perfect time for Southerners to experiment with pure totalitarianism. The Mississippi frontier was the perfect spot to make violence unlimited.[20] Immediate abolitionism had just been proposed in the North. The move for permanent slavery had not yet swept the South. A runaway expansionism had recently swirled through central Mississippi, then the South's wildest west. Unruly residents of Hinds and Madison counties in central Mississippi possessed maximum inclination to gun down their enemies.

Between 1830 and 1840, these two counties' slave proportion exploded from 39 to 69%. On this newly opened frontier, churches and schools were few. Duels were frequent. This brawling world was replete with remorseless slaveowners and surly slaves, jealous rednecks and frontier hangers-on. A violent-prone region with an unruly constituency was just the place to pour conformity down nonconformist throats.

Throats first became endangered in Madison County immediately before liberty's birthday, July 4, 1835. Rumors of slaves plotting a new Independence Day caused appointment of the usual extralegal committee of investigation. A slaveowner reported to the committee that his slave, under heavy lashing, had implicated one of Ruel Blake's slaves.

Blake refused to let investigating whites lash *his* slaves. When an accuser complained that Blake was too much a nigger-lover to whip forth the truth, a brawl ensued. Blake fled. He was captured. More slave confessions jailed other whites. Thousands of lashes slicing dozens of blacks yielded the story whites wished (and dreaded) to hear. Slaves accused not only the "soft" Ruel Blake but also the hardbitten Drs. Joshua Cotton and William Saunders of plotting insurrection.

The two seedy white doctors epitomized disreputable types omnipresent on a not-quite-reputable frontier. Cotton and Saunders practiced the slightly quack profession of "steam doctoring," promising miracles from hot applications. The shady miracle workers had long been suspected of unseemly rendezvous with blacks. Saunders had been so dissipated as to be expelled from a disreputable boarding house.

Madison County folks, realizing that white courts would not admit black testimony against whites, still wished accused whites to have "something like a *trial,* if not *formal,* at least *substantial.*" A new committee of safety, composed of the customary "richest and most respectable," was appointed. The committee's members owned an average of 44 slaves. The only nonslaveholder "trying" the quack doctors was the town's most respectable physician.

After rounding up, torturing, and "trying" Blake, Cotton, and Saunders, lawbreaking law enforcers elicited a frightful plot "justifying" a frightful inquisition. The two quack doctors were allegedly implicated in John Murrell's gang of Tennessee white desperadoes, who allegedly sought to free every southern slave.[21] The revelation about Tennessee satisfyingly blamed agitation on outsiders even further outside the nexus of Mississippi respectable folk than these disreputable quacks.

More horrifying, and not at all so satisfying, was proof that Ruel Blake, the man so soft as not to whip slaves hard, was indeed "sickly sentimental" on slavery. Just before swinging from the gallows, this "traitor" freed all his blacks. Most horrifying of all, some blacks "confessed" intention to slay "all the whites, except some of the most beautiful women, who they intended to keep as wives," as "white men had told them they might do."

The many-layered horror of outside agitators, inside softhearts, and defiled color lines threw Madison County into hysteria. Women and children were gathered up and garrisoned. Blacks and whites were hunted down and savaged. White after white, seven in all, the all-time antebellum southern record, swung from the gallows. Many more than seven blacks hung lifeless in the sky.

What ultimately stopped this terroristic purification was Madison County's attempt to purify Hinds County. Among the over 50 alleged insurgents named by Saunders and Cotton were two nonslaveholders who lived across the county line in Hinds, outside the turf Madison County mobs could "legitimately" intimidate. The Madison County Committee of the Respectable, seeking to pass respectable limits, dispatched its cavalry. Armed Madison horsemen, led by a small slaveholder named Hiram Perkins, demanded the right to extradite accused nonslaveholders over the county line.

At stake in Madison County's demand on Hinds County was the right to terrorize beyond local limits. At stake in Hinds County's response was the southern belief that only local folk could coerce each other. Patrick Sharkey, a powerful Hinds County slaveholder and justice of the peace, moved to take care of his folk, black and white. The justice of the peace declared *his* neighboring whites innocent. He sent Hiram Perkins and friends emptyhanded back to *their* folk.

The returning horsemen's tale enraged Madison County's Committee of the Respectable. The kangaroo court ordered a beefed-up cavalry to procure the accused "at all hazards." Patrick Sharkey also must be extradited for "trial." A man so protective of suspected insurrectionists was probably "soft on slavery" and an "enemy of Mississippi."

Patrick Sharkey proved not soft on anything. Such incredible suspicions of such a credible Southron illustrated why democrats demanded restraints on terrorists. Justice of the Peace Patrick Sharkey's cousin was William Sharkey, chief justice of Mississippi's highest court. Both Sharkeys exemplified a ruling class determined to rule its turf.

Patrick Sharkey placed his fight for local folks' turf and for private dictators' *noblesse oblige* in a strange garrison. Or rather, Sharkey's fort was appropriate for a class sometimes equating mob justice with privies. The justice of the peace barricaded himself and his family in his outhouse. There he waited to ambush invading horsemen.

Hiram Perkins and his Madison County gang galloped onto Sharkey's property. Perkins trotted past an outhouse window. Sharkey fired. Perkins tumbled. The battle of the privy was on.

Madison County cavalrymen poured bullets in the offending window. The offended Hinds County patrician stuck out his gun and returned fire. A blast shattered Sharkey's gun hand. Shifting hands, he fired, fired, fired. One victim, thigh gushing, tumbled almost atop the dying Hiram Powers. Another invader, collar ripped off his coat, had reason to thank heaven for losing but a garment. Another half-inch and the chief justice's cousin's bullet would have ripped the governor's nephew's jugular.

Invaders had seen enough of the gunman of the outhouse. Picking up dying commander and wounded fellows, they retreated across the county line. Sharkey knew they would return. He rode over to his county seat to request protection from his folk.

Hinds County's own "Committee of Safety" moved to "try" Patrick Sharkey, its own alleged traitor. Madison County citizens rode over to demand extradition of the accused. Chief Justice William Sharkey moved in to represent his cousin. The chief justice lamented his court's temporary powerlessness. He urged Hinds County folk to protect "citizens of their own county from trial beyond its confines," until regular courts could reconvene. Sharkey's neighborhood, rallying behind its own, armed to defend. Madison citizens armed to lynch. "A civil war must ensue," cried a handwringing observer.

The imminent showdown, no longer a pitched battle between the chief justice's and the governor's folk, would be a brothers' war between two slaveholding communities. The contest would involve not whether one slaveholder was loyal to slavery but whether folk could violate other folk. The warfare might indicate whether violent means of social control would be narrowly confined to a neighborhood or pass beyond county lines.

The battle became the most significant war never fought in the Old South. Vigilantes never passed that county line. Madison County citizens, although bent on blood revenge, ultimately honored local limits on folk bloodletting. They disarmed. Hysteria ended. Tyranny over whites could not be extended to other folks' terrain.

Madison residents subsequently discovered that they had gone further than democratic despotism could sanction. Once Chief Justice William Sharkey's court system resumed operations, Justice of the Peace Patrick Sharkey strode inside the courthouse. The commander of the outhouse sued Madison County assailants for damages. Through the legal system, Sharkey could exert leverage across county lines, the very power extralegal mobs lacked.

Sharkey won. His assailants had to pay $10,000. Whether in Mississippi in the 1830s or Tennessee in the 1850s, whether victims were disreputable grocers or respectable titans, extralegal terrorists might find violating democratic law to be very expensive.

– 10 –

The most notorious antebellum example of supposed forced exile illuminated the same principle. According to James Birney of Kentucky, unlimited mob power drove him to the North in 1835. The half-truth helped Birney gain nomination in 1840 and again in 1844 as a northern antislavery party's first presidential candidate. For a historic nominee, the candidate was drab, unemotional, colorless—in a word, unhistoric.[22]

But Birney had made himself an epic symbol of slavery gutting democracy. The Kentuckian projected the image of a native Southerner and emancipating slaveholder who had fled his region because he was to be lynched. What really happened was more complex and revealing.

James Birney was almost bred to wonder if despotism and democracy were compatible. Doubts about slavery had led Birney's slaveholding father to ask the Kentucky legislature to abolish it. The senior Birney, an Irish immigrant, had come to the Kentucky frontier not to abolish slavery but to rise in the ranks of its gentry. Starting out as a lowly peddler, he had ascended to a plush Bluegrass estate. His white Georgian mansion, up the hill from Danville's developing society, was proof of the newcomer arrived. That a proud climber should deplore the fruits of his climb illustrated how sincere Border South qualms about slavery could be.

The senior Birney also displayed the conservatism balancing the qualms. He intended to retain his slaves until the government instructed him to emancipate. Government never came close to so instructing. James Birney, Jr., future slaveholder and emancipator both, was raised not only to free but also to own slaves and to know how profoundly James Birney, Sr., was involved in having it both ways.

Birney the younger could not succeed at enslaving or freeing until he overcame the effects of his father's indulgent pampering. Given a black playmate
when he was only six, the spoiled young heir descended on Princeton University
in his teens, armed with fancy clothes and blooded horses and crammed wallet.
He drank, caroused, partied his way to two suspensions before graduating.

Neither undergraduate suspensions nor postgraduate law studies under Philadelphia conservatives dulled Birney's raw edges. Home from the staid North,
he marched on the swashbuckling South. In the 1820s on the Alabama frontier,
Birney gambled away his fortune playing cards with frontier sharks. Before he
could catch himself, he had to sell his plantation and almost all his 40 slaves.
Merchandizing those "family friends" helped reduce Birney to the self-loathing
necessary for spiritual conversion.

He was converted to the Do-Good Christianity rampant in the American
1820s. The new teetotaler began his career in disinterested benevolence by urging everyone else to stop drinking. The old slaveholder then embarked upon an
antislavery career. In 1832, he became agent of the American Colonization Society. He was paid $1000 a year to publicize colonization of blacks in Africa,
which he considered a viable mode of antislavery.

Birney left antislavery outside his colonization pitch to Alabamians. He
instead urged that the Border South's favorite reform would conserve the Deep
South social order. The dissimulating reformer explained that the Border South
could not use slaves as profitably as the Deep South. Witness the sale of blacks
southward. But because the Border South retained some blacks, white frontiersmen preferred the Border North. Before long, Birney warned Alabamians,
Upper South developers would expel their insufficient number of blacks to gain
sufficient numbers of white.

Blacks expelled would be either dumped South or deported to Africa. Your
interests, said the ex-Kentuckian to fellow nouveau Alabama slaveholders, is
that my old area not drown our new area in excesses of resentful blacks. Join
with me, then, climaxed the Kentuckian turned Alabamian, in turning Kentucky blacks towards freedom in Africa rather than towards insurrection in
Alabama.

In private, Birney whispered other purposes. Slavery, secretly wrote this
public champion of strengthened slavery in Alabama, is an "odious relation
which my soul hates." The paternalist was "fully convinced of the corrupting
influences of slavery" on children, "especially those of our own sex." He had
six boys. He wanted to raise them in virtuous Illinois.[23]

Then why stay in depraved Alabama and agitate to consolidate depravity?
Because a native son hiding his real purposes could best talk to touchy Southerners. If slaveholders could now be convinced that colonization would "give
them a more quiet and undisturbed *possession* of their slaves," they would subsequently discover that colonization also offered a "quiet and undisturbed" way
to terminate bondage.[24]

Birney's position illustrated the way a clever faker, black or white, could
slide around slaveholders. His problem, like Cuffee's, was whether resistance so

disguised could effectively destroy. The answer was that as destructive agitation, Birney's camouflaged heresy was ahead of its time. Although the Kentuckian hardly invented the arguments, he here presciently advocated two ideas destined to be dangerously stimulating a decade later: the Border South economic argument for deporting slaves down south and the Deep South racist fear of being imprisoned with hordes of blacks arrived from up north.

In the early 1830s, Birney's Alabama auditioners found these visions too remote to be scary. By hiding antislavery in a speculation that some economic crisis somewhere up north might someday bring too many blacks down south, Birney became a bore. His Mobile harangue led to "great satisfaction at my manner of treating the subject"—but few friends for the cause. His Tuscaloosa and Huntsville exertions led to an "altogether discouraging . . . deadness to the subject." His address in New Orleans left a large audience "deplorably inert." His almost desperate arguments in Nashville were "so much bolder" that he expected complaint. None developed.[25]

This allegedly practical politician's career seemed impractical whatever he did. If he hid behind colonization, everyone yawned. If he dropped the camouflage, mobs might mass. Since nothing effective could "be done *South* of Tennessee," Birney decided to move north to Kentucky.[26]

Within a year of returning home, James Birney publicly renounced colonization and embraced abolition. Emancipation, he explained, when conditional on not-yet-achieved colonization, encouraged sinners to continue sinning. Say to a slaveholder he may in "*present circumstances* hold slaves" and you supply "an opiate to the consciences." Unless future colonization gave way to immediate emancipation, those preaching benevolence in a slaveholding ocean would have the impact "of a popgun on the beach."[27]

The new immediate emancipator remained armed with popguns. After dropping colonization disguises, he became even more wary of mobs. But he still produced mostly yawns. Antislavery in Kentucky, if more thinkable than in Alabama, remained too apparently remote to provoke excitement here and now.

The careerist had at least not lost a career by renouncing colonization. Having quit the pay of the American Colonization Society, he now cashed checks from the American Antislavery Society. The renowned Yankee philanthropist, Arthur Tappan, signed over the funds. Alabamians would not have tolerated Tappan's salaried organizer. Yet in Kentucky, abolitionists' undisguised employee organized a Kentucky State Antislavery Society. He audaciously called it "Auxiliary to the American Antislavery Society." The "proceedings," reported Birney, were "harmonious among ourselves and uninterrupted from without."[28]

Then Birney inspired some excitement in the neutralist Border South. In the summer of 1835, he announced an August inaugural issue of the *Philanthropist*. The weekly newspaper would urge immediate abolition. Samuel S. Dimukee, an experienced printer, would own the press.

Some powerful Kentuckians preferred to coerce James Birney. The usual public committee of the "most prominent and influential" organized the usual mass meeting. Vigilantes urged Birney to suspend publication for several months. These opponents conceded that slavery was "a moral and political evil," albeit a "temporary necessity." They simply asked "outside agitators'" paid agent to delay his legal publication until the state legislature could reconsider the law.[29]

A Deep South slave community would have shunned such delaying apologetics. But Alabamians could not coercively lay down rules for consent in Kentucky, any more than Madison County, Mississippi, residents could establish codes for folks in Hinds County, Mississippi. Each neighborhood mob had to obey its community's sense of legitimate coercion.

In Kentucky, the anti-Birney mob delayed partly because no neighborhood consensus developed. After one mob formed to lynch Birney, another formed to lynch the lynchers. Violate James Birney, said the ultra respectable Joseph J. Bullock, and you must mob *me* and hundreds of others. In the "case" of James Birney, as in the "case" of Patrick Sharkey, two kangaroo courts ended up stymied against each other.[30]

Birney became judge of last resort. His publisher, Samuel Dimukee, having lately procured the press from one J. J. Polk, still owed Polk part of the purchase price. The press was Polk's collateral. Neither Dimukee nor Polk felt comfortable betting their dollars on Birney's future. Such mercenary considerations led Dimukee to sell the press back to Polk and Polk to propose a resale to Birney, if Birney still wished to publish.

Everything about this practical agitator mitigated against gambling his cash on so risky a venture. Despite experiments with camouflaged antislavery in the Deep South, despite espousing uncamouflaged abolitionism in the Border South, Birney had nowhere moved southern masses. Better finances, more followers, less mobs, and a more moral upbringing for his children might reward his decision not to buy out J. J. Polk. He decided to shut up—in the frustrating, perhaps lynching, Southland. He decided to let others put up—in the freer North.[31]

Birney spent several months arranging what he called "exile." In the interim, he anticipated an attack. None transpired. A mob had only asked him to delay. After he decided not to publish at once, he could freely go or stay.

– 11 –

The decision to leave was hardly cowardly and assuredly productive. James Birney could never have run for the White House from his homeland. He could never have been an influence at home unless he renounced Arthur Tappan's cash. He might have been tarred and feathered even if he had repudiated Tappan's funding.

On the other hand, Birney's neighbors might have protected him. If he had been lynched, he might have received damages in court. All these *mights* indicate that in the case of James Birney versus the never-lynching-mob, final cards were never played.

Enough tactics were deployed to show that undemocratic pressures had limited Birney's prospects. Southern coercers' most determined drive was always to cordon off outsiders, lest cautious insiders grew bolder. Antebellum Northerners could theoretically move South and help agitate from within. Southerners could theoretically stay South and accept outsiders' paychecks.

Southern violence squashed those theories. Yankees come South had to watch every word, as Levi H. Harris could testify. The Southerner paid by Yankees had to risk his own cash, as James Birney prudently refused to do. Given all these and more impositions on attempts to persuade, was not the Old South a closed society?

A somewhat closed society the South assuredly was. But the slavocracy could not quite keep insiders from ducking and weaving and continuing to fight. In Kentucky in the mid-1830s, James Birney could have resumed national colonization alliances, if he had cut his ties to Arthur Tappan. Birney also could have returned to his Alabama pretenses, preaching that slavery violated Kentucky whites' economic interests. We will watch Cassius Clay seize these positions in the same state—and stare down all mobs.[32]

We will also watch coercion influence Clay's no less than Birney's decisions. Physical and especially verbal violence would get to Cassius Clay's followers, pushing less committed admirers into hiding. But frustrated reform leaders still retained choices. Birney chose to leave. He ended up running for president. Clay chose to stay. He ended up running for governor.

Clay could have run for nothing in the Deep South. But Deep South lynchers could not touch the Border South. No dictatorial violence ousted Cassius Clay, or deterred him from seeking collaborators up north, or prevented timid followers from lying in wait for northern support to develop. The world of the democratic despot remained a somewhat open society, particularly at the South's northern extremities.

– 12 –

That vulnerability aside, slaveholders achieved vast social control over the democratic/despotic South. Such antithetical governing systems as egalitarian republicanism and perpetual slavery theoretically needed total separation to coexist, which helps explain why the southern color line was so sacred and miscegenation such a horror. But a little unsanctioned mixing of theoretically unmixable regimes actually somewhat consolidated ruling class control. Coercive lynching helped split white dissenters from outside agitators, just as genial persuasion helped split loyal servants from black rebels. Only where areas were whiter, despotic sanctions softer, and slave removal more plausible did slaveholders' power begin to fray.

An intriguing comparison across the color line sums up the large strength and uncertain weakness in ruling class power. Differences abounded between the border's James Birney, the white citizen supposedly hounded off tyrants' turf, and the border's Frederick Douglass, the supposed black dashing beyond tyrants' grasps. Dissimilarities, however, obscured revealing similarities. Douglass's skin color, allegedly black, was actually halfway towards Birney's whiteness. Birney's real reason for leaving, somewhere between the half-push of dictatorial mobs and the half-pull of democratic opportunity, blurred with Douglass's successful run from loose enslavement.

Both dissenters were most hapless when furthest south. Douglass, symbol of the fugitive slave danger, ran from Edward Covey only to Massa when down in southern Maryland. Birney, epitome of northern cash infecting southern politics, could not dent public consciousness down in Alabama. Both began to break free only after moving to the South's northern edge.

Birney and Douglass still decided that the system at its most open remained too closed. Both learned that the confused mix of the democratic and despotic could prevent as well as invite resistance. Douglass's attempt to rally group runaways collided with both slaves' fear of white coercion and a betrayer's retreat to white patronage. Birney's attempt to rally white dissent encountered difficulties both in persuading citizens and in defying mobs. Douglass and Birney came to the same conclusion: freedom required departure.

Other dissenters stayed. Immersion in democracy abroad, they hoped, might someday lessen Border South despots' not-quite-total control at home. Yankee allies, especially if constructively conservative, might yet lead more Frederick Douglasses to risk liberating flight, and/or more Cassius Clay sympathizers to defy physical and verbal abuse, and/or more border slaveholders to sell slaves southwards. A not-so-open Border South world might then prove too little closed for comfort.

Partly to guard against that shift in the nature of their social control, some strategically placed border masters eventually demanded Fugitive Slave and Kansas-Nebraska laws. These attempts to shutter off slaveholders' exposed northern boundary arguably involved anti-republican impositions on northern whites. Southern impositions still prevailed in Congress because enough Yankees cared most about preserving federal Union and national parties.

Many northern—and some southern—egalitarian republicans, however, resented Slavepower bullying, minority dictation, and dubiously republican law. If democrats' resentment of the imperious Slavepower ever exceeded willingness to appease it, slaveholders might have to chance a more open republican world at home—or might have to dissolve the egalitarian republic abroad.

PART III

CONDITIONAL TERMINATION
IN THE EARLY UPPER SOUTH

From the beginning of national politics, the more northern South's political leaders sporadically, tentatively considered terminating slavery. The tentativeness enabled slaveholding zealots to shout down softhearts. But hardhearts did have to shout. Those who believed in slavery also had to wonder if those who preferred the institution's termination would crusade uncompromisingly for its perpetuation. These problems began with Thomas Jefferson and the Founding Fathers, persisted in and beyond the Missouri Controversy, and came to an early climax with indecisive debates about slavery's future throughout the Chesapeake Bay in the late 1820s and early 1830s.

CHAPTER 7

Conditional Termination in the Early Republic

The most dominating Southerner as late as 1860 was not Jefferson Davis or William L. Yancey or any other Founding Father of the southern nation. The most critical slaveholder to Southrons who marched off to Civil War was not John C. Calhoun or Andrew Jackson or any other statesman who had ruled one generation before. The master who mattered most had been buried at Monticello a third of a century before slaveholders rose in rebellion.

In death even more than in life, Thomas Jefferson dominated because of the persistent "antislavery"(?) tradition he epitomized. To mid-nineteenth-century Southerners who unhappily apologized for the system, Jefferson's conditional strategy for terminating slavery remained the best hope that the institution would slowly fade. To latter-day reactionaries, the Virginian's tentative program remained the best reason to worry about apologists. The history of southern extremism from Jefferson's day to Jefferson Davis's could be summed up as one long, losing campaign to extinguish Monticello's master's vision in more northern sections of the South.

Recent historical wisdom makes these fire-eaters' concern unfathomable. Jefferson's way of awakening to the problem of slavery is currently seen as hypocrisy personified: much talk, little sacrifice of his own property, less done to sabotage his class, something perhaps done to sire his slaves, and, at the end of his life, supposedly a whining plea for a South forged to John C. Calhoun's South Carolina specifications.[1] Against this latter-day standard of realism, the Calhouns who stewed about the Jeffersons become unrealistic abstractionists.

Latter-day commentators who dismiss the Jeffersons' indecisive yearnings are not so realistic themselves. Attempts at cautious reform will indeed not advance very far, if reactionaries resolutely deter reformers. But that "if" is critical—and the necessity for vigilance has highly realistic effects. Worse, reactionary consolidation cannot proceed very far either, if apologists remain numerous and unconvinced.

Those lessons were everywhere learned during the American republic's first age of slavery politics. Those who would perpetuate slavery early discovered that as long as they threatened creditably, the South's tremulous Jeffersons would fall silent. But perpetualists also early discovered that apologists could neither be forced into consolidations of the institution nor forced away from increasing its vulnerabilities. The result was early loss of proslavery opportunities and early emergence of a crimped and contained Slavepower.

The second and third generation of slaveholding perpetualists drew the proper conclusion. If the South was ever to be *a* South, actively warring against antislavery, Jeffersonians' passive failure to man the barricades had to be contested as aggressively as apologists' tame attempts to chip away at the institution. Thomas Jefferson epitomized why fire-eaters had to rally the irresolute. Such necessity profoundly shaped southern extremist politics.

– 1 –

Faulty analysis and faulty semantics both have contributed to the late twentieth century's dismissal of Jeffersonian "antislavery." Linguistic and analytical problems are related. Changing words will not rescue meanings. But fresh linguistic symbols may jar sensibilities towards subtler understandings.[2]

The word "antislavery" has accordingly been barred from this analysis of southern uneasiness with slavery. That linguistic symbol, because connoting both an attitude and an action, has fallen victim to latter-day tendencies to conflate different characteristics. Once upon a time, analysts knew that not every sincere attitude led immediately to action. Back then, a Jefferson who obviously harbored "antislavery" beliefs and equally obviously was chary of "antislavery" action could be called some species of "antislavery."

Not now. Up-to-speed cynics, most cynical about political rhetoric, deploy an all-or-nothing test of politicians' language. Politicos who believe supposedly act to implement their beliefs. Those cautious about acting cannot sincerely believe. Against that conception of belief and action, Jefferson the "antislavery" man becomes the great American hypocrite.

Understanding slavery politics requires a more subtle conception of colliding attitudes. People have many wishes, some more dear, some less, each capable of yielding action if some more cherished desire does not bar the way. Thomas Jefferson, true to the species, was a bundle of relative priorities. He wished to end slavery. He wished other things more. He sought to ease bondage away whenever he thought higher priorities might permit. He shied from a lower priority when conditions seemed to him to threaten greater goals.

New words are needed to describe the apologist who desired to terminate slavery, but only when conditions were favorable. Jefferson was a prime example of that Upper South tradition hereby dubbed Conditional Termination. He would terminate nothing—would be only privately and impotently "antislavery"—if conditions seemed to him wrong. But this ruler would nudge his class towards termination, assuming conditions seemed safe. Unless Unconditional Perpetualists denied the Conditional Terminator his conditions, this reformer could—did—cautiously start something capable of growing out of hand. *That*

Jefferson—that often subterranean but never absent wish that blacks and slaves might, under the right conditions, diffuse away—helped provoke southern extremists over many decades into secession and civil war.

– 2 –

Scoffers might more readily reconsider the beginning of this process if the word "Jefferson" no less than the word "antislavery" could be erased from "Jeffersonian antislavery." Thomas Jefferson's attitudes and actions towards blacks are so repugnant these days that connecting this Southerner with Conditional Termination almost cements the notion that "Jefferson antislavery" never could and never did threaten anything. Furthermore, by putting Jefferson front and center, an analyst risks conflating a man who wavered with a national generation which acted most unwaveringly in northern areas where his irresolution was least present.[3]

These difficulties cannot be short-circuited by abolishing Jefferson, for to his generation and the next, he remained centrally connected to the hope of finding conditions under which slavery might fade away. To obliterate this persistent symbol of an attitude is to erase a historical fact. But the relationship between man and movement was one of symbol, not cause.

Thomas Jefferson's role in southern thought about slavery resembled his role as an American Revolutionary. Jefferson was not an epic figure in 1776 because he made the revolution happen. Events would have occurred the same way had he never lived. Nor did Jefferson, as author of the Declaration of Independence, create a new intellectual design. Instead, he luminously expressed pre-existing American beliefs.

Jefferson made equally little happen about bondage during the first generation of slavery politics. Nothing done or left undone would have transpired any differently had he never lived. Nor did Jefferson formulate the Upper South's world view. In tortured writings on slavery, he only applied an elegant veneer to an ugly indecision that was already the essence of the Upper South mentality.

Thomas Jefferson was an elaborator. He had an extraordinary gift of lending grace to conventionalities. The conventionalities are the point. Jefferson was not creator of Conditional Termination but the symbol of the conventionality and the most notorious man who acted out the creed—which meant most often that he shuddered to act.

Jefferson emerged from his, to us, unbearably slow actions to appear, to us, as hatefully nonheroic and nonprogressive. But he did emerge, with the tradition he epitomized intact, to inspire others to move towards termination of bondage, should slaveholding perpetualists be so stupid as to allow subsequent procrastinators the requisite conditions.

– 3 –

While the slaveholding democrat's predicament intensified as nineteenth-century egalitarian republicanism took hold, the South's discomfort with slavery began 50 years earlier, in an era of elitist republicanism—and for good elitist reasons. As the historian David Brion Davis has superbly taught us, for over two thousand years mainstream thinkers had called bondage as natural as breathing.[4] Then in the mid-eighteenth-century Age of Enlightenment, sensibility shifted. Southern "enlightened" slaveholders were among the first Americans to see forced labor as a problem and to thrust the issue into politics.

The American Revolution, by focusing American Enlightenment thought on the problem of tyranny and liberty, raised to higher consciousness the new awareness of slavery as an evil. Thus in his first draft of the Declaration of Independence, Thomas Jefferson accused King George of waging "cruel war against human nature itself, violating its most sacred rights of life and liberty in the persons of a distant people," carried by an "execrable commerce" into that "assemblage of horrors," "slavery in another Hemisphere."[5]

The enlightened planter who called his own labor system an assemblage of horrors was especially addicted to one enlightened virtue: balance. How Jefferson adored the concept. With that love affair, he epitomized his era. For a passing instant as the eighteenth century eased into the nineteenth and Americans increasingly recognized slavery as an unbalanced institution, enlightened gentlemen believed that rationality would balance irrationality, the head balance the heart, serenity balance chaos. The best men could bring the world to equilibrium. The balanced mind could everywhere keep the scales from tipping.

Jefferson, as he poised himself to be seen in Monticello's drawing room, personified that conception. His flowing red hair, which another man would have made a symbol of eccentric genius, he stylized into structured order. He was never seen in public without his rebellious locks combed into control—unless he covered the chaos with a gentleman's immaculate wig. Disbalancing bulges rarely disfigured his figure. His silks appeared never to show discoloring smudges. His house was swept clean of dust, dirt, disarray. His furniture was arranged in balanced pairs. His favorite posture, seated at his leisure, balanced deftly on a hip, the public face rarely wrenched by hilarious laughter or by ferocious frown, invited a conversation as symmetrical as the setting.

Such a man's creations were variations on a theme. What was the blueprint for enlightened republics? The free exercise of rationality everywhere protected—with every power harmoniously balanced by some other. What was the blueprint for enlightened buildings? A variation on the rationality of the Greeks—with every window, wing, wainscotting harmoniously balanced by another. What was the blueprint for an enlightened declaration to mankind? A catalogue of universal rational laws—with every proclamation, paragraph, phrase harmoniously balanced. What was the blueprint for telling an enlightened lady of one's lusts? A poetic dialogue between cool mind and convulsed heart—with rational intelligence balancing rapacious passions.

Still, beneath Jefferson's fastidious equilibriums lay unbalanced emotions he was loath to reveal. When he lost his beloved poise, as in his diatribes against "demonic" Federalist opponents, he sounded like some raving Andrew Jackson. He then appeared to revel not in tempered rationality but in temper tantrums.

What threatened Jefferson's temper most was not Federalism abroad but foundations at home. Thomas Jefferson knew that his leisure to balance on his hip, calming the universe with balanced statemanship, balanced buildings, balanced sentences stemmed from a relationship unbalanced and unbalanceable. As much as this very large slaveholder loathed what slavery did to the slave—and Jefferson oft expressed his hatred—he even more despised what despotism did to rulers. Slavery unbalanced the slaveholding elite, thus unbalanced the aristocratic republic, and thus unbalanced the future of the white race. To this adorer of symmetry, slavery threatened to make unsymmetrical the best rulers of the best hope of mankind.

Slavery, Jefferson cursed in his most famous and heartfelt diatribe, taught white children "perpetual exercise of the most boisterous passions." Master "storms," his offspring "looks on, catches the lineaments of wrath," and proceeds to loosen "the worst of passions." Slavery taught young white aristocrats to be sexually licentious, to be irresponsibly lazy, to be odiously tyrannical. The gentleman "must be a prodigy who can retain his manners and morals undepraved by such circumstances."[6]

Gentlemen's unnatural attempt to preserve an unbalanced class foundation would lead to lower-class revolt. Upper-class whites had to choose, so Jefferson believed, between giving blacks freedom or suffering black insurrection. "If something is not done, and soon done," he wrote, "we shall be the murderers of our own children." The world was moving too surely towards progress. Nature's God was too surely just. Slaves deprived of nature's rights would too surely seize arms after their own Declaration of Independence. "Nothing is more certainly written in the book of fate," he declared, "than that these people are to be free."[7]

A balanced achievement of freedom would remove freedmen from the South. "It is still in our power," wrote Jefferson, to effect "emancipation and deportation peaceably," so "that the evil will wear off insensibly."[8] Africans coming to Virginia tipped the balance scale in the wrong direction. The balance had to be slowly tipped right. After Virginia barred the inflow of new Africans, the state should slowly send blacks away, perhaps to Africa, more likely to the Caribbean. Then white laborers would slowly migrate to Virginia. This reversed population flow would yield triple salvation. Despotic whites would no longer degrade blacks. Degraded slaves would no longer despoil aristocrats. Degenerate despotism would no longer deter white migrants.

But freeing slaves without removing blacks was unthinkable. Jefferson suspected (though he thought himself broadminded to invite black intellectuals to change his mind) that blacks were mentally inferior. He never invited anyone to change his opinions that blacks were naturally uglier; that natural secretions gave them "a very strong and disagreeable odour"; that black males were naturally "more ardent after their female"; that their natural lusts were "more an eager desire than a tender delicate mixture of sentiment and sensation"; that their griefs were "transient," both "less felt and sooner forgotten."[9]

His own prejudices helped convince Jefferson that prejudiced whites would never accept blacks as equals. Freed blacks could not be retained in America because "deep-rooted prejudices entertained by the whites" and "ten thousand recollections by the blacks, of the injuries they have sustained" would "divide us into parties, and produce convulsions, which will probably never end but in the extermination of one or the other race."[10]

Hasty emancipation would as surely produce "convulsions" and "exterminations." Premature agitation would unbalance blacks and whites alike, leading to slave insurrections and white intransigence. Slaves, ever angry because deprived of natural rights, would rise up. Aristocrats, ever fearful of slave revolts, would violently counterattack. The white government, its balance ever precarious because of unnatural black enslavement, would be torn apart by angry recriminations and awful reprisals.

The balanced way required not blustery belligerence in legislative halls but calm conversation in drawing rooms. When gentlemen came together, soothed by dining and comforted by madeira, they could exchange opinions about what must be done. When the natural aristocrat was privately converted, it would be time—it would be safe—to go public.

Private manumission could set the tone of public emancipation. Enlightened aristocrats might free slaves in last wills and testaments, after educating blacks for freedom. Alternatively, sensible manumission might proceed one uplifted family at a time, with transportation to a land where former dependents would be fully free. If some cynic saw such plans as hypocrisy, crassly enjoying a rich slaveholder's lifestyle while cunningly posing as some distant liberator, Jefferson would have hotly denied the charge. It was rather, he would have insisted, a question of enlightened trusteeship, of remaining responsible for the irresponsible until children were educated to be adults.

Jefferson's plan of public emancipation, modeled after his blueprint for private trusteeship, involved manumission only of those born hereafter and only after they were 21, with colonization required after the new generation was educated. This so-called *post-nati* principle was fundamental. Unless emancipation was restricted to those born hereafter, natural rights philosophy could bankrupt natural rights governments. Natural rights to property mandated state compensation for property seized, even if the property was an unnatural slave.

Post-nati freeing of future children, as opposed to immediate freeing of present adults, made expenses natural. At worst, the state would have to offer compensation only for less expensive offspring, not for more expensive field hands and breeding "wenches." At best, the state might not have to compensate, since masters' property rights, it could be argued, extended only to slaves heretofore purchased, not to slaves hereafter born. Alternatively, slave children could work for master long enough to pay for their value, upbringing, and deportation. In any event, payments for manumission and deportation would be stretched over many decades, balancing whites' budgets and their apprehensions. No black would be freed for 21 years. No white would be deprived of a slave now on earth. No state would be freed of slavery for several generations.

Jefferson's ideal was a nationally financed scheme of reversed black population flow. During the pre-Revolutionary era, he scored the English for permitting Africans to be dispatched to America. During the post-Revolutionary period, he urged Congress to stop fresh Africans from flowing to America and to prevent slaves from streaming into unenslaved new American areas. The population flow, once stopped, should be reversed. The nation should find the best overseas colony for freedmen and finance post-nati deportation.

Nationally as locally, public opinion must be slowly prepared. When proposals provoked a sizable segment of the population to unbalanced defensiveness, the time was not right. Proposals offered in a holier-than-thou spirit were always wrong. But if Northerners approached Southerners in the right spirit at the right time, a national coalition could turn black population flow around.[11] Some glorious distant day, all blacks would reside outside a lily-white and altogether free America.

Jefferson's emphasis on averting public clamor, on agitation dropped if anger ensued, on emancipation scuttled if deportation was impossible, on balanced opinions and balanced tempers and balanced budgets and balanced migrations—all these shrinkings from unbalanced consequences indicate a reformer trembling at reforms. The fastidious Mr. Jefferson would touch the Domestic Institution only when the issue was domesticated. But the procrastinator trembled also that the institution was not domesticated. White republicanism would be unsafe until the slavery issue was removed. Future generations would be endangered if slaves were left to free themselves. Everywhere, Jefferson worried, the evil might yield bloodshed, whether men sought to make slavery unnaturally permanent, or sought to terminate it unnaturally soon, or sought to do too much or too little of anything at all.

In one unforgettable sentence, this leader of a class expressed the quiver his version of ruling-class ideology inspired. "We have the wolf by the ears," Jefferson wrote, "and we can neither hold him, nor safely let him go."[12] Anyone who realizes the terror in that summary of a world view is prepared to understand Jefferson's hemming and hawing about surrendering whites' hold on blacks. But this enlightened gentleman, who saw his very existence in terms of clinging to the slippery ears of a runaway beast, also needed to pretend, not least to himself, that life was as smooth, as serene, as symmetrical as a canter through rolling hills.

– 4 –

No wonder that posterity scorns this procrastinator. By making expulsion of Afro-Americans a prerequisite for ending American slavery, Jefferson loaded "antislavery" with a condition considered crushing at the time and outrageous now. By calling slaveholders' right to property as natural as slaves' right to freedom, Monticello's master slowed termination of bondage to a crawl. By urging that apologists shush if proslavery warriors roared, Jefferson invited his whisper to be drowned out. All those conditions saddled the most difficult social revolution this nation has ever attempted with the most superb excuses for delay. At best, Jefferson's conditions could only lead to tortuous progress. At worst—and Conditional Termination sometimes operated this horridly—the attitude was an excuse for relishing the fruits of slavery, while taking self-serving pride in not acting too soon. And yet Jefferson really did think if action came too late, his children and his children's children would drown in the bloodbath.

Such conflicted priorities invite a classic psychological pattern. One seeks to avoid the unavoidable, to repress the irrepressible, to reconcile the unreconcilable by willing it out of mind. Thomas Jefferson mastered dissimulation. He developed fantastic powers of avoidance, of not letting the public see, of not letting himself see, how distressed he was by slavery. His distress nevertheless remained acute enough to yield a little action. Both the small amount done and the huge amount avoided were as obvious at Monticello as in the White House.

Jefferson's world view demanded two activities while directing Monticello. First, this owner of over a hundred slaves charged himself with being an enlightened trustee, correcting present contaminations and preparing future freedmen. Second, he obligated himself to free those properly prepared. Jefferson, true to his character, usually managed to avoid thinking about these mandates. Equally characteristically, he managed to live up to his world view occasionally—disastrously seldom from one perspective, dangerously often from another.

One episode at Monticello illustrates the master's genius at evasion. Sally Hemings, Monticello's most celebrated slave, put Jefferson to the test as few trustees have been tested.[13] No trustee more successfully evaded his examination. Most historians, emulating Jefferson's contemporaries, have narrowed the Sally Hemings issue to one question: Did Jefferson sire her five mulatto children?

The circumstantial evidence does not serve Jefferson well. Hemings, whitish daughter of Jefferson's father-in-law, was long a household servant within the Big House. Jefferson was always in residence nine months before she gave birth. Jefferson manumitted some of her children and freed no black without a Hemings connection.

This evidence, to some, will always convict Jefferson. Others will urge that these circumstances could point towards other member(s) of Jefferson's white family as sire(s). Furthermore, the fact (at last a fact!) that Jefferson's father-in-law sired Sally Hemings perhaps explains why only Hemingses were manumitted.

This futile debate over circumstances obscures the undebatable point about dissimulation. Jefferson never faced or resolved the moral mess in his mansion, whether he and/or other white relative(s) joined Sally Hemings in multiplying the morass. And morass miscegenation was, as Jefferson defined morass, the most "unnatural" morass infecting the "natural aristocracy."

As Jefferson knew, miscegenation, however common in the Old South, was not commonly *that* luxuriant in southern Big Houses. Multiplying mulattoes were also uncommonly "obscene" in so uncommon a mansion as Monticello.

This was supposedly the utopian Big House, the model on the mountain for an adoring South to emulate. A morally enlightened trustee would have had to act, however unpleasant the action.

Jefferson preferred to avoid the unpleasant. He probably could not bear the emotional cost of confrontation, the unbalancing and horrid scenes which would have punctured the gorgeous symmetry at Monticello. The exquisitely balanced owner would have had to confront and cast away a slave he likely saw as lustily unbalanced. He would also have had to confront and correct his own "unbalanced" lusts, if he had indeed been once or many times the father. Alternatively, he would have had to face and castigate the nephew and/or other white relative(s) who had so "unnaturally polluted" the plantation. Finally, he would have had to embarrass himself before the man who took Sally Hemings off his hands, for he could not morally separate those whitened children with the tell-tale faces from their mother. Such nasty confrontations would have broadcast that Monticello had become a miasma.

Jefferson chose to do nothing. Or more accurately, he probably never allowed himself to think about the choices. Decades passed. Mulattoes multiplied. This procrastinator continued to allow the world—perchance himself—to believe Monticello's balanced surface was reality.

Jefferson's love of balanced surfaces and inclinations to forget unbalanced foundations explain why he failed almost as much as manumitter as he failed as Sally Hemings's trustee. That "almost" is crucial. Jefferson freed some 10% of his over 100 slaves. Ten percent per generation could water down slavery. So too, Jefferson's voluntary surrender of 10% of his property shows some commitment. Latter-day intellectuals who can see only commitment to slavery might ask themselves how often *they* have sacrificed 10% for their ideas.

Yet 90% still enslaved left the master class its power and prerequisites. Jefferson sustained his brilliant life-style by selling some 50 bondsmen. His executors, forced to sell more of his slaves to pay his debts, had few bondsmen left to free, whatever the last will and testament said.

To free expensive slaves more extensively, Jefferson would have had to repudiate his expensive dream of making Monticello the most elegant American mansion. Jefferson probably never gave the option a thought. Retrenchment never had a chance not so much because Jefferson preferred his artistry to his morality as because he had a constitutional inability to confront those hard choices his ideology demanded. The man who probably managed to overlook Sally Hemings probably also managed not to notice that the newest sublime decoration at Monticello was condemning another soul to another year of slavery.

Given the hard and disagreeable path American abolitionists faced, could a man so adept at avoiding hard and disagreeable thoughts ever have damaged his class's position? One answer is that Jefferson faced the disagreeable often enough to free 10%, and 10% was a beginning. An uncertain master class, proslavery zealots feared, might swell that beginning. Those in revolt against Jefferson also noticed that in minor terminations, as in massive dissimulations, life at Monticello was a model for what Jefferson accomplished—and evaded—during the first era of slavery politics.

– 5 –

Abroad as at home, Jefferson was timid about confronting slavery's problems, eager to maintain surface balances and to avoid unbalancing thoughts, determined to abort unbalancing reform. Yet abroad as at home, this adorer of symmetry helped knock slavery slightly off stride. He succeeded in working beneath the surface on proposals he prayed—others feared—would yield his master plan for ending slavery: turn the black population flow away from America.

He did work beneath the surface. Jefferson blasted bondage only in *private* correspondence and in his published *Notes on Virginia*—published anonymously, characteristically, "lest it produce an irritation." When Jefferson the President was asked to endorse an antislavery poem publicly, he refused lest he lose his influence. "I have most carefully avoided every public act and manifestation on that subject," he had earned the right to brag. He promised to "interpose with decisive effect" whenever emancipation became practical. Until then, going public would merely "lessen my powers of doing . . . good in the other great relations to which I stand to the public."[14]

The formula might seem to require the ex-President to go public on emancipation after he retired from public life and had no "other great relations . . . to the public" left to lose. So thought Edward Coles, a Virginian of a younger generation. Coles was soon to earn the right to press older statesmen to go public on antislavery. Frustrated in efforts to free slaves in Virginia, he would migrate to Illinois. There he would sacrifice his inheritance by manumitting his bondsmen and use his influence as governor to keep his state free soil. In 1814, Coles wrote Jefferson, begging the legendary old man to crusade for abolition.[15]

Jefferson begged off. "This enterprise is for the young," lectured the elder. As for young Coles, Jefferson instructed, he should keep slaves enslaved in Virginia. Otherwise, poorly prepared serviles might not have enough to eat. Coles should also remain publicly silent on abolition. The best way was to "insinuate and inculcate it softly" and privately, until a "phalanx is formed." Cole's reply was painfully apt: "Doctor Franklin, to whom, by the way, Pennsylvania owes her early riddance of the evils of slavery, was as actively and usefully employed . . . after he had past your age."[16]

Jefferson never forgot his youthful effort to suggest abolition to the Virginia legislature. In 1784, when working on a new state constitution, Jefferson penned a draft amendment, declaring the post-nati principle that those born after 1800 would be someday freed. He then, characteristically, put someone else up to proposing the amendment in public. A quarter-century later, Jefferson was still shuddering that his front man "was denounced as an enemy of his country and treated with the grossest indecorum." Jefferson, having decorously seconded the motion, was "more spared in the debate." He ever after privately whispered that it was "not yet time" if slaveholders denounced agitators as traitors.[17]

For the rest of his life, Jefferson never thought the time had arrived. With legislative talk delayed and legislative action stalled, Jefferson's Virginia emancipated only in silent last wills and testaments. The process state-wide freed slaves slower than Monticello's creeping pace. In 1806, Virginia legislators further thwarted the process by restricting manumissions. Jefferson, characteristically, never denounced the restrictions.

In national as in state politics, Jefferson cautiously sought to diffuse away slavery. But his tentative gestures occurred usually in private and never at the expense of unbalancing his higher priorities: controlling blacks, sustaining the white republic, and furthering his republican career. Not that Jefferson had to suffer the unpleasant opinion that he was sacrificing priorities. He believed that if he evaded decision, the necessity for choice would evaporate. Once national public opinion on emancipation became as balanced as Jefferson congratulated himself on being, the national government would ease bondage—and blacks— outside the white man's republic.

– 6 –

Two of the three centers of public opinion on slavery in Jefferson's era made his hope of balanced termination by redirected population flow somewhat feasible. The first slightly hopeful area, Jefferson's own Upper South, Chesapeake Bay, tobacco-growing region usually shared Jefferson's world view. Virginians, Marylanders, and Delawarians usually favored stopping the flow of Africans to America. Many Chesapeake Bay masters would also have favored a suitably slow and ultra-cautious way to experiment with sending post-nati slaves to Africa or Latin America.

On the practical question of when and how reform could begin, Jefferson was somewhere in the middle of Chesapeake Bay disagreement. In the demographically blacker Lower Chesapeake state of Virginia, masters were manumitting a tad slower than Jefferson's pace, while echoing his insistence on removal. By 1820, Virginians had freed only 8% of their 462,042 slaves. In the demographically whiter Upper Chesapeake states of Delaware and Maryland, masters were manumitting three times faster than did Jefferson, while implicitly wondering whether removal was necessary. By 1820, 43% of these two states' 164,594 blacks were freed.

While the Upper South moved towards ending its admitted evil somewhere between slowly and more slowly still, the second great center of public opinion, the North, moved a little faster, but with some Jefferson-like conditions. Northern insistence on proper circumstances before ending slavery is integral to the southern story, for the "North" was then the hinterland of the slavocracy. By "North," posterity usually means the states possessing no slaves by 1860. But what became the most southern North of 1860 was the most northern South in 1776, if "southern" means possession of significant numbers of slaves.[18] In New York, the percentage of inhabitants enslaved in the mid-eighteenth century hovered around 14%, a figure slightly above the Border South's percentage in 1860. Colonial New Jersey's slave percentage was only a little lower, Pennsylvania's only a little lower still.

In terms of absolute number of slaves, the someday-to-be-northern Mid-Atlantic region was surprisingly southern at the time slavery was first considered an American problem. In 1790, the state of New York possessed the sixth largest number of slaves, ahead of Kentucky; New Jersey was eighth, ahead of Delaware; Pennsylvania was tenth, ahead of Tennessee. New York, New Jersey, and Pennsylvania, taken together, contained one and a half times more slaves than did Georgia.

Still, this then-most-northern South already possessed in 1776 the key condition for southern Conditional Termination: a low and declining percentage of blacks.[19] Mid-Atlantic white population grew much faster than the region's black inhabitants. New York was 14% black in 1756, 12% in 1771, 6% in 1790. This eighteenth-century process in Mid-Atlantic states was a rehearsal for slower nineteenth-century drifts of the Border South towards black percentages under 10%, that magic plateau which in both centuries established the first condition for seriously considering abolition.

One condition still delayed emancipation in the then-most-northern South. In a nation equating life, liberty, and the pursuit of happiness with life, liberty, and the protection of property, liberty for slaves required payoff to property owners. The problem made post-nati emancipation particularly attractive. If only slaves not yet born were freed, perhaps no payoff would be necessary.

Mid-Atlantic slaveholders begged to differ. They had paid for the perpetual labor of slaves unborn in the high purchase price of slave "wenches." State seizure of the afterborn might also be an entering wedge. Reformers might move on to freeing those born before the arbitrary date.

Such intransigent defense of slave investment might sound too southern to be northern. Northerners supposedly only emancipated because slavery did not pay in colder climes. But Mid-Atlantic states are in the same climatic zone as the Border South, and some northern slaveholders fought for their investment for as many decades as did William Lowndes Yancey. Planters in eastern New Jersey and along New York's Hudson River, where slaves in some spots comprised as much as 30% of the population, were tolerably pleased with their profits and intolerably outraged that slaves could be seized when each was still worth several hundred dollars. Our strongest opponents, a New York proponent of black freedom later remembered, "were chiefly Dutch. They raved and swore by *dunder* and *blixen* that we were robbing them of their property."[20]

New York and New Jersey slaveholders who raved and swore still differed significantly from 1861 secessionists. While all these reactionaries wished to protect a valuable investment, New York and New Jersey slaveholders considered property in labor neither economically indispensable nor racially necessary. Believing a few blacks easy to control, they primarily wished to be paid to be virtuous. Their tactics were not to stand and deliver on some Civil War battle-field but to stall for more years of profits, then to raise the ante for giving up the profitable. The great Yankee battle was not so much over whether the post-nati would be freed but when, at age 21 or 28? Seven years of delay made some difference to capitalists—and enormous difference to bondsmen.

Emancipation after the American Revolution occurred without slaveholder-enforced delays only in the almost-slaveless, northernmost New England states of Massachusetts, New Hampshire, and Vermont. In more southerly Rhode Island, where 6% of the population was enslaved in 1776, post-nati emancipa-tion was delayed until 1784. Freedom for those born earlier was never passed; 108 slaves remained in Rhode Island in 1810. In Connecticut, where 5% of the population was enslaved in 1790, post-nati emancipation was put off until 1794 and freedom for other slaves not decreed until 1848.[21]

In Pennsylvania, where over 10,000 blacks resided, a powerful Quaker anti-slavery faction secured the first American post-nati law in 1780. The vote was close, 34–23. The law delayed freedom for the afterborn until age 28, a conces-sion to slaveholders who had called the initial bill, freeing females at 18 and males at 21, a violation of property holders' liberty. The Pennsylvania legisla-ture never decreed liberation for blacks born before 1780. Over 400 blacks remained enslaved in the Quaker State in 1830.[22]

New Jersey's slaves, 11,423 in 1790, had to wait longer for legislative relief. In 1804, the legislature freed those born thereafter, males at age 25, females at 21. At slaveholders' insistence, legislators allowed masters to "abandon" after-born black children, then be paid by the state to raise (and work) those "aban-doned." These payments comprised over a third of the state's nonpenal and nonmilitary budget.

New Jersey repealed the budget-busting abandonment policy in 1811. Slave-holders then could re-enslave those "abandoned," as if not a cent had been paid. Over 7500 slaves remained in New Jersey in 1820, over 2200 in 1830. Eighteen lifelong black apprentices remained in 1860 to cheer the election of the Great Emancipator, whose war against the Slavepower finally ended slavery in the North.[23]

In New York, slaveholders stalled off post-nati emancipation until 1799. They then secured the right to keep the afterborn until ages 28 (males) and 25 (females). Slaveholders also enjoyed more liberal "abandonment" bounties than New Jersey would later provide. Twenty thousand New York blacks remained enslaved in 1800, 15,000 in 1810, 10,000 in 1820. The institution was not wiped out of the Empire State until 1827.[24]

Thousands of New York and New Jersey post-nati slaves, although sup-posed to be freed on designated birthdays, remained perpetually enslaved. Post-nati emancipation laws almost invited masters to sell afterborn slave children south, before the emancipating birthday. Both New York and New Jersey early forbade this cynical practice. But both states initially provided too mild penal-ties to stop the travesty. Both waived penalties if slaves "consented" to transfers. Both allowed state officials to save prison expenses by selling convicted slave "criminals" to Dixie. One historian estimates that twice as many New York slaves were ultimately sold down south as were freed.[25]

These evasions yielded notorious stories and a public outcry. Both states closed post-nati loopholes within two decades of emancipation. Antebellum New Jersey, however, never ceased cashing in black "criminals" at New Orleans slave auctions. And immediately before New Jersey's crackdown on selling post-nati slave children down south, a Dutchman named Nicholas Van Wickle received permission to cash in his 60 slaves in Louisiana, based on their "consent" to forgo freedom.[26]

Van Wickle's grotesque culmination serves as climactic symbol of delays and evasions in what became the most southern layer of free states. An end to Yankee slavery at last came, not because slaveholders were going broke but because the huge nonslaveholding majority finally acted to eliminate the institution. The somewhat encouraging lesson of the sadly slow reform was clear. Assuming that low free black concentrations and modest compensations to slaveholders could be achieved, Conditional Terminators could eventually meet other conditions.

The now-most-northern South learned a less savory lesson. To reduce costs of emancipation, southern legislatures could decree post-nati abolition, then allow slaveholders to sell post-nati blacks into permanent Deep South thralldom before the liberating birthday. Still, despite slaveholder stalling and slaves enslaved elsewhere, a tier of somewhat enslaved states had been liberated at the slavocracy's northern extremity. Whites in tropical black belts were well aware that their next layer of northern protection, the Border South, possessed not-so-high concentrations of slaves, had few qualms about blacks being sold southward, and indeed might be prepared to dump blacks more swiftly southward, so that termination could proceed in another South-become-North.

– 7 –

In the first era of slavery politics, while what was becoming the North was ending slavery without trauma, its posture towards what was becoming a peculiar South remained nonprovoking. New England Puritans, for reasons New England historians have yet to clarify, were strangely quiet on slavery while thundering about other national sins in the early nineteenth century. Only John Woolman's northern voice echoed in the South. Woolman, Pennsylvania leader of the Middle Atlantic's Quaker abolitionist movement, never flaunted his virtue. He softly knocked on slaveholders' doors and humbly slipped into their parlors to discourse between thee and thou on the inner spirit abolitionist and slaveholder shared with slaves. Woolman's successor, Benjamin Lundy, often balanced non-holier-than-thou Quaker attitudes with African colonization remedies in his *The Genius of Universal Emancipation,* the most important North American antislavery newspaper of the 1820s.[27]

Unfortunately for Woolman and Lundy, the third important center of American public opinion on slavery, South Carolina, differed with the procrastinating Upper South and the gradually emancipating North. South Carolina leaders never much doubted that the institution, whether good or evil, was permanently necessary. For four years in the early nineteenth century, they reopened the flow of Africans to America.

The difference between South Carolina and the Chesapeake had deep roots in geography and in the colonial past. The Old Dominion, settled early in the seventeenth century by Englishmen with no experience as slaveholders, had originally imported blacks as short-term indentured servants. South Carolina, settled late in the same century in part by experienced West Indian slaveholders, had opted for permanent bondage from the beginning. In the early eighteenth century, the deadly Carolina rice swamps, compared with the healthy Virginia tobacco-producing Tidewater, needed far higher percentages of blacks.

Then late in the eighteenth century, while Virginia's declining tobacco profits coincided with rising Enlightenment antislavery, South Carolina's slave economy dramatically took off. Virginia's planters survived by growing less tobacco to market abroad, raising more grains to trade locally, and selling slaves to finance this smaller but safer mixed economy. Such economic shrinkage encouraged thought about black population shrinkage.

Meanwhile, South Carolina's expansion inspired thoughts of burgeoning black population. In the Age of Enlightenment antislavery, Carolina rice fields, in contrast to Virginia tobacco acres, were as productive as ever. Rice, unlike tobacco, also sold at as high a price as ever. On top of this lowcountry economic base in rice, the Carolina upcountry became, at the turn of the nineteenth century, America's first cotton kingdom, and the Carolina sea islands off the coast became a center of luxury cotton production. South Carolina, for a passing moment, needed more slaves, not less. Carolinians had long since decided that malarial swamps would be unworkable without permanent slaves.[28]

South Carolina aside, the North and Upper South, taken together, represented a huge majority abstractly hoping that their complicity in bondage might fade. But Carolina's intransigent fragment had leverage, for Americans wished a Union of all fragments. Allowing any colony to become its own nation raised the specter of a New World as balkanized as the Old World, of tyrannical Europe gutting republican America by playing off new nations against each other. Almost all the Founding Fathers believed that nothing done about slavery should jeopardize Union. Here was another condition blocking an end to slavery, a massive condition so long as southern hardhearts remembered to shout down softhearts.

South Carolinians first shouted down a whispering Virginian before the American Revolution began. When drafting the Declaration of Independence, Thomas Jefferson, it will be remembered, denounced the king for permitting the evil to spread to America. South Carolinians, characteristically, bridled. Jefferson, characteristically, deleted the draft paragraph.[29]

Jefferson was in Europe and thus not present to cave in when South Carolina threatened not to join the Union if the Constitutional Convention of 1787 empowered Congress to end the African slave trade immediately.[30] Jefferson, characteristically, never publicly denounced the eventual compromise, which bribed South Carolina to participate in Union by barring congressional prohibition of the African slave trade until 1807. Nor did Jefferson, characteristically, publicly lambast the cost. Between 1803 and 1807, South Carolina reopened the overseas trade and enslaved some 40,000 more Africans. Shades of Nicholas Van Wickle consigning soon-to-be freed New Jerseyites to Louisiana slave auctions right up to the deadline.

Only a fraction of wealthy Carolinians relished those 40,000 more Africans. Rice planters, Carolina's most powerful slaveholding group, thought their black concentrations already nervously high. Most of them voted against reopening the slave trade. Reopening passed the Carolina legislature in 1803 because the new Carolina Cotton Kingdom supported it. Cotton planters on the coast and in the upcountry wanted more blacks to raise more cotton.[31]

Cotton producers who would fortify slavery with more slaves could win one state legislative vote. Still, the ancient rice gentry was too powerful in the Carolina congressional delegation for nouveau adventurers to produce the usual Carolina kicking and screaming against national prohibition of the trade. In 1807, the first year Congress could end importations from Africa, aggressive southern imperialists were too few and too cornered to stymie those who would reverse black population flow.

America's most famous procrastinator was delighted with the occasion. In his Annual Message of December 1806, President Jefferson asked Congress to abolish the noxious commerce at the first possible constitutional moment. With South Carolina for once willing to allow something about slavery to be ended, Congress sped the bill abolishing the African slave trade to the White House. By applying his presidential signature, Jefferson brought to completion his own proposed first step towards turning the flow of black population around.

The law comes across in textbooks as a non-event. Southerners who fought to reopen the African slave trade in the 1850s knew better. The closure of the African slave trade was probably the most important slavery legislation Congress ever passed and among the most important American laws on any subject. The importance to Africans who would otherwise have become enslaved Afro-Americans needs no discussion. Only a little less obvious is the law's importance to Afro-Americans and their masters. The Man and and his bondsmen would have together developed a far less *Peculiar* Institution if a million or so "raw Africans" had been present to encourage despots' reliance on coercive violence, to discourage their thoughts that Cuffees familiarly consented, and to preclude their conception that only decent medicine, shelter, and food could increase the size of their labor force. This one law by itself justifies a critical assumption behind this volume: that the "new" social history must not be divorced from the "new" political history, for politicians' headline events shape, and are shaped by, the very ground rules of day-to-day social life, among the lordly and the lowly alike.

African slave trade closure also established critical ground rules for the imminent North American sectional controversy. After the North American prohibition, Cuban and Brazilian regimes together imported over a million and a half Africans, largely to stock sugar and coffee plantations. The North American Lower South could have productively paid the then prevailing price for at least that many imports, to stock new southwestern sugar and cotton plantations. Instead, the Lower South purchased fewer blacks at higher prices from the Upper South.[32] One critical result: the relatively blacker and more committed to slavery Lower South black belts became, the relatively whiter and less committed such areas as Delaware and Maryland became. The southern regime, considered as a whole, not only became politically weaker in one area when stronger in another but also was deprived of the added political representation in the national House of Representatives which a million or so more blacks would have brought.

The slave trade closure's short-run impact was the same as its long-run ramifications. In Jefferson's day as in Jackson's as in Lincoln's, the slavery issue in American politics characteristically focused on whether the system could survive at the slavocracy's edges. In Jefferson's era as later, slavery was usually weakest because most sparse at its northernmost extensions. But even in New Jersey, the system still retained enough staying power to make its death struggle long and arduous. An inpouring of Africans might have bolstered slaveholders ready and willing to save themselves.

That historical fantasy, of course, is unthinkable. The unthinkability is the point. The end of the African slave trade institutionalized the thought, southern and northern, that slavery should be conditionally terminated, not perpetually consolidated. African slave trade closure, more than any other action on that thought, diluted slavery where the system was thin, limited expansion where the institution was thick, and invited a North swollen by millions of immigrants from Europe to grow much faster than a South denied a legal soul from Africa. No other early action so shaped the later slavery controversy, which is one reason why in the 1850s southern extremists attempted to repeal the critical initial termination.

Cynics have argued that Jefferson's generation's crass materialism and racism, not their republican distaste for tyranny, led to this step forward. Most slaveholders, so cynics insist, wanted to maintain slave prices. Reopening the African slave trade would drive slave values downward. So too, racist Americans hardly wanted more "niggers" around.

This realism usefully emphasizes that the Founding Fathers were no purists, obsessed with "antislavery" exaltations. Their best-of-American belief that slavery polluted republics came heavily freighted with worst-of-American conceptions that white republics should be rid of blacks and that riddance must not strain Union or pocketbooks. Still, ending the flow of Africans towards "the land of liberty" had its obvious ideological appeal. These Founding Fathers were proud of leading the world towards human freedom and uneasy that their utopian blueprint contained so despotic an institution. Closure of the African slave trade illustrated the moment tremulous visionaries could be invincible: the moment when racial, political, and economic practicalities furthered rather than blocked their lesser but cherished vision of undercutting their most anti-republican institution.

– 8 –

While prohibiting African importations always seemed the vital first step towards emancipation, slavery apologists at first embraced but would soon renounce an apparent corollary: that stopping the institution's spread onto uninfected American turf would also further abolition. In 1784, Jefferson himself struck uncharacteristically boldly against the expansion of slavery into new territories. He joined several others in proposing to the Continental Congress that all new American territory, North and South, be closed to slavery after 1800. This proposed Ordinance of 1784 would have barred bondage from Alabama and Mississippi no less than from Illinois and Indiana 16 years hence.

Free soilers failed to secure the edict largely because only one other southern delegate stood behind Jefferson. Nonextension would still have won a congressional majority if one New Jersey delegate had not been ill in his dwelling. "The fate of millions unborn," Jefferson later wrote, was "hanging on the tongue of one man, and heaven was silent in that awful moment."[33]

The Ordinance of 1784 would not necessarily have been that awful for slaveholding perpetualists. Because of Jefferson's characteristic caution about premature reform, his law would have delayed emancipation in the territories for 16 years. In the interim, planters, cotton, and slaves would likely have invaded Alabama and Mississippi. In 1800, an established regime would have likely resisted congressional attempts to implement the 1784 Ordinance. South Carolina would have likely backed resisting slaveholders. The Jeffersons, as usual, would have likely caved in before Carolina.[34] Still, in his Ordinance of 1784, Jefferson demonstrated the history he would have preferred to make, if Unconditional Perpetualists had allowed Conditional Terminators to pass and enforce a reforming script.

Reformers' next favorite script was the Northwest Ordinance of 1787. Article VI of this famous Ordinance barred slavery from a huge midwestern area, comprising the future states of Illinois, Indiana, Ohio, Michigan, and Wisconsin. Article VI, like closure of the African slave trade, passed Congress because economic and racial conditions helped republican distaste for bondage to flourish. Southerners already possessed huge empty spaces to their west, in Kentucky, south of the Ohio River. A northern nonslaveholder migration to empty spaces north of the river might actually serve southern slaveholders' pecuniary interests. Yankees without slaves would not grow southern staples and thereby flood slaveholders' market. The midwestern-slavery-barring Article VI "was agreed to by the southern members," conceded William Grayson of Virginia, temporary presiding officer of the Continental Congress, partially to prevent "tobacco and indigo from being made on the NW side of the Ohio."[35]

But in the Northwest Territories after 1787, as in many northern states for the next half-century, some slaveholders, convinced that bondage could be profitable, still sought to save the institution. French Canadian planters had entered the Midwest before Congress passed the Northwest Ordinance. Could the Ordinance after the fact seize these long-time settlers' few slaves? Only if Congress passed bureaucratic mechanisms for seizing property. Congress, led at a crucial moment by Jefferson's favorite politician, James Madison, refrained from doing anything so in violation of property rights. The Midwest was left with the fact of a few old slaves, the few new words declaring antislavery, and no decisive congressional action to arbitrate between words and facts.

Into this vacuum where Jeffersonian procrastinators feared to tread stepped the most powerful economic interest in any new American territory: land speculators. These entrepreneurs bought unsettled land for pennies. They would make millions if settlers came. In 1787, land speculators, like congressmen, expected Yankees massively to migrate to the Midwest.

Instead, Northerners at first dribbled into northwestern territories. Meanwhile, Virginia slaveholders exploded into Kentucky, and Carolina slaveholders drove into Alabama and Mississippi. For a passing moment, slavery seemed a more expansive institution than free labor. The Illinois territory, located at its southernmost extreme in the same latitude as Richmond, Virginia, and bordering on the slavery-enticing Mississippi River, seemed as capable of exporting cash crops as was the Hudson River slaveholding area. Midwestern land speculators in the first decade of the nineteenth century, seeking to deflect the southern population surge their way, petitioned Congress again and again to repeal Article VI and thus encourage slaveholders to settle in Illinois and Indiana.[36]

Land speculators' petitions, like New York and New Jersey's slaveholders' resistances, demonstrate that northern slavery hardly died because capitalists believed climate barred the institution. Rather, slavery was crippled because a law banned what entrepreneurs believed climate encouraged. Especially in southern Illinois's Mississippi Valley, slavery would have been even more enticing if another law, barring fresh African imports, had not lowered the potential number of slaves available.

Missouri's early history reinforced land speculators' judgment that only law stopped slavery from entering midwestern latitudes. The same climate prevailed in those two Mississippi River neighbors, Illinois and Missouri. Both territories contained capitalists using slaves and eager for more. The difference was that Illinois came under the Northwest Ordinance, theoretically barring slavery, while Missourians, because in the Louisiana Purchase Territory, were free to import slaves. So midwestern settlers who wished to use slaves usually went to Missouri rather than to Illinois. Only your infernal edict, Illinois land speculators cursed to Congress in the early nineteenth century, restrains slaveholding settlers from stopping here rather than there and making us rich.

Congress refused Illinoians' petitions to repeal the Northwest Ordinance, just as congressmen had refused to pass legislation to seize the territory's preexisting slaves. The latest non-action threw both sides of southern apologists' inhibitions in the path of slaveholding expansionists. Having tremulously passed a bar to slavery, apologists now passively refused to shore up a vulnerable institution.

In this case, doing nothing was doing something. Congressional non-action left slavery's fate up to Illinois settlers to decide. Slaveholders were reluctant to gamble expensive slave property in defiance of the Northwest Ordinance, especially when slavery in neighboring Missouri required no defiance at all. Advantage thus passed to nonslaveholders.

Barely. Illinois slaveholders brave enough to try the system despite the Northwest Ordinance secured "apprentice" laws in the territorial legislature, allowing slavery in everything but name. Under these laws, black apprentices alias slaves grew from 168 in 1810 to approximately 900 in 1818, the year Illinois became a state and thus escaped the Northwest Ordinance's territorial prohibitions. In 1824, slaveholders staged a critical battle to make Illinois an uncamouflaged slaveholding state.

Nonslaveholders rallied behind the Illinois governor, who was none other than Edward Coles, the young Virginian who had a few years earlier urged the aging Jefferson to fight publicly against slavery. Jefferson had answered that Coles should remain a slaveholder in Virginia and refrain from anything louder than quiet and private antislavery discussions. Coles had instead transported his black Virginians to the Illinois prairie, freed them immediately, and given each black family a 160-acre farm on Mississippi River bottom land.[37] The governor now saw the fight to oust slavery from Illinois as his climactic struggle to be truer than Jefferson to "the principles which gave birth to the American Revolution."[38]

In this bitter and historic 18-month-long showdown over slavery's fate in Illinois, republican distaste for slavery was often emphasized, as was whites' distate for blacks. Argument especially raged over rival solutions to frontier population shortage. Who would supply most laborers to work the empty Illinois prairies, Southerners or Northerners? Proponents of slavery urged that the Northwest Ordinance's ban on slavery had directly caused Illinois's "torpid" growth. Slaveholders, if now legally invited to come, would especially be attracted to the state's lush Mississippi River shores. Coles's supporters answered that northern free laborers would come faster, unless repelled by the "idleness, vanity, luxury" of that aristocrat "of the worst species," the southern slaveholder.

Fortunately for Coles, late population surges gave new credibility to the old notion that Yankee nonslaveholders would people Illinois more swiftly than southern slaveholders. After the War of 1812, southern migratory patterns pointed southwest, towards the Cotton Kingdom. Meanwhile, the great northern push westward, which authors of the Northwest Ordinance had been expecting in 1787, at last developed—and with a vengeance.

The new population trends emphasized that apologetic slaveholders had tossed away what no chancy venture can afford to lose: a passing opportunity. Earlier in the century, land speculators, disappointed with the lack of northern settlers and impressed with southern population movements, had done their best to remove the Northwest Ordinance's leaky ban on slavery. Repeal of Article VI two decades before 1824 might have left the institution in Illinois, as in contiguous Missouri, if not massively omnipresent, at least present enough to withstand the Edward Coleses.

But now Conditional Termination's moment had arrived, as it had with the closure of the African slave trade. When creditable racial and economic arguments augmented democrats' distaste for tyranny, and when no South Carolina disunionist ultimatum made reformers pause, the reforming mentality was hard to beat. Coles and antislavery won the election of 1824 by a vote of 6,822 to 4,950. The margin, while clear-cut, also showed that softhearts' procrastinations had allowed the thought of slavery in Illinois to become all-too-widely thinkable.

History here repeated itself. Just as the decision to close the African slave trade at last occurred 30 years after Jefferson deleted the matter from the Declaration, so Illinoians finally secured a free soil future 40 years after Jefferson lost the Ordinance of 1784. Just as South Carolina cotton planters used the delay to import 40,000 more Africans, so Illinois slaveholders used the procrastination to apprentice a thousand blacks and to come within 8% of winning a referendum on bondage. Even after the 1824 referendum, a few black apprentices would serve Illinois masters for two decades. The same pattern of long delay, more black suffering, and ultimate containment occurred in New York and New Jersey. The pattern was clear. Not-very-aggressive reformers could end slavery where black population ratios were low, the economy right, and disunion no possibility. But the condition that property rights must be honored still made the cornering of slavery a delayed and close call—and the call became closer when perpetualists aggressively sought to spread slavery.

– 9 –

Less-than-aggressive termination of bondage in whitened areas further north helps explain why slaveholding apologists avoided action in blacker areas further south. President Jefferson purchased the vast Louisiana Territory from the French in 1803. His good friend President James Monroe of Virginia later purchased the vast Deep South territory of Florida from the Spanish. Both Virginians managed to forget about barring slavery in these new Deep South territories, in part because Deep South states might disrupt any such attempts. Shades of slaveholding apologists managing to forget about South Carolina's 40,000 new Africans. Shades of Thomas Jefferson managing to forget about Sally Hemings.

These tendencies to forget directed the surge of black population towards American areas least likely to reverse the flow. Apologists tremulously helped bar the spread of slavery into the Northwest Territories, where nontropical climate made the institution relatively harder to consolidate, and boldly secured Louisiana and Florida, where tropical habitats made bondage relatively more profitable. Furthermore, inclinations not to dare a controversy over slavery in the Louisiana Purchase Territory permitted the institution inside one area where termination was feasible. The future state of Missouri no less than the future state of Louisiana was in the Louisiana Purchase Territory. By saying nothing about slavery in the Louisiana Purchase Territory after banning slavery in the Northwest Territory, Congress invited slaveholders to flow into the midwestern area of Missouri rather than into the neighboring area of Illinois. The result by 1820: Missouri's 10,222 slaves constituted 15.8% of its population, while Illinois's 917 apprentices alias slaves constituted 1.7% of its population.

In both Missouri and Illinois, apologists' tendency not to confront slavery made problems worse. Early failure to oust the few dozen slaveholders residing in the Northwest Territories ultimately led to a bitter and rather close local confrontation over enslaving the free state of Illinois. So too, President Jefferson's early failure to bar potential slavery in Missouri Territory would soon lead to a national crisis over freeing the enslaved state of Missouri. We will watch Thomas Jefferson unhappily foresee that the Missouri Controversy was the first signpost on the road to disunion. But this apologizing procrastinator would typically fail to see that his tendency to shield his eyes had helped create a crisis of prophetic proportions.

– 10 –

This appropriate climax to the first famous Conditional Terminator's wavering approach epitomized the first generation of slavery politics. The lesson of Thomas Jefferson's not-so-bold sideswipes against slavery was curiously similar to the lesson of Denmark Vesey's very bold confrontationism. Camouflaged Jeffersons, like disguised slave rebels, could attack if the establishment went to sleep. Perpetualists who had the sense to guard their rifles, however, could keep dissemblers from massively assaulting.

Still, bullets and bullying could not prevent stealthful resistance. Just as Cuffees could slip a little poison into water wells, so slaveholding apologists' passive unwillingness to fight for more slave territories and more Africans had undercut sectional consolidation. If Latin American-like lust for millions of more Africans plus midwestern land speculators' greed for a rapacious slaveholder frontier had overcome republican distaste for tyranny, North American slavery might have emerged from the first generation of slavery politics as a booming national institution with an imperialistic slaveholding class. Instead, slaveholder republicans' wary acquiescence in containment helped transform the Slavepower, in one generation, into the national republic's most apologetic and cornered power structure.

The trapped Slavepower remained powerful, however, not least because past retreats at the fringes generated greater intransigence inside the southern center. A national institution had been contained in a peculiar section. But whites trapped with blacks were more susceptible to racial anxiety and thus more opposed to a still narrower containment. Again, a sectional institution had been barred from receiving overseas recruits. But rulers of an institution deemed too poisonous to grow could become more aggressively defensive when challenged by a rapidly growing North.

Could reformers so tentative in a period of little outside attack confront external assault without becoming rabidly defensive? Could a reform mentality that operated so tremulously in the somewhat whiter Mid-Atlantic and Mid-west dare to attack the somewhat blacker Border South? Could reformers who had barely nudged slavery in the Middle and Lower Souths ever force blacks out of America's blackest domains? Apologists had had difficulty scoring relatively easy early victories over slavery. Harder tests of the soft mentality lay just ahead.

CHAPTER 8

The Missouri Controversy

According to the current conventional wisdom, the South gave up the attempt to abolish slavery after reformers' first real test. The Missouri Controversy of 1819–20 supposedly annihilated "Jeffersonian antislavery," with Thomas Jefferson himself slaying his offspring. Jefferson's 1820 letter after the Missouri Compromise to Congressman John Holmes is the supposed critical proof that the Sage of Monticello drew close to John C. Calhoun.

Jefferson's Holmes letter does reveal revised tactics. But this and other evidence hardly shows that southern apologists became warriors for slavery's perpetuation. Instead, the Missouri Controversy scared the Jeffersons towards new efforts to remove slaves from America.

– 1 –

The Missouri Controversy differed from almost every pre-Civil War congressional crisis in that a Northerner attacked first. On the unlucky (for the Union) 13th of February, 1819, James Tallmadge, Jr., congressman from New York, moved twin amendments to a bill enabling enslaved Missouri to write a constitution and then be admitted into the Union. The first amendment would bar future slaves from entering the admitted state. The second amendment would free Missouri slaves born after admission at age 25.[1]

Tallmadge was the man and Missouri was the place to spread abolition achieved in the North down to the Border South. In 1817, the congressman had helped secure New York's final emancipation act, freeing all slaves ten years hence. In 1819, the Tallmadge Amendments proposed a more limited abolition, reserved exclusively for slaves thereafter born in Missouri. Tallmadge's proposed age for freeing post-nati slaves in Missouri, 25, was exactly what New York had enacted in 1799 for post-nati black females (New York post-nati males had been declared freed at 28). In 1819, Missouri had about the same small number of blacks, around 10,000, as did New York. Missouri's relatively

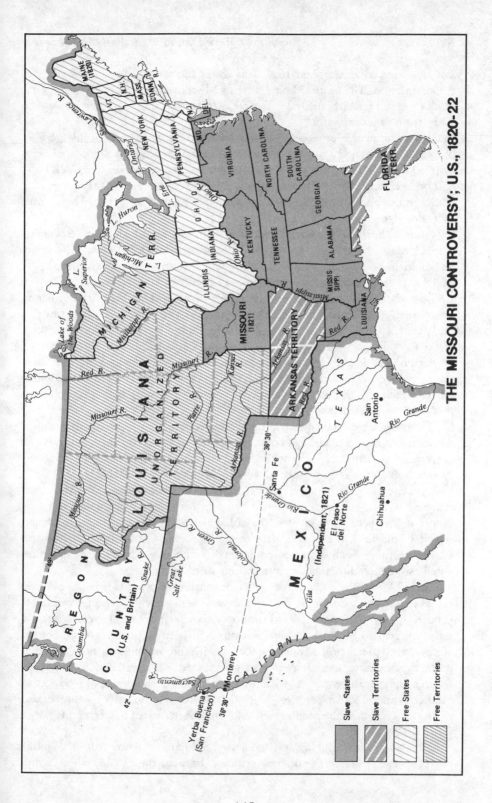

THE MISSOURI CONTROVERSY; U.S., 1820-22

Slave States

Slave Territories

Free States

Free Territories

low slave percentage, around 16%, was about the same as New York's in the colonial period. The proposed new state of Missouri, not very enslaved or very black or very far south, invited a Yankee attempt to nudge southern apologists away from procrastination.

James Tallmadge proposed Thomas Jefferson's sort of gingerly nudge. No black born before 1820 would be freed. No slave born after the law passed need be freed before 1844, or indeed ever. Nor need a large Missouri free black population ever exist. Black ratios were low, no slave could enter in the future, and blacks could be sold down river before emancipating birthdays, as had been done in Tallmadge's state.

James Tallmadge, Jr., was a Republican. But northern Federalists, especially Rufus King of New York, supported Tallmadge with special venom. Shocked slaveholders no longer faced John Woolman's tactful probing. Yankees now urged that the South was too depraved to expand.

Behind the new vituperation lay an old wound. The Tallmadge Amendments revived and brought center stage an important secondary issue in the Philadelphia Convention of 1787. At the historic conclave where the United States Constitution was designed, North and South had differed over how to apportion seats in the House of Representatives. Northerners would base each state's number of representatives solely on its percentage of the nation's white citizenry. Southerners would swell their power by counting both white citizens *and* black noncitizens.

The issue's importance transcended the House. Sway over the entire government was at stake. The less-populated South was already scheduled to wield power disproportionate to its white numbers in the Senate, for each state, no matter how extensively populated, would elect two senators. In the Electoral College, each state would receive one presidential elector for each senator and representative. Thus extra southern power in the House, when added to extra power in the Senate, would lead to enhanced power in selecting Presidents, which would lead to added control over a Supreme Court nominated by the Chief Executive. Such special leverage, over and above a one-white-man, one-vote basis, denoted that loaded antebellum word, Slavepower.

In 1787, when the Constitutional Convention resolved this issue, conventional republican wisdom justified the Slavepower's right to extra power. Independent gentlemen were expected to supply civic virtue from above. Dependent plebeians had to be blocked from seizing their betters' property from below. Slaves were special property but property still and arguably in need of extra protection because special. A properly balanced elitist republic, argued the South's eighteenth-century patricians, must give slaveholders extra power to balance nonslaveholders, just as the ideal constitution must give the propertied extra power against the propertyless and small states extra power against large states.

Northern elitist republicans still objected to augmented power for the southern propertied elite in the one government branch, the House, where white numbers alone were supposed to dictate each state's sway. Both North and South had to give in a little if aristocratic Union was to begin. Hence the resulting compromise, with each white counting as one soul and each slave as three-fifths of a human when apportioning each state's share of House seats. Slaves were also made to count as three-fifths of persons in determining each state's proportion of those "direct taxes" Congress was authorized to charge state governments. The Slavepower was to pay extra dollars for extra power.[2]

The three-fifths clause only slightly boosted the Slavepower's power. In 1790, southern states, possessing around 40% of the nation's white population, controlled around 47% of the House and Electoral College. That small expanded leverage became decisive only in the closest presidential and House votes. In the most important political contest in the early republic, the Election of 1800, the three-fifths clause probably turned what might otherwise have been the Age of Adams into the Age of Jefferson. In an Electoral College where the three-fifths clause gave Southerners 14 extra electors, the Republicans' Thomas Jefferson defeated the Federalists' John Adams, 73–65. Jefferson swept the South's extra electors, 12–2. If no three-fifths clause had existed and House apportionment had been based strictly on white numbers, Adams would have likely squeaked by, 63–61.

So ended Massachusetts's Adams's one-term interruption in Virginia slave-holders' dominion over the White House. Thomas Jefferson served out two presidential terms, as had George Washington before Adams and as would James Madison and James Monroe after Jefferson. Virginia's elite thus controlled the new nation's highest office for 32 of the republic's first 36 years: truly a Virginia Dynasty.

Partisans of the Virginia Dynasty often charged that Federalists were dangerously undemocratic. Younger Federalists, not a tad less democratic than Jeffersonians, especially resented the slur on their democratic sensibilities, particularly since the very establishment of the Age of Jefferson had depended on the arguably undemocratic three-fifths clause. Dynastic aspects of the Virginia Dynasty bothered Federalists' opponents too. Northern Republicans such as James Tallmadge, Jr., resented Virginians for monopolizing high office. The Jeffersons, Madisons, and Monroes passed power to each other as if only slave-holders possessed republican virtue. But did the Virginia Dynasty, spawned by the three-fifths clause, begin its reign democratically?[3]

That question became increasingly disturbing as the American definition of legitimate republicanism shifted. The nineteenth-century change from elitist to egalitarian republican sensibilities best explains why the first mainstream northern assault on the Slavepower came not after the American Revolution but 40 years later, during the transition from the Age of Jefferson to the Age of Jackson. The three-fifths clause, which seemed republican according to aristocratic assumptions of the Age of the American Revolution, became anti-republican according to egalitarian assumptions of the Age of the Common Man. In state legislatures, city councils, and national presidential elections, leaders and followers insisted that the people, not the propertied, must rule. "The people" meant adult white males, ruling on a one-citizen, one-vote base. The three-fifths clause, awarding the Slavepower extra representatives for enslaved noncitizens, was the most anti-republican relic of a repudiated political outlook.

The three-fifths clause seemed outmoded in a crasser way. The Slavepower's constitutionally prescribed bargain, larger taxes for larger power, had grown anachronistic. Before 1787, requisitions charged to each state supplied federal revenues. The Constitution established each state's share of such direct taxes on the federal basis: whites plus three-fifths of slaves. In 1798, a federal direct tax charged the Slavepower three-fifths extra for its three-fifths extra power. But in the nineteenth century, taxes levied directly on states were no longer needed. Instead, Congress secured money through land sales and external tariffs. The Slavepower, having contracted to pay extra dollars for extra House seats, now had to pay not one cent.

Missouri's bid to enter the Union brought such bitter thoughts, or if you will, resentful sour grapes, to the fore. Another southern state, Yankees argued, meant more illegitimate political power for the South, more slaveholding Presidents, more northern politicians relegated to undeservedly inferior positions. The North was not yet ready to slice the three-fifths clause from an otherwise healthy Constitution. The better remedy earlier seemed to be containment of the disease. James Tallmadge would slowly eliminate a new state's slaves and thus prevent the three-fifths clause from swelling the Slavepower. This proposal showed no concern for blacks. Instead, for the first of many times, Northerners demanded their own liberation from slaveholders' unrepublican rule.

Proponents of Tallmadge's Amendments admitted that they sought only white men's egalitarianism. I have no business with slavery as a social system over blacks, Rufus King declared. I oppose slavery's expansion because it bears upon whites' "great political interests." The three-fifths clause would rob Northerners of all "political power or influence in the Union. The slave region will parcel out the great offices, will determine all questions," and will forever "remain our Masters."

Rufus King argued that the three-fifths clause had been only a temporary bargain, exclusively between old states. "Extension of this disproportionate power to the new states," he said, "would be unjust and odious." New as opposed to old enslaved states, added James Tallmadge, "had no claim to such an unequal representation, unjust in its results upon the other States," as the three-fifths clause.[4]

Southerners answered that jealous Rufus Kings and James Tallmadges sought the White House, not equality for whites. That cynicism both shrewdly diagnosed and partially ignored northern malaise. Yankees assuredly resented Virginians' power. But Northerners' sorest point was that the Slavepower's unequal ascendency defied the new egalitarian wisdom. If black slaves were allowed to spread, areas of white men's egalitarianism would further shrink: that was the political fire ignited in the North.[5]

– 2 –

The Tallmadge Amendments initially received bipartisan support from the North and bipartisan condemnation from the South. Tallmadge's least radical motion, to forbid entrance of future slaves into Missouri, passed the House 87–76. The North voted 86–10 aye, the South 66–1 against. Tallmadge's most radical motion, to free slaves born thereafter in Missouri at age 25, squeaked by more narrowly, 82–78. The North voted 80–14 for, the South 64–2 nay.[6]

Those two southern "traitors," both from the Border South, secured Tallmadge's most anti-southern amendment in the House. If the pair had voted their southern brethren's way, an 82–78 victory for post-nati emancipation would have lost on an 80–80 tie vote. Tallmadge's proposal to bar future slaves from entering Missouri would have still passed the House and inspired a Missouri Controversy. But on these first roll calls of the first great nineteenth-century slavery crisis, a specter emerged never to cease troubling slaveholding perpetualists: that at critical moments, too many border neutrals would side with the North.

House passage of both Tallmadge Amendments raised another perpetual southern concern: that a permanent northern numerical majority could control the House. The long-term southern antidote would be to control the Senate. In 1819, the Union ostensibly contained 11 free states, 10 slave states. But one so-called free state, Illinois, was still five years away from abolishing black apprenticeship alias slavery. Its two senators, both southern natives, once had or now did command apprentices. On the critical Senate roll call, the Tallmadge Amendments lost 22–16, with three northern senators voting with the two Illinois southern-sympathizers and a unanimous South.[7]

The impasse between the North-controlled House, insisting on the Tallmadge Amendments, and the South-controlled Senate, demanding admission of enslaved Missouri without Tallmadge's dual restrictions, could not be broken in 1819. Meanwhile another impasse, though broken, reinforced southern concern about Missouri. The Louisiana Purchase Territory south of Missouri contained the future areas of Arkansas and Oklahoma. In 1819, northern congressmen sought to bar bondage in this so-called Arkansas Territory. The area, though in the latitude of the Middle South, was then less enslaved than Border South Missouri. The Missouri Territory had around 16% slaves, the Arkansas Territory around 11% slaves. The Yankee assault on Arkansas Territory thus sought limits on slavery further south than anything since Jefferson's Ordinance of 1784, in a southern hinterland as spottily enslaved as colonial New York had been.

The South turned back this invasion of its Middle South fringes, barely. The House expunged the antislavery requirement from the Arkansas Territory bill, 89–87, with Southerners voting for slavery 74–1 and Northerners against it 86–15. Nonextension of slavery in Arkansas Territory also lost in the South-dominated Senate, 19–14, with four Yankees voting the South's way and no Southerner voting the North's way. Having narrowly retained the not-very-enslaved Arkansas Territory, southern congressmen went home in 1819, depressed that the next session might bring no such retention of the not-much-more-enslaved proposed state of Missouri.[8]

– 3 –

The ensuing southern public debate, mirroring southern congressional speeches, demonstrated a section set against both permanent slavery and outside impositions to end temporary slavery. Only in South Carolina—so often, only in South Carolina—did a southern leader advocate perpetual slavery. United States Senator William Smith, anticipating later proslavery polemics, called slavery universal throughout history, sanctioned by the Bible, honored by the Greeks, needed by infantile blacks, and exalted by the South into a patriarchal relationship between master and slave. "No class of laboring people in any country upon the globe," soared Smith, "are better clothed, better fed, or more cheerful, or labor less" than our indulged serviles.[9]

Southerners outside South Carolina could not muster that enthusiasm, not even when resenting Yankees' slurs. Thomas Ritchie, renowned editor of Virginia's prestigious *Richmond Enquirer,* asked Yankees to remember "how difficult it is for us to get rid of" slavery. But "we do not vindicate servitude; we wish no slave had touched our soil; we wish it could be terminated."[10] Such wishes emanated from the Deep South too—always excepting South Carolina. Robert Reid of Georgia told Congress that "'[I] hate the touch of servile hands; I loathe the slaves who cringe around'; and I would hail that day as the most glorious" when blacks shall be "placed upon the high eminence of equal rights."[11]

Southerners who called slavery wrong might be thought amenable to Tallmadge's proposed way to set things right. James Tallmadge would ease bondage away Jefferson's soothing old post-nati way, with a soothing old Yankee addition: allow the afterborn to be sold, before emancipating birthdays, into perpetual bondage down south. Still, the New Yorker's southern-style remedy came accompanied with an anti-southern moral attack, an anti-southern bid for power, and the anti-southern idea that outsiders, not insiders, should decide slavery's fate. Tallmadge would furthermore abolish slavery not during the territorial phase of a region's development, as southern nonextensionists had previously proposed, but during the statehood process. The shift in timing violated southern insistence that each state must decide for itself about slavery.

Southern attack on this Yankee poisoning of southern conceptions came accompanied with a crucial swerve in slaveholder thought. Speaker after southern speaker, in Congress and out, urged that spreading, not containing the institution would best create conditions for terminating bondage. This important so-called diffusion argument was not so much new as newly accepted. Land speculators, when seeking repeal of the Northwest Ordinance's ban on slavery extension, had urged that diffusing blacks over midwestern areas would dilute southern racial anxieties and thus further racial reform. Most midwestern and southern proponents of the Northwest Ordinance had scoffed at this "liberalism."

The Missouri trauma turned scoffers around. Their revised thoughts would long remain important, especially during the Texas Annexation Controversy. The Southerner who best defended diffusion during the Missouri Crisis would become a key actor in the Texas epic. John Tyler of Virginia was a member of the House of Representatives in the 1820s, President of the United States in the early 1840s. The President would never recover from the congressman's sudden vision that diffusing blacks, not containing them, offered better conditions for bringing slavery to an end.

Confining black masses within ever blacker black belts, Tyler explained to Congress, would encourage slave insurrection and discourage racial reform. But diffusing the black plague would ease apprehensions and invite abolition. Would you "suffer" the "dark cloud" of slavery "to increase in its darkness over a particular portion of this land until its horrors shall burst?" Or would it "be well to disperse" the blackness and "reduce it to a summer's cloud?"

Tyler called his dark cloud/summer cloud image a metaphor for slavery's recent history. Where the cloud was black, no reform had been accomplished. Where blacks were diffuse, much progress had been made. "What enabled New York, Pennsylvania, and other states to adopt the language of universal emancipation? Rely on it, nothing but the paucity of the number of their slaves. That which it would have been criminal in these states not to have done would be an act of political suicide in Georgia or South Carolina." By repudiating nonextension, by rejecting Tallmadge, by diffusing slaves onto Missouri's plains, "you add much to the prospect of emancipation and the total extinction of slavery."[12]

Is posterity supposed to believe that Southerners believed this stuff? That expanding slavery could best end it?! That saving the institution in Missouri could best eliminate it elsewhere?! These propositions the more strain credulity because they functioned so self-servingly. What a wonderful way to feel good about a supposedly evil way to make profits: expand the profits and you will end the evil!

The diffusion argument, for some Southerners all the time and for all Southerners some of the time, operated as just this kind of noxious sedative. More than a few Southrons furthermore cynically used the notion of diffusion to block northern power. But to dismiss diffusion as entirely cynical or self-serving is to miss a revelation of the southern mentality. From posterity's perspective, as from James Tallmadge's, stopping slavery from expanding seems the path towards ending it, while allowing slavery to spread seems the trail towards saving the institution. But neither Tallmadge nor posterity lived in the race-haunted Old South, where high black ratios seemed to force the wolf to be held by the ears and low black ratios seemed to allow grasps to loosen. Jefferson, whose trembling metaphor defined that world, had previously concluded that emancipation by reversed population flow required containing the flow of the enslaved to new areas.

He erred. Nonexpansion follows from our assumptions, not his. Error is uncovered most quickly when tested most traumatically, and traumatic Tallmadge Amendments jarred Southerners' mentality towards the truth that nonextension destroyed their prime condition for terminating the institution. Spreading out blacks, not concentrating them, best produced low black ratios. Diffusion was another name for the slave drain, that process of moving slaves down to the more enslaved tropics which made the more northern South more amenable to termination of the institution. Diffusion sanctified the emancipation process in New York and New Jersey, where low black ratios and dumping blacks down river allowed other conditions for ending slavery to be met. Diffusion offered the hope of moving enough blacks out of Virginia so that tremulous Jeffersons might dare to go public.

The Conditional Termination mentality was a vision of getting blacks safely out, of whitening a world, of removing the race to other plains. The Tallmadge Amendments smashed the vision, leaving the mirage of whites and blacks packed together more tightly. With diffusion, claustrophobic slaveholders grasped at the fading light beyond Mr. Tallmadge's darkening jail.

– 4 –

When Congress returned in 1820, a southern native who represented Northerners sought to unite North and South behind diffusion of slaves to Missouri. United States Senator Jesse B. Thomas of Illinois, formerly of Maryland, now owner of five black apprentices, alias slaves, was eager to save his fellow slaveholders without antagonizing his northern constituents. He would secure enslaved Missouri by bribing Yankees to drop Tallmadge's proposals.

One bribe was already operating before Jesse Thomas concoted another. A bill to admit Maine without slavery had been coupled with the Senate's bill to admit Missouri with slavery. On February 16, 1820, Thomas moved to link to the Maine-Missouri linkage a bill outlawing slavery in the Louisiana Purchase Territory north of the 36°30' line. Only future Arkansas and Oklahoma lay south of the line in the remaining Louisiana Purchase territorial domain. Both future states were in the so-called Arkansas Territory. Southerners had defeated antislavery in this territory at the previous session. Thomas's 36°30' line thus would allow Southerners to keep the crumb previously saved. The North would receive the rest of the enormous Louisiana Purchase territorial land mass, meaning most of the area of nine future states, including the future area of Kansas, due west of Missouri.[13]

The Thomas plan angered some Southerners. They denounced the unequal division of turf and the constitutional precedent. "To compromise" on Jesse Thomas's basis, wrote Senator Nathaniel Macon of North Carolina, "is to acknowledge the right of Congress to interfere" with slavery in future territories. By guaranteeing the North so many future states, William Smith of South Carolina added, the South would surrender senatorial parity.[14]

Other southern senators would let the future take care of itself. For the present, the Thomas proposal might save slavery in Missouri. When roll call time came, Jesse Thomas's three linked bills passed the Senate, 24–20.[15] The senatorial roll call lineup almost matched the 22–16 defeat of the post-nati Tallmadge Amendment in the previous session, with all Southerners and several Yankee defectors defeating most Northerners.

The Thomas plan faced rougher treatment in the House. In that chamber, more Yankees and all Southerners would have to turn south for Southerners to win. Northerners relished prospects both of free Maine and of free territories north of 36°30′. Still, few Yankees were willing to overturn the last session's 82–78 vote for post-nati freedom in Missouri. Nor were southern congressmen, especially from the Deep South, unanimously agreed on selling out slavery's future above 36°30′. With some Southerners and most Northerners against various parts of Jesse Thomas's proposals, the linked bills could not pass the House.

A Senate-House conference committee developed an alternate strategy. The committee unlinked the bills and proposed separate passage of each. In a vote on just the 36°30′ line for the Louisiana Purchase territories, the southern minority could safely take out its ire on the "sellout," for the northern majority could secure the emancipating line anyway. Then hopefully all Southerners and a few Northerners could admit Missouri without the Tallmadge Amendments.

The ploy worked. Abolition above 36°30′ passed the House 134–42, with the North affirming 95–5 and the South splitting 39 aye, 37 nay. Then enslaved Missouri was given permission to write its constitution, without the Tallmadge conditions, 90–87. On the latter vote, every Southerner and 14 Yankees overcame 87 Northerners.[16] Four other northern congressmen who could have overturned the South's three-vote victory over Tallmadge instead abstained.

Of the 18 Yankees who either voted the South's way or (as helpfully) voted not at all, only one was a Federalist. The 17 northern Republicans who leaned southwards talked publicly of saving the Union. They also feared privately that a Rufus King triumph on Missouri might revitalize the Federalist Party. Their attitudes, partisan and nonpartisan, prefigured the opportunity the minority South would seize again and again to control the North-dominated House of Representatives in pre-Civil War crises. In the Missouri Controversy, as later, the minority South could secure no concessions on slavery from northern nationalists, Federalist or Whig. But appeals to Union and party could attract some saving Yankee states' righters, Jeffersonian or Jacksonian.

In the Missouri Controversy, as later, the South needed only a few Yankee allies because the Slavepower possessed extra House power. The three-fifths clause, the most important reason why the James Tallmadges fought the enslavement of Missouri, ultimately defeated the Tallmadge Amendments. In a House apportioned sheerly on white numbers, the South would have had 17 fewer members in 1820. The Slavepower needed almost all those 17 boosts in power to defeat Tallmadge by three votes.

The Slavepower still had to wield its extra power unanimously. At the previous session, two border Southerners, by voting for the post-nati Tallmadge Amendment, had secured Yankee victory in the House. But this time, these two

Southerners voted the South's way, giving slavery in Missouri its House victory. At least at this session, *a* South existed, whatever its various ideologies, on letting new states decide on their own labor system.

No South existed on whether Congress could bar slavery from territories which were not yet ready to become states. Border South congressmen, representing the least enslaved and most apologetic region of the South, voted 16–2 to ban bondage north of 36°30′ in the Louisiana Purchase Territory. The rest of the South protested against the congressional bar, 35–23.

Border South neutrals saw nothing wrong with voting the North's way. Since the South could not stop the northern majority from passing 36°30′ anyway, why not throw a sectional blessing on the continued Union? Borderites also saw no harm in barring diffusion of slaves to new areas up north, for they could dump blacks on old states further south. As for slaveholders further south, they wished to keep open a racial safety valve for blacks diffused upon them. In their vote to close off slavery at 36°30′, Border Southerners sided with the North against the tropical South.

The borderland, the southern region least under slaveholders' control, had been the appropriate locale of the first national slavery crisis, as it would be the arena of many future controversies. In this case, the border commodity sacrificed, possible slave expansion above 36°30′, endangered the border regime saved, Missouri's. The 36°30′ line, declaring slavery off-limits in new territories northwards, ran across the *southern* border of Missouri. So southerly a geographic signpost indirectly pronounced that Missouri and the whole Border South—Kentucky, western Virginia, Maryland, Delaware—were geographically too far north for slavery, just as New York and New Jersey had been before.

This vote to ban slavery west of the most northern South hardly doomed the institution eastwards, in the border states themselves. But border congressmen had gratuitously accepted a free labor western border for Missouri. To the north and east, free labor areas already bordered the lightly enslaved new state. The surrender to the west thus re-emphasized one of the Missouri Controversy's overriding issues: did the more northern, less enslaved border area have a permanent slaveholding future? The temporary answer was that Missouri's relatively few slaveholders could persist on condition that they could tolerate free labor encirclement. A third of a century later, in Kansas-Nebraska times, Missouri's slaveholders would find that condition intolerable. Their movement to repeal the Missouri Controversy's ban on slavery west of the borderland would then make the crisis of 1819–21 look tame.

– 5 –

The allegedly soothing Missouri Compromise not only ultimately led to the destructive Kansas-Nebraska Controversy but also immediately destroyed one basis for a national reform coalition. Yankees and Southerners had once united to bar slavery from the Midwest. They now divided over diffusing slavery to

Missouri. Yet despite the North-South fracture on where blacks should be allowed in America, North and Upper South might still unite on sending Afro-Americans out of America. No man better summed up national possibilities lost as well as national possibilities retained than did Thomas Jefferson.

Jefferson's key letter on the subject went to Congressman John Holmes on April 22, 1820. Holmes, a New England Jeffersonian Republican, was one of only five northern congressmen who had always voted with the South on the Tallmadge Amendments. Writing this helpful Yankee, Jefferson could be candid.

Jefferson found vivid metaphors for abstract anxieties. This was the letter where he likened slavery to the wolf held by the ears and called the northern assault "like a fire bell in the night," "hushed" only "for the moment." The North-South "geographical line, coinciding with a marked principle, moral and political, once conceived and held up to the angry passions of men, will never be obliterated; and every new irritation will mark it deeper and deeper." To this all-too-true prophesy, Jefferson added the dirge of the old man who mourns for life's labor lost: "I regret that I am now to die in the belief, that the useless sacrifice of themselves by the generation of 1776, to acquire self-government and happiness to their country, is to be thrown away by the unwise and unworthy passions of their sons, and that my only consolation is to be, that I live not to weep over it."

Jefferson moved from patriarchal gloom to parochial attack on outsiders who meddled with states' internal affairs. These phrases, according to the current conventional wisdom, announced Jefferson's transformation into Calhoun. Jefferson declared that Congress could not "regulate the condition of the different descriptions of men composing a State." Decisions on slavery's future were the "exclusive right of every State, which nothing in the Constitution has taken from them." Calhoun never said it better. But then again, no American in the Age of the Founding Fathers believed that the federal government could abolish slavery in *states*.

Jefferson's Holmes letter did break new ground, Calhoun's ground, in repudiating the former Jeffersonian gospel that the federal government should bar expansion of slavery in *territories*. The Virginian never could have penned the Ordinance of 1784 if he had then believed, as he wrote Holmes in 1820, that "diffusion over a greater surface" would make slaves "individually happier, and proportionately facilitate the accomplishment of their emancipation" by spreading blacks thinly. Here we have the smoking gun which supposedly proves that Conditional Termination had been unconditionally terminated. "When the chips were down, as in the Missouri crisis," concludes Jefferson's most brilliant latter-day critic, the ex-President "threw his weight behind slavery's expansion, and bequeathed to the South the image of antislavery as a Federalist mask for political and economic exploitation."[17]

Jefferson did indeed emerge from the Missouri Controversy as a territorial expansionist, or better, diffusionist. The Virginian did indeed misconstrue northern condemnation of the three-fifths clause as just a crass quest for power.

But Thomas Jefferson remained as far from John C. Calhoun as Virginia was from South Carolina. Calhoun would expand slavery to perpetuate it. Jefferson would diffuse the institution to end it. Calhoun would destroy the Union, assuming destruction of slavery was the alternative. Jefferson would use the Union to diffuse slaves onto the prairies and then beyond American shores. "I can say, with conscious truth," a Jefferson without Calhoun's consciousness wrote Holmes, that no "man on earth ... would sacrifice more than I would to relieve us from this heavy reproach, in any *practicable* way." A "general emancipation and *expatriation* ... would not cost me a second thought" if effected "gradually, and with due sacrifices, I think it might be." The Tallmadge agitation was democratic "suicide ... and treason against the hopes of the world" not least because it threw away an end to slavery "more likely to be effected by Union than by secession."

Jefferson explained more fully to Albert Gallatin, his former Secretary of the Treasury, how the Union might expatriate blacks. Out of the "evil" of Missouri, Jefferson was "glad to see one good effect." Calhoun deemed the effect horrid. The national crisis, cheered Jefferson, "has brought the necessity of some general plan of emancipation and deportation more home to the minds of our people than it has ever been before." Virginia's governor, noted Jefferson, "has ventured to propose" an emancipation scheme.[18]

The governor in question was Jefferson's son-in-law, Thomas Mann Randolph. Governor Randolph had lately informed his legislature that introducing slavery was "a deplorable error." He had urged the "magnanimity" and "sound policy" of appropriating "the whole revenue now derived from our Treasury from slaves to the purchase" and "deportation" of bondsmen "at the age of puberty." The governor would deport twice as many females as males, "at least for a considerable length of time," thereby halving the natural increase of blacks to be deported thereafter.[19]

Jefferson wrote Albert Gallatin that Virginia would and should reject its governor's plan. His son-in-law's proposed use of "one-third of the revenue of the State" for emancipation and deportation "would not reach one-tenth of the annual increase." Annual proceeds of the federal land office, on the other hand, would bring "deporation within the possible means of taxation." The nation must help each state to become lilywhite.

Jefferson's true "final" word on slavery was written neither to John Holmes nor to Albert Gallatin but to Jared Sparks, a Federalist from Massachusetts, four years after the Missouri Crisis. The Sparks letter, following up themes in the Gallatin and Holmes letters, implicitly conceded that outsiders must help slaveholders abolish slavery, at insiders' invitation of course. Jefferson would not have appreciated the ugly term for seeking outside aid. The word nevertheless sums up a central reason why southern zealots feared southern apologists. The Virginian was potentially a collaborator.

Jefferson's basis of collaboration with Northerners to end slavery demanded deportation of blacks. Jefferson gently chided Sparks for advocating diffusion to Africa. That colonizing distance was too far, the transportation expense too great. Rather, Jefferson urged dispatching blacks to Saint Domingue. (HAITI, one can imagine Calhoun storming!)

Jefferson pressed on Sparks "my reflections on the subject five and forty years ago." He would emancipate "the afterborn," and deport them at "a proper age." The federal government should pay for deporting blacks by selling "lands which have been ceded by the very states now needing this relief." Granted, "this subject involves some constitutional scruples. But a liberal construction, justified by the object, may go far, and an amendment of the constitution, the whole length." (Calhoun?!)

Jefferson's "whole length" would take time, more time than Jefferson had left. Only those born hereafter should be freed and removed. The "old stock" would have to "die off in the ordinary course of nature." Still, the very slowness of "final disappearance" made reform "blessed." The final "beatitude" was "forbidden to my age." But he left posterity "with this admonition, to rise and be doing."[20]

Of course Jefferson left behind another admonition. He would shrink back and do nothing if conditions were wrong. His twin conditions remained race removal and perpetual Union. By threatening disunion, South Carolinians could make Jefferson's conditions unreachable. The fatal weakness of Jeffersonian apologetics was that moderation must collapse before determined extremism.

But extremists did have to be determined, now more than ever. Despite the first Yankee onslaught, Jefferson's Upper South world still yearned to use reversed population flow to diffuse away a "curse." While the old strategy of damning up the flow of slaves in America had been repudiated, the Jeffersons more than ever sought to diffuse blacks from America. The final lesson of Jefferson's life was that unless slaveholding watchmen rang their own fire bell in the night, a national collaboration of Yankees and Southerners might tremulously seek to free—and to whiten—the United States.

– 6 –

Jefferson's last words summed up the revived thrust of southern apologetics. That old trio of legacies of the American Revolution—that slavery was a problem, that its solution required right conditions, and that the first condition was a low ratio of blacks to whites—outlasted the Missouri trauma as it would survive every other crisis on the road to disunion. Rufus King's attack produced no alarmed consolidation of *a* South. Instead, post-Missouri Compromise slavery politics featured a battle between Upper and Lower Souths over whether to enlist the national government in removing blacks from America.

This new phase of struggle within the South really began before the Missouri Controversy, with the founding of the American Colonization Society in 1817. The Society, dedicated to sending American blacks back to Africa, sought to build on the greatest accomplishment of the first generation of slavery politics: stopping the migration of Africans to America. In ensuing decades, the Society succeeded in securing land for its Liberia colony and in stocking the new republic with some 12,000 ex-American blacks. The success measured up poorly against crushing troubles. Trouble began in Africa, where a "stranger's fever" killed many seeking a new life. Periodic wars maimed or murdered many more.

Peril in Liberia helped produce paralysis in America. The American Colonization Society could convince less than 2% of American free blacks to volunteer for a bout with the stranger's fever. Nor would free whites volunteer enough funds to send over many more. Nor could the Society find a national platform to encourage nationwide contributions. Some Deep South contributors wished to consolidate slavery by deporting free blacks. Many northern and Upper South contributors wanted to exile all blacks, slave and free. The Society's officials, eager for voluntary contributions, fudged the issue, pleasing no one.[21]

One trouble was that support, black and white, had to be voluntary. But so gigantic a task of social engineering almost demanded that government compel blacks to leave and whites to finance deportation. The American Colonization Society, sensing the crippling limits of voluntarism, set up initial headquarters neither in Boston, where voluntary benevolence most thrived, nor in New York, where wealthy contributors were most concentrated, but in the scarcely inhabited mudhole of Washington, D.C. In 1827, the Society met, appropriately, in the chambers of the National House of Representatives to vote on sending its first colonization petition to Congress. In a major address to the Society, the Border South's most powerful politician welcomed the foray.

Henry Clay of Kentucky, now American Secretary of State, told colonizationists that invoking "the public aid in execution of the great scheme" was the "sure road to ultimate success." Clay called slavery the "deepest stain," the foulest "blot," the "greatest of human evils." To emancipate "the unhappy portion of our race doomed to bondage" would be grander than "all the triumphs ever decreed to the most successful conqueror."

While only states had constitutional power to conquer slavery, Clay argued, the national government must enable states to act. High ratios of blacks to whites, the condition preventing state emancipation, was a national evil demanding a "common remedy." The federal government must reduce blacks to a fraction of the white population. Then history had shown that states would act. Witness New Jersey and New York.

Clay would enable the now most northern South to emulate the now most southern North by using national funds to colonize the natural increase of slaves each year. He estimated that colonizing the requisite 50,000 blacks a year would cost an affordable $1,000,000. With white population increasing and black population departing, a nation now one-seventh black would become one-tenth, then swiftly one-twentieth black. National colonization would enable state governments "to bear" emancipation, "without danger and without suffering."[22]

Henry Clay's logic resembled Thomas Mann Randolph's reasoning to the Virginia legislature seven years earlier. The Kentuckian refrained from Randolph's suggestion that breeding "wenches" should be exported twice as fast as males. But both Upper South establishment leaders would lessen whites' apprehension about reform by shipping out blacks' natural increase. An expanding white population would then make non-increasing blacks inconsequential. Emancipation might follow. This was social change with the brakes on, the budget saved, blacks deported, and slavery continuing for many decades. But swift and radical and color-blind the Conditional Termination vision had never remotely been.

Henry Clay's version of the traditional caution was more practical than Governor Randolph's. Thomas Jefferson had pointed out that his son-in-law's scheme would strain Virginia's budget. Clay's plan would not strain national finances. The national government was heading towards its first (and last!) national surplus in history. Nationalists of Clay's ilk, North and South, would use excess funds to solve national problems.

No problem was greater than slavery, no approach more popular than colonization. A list of colonization advocates would include just about every American political hero from 1790 to 1860, including Jefferson and Jackson, Washington and Lincoln, excluding only those typical exceptions, the Adamses, father and son, and John C. Calhoun. The notion of sending Afro-Americans back to Africa, like the notion of stopping Africans from coming to America, was all too mainstream an American conception for slaveholding zealots' comfort.

If most Americans, North and South, found national whitening experiments intriguing, disagreements abounded on how to experiment. Most Southerners preferred to begin by colonizing free blacks. Most Northerners would commence by removing slaves. Again, many colonizationists wanted government to force unwilling blacks out. Forcible deportation, however, troubled many American democrats. Any of these experimental "details" could have aborted a national law or hindered an enacted experiment.

The nation, however, never arrived at the stage of deciding on experimental details, for the usual obstructionist minority would not allow consideration of the experiment. Back in 1787, South Carolinians had warned the national majority that an immediate end to the African slave trade would preclude Carolina participation in the proposed nation. Throughout the 1820s, Carolinians warned that if the nation deported Afro-Americans, they would depart the Union.

In January 1824, the Ohio legislature urged on Congress a Jefferson-like scheme to terminate slavery. Ohioans called slavery a "national" evil and accepted their obligation "to participate in the duties and burdens of removing it." A national edict should free slaves born after enactment when the afterborn reached 21 if they agreed to federally financed foreign colonization. Eight northern states endorsed Ohio's post-nati scheme. In 1825, United States Senator Rufus King, whom Jefferson loathed as a prime instigator of the Missouri Controversy, moved towards Jefferson's position by urging use of public land revenues to finance emancipation.[23]

King's and Ohio's attempt to get the nation moving on removing blacks produced a new ultimatum from the old foe of the Upper South's favorite solution to slavery. South Carolina Governor John Wilson, upon sending the Ohio Resolutions to his legislature in 1824, urged "a firm determination to resist, at the threshold, every invasion." The Carolina Senate, needing no urging, resolved against "any claim of right, of the United States, to interfere in any manner." A year later, Rufus King's Senate effort provoked similar Carolina warnings.[24]

The American Colonization Society's petition to Congress met the same negative response in 1827. United States Senator Robert Y. Hayne warned Congress to keep hands off slavery or else. Slaveholder safety, said Hayne, lies "in the want of" federal power "to touch the subject at all." Let Congress not heed Hayne's warning, resolved the South Carolina legislature at the end of the year, and Carolinians would unite "with a firm determination not to submit."[25]

That South Carolina would not submit to a national colonization experiment may seem incredible to posterity. In the late twentieth century, deporting blacks seems so immoral, the American Colonization Society so impotent, removing millions so farfetched as to be unworthy of serious consideration. Nineteenth-century South Carolinians scoffed at African colonization too. But these warriors conceived that nationally financed colonization experiments could succeed in the failing. The precedent of attempted federal action might lead to the next, maybe not-so-impractical experiment with removing blacks.

South Carolinians also found sufficient danger in a string of failures. White men's talk in Congress demonstrably produced black talk about insurrection. Charleston's Denmark Vesey Conspiracy of 1822 had come on the heels of the Missouri debates. Vesey had failed. So would subsequent attempts.

Failed slave revolts still took the domestic out of domestic slavery and the serenity out of domestic serenity. Some pretend Cuffees, Carolinians never forget, had turned out to be Vesey Conspirators who had threatened to rape our daughters and throw-our-guts-in-our-face. A future Carolina congressman regretted that we should be subjected "to a jealous police, and view with distrust and severity, those whom we are disposed to regard with confidence and kindness. It is no little grievance, that the weaker individuals among us, are harassed and alarmed. . . . It is with no pleasant feeling, that we see members of our families turn pale at observing a pamphlet of the [Colonization] Society on our tables."[26]

Carolinians had lately grown pale watching whites no less than blacks throw off masks. Carolina country gentlemen, more than other southern squires, read London journals, kept up with London gossip, winced or rejoiced over English politics. In late 1827, these Anglophiles worried that William Wilberforce's earlier, allegedly "innocuous" law, closing the African slave trade, was leading towards abolition of slavery in the British West Indies. When Wilberforce proposed the initial action in the early nineteenth century, he was "even *more cautious* than the Colonization Society. He took especial care not to profess that the abolition of the slave trade was but the *first* step."

Now look! Parliament would imminently end slavery in the British Empire. If Carolina did not meet colonization experiments at the threshold, we will end up "like the weak, the dependent, and the unfortunate colonists of the West

Indies," dragging in "a miserable state of political existence, constantly vibrating between our hopes and our fears as to what a distant Congress may do towards us."[27]

Carolinians saw other Southerners as blind to dangers in congressional black deportation schemes, just as West Indians had been blind to dangers in Wilberforce's first step. "Open and direct" abolitionists could never influence the South. But abolition was hidden under the genial façade of colonizing blacks, just as Rolla Bennett's fantasy of raping Massa's daughter was hidden under the façade of happy Cuffee. "If slave property is made insecure—if the quiet and content of the negro is chased away—if the timid, among our people, catch the alarm, and by their weakness, assist the effect of injuring our property and lessening our safety—we owe it not to the wild fanatics, whose notions our people can in no sort adopt—but to that other and subtler plan, which while equally impractical as to what it pretends to aim at, yet allures men into it, merely by seeming to offer a middle way."[28]

Imagine a best-case scenario, Carolinians urged. Suppose that colonization experiments fail and fail. Will planters buy slaves, Robert Y. Hayne asked the United States Senate in 1827, while the government experiments with terminating slavery, any more than capitalists will buy bank stock while the government experiments with terminating banks? Will slaves labor docilely while their fellows are off experimenting with freedom? The South would dissolve into bankrupt slaveholders running away from angry slaves, while "innocuous" colonization experiments failed.

South Carolina had long since discovered how minorities make majorities abort experiments. They once again threatened so ominously as to silence the fastidious. Carolinians' disunion ultimatum thus became the key practicality making a full-scale congressional debate on colonization impractical. As to whether endless talk in Congress and/or an enacted experiment, however faulty, might have damaged a *domestic* institution—well, was Carolina's imagined scenario so preposterous?

– 7 –

In 1827, as so often in the past, uncertain Upper South apologists submitted to Carolina certainty. But in the late 1820s, conflict between the northern and southern older Souths, now half a century old, was escalating. Disagreements over transporting Africans to America were giving way to confrontations over returning Afro-Americans to Africa. The American Colonization Society, Jefferson's plea to Jared Sparks for a national colonization coalition, the Ohio and Rufus King proposals, Henry Clay's address—all these deportation schemes portended southern collaboration with sympathetic Northerners to whiten America. South Carolina's ultimatums on colonization portended escalating pressure to scare Upper South apologists into renewed procrastination. Jefferson, epitome of procrastination, was dead. The battle over diffusing blacks and slaves was entering a new phase.

CHAPTER 9

Class Revolt in Virginia, I:
Anti-Egalitarianism Attacked

The Upper South dream of sending blacks away, having survived the national Missouri Controversy, swiftly faced two local tests. Between 1829 and 1832, twin lower-class challenges threatened the Virginia ruling class. Nat Turner's slave revolt against slaveholders' social power, coming almost in lockstep after a nonslaveholder assault on the Slavepower's political power, led to the most famous southern legislative debate over ending slavery.

Once again, the historical myth is that Virginians surrendered their vision of diffusing slavery away. After successive challenges from white and black underclasses, the upper class supposedly repudiated old apologetics. All southern whites then supposedly hunkered down to perpetuating their newfound blessing.

But Old Virginia could not turn itself instantly modern. While some elitists at the Virginia Constitutional Convention of 1829 yielded a little to white commoners' demand for an egalitarian state government, the revised constitution still retained anti-egalitarian power for the Slavepower. Three years later, lower-class resentment plus some upper-class wavering led to a rather close call on a rather wispy legislative resolution to end slavery. But the very slaveholders who saved the institution still voiced hope that blacks and slaves would someday diffuse from Virginia.

– 1 –

In 1829, Virginia, like the entire Atlantic Seaboard South, lived under a late eighteenth-century state constitution. The state's basic laws followed the elitist logic underlying the federal three-fifths clause. Nationally and locally, the late eighteenth-century Anglo-American establishment assumed that those richer and wiser and more virtuous should govern those lesser. The domineering sensibility built into southern slaveholders' control over blacks here extended into dominance over white citizens as well.

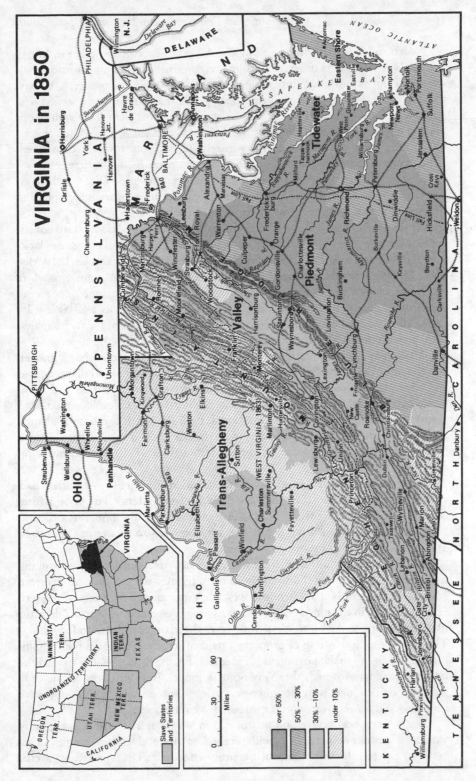

VIRGINIA in 1850

Slave States and Territories

Miles
60
30
0

over 50%
50% – 30%
30% –10%
under 10%

163

North and South of Virginia along the Altantic Seaboard, whether in Maryland or North Carolina or South Carolina, eighteenth-century constitutions bolstered the elite's control. White males, to vote, had to possess property. Voters, to hold office, had to possess more property still. Eastern districts, settled first and blackest with slaves, possessed more state legislators than their white population justified. Western districts, settled later and more lily-white, elected fewer representatives than the one-white-man, one-vote formula demanded. Legislatures apportioned according to white numbers *plus* property—the so-called mixed basis—selected governors and judges. Undemocratic? On the contrary, as ideally republican, according to the eighteenth-century understanding of ideal republics, as the federal three-fifths clause.

As republican ideals shifted from elitist to egalitarian notions, state constitutions were revised too. Constitutional changes came fastest in new states lacking old attitudes and institutions. Alabama, entering the Union in 1819, displayed in its constitution none of the Old Order. In nouveau Alabama, all white males could vote and hold office. The legislature was apportioned on a one-white-man, one-vote basis. The electorate elected governors as well as legislatures. Here was the new herrenvolk order: pure egalitarianism for white males, pure servility for blacks, the constitution itself guarding the color line.[1]

After 1819, southwestern states copied and perfected the Alabama model. By the mid-1830s, not only Alabama but also Mississippi, Tennessee, and Arkansas were ruled on the one-white-man, one-vote basis. Florida and Louisiana entered the Union on close to the egalitarian republican formula, and Georgia was swiftly approaching that ideal. If all the South had been Alabama, as indeed most of the Lower South was, the Slavepower would have always based its state constitutions and ruling group attitudes on race and never on class.[2]

But the oldest South was not Alabama. Gentlemen along the Atlantic Coast called unnatural the posture that poor blacks were inferior but poor whites equal to superiors in big white houses. A mobocracy, as traditionalists called it, also seemed dangerous. What a way for a master class to master its destiny, to allow another class to master government.

The ranker class, unfortunately for upper-class reactionaries, was swelling inside the oldest South. Nonslaveholding migrants were filling up western Maryland, western North Carolina, western Virginia, and even bits of western South Carolina in the nineteenth century. These Westerners inside the Old East, like immigrants to the New West, wanted egalitarian republicanism for whites. They sought a dismantling of property qualifications for voting and officeholding and an end to malapportioned legislatures. Egalitarians' pressure moved the Old South slowly towards the New South's model. But "progress" came only after gentlemen massively fought—sometimes successfully fought—to save their unequal power over whites no less than over blacks.

Fights were most severe and protracted in Virginia. The state's topography was as if custom-designed to yield pitched battles and uneasy compromises between eighteenth- and nineteenth-century conceptions of republican government. Old Virginia conservatives, located in the middle of the oldest South, were both more intransigent than egalitarians further north and more compromising than elitists further south. Above Virginia, the Maryland gentry showed a weaker devotion to slavery and to the authoritarian values slavery continued to make relevant. Below Virginia, South Carolina commanders retained more entrenched autocratic sensibilities. Virginia's ancient gentry, producing proportionately more export crops than Marylanders with proportionately fewer slaves than South Carolinians, retained enough outmoded sensibility to provoke newer Virginians. But they were not quite prepared to stonewall against those they provoked.

In addition to being situated too near the middle of the South to attain full extremist consciousness, Virginia's rulers were too divided from other classes and from each other to consolidate the state's Old Order. Two mountain chains, the more eastern Blue Ridge and the more western Alleghenies, run parallel to each other, north-south down the Old Dominion. East of the easterly Blue Ridge, sloping south and east towards the Atlantic Ocean, lies the Piedmont and Tidewater. Most counties in this locale of Old Virginia possessed over 40% slaves. At eastern Virginia's southern extreme, in so-called Southside Virginia, black proportions passed 50%.

West of the westerly Alleghenies, sloping north and west towards the Ohio River, lies the Trans-Allegheny West. Most antebellum counties in this locale possessed under 10% slaves. At its northern extreme, in the so-called Panhandle, western Virginia counties contained only 1 to 5% slaves. Most western Virginians were Pennsylvania Germans or Scotch Irish or other opportunistic Northerners who had lately streamed south through Allegheny Mountain passes. They had seen themselves as going not south but west. They had stopped in Trans-Allegheny Virginia because mountainous terrain invited a free labor rather than slave labor culture. By 1830, few extensively settled portions of the South were so northern, so egalitarian, so free labor, so antithetical, in short, to eighteenth-century elitist sensibilities.

The Valley of Virginia, between the Blue Ridge and Alleghenies, drew settlers from both old supporters and new opponents of fading notions that civic virtue must be imposed from above. Migrants from eastern Virginia, largely of English ancestry, found good prospects for slaveholding in river valleys west of the Blue Ridge. Migrants from western Virginia, often of Scotch or German ancestry, found good conditions for nonslaveholding farming in hilly terrain east of the Alleghenies. The Valley's resulting slave percentages were in the middling 25% area. Nothing like so massive a neutral zone divided colliding regimes elsewhere in the older South.

The mixed regime in the Valley possessed the balance of power because eastern Virginia, with an unbalanced plurality of constitutional power, lacked the social purity to exert its authority unanimously. Seepage of western attitudes into eastern strongholds went furthest in cities. Here white nonslaveholding laborers, called wage slaves in the proslavery argument, loathed black slaves and resented scornful squires. A rural equivalent existed northwards in eastern Virginia. Northwestern Piedmont and northern Tidewater areas near mountains or near Washington, D.C., possessed fewer slaves and more egalitarian attitudes.

Eastern Virginia attitudes also seeped west, making the newest Virginia as impurely new as Old Virginia was impurely ancient. In the southern Trans-Allegheny, particularly along the Greenbrier River, 25% of inhabitants were enslaved. These rather blackish belts sometimes defended elitist attitudes, unlike whiter, more northern Trans-Allegheny counties. The Panhandle, the most northern area not only of western Virginia but of the whole South, spawned the most uncompromisingly egalitarian version of Virginia republicanism.

Virginia, in short, not only split east/west, with appeasers occupying the Valley between, but also north/south, with compromisers infiltrating uncompromising eastern and western areas. Or to express reactionary vulnerability a more telling way, Virginia stonewallers confronted more than Virginia progressives two mountains and a valley removed. The Old Order also faced faltering views on its own side of the mountain and within its own mansions. Here, as so often, sprawling Virginia was a microcosm of diverse Souths; and here, more than anywhere, the Old Dominion exemplified a southern history not of confident class rule but of division and drift, within and without ruling mansions.[3]

– 2 –

Those mansions—or rather that division about whether leaders ought to live in mansions—epitomized Virginia's disagreement over proper authority. Homes, to leaders of nineteenth-century folk neighborhoods, were more than dwellings for intimates. Houses were also places to receive non-family folk and, as such, projections of appropriate leadership.

An elitist's palatial house symbolized a world in which betters ruled lessers of all races. Poorer visitors came to grand mansions with a deferential attitude. An egalitarian's house, on the other hand, signaled a world where no one dominated. Visitors came to humble huts on equal terms.

Trans-Allegheny leaders' residences were usually rural log cabins. When leaders lived in cities, in Ohio River towns high in the Panhandle, they resided in the city equivalent, simple brick houses. Unassuming dwellings, whether of rough old logs or shiny new brick, epitomized an unassuming community where comforts were crude and where all (white) folks considered themselves roughly the same.

A visit with an eastern Virginia swell was more like an audience with a lord. The mansions, ancient thick brick relics of English times, stood for lords who had ruled for generations. The first view of these dwellings denoted imposing rulers. Long avenues of ancient oaks, service buildings joined to or near the ancient mansion, the multi-story eminence of the lordly residence—all of this displayed encrusted prerogative. Here some were too rude to be welcome.

In middle Virginia, the leader's house epitomized those drifting between elitist and egalitarian regimes. The most notorious drifter was, of course, Thomas Jefferson, and his lovely house exquisitely expressed competing conceptions of how republicans should lead. Anyone who wishes illustration of the middle ground between the state's eastern and western extremes has only to experience Monticello.[4]

The word "Monticello," meaning "little mountain," expressed in itself a compromise. Jefferson and Monticello were of that eastern Virginia hilly area rising towards western Virginia mountains. Jefferson's Albemarle County, while containing some 50% slaves, was located in Blue Ridge foothills, leading to regions where few were enslaved. The magnificent view from Monticello, looking over western mountains dominated by nonslaveholders, left Thomas Jefferson no illusions about being able to dictate to egalitarians. At the eastern extreme of Virginia, in contrast, the equally magnificent view from Mount Vernon, looking down on a Potomac River dominated by slaveholders, left the nation's most famous surveyor every reason to think he could master more worlds than he could survey.

The first view of Mount Vernon, as one enters through endless flat acres, is of a typical eastern Virginia ruling mansion. George Washington's Georgian expanse stretches from lordly residential quarters toward kitchen, carriage house, smoke house, and other comforts. In contrast, the first impression of Monticello, as one reaches the summit of the little mountain, is confusion about whether the house is lordly. Trick windows create confusion. A three-story palace looks like a single-story home because of windows faked to look as if only one tall floor exists.

Extensions of the residence to each side, because initially invisible, enhance initial impressions of anti-grandeur. A sweeping three-part complex, with paired wings connecting the central living quarters to service units, has been camouflaged to look at first like a one-part house. Jefferson accomplished the trick by placing his service wings underground out front, only visibly above ground out back.

Inside, antebellum servants were almost as invisible as service wings had been in front. Instead of blacks cleaning, cooking, and scurrying underfoot, in the normal way of southern grandeur, the residence seemed reserved for self-sufficient whites. Trick devices, not slaves, connected residents with comforts. No liveried servant opened the paired doors. Instead, the pressure of a visitor's hand on one also opened the other. No slave brought food or drink. Instead, pivoting windows delivered treats. It was as if some magician had created not a showpiece for slavery but a democrat hiding slaves.

The overall effect was less of magical contrivance than of aristocratic slaveholder and egalitarian republican affecting a balance. Nowhere else in the South could one find such aristocratic hauteur seeking such democratic simplicity, such a luxuriously pampered squire served by so many invisible slaves, such imposing decoration affecting commonplace use. The secret of straddling the

Monticello and its trick windows. Courtesy, Thomas Jefferson Memorial Foundation, Inc./James Tkatch.

eighteenth and nineteenth centuries, as expressed in the bricks and mortar and especially the trick windows of Monticello, was to be seen as somehow above, yet somewhat of the masses. Jefferson, who lived closer to American nonslaveholders than did most Virginia titans, wished to be seen as a personage both superior and equal. His house announced a host who humbly heard—and who imperiously instructed too.

So strained an amalgam was easier to announce in trick windows than in straightforward prose. Jefferson's political theory was a labyrinth seeking a juncture between warring viewpoints. Not for him was the straightforward, class-infested ideology of eighteenth-century elitist republicans to Monticello's east, who based upper-class prerogative on denial of human equality, white or black. Nor was he ready for the straightforward, race-infested ideology of nine-teenth-century slaveholders to Virginia's west, who used the color line to rec-oncile white egalitarianism with black inequality. Jefferson, ever in between, erected his political ideology, like his mansion, on the foundation that white equality was truth—and error too.

He began where more reactionary Virginians ended, with the concept of a natural aristocracy. As a domineering slaveholder raised in a century presuming that the propertied must dominate, he believed enlightened gentlemen must control enlightened government. The best should rule, dispersing civic virtue. The worst should follow, lest civic vice predominate. Orthodox eastern Virginia opinion, all of that.

Where he broke with easterly fossils—where he edged towards neighboring newcomers—was in assuming that commoners had sufficient civic virtue to select governors. No need to assure reign of natural aristocrats by disenfran-chising and gerrymandering. Lessers would elect right superiors. Then inferiors would defer.[5]

The potential flaw in that formulation—the place Jefferson's natural aris-tocracy unnaturally deviated from the aristocratic lesson of slavery—was that superiors' wise government depended on inferiors' wisdom. Lessers must be wise enough to elect right superiors. Much of the balanced Mr. Jefferson's unbal-anced temper stemmed from awareness of that flaw. He feared that his Feder-alist opponents' demagoguery would render his trusted electorate untrustwor-thy. Aristocratic uneasiness led to Jefferson's darker record on civil liberties, including advocating laws against "seditious" libel. Books were also known to be censored at the University of Virginia, which he founded.[6] But while this aristocrat occasionally sought to jail dissenters and screen information, he never sanctioned Virginia's undemocratic electorate and unrepresentative legislature. He called Virginia's eighteenth-century constitution, giving some men unequal privileges, "a gross departure from genuine republican canons."[7]

Further eastward, Virginia squires considered Jefferson's attack a gross departure from responsible class domination. Not for them were tricks making a superior's palace less palatial. Nor would they tolerate Jefferson's concern over whether inferiors really would elect the right superiors. They would not give inferiors the chance to fail. They would ensure the reign of the best in the con-stitution—unless compromised by faltering leaders inside more northern and more western Piedmont regions.

– 3 –

Statistics illustrate how a Virginia constitution half a century old was, despite Jefferson, perpetuating an eighteenth-century regime thirty years into the nine-teenth century. By 1830, the old suffrage requirement of owning 50 acres or an equivalent still disenfranchised perhaps half of Virginia's adult white males. The anti-egalitarian apportionment of the tax-initiating lower house also still gave extra power to Virginia's eastern establishment. In the 1820s, the first Virginia, the encrusted Tidewater, with but 26% of the white population, had 35% of Virginia's lower house delegates. At the same time, Virginians come lately in the Valley and Trans-Allegheny, with 44% of the white population, had only 37% of the delegates. These disproportions in Virginia's House of Delegates paralleled disproportions in the national House of Representatives, product of that elitist relic, the three-fifths clause.[8]

The Slavepower had still more disproportionate power, in Virginia as in the federal government, in the upper house. Locally as nationally, however, an eighteenth-century Slavepower with some extra power possessed nothing like absolute sway. Virginia's slaveholding elite had only enough undemocratic power to save itself in close legislative votes—and to irritate egalitarian republicans mightily.

As the nineteenth century progressed, population movement made the Slavepower's undemocratic share of power ever more irritatingly anti-republican. The Tidewater experienced almost zero population growth in the nineteenth century. The Trans-Allegheny, with a 500% growth rate between 1790 and 1830, grew faster than all other parts of the state put together. Thus the Trans-Allegheny, possessing less than half the Tidewater's white population in 1810, had 10% more white inhabitants by 1829—and a frozen two-thirds fewer lower house delegates.

That slide away from one-white-man, one-vote republicanism led increasingly irate Westerners to demand a constitutional convention throughout the 1820s. By the end of the decade, Easterners sought to ease pressure by a concession meant to concede little. The eastern legislative majority sanctioned a popular vote on whether to call a convention. But the popular vote would poll an undemocratic populace, since only half of white male adults could vote. Should the people approve constitutional reconsideration, the malapportioned legislature could malapportion convention seats.

The people approved for a reason ominous to the Old Order. Eastern Virginia, with the votes to block a convention, lost because some of its own defected. One-fourth of Tidewater voters, heavily in cities peopled heavily by jealous nonslaveholders, voted for reconsideration of elitist republicanism. More important, 45% of Piedmont voters, largely in Jefferson's northwestern Piedmont, defected from eastern reactionaries. A unanimous Tidewater and Piedmont could have defeated the convention call by approximately 24,000 to 15,000. Instead, the referendum won, 21,896 to 16,632.

When the legislature voted on convention apportionment, the northwestern Piedmont's representatives again defected to give the East a few less convention than legislative seats. But the few elitist defectors stopped short of voting for an altogether egalitarian convention. Eastern Virginia was awarded nine more delegates than its white population warranted. Easterners, with a bare majority of Virginia whites, would have a swollen two-thirds' majority of the Convention.[9] Eastern oligarchs could still save the Old Order—if they could straighten out gentlemen's confusion about how gentlemen should dominate.

– 4 –

Easterners and Westerners descended on Richmond for the Convention of 1829 as if dressed for war between Old and New orders. The eastern old guard— Monroe, Madison, John Randolph of Roanoke, Benjamin Watkins Leigh—bore the look of eighteenth-century drawing rooms. Their white wigs were scrupulously powdered. Their velvet cravats were fastidiously tied. Their knee britches and silk stockings were meticulously married. When their lordly leader, John Randolph of Roanoke, descended to endure the Convention, he came down from his imported English coach drawn by his imported English horses, snapping open his imported English watch to make sure he would suffer no extra moments among the riff-raff.

Randolph smirked at the opposition. Westerners arrived not fit to ride to hounds but fitted out for nineteenth-century enterprise. Their heads were topped with hair crudely cut. Their string ties were askew. Their homespun coats and pants were mismatched. They crudely dismounted from rudely bred horses and tramped on into the Convention.

Old-fashioned squires found noises emanating from trampers as boorish as the sight. United States Congressman Phillip Doddridge, leader of western reformers, sounded to tittering gentlemen like he belonged back in Scotland. Doddridge's Scotch Irish twang seemed proof that gauche upstarts now presumed to tell Virginia's first families what Virginia's traditions involved.

Doddridge spoke for the newest North come to reside within the oldest South. The enterprising attorney, born and educated in Pennsylvania and scion of immigrant parents, had settled in the Ohio River town of Wellsburg, high in the Virginia Panhandle. His new neighborhood was as far north as Philadelphia. His neighbors were usually as little disposed as Philadelphians to own slaves.

But Doddridge was no more Yankee than that huge fourth of the South which cared more about other priorities than slavery. Like so many borderites, Doddridge had no intention of stripping slaveholders of black slaves, unless gentlemen stripped commoners of white egalitarianism. Mountaineers cared little, most of them, whether gentlemen owned "niggers." They cared passionately, all of them, whether democratic Union was perpetuated and whether state government was democratic. Geographically isolated from Southerners who thought the enslaved South the only South, socially allied with Northerners who thought egalitarian republicans the truest Americans, theirs were priorities which slaveholding reactionaries considered insidiously anti-southern.

At the Convention, Phillip Doddridge's oration struck reactionaries as proof of commitments askew. Slaveholders, marveled Doddridge, would "exalt a minority into rule, and require a majority of free citizens to submit." Such slaveholding "doctrine makes me a slave." No matter if Doddridge could "pursue my own business and obey my own inclinations." If "you hold political dominion over me, I am" in chains.

Doddridge claimed he sought only to snap chains ensnaring whites. But his language hinted at someday breaking all men's bonds. Doddridge sought to allay eastern gentlemen's "uneasiness, in some degree," on western distaste for slavery. Although he had "no desire to see the slave population of my country increase," he predicted that slaves would be sold, "to some extent, in western Virginia."

Easterners compared Doddridge's "some degrees" and "some extents" and "no desires" with his unconditional desire for western power over the East. In 1790, pointed out the Westerner, the area of Virginia east of the Blue Ridge had contained 186,000 more whites than the area west. In 1829, the East's white majority had shrunk to 43,000. The majority, Doddridge declared, would "soon" reside westward "and there increase forever." Westerners were the new Virginia. But outmoded Virginians sought "our perpetual slavery." Well, "feeble" slaveholders had better not risk our "violence," warned this non-Cuffee. "A race is rising up" west, "with astonishing rapidity, sufficiently strong and powerful to burst assunder any chain by which you may attempt to bind them, with as much ease as the thread parts in a candle blaze."[10]

If anything could enrage supposed masters more than images of hapless slaveholders consumed in flames, it was a supposed friend urging helpless surrender. Chapman Johnson, a slaveholding Richmond lawyer representing a Valley county near Thomas Jefferson's little mountain, resurrected the specter of a besieged class divided against itself. Johnson urged imperial slaveholders to save black slavery by surrendering white imperiousness.

The Valley representative called western opposition to slavery still only potential. Blocking western priorities would make western antislavery actual. Gentlemen must not dare, warned Johnson, openly avow and adopt "as a principle of your Constitution" that Westerners "must pay for the protection of your slaves" with "the surrender of their power." You would then hand your strongest potential enemies "the strongest of possible temptations to make constant war" upon you.

The war would be more one-sided, gloomed Chapman Johnson, than stagnating East against vigorous West. True, the area west of the Blue Ridge would soon contain the white majority. But even worse, western enemies would find "many ardent auxiliaries in the bosom of your own society. Eastern white menials, owning none of that property, and doomed to the laborious offices of life," feel themselves degraded when laboring "in common with the slave." White wage slaves also harbor a "sentiment of envy towards" slaveholders. East and west, concluded Johnson, a nonslaveholder majority which cared more about white egalitarianism than about black slavery should be given the racist regime it wants. Then you will "inspire a feeling of affection—and justice."[11]

Johnson here championed a classic minority strategy when a majority still remained only potentially an enemy. Johnson would soothe, appease, avoid awakening hostility. Like southern appeasers to follow, Johnson conceived that actions intolerable to majorities would drive egalitarians towards antislavery. Johnson was for utopia, herrenvolk Alabama style: sheer democracy for whites, sheer despotism for blacks, no crossing over the color line.

The classic alternative minority strategy, that the few must dominate not through appeasement but by dictation, had three brilliant advocates in the 1829 Convention: Benjamin Watkins Leigh, John Randolph of Roanoke, and Judge Abel P. Upshur. The trio remained convinced that the powerful had always, would always, and should always command. Their stonewalling strategy, like that of reactionaries for the next 30 years, required the upper class to come to full consciousness and to stop a potential antislavery majority from realizing a countervailing consciousness. Tidewater reactionaries favored utopia, anti-her-renvolk South Carolina style: elitist republicans dominating poorer folk, black and white.[12]

Stonewalling had to begin with a minority convinced that majority rule was wrong. To Randolph, the "principle that Numbers and Numbers alone, are to regulate all things" was "monstrous tyranny." Majority rule was, in Leigh's words, "the end of free government."

None of the trio could see natural or rightful reason for the herd to rule the herdsman. In a state of nature, they pointed out, a few powerful beasts "naturally" prey on those weaker. The powerful would not be so unnatural as to enter society to be preyed on by the powerless. Rather, "those who have the greatest stake" of social wealth must possess "the greatest share" of political power. Benjamin Leigh had none of Thomas Jefferson's nervous faith that the rabble would elect proper aristocrats. Power given unnaturally to the mob would result in demagoguery, "corruption," "violence," ending "in military despotism. All the Republics in the world have died this death."[13]

A viable republic must ensure the constitutional rule of the civically virtuous—alias legal reign of the wealthy. White "peasants," no less than black, must accept their betters' rule. Not that the "hardy peasantry of the mountains" are comparable to black slaves, Leigh condescendingly conceded, "in intellectual power, in moral worth, in all that "raises man" above the brute. . . . But I ask gentlemen to say," Leigh sniffed, whether those "obliged to depend on their daily labor for daily subsistence, can, or do ever enter into political affairs. They never do—never will—never can. . . . So far as mind is concerned," the "peasantry of the west" lacked capacity to govern.[14]

Peasantry of the West. How that contempt did enrage egalitarian republicans such as Phillip Doddridge. How Leigh did delight in their outrage. At that pristine moment of hatred, grandees and commoners knew what history would take 30 more years to reveal—that Virginia, the pivotal state in the middle of the South, could not forever find a middle way.

The extremes already preferred separation to submission. Doddridge conceived that gentlemen's "immoral" denial that we are "your equals in intelligence and virtue" and their "corrupt" demand that government confer "power . . . on wealth" ought to create a new 1776. Randolph believed that the mob's nonsense that "a bare majority may plunder the minority" and their "demand to divorce property from power" would fashion "a new despotism." Were he but mercifully younger, squeaked the aging relic, "I would, in case this monstrous tyranny shall be imposed upon us, do what a few years ago I should have thought parricidal. I would withdraw from your jurisdiction. I would not live under King Numbers."[15]

The worst "stupidity" an enemy of King Numbers had to endure in the Convention, Randolph added, was Chapman Johnson's nonsense that the East's "unnecessary" attacks on majority rule created the West's "unnecessary" attacks on minority enslavement. Rather, rival social structures necessarily produced rival political ideologies. Just as the East's aristocratic politics grew out of an aristocratic institution, so the West's egalitarian politics grew out of an egalitarian culture. The very "habits" of yeoman culture, added Upshur, especially the "personal exertion" of the individual free to make his own world, created "a rooted antipathy" to inequality, both social and political. Surrender the war for political inequality and a war against social inequality would follow.[16]

Easterners expected the war to begin as battle over taxation and appropriations. Westerners believed that mountains blocked western prosperity. Build canals and roads through the towering ranges, so conceived isolated Appalachian laborers, and free labor markets would absorb mountaineers' products. State internal improvements could liberate free labor energies.

Benjamin Watkins Leigh answered that nonslaveholders would then enslave the rich. The mob would finance its roads and canals by passing soak-the-slaveholders taxation. Nor would slaveholders' enslavement end with towering taxes on slaves. "Oppressive taxation," a critical "interference" with "our slave property," would lead to the ultimate interference. "When men's minds once take this direction, they pursue it as steadily as man pursues his course to the grave."[17]

When men's minds take this direction. Benjamin Leigh's words echoed Chapman Johnson's diagnosis of "the enemy." For all Leigh's talk of war of worlds, he saw no enemy mentality absolutely committed to antislavery. He saw the same phenomenon Johnson spotted—an egalitarian world with tendencies, still unknown even to itself, to perpetuate egalitarianism by abolishing slavery. Johnson, by appeasing on the matter of white rule, would keep that other mind from awakening to its tendencies against black despotism. Leigh, by stonewalling on legislative power, would bring his class to full elitist consciousness and block that other class from evolving towards a countervailing consciousness. Johnson, like southern moderates in coming decades, preferred to ignore tendencies only implicit. Leigh, like southern extremists in years ahead, preferred to assault implicit tendencies at the threshold.

But a minority class stonewalling at the threshold must be a class, awakened and consolidated. Chapman Johnson was right that a minority barring majority rule had better possess overweening determination, now and at all future conventions, to crush what it stirred up. Since the upper class still controlled a malapportioned legislature, and malapportioned legislatures could malapportion conventions, and malapportioned conventions could malapportion legislatures, the ruling class had perpetual theoretical power—if it thought and acted like a class. But let the class crack, Randolph warned, and "'the waters are out" and "a rat hole will let in the ocean.'"[18]

Upper-class consciousness was not up to the requirements. One trouble, diagnosed stonewallers, was that geographic priorities transcended class priorities. "The slaveholder of the East," regretted Abel P. Upshur, "cannot calculate on the cooperation of the slaveholder West, in any measure calculated to protect that species of property." On the issue of taxing slaves to build western roads, for example, the western slaveholder would discover he was more Westerner than slaveholder. Only in eastern Virginia did slaves "constitute the leading and most important interest."[19]

To Upshur's picture of a class geographically divided in priorities East from West, Randolph added a portrait of slaveholders divided against themselves even in the East. One-white-man, one-vote fanaticism, said Randolph, was a sword above gentlemen's necks. And "from what quarter" does the swordsman come? "From the corn and oat growers on the Eastern Shore? ... From the fishermen on the Chesapeake? The pilots of Elizabeth City? No, Sir, from ourselves—from the great slaveholding and tobacco planting districts!" Randolph professed he never would have believed that Chapman Johnson or any "slaveholder of Virginia" would display "so great a degree of infatuation."[20]

John Randolph of Roanoke, one of the nation's most famous Jeffersonian Republicans, was surely faking surprise that an upper-class compromiser had surfaced. The reactionary chose not to tell the Convention that Piedmont deviations from the gospel of malapportioned legislatures were Thomas Jefferson re-emerged. Randolph also chose not to say that he and delegates more tough-minded than Jefferson on authority over whites were Jeffersonian softhearts on authority over blacks. Benjamin Leigh confessed to the Convention he wished he "had been born in a land where domestic and negro slavery is unknown." Heaven forbid he had been nurtured outside of Mother Virginia. But he wished Providence had spared "my country [i.e. his state!] this moral and political evil."[21]

Abel P. Upshur was at no less pains to assure his friends that "I abhor slavery." Upshur would leave termination of the abhorrent, he privately wrote, "to the slow operation of moral causes." But since termination of bondage must not "be suddenly effected," he "would not make" legislative emancipation "possible in our Constitution." As for John Randolph of Roanoke, his secret last will and testament offered freedom to his slaves.[22]

An impartial observer, hearing Leigh's public apologetics or spying on Upshur's private confessions or reading Randolph's will, had to wonder whether rulers sorry about the slaveholding foundation of superior power would always wage all-out war for prerogative. The hidebound Mr. Leigh, the sneering Mr. Upshur, and the ferocious Mr. Randolph were tougher fighters for authoritarian views than were Thomas Jefferson or Chapman Johnson or any leader of Old Maryland and Old Delaware up north. But the toughest Virginian was compromised compared with Carolinians further south—and he was facing a more uncompromising egalitarian challenge. Was any Virginian, was any ruling establishment in the Upper South, tough enough to stonewall against Chapman Johnson's appeasements?

The Convention's ballots showed, as Randolph feared, that too many authoritarians favored surrender of authority. Too many Chapman Johnsons, based too securely in Thomas Jefferson's northwestern Piedmont, would appease the new egalitarians rather than stonewall for ancient elitism. The key vote came on Leigh's proposal to structure the tax-initiating lower house on the "mixed" basis of property and numbers. Leigh's formula, basing a district's legislative apportionment equally on numbers of whites residing and dollars of taxes paid, would have given the Tidewater and Piedmont, with 54% of whites in 1830, control over 65% of the tax-initiating House of Delegates. Leigh's mixed basis formula lost, 49-47. Defeat came because 13 Easterners, largely northwestern Piedmont delegates and including representatives from Jefferson's Albemarle County, deserted to join unanimous Valley and Trans-Allegheny contingents.[23]

With property knocked out of Leigh's property-plus-numbers formula, the question became when the numbers would be counted. Since western white population was growing proportionately faster than eastern, Westerners wanted the Convention of 1829 to base apportionment on the 1830 census. Egalitarians also wanted periodic reapportionment, so that the West's share of legislative seats would periodically increase with its white numbers. Reactionaries demanded apportionment based on the 1820 census and no reapportionment thereafter.

The East won this round because the upper class acted slightly more like a class. Apportionment based on 1820 won over 1830 when three of the 13 Easterners who had defected to defeat Leigh's mixed basis returned to uphold apportionment based on outmoded numbers. Phillip Doddridge's motion to reapportion in 1840 also barely lost, this time because one of the 13 eastern defectors wished to freeze apportionment on the unequal 1820 basis.

The 13 eastern wanderers ultimately secured something of a compromise. Where Leigh's mixed basis of property and numbers would have given the Tidewater and Piedmont 65% of lower house delegates, and an apportionment based on 1830 numbers would have given the slaveholders' region 54%, apportionment based on 1820 numbers gave the Slavepower 57%. Democratic despots, as usual, were despotic enough to enrage, too democratic to mash those enraged.[24]

Egalitarian Virginians raged primarily about an ever more elitist future. The defeat of future reapportionment left political power frozen to a formula already nine years anachronistic and sure to grow ever more anti-egalitarian. Such perpetual Slavepower, Doddridge warned, looks to freemen's "perpetual slavery."[25]

Other Convention compromises, Doddridge believed, also enslaved whites. The requirement that voters must have $50 worth of land was neither eliminated, as the West wished, nor kept sacrosanct, as the East desired. Instead, the $50 was reduced to $25, reducing the disenfranchised from about half to about a third of white freemen. The upper house would remain even less democratically apportioned than the lower. The two malapportioned legislative houses would continue to elect state executive and judicial officials.

Westerners went away muttering that white democracy and black slavery were incompatible. Easterners went away wondering whether rulers divided and apologetic about their authority could survive anti-authoritarian opposition. A thousand days later, Nat Turner would press another test of upper-class resolve—and white nonslaveholders would add the most searching test yet.

CHAPTER 10

Class Revolt in Virginia, II:
Slavery Besieged

Nat Turner, that most successful of North American slave insurrectionists, terrified the slaveholding establishment into an historical debate over emancipation!

How a dramatic chronicler would love that introduction to a tale of murder begetting reform. Perhaps a novelist would prefer the fable that John Brown's famous Harper's Ferry raid in 1859 scared the South out of the Union in 1860. But epic possibilities abound in the saga of how Nat Turner's uprising in 1831 frightened Virginians into the most massive reconsideration of slavery that ever occurred in a North American black belt.

So much for epic possibility. Most Virginians, like most Southerners, were only fleetingly panicky about whether blacks would murder whites. For either Nat Turner or John Brown to touch off lasting crisis, terror had to touch more sustained anxieties. In both 1831 and 1859, passing doubts about whether whites could control blacks quickly gave way to these masters' greater worry: whether slaveholders could count on nonslaveholders, especially nonslaveholders two mountain ranges removed.

We will see that John Brown's Harper's Ferry raid in 1859 is an overrated cause of southern secession in 1860, not least because too little substantiated initial fears that slave revolt would inspire nonslaveholder uprising. In 1832 that deadly sequence transpired. Virginia's legislative showdown over slavery, following in the wake not just of Nat Turner but also of the Convention of 1829, stemmed far more from white egalitarians' fury at elitist republicanism than from slaveholders' fear of black insurrection.

Still, Nat Turner's uprising bestowed one boon on western egalitarians who would deflate eastern elitists. In the malapportioned Virginia legislature of 1832, as in the malapportioned Virginia Convention of 1829, a unanimous eastern establishment could have stymied western nonslaveholders. But Turner widened cracks at the top. A small fraction of eastern slaveholders, alarmed at Turner's revolt, initiated debate on how to ease slavery out of Virginia.

– 1 –

Why did a few strategically placed slaveholders cave in before Nat Turner? The answer is not obvious, for Turner was never close to victorious. William Styron's rather implausible novel, *The Confessions of Nat Turner,* is most plausible in asking the question (its misleading answers aside) why Turner and friends did not brutalize more broadly. A novelist's problem in turning a few dozen assassinations into an epic of assassination parallels the historian's problem in explaining why an easily controlled rebellion demoralized a few critical slaveholding legislators.

Turner's revolt is replete with ironies of a historic, frightening killer who looked not all that frightening and whose killings were not necessarily numerous enough to slay several significant slaveholders' will to continue.[2] Nat Turner was not an eerie dwarf, such as Gullah Jack, the witch doctor in Charleston's Denmark Vesey Conspiracy of 1822. Nor was Turner an intimidating giant, such as the towering General Vesey. General Nat was ordinary in size.

Nor was Nat's owner of historic stature. The "master" was one Putnam, an infant. Putnam, having inherited "his" black from his lately deceased father, had lately been brought with "his" slave to live under his new stepfather, Joseph Travis. Nat Turner, least mastered of North American slaves, had master and step-master both.

Nor was Turner's capture accomplished in the epic manner of John Brown's at Harper's Ferry. No establishment army smashed into a rebel-occupied arsenal, braving a fusillade of bullets. Rather, an impoverished nonslaveholder snatched the starving rebel from a heap of pinebrush. Previously, a slave's dog had chased the fugitive from a cave and a bullet through the hat had driven him from a corn-fodder stack.

Nor did Turner orchestrate a grande finale in the manner of John Brown at the gallows. No righteous warrior here told his killers that the meek would murder the mighty. Rather, the slave capped an uneventful hanging by not moving a muscle before expiring.

Nor had General Nat's 60 black warriors almost conducted a successful coup d'état. The Virginia militia, upon racing to the scene, could find only whites brutalizing blacks. Those who subsequently searched for brutalized white bodies found that fire had consumed some human remains. Wolves had devoured others. But even fantasies agitated by these horrors could not conceive of more than 70 whites slain.

Sixty rebels could not massacre many whites in so short a time in so isolated a setting. Nat Turner's locale was not the crowded stage of a Vesey in Charleston, where thousands of throats were present to be sliced. Turner's army victimized a scarcely populated speck of southernmost Virginia near the uninhabitable North Carolina Dismal Swamp. Turner terrorized this remote turf for 48 hours. His uprising was effectively over after one evening. In the morning, one brief barrage from six whites sliced the rebels' ranks in half. Another brief burst shrunk Nat's army to Nat hiding alone. Only Southampton County of Virginia's hundreds of counties experienced the uprising. Less than 1% of Southampton's territory was touched. Turner's crudely armed followers had to march 10 miles to gain an arsenal. Rebels traversed only five.

If that sort of rural uprising had inevitably caused all to quake, Latin American slaveholders would have been constantly trembling. Hundreds of Latin American revolts spread thousands of times more viciousness than did Nat Turner's spree. Latin Americans did not almost do in slavery every time—any time—thousands of bondsmen marauded and murdered. They would have been incredulous that 60 rebels could almost crack an establishment. But then again they knew despots must live and die by the sword. They were not democrats who needed to believe that familial slaves willingly consented to slavery.

Nat Turner's anti-familial assault killed something more vulnerable than some 70 white dependents. Nat Turner murdered slaveholders' domestic illusion. One question summed up why Nat Turner himself particularly threatened a Domestic Institution. Since Turner was a family assassin, what "family friend" could be trusted? Nat Turner had always posed as loving "boy," grateful for patriarchal guidance. Why lock doors against Nat Turner? He would protect his Massa, little Putnam.

How little they knew, Virginians shuddered after Nat Turner threw off the disguise, what transpired behind *their* Cuffee's mask. While Turner's body had been performing Cuffee, his mind had been savouring the Holy Spirit. This domestic servant came to his mission after a vision "of white spirits and black spirits engaged in battle, and the sun was darkened, the thunder rolled in the Heavens, and blood flowed in the streams." At first Nat Turner thought the white's anniversary of freedom was the appropriate day to slaughter despots and their families. But as July 4 approached, his black body ached. His illness seemed a sign that blacks must follow their own calendar. Then in mid-August, a black spot obliterated a sun made silvery-white by the fog, and the sky turned bloody crimson. The black knew the time to redden "his" white folks had come.

Past midnight on August 22, 1831, Nat Turner's stepmaster, Joseph Travis, slept on the second floor with his wife and three children. The general put a ladder to a window, climbed inside, tiptoed downstairs, and let in six privates. Rebels, sneaking into the bedrooms, swung first at Massa Travis. The stepmaster was decapitated. His wife's neck was severed. One blow beheaded two sons sleeping together. Gore-splattered warriors then splintered furniture and smashed china, apparently leaving no semblance of home intact.

They rushed into the August night. They remembered something intact. Putnam lived. They slipped back. They crept to his crib. They slit off his head. They fed his spurting body to the flames. Nat Turner, "infantilized" slave of an infant, was "childish" domestic no more.

Turner had planned, after gutting his own "home," to march on the town of Jerusalem, ten miles north. He would there capture guns to replace hatchets. He may have anticipated marching back south and hiding gunmen in the Dismal Swamp.

He never made it up to the Promised City, much less down to the saving swamp. His army spent too much time and awakened too many alarms slaughtering sleeping families. Perhaps rebels thought domestic bloodletting would attract recruits. Perhaps vengeance waylaid strategy. Most likely the devout leader based his strategy on those heavenly signs of reddened whites. Whatever the reason, Nat Turner's army savaged every white domicile en route.

A spree less heavy on domestic savagery might have been harder to put down. The general might have slipped his army past sleeping homes, murdering only if someone noticed. His troops might have raced to Jerusalem, ambushed the town, seized guns, and rushed back towards the Dismal Swamp, with hours of night still to pass. That raid would have combined Denmark Vesey's surprise attack on The Man's guns with Frederick Douglass's dash beyond The Man's grasp.

The preacher saw a more anti-domestic coup written in a crimson sky. Nat Turner's crew did not restrict its savagery to resisting males. At their most notorious stop, the Waller home, instead of hunting down a patriarch fleeing to awaken the community, they massacred his wife and ten school children sleeping at his house. Black warriors then made a heap of the headless white dependents.

One best counts victims not by heads but by homes. The Francis home: wiped out, including one woman and three children. The William Williams home: wiped out, including one woman and two children. The Jacob Williams home: wiped out, including two women and five children. The Vaughan home: wiped out, including a widow and two children. In all, less than ten white men were killed. Twice as many women were savaged. Twice again as many children were massacred.

In a reversal typical during southern insurrection scares and especially understandable this time, panicky whites briefly turned the Domestic Institution into an anti-domestic prison. Homes were abandoned. Women and children were garrisoned. Men marched in front of un-family-like forts, as if guarding jails. Having previously assumed, albeit with occasional qualms, that hearths and firesides were safe from midnight assassins, slaveholders now assumed the unmentionable reverse: that every domestic could be an executioner. Having previously assumed, albeit with some brutal lashings, that fatherly cuffs would keep slaves laboring, patriarchs now slaughtered dozens of suspected blacks, put bodyless heads and headless bodies on display, savagely reminded Cuffee of the price for not obeying Massa.[3]

That anti-domestic violence had to dissipate. Patriarchs could not routinely be executioners. Families could not reside in garrisons. "Family friends" could not be locked outside homes. But the domestic charade, once resumed, had lost its verisimilitude. Democrats wanted no more garrisons. But could they believe their domestic slaves consented?

– 2 –

One important matriarch could not. Jane Randolph was the wife of Thomas Jefferson Randolph. Her husband was son of Thomas Mann Randolph, the governor who had urged the Virginia legislature to deport blacks after the Missouri

Controversy, and thus grandson of Thomas Jefferson, who had called state deportation less practicable than national action. Thomas Jefferson Randolph, his grandfather's namesake and executor, was to the manor born when it came to Conditional Termination.

Mrs. Randolph saw the Turner insurrection as a sign to start terminating slavery. The Southampton "horrors," Mrs. Randolph wrote her sister, have "aroused all my fears which had nearly become dormant, and indeed have increased them to the most agonizing degree." The "horrible slaughter" was no more "torturing" than "appalling precautions" now necessary "even up here," hundreds of miles from Southampton. Nothing should "induce persons who can get a home elsewhere to remain." She was "using all my efforts with Jefferson," as she called her husband, "to quit at once and move North." She would make "Jefferson . . . think on this subject as I do."⁴

"Jefferson" thought about insurrection the way his grandfather had. Thomas Jefferson Randolph tried to calm his wife. Cuffee, he claimed, for now, is too lazy to kill. National, state, and local armies, for now, could crush any uprising.⁵

For now. For now. How this "Jefferson" sounded like his grandfather. Thomas Jefferson had always deflected his nightmare onto generations unborn. If we do not do something, he had warned, our children's children will be murdered. By placing danger in the distant future, Monticello's master had eased necessity for instant action. A conception of danger nonexistent until the living are dead invites the thought that the Thomas Jeffersons would never act.

The grandson proved otherwise. Procrastinators are especially tested when future fears receive present substantiation. Those timorous about generations yet unborn may build bulwarks against danger. Or edgy procrastinators may seek termination of a dangerous institution. Thomas Jefferson Randolph nervously stepped forward where his grandfather had faltered back. "The danger," Thomas Jefferson Randolph wrote his terrified wife, "is to our children's children 40 or 50 years hence, not to us."⁶

But true patriarchs must save future families. In his speech in the Virginia House of Delegates on January 16, 1832, initiating the legislature's historic debate, Thomas Jefferson's grandson predicted how his slaves would murder his grandchildren.⁷ Randolph foresaw "a dissolution of this Union." A northern "invasion, . . . in part with black troops," would offer "arms and asylum" to slaves. When white males "shall march to repel" Yankees, "their families" would be "butchered and their homes desolated in the rear."

This familial patriarch, wishing "better prospects" for our progeny, pressed hard for a version of the post-nati plan which his grandfather had softly suggested. Thomas Jefferson Randolph urged a legislative decree that Virginia slaves born on or after July 4, 1840, would be freed after they became adults— women at 18, men at 21. All those freed must then be deported to Africa.

Randolph's plan would free no slaves born on or before July 3, 1840. No slave woman born on or after July 4, 1840, would be freed before 1858; no slave male before 1861. Indeed, no slave born in Virginia need ever be freed. Masters could sell otherwise-to-be-freedmen into perpetual slavery down south before emancipating birthdays. Thomas Jefferson's grandson would make New York's illegal form of black removal legal, even moral in Virginia, just as New York's James Tallmadge, Jr., had proposed for Missouri.

The Virginia government, cheered Randolph, need not compensate masters for potentially unemancipating post-nati emancipation. Future mothers would be the only relevant property owned at the moment future emancipation was decreed. That property would always remain Massa's. As for future offspring, they could be sold down river if slaveowners wished compensation. Nor would Randolph charge public coffers for freedmen's deportation to Africa. Young adults would be required to labor long enough to finance their journey towards freedom. The consequence, for Virginian grandchildren of Jefferson's grand-child, would be priceless, costless absence of blacks.

Eastern Virginians' leading newspapers cheered Randolph's proposal. The Democrats' *Richmond Enquirer* hailed the "unprecedented event" and, urged "one *last appeal* for emancipation." The *Enquirer*'s most important newspaper rival, the Richmond *Constitutional Whig,* denied this legislative debate would be the last. "This year may not see the vast work commenced. . . . A half cen-tury may not see it completed." But no philanthropist could "calculate the ben-efits to mankind of Virginia's . . . abolition."[8]

Virginia's governor concurred. Governor John Floyd, a slaveholder, had in November 1831 timidly initiated what he prayed would be a south-wide move-ment to remove his property. He privately informed South Carolina's and Geor-gia's governors that his annual message would urge "a first step to emancipa-tion." His proposal, Floyd reassured South Carolina Governor James Hamilton, Jr., "will of course be tenderly and cautiously managed, and will be urged or delayed as your State and Georgia may be disposed to cooperate."[9]

Hamilton's reply evidently has not survived. What a loss. The South Caro-lina governor must have penned a memorable command from the Lower South to the Upper South to measure up to being a Southerner. The South Carolina Nullifier, deep in a fight to nullify the legal basis for future antislavery, would hardly join a Slavepower Conspiracy to abolish slavery. Perhaps given pause by South Carolina's "Little Jimmy," Governor Floyd was circumspect in recom-mending legislative action. But Randolph's debate had the governor's sanction. At last, a fraction of the Virginia establishment encouraged a "Jefferson" to act.

A handful of key slaveholding legislators affirmed Thomas Jefferson Ran-dolph's conception that the safety of southern homes demanded removal of slav-ery. James McDowell, Jr., a Valley slaveholder and a future governor of the state, called this "domestic institution" an inseparable union of "danger and slavery." In patriarchal Virginia, "peculiarly," McDowell claimed, "attachment of the slave to his owner is common." But this very "humanity of our people" was the "principal cause of apprehension." Paternalists who "improve" a slave's "intellect" and "lift up" his "condition" thereby "bring him in nearer contact with the liberty he has lost." Patriarchs proud of the "privileged condition of their slaves" had created "a mask of mischief," hiding a "future explosion."

Domestic servitude, warned McDowell, is the worst "conceivable" form of slavery. "Nothing can be done" to ensure "domestic defense," for our "dwelling is at all times accessible" to our "enemy." The "defenseless situation of the master and the sense of injured right of the slave" are "the best possible preparative for conflict."[10]

William Henry Brodnax, another large slaveholder and representative of a heavily enslaved district, added another theory on why Nat Turner's rebellion necessitated deportation of domestic servants. General Brodnax, commander of militia units during the Southampton Insurrection, had dashed to the scene, thousands at his command, only to discover no insurrection to conquer. Midnight assassins had scattered the moment they could no longer advance "unseen and unopposed."

The general, although finding no enemy to conquer, had experienced one almost unconquerable difficulty. "The public mind was excited almost to frenzy by seeing the mangled corpses of helpless females and unoffending infants devoured by dogs and vultures." His army had "the greatest difficulty" stopping "indiscriminate slaughter of the blacks." Some "Domestic Institution" this, where the commander sent to prevent Cuffee from decapitating Massa had instead to prevent patriarchs from massacring blacks.

William Henry Brodnax was "not without *my* fears." Within "insulated neighborhoods, a few misguided fanatics, like Nat Turner," could recommence "partial excesses of pillage and massacre." Midnight ambushes, "the real extent of the danger," were "bad enough." What matter to the mutilated family whether others were slaughtered? "To the wretched individuals assailed," a revolt against their household was as critical "as if all the world was involved."

Brodnax believed that another insurrection anytime "soon" would yield "indiscriminate slaughter of all the blacks." The more probable event, several "*partial* attempts" at "intervals of many years," would still provoke white avengers. A responsible paternalist must protect his blacks against likely massacre—and his whites against not-so-likely beheadings.[11]

Brodnax and the few other slaveholding reformers in the legislature called the Domestic Institution detrimental to economic prosperity as well as to domestic safety. "Virginia," complained McDowell, "has greatly declined." Slave labor's "improvidence," "inactivity," and "apathy" have yielded "our desolated fields, our torpid enterprise, and . . . our humbled impotence."[12] "Who can doubt," added Brodnax, that "*slavery*" is "principally" the cause of Virginia's pecuniary decline?[13]

On what should be done about this "mildew," this "incubus," this "transcendent evil," William Henry Brodnax turned on Thomas Jefferson Randolph with that viciousness reformers reserve for each other. "Monstrous," "dangerous," "*revolutionary,*" "*immoral*"—that is what Brodnax thought of this latest "Jefferson." Randolph's notion that the state would owe masters nothing for children seized, Brodnax scoffed, displayed "very absurd" understanding of why masters paid premiums for breeding "wenches." "Jefferson's" conception of obviating "impending *dangers*" with a plan commening 30 years hence, marveled the white commander who had marched on Nat Turner, left criminally vague "what is to become of . . . our safety . . . in the meantime." In "dark and uncertain" years before the "day of jubilee," Virginia legislatures would spend "winter after winter" causing "dangerous excitement" by considering repeal of the Jacobinical law. No less certain to lead to "lawless efforts and insurrection" was Randolph's proposed mix of blacks to be freed because born on or after July 4, 1840, and blacks always to be enslaved because born on or before July 3, 1840.

To further disrupt the domestic realm, Randolph's proposal would give every gentleman "the strongest temptation . . . to convert himself into a negro-trader." Owners could "sell and pocket the value of every one of these post-nati, up to the very hour" of adulthood. Under "this fanciful" emancipation, where not "one single negro ever would be liberated," blacks would rise like madmen when sold down river in the final hour. Randolph's chimera was thus a scheme of liberation destined to free no one, a preservation of domestic peace destined to produce 30 years of domestic warfare, a maturation of Virginia paternalism destined to make every patriarch a child-seller.[14]

William Henry Brodnax proposed instead that deportation be commenced immediately and emancipation soon. He would begin by exiling 6,000 free blacks a year, at state or federal expense. "Within ten years," no free black would remain. After this "process . . . shall have demonstrated the practicality . . . of gradual deportation," Virginia should move on to deporting 10,000 slaves a year, with compensation to masters. "In less than 80 years," not one slave would blacken lily-white Virginia.[15] Expensive? Certainly. But less costly and more moral than the alternative: slaughtering domestics during the next insurrection panic, a catastrophe Thomas Jefferson Randolph's proposal would hasten.

– 3 –

Most Virginia slaveholders and most of their representatives saw a better upper-class solution than Brodnax's or Randolph's. Rulers of blacks should shut up and do nothing. Nat Turner's rebellion, said slaveholding conservatives, would remain too exceptional to ruin domestic slavery, unless legislative speeches provoked more domestic savagery. No legislative talk should occur, for no effective law was possible. Legislative action against slavery required government-financed compensation to slaveholders and deportation for slaves. Virginia could not afford remedies so expensive.

But no legislator called slavery good or permanent. All assumed the posture of Benjamin Watkins Leigh, demanding no legislative interference with the "evil." Everyone found some way to call bondage a "curse," a "poisoned chalice," indefensible "in the abstract."

These not-very-proslavery opponents of legislative action saluted a safer way of cleansing the Chesapeake of bondsmen. Worldwide demand for cotton, urged Randolph's and Brodnax's opponents, would slowly drain Virginia slaves towards the cotton-producing Deep South. As slaves diffused out, whites would come in. "Natural causes," trumpeted William O. Goode, would gradually, peacefully achieve "removal of slavery from Virginia."[16]

With most slaveholders preferring "natural" termination by slave sales, "unnatural" legislative termination had no chance, if the issue was the upper class's to determine. The danger of ruling-class division remained what it would ever be: lethal only if nonslaveholding locales, North or South, made the fate of slavery their business too. Thomas Jefferson Randolph, like his grandfather, favored proper collaborations with other regions and classes to achieve blacks' removal. In 1824, Thomas Jefferson had sought alliance with a northern non-slaveholder, Jared Sparks, to achieve through national legislation what state legislatures could not afford. Now Thomas Jefferson Randolph sought alliance with Virginia nonslaveholders to secure a legislative interference most slaveholders could not abide.

Brodnax called Randolph's proposed collaboration treason. Letting non-slaveholders decide about slavery would undo the work of the 1829 Convention. Virginia's minority of slaveholders had then secured protection against King Numbers. Now, allowing a nonslaveholding majority to determine whether, when, and how slaveholders' property shall be seized would re-enact "the dark and bloody scenes of the French Revolution."[17]

Randolph answered Brodnax with a metaphor. Suppose dogs bit citizens. Should only "dogholders" determine "whether the dogs should be destroyed?" Is not the family "of the non-dogholder as likely to be bitten and to die . . . as the family of the dogholder?"[18]

With that metaphor, Randolph caught the possible danger in the division of Virginia's upper class. When have-nots meddled with what they did not have, a split among the haves could be disastrous. If Nat Turner had commenced a series of events destined to topple the establishment, nonslaveholders would have to make Virginia slaveholders pay for division at the top. The West had failed, despite Thomas Jefferson's invitation and eastern divisions, in 1829. Now a new "Jefferson" was renewing the invitation for a historic collaboration.

– 4 –

Yeomen needed no invitation. They accepted anyway. So-called outsiders gained delicious legitimacy by following insiders. Eastern slaveholders, pointed out the West's George Summers, initiated antislavery debate and "called for assistance." Western nonslaveholders came "at their request, . . . to labor side by side with them."[19]

They labored side by side with Randolph because slavery was not just slave-holders' business. Back in 1829, Phillip Doddridge had regretfully predicted that slaves might be sold west. The Nat Turner affair, warned western legislators in 1832, increased the prospect that the "black vomit" would spew upon them. Eastern Virginia, diagnosed Westerners, had too many slaves. Other southern states would bar Turner-crazed serviles. Where would that leave western Virginia's fertile valleys? The only outlet for diffusion of eastern Virginia's slaves! Cursed by a "disease . . . we can establish not even a QUARANTINE" against.[20]

Most Westerners, like their handful of eastern legislative allies, wished to quarantine themselves against Turner-like domestic dangers. No one wants to live, noted Charles Faulkner of the Valley, in a home where "such an evil *may* occur"; and where no "vigilance of your police can prevent its recurrence." No one wishes to reside, added George Summers of the Trans-Allegheny, in a household where "a daring and desperate spirit" masks the "murder in his heart" with "smiles upon his face" as he "leaps upon his devoted victims."[21]

Still, Westerners attacked slavery less because of dread of slave rebellion than because of desire for political power. Like Rufus King at the time of the Missouri Controversy, nonslaveholders argued that because slaveholders demanded more than one-white-man, one-vote, achieving white political equality required containing black slavery. A tyrannical institution had spawned a tyrannical constitution, based "on the odious doctrine that wealth is the proper basis of Representation." Social tyranny, having begotten political tyranny, would furthermore spawn economic tyranny. The eastern minority, alias the anti-republican legislative majority, would defeat "railways, canals, and all other magnificent projects" of the western majority, alias hapless legislative minority.

Westerners held down politically and thus economically by the Slavepower would be still more economically shackled, they declared, if slavery poured over the mountains. Trans-Allegheny legislators, echoing again eastern critics of the system, called slavery the sure route to economic stagnation. Free labor was the key to economic growth. Independent republicans who freely consented to labor outperformed dependent slaves lashed into exertion. A single poor Westerner, working a minuscule "patch of corn," displayed more "boldness of invention" than 10,000 lazy slaves or 1000 idle owners.[22]

The argument demonstrated that just as economic systems yield political ideology, so political systems generate economic ideology. Republican and capitalistic assumptions here fused into an ideological passion for consent, whether to labor or to be ruled, a passion beyond what mere politics or mere economics alone could have inspired. Benjamin Watkins Leigh's point at the Virgina Convention was proving to be all too right: egalitarians aroused to full consciousness could turn against all forms of coercive inequality. With Westerners' desire for consenting and equal laborers fusing with their desire for consenting and equal citizens, Easterners would need every unequal constitutional advantage which Leigh had lately helped secure.

– 5 –

Westerners preferred Randolph's way of clipping the Slavepower's dominance to Brodnax's. Nonslaveholders would rather begin by removing slaves than by deporting free blacks. But rather than losing reform in a squabble with each other, reformers coalesced behind an abstract proclamation that legislative action against slavery was "expedient." Conservatives coalesced behind a motion to table the subject.

Virginia proved, as usual, too divided for so clear-cut a choice. The resolution declaring legislative action against slavery "expedient" lost, 73-58. The vote revealed a geographically remote nonslaveholder class almost unanimously eager to challenge the Slavepower. The Trans-Allegheny declared legislative reform expedient, 31-0. The Valley concurred, 18-6. The half-dozen valleyites who voted with eastern slaveholders all lived in slavery's few southern Valley bastions.

Only the East's extra legislative seats prevented nonslaveholder power from truly menancing the Slavepower. The legislative malapportionment of 1829 gave western Virginia seven less, eastern Virginia seven more delegates than a one-white-man, one-vote apportionment would have provided. A shift of seven votes would have narrowed a rather substantial 73-58 vote against the expediency of legislative termination into a razor-thin 66-65 defeat for nonslaveholders. Virginia, with one and a half times more slaves than any other southern state in 1830, barely had a majority mandate to continue despotism, at least according to the egalitarian republican way of measuring mandates.

The legislative vote also illustrated continued dissent inside the slaveholders' section. Nine eastern delegates voted for the expediency of legislative action against slavery. Two defectors represented Tidewater cities, home of nonslaveholding laborers; one represented the Tidewater's Accomac County, bastion of nonslaveholding fishermen; six represented areas near Monticello, locale of planters geographically and ideologically close to western Virginia antagonists. This fraction of slaveholders, when added to the nonslaveholding majority, could indeed have endangered slavery—if King Numbers had ruled the Old Dominion.

The malapportioned legislature, having resolved against legislative interference, next voted on tabling further discussion. On that roll call, the crack in the eastern ruling class widened. Eleven eastern delegates who had voted down the expediency of legislative interference joined the nine eastern "traitors" who had voted up legislative termination to provide 20 eastern votes against terminating the debate. Too few Easterners stood ready to silence western insurgents.[23]

Wavering legislators, having voted against terminating the discussion and the institution, now had to terminate something. The foggy solution came from an indistinct figure. Archibald Bryce, Jr., a representative from the northwestern Piedmont, moved that the legislature take the "first step" of colonizing free blacks. The second step, of colonizing enslaved blacks, "should await more definite development of public opinion."

Since slaveholders wished *free* blacks out, Bryce's middle ground might seem tilted toward perpetuating slavery. But Bryce inclined towards ending slavery. He called his resolution an "entering wedge," a signal to "the world" that Virginians "look forward to the final abolition of slavery . . . and that we will go on, step by step, to that great end." Virginians believed that ending slavery required removing blacks. Let us prove, urged Bryce, that colonizing free blacks would work. Then terminating bondage would follow.[24]

The vote on the Bryce Preamble showed that most legislators read Bryce's language Bryce's way. Of the 73 conservatives who had previously voted that legislative termination of slavery was "inexpedient," 58 now voted that Bryce's "entering wedge" was also inexpedient. Of the 58 reformers who had affirmed legislative action as "expedient," 52 now accepted Bryce's experiment to prove that removing blacks was expedient. The Bryce Preamble passed because those eastern moderates who had voted against terminating *both* the discussion and the institution joined 90% of the legislative termination coalition in hoping that colonization now would make action against slavery expedient later. Almost all members of the swing group of eastern moderates represented counties with over 40% slaves.[25] An irresolute ruling class had pushed an irresolute resolution over the top.

– 6 –

Thomas Jefferson Randolph cheered Archibald Bryce's one-quarter loaf. "A revolution has commenced," he wrote his wife, "which cannot go backwards." A key legislative supporter agreed. "Do not fear any plan of abolition that proposed *less* than yours," wrote James McDowell. "The first step is everything." Let "the legislature once decree" a shipment of 100 negroes. Then "our objective is achieved—achieved because the value of the negro as a property for speculation" will be "gone & because the moral sentiment of the community will eschew" so besieged a property.[26]

McDowell's victory statement echoed Robert Y. Hayne's warning, back in 1827, that slavery would be lost if Congress so much as debated colonization. The Virginia apologist and the Carolina perpetualist agreed that the slightest slaveholder submission to government meddling would nurture uneasiness in the Big House, unrest in the quarters, uncertainty at slave auctions. The Bryce Preamble could be an "entering wedge" if it sliced a smidgeon into masters' dominance.

But Archibald Bryce's language could not cut fudge unless the Virginia legislature proved it meant to ship out blacks. The declaration that the government meant to deport would be empty without a law to effect deportation. To guarantee McDowell's first boatload of 100 blacks, the Virginia government had to provide 100 tickets and ensure 100 souls on board.

Irresolution reigned again over how to ensure passengers. Archibald Bryce wished to begin with free blacks. But would free blacks freely consent to go? General William Henry Brodnax, the white who had coerced Nat Turner's blacks, answered that he would *make* free blacks go.[27]

This deportationist was too toughminded for most Virginia softhearts. Some Virginia blacks had been incongruously freed, even if all blacks were supposed to be slaves, because ex-slaves' ex-masters no longer consented to coerce "their people." The resulting freedmen owned land. Could a property-loving republic dictatorially seize property by despotically expelling property owners? Free blacks had enslaved mates and children. Could a domestic regime savage homes by exiling husbands?

The Virginia majority could not. To deport a "whole class . . . of free men," urged the Richmond *Constitutional Whig,* would "stain the Statute Book of Republican Virginia with a law which would disgrace Turkey."[28] Such attitudes left only slaves eligible to be forced aboard ship. Few doubted that coerced slaves could be coercively deported. But eastern Virginians preferred that free rather than enslaved blacks be the first removed.

The House finally narrowly passed financing to deport slaves who masters wished to free, with Archibald Bryce's majority at last honing an edge on his entering wedge. But the Senate narrowly refused to concur in the appropriation bill, largely because eastern Virginians had even more seats proportionately in the upper house than in the lower. The Slavepower's extra power in the Senate thus narrowly defeated state-financed deportation of slaves about to be freed, just as the East's extra seats in the House of Delegates had widened the margin against the expediency of legislative action. The malapportioned legislature of 1832 adjourned, having brought forth only Archibald Bryce's abstract affirmation of colonization as an entering wedge, and having authorized not one of James McDowell's 100 proofs that the legislature meant to act on the abstraction.[29]

– 7 –

The Virginia Slavery Debate exposed a regime in need of new vocabulary, new thought, new action to consolidate slavery. Upper-class rulers who called slavery dishonorable almost invited renewed efforts to cure dishonor. Procrastinating Virginians needed at least a rationale for further procrastination. Zeal to perpetuate slavery would have yielded still more comfort.

Historians, sensing slaveholders' discomfort, have written as if Virginia's historic debate of 1832 spawned a Great Reaction immediately thereafter. An escalating move to call slavery blessedly permanent supposedly dissolved ancient differences between Old Virginia and Old Carolina. Thirty years before the Civil War, the Old South confidently united on confident reactionaries' terms.

Alas for reactionary confidence. So much for posterity's confident logic. The Old Dominion mentality evolved within its own logic, which meant never far from old assumptions. Instead of immediately rallying behind South Carolina's Unconditional Perpetualism, procrastinating upper-class Virginians needed another 20 years to repudiate Conditional Termination. Even then, the greatest theorists would stumble over the same ideological traps which prevented earlier Virginia polemicists from calling slavery a perpetual blessing.

Thomas Roderick Dew, the most famous Virginia writer on slavery in the aftermath of the slavery debate, supposedly proves that the Old Dominion immediately repudiated the viewpoint that slavery was evil and should be ended. Some of Dew's positions did anticipate later arguments that slavery was a permanent good. But Dew lived in the wrong place and at the wrong time to clear his voice of Virginia apologetics. This key writer is the so-called exception proving the rule that Old Dominion reactionaries remained drifting Virginians rather than consolidating South Carolinians.

Thomas Dew came naturally by Old Virginia's procrastination. He was both scion of an old Tidewater family and professor at William and Mary College in Williamsburg, once Old Virginia's capital. His *Review of the Debates in the Virginia Legislature*, published several months after the debate, reiterated what had passed for "proslavery" in the debate itself, which was never defense of perpetual slavery.[30]

The professor attacked the Virginia legislature for dangerous talk and disastrous solutions.[31] Every remedy for slavery proposed, urged the young Tidewater political economist, would collapse the commonwealth. Liberating and deporting every black would cost one-third of the state's wealth. The other two-thirds of Virginia's financial power, largely based on the slave economy, would dissolve without slavery. Thomas Jefferson Randolph's trickle of post-nati blacks in exile would infuriate blacks not exiled. William Henry Brodnax's larger trickle of deported free blacks would overwhelm tiny Liberia.

The professor was more interesting when he moved past such by now stale arguments. Many passages in his *Review* and in essays published soon thereafter prefigured later arguments that laborers of all races in all nations should be enslaved. An upper-class Virginian of Dew's ilk was trained to distrust Alabama's herrenvolk model: only slavery for blacks, only egalitarianism for whites. Upper-class domination over poorer folk, black and white, was written into the Virginia government. Dew sometimes wrote color-blind dominance into his proslavery argument.

Dew thus called slavery the remedy for modern industrialists' exploitation of all races. Wage slaves, always underpaid and often fired, would be better off as chattel slaves of protective paternalists. "At this very moment," Dew claimed, "in every densely populated country, hundreds would be willing to sell themselves" into chattel slavery "if the laws would permit." "A merrier being does not exist on the face of the globe," Dew soared, "than the negro slave of the U. States."[32]

In his other writings in the mid-1830s, Thomas R. Dew occasionally picked up a point left implicit here, that wage slaves would eventually rise in revolution, unless chattel slavery saved Western Civilization. America, argued Dew, because not yet densely populated, would be among the last nations to suffer lower-class revolt. But even here, "the time must come." Eventually, "millions shall be crowded into our manufactories and commercial cities." When the urban poor shall "form the numerical majority," then a French "reign of terror" would devastate the American social order. Only paternalistic slavery could "ward off the evil of this agrarian spirit."[33]

But this Virginia prophet, the first to call slavery best for all races, always dropped the argument for color-blind bondage after a few paragraphs. Elaborate proof that Hebrews and Christians maintained color-blind slavery, for example, came coupled with the admission "that slavery is against the spirit of Christianity." Dew's excuse for supporting an anti-Christian institution: the "evil" has been "entailed upon us by no fault of ours," and we must not "shrink from the charge."[34]

So too when discussing economic relations, this occasional advocate of enslaving all laborers usually called free labor the fast lane to prosperity. Adam Smith's *Wealth of Nations* was Dew's favorite economic treatise. The Virginian agreed "in the main" with the Scot that "desire to accumulate" leads free citizens to "much more efficient and constant exertions" than the lash can draw from slaves. Like Smith, Dew trusted the Invisible Hand of free labor's ambitions more than the heavy hand of government.[35]

A man usually so fond of Adam Smith's free labor ideology could only call coerced labor sublime under exceptional circumstances. Dew attacked Smith for ignoring two exceptions. First of all, Adam Smith had erroneously considered "desire to accumulate and better our condition" a human universal. Yet among red and especially black men, the "principle of idleness triumphed over the desire for accumulation," unless "the strong arm of authority" coerced. Thomas R. Dew's universal slavery here narrowed towards what a later school of color-blind proslavery writers would deride as "mere negro slavery," servitude as good only for supposedly lower, lazy races.

Dew escaped "mere negro slavery"—and further constricted bondage—in his second exception to Adam Smith's universals. Smith erred, thought Dew, not only in thinking exertion exceeds laziness in all races but also in presuming that hard work is more attractive than indolent leisure in all climates. In steaming southern habitats, "idleness is very apt to predominate," even amongst the highest races, "over the desire to accumulate." Whites in "very warm or tropical latitudes" have always displayed "signal deterioration of character, attended with an unconquerable aversion to labor." Only color-blind "slavery can remedy this otherwise inevitable tendency" in oppressive tropics.[36]

Dew's geographical and racial exceptions to Adam Smith led to a dual map of utopia. Inferior races should be forced to labor in torrid zones. Superior races should be at liberty for exertion in cooler climes. An Invisible Hand more subtle than Adam Smith's had already produced that happy result in the United States. "To the North, negro slavery has everywhere disappeared, while to the South it has maintained its ground against free labor."

So where was Virginia, key state of the Middle South? Dew answered with three critical words. Virginia, like Maryland, was "too far North" for slaves. Free whites, better workers than coerced blacks in cooler climes, would outproduce slaves in coolish Virginia. Coerced blacks, better laborers than consenting whites in humid zones, would be called to the Lower South. Slave sales would naturally accomplish what meddling legislatures would make impossible.[37]

The Dew who would keep government hands off blacks still wanted government hands on the economy, to hasten economic preconditions for deporting blacks. He wished the Virginia legislature to build canals and roads past mountain barriers. New western opportunities to ship produce to eastern seaboard cities would draw grain farmers. Newly burgeoning eastern cities would attract free laborers. New floods of productive white workers would push less productive blacks southward. An institution imposed unnaturally too far north would drain to its natural Lower South home. Virginia, shorn of the "evil," would ascend into modernity.[38]

Thomas R. Dew here completed a wild ideological tour. This "proslavery" Easterner thought eastern Virginia too far north for slavery. This proponent of progress through individual rather than governmental exertion urged the state legislature to build western internal improvements and thus hasten the departure of Virginia's slaves. This supporter of slavery as the solution for advanced industrial economies wished free labor to propel Virginia into the industrial age. This defender of slavery as biblically sanctioned called slavery anti-Christian in spirit and unfit for nontropical Christians. This prophet who supposedly spawned a Great Reaction for a consolidated South divided the southland north and south and wished *his* South to go the way of New York and New Jersey. Thomas Dew ultimately proves that *all* Virginians in the 1830s, even the one who flirted with slavery-blessed-for-all-races, hoped the Upper South would someday contain no more slaves—and only the white race.

– 8 –

Thomas R. Dew was understandably on the minds of Virginians who consolidated proslavery later. Theorists in the 1850s called Dew's publication of the 1830s the most important book they had read. To build upon Dew's position that slavery was best for all laborers, black or white, Virginia intellectuals 20 years later would have to pick and choose among the professor's sentences. But expunge Dew's slavery based merely on race and geography, spike the notion that slaveholding was unchristian in spirit, bury the cry that Virginia was too far north. Then the pieces put together weirdly in the 1830s could help build the case for universal slavery in the 1850s—if the George Fitzhughs could avoid their own dizzy spin through the difficulties beyond "mere negro" slavery.

Historians label those who prefigure as transition figures. The trouble with seeing Dew as transitional is that no transition took place. The professor did not lead a school of his Virginia contemporaries halfway towards the 1850s. In his state, he worked largely alone. Benjamin Watkins Leigh published a short proslavery pamphlet in 1833. Abel P. Upshur struggled with the political side of proslavery polemics in the later 1830s. But the great Virginia proslavery writers—George Fitzhugh, William R. Smith, Thornton Stringfellow, and so on—were all luminaries of the 1850s. All were conscious they were attempting something fresh. In all of Virginia's past publications, they found little useful precedent. Thomas R. Dew's bits of clarity, although imbedded in contradiction, were the only useful tradition handed down from an era when not even Dew wished a transition from Conditional Termination.

- 9 -

Dew was not the commanding author even in his publishing season. In 1833, while Dew urged state internal improvements to escalate diffusion of Virginia's slaves southwards, his ideological opponent championed a different diffusion. In *The Slave Question in Virginia,* published within weeks of Dew's *Review of the Debates,* Jesse Burton Harrison urged the Virginia legislature to deport blacks to Africa.

Harrison, friend of Thomas Jefferson and cousin of Henry Clay, was a personal link between the tradition of federally financed colonization/termination that Jefferson had proposed and that Clay would perpetuate. But for now, in his *The Slavery Question in Virginia,* Harrison urged not federal but state-financed deportation to Africa. Like the Dew who called Virginia too far north, Harrison termed his arguments against Upper South slavery "very little" applicable to the Deep South. Virginia, however, *"possesses scarcely a single requisite to make a prosperous slave-labor state."* A state so far north, by sending blacks "home" to tropical Africa, would become home for free whites.[39]

In the 1833 legislature, Virginia's establishment favored Harrison over Dew. The legislature authorized $18,000 a year for five years to colonize free blacks. At last, the state had decided how Archibald Bryce's "entering wedge" might enter something.[40]

The entering wedge still could not necessarily remove one black from the commonwealth. Colonization of slaves was not authorized. Coerced deportation of free blacks also was not enacted. Free blacks could freely decide whether to accept the state's free tickets to Africa.

Blacks largely decided to stay. Their families, their jobs, much of their culture was American. Migration to Africa was a flight from the known and the understood. The Virginia government could keep its money. Afro-Americans would consent to make America their home.[41]

Blacks' decision to stay and whites' indecision about deportation together gutted the vital condition for termination of slavery: that free blacks would leave. James McDowell's 100 blacks had never stepped aboard ship. These legislators' waverings had left slavery in Virginia no closer to termination.

- 10 -

Much was lost and little gained in the Virginia "Antislavery" Debate. Lost was any prospect that New York's or New Jersey's legislatively induced slave sales to the Lower South could be achieved in the Middle South. Virginia solons had ruled that their state, if too far north for perpetual slavery, was too far south for that much legislative interference. Furthermore, state government-financed colonization, that popular conception up in Henry Clay's Border South, had won so indecisively down in the Middle South as to be lost.

Middle South reformers' failures might seem to make Middle South slaves the greatest losers. But black freedom would likely have been lost no matter who won among Virginia whites. Another traditional title for this episode, the Virginia "Antislavery" Debate, shows how inappropriate is that word "anti-slavery." A better title would be the Virginia Deportation Debate. The issue was less how to liberate slaves than how to move blacks elsewhere—most often to slavery elsewhere. Most western Virginians favored legislatively induced removal of slaves, lest blacks be marketed across the mountains. Most eastern Virginians would rely exclusively on private sales to diffuse slaves to more trop-ical climates. Thomas Jefferson Randolph would escalate slave removal with post-nati threats. General Brodnax would expel blacks to Africa. Thomas R. Dew would use internal improvements to quicken slave sales southward. But all these opponents implicitly concurred that households would be safer and labor more productive if Virginia's blacks could be diffused away. That consen-sus helps explain why the diffusion argument had emerged in the Missouri Con-troversy of the 1820s and would remain in the Texas Controversy of the 1840s as the natural outcome of southern apologetics, more natural than Jefferson's attempts to bar diffusion of slaves to new territories during the 1780s.

While state government-accelerated diffusion lost in 1832–3 and slaves who were not diffused neither won nor lost, reactionaries secured a shaky victory. Western Virginia nonslaveholders, angry about their second political defeat in three years, were more determined than ever to secure a one-white-man, one-vote, democratically apportioned state legislature. If egalitarian republicans won the next constitutional controversy over apportionment, the next deter-mination of slavery's fate might occur in a Virginia legislature elected on an up-to-date count of where citizens lived. Then the burgeoning West could dic-tate to the stagnating East. The key issue in these Virginia controversies, as in the Missouri Controversy, remained undecided: Could slaveholders' quest for unequal protection and nonslaveholders' drive for equal power yield a political solution acceptable to both— and safe for slavery?

Virginia's compromised Slavepower seemed in no position to master the answer. The slaveholding establishment had been too divided to table reformers' call for action. Conservatives had also been too split to defeat Archibald Bryce's entering wedge. Bryce's removal scheme had failed not because hardheaded reactionaries were too powerful but because reformers were too softhearted to support coercive deportation. As for slaveholders who cheered these failures, they hoped to continue diffusing their Peculiar Institution to buyers southward, to the very buyers who wished to possess a permanent slavocracy northward. Furthermore, many of the Virginians who called African colonization sure to bankrupt the state also hoped the richer national government would pay for the experiment.

South Carolina called these antics folly, unbelievable folly, cowardice indi-cating that irresolution in the Middle South demanded resolute action in the Lower South. No reliable slavocracy could counter slave rebels and rebellious nonslaveholders with loose talk in the legislature and with loose agreement that removal of slaves would be salutory. Nor could a regime hoping to remove its slaves be counted on to crusade forever for slavery.

Still worse from the Carolina perspective than irresolute apologetics in Virginia, apologists were massing more resolutely in the tier of states further north. In the Border South, where low black ratios, the key condition for Conditional Termination, were more achievable than in the Middle South, another debate over terminating slavery was transpiring in the wake of Nat Turner.

CHAPTER 11

Not-So-Conditional Termination
in the Northern Chesapeake

Attitudes about ending slavery in the Chesapeake Bay area during the Nat Turner era, like most things southern, varied with geographical location. Furthest south in this oldest enslaved area, the post-Turner Virginia legislature considered the state too far south for government "unnaturally" to remove blacks. Furthest north in the Chesapeake, legislative action on removal was considered more natural. Ending slavery without removing blacks was also considered more possible. In the mid-1840s, Delaware's legislature even decided that private manumissions without removal of blacks was proceeding so famously that public action was irrelevant.

Delaware solons were right, at least about Delaware. Individual manumissions were eroding the institution rather totally in Delaware, rather swiftly in northern Maryland, rather slowly in southern Maryland. Wherever irresolute masters might drift in Virginia, slavery was slowly drifting from the northern Chesapeake. Meanwhile, freed blacks were staying.

Maryland slaveholders were not upset that slavery was weakening. But the establishment, distressed that free blacks were remaining, initiated another legislative slavery debate in the wake of Nat Turner. That revealing Maryland story makes the more famous Virginia Slavery Debate of 1832 no southern exception—not even in 1832.

– 1 –

The Maryland Slavery Debate of 1832 is especially important because it did not occur in some white-belt area such as Delaware or western Virginia or eastern Tennessee, where slavery was never massively present. Maryland, an early bulwark of the North American Slavepower, retained as widespread a black belt as existed in the northern third of the South. If Maryland, and especially southern Maryland, was not southern, then nothing was southern except the Deep South. Lower South planters feared precisely that possibility.

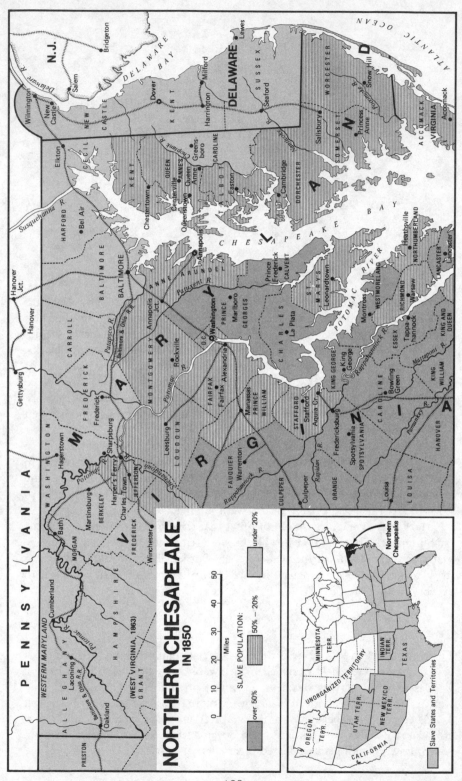

NORTHERN CHESAPEAKE
IN 1850

SLAVE POPULATION:

- over 50%
- 50% – 20%
- under 20%

Miles
0 10 20 30 40 50

Slave States and Territories

Northern Chesapeake

No such fear existed when the American nation was founded. In 1790, about one out of six southern slaves lived in Maryland. Almost one out of three Maryland inhabitants were slaves, a ratio a little under Georgia's (35%) and a half fatter than any Border South state's percentage would be in 1860 (Kentucky would be the leader at 19%).

Early national Maryland and Virginia were comparable in many ways. In 1790, the two Chesapeake Bay regimes both had low percentages of free to enslaved blacks (Maryland 7%, Virginia 4%) Each state contained a wealthy tobacco-exporting squirearchy, which was most extensive south in each commonwealth. This Slavepower disproportionately dominated both states' legislatures.

Still, if similar Chesapeake Bay topography made for similar eighteenth-century beginnings, two geographical differences made for different nineteenth-century outcomes. First of all, Maryland possessed an almost exclusively Atlantic Seaboard locale. Only one Maryland county, significantly called Allegheny, jutted significantly into the mountains. Maryland slaveholders never had to endure Virginia planters' nemesis: nonslaveholders assaulting from across the Alleghenies.

But Maryland's more northern locale was as antithetical to slavery as was Virginia's more western extension. Free labor Pennsylvania spread across Maryland's entire northern border. In the Old Dominion, only largely nonslaveholding western Virginia had a nonslaveholding northern neighbor.

Maryland's more northern locale lent greater opportunity to observe northern-style racial control. Southern whites usually supposed that racial control required either enslaving or removing blacks. Some Yankess had once thought in those terms. New York and New Jersey slaveholders often chose to dump slaves south before post-nati emancipation could occur. But northern states, by ultimately outlawing that unseemly form of removing blacks, indirectly ruled that freedmen who stayed could be easily controlled. Disenfranchisement, job discrimination, segregation—those sufficed for white safety, north of slavery.

Southerners scoffed that northern racial control worked because the North had few blacks to control. Maryland put scoffing to the test. The state was far enough north to find northern ways tantalizing but sufficiently southern to have dense black populations to control.

Enthusiasm for northern solutions was greatest in Maryland's northernmost sections. North Maryland, here defined as the most northern tier of Maryland counties, bordered on Pennsylvania. All five North Maryland counties were north of the Chesapeake Bay. Only one county, and that one but briefly, ever contained more than 20% slaves. Blacks comprised only 18.5% of North Maryland's population in 1790, only 13.7% in 1860. Such northern-style racial ratios invited northern-style racial experiments.

Still, North Maryland was far enough south to be something of a slave society—especially in the beginning. In 1790, the area possessed 21,000 slaves, three-fourths as many as Georgia. Slaves comprised 17% of the population, as high a percentage as Kentucky's. Even Baltimore City was 9% enslaved—with more slaves than lived in Richmond.

Marylanders closer to the tropics possessed many more slaves. South Maryland, here defined as the entire state below the northern tier of counties, was in the north-south latitude of, and usually close by, the Chesapeake Bay. The Eastern Shore of the Bay was locale of Maryland's most famous plantation area and home of the Bay State's most renowned slaveholding families: Bennetts, Chamberlains, Goldsboroughs, above all Lloyds, owners of that exquisite Talbot County plantation mansion, Wye House.

Maryland counties on the less famous Western Shore of the Chesapeake could never match the grace, power, and confidence Wye House exuded. But the Eastern Shore could not match the Western Shore's proportion of slaves. Charles County of the Western Shore topped all Maryland counties in 1790 with 49% slaves. Counting both thickly enslaved shores, 11 of the 13 South Maryland counties had over 30% slaves in 1790. South Maryland's 82,000 slaves then comprised 43% of its population, a percentage equal to, yes equal to, South Carolina's.

But just as North Maryland, although largely a free white society, was something of a slave area, so South Maryland, while heavily enslaved, was something of a free labor commonwealth. Much of South Maryland was within the North's trading system. The Eastern Shore early became Philadelphia's trading hinterland through Delaware River connections. Later, increasingly free labor Baltimore marketed increasing proportions of Eastern and Western Shore products.

Easy access to urban markets gave South Maryland producers early incentive to diversify crops. In the middle of the eighteenth century, Maryland planters, while still prosperous from tobacco, profitably switched many acres to wheat. Virginians, farther from big-city wheat markets, made the transition later in the century, less thoroughly, and only after tobacco prices turned sour. Belated flight to mixed agriculture saved many Virginia titans from bankruptcy. But diversification never proceeded far enough to bring Maryland-style bonanza. Virginia planters could help feed immediate neighborhoods. Maryland planters could help feed hundreds of thousands in Baltimore and Philadelphia.

South Maryland's greater access to urban markets and greater amount of wheat production had two northernizing results. First of all, grain farming made slavery seem less necessary. While slaves worked wheat and nonslaveholders grew tobacco, profit margins from using slaves in tobacco, a more labor-intensive crop, were objectively larger. More subjectively, grain farming seemed in the North American perspective more "natural" to free labor family farmers. Subjective assumption joined objective coin in inviting South Marylanders' Yankee-style dreams.

Close connection with Philadelphia and Baltimore marketeers furthermore gave upper-class Maryland agrarians something of northern merchants' mentality. Lloyds and Goldsboroughs, unlike planters further south, operated simultaneously as large-scale farmers and large-scale merchandisers. They served as mercantile outposts for Philadelphia and Baltimore traders. They handled their own factoring, buying, selling. They also started neighbors' crops off to market.

These merchants-as-planters and planters-as-merchants gained dual values along with doubled wealth. They internalized Philadelphia norms—confidence in free labor, desire for free education, zeal for unhindered capitalistic growth. Just as wheat production made slave owners conceive South Maryland could do without slaves, so mercantile endeavors led planters to comprehend free labor entrepreneurial advantages.[1]

Heavily enslaved South Maryland displayed northern inclinations by joining North Maryland in post-Revolutionary War experiments with the northern race relations option. During the national republic's first two decades, while contiguous Middle Atlantic states were passing post-nati emancipation, Marylanders freed almost 25% of their blacks. By 1810, 30% of North Maryland's blacks were free, as were 20% of South Maryland's. Neither half of enslaved Maryland could evolve farther towards freedom and remain much of a slave area.

At this critical juncture, North Maryland sped past the halfway point towards becoming a northern racial order, while South Maryland's transition almost stopped. Between 1810 and 1830, South Maryland's free black population increased from 21,167 to 25,071. That 1% growth rate annually, under the southern norm for natural increase of blacks, indicated few manumissions. In contrast, North Maryland's free black population jumped from 12,760 to 27,867, indicating many manumissions. Between 1810 and 1830 the proportion of South Maryland blacks who were free increased inconsequentially, from 20.4 to 24.7%, while the North Maryland proportion shot from 30.8 to 51.3%, halfway towards freedom.

By 1830, over half of North Maryland's free blacks lived in Baltimore. Over three-fourths of the city's blacks were free, up from one-fifth in 1790. In 1830, slaves comprised 6% of Baltimore's total population, down from 9% in 1790 and heading down under 2% in 1850 and barely 1% in 1860. North Maryland's dominating metropolis, the South's largest city, was far more a free black than an enslaved black zone and far more dependent on free white wage earners than on any black laborers.

Slavery was decaying almost as fast in the North Maryland countryside. In 1830, 35% of North Maryland's non-Baltimore blacks were free, up from 19% in 1790 and escalating towards 55% in 1850 and 63% in 1860. This freeing of slaves came naturally to a countryside, like a city, close enough to the North's migrating white population to gain an alternative labor source. Between 1790 and 1830, rural North Maryland whites increased almost 50%, modest compared with the quadrupling of Baltimore's whites but massive compared with South Maryland's zero white population growth.[2]

This northern-style white population growth, in the region of Maryland halfway towards adopting northern-style race relations in 1830, made stagnating South Maryland politically vulnerable. Back in 1790, South Maryland had contained slightly less than 50% of the state's whites. By 1830, the Slavepower's region still retained its former 60% of the state's malapportioned legislative seats but could claim only 35% of the state's whites. If pressure for a one-white-man, one-vote legislative reapportionment, à la Virginia, proved irresistible in Maryland—and pressure was building—North Maryland might gain the power to reaccelerate South Maryland's now barely moving evolution from slavery to freedom.

A third of the way into the nineteenth century, South Marylanders, despite having slowed their transition towards a free society, could not be confident that the slowdown would continue. The area's entrepreneurial titans, influenced by Philadelphia mentalities, possessed dubious ideological resources to fight northern world views. The region contained many free blacks, potential sources of all kinds of trouble. In the wake of Nat Turner and the Virginia Slavery Debate, South Marylanders, still controlling the malapportioned legislature, saw need to act before no action would help.

– 2 –

In Maryland as in Virginia, citizens petitioned the legislature meeting after the Nat Turner revolt, asking that slavery be debated. Maryland petitions ranged from the extreme northern position that slavery was "unholy" and free blacks "well-ordered" to the extreme southern position that "liberation of slaves was repugnant" and free blacks "incompatible with the welfare, happiness, and prosperity of this state." Petitions were referred to a joint committee of the two legislative houses.[3]

Slaveholders ran the committee. All members save one represented South Maryland. The North Marylander owned six slaves. The chairman and dominant member of the committee, Henry Brawner, was a large southern slaveholder who represented a dominant slaveholding community. Brawner owned 58 slaves worth some $30,000, putting him in the top 2% of North American masters.[4] His area, Charles County at the southern extreme of the Western Shore, possessed 57% slaves in 1830, the highest percentage in Maryland and in the top 1% of southern counties. In Brawner's committee and especially in Brawner personally lay whatever potential existed for a Maryland counter-revolution, Deep South-style.

The Brawner committee report urged a halt to North Maryland's evolution towards a free black society.[5] But instead of pushing North Maryland backwards towards slavery, Henry Brawner would push all blacks, slave and free, outside of Maryland. This large slaveholder desired a white, free-labor utopia.

Brawner called slavery "an admitted and awful evil." In addition to wearing out the word "evil"—he used it nine different times—Brawner sought synonyms. "Injurious," "infected," "destructive," the "blighting cause" of "the stain upon" Maryland's "otherwise bright escutcheon"—on and on went the abolitionist vocabulary.

Brawner especially hated slavery for halting white migration to Maryland. "The most careless observer," wrote Brawner, could see that North Maryland counties with a "slight degree" of slavery drew more whites and were thus more prosperous than South Maryland counties, all "largely infected" with slavery.

Brawner pointed out that neighboring Pennsylvania, altogether free of the "curse," had expanded nine times faster than Maryland since 1790.

In underpopulated America, Brawner continued, zero population growth left everything impaired. South Maryland's sparse white population presented "an insuperable obstacle" to "almost every species of improvement," including free public education and all "higher cultivation." But remove slavery, that "obstacle to the march of mind," and Maryland would gain the white migrants to rival northern states "not only in population, prosperity, and wealth, but in the higher and more noble endowment of intellectual and scientific attainments."

Brawner's argument tossed away North Americans' central reason for adopting slavery. Brawner's ancestors had brought Africans to the Chesapeake to solve *the* American problem: too much land, too few laborers. But that momentous so-called non-event, African slave trade closure, plus that obviously momentous event, the explosive growth of the cotton frontier, had removed many Chesapeake blacks to the Cotton Kingdom. Deep South land speculators and planters still found, as had Chesapeake entrepreneurs a century earlier, that gangs of slaves best brought labor to virgin resources.

Henry Brawner called free wage earners the better alternative in areas selling off slaves. He here repeated the theory about drawing laborers to less tropical climates which had helped rally an Illinois majority against slavery. Four decades earlier, some midwestern capitalists, speculating that slaveholders might surge to the Midwest, had urged repeal of the Northwest Ordinance's barrier against slavery. In the early 1820s, at showdown time for slaveholders who had sneaked black apprentices through the Ordinance's loopholes, Governor Edward Coles of Illinois had countered that Yankee free laborers would populate the prairies fastest, if only the state totally barred slaveholders. Now in 1832 in Maryland, Henry Brawner applied Coles's logic to the next tier of states southwards. By calling slave labor detrimental to increased labor, he summoned the most lethal argument against slavery in labor-starved, development-crazed America.

Brawner prayed that South Maryland might "be delivered" from slavery, but not in North Maryland's "unfortunate way." "Removal" of freed blacks he called "essential." The Maryland legislature should encourage emancipation and insist on deportation. Pushing blacks out would reduce and eventually eliminate both South Maryland's quantities of slaves and North Maryland's quantities of free blacks.

Removal of blacks, declared Brawner, would be cheap and easy, for "slavery in our state has been wearing out of itself." Many slaves, this large slaveholder cheered, "have heretofore been sold away, and no doubt this will still continue." The South Maryland leader could not however abide Maryland masters who have "emancipated one-third of their slaves" without removal. That sort of freedom was "to say the least of it, of most doubtful benefit," to blacks as well as whites.

Brawner urged the legislature to require and pay for deportation to Africa after emancipation. The prospect of sending "family friends" where blacks could be truly free, plus the vision of giving white families freedom from a black presence, would escalate voluntary manumissions. The "evil," after being "greatly reduced by the free will offerings of patriotism and benevolence," would become "a light burden," if state aid became "necessary in its final extinction." To Maryland's Brawner even more explicitly than to Virginia's Archibald Bryce, state-financed colonization was meant to be an "entering wedge," removing first free blacks, then black slaves, and in the process attracting white migrants to boost the area's wealth.

Henry Brawner's entering wedge was sharper than Archibald Bryce's. In Bryce's Virginia, *compulsory* deportation of blacks was defeated. The indecisive Old Dominion legislature had left freed slaves free to reject their free ticket to Africa, to the disgust of Henry Brodnax. Maryland's Brawner agreed with Virginia's Brodnax. The legislature must make sure the experiment began by forcing some blacks to leave. Brawner's committee report urged cash and sanctions to make deportation a condition of future manumission.

When massing behind the Brawner report, South Marylanders sought to commit the state to ending slavery by colonizing blacks. By seeking to kill the Brawner report, North Marylanders sought to continue manumissions without removal. North Maryland wished to resume marching towards a North where freed blacks were easily controlled. South Marylanders wished to commence marching towards the "better" sort of North where no blacks were present.

Legislative malapportionment made this phase of the clash no contest. South Maryland, with 35% of Maryland's white population, had over 60% of the legislative votes. Brawner's bill thus passed 37-23. South Maryland voted for it, 31-6. North Maryland voted against it, 17-6.[6]

The act appropriated up to $20,000 in any one year, and up to $200,000 in twenty years, to facilitate emancipation-colonization. The money could be used to finance passage to Africa, to develop an African area to receive Maryland blacks, and to advertise Africa as a mecca for free blacks. Slaves manumitted in the future were required to leave, unless a court gave those with "extraordinary good conduct and character" an annual license to stay. Each county clerk had to report any new manumission within five days. A clerk failing to comply was fined $10. A $5 reward went to any informer who tattled on a non-complying clerk. Thus did South Maryland seek to put teeth in its effort to stop North Maryland's racial evolution.[7]

– 3 –

The teeth were too blunt, for the act sought to violate the southern understanding that each locality should determine its own affairs. South Maryland's attempt to dictate communal mores and customs to North Maryland was like Madison County, Mississippi, trying to dictate lynch law to Hinds County. But this time no armed mob was crossing county lines and no Patrick Sharkey had to transform an outhouse into a fortress. This time, $5 and $10 fines were the only firepower sustaining imposition of the invading locale's will on the invaded.

North Marylanders proved unwilling to surrender values for pennies. North Maryland clerks usually failed to report manumissions. North Marylanders usually failed to tattle on offending clerks. When a stray North Maryland clerk sent in names of manumitted slaves, North Maryland judges usually gave new freedmen annual license to stay. Forcible deportation of freed slaves forced few to leave.[8]

The debacle measured the weakness of South Maryland's counterrevolution. Only massive sanctions can force social movements backward. $10,000 fines for nonperformance of lawful duty and $5,000 bribes for ratting on illegal noncompliance might have forced North Marylanders to obey South Marylanders' edict. Instead, the largest loophole in South Maryland's law, allowing North Maryland judges to give any freed black annual license to stay, permitted legal, cost-free nullification. Five- and ten-dollar fines hardly deterred more illegal nullifications.

South Marylanders continued to display their irresolution by failing to pass tougher statutes when their weak law was nullified. No regime can allow a rule designed to save its conception of social control to be flouted. South Maryland had imposed its will, as expressed in law, against North Maryland's will, as expressed in its willingness to obey. In this confrontation, South Marylanders did not so much blink as close their eyes when North Marylanders ignored milktoast sanctions. South Marylanders never piled on new laws forcing removal. North Marylanders continued freeing slaves without removal. No fresh Maryland slavery debate would occur until the eve of the Civil War. Then the Maryland Debate over Re-enslavement would provide another measure of South Maryland's uncertainty.

The loopholes in the 1833 deportation law and South Maryland's failure to close them hinted that despite his righteous rhetoric, Henry Brawner believed North Maryland not altogether wrong to let at least some blacks stay. By 1830, 25% of *South* Maryland's blacks were free. The freedmen produced needed labor rather than convulsive insurrection in the months after Nat Turner. Indeed, two blacks on Brawner's plantation were free. No disorder resulted. South Marylanders, in truth, respected many of "their" free blacks, which is why they decreed that courts should allow respected freedmen to remain.

Maryland's most enslaved area, in sum, was too free itself to insist very strongly that freer areas force manumitted slaves on African-bound galley ships. Henry Brawner, Maryland's excuse for a reactionary, disliked coercive slavery himself too much to coerce free blacks remorselessly. His South Maryland area, despite black ratios in Lower South ranges, was too akin to Philadelphia to act like Charleston. And South Carolinians thought Virginia's upper class could not be counted on!

– 4 –

Just as Marylanders went farther (but not much farther) than Virginians in forcing slaves and blacks out, so the Maryland legislature went farther (but again, not much farther) than the Virginia legislature in seeking to convince blacks freed in the past to remove themselves. Virginia appropriated $30,000 for five years, solely for blacks' free tickets to Africa. Maryland appropriated $200,000 for 20 years, to be used, in part, to convince blacks to accept free tickets.[9]

As Marylanders saw it, free blacks would reject transportation to the American Colonization Society's dismal Liberia colony. So while most of Virginia's $30,000 went unspent, most of Maryland's $200,000 was spent on developing a colony supposedly worthy of crossing oceans. The Maryland Colonization Society, in the years after 1832, lavished funds on its own New World mecca, Maryland in Africa, a colony near Liberia.

The rest of Maryland's $200,000 appropriation was largely spent on agents to advertise utopia. Lecturers offered free blacks not only free passage but also a headstart upon arrival. Migrants were promised rent and board for six months, five acres to farm for life, and a low-interest loan for improving the farm, to be forgiven if the pilgrim remained in paradise. New arrivals also received immediate citizenship. Entrepreneurial democracy, American-style, would come to Afro-Americans willing to desert America.

To load the choice for libertarian Africa still more, the Maryland legislature of 1832 sliced back free blacks' life-style in enslaved America. Free persons of color in Maryland could not vote, serve on juries, or hold offices. Any free black caught without "visible" means of support could be hired out for a year. If unemployed ten days after service was over, sheriffs could again sell the vagrant "as a slave" for a year. The white sheriff "deciding" a free black was "idle" received 6% of the year's "wages."[10]

With a choice between restricted freedom in Maryland and total freedom in Maryland in Africa, white Marylanders were convinced black Marylanders would consent to migrate. This worst of American problems would then be solved in a classic American way. Afro-Americans would choose to leave their bad Old World, in this case America, for liberty and opportunity in a new world across the sea. The richest American black, wrote the Reverend Mr. Richard Fuller of Baltimore, like the poorest European white, "lives and moves and has his being amidst humiliation." But in Maryland in Africa, boomed the Reverend Mr. James B. Hall, blacks could vote, sit on juries, prosper, become "MEN, in the largest sense of the word."[11]

The magnitude of that promise, urged John H. B. Latrobe, insured success. Latrobe, for two decades president of the Maryland Colonization Society and subsequently president of the American Colonization Society, was fond of denouncing as "unfriends" friends who relied solely on colonization societies. If black removal depended only "upon the American Colonization Society, even though Congress threw open to it the treasury of the nation, the work would never be accomplished." Money starts but does not build colonies. Successful new worlds flourish because of that common impulse "of humanity—THE DESIRE TO BETTER ONE'S CONDITION." The lure of better conditions, having brought Europeans to America and taken "Englishmen to Asia," will carry "EVERY FREE PERSON OF COLOR" to Africa.[12]

Maryland free blacks made Latrobe a poor prophet. They joined Virginia brethren in considering Africa more like Siberia. Despite enticements of free passage, free land, free citizenship, despite being lectured at about wondrous mangroves and Tanh trees and chandelier lilies, Maryland free blacks preferred semi-freedom in baleful Baltimore. Less than 1% of Maryland free blacks ever accepted their free bout with the stranger's fever. Maryland in Africa, barely a thousand souls strong, could barely hold off hostile African tribes. In the 1850s, the colony gratefully accepted Liberia's offer of annexation.

The demise of Maryland's $200,000 paradise, together with Maryland's failure to force non-volunteers to voyage, undermined Henry Brawner's not-very-reactionary reaction. South Maryland had done nothing effectual to stop North Maryland from evolving toward a realm of freemen, black and white. By 1850, 71% of blacks in North Maryland and 30% of blacks in South Maryland were free. The whole state was 45% emancipated. Here at last, Conditional Terminators seemed to put termination ahead of conditions. But even here, manumission was proceeding at a glacial pace.

– 5 –

Delaware moved faster towards manumitting slaves without removing blacks. The almost-emancipated state was the last reminder of days when slavery had tolerably flourished in the Mid-Atlantic region. Back in 1790, at the first federal census, New York had reported 21,000 slaves, New Jersey 11,000, Delaware 8,887, or 15% of its population. At that time, Delaware had only 3,899 free blacks, 7% of its population.

During the early nineteenth century, Delaware joined more northern Mid-Atlantic areas in undercutting the institution. By 1830, Delawareans owned only 3,292 slaves, or 4% of the state's population. Meanwhile, the state contained 15,855 free blacks, or almost 21% of its population. Almost five times more blacks were free than enslaved in "slaveholding" Delaware, a state with a higher percentage of blacks than Kentucky, Missouri, or Tennessee.

Despite southern-style black ratios, Delaware's almost-emancipation might be dismissed as another northern state's abolition, except that Delaware's most slaveholding area was geographically in the same latitude as heavily enslaved South Maryland. Two-thirds of Delaware's slaves were concentrated in Sussex, the most southern of Delaware's three counties. Sussex, due west of Maryland's Eastern Shore, contained as fine soil. The county dispatched some tobacco and more wheat up the Delaware River system to Wilmington and Philadelphia. The difference between Eastern Shore Delaware and Eastern Shore Maryland was that Sussex County, Delaware, contained three times as many free blacks as slaves, while neighboring South Maryland counties contained twice as many slaves as free blacks.

In Delaware's Sussex County, with its not-so-small 24% black ratio, planters easily controlled free blacks without slavery. Justices of the peace could hire out free blacks who supposedly lacked "good and industrious habits." Employers received "all the rights of a master." With quasi-slavery coercing the exceptional Delaware free black who did not consent to labor, even Delawareans who disliked free blacks conceded "that they supply too much . . . labor to be dispensed with." Why, then, impose conditions on termination, at least in areas with Border or Middle South type black ratios?[13]

- 6 -

Delaware's free black regime raised yet another question about South Maryland's enslaved society. Could so densely enslaved a black belt survive so close to so much black liberty? On Maryland's Eastern Shore, slaves did not have to flee across some wide Ohio River to find most blacks practicing freedom. Almost-emancipated Delaware was a step on hard ground away. Or to put this fugitive slave problem in perspective, in addition to South Maryland's difficulties having increasingly free black North Maryland in the same state, most of Maryland's Eastern Shore had to tolerate a largely free Delaware neighbor.

Eastern Shore slaveholders, while brooding about the regime next door, at least were encouraged that Delawareans had staved off legislative emancipation. As early as 1803, the Delaware House of Representatives came within a tie vote of abolishing slavery. In 1847, in another example of the nonsense involved in calling the Virginia Slavery Debate of 1832 the only or last southern reconsideration of slavery, the Delaware legislature again drew close to abolition. A bill in the classic post-nati vein, freeing Delaware slaves born after 1860, sailed through the House of Representatives, only to lose by a single vote in the Senate. In both chambers, Delaware's two northernmost counties voted 80% aye. The unanimous Sussex County delegation had just enough support in the Senate to stave off the guillotine.[14]

Legislative near-miss, which had been like an earthquake in Virginia, caused nary a tremor in Delaware. "Never," reported the *Delaware Gazette*, "have we seen so important a measure produce so small a sensation." Postponing legislative emancipation until 1860 left time "enough for all the Negroes to run away."[15]

The *Gazette*, Democrats' chief Delaware newspaper, called legislative emancipation unnecessary for a complementary reason: because masters were running away from slaves. "Slave labor is far more unprofitable in Delaware, Maryland, and parts of Virginia, than free labor." Slaveholders half a continent from the Cotton Kingdom profited more from money in the bank. Banks did not run away. Emancipation would come "by the very process which is continually going on, viz the gradual emancipation of slaves by their masters."[16]

The *Delaware Republican,* Whigs' chief newspaper, pointed to another gradual process. Diffusion of free white laborers into the Border South and of black slave laborers into the Lower South "operates as certainly and as surely as any of the laws which govern our bodies. We cannot escape it if we would." In grain states, where "climate is congenial, free labor is obtaining the mastery over slave labor, and the system of chattel slavery is dying out. This is the case in Delaware, in Maryland, Kentucky, and Missouri, or at least in some portion of each of them." This truth was "as incontrovertible as that the earth itself exists."[17]

With Delawareans calling Thomas R. Dew's too far north truth incontrovertible, Lower South warriors in the late antebellum period hoped that "another truth might be universally understood." Slaveholders should understand "that instead of having fifteen slave states, they really had only fourteen."[18] Or, because of Maryland, was the pre-Civil War Slavepower only thirteen states strong?

– 7 –

The answer was obscure. Conditional Termination, true to its irresolute nature, had eroded but not eliminated slavery in the Northern Chesapeake. At the creeping pace of the first half of the nineteenth century, North Maryland figured to be just about emancipated around the beginning of the twentieth century. South Maryland figured to take longer to be free. Nineteenth-century Delaware indicated that, even at those remote moments, a Maryland almost manumitted might cling to vestiges of the institution.

Maryland's Henry Brawner, whose moment on southern center stage was one of the briefest and most illuminating, epitomized why slavery's fate too far north was working itself out so slowly. The man was as divided as his class and his state. Brawner developed the lethal argument that a lily-white Maryland would have more laborers. Yet his less-than-lethal law hardly stopped North Maryland's evolution towards a white-migrant-repelling, free black commonwealth. Furthermore, this reformer who believed free whites outlabored slaves and that black slaves outlabored free blacks still worked his own plantation with 58 slaves and two free blacks. No wonder slavery's fate was obscure in the state where compromised Henry Brawners governed.

The North Chesapeake, the exceptional area where apologetics produced extensive manumissions, ended up being the exception proving an important rule: Conditional Termination was more corrosive for the perpetualist zeal it compromised than for the emancipationist victory it hastened. Zeal, for or against slavery, was the antithesis of this compromised mentality, as was haste to decide either way. In Archibald Bryce's Virginia and in Henry Brawner's Maryland in the aftermath of Nat Turner, apologetic mentalities drew drifting establishments towards the middle, against doing or dying for perpetuation or for termination. Men geographically and ideologically adrift in the middle, especially men who prayed that slavery would ease away and the Union would endure forever, would not hasten a showdown that would leave them crunched between fanatical Northerners above and rabid Southerners below.

This long-term local drift had an important short-term national consequence. Maryland and Virginia, while struggling towards state colonization experiments in 1832–3, were simultaneously willing to consider better financed federal experiments. The old nay-sayer was determined to nullify such considerations. Lest Chesapeake Bay apologists attempt to use federal authority to remove blacks, important South Carolinians felt compelled to render that alleged authority null and void.

PART IV

NONDECISIVE DECISION
IN SOUTH CAROLINA

Antebellum South Carolinians who would control Upper South apologists faced the classic extremist's problem in a democracy: how to command a non-extreme mainstream. The classic democratic answer, persuade those less fervent, offered these zealots too little satisfaction. Carolina intransigents were usually too far out to convince a southern majority.

Coercive tactics offered little more chance of success. Lynching, the only extralegal form of coercing whites that was considered at all legitimate in this despots' democracy, became illegitimate if mobs marauded on other folks' turf. That left geographically isolated ultras only one point of leverage over far-off moderates. A majority in one southern state, by disobeying national laws, could force an armed showdown. Indecisive moderates would be forced to shoot rather than talk.

Still, resentful southern moderates might aim their guns at precipitous rebels rather than at national law enforcers. Did Carolinians dare take the chance?

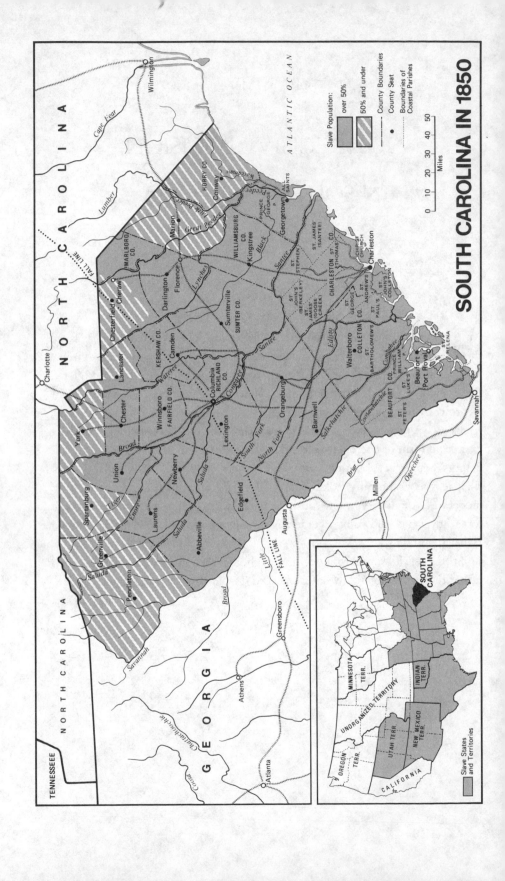

SOUTH CAROLINA IN 1850

Slave Population:
- over 50%
- 50% and under

— County Boundaries
• County Seat
····· Boundaries of Coastal Parishes

Miles
0 10 20 30 40 50

TENNESSEE

NORTH CAROLINA

N O R T H   C A R O L I N A

G E O R G I A

ATLANTIC OCEAN

Wilmington

Cape Fear

Lumber

Charlotte

FALL LINE

Cheraw

CHESTERFIELD CO.

Lancaster

York

Chester

Union

Spartanburg

Greenville

Pendleton

Saluda

Saluda

Broad

Enoree

Tyger

Laurens

Abbeville

Newberry

Winnsboro
FAIRFIELD CO.

KERSHAW CO.

Camden

Columbia
RICHLAND CO.

Lexington

Edgefield

Saluda

Savannah

Little

FALL LINE

Greensboro

Augusta

Athens

Atlanta

Chattahoochee

Oostanaula

Coosa

Ogeechee

Millen

Briar Cr.

Savannah

Broad

Coosawhatchie

Salkehatchie

Edisto

MARLBORO CO.

Darlington

Florence

Lynches

Sumterville
SUMTER CO.

Wateree

Congaree

Santee

Orangeburg

Barnwell

Marion

Great Peedee

Little Peedee

HORRY CO.

Conway

Waccamaw

Peedee

WILLIAMSBURG CO.

Kingstree

Black

PRINCE
GEORGE

Georgetown
ALL
SAINTS

ST. JAMES'
(SANTEE)

ST.
STEPHEN

ST. JOHN'S
(BERKELEY)

ST. THOMAS

CHARLESTON ST. CO.

ST. JAMES'
GOOSE
CREEK

ST.
GEORGE'S

ST. ANDREW'S

Charleston

ST. JOHN'S
(COLLETON)

ST. PAUL'S

ST.
BARTHOLOMEW'S

COLLETON
CO.

Walterboro

Combahee

PRINCE
WILLIAM

ST. PETER'S

ST.
LUKE'S

BEAUFORT
CO.

Beaufort
Port Royal

ST. HELENA

Santee

South Fork

North Fork

Wateree

CHAPTER 12

Origins of
South Carolina Eccentricity, I:
Economic and Political Foundations

Disagreement between South Carolina extremists and Chesapeake Bay moderates emerged more sharply than ever in 1832. While western Virginians demanded expulsion of black slaves, partly to establish white egalitarianism, South Carolinians demanded a veto by a national minority, partly to perpetuate slaveholding elitism. In the Nullification Controversy, John C. Calhoun's state went to the brink, seeking to stop King Numbers from destroying old-fashioned slaveholders. Then, just when South Carolina's eighteenth-century world view seemed destined to carry the Old Order out of nineteenth-century democracy, the state's oligarchs stepped back. They became republicans who were willing to compromise.

The pattern of charge and retreat in the Nullification Controversy would remain antebellum South Carolina's signature. Seldom has so geographically concentrated a revolutionary fringe group been so early committed to revolution. Seldom have such committed revolutionaries been so chary about rebellion. These extremists were long unable to sustain the historical role they cherished, unable to capture the identity they craved. They were like T. S. Eliot's *Hollow Men*, groping "between the idea and the reality, . . . between the conception and the creation, . . . between the desire and the spasm"—until finally, holding their breath, they precipitated a rebellion others had to encourage them to begin.[1]

– 1 –

Why were South Carolina squires more extreme than other Southerners—and why so much sooner? Why were these arch-extremists so frightened of extremism—even so late? Few questions about Civil War causation are more important. None require subtler answers. At times, South Carolina masters flashed signs of uncertainty, fear, inferiority complex—the stridency of false posturing. The next moment, the same people emitted signals of cockiness, fearlessness,

213

felt superiority—the rhetoric of true believers. Outsiders, intrigued by this schizophrenic sphinx, were wise to be puzzled about where Carolina's confidence ended and doubt began.

Posterity can be more certain what made for both confidence and doubt. No other southern regime was so committed to eighteenth-century elitist principles or so resistant to nineteenth-century egalitarian republicanism. South Carolina's balance of despotism and democracy, tipping unusually far toward old-fashioned imperiousness, gave its masters strong confidence in contained, hierarchial dominance and special contempt for sprawling, leveling "mobocracies."

Still, even those Old English fogies could not escape the influence of the American nineteenth century. The resulting Carolinians saw themselves partly as fine fellows, but partly, too, as foolish hypocrites. Even in South Carolina, patriarchs could not maintain cocksure certainty without being dismayingly conscious of belonging to another world. Somewhere between the cockiness and the dismay stood a snob not quite at ease with his own snobbishness.

– 2 –

Carolina snobbishness began and remained most rampant in the malarial-infested coastal swamps. No extensively settled southern habitat was so forbidding to white migrants. Yet at least until the heyday of Louisiana sugar fields in the 1850s, no region offered such fabulous fortunes to whites who dared to come. Nowhere in the South were alternatives so stark. Either a few rich whites would continue to force many slaves to develop this deadly El Dorado, or the miasmic swamps would become too inhuman for development.

The area's peculiar wetlands at first attracted a peculiar settler. Compared with emigrants to the Chesapeake, early Carolinians came not from England, with its lack of a slaveholding establishment, but from Barbados, with its consolidated slave regime. Wealthy Latin American types came prepared to press an especially large black population on the only area of coastal America geographically repellant to a large white population.

Carolina slaveholders still needed a tropical crop fit for slaveholding labor. Carolina's coastal slop, too far north for Latin America's sugar and coffee, was too mucky for the Chesapeake's tobacco. Slavery could not be viable in the swamps until whites found an alternative.

Historians' guess is that slaves taught slaveholders what to grow. Bondsmen, having cultivated rice in Africa, knew that swamps laced with tidal streams would sustain the golden grain. Cuffee was apparently here exhilarated professor and Massa obliging student.[2]

How latter-day celebrants of black creativity do miss the irony in celebrating this black contribution to American inventiveness. How blacks did pay for what whites learned. Payments began with the inch-by-inch clearing of overgrown jungles. Isolated specks of turf, once cleared, had to be irrigated. Slaves slipped and slid in the muck, digging deep parallel canals from the river through the clearing. Shallower, perpendicular ditches connected canals. Along river beds, across new canals, black laborers fashioned dams and sluices. Masters could then boss the tide, flooding fields so rice could sprout, draining water off so slaves could weed.

Because rice fields were so expensive to develop, rice plantations cost several times more than settled turf elsewhere in North America. Posh acres, once expensively developed, became almost worthless without expensive slaves. Vulnerable sluices and dams had to be incessantly repaired. Thick soils had to be constantly weeded. Golden grains had to be quickly harvested. Compared with tobacco and cotton black belts, rice swamps, even after development, never attracted as many yeomen nonslaveholders.[3]

Nor were as many poor whites available to work as tenants or day laborers on rich men's estates. Even after being cleared, Carolina swamps remained sickly, largely because malarial mosquitoes remained omnipresent. Blacks alone could be forced to risk what relatively few whites would chance.

Slaves could be risked because black bodies were less susceptible to malaria's killing fever. Africans often had special blood cells, making them specially vulnerable to sickle cell anemia as well as specially able to fight malaria. Slaves usually caught swamp fevers, then usually survived the raging temperatures. The "only" danger tended to be a frightful convalescence and a debilitated physical system for months or years thereafter.[4]

Because rice cultivation demanded many laborers and the sickly habitat repelled many whites, the region developed an unusually black population. In 1830, lowcountry inhabitants were 85% slaves. Many sorts of blackness surrounded Carolina's unusually isolated and especially outnumbered white fraction. Elsewhere in the South, plantation areas were cleared to the edge of the horizon. Farmers could usually see endless white men's properties. Here, clearings tended to end at each developed property. Owners could usually see only surrounding jungles. Elsewhere, bright blue rivers connected planters to the world. Here, unconnected swamp pools were blackest black. Elsewhere, black slaves, barely if at all outnumbering whites, talked with white men's drawls. Here, massive quantities of blacks, comparatively isolated from whites, characteristically employed Gullah linguistic traits. Here a planter wrote that "I am actually so startled at the sight of a white face that I avoid my own . . . in the glass in the morning." No planter elsewhere in North America could have written that incredible sentence.[5]

The black jungle infiltrated all aspects of white thought. In coastal Virginia, Thomas Dew speculated about selling blacks south and attracting white migrants. South Carolinians conceived that without slaves to risk the miasma, Carolina swamps would revert to wilderness. In North Maryland, many masters did not fear to free Afro-Americans, who retained relatively little African culture. In coastal Carolina, whites feared that Afro-Americans short on American acculturization, if freed, would Africanize the lowlands. In other parts of the Lower South, slaveholders expanded on endless terrain. In wetland South Carolina, planters sought to retain bits of clearing.

Or, to be more accurate, South Carolina's gentlemen dreamed of vacations from confined jungles. Whites sought to make such a financial windfall as to flee during the murderous malaria season. In the middle of the eighteenth century, absenteeism became widely attainable. Planters gained decent profits from the golden grain. They then secured supplemental treasure. British merchants craved indigo, a putrid dye turning dull cloth lush blue. Planters discovered that hills above flooded swamps could spawn the unseemly stuff. Slaves, when not needed in rice fields, could be forced up above to endure the stench, double Massa's profits, and help finance Massa's vacation.

By 1760, South Carolina absentees had become perhaps the richest American entrepreneurs and the only ones often not directing their enterprises.[6] Even a semi-competent overseer who brought in three-quarter crops mined enough treasure to support planters' vacations. If no resourceful overseer could be found, a decent overseer could be shared. Such white supervisors checked in with black drivers periodically. Other planters dispensed with this mock white supervision. Such masters appointed a black driver to be Massa from the time malarial mosquitos first attacked in April to the time frost killed off the bugs in October.

Thus did a class unusually independent of their plantations become unusually dependent on slaves. Thus did a region 85% black when whites were most resident become 98% black when white businesses were most active. No other North American black belt was remotely this black—a spur to South Carolina whites' special ferocity. No other southern rulers were such idle aristocrats—a source of Carolina's oligarchic hauteur. Few slaveholders had larger fortunes at risk in improved land values and in huge slave gangs—the crassest source of South Carolina's peculiar extremism. Perhaps most important of all, no other southern leaders saw such stark alternatives. Either slavery would enable masters to frolic beyond killing fevers, or emancipation, gentlemen feared, would force whites to flee a slaughtering unprecedented even in this deadly area.[7]

– 3 –

With all the world a possible semi-annual residence, South Carolina's newly rich gentry often settled a few dozen miles from home. In Charleston, they found a relatively healthy mecca. Not until the heyday of Natchez, Mississippi, in the late antebellum era would residents so scornful of urban entrepreneurship so dominate a southern city. Not even Natchezites, who directed nearby cotton plantation enterprises, scorned enterprise itself. Charleston was as close to an anti-entrepreneurial city as any enterprising city could be.[8]

The very setting of lowcountry planters' urban paradise seemed alien to enterprise. Charleston was not situated on Carolina's largest streams: not on the Savannah or the Santee or the Great Pee Dee, long rivers flowing down from the expanding upcountry and from other swelling southern states. Charleston instead guarded the point where little rivers serving only the contracting lowcountry met the sea. The Ashley and Cooper rivers, prime avenues of the rice aristocracy and free of the "contamination" of touching another state, form a narrow peninsula where they condescend to enter the Atlantic Ocean. The spit of land sandwiched between expiring rivers looks like a tongue stuck out at the world. At the tip of the tongue, where North America gives out, Charlestonians filled in the sea to form a lovely city park. At this so-called Battery, lower- and middle-class Charlestonians could glimpse gentlemen and ladies gazing England's way.

Squires shunned other contacts with commoners. Long, broad, largely business streets ran down the length of the Charleston tongue. Short, narrow, largely residential avenues ran from river to river across the width. An insular illusion resulted. Out on planters' urban porches, all light, air, and cooling breeze seemed emanating from Carolina's exclusive Ashley and Cooper rivers.

Charleston's imposing front doors, cut in walls apparently high and antiquated enough for English castles, provided another revealing illusion. The apparent house door provided access only to the garden, invisible from the street. To reach a gentleman's presence, one had to follow the exquisitely ruffled slave past the street door, across the secluded garden, inside the real house door, and up steep stairs to the regal drawing room. Charleston's trick doors, a means of making exclusiveness seem more extreme, contrasted with Monticello's trick windows, a means of making the exclusive seem more egalitarian. The Charleston gentry's houses echoed Hugh Legare's classic pronouncement: "The politics of the immortal Jefferson. Pish!"[9]

Everything about the Charleston visible out of doors seemed to wish a pish and a plague on more Americans than Mr. Jefferson. Ever-present brick walls, stuccoed and stylishly colored every tint in the rainbow, together with omnipresent piazzas, those gracious two-layered balconies turning icy shoulders to cobblestone streets, reverberated with memories of West Indian potentates. Intricate lacy ironwork guarding balconies, together with massive iron gates sealing off gardens, hinted at barriers guarding ancient French princes. The dominant Adams-style architecture, with its sweeping bay windows and rococo carved doors, made the clock seem to stop at late eighteenth-century England. The two dominating steeples, hallmark of St. Phillip's and St. Michael's churches, made the heavens seem monopolized by an Episcopalian God.

Anything English seemed holy in this province. Streets were named King and Queen. Poets worshipped Dryden and Pope. John Locke drafted an early state constitution. St. Michael's Church looked as if designed by Sir Christopher Wren.

Away from the masses, inside rich men's mansions, furnishings the more celebrated English genius. In every significant late colonial American city except Charleston, furniture makers carved their Chippendale case pieces with an American twist. The most widespread American deviation from English designs yielded what posterity calls the highboy. That elegant tower of mahogany rises sleekly on tall, curved legs to banks of drawers, then rises over the drawers to a curved top. This earliest rendition of an *American* style expressed Revolutionaries' aristocratic ideal: style without ostentation, power without heavyhandedness, soaring sophistication lightly and delicately deployed.

A classic American-style "Highboy," made in New England. Courtesy, Israel Sack Inc., New York City.

A classic English-style "Tallboy," made in Charleston. Courtesy, The Charleston Museum, Charleston, South Carolina

The contemporaneous English high chest, which posterity calls a tallboy, employs a different aesthetic to announce a different aristocracy. The tallboy is massive, heavy, imposing, meant to sink rectangularly, not soar curvaceously. Rich Englishmen's favorite chest, with its squat feet and its drawers descending close to the ground and its heavily-carved moldings on the squared-off top, epitomized an aristocracy weightily commanding.

Among American cabinetmakers, only Charleston craftsmen failed to make fully developed American highboys. In America, only Charleston cabinetmakers turned out English-style tallboys. The very furniture containing Massa's London-made shirts declared that at the moment of their economic ascendancy, these rulers aspired to be English-like commanders.[10]

An English visitor who dined with these "Englishmen" found that aspiration in every scrap of food and conversation. The voyager feasted on a saddle of mutton, served on English china. He heard that South Carolina's legislature was like the British Houses of Lords and Commons. He listened to sneers about boorish pols governing in Washington. "There never can be a good government," he was assured, "if it is not administered by gentlemen." He was also treated to contempt for money-making and money-grubbing. "The greatest absurdity in the world," ran the sneer, "is a 'Liverpool gentleman.'" When Carolina gentlemen imbibed too much champagne and claret cobblers, their hyperbole could veer toward re-embracing the Empire and reclaiming a king. They wished to be seen as returned expatriates, back in London with English identity intact after a tour of duty in the provinces.[11]

Or rather, they affected airs of tarrying in the metropolis only for horse races and social seasons before resuming residence in the English countryside. During the late heyday of the Anglo-American connection, twice as many South Carolinians as all other North Americans combined had secured educations in England's schools. From that and other sojourns in London, and from reading agrarians such as Bollingbroke, Charleston squires came to consciousness of what they took to be an English country squire's persona and world view. By nullification times, that consciousness was seventy years old, plenty of time for an aristocracy to mature into comfortable confidence in its own identity.

Throughout the antebellum period, much of the talk in Charleston's drawing rooms aimed at demonstrating that seasoned provincials ran their affairs like London cosmopolitans. Just as English lords disdained frantic hustle, so absentee planters avoided gauche exertion. Just as English gentlemen lived off land rents which their staff collected from tenants, so the rice gentry lived off crops which their overseers gleaned from slaves. Just as English titans sometimes forgave rents and debts of poorer tenants in poorer times, so patriarchal masters aided less affluent neighbors and provided for slaves. Just as grateful tenants elected disinterested squires to Parliament, so patriarchal masters expected deferential yeomen to call them to the state legislature.

Charlestonians sometimes saw themselves as out-Englishing the English. In 1832, British lords gave in a trifle to majoritarian democracy in the English

Reform Bill. At almost the same instant, Carolina gentlemen vetoed majority action in the Nullification Controversy. Charleston gentlemen would preserve not the compromised Englishness of the nineteenth century but Old World republicanism as it used to exist before the American Revolution.

– 4 –

Before Charleston could command a Carolina march backward, the more progressive portion of the state would have to relish retreat and confinement. Nothing had been confined, in the late eighteenth century, about the sprawling backcountry above coastal swamps. South Carolina's seaboard gentlemen, compared with Virginia Tidewater planters, felt less inclination to spread past the coast. The Virginia Piedmont and Tidewater quickly became Siamese twins of eastern Virginia because Tidewater farmers could use Piedmont soil to pursue the same tobacco endeavors. Backcountry South Carolina, in contrast, long offered would-be English country gentlemen an alien frontier. No rice cultivation would prosper above the swamps. With lowcountry patricians usually uninterested in migrating, backcountry Carolina settlers, like Trans-Allegheny Virginia settlers, came largely from Scotch Irish and other ethnic sorts streaming down from western foothills.

Newcomers found more opportunities for slaveholding than existed in the Virginia Trans-Allegheny. The backcountry above the swamp offered fertile land for indigo, tobacco, and grain plantations. By the late eighteenth century a mixed small slaveholder/yeoman nonslaveholder society had developed that resembled the Virginia Valley's. Like Valley squires, backcountry Carolina slaveholders disliked coastal snobs for being heavyhanded, ostentatious, overly English. At the turn of the nineteenth century, the New South inside Old South Carolina demanded an egalitarian constitution for white men.[12]

This demand collided with the state's sacrosanct eighteenth-century legislative malapportionment. Rice districts, with their tiny white population and small fraction of the state's landed area, controlled both houses of the state legislature. Substantial property qualifications for voting and higher property qualifications for legislative service ensured that commoners would not interfere with their betters. The best men, in legislature assembled, elected the rest of the government.

The backcountry's crusade for an egalitarian version of slaveholder republicanism briefly threatened to make South Carolina, rather than Virginia, the battleground between Old and New Souths. But this conflict over egalitarianism swiftly turned into a consensus on elitism. After 1794, Eli Whitney's cotton gin helped turn the backcountry population from alien to ally. Upland Carolina, because it was the Lower South area geographically closest to the Atlantic, was the first to experience cotton mania. Slaves by the tens of thousands were pushed onto the red clay. Almost all of South Carolina soon became a black belt. In 1790, about five-sixths of the state's slaves had lived in the lowcountry. By 1830, over three-fourths of them toiled in the upcountry. Two-thirds of

Carolina counties then contained over 40% slaves and only two possessed under 30%. The twin exceptions, each with a not-so-unblack 23% blacks, approximated the average of Middle South states. It was as if eastern Virginia aristocrats had wiped out the Trans-Allegheny and only had to control the compromising Valley. No other southern elite faced so weak a pressure to compromise with nonslaveholding egalitarians.

When slaves first spread over all of South Carolina, different black belts in different geographic settings made for different upper classes. At the beginning of the nineteenth century, upcountry planters, expanding over seemingly limitless acres, exuded that coarseness so typical of new societies and so ridiculed in Charleston drawing rooms. Brawling, gambling, whoring, contemptuous of culture and bent on amassing millions, cotton upstarts were as much like rice patricians as hustling young tycoons are like fading grandfathers.

Geographical factors quickly aged the adolescent.[13] South Carolina's large place in pre-Civil War annals belies its small size. Worldwide demand for cotton was huge. Virgin soil to the Southwest was farflung. South Carolinians' exhaustive cotton cultivation soon corrupted the upcountry's red clay. Carolinians then spilled beyond the state. Migrants deserted acres choked with broomsedge and briar. Ex-South Carolinians also left behind planters soberly aware of Carolina's limits. By 1830, those who stayed in Mother Carolina characteristically no longer tilled virgin lands. Instead, stay-at-homes struggled to save debilitated acres. The upcountry cotton planter who was surrounded by deserted plantations, like the lowcountry rice planter who was surrounded by impenetrable swamps, would have to make confinement a virtue.

Carolina cotton magnates sometimes stayed behind because lowcountry virtues seemed newly attractive. In Carolina, New and Old South types were not an isolating thousand miles apart, as would be the case with imperialistic New Orleans and anti-imperialistic Charleston. Upcountry and lowcountry gentries went to South Carolina College together, ruled in the same state legislature, traveled to the same summer resorts, married and buried each other. Those interactions soon led to a meeting of minds. The upcountry upstart, when shunning another crass start in the "vulgar" Southwest, often self-consciously voted for old ways. He too would become an English country gentleman. He too would sneer at the cotton boobacracy. The man once on the make, now proud to understand that life must transcend mere greed, would live for culture and horses and consolidating the regime. "I did not wish," sniffed James Hammond, "to remove from my native state and carry a family into the semi-barbarous west."[14]

The cotton revolution spawned one more enclave of reaction. Sea islands along the coast proved fertile for a luxury sort of silky fiber called, appropriately, sea island cotton. The crop added a third staple and a third group of "English country gentlemen" to the Carolina contingent.[15]

A decade into the nineteenth century, clashes over legislative representation seemed no longer worth pursuing. Lowcountry gentlemen increasingly felt upcountry tycoons could be trusted. Upcountry entrepreneurs increasingly felt lowcountry gentlemen would use Slavepower admirably. The result was the so-called Compromise of 1808—so called because the upper crust compromised so little. The settlement was called a compromise because the minority lowcountry almost controlled the Senate, while the majority upcountry thoroughly dominated the House.

But this *quid pro quo* compromised nothing of aristocratic sway, since aristocrats controlled upcountry and lowcountry both. Not even the body rewriting or reratifying the Constitution was popular. The gentlemen's legislature simply called itself into special session. Patricians then apportioned each county's share of House seats half on the basis of taxes paid, half on the basis of white population: the very "mixed" basis for Slavepower control which Benjamin Watkins Leigh would fail to push through the Virginia Convention of 1829. A tougher version of the federal three-fifths clause was alive and well in the Federal Union's imminent nemesis, South Carolina.

In 1810, in another compromise changing next to nothing, the Carolina legislature extended suffrage to all adult white males. The gentry retained the highest North American property restrictions for office holders. In no other southern legislature in the 1850s did slaveholders occupy a majority of seats. In no other American state in 1860 did the legislature elect the governor, all judges, and presidential electors.

A governor could not interfere with his legislative selectors. The state's chief executive, more a figurehead than the English king, could neither appoint subordinate officials nor veto legislative law.[16] The Carolina legislature, having out-Englished the English in establishing "parliamentary" power, copied every thread of English parliamentary costumes when garbing presiding officials. The speaker of the Carolina House, alias Speaker of the House of Commons, carried in a duplicate of the English mace. According to immemorial custom, Carolina legislative activity, like the English, began in late autumn and halted before Christmas, so lords could holiday on their acres.[17]

Immemorial custom also usually kept electioneering from Americanizing this "English Parliament," except in the newest, least enslaved western portions of the upcountry. Nothing could be more anti-English than Carolina's giving all adult white males the vote. But nothing was more un-American than Carolina's leaders' unofficially restraining voters from making legislative policy. Elsewhere in nineteenth-century North America, campaigning and electioneering, when combined with universal white suffrage, gave the masses indirect legislative power. Rival candidates, by wooing voters with rival programs, asked citizens to set policy.

But everywhere in the lowcountry and most places in the upcountry, the gentry continued to insist on the Anglo-American, eighteenth-century orthodoxy that independent gentlemen should filter poorer folks' opinions. Few campaigned in South Carolina. No two-party system existed. Few platforms were announced. Commoners usually voted for gentlemen's unopposed nominee. Gentlemen then made decisions for the state before their God and the mace.[18]

William Porcher Mile's noncampaign, on the occasion of his being anointed the lowcountry's leading lord of the 1850s, exemplifies how campaigning was usually eschewed. Miles, scion of an important lowcountry family and a college teacher who pounded old verities at young gentlemen, was called to Charleston's seat in Congress in 1855. Outside Carolina, and at upper extensions of Carolina itself, candidates would have earned voters' call by expounding and gesticulating, promising and pandering.

Miles earned his call by fleeing from lowcountry voters. Upon hearing that a murderous epidemic afflicted Norfolk, Virginia, the professor dashed north to nurse the sick. His spontaneous gesture of "duty regardless of selfish outside consideration" led "the whole body of substantial propertyholders" to nominate him for Congress.[19]

Voters still had to ratify the elite's choice. Miles was instructed to eschew "any part" in canvassing. He should "remain in Norfolk until your appointed time for return—then come back to your Professorship and go to College as usual."[20]

Until the Civil War, the professor who "campaigned" by nursing elsewhere went back to Congress per usual. His congressional positions were erratic. Other Charlestonians were his superior in "points of culture." But chummy lords who had known him since "Sunday School days" knew him to be superior in "independence, justice, courtesy, unwearying sense of duty." Those qualities mattered most when country gentlemen decided which of their own the crowd should elect.[21]

By the middle of the nineteenth century, in the middle of the most rampantly democratic (for whites) nation in the world, white South Carolinians could rightly brag about as aristocratic a government as ever took a democratic form. The South Carolina "legislature," exulted James Hammond, "has all power. The Executive has none. The people have none beyond electing members of the legislature, a power very negligently exercised from time immemorial." "The people," added James Hamilton, Jr., "expect that their leader in whose . . . public spirit they have confidence will think for them—and that they will be prepared to *act* as their leaders *think*."[22]

White commoners joining black slaves in acting as Massa *thinks*—how that formula did defuse the clash between aristocratic slavery and egalitarian republicanism. South Carolina, the state most responsible for making a southern nation, was the exception disproving the rule that herrenvolk democracy was the key to southern nationalism. In South Carolina, gentlemen usually reigned according to the principle of slavery: that the best should direct and bestow civic virtue from above. Everywhere else in the nineteenth-century South, including in eastern Virginia realms where elitism remained highly valued, eighteenth-century formulas had to be clipped and compromised. In oldest Carolina, and in much of Carolina newly old too, the country squire, alias English country gentleman, confidently rejoiced that at least in one state, the rich and talented could veto King Numbers.[23]

– 5 –

Still, the more one observed the Carolina gentry, the more such bravado seemed forced. Beyond the confidence lay echoes of sham—shame too. Carolinians were especially ashamed about their declining economic power. Charleston epitomized waning upper-class wealth. A low-lying black cloud, physically and metaphorically, hung over the city. From afar, the mysterious darkening above, even more than front doors alias reserve walls shielding gentlemen from the streets, hinted at the mood of this place.

The discolored stain hovered over the most vigorous spot in nineteenth-century South Carolina—and the place where gentlemen's vigor was most impaired. Charleston contained the wildest open-air retail market in North America. Several city squares were crammed with enticing produce, screaming hawkers, shoving crowds. Up close, the black shadow above turned out to be Charleston's flock of turkey buzzards. Vultures periodically dove down to snatch discards. The fowl then planted themselves like lords owning the turf.

Only Charleston's retailers battled the black birds. Battlers were themselves usually black. Negresses and so-called "unkies" reigned over the stalls. Black women sucked on huge pipes. Their hair was wrapped in multi-colored bandannas. Their men, kicking and hollering, drove black buzzards inch by inch out of white customers' way.

Beginning in the second decade of the nineteenth century, customers grew pickier about proffered fares. Prized hares and wild turkeys and she-crabs were a little too contemptuously disdained. Imperfect morsels discounted for quick sale were a little too impetuously snatched up. Wallets unfolded to pay for bargains were a little too lacking in padding.

Scant white dollars intensified retailers' competition. Many competitors were free blacks. They strove to be richer than whites in the capital of the realm dedicated to enslaving blacks. Other marketplace princes were slaves. They strove to disprove their owners' claim that "inferior" blacks needed a master. With whites' scarce cash draining into blacks' pockets and blacks' successful merchandising mocking whites' racist assumptions, gentlemen were doubly paying for holding themselves above scummy marketeering.

Potential costs escalated every Saturday at dusk, when country slaves descended on the city. Black boatmen bore Massa's produce for black retailers to sell. After anchoring crafts, country slaves moved towards the city market, immense loads balanced somehow on their heads. Shuffling along, their skin blackest black, their Gullah chants soaring, they almost seemed retainers of some God alien to this place.

Once, in a long night of terror never forgotten between the Ashley and the Cooper, Saturday night invaders had been called Denmark Vesey's soldiers. Perhaps the most frightening rumor amidst Charleston's Vesey Insurrection Scare of 1822 was that the rebel chieftain had traveled through the lowcountry, recruiting blacks who weekly paddled into white men's city. What an ambush these Cuffees could have staged, if anti-Cuffees they had indeed become.

The rumor was never confirmed. Planters continued to trust "their people" with their cargo. Masters claimed never to think that this largest concentration of the least Americanized blacks would take advantage of the most vulnerable slave city outside Haiti.

Their action indicated otherwise. Ever after Denmark Vesey, bells in St. Michael's belfrey sounded at 9:15 p.m., warning blacks to depart the streets until daylight. A hundred white cavalrymen nightly enforced the curfew. They made local gentlemen a little less dependent on independent blacks.

The theme of precarious independence could not be kept outside Charleston drawing rooms. Tales of fraying fortunes dominated mid-nineteenth-century Charleston gossip. The financial foundation for high living had obviously turned shaky sometime after the American Revolution. The swirl of chatter included tales of Nathaniel Russell going bankrupt building a free-flying spiral staircase, of Jimmy Hamilton's son becoming a common clerk, of Widow Heywood emptying the bottle amidst seedy splendor. The lowcounty's prime crops, moving a little slower than formerly off East Bay wharves, also hinted at a substructure gone soft. Carolina's lovely long-grained rice and lacy long-staple cotton were fashionable estates' appropriate products. Elegant staples also yearly patched up many a precarious fortune. But such luxury yield could not compare with crude cotton in producing economic expansion. Next to raucous New Orleans and galloping St. Louis, fastidious Charleston was frozen at a standstill.[24]

Lowcountry planters had lost the materialistic bases of being English country gentlemen the moment they quit the British Empire. In Carolina's most prosperous colonial days, English indigo bounties, when added to rice profits, had created a business profitable enough to require little management. But by departing the Empire, Carolina's "Englishmen" forfeited the English bounty, lost the prop making indigo planting profitable, and thus undercut their way of sending heirs to London schools.

Removal of the indigo crutch revealed the artificial economic foundation of Carolinians' claim to be English country gentlemen. English country landlords, unlike slaveowners emulating them, could afford not to work. English lands could yield no more than tenants' rents. Most rents were fixed for tenants' lifetime.

In contrast, the rice planter, with no prefixed annual income, could ignore business management only so long as plantation income soared without his direction. Rice cultivation before indigo had rarely been a wildly soaring business. Rice plantations after indigo could rarely be more than decently profitable—and only if decently managed.

Well-managed rice plantations were more stable than other southern enterprises. Rice soil, compared with cotton and tobacco acres, wore out less often. Flooding rivers usually replenished marsh muds. When soils ran chalky, clay applications usually renewed fertility. Nor did any world-wide rice glut develop, akin to cotton or tobacco gluts. Rice prices were more stable than prices for any other southern staple.

On a badly run plantation, however, rice yields could drop disastrously. The enterprise's tricky schedule and equipment demanded entrepreneurial expertise even more than did tobacco or cotton cultivation. Duplicitous blacks had to work hard on key hoeing and cultivating days. Cuffees, pretend or otherwise, had to keep intricate dams and sluices ready for key moments when fields had to be flooded or drained. Some expert had to calibrate precisely when to hold back or welcome the tides.

After indigo, rice planters were wise to be their own calibrators. Responsible overseers in uninhabitable swamps, unlike responsive English rent collectors, remained hard to hire. The few responsible overseers, more than the multitude of responsible English accountants, could reasonably aspire to enter the ruling class. Frugal white hirelings could buy up ruined estates of dissolute spenders. If post-English Empire Carolinians persisted in copying English landlords, they would trade places with overseers they should have been overseeing.

Nineteenth-century heirs destroyed their remaining chance to live like eighteenth-century English gentlemen by repealing the legal foundation of the English aristocracy. Nothing better shows how the American democratic world infected these "English" squires than Carolina's abolition of primogeniture and entail after the American Revolution. Legal preservation of entire ancestral estates, with eldest sons inheriting everything, seemed undemocratic in even this most aristocratic part of America. As a result, fortunes were "separated into lesser parcels, distributed among numerous families," with each given "but a bare maintenance if properly economized."[25]

Bare maintenance and proper economy required that Carolina slaveowners become not English but Virginia country gentlemen. Even in plusher days, Virginia's finest had only been absentees when residing in the White House or some such temporary locale of aristocratic duty. After 1824, with the nation no longer calling for their dynasty, with primogeniture and entail no longer preserving estates whole, and with the world not paying high prices for tobacco, Virginia gentlemen had to become entrepreneurial homebodies. By economizing, fertilizing, diversifying, they clung to shreds of ancestral estates.

Carolina coastal squires often scorned Virginia-style clinging. Absenteeism, rooted in both dread of swamp disease and love of Charleston idling, remained treasured. "Our ancestors," lamented Francis D. Quash in 1831, are our "worst enemies." Our generation, "rocked in the cradle of wealth," underfinanced after "divisions of property," faces "the grim visage of bankruptcy." Yet capital and time are "withheld" from shrinking estates "to answer the exactions of the ghosts of departed city joys." Carolina's young men," added another city observer, are "too apt to be above" business, "which their false pride tells them is not gentlemenlike." These "lavish" spenders gave in "to idleness and dissipation." The "evil" was "progressing to an alarming degree."[26]

William Heyward was an alarming case. His eighteenth-century father, Judge Heyward, had spent the productive growing season on the Charleston party scene and the nonproductive winter season on his Georgetown rice estate. In 1808, an observer found the nineteenth-century heir still in Charleston in December, long after the killing frost. Billy Heyward was "lounging away his mornings," and "drinking away his afternoons." The young sport seemed "not satisfied himself with his mode of existence." He planned to go to his plantation "in a few days to see how things are going on there." But "he confessed to me that he hated to have anything to do with negroes."[27]

A half-century later, Robert F. W. Allston, Georgetown's most prominent rice planter, reported the result of Heyward's distaste for management and taste for dissipation. Mrs. Heyward had recently died of alcoholism. An ex-overseer owned Billy Heyward's fine mansion and 40,000 acres. Weeds "covered up" old orange and lemon and olive groves. "Pride and vanity" had demolished "princely wealth and splendor."

Allston was "filled with melancholy reflections at the decay of families. . . . Here are two Cuthberts who have run through everything left to them and are now loafers spunging on anybody who will suffer them." There were the Hazards, the son a suicide, the old man's estate now owned by an ex-overseer. So too, "the residence of poor Ben Allston is burned down and planted over—there is nothing of him or his left."[28]

At the other end of the swamp, near the Georgia border, Charles Manigault reported equally little left of an ancient gentry. In the 1830s and 1840s, he had seen 40 to 50 plantations sold, on which an "ordinary practical man," exercising "prudence & industry & . . . self denial & economy" could prosper. Instead, "for *want* of *this prudence* . . . all the old families who formerly owned *these plantations* have disappeared, . . . while overseers & aliens to our climate & to our society take possession of the soil." Manigault had bought his plantation from an overseer; his two neighbors were ex-overseers; and another ex-overseer owned the plantation across the river.[29]

Manigault's and Allston's swamps, locale of much anti-entrepreneurial fastidiousness, had become the site of entrepreneurial mobility. This least American area may have been America's best example of spent capitalists falling and raw capitalists rising. All the great aristocratic names at the time of the Revolution of 1776—Lowndes, Rutledges, Pinckneys, et al.—were nowhere to be found leading the Revolution of 1860. Instead, names so Yankee as Robert Barnwell Smith (he changed his last name to the wonderfully Carolinian Rhett) led the old order out of the new century.

Old families who saved estates by practicing Yankee virtues were not heroes of this anti-Yankee culture. Charles Manigault, for example, when missed in chattering Charleston, could be found "jogging off in the old sulky & my bobtailed horse, travelling to the Savannah River, putting my horse up at a log hut in the pine barren, then footing it thru a two mile swamp and crossing in a canoe to my Island plantation." There he spent "the best years of my life clearing its swamp."[30] By resourceful management, he made around 8% a year. The profit was decent enough to indicate how resourceful overseers could rise. An 8% margin was also slim enough to indicate why unresourceful absentees failed.

For his pains, Manigault experienced his family's contempt for being too capitalistic. His friends twitted him for crediting his prosperity to Yankee exertion instead of ancient inheritance. But Manigault could stridently answer (and he was revealingly strident about it) that without money-grubbing exertion, heirs would trade places with overseers.

Robert F. W. Allston was also mocked for capitalistic crudity instead of praised for capitalistic success. Allston too made around 8% a year on rice by cherishing "habits of thorough investigation." He believed even daughters "ought to learn some trade." While he was proudly acquiring "the reputation of a man of business" by improving "my paternal estate," his wife was off in the "wicked" city, where he feared his children would "acquire habits" of "luxury." He preferred they acquire habits "of Dr. Franklin."[31]

Benjamin Franklin indeed! Allston's wife ridiculed his "Poor Richard" practicalities. Allston writhed at her ridicule, just as Manigault winced at his family's displeasure. No lowcountry scion of an old family could escape unease, whether he saved estates by becoming a managerial capitalist or lost his inheritance by shunning management. Either way, his was the pain of an old order unable to afford Old English values.

– 6 –

Carolina upcountry cotton planters faced similar problems for different reasons. Since absenteeism had never been rife in the more healthy upcountry, expenses of second homes and consequences of non-entrepreneurial idling seldom occurred above the swamps. But upcountry managers suffered other economic troubles. Planters whose slaves worked tired soil ended up with straggly crops of cotton, especially compared with lush yields oozing from fresh Alabama or Mississippi acres. When world-wide cotton markets turned down, as happened in 1826–32 and 1837–49, poor yields piled atop poor prices bankrupted many an upcountry planter. When cotton prices shot up, as they did briefly in the mid-1830s and extensively in the late 1850s, times were better in Carolina but not as flush as in Alabama.[32]

Economic stagnation in the upcountry, with its tired cotton fields, and economic squeeze in the lowcountry, with its gentry living too high on inheritances too divided, led to a mass exodus from Carolina for the virgin West. Few migrants came to replace those leaving. By 1860, 96.6% of South Carolinians were Carolina-born, a degree of insularity unheard of elsewhere in the highly insular Old South. Yet 42% of those born in Carolina lived elsewhere, another incredible Old South number.[33]

The little world limping behind could crab all it pleased about vulgarians who deserted it. But these "eighteenth-century Englishmen" were sufficiently nineteenth-century Americans to suspect that those who failed to grow would sink. With the adventurous half of Old Carolina voting with their feet for expanding America while the contemptuous half stagnated in ancient rice parishes and aging cotton districts, how could those remaining summon the energy, much less the power, to save the Old South and lead the New? That question by itself made these gentlemen desperate enough to be revolutionaries—and made them wonder if they could sustain any revolution at all.

CHAPTER 13

Origins of
South Carolina Eccentricity, II:
Cultural Foundations

Economic historians, Marxist and otherwise, have recently emphasized that materialistic factors generate cultural factors that take on causal power of their own. So too, cultural imperatives join economic imperatives to create political imperatives. Particularly in antebellum Charleston, where an important cultural renaissance occurred simultaneously with important political strivings, the politics bore on the culture and the culture helps explain the politics.

Carolinians thought themselves culturally special for three related reasons. Because they were of the oldest South, they supposedly took more patriarchal care of "their people" than did southwestern upstarts. Because they outdid other Old South gentries in recreating Old English customs and politics, they were allegedly truer English country gentlemen. Because absenteeism maximized opportunity for nonmateralistic concerns, they were supposedly creative intellectuals. These three claims led to soaring senses of self-worth—and invited gentlemen's suspicion that they were not as worthy as claimed.

– 1 –

South Carolinians' first claim to superiority, their allegedly especially patriarchal treatment of slaves, was both true and false. Paternalism was especially plausible inside Charleston homes, for household servants were easiest to consider part of a *Domestic* Institution. Nowhere in the South were domestic servants more separated from agrarian toil than in the weeks and months when Massa and household slaves shared Charleston town houses, far away from field hands.

But those field hands, particularly on large and impersonal plantations, belied notions of paternalism and domesticity. Carolinians who thrust blacks into miasmic jungles used up "their people" at a pace unthinkable on healthy frontiers. Only this deadly North American region rivaled "exploitative" Latin Americans in sometimes killing off slaves as fast or faster than slaves reproduced themselves. Sensitivity on the subject led to endless attempts to prove what swamp lords knew to be false: that blacks partially immune from malaria were totally safe in a deadly habitat.

Swamp environs precluded other essentials for a paternalistic regime. Lowcountry patriarchs, because absent so many months, could not influence blacks culturally as extensively as could resident planters elsewhere. Because swamp slaves retained peculiarly persistent African linguistic traits and customs, they seemed less part of an American family. The Carolina lowcountry, having opened its African slave trade latest and Americanized its Gullah-speaking blacks least, having the largest relative percentage of absentee planters and big plantations, was the North American regime most like impersonal Latin America.

Swamp planters were likely of two types. Neither type exemplified paternalism. The classic lowcountry tycoons were absentee heirs of old families, hiring agents to force Gullah-speaking workers to endure swamp fevers. But often owners were ex-overseers and hard-driving swamp managers, *nouveau* southwestern style.

No Mississippian battled blacks more resolutely than did poor men newly arrived as masters in supposedly patriarchal South Carolina. My first year of planting, confessed that ultimate *arrivé,* James Hammond, required a "severity which cost me infinite pain and gained a name which I detest of all others to subdue" my slaves. The detested name, perhaps "nigger-driver" and assuredly not "paternalist," remained appropriate for many years. James Kirk, a successfully climbing ex-overseer, told a visitor that "if he lives 10 or 15 yrs. longer," his slaves would "gain ascendency over him. . . . [He] is sensible they are gaining on him: confesses whips in a passion & half the time unjustly." There was a man with attitudes that a South Carolinian was not supposed to have.[1]

Those 9:15 curfew bells in Charleston also rang out of a strained sensibility. The subsequent patrol pounding the streets announced that domestic slavery did not seem domestically safe. Fathers do not muster armed guard against "boys." These patriarchs sensed they needed protection against "family friends." That armed protection, nightly greater in Charleston than elsewhere in the Old South, made Charleston's allegedly greater paternalism more than a little suspect.

– 2 –

The Carolina gentlemen's performances as English country gentlemen were as true and as strained as postures of patriarchal slaveholders. Like their counterparts in England, they were supposed to relish the outdoors. They indeed loved sports. But when the climes beckoned them out of doors, they were often in Charleston. In the stuffy city, they were outside mostly on secluded porches, where they regaled each other with stories of sport they played on their departed plantations.

They loved English-style riding. Foxhunting was a favorite recreation. Race week in Charleston, like race week in London, was their supreme moment of sport. But few coastal squires kept hunters and fewer owned race horses. They knew that hunts could hardly penetrate the tangled lowcountry brush. They knew that a handful of upcountry outdoorsmen owned most of the Carolina race horses. Lowcountry "Englishmen"'s sport, when showed off to bewildered English visitors, consisted of black gangs dressed up in coat and cravat and panting like hounds as they rowed off to chase that lowcountry water monster, the devilfish.[2]

English?

Again, these "transplanted Englishmen" had supposedly consolidated North America's only House of Parliament. Their state regime came closer to that ideal than any other in the United States. But their not-altogether-English state constitution gave all white men the vote. Their state also contained one threatening area not happy with their English-style House of Commons. Semi-mountainous western regions of Carolina sustained a largely nonslaveholder culture restive about the Compromise of 1808. These folks periodically urged that a one-white-man, one-vote reapportionment should undermine coastal "rotten-boroughs."

Democratic America intruded even more when Carolinians participated in federal politics. John C. Calhoun, Mr. South Carolina, periodically plunged into the "digusting" two-party system. The upcountry's James L. Orr, South Carolina's most ascendent politician after Calhoun died, frequently urged South Carolinians to save themselves inside the "vulgar" National Democratic Party. With Orr, of all people, threatening to replace Calhoun as Mr. South Carolina, Carolina was threatening to join, of all things, the American nineteenth century.[3]

– 3 –

Because absentee slaveholders suspected they were neither altogether paternalistic nor sufficiently English country gentlemen, they craved their own cultural identity. That imperative created the critical Carolina pretense: that slaves freed slaveholders to develop a high culture. The posture had a large reality. The South Carolina lowcountry in general and its queen city, Charleston, in particular, sustained a revealing antebellum cultural renaissance. No other southern center, urban or otherwise, demonstrated such intellectual vitality until long after the Civil War.

Carolina's downturn of economic production ironically generated and helped define this cultural upsurge. The Old Charleston of the Age of American Revolution, a locale ripe with materialistic prosperity, had concentrated on material ornaments. Wealthy urbanites had supported superb architects, resourceful stucco molders, stylish cabinetmakers. As the decaying Charleston of the nineteenth century emerged, the economy declined, artistry with materials slowed, and creativity with words soared. At the very time the booming Southwest was draining away lowcountrymen, Charlestonians were expanding their beloved Library Society, establishing their own college, creating their own medical school, founding their own literary journals and publishing millions of words on local fauna and national history, parochial diseases and universal theologies, law and classics, politics and social structure. Whatever else Charleston gentlemen cut back on, their consumption of paper and ink knew no limits.[4]

This conjunction of a rise in verbal creativity and a decline in economic power produced among intellectuals a certain refined despair. The unlovely world outside was not listening to the fraying old city with its newly lovely literature; and smallish Charleston contained too few intellectuals, especially compared with New York or Boston or Philadelphia, to generate enough patrons at home to satisfy its new literati.

The best way to seek wider audiences was to leave Charleston. For a city obsessed with stopping its drain of dollars and people to the philistine world outside, Charleston generated a surprising number of cultivated exiles, as well as an inclination in those who stayed to write obsessively about expatriation. Of those who could neither bear to leave nor bear to stop writing about departing, the greatest was William Gilmore Simms, leader of the Charleston Renaissance. Of those who departed and used their cultural distance to bring Carolina assumptions to the richest artistic achievement, the most remarkable was Washington Allston.[5]

Allston, who bore one of the lowcountry's most prominent names, became the leading American painter of his turn-of-the-nineteenth-century generation. He would make any list of the top ten American painters of any generation and should top any ranking of the most creative Carolinians. Hence the importance of Allston's decision to create elsewhere. The painter, like many American artists, early deserted his ancestral area to study in the North and Europe. Most great American painters came home again. Allston returned to sell off his inheritance, thereby gaining the wherewithal to leave forever. All his canvases were painted far away from the South and in the early nineteenth century, before Southerners established regional identity.

His dominant style was of the cosmopolitan world he entered, with only traces of the province he deserted. His greatest paintings were often in the mainstream Anglo-American, late eighteenth-century tradition of art as recreation of historic events. All great American painters of the period adopted the art-as-history conception, often to recreate epic American Revolutionary scenes. Allston, who had retreated from South Carolina, also retreated so far from American patriotic concerns as to paint only epic Bible scenes when working in the historic genre. Allston's renditions of sacred history usually have nothing recognizably Carolinian about them.

Nor do Allston's landscapes, his other favorite mode of painting, usually betray Carolina roots. His nature paintings were an early development of what would come to be the dominant mid-nineteenth-century American art tradition. Mid-nineteenth-century American landscapes characteristically convey nature as sleeping beauty. Lush valleys lead to majestic mountains and blood-red twilight skies. Only a blasted tree trunk in the foreground hints at nature's fury. In the rest of the canvas, nature's beneficence usually transcends the casualty.[6]

We have come to call this usually smiling landscape tradition the Hudson River School. But Washington Allston perfected the genre in the earliest nineteenth century, over thirty years before Thomas Cole or Thomas Doughty or Asher Durand or Frederick Church painted the Hudson River. Allston's nature scenes are usually lushly beneficent. His *Landscape with a Lake* (1804) has what would come to be the obligatory blasted tree trunk in the foreground. Tragedy fleetingly acknowledged, the landscape ascends a path up the picture, through healthy trees to a luminous lake, to sublime mountains, to happy skies. So too Allston's gorgeous *Moonlit Landscape* (1819) conveys a luminously lit natural paradise. The canvas exudes that fascination with clean, rich light which would define, a generation later, the American Luminist Tradition.

Allston's precociously early American landscapes, like later American nature canvases, tend to have the defects of their virtues. They usually capture nature's peak moments of luminosity. They characteristically miss the ferocity when black clouds block the clean light.

But the fascination of Washington Allston as precursor of the imminent American landscape school is that, unlike most successors, he occasionally reversed the emphasis. As history painter, this South Carolina exile had been far enough outside the American mainstream to escape painting the American Revolution. So too, as nature painter, this product of malevolent swamps was far enough outside the American consensus to reject, occasionally, American conceptions of benevolent nature.

Allston vividly remembered his "favorite" childhood "amusement," drawing "little landscapes about the roots of an old tree." Such lowcountry "delights would sometimes give way to a stronger love for the wild and the marvelous." The future artist "delighted in being terrified by the tales of witches and hags, which the Negroes used to tell." With "much pleasure I recalled these feelings on my return to Carolina; especially on revisiting a gigantic wild grapevine in the woods, which had been the favorite swing of one of these witches."[7]

Washington Allston's darkest landscapes are full of this mood in these jungles, where towering trees usually block the sunlight and eerie blackness looms. Allston's greatest canvas in the darker vein, *Elijah in the Desert* (1817–18), contains the obligatory blasted tree. But this time the savaged growth stands front and center, as if ready for revenge. The tree's two grotesque arms reach towards a violent sky. A black raven, who looks much like Charleston's turkey buzzards, clutches a limb, while another hovers closer. Allston's dark fowl, bearing food, can alone nurture the isolated white Elijah, who lies helplessly beneath the forbidding tree.

The theme of whites at the mercy of blackness is also conveyed in Allston's under-appreciated *Ship in a Squall* (before 1837). This frightening work features alarming black skies and waters which surround a solitary white ship, rendered in chalk. The besieged ship on the soulless sea seems reminiscent of Allston's homeland, with its huge concentrations of blacks and the isolated planter star-

Washington Allston's "Landscape with a Lake." Courtesy, Museum of Fine Arts, Boston, Gift of Mr. and Mrs. Maxim Karolik.

Allston's "Moonlit Landscape." Courtesy, Museum of Fine Arts, Boston, Gift of William Sturgis Bigelow.

Allston's "Elijah in the Desert." Courtesy, Museum of Fine Arts, Boston, Gift of Mrs. Samuel Hooper and Miss Alice Hooper.

Allston's "Ship in a Squall." Courtesy, Fogg Art Museum, Harvard University, Cambridge, Massachusetts, Washington Allston Trust.

tled to see a white face in the mirror. Allston, the Carolinian as American who foreshadowed the coming American school of painting, could not have better conveyed a world grimly, dangerously outside the American consensus. For a fleeting moment, the Carolina insider who deserted to become an American insider exquisitely expressed his world's special identity.

But art historians have only dimly recognized Allston's Jekyll and Hyde development of the American landscape tradition. They have even more dimly seen the relationship between Allston's divided vision and a soul slightly too Carolinian to be undividedly American. Such latter-day dimness has a long tradition. Charleston barely noticed Allston.

– 4 –

While Washington Allston was the insider who happily left, carrying away liberating perspectives on the world outside, William Gilmore Simms was the semi-outsider who traumatically stayed, trapped with an anti-exile's stereotypes about glories within and horrors without. Simms, the Old South's greatest novelist, was one-man proof that a Charleston Renaissance paralleled the American Renaissance. His best works sought to turn rejection of mainstream American themes into great American fiction. His trouble was that the very Carolina orthodoxies which inspired a dissenting angle on the American Renaissance stymied full artistic exploration of the deviant counterculture.

The lowcountry's stimulating, narrowing cants captured the future novelist's imagination amidst a real-life scene few novelists could make realistic. The shocking event, occurring when young Simms was an impressionable 12-year-old, climaxed a traumatic upbringing. William Gilmore had been only two when his mother, offspring of an old Carolina family, died. Simm's father, an emigrant from Ireland who had temporarily flourished in Charleston mercantile circles, lost fortune and wife about the same time. Père Simms, crushed, emigrated again, this time to the southwestern frontier. The adventurer left William Gilmore with the boy's maternal grandmother.

A decade later, Simms's father, arrived back in Charleston, determined to summon his son to the wilds. The grandmother would not surrender "her" boy. The father sought to capture the twelve-year-old on the street. William Gilmore, rolling and kicking over the Charleston cobblestones, shrieked that he would not go. Sympathetic Charlestonians gathered. They tore the lad from the outlander's grasp. They insisted that a Charleston judge decide whether the frontier could swallow up another of Charleston's offspring. The judge let the youngster decide. The future novelist opted for Charleston, as would his every novel.

A decade later, Simms reaffirmed his decision. He visited his father for several months in Mississippi. The elder Simms, who had left Charleston penniless and had made himself a frontier titan, promised his son fame and fortune if he would stay out West. Young Simms refused. "Return to Charleston!" exclaimed the father. "Your talents . . . will there be poured out like water on the sands. Charleston! *I know it only as a place of tombs.*"[8]

Simms came back determined to make Charleston's tombs an inspiration. Charleston's would-be inspirer cherished the historical novel, or the romance, as he preferred to call it. For Simms, as for the later and greater southern novelist, William Faulkner, the past was not dead. It was not even past. Simms declared "history" to be "the most lovely" and "the most legitimate daughter of heaven," for through her "the past lives to the counselling and direction of the future."[9]

Simms pronounced historical romancers more important than political actors in directing Carolina backwards toward reactionary glory. "The statesman" would die and become "dust." But "the glorious record of the past, preserved to the future, only by the interposition of creative art . . . still speaks."[10] This determination to be Carolina's hero invited frustration. Simms often groused that Charlestonians lionized him too little.[11] The city's not-so-many intellectuals in fact praised him much. But his tomb, as his father had predicted, would never outshadow others in politically obsessed Charleston.

The oft-embittered Simms oft complained that he would have been better off in cosmopolitan New York or even in the Wild West. But he stayed on in the decaying province. His endeavor to be the first Charleston writer who supported his family and inspired his culture through scribbling ultimately yielded a soaring pile of 65 books, including essays, dramas, poetry, histories, biographies, geographies, and especially the over two dozen novels. His private library was the largest in Carolina; his literary contacts with New York City pundits exceeded any Southerner's; his calls for an *American* literature were as compelling as any Yankee's; he edited literary journals of national importance. Could Old South intellectuals write anything more interesting than proslavery pamphlets? Let us consider the intriguing Simms, who wrote 150 pages of proslavery propaganda and 20,000 pages of just about everything else.

Simms placed his fictional characters in a curious setting for an author so dead-set against the wilderness. His protagonists almost always departed civilization for adventures amidst the lawless. His was a variation on the dominant American theme of an old civilization moving out onto untamed nature.

Simms's rendition was indeed a variation, for he reversed the usual American outcome. Northern writers often made the individual divorced from community, severed from familial origins out in space, the American seer. To New England Transcendentalists such as Ralph Waldo Emerson and Henry David Thoreau, sublimity was best found alone and apart, with feet trailing in the dewy grass.

Transcendentalists' major Yankee literary opponents, Herman Melville and Nathaniel Hawthorne, retorted that nature can be more terrible than dewy grass. Melville's white whale in *Moby-Dick,* whatever else the enigma may represent, shows that nature, when sought monomaniacally, will destroy the exile from civilization. Ishmael, the only whale-seeker who declares himself but temporarily at sea, is the only pilgrim who returns safely to land.

So too, Hawthorne's Hester Prynne, heroine of *The Scarlet Letter,* ultimately lives on the edge of both forest and town. Although unrepentant about her impassioned adultery in the wilderness, she willingly wears the scarlet "A" decreed by civilization. Emersonian opponents thus honored quests for meaning beyond the settlement while also insisting that a total severing from civilization has costs. The northern novelist who came closer to minimizing the costs, James Fenimore Cooper, made his frontier heroes, variously called Hawkeye or Leatherstocking or Natty Bumpo, into uncivilized natural men, alias that new hero, The American.[12]

Simms thought Cooper created dubious heroes. "We admire" Cooper's natural frontiersmen, sniffed Simms, but "love them we do not." The South Carolinian criticized Natty Bumpo's inventor for failing "to hit the true line that divides the simplicity of nature from the puerility of ignorance." Cooper mistook backwoodsmen's "burly defiance . . . for the calm, manly tone of gentlemanly independence."[13]

Simms's so-called Border Tales, his frontier romances closest to Cooper's, revolve around gentlemen of manly independence who dangerously wander into burly domains. Where other writers of the American Renaissance saw flight from civilization as the route toward discovery, Simms painted life on frontiers as nasty, brutish, and short. Cutthroats, fleeing disappointments or disasters back east, abounded. Better sorts, misplaced inside lawless and cultureless wastelands, only learned how to battle better against bandits. Personal growth demanded rejecting the uncouth West and returning to the cultivated seaboard.[14]

The stance especially slashed at that most irresponsible Carolina aristocrat, the one who deserted Carolina. In *Richard Hurdis,* for example, Richard is the restless, hot-tempered, young Carolina blade who, when disappointed in love, wishes a "'better place'" out West. "'Better place!'" explodes Richard Hurdis's mother. Your ancestral home is "'good enough.'" The matriarch turns out to be right. A frontier "reported to be rich as cream" reduces "Mississippi-mad" pioneers to "the savage feebleness of the Indians."

The only redeeming character amidst the "license of the wilderness" is Colonel Grafton, an old friend of the Hurdis family, who has imposed a speck of order on disorderly frontiers. Grafton is one of the responsible older aristocrats Simms constantly pits against irresponsible young gentlemen. With Grafton's help, Richard Hurdis learns responsibility by routing outlaws. Hurdis completes the lesson by returning to his ancestral estate.[15]

Simms's better known Revolutionary War romances and his most famous volume, *The Yamassee,* resemble the Border Tales in being set outside civilization. Whether fighting Indians in the early eighteenth century in *The Yamassee* or battling Englishmen later in the century in such Revolutionary War historical romances as *The Partisan,* responsible Carolina squires bring order to the Carolina backcountry. The difference from the Border Tales is that upper-class duty here demands temporary exile from cultivated parishes. During a war of revolution, squires must move out to turn revolutionary chaos into structured hierarchy. They then must return to reassume hierarchical responsibility in the parishes.

Again and again Simms pits the wise, even-tempered patriarch against the selfish, hot-tempered squire. *The Partisan's* hero is Major Robert Singleton, Singleton being Simms's mother's family name, a patriarch "finely intelligent and tolerably handsome." Singleton, under the command of Carolina's Swamp Fox, the famous guerrilla warrior, Francis Marion, would transform a necessary revolution and a necessary guerrilla strategy of fighting into a mechanism for ordering a wilderness. Singleton's antithesis is his uncle, Colonial Walton, "a gentlemen in every sense of the word," who irresponsibly prefers luxuries on his plantation to temporary obligation in the wilds.[16]

So too in *The Yamassee*, the hero is Governor Charles Craven, alias Gabriel Harrison, who comes out from civilization to tame Indians. Harrison's antithesis is Hugh Grayson, an overly fiery and dissolute aristocrat, who for a time boorishly helps contribute to the frontier chaos Harrison would control. Just as Colonel Grafton eventually educates Richard Hurdis in patriarchal duty, so Harrison eventually lifts up Grayson and Singleton elevates Walton. The ever wise and newly wise patriarchs make the wilds a little less wild and then go home again.[17]

Simms's development of the nature/civilization theme makes one bow in James Fenimore Cooper's direction. Usually, wise upper-class types teach dissolute aristocrats how to be crafty in nature and responsible upon returning home. Occasionally, however, a classless natural product of the forest, à la Cooper's Natty Bumpo, becomes the agent of upper-class uplift. In the Border Tale *Guy Rivers*, for example, Mark Forrester, a "natural noble" of the forest, deflates the pomposity and guides the obligations of the hot-tempered young squire Ralph Colleton, who has unfortunately exiled himself from a lowcountry parish "famous for its wealth, lofty pride, polished manners, and nobel and considerate hospitality." So too, the frontier scout Thumbscrew Witherspoon elevates the fiery young gentleman, Ernest Mellichampe, in the Revolutionary War romance, *Mellichampe*.[18] But compared with Cooper's frequent uncivilized redeemers, these figures are not very uncivilized (they are usually vaguely related to uncivil civilized sorts they help civilize) and never the ultimate heroes (they usually are killed off too early to see those they have uplifted triumph and return). No man with a dialect can be William Gilmore Simms's hero. A Carolinian speaking the King's English must save patriarchal Carolina.

Simms's endless vote for civilized parishes served personal, parochial, and cosmopolitan needs. The obligation to come home again justified that screaming future novelist, who had made a scene on the streets rather than be hauled off to papa's wilds. Simms's Border Tales in particular also filled the Carolina imperative, at a time of destructive depopulation and dissolute idling, of calling upon the Carolina aristocrat to stay home, set to work, and summon the energy to lead the uncivil South. So too, Simms's Revolutionary War romances, celebrations of hierarchical order amidst disorderly guerrilla combat, served nineteenth-century Carolina's quest for a slaveholders' revolution aimed at reactionary conservation.

Best of all, Simms's tales turned provincial need into sophisticated reformulation of the American Renaissance. An American literature, as Simms wrote it, did not glorify escape from civilization in the New World wilderness. Simms instead made the American mission a reassertion of cultivation, hierarchy, and order in defiance of dangerously close, fearfully seductive wilds. This definition of Carolina identity offered as promising a slant on Emerson's dewy optimism and Cooper's Natty Bumpo as did Melville's or Hawthorne's perspectives.

Unfortunately, Simms's novelistic inventions were not up to the potential of his message. The problem lay not in the inventor's literary skills. Simms at his best was a superb crafter of sentences, deviser of characters, imaginer of scenes and—rare talent—concocter of humor. His defect was a tendency to stereotype characters, thereby bringing frontier melodrama to full absurdity.

Behind this tendency lay a worried South Carolinian's stereotyped inclination to see Southerners outside as uncouth barbarians and gentlemen within as either heroes or betrayers. Simms's frontier villains are irredeemably malign. His aristocrats are either calm, sensible, responsible—in a word, sublime—or wild spenders, fiery in temperament, erratic in judgment—in a word, betrayers. Shove these good guys and bad guys into the full trappings of the hair-raising, gun-toting, rescue and murder, Walter Scott-James Fenimore Cooper romance and you have, let us be kind, a certain amiable preposterousness.

Simms is not amiable when his stereotypes pass beyond white men to portray other races and the other sex. The defect is rampant in *The Yamassee,* unfortunately Simms's most widely read novel nowadays. This melodramatic tearjerker revolves around Indians in the Carolina backcountry, on the warpath against encroaching whites. When the "higher race" circumscribes red men's hunting grounds, inferiors, raging at dependency, strike back. The "best thing" whites "can do for them is to send them as far as possible from communion with our people."[19]

Simms's whites allegedly do better by blacks. Slaves seldom appear in Simms's many novels about planters temporarily away from plantations. The few slaves who accompany patriarchs to the wilds are always adoring body servants. These ultra-Cuffees repeatedly stage what Simms obviously thought was an affecting renunciation scene. Renouncing offers of freedom, they pronounce themselves happily enslaved.

In *The Yamassee,* Simms used his stock renunciation scene to reemphasize why racial inferiors without patriarchal protectors necessarily become hapless barbarians. After routing Indian savages, the hero, Gilbert Harrison, offers manumission to his ultraloyal bodyservant, Hector. "'I give you your freedom, old fellow. Here is money, too, and in Charleston you shall have a house to live in for yourself.' 'No maussa; I can't go; I can't be free,'" replied the negro. "'You want Hector for eat acorn wid de hogs, and take de swamp wid de Injin?'" Inferiors deprived of a superior must "'git drunk and lie in de ditch. . . . You come in de morning, Hector dead.'" Better to adore maussa than to be a dead Injin.[20]

Adoring white belles are no less hapless in *The Yamassee.* Such helpless white angels abound in almost all Simms's tales. The stock weak beauty this time is Beth Mathews, who stages a stock Simms fainting scene before a rattlesnake. "She sees him approach," the reptile's neck "arched beautifully like that of a wild horse," his "huge jaws unclosing almost directly above her, the long tubulated fang, charged with venom, protruding from the cavernous mouth— and sees no more!" The senseless lass does not see a lad slaughter the reptile just in time or see the snake "throw himself over with a single convulsion, and, a moment after, lay dead besides the utterly unconscious maiden."[21]

Such melodramatic stereotyping of ladies and blacks helps explain why a writer so immovably against moving out of lowcountry South Carolina was artistically compelled to create scenes of exile. If Simms had set his stories inside settled parishes or plantations or the Big House, he would have had to move females and slaves into the center of his narrative. One-dimensional dependents as stars of the story would have ensured sappy novels, as almost always occurred in antebellum southern domestic fiction.

In contrast, Simm's tales of white males seeking aristocratic identity and hierarchical order on a relatively homeless and villian-infested frontier, for all the stereotyping of good guys and bad, relegated still more stereotypic loving Cuffees and docile ladies to the background. Moreover, males' camaraderie in the army camp created in itself a community of strong characters, lovingly together in their mission, separately ranked in their army stations. The campfire hierarchy, with its aristocratic elegance on top and its animal energy below, had the vitality to rout outlaws and civilize savages. In contrast, the ideal domestic hierarchy at home, with cultivated gentlemen bossing sugary-sweet belles and sycophant darkies, had elegance without energy–precisely decaying Charleston's problem in its age of literary flowering. No wonder William Gilmore Simms, while forever sending patriarchs back home with frontier mission accomplished, almost always kept homecomings offstage.

Almost always. The problem of how returning patriarchs applied wilderness lessons to parish life could not be forever ignored, not by an author so committed to literature as mechanism of patriarchal uplift. This anti-expatriate's urge to center a fiction on return from expatriation became overwhelming after publication of Harriet Beecher Stowe's *Uncle Tom's Cabin*. Mrs. Stowe attacked the elegant southern plantation especially for its inelegant vulnerability to expatriation. Refined gentlemen without cash, Stowe made clear, had to sell slaves down river to pay for refinements, even if the price was Uncle Tom's smashed home.

Simms rushed his novelistic answer into print almost as fast as Mrs. Stowe's chapters appeared.[22] Despite the haste and the problems a domestic scenario posed to an author who had avoided his most obvious subject, Simms's new fiction was by far his best novel. Its virtues indicate that Mrs. Stowe had catalyzed the production of a fable long simmering in the fablist's consciousness.

Woodcraft features Captain Porgy, easily Simms's finest male character, who comes home from the Revolutionary War to cavort with the Widow Eveleigh, easily Simms's finest female character. Porgy and the Widow are allied against slave snatchers, who have stolen their bondsmen during the Revolutionary War. One hardscrabble thief is a nonslaveholder squatting on Eveleigh's land. Another richer villian has a mortgage on Porgy's land, a debt incurred because Porgy had been a dissolute prewar aristocrat. The Captain returns to his delapidated plantation much reformed but almost penniless; like Harriet Beecher Stowe's planters of genteel poverty, he may have to sell his black friends, even if he can wrest them from thieves. In *Woodcraft's* main action, Porgy and Eveleigh rescue their slaves and each other from villains, stall off the sheriff, hound the mortgage-holder into suicide by exposing his crimes, and ultimately decide whether they can live happily together as man and wife.

Simms's readers have had the delight of meeting Captain, sometimes Lieutenant, Porgy before. In the Carolina novelist's Revolutionary War series, as in William Faulkner's Yoknapatawpha saga, some characters reappear in various volumes. Porgy's reappearances are always welcome. This gargantuan warrior with the colossal belly and zesty taste for Shakespeare has the traditional fat man's virtue: great good humor. His capers are usually worth a chuckle and sometimes productive of guffaws, whether he is crying for help to hoist himself onto his feet or slurping his lowcountry feast of *alerta* and *lagarta,* alias frogs' legs and baby alligators.

Porgy is yet another of Simms's once-decadent, now-reformed aristocrats. But the fat humorist stands alone in having some former vices mixed up with considerable new virtue. He is too irredeemably huge and greedy to become some chaste exemplar of morality regained. Simms calls him an epicurean. But Porgy is never too finicky to chomp. He never saw a third course he could refuse. "'By St. Bacchus,'" he bellows, "'I must drink—I must eat—I must be guilty of some fleshly indulgence.'"[23] He fights like blazes for the cause, then filches some poor compatriot's blanket for his snooze. He is the reformed sinner as reborn overeater and thus that unprecedented Simms character—the well-rounded—no, widely rounded—hero.

Porgy's escapades often turn Simms's melodramatic absurdities into believable comedy. In one pre-*Woodcraft* moment of battle, the immense fellow demoralizes his opponent by laying on him. "'Your faith may move mountains,'" the fat man says to the flattened fellow below."'But your surrender only shall remove me.'" "'Can't someone relieve me from this elephant,'" gasped the half-strangled victim. "'Elephant,'" roared Porgy. I'll have at you with, what else, "'my grinders.'" Porgy, after being mercifully removed before he could sink his teeth, complains that the enemy "'called me an elephant! Me! Me an elephant.' 'He had need to do so,'" replies Porgy's commander.[24]

Such incidents, like all Porgy's appearances before *Woodcraft,* are sadly brief. In *Woodcraft,* Porgy happily dominates the text. In the most delightfully outrageous scene, Porgy and camp followers demoralize the deputy sheriff by shaving off the law enforcer's beard. As lather routs law, Porgy warns the wielder of the razor not to "'cut off his nose. . . . This class of animals seldom have much to spare; and the loss of such a member would really disfigure the face terribly.'"[25]

Simms's melodramatic skirmishes work better in *Woodcraft* not only because Porgy is a more human hero but also because villains are more believable. This time, the author cannot fall back on the cant that men outside civilization, and especially inferior races, incline toward barbarism. The scene is at last inside civilized parish life, which must generate its own malignity. To Simms's credit, even though he was writing an answer to *Uncle Tom's Cabin,* he rooted his evil men in flaws of his best society.[26] Just as the pre-Revolutionary War Porgy was the Carolina planter as dissolute wastrel, so the slave-stealing nonslaveholder is the resentful neighbor as steaming plebeian. Although squatting for free on the Widow Eveleigh's land and the object of her cheery charity, the ragged villain resents her and her class's wealthy condescension. He would steal slaves who call him, though a white man, trashy "buckrah."

The jealous squatter's boss in criminality, the mortgage-holding, nouveau-riche capitalist, is no less believable. In Simms's South Carolina, new men were snapping up estates of dissolute old families. Simms grieved with every snap. Restless, cultureless, rootless souls like his father might seize everything vital from genteel souls like his grandmother. Cosmopolitan gentlemen such as Porgy have to summon dynamism about more than eating. Otherwise, contemptible money-grubbers above and corrosive beggars below will consume gentlemen's estates like so many sandwiches.

The Widow Eveleigh, who summons more consistent energy than does the sporadically heroic Porgy, is as much an improvement over Simms's previous ladies as *Woodcraft*'s villains are improvements over previous frontier scoundrels. Nothing about this high-toned battler suggests pale angels who faint before rattlesnakes. She is intelligent and brave, as manly as any man. She is a surprising creation for an author who has written over two dozen novels, preaching that everything, especially docile ladies, must be frozen in hierarchical niches.

The very act of writing a domestic novel, one suspects, forced Simms to transcend Charleston's stereotypic, angelic lady, whose passivity would deaden the tale. Charleston's reality served Simms's literary needs better than did the cardboard myth. Ladies in Simms's lowcountry were willful in the household, if not as fully as in the ideal Yankee home, still too powerfully for haughty southern patriarchs' comfort. Simms knew all about tensions in houses such as Robert R. F. W. Allston's and Thomas Chaplin's. Much of the plot of *Woodcraft* concerns whether an independently powerful lady such as Eveleigh and an independently powerful patriarch such as Porgy should marry at all. With the creation of such a lady, Simms at last broke free from at least one lowcountry cant.

He could not go farther, which meant he could not go far enough. Porgy's homecoming, especially as an answer to *Uncle Tom's Cabin,* involves not just saving the hearth and chosing a lady but also ruling slaves. Here Simms fell back on his worst stereotypes. Once again one of those please-don't-free-me-Massa scenes epitomizes Simms's rendition of Cuffee. Porgy's favorite slave Tom (who is, of course, the fat patriarch's cook!) announces that "'I no guine to be free no way yo kin fix it; so, maussa, don't you bodder me wid dis nonsense t'ing 'bout free papers.'" A "'free nigger,'" as Tom puts it, "'no hab any body for'" finding him food; "'he's a d—n pretickilar great big fool, for let he maussa off from keep 'em.'"[27]

No slave in *Woodcraft* lets Porgy off from keeping 'em. When Massa leaves for war, darkies run off and hide from the patriarch's enemies. They race adoringly back when he returns, screaming, "'De Lord be praise, maussa, you come home at las'!'" Thereafter, announces Simms, "the negroes, glad once more to find themselves" with home, and "provisions, and the protection of a white man," slaved "with a hearty will and cheerfulness which have amply made up for lost time." Anyone who finds that incredible, says the novelist, does not "know what a Carolina plantation is—one of the old school—one of ancient settlement—where father and son, for successive generations, have grown up, indissolubly mingled with the proprietor and his children for a hundred years."[28]

Simms knew better. At the very time he wrote this orthodox pablum, his best friend, James Hammond, was befouling a marriage by indulging in particularly rank miscegenation, a license Simms loathed and had publicly pronounced disgustingly common.[29] The responsible patriarch had to avoid temptation, while blending terrorizing and cajoling with a subtle hand. Simms, the writer who would teach his class its duty, could write realistically about every aspect of patriarchal obligations, save the most important duty.

Simms proceeded to do the next best thing: He relegated cardboard slaves to the sidelines. With the Domestic Institution usually offstage, this novel about return to responsible domesticity usually centers on the Widow's and Porgy's campaign to save Porgy's home and slaves from villains. That objective accomplished, the domestic problem involves whether hero and heroine should marry. Here again, Simms's unorthodoxy could only go so far. The fiercely independent woman could be imagined—but not imagined happily wed. The Widow turns down Porgy "'because I have a certain spice of independence in my temper,'" while you "'have a certain imperative mood which would make you very despotic, should you meet with resistance.'" Porgy, who had been attracted to but also repelled by women "'quite too masculine,'" gladly accepts her diagnosis. He is also just as glad when another possible wife, this time quite too feminine, chooses someone else.[30]

With slaves offstage and Porgy's home without a lady, the expatriate returned happily settles for an alternative domestic institution. He resurrects his home away from home. He renews campfire camaraderie. His permanent family will be his male retinue of wilderness warriors.

This bizarre conclusion is revealingly appropriate. From the beginning of the novel, Porgy laments that his flight toward responsibility in the backcountry is over, that he may not be successfully responsible back home. From the beginning of his career, Simms had written about the civilized man learning to be responsibly civil in the wilds. He had thus avoided problems of writing a domestic novel within Charleston's domestic stereotypes. When this anti-expatriate finally wrote about the expatriate returned, the domestic problem was finessed. Skills at woodcraft rescue slaves from the villains, stall off the sheriff, and ultimately supply a model of the ideal domestic home. A house not for children or for slaves but for woodcrafters is saved.

This conclusion can lead to no new beginnings. Parish civilization has been ennobled without noble men and women joining; no noble heirs can follow. "Charleston," the father had said long ago, *"I know it only as a place of tombs."* His anti-expatriate son, having at last written something other than fables about temporary expatriation, left returned expatriates with nothing ahead but the grave. *Woodcraft's* climax eerily echoes the tortured elegy of yet another South Carolina expatriate intellectual, the essayist and classicist Hugh Swinton Legaré: "We are (I am sure) the *last* of the *race* of South Carolina; I see nothing before us but decay and downfall."[31]

Still, the father had been wrong that in decaying Charleston, Simms's talents would "be poured out like water on the sands." Simms vividly rendered everything that made Carolina dangerously important: its ache for energy to save its elegance, its fright about and disgust for a New South that was depopulating the Old, its urge for and apprehension about a nonrevolutionary revolution, its determination to model an anti-egalitarian future on an aristocratic past.[32]

A failed literary effort is also worth remembering when its very failures occur after interesting struggles and for important reasons. In *Woodcraft,* his supreme effort to evade hometown rigidities and home-exaggerated melodrama, Simms was almost himself the desperate woodsman, dodging obstacles he never before had evaded, until the lowcountry brush became too thick for a loyal son to handle. If he finally was trapped into stereotype and had to settle for sterility, his downfall illuminated that elegant despair at the core of a cultural moment he could not be dragged away from personifying.

– 5 –

Posterity enjoys Mary Boykin Chesnut's diary more than William Gilmore Simms's novels. Chesnut's journal of the Civil War years is less stereotyped than anything Simms or any other antebellum Carolina male wrote—a fitting accomplishment for a female who had her hates for patriarchal stereotypes. But the Chesnut diary, if the apex of Carolina literary achievements, also illuminates the limits of that achievement. Mrs. Chesnut strikes fleetingly, then retreats. She describes supremely, then spreads trivia. She announces bold position, then settles for pampered indolence. She could have been reviewing her book when lampooning Carolina masters. "Our planters," she observes, are "impulsive but hard to keep moving. They are wonderful for a spurt." They then "like to rest."[33]

Mary Chesnut did not live to publish her fitful diary. A decade and more after her death, editors found the manuscript and published part of it. The published segment was long thought to be Chesnut's diary as she wrote it during the Civil War. The historian C. Vann Woodward has recently taught us, however, that the published diary was actually a rewrite of a Civil War journal. In the 1870s, and again in the 1880s, Chesnut reworked her diary of the 1860s.

She aspired to bring people alive, to make events vital, to give us after the fact a Civil War epic.[34]

While Simms chose the form of the Sir Walter Scott epic romance, Chesnut chose the mode of the drawing-room drama. For a frustrated female novelist in the nineteenth century, tea party tales came naturally. The greatest women novelists, such as Jane Austen and George Eliot, were turning sagas of barbs and surprises in the drawing room into witty and ironic recreations.

Mary Chesnut's experience lent credence to Jane Austen's settings. This South Carolina belle, offspring of one wealthy upcountry clan, had married into another. Her husband, James Chesnut, Jr., was United States senator from South Carolina at the time of secession. While the husband drove ahead in politics and grew richer driving slaves, he expected his petticoated belle to be queen of his parlor. Because of her husband's position, the wife had access to tea parties in Charleston when Civil War broke out and to Mrs. Jefferson Davis's salons during the war. To this good fortune in being at the right parties at the right times, Chesnut added an Austen-Eliot understanding of partygoers' ironic foibles. A superb capacity to spin a phrase, when added to personal experience with materials of a great literary convention, gave Chesnut every chance to fashion a drawing-room epic.

Chesnut draws readers straight into upper-class parlors, with "so many pleasant people, so much good talk . . . talk, talk, talk, a la Carolina du Sud." The gentle folk eat "goods the Gods provide," from "English grouse" to "venison from the west" to "salmon from the Lakes." Feasters are so "*well* bred, nobody disagreeable, nobody unkind, all clever, some remarkably so." Ladies, even married ones, flirt with other ladies' husbands. Husbands, even nonflirters, speculate on whose wife is most fetching. Latest rumors on whose child might have been born a trifle quick after nuptials are eagerly pursued. Latest information on which belle will choose which cavalier is hungrily consumed. Mary Chesnut's is "such a busy, happy life—so many friends, . . . so clever, so charming."[35] Chesnut's merry aristocrats usually have all the stereotypic beatitude of Simms's good guys—and of Allston's most harmless landscapes.

Still, Chesnut's best scenes can be sublime, precisely because the diarist, unlike Simms but like Allston, sometimes squarely faces the most dismal message of her materials. Just beyond "such beautiful grounds, . . . such delightful dinners, such pleasant drives, such jolly talks" lies "this horrid war" which "poisons everything." Ugly battlefront news pours in on ladies pouring tea, tidings of arms annihilated, legs lost, brains battered. "Those poor boys of between 18 and 20 years of age," cringes Chesnut, "—Haynes, Trezevants, Taylors, Rhetts, etc., etc.—they are washed away, literally, in a tide of blood. There is nothing to show they were ever on earth."[36]

Chesnut's sustained contrast of gossipy chatter and grotesque war, however, highlights her inability to sustain a viewpoint on the bloodletting culture. For a sentence, a paragraph, a page, the Carolina belle exposes upper-class foundations with a sensitivity worthy of Jane Austen and an honesty Simms could not muster. She then lapses for pages into celebration of the society she has just savaged.

A couple of times, for example, Mary Chesnut reveals her so-called friends, family slaves, to be perhaps not so friendly. Her darkies go on serving as if oblivious to the war outside. They apparently care nothing about whether General Sherman will bring freedom. But their mistress occasionally wonders what lies behind the "shiny black mask."[37] Simms's novels never hint that Cuffeeness might be a façade.

Chesnut could not, however, sustain an epic built on slaveowners not knowing what they most had to know. Like William Gilmore Simms, she needed to believe that Cuffees' cheery docility was no mask. So Mary Chesnut's slaves characteristically emerge as true-blue serviles—and less interesting than on the couple of occasions when the writer calls blacks "sphinxs."[38]

Again, for three wonderful pages, Chesnut's journal recreates a slave insurrection. Her description of slaves' slaying of her cousin, Mary Witherspoon, is as vivid a vignette as any episode in Herman Melville's *Benito Cereno.* Mrs. Witherspoon, like the master in Melville's masterful tale of slave insurrection, emerges as the permissive slaveholder who could not believe pampered servants would murder. When the overly permissive lady suddenly removes privileges, Cuffees lash back, slaughtering Missus in her bed. Mrs. Witherspoon's corpse is found the next day, her white face and neck "black and blue," her sheets and nightgown saturated with gore. "We ought to be grateful that any of us is alive," cringes the spinner of this "bloody story that haunts me night and day."[39]

Then, as swiftly as it came, the cringing vanishes. Mary Chesnut regains her nerve. She announces that she will "go down on the plantation tomorrow and stay there," even without a "white person in twenty miles." Why should she trust blacks she just called "horrid brutes—savages, monsters"? Because "my Molly and half a dozen others that I *know* [emphasis hers]—and all the rest I *believe* [emphasis mine]—would keep me as safe as I should be in the Tower of London."[40] Betwixt that *know* and that *believe* lay the patriarchal charade. But the great theme, never seen in a Simms novel, vanishes from Chesnut's pages as if Mary Witherspoon had never appeared.

Again, Chesnut's occasional passages on slavery's immorality rival anything in antislavery literature. She particularly comes down hard, momentarily, on miscegenation. She suspects her father-in-law of fathering several whitish blacks. "God forgive us," she winces, "but ours is a *monstrous* system."[41] Simms thought miscegenation was monstrous too—but the monster never appears in his novels.

The horror drops off Chesnut's pages too quickly. Delight in slavery's benefits replaces outrage at slavery's travesties. "Those old gray-haired darkies and their automatic noiseless perfection of training," praises the lady, "one does miss that sort of thing. Your own servants think for you, they know your ways and your wants"; they assure "all responsibility" for your "ease and well being."[42] No proslavery writer—not even William Gilmore Simms—said it better.

Again, in several marvelous passages, Mrs. Chesnut sounds faintly like a modern feminist ripping at patriarchal dictators. She writhes under Mr. Chesnut's orders. He demands that she play the empty-headed charmer. He forces her to live in places she finds grotesquely uncharming. "No slave," she storms, is as enslaved "as a wife."[43] Simms's Widow Eveleigh could have written that.

But just as Chesnut, occasional hater of slavery, was too implicated in slave-holding mentalities to be much a part of antislavery, so the diarist who occasionally blasted women's place was too implicated in male-made ideologies to be confused with Eveleigh. Mary Chesnut, loather of phony pedestals, made herself the wittiest gossiper and charmer in her diary. The Widow Eveleigh, because fearing just such an empty fate, refused the imperious Porgy.

And then again, in one fine passage, Chesnut denounces as ridiculous all her wifely chatter. "Flirtation," she scoffs, "the business of society," is but "playing at lovemaking. It begins in vanity—it ends in vanity. It is spurred on by idleness and a want of any other excitement." It seems to burn fingers but breaks no hearts. "Each party in a flirtation has secured a sympathetic listener to whom they can talk of themselves." They can brag incessantly to someone "who for the time admires them exclusively. . . . It is a pleasant but very foolish game—and so to bed."[44]

This ironic theme is worthy of Jane Austen: a tea party society lovingly depicted, only to be relentlessly revealed as deceptive and worse. But Mary Chesnut lacked the relentlessly ironic point of view of a Jane Austen. Mary Chesnut's diary reveals her getting up the next day, to give her life over again to the not very pleasant game she had fleetingly despised.

When drawing other characters, as in presentation of her viewpoint, Chesnut displays finer ability to render subtleties in a paragraph than to sustain insight throughout a book. Her few lines on her aging father-in-law, for example, are a glorious snapshot of the southern patriarch. She describes old man Chesnut as "partly patriarch, partly grand seigneur," wholly "a splendid wreck." Blinded now physically, he had long been blinded spiritually by his chauvinism, his materialism, his arrogance. The aging dictator does not "believe anybody," will not "trust anybody," would never "leave me alone in his wine cellar." Underneath his "smooth exterior" lies "the grip of a tyrant whose will has never been crossed."

Mary Chesnut adds that "in this house" reside "three very distinct" tyrants—"three generations of gentlemen, each utterly different from the other—father, son, grandson."[45] Here is a theme of family declension worthy of the novelist's extended portraiture. With such material and with honesty about miscegenation, William Faulkner would transcend William Gilmore Simms's achievement.

Mary Chesnut, however, could do no more than announce the road past Simms. Her conception requires three generations of characters to become ever more clearly different as tragedy drives towards resolution. But her old man Chesnut, marvelously introduced, never progresses beyond the introduction. The aging tyrant's son, Mary Chesnut's husband, wanders in and out of the diary, vague except for a male tyranny akin to the old man's. The third generation emerges vaguer still. The only relentlessly clear Chesnut is Mary Chesnut's wandering self.

Characters who play bit parts are even more faceless. Gentlefolk step in and out of Mary Chesnut's parlors, their names dropped, backgrounds mysterious, missions obscure. So too, when telling of her reading, Chesnut rarely describes how books are molding her vision. She instead constantly drops in unidentified textual fragments. Between bit characters left to be identified and bit quotes left to be given a context, Chesnut's revision, to be wholly intelligible, demands C. Vann Woodward's twentieth-century editorial annotation.

In another of her occasional superb phrases, Chesnut describes South Carolinians as all too "ready to begin a fight—but then, we flap our wings and crow so."[46] Her revised journal does flap and crow so. The fleeting abolitionist must swallow antislavery and enjoy slaveholding. The not very feminist female must swallow feminism and tensely tolerate her man. The would-be heroine must preside over a tea party not worthy of heroes. The would-be novelist must leave behind a revised journal, with people and phrases strewn around as if in an unrevised diary. In addition to its brilliant moments, Chesnut's revised journal is valuable for inadvertently displaying a writer imprisoned in nervous dissatisfaction.

A comparison of Washington Allston, William Gilmore Simms, and Mary Boykin Chesnut is instructive on the Carolina cultural predicament. Simms, working within South Carolina in the slaveholder's era, had more trouble transcending orthodoxy. Allston and Chesnut, when removed from antebellum Carolina, better escaped stereotypical artistry. Allston left for the North and Europe. Chesnut's revision occurred two decades after emancipation.

Even at a distance, neither relentlessly explored Carolina's cultural identity. Allston's several dark and gloomy paintings, so different from his hundreds of un-Carolinian oeuvres, remind one of Chesnut's occasional relentless probings, so different from her hundreds of pages of restless commonplaces. Slaveholders' world, supposedly freeing master to be creative, usually so buried artists under cultural stereotype as to stymie creativity. Nonstereotyped art almost required exile, in the manner of Washington Allston. Then the Carolina genius could brilliantly throw perspective on other worlds and other traditions.

– 6 –

Chesnut's frustration with creativity unfulfilled no less hung over Carolina's male essayists. Gentlemen, like the lady on the pedestal, could climb up to rarified drawing rooms and consume rare roasts and exchange rich witticisms. But they could only talk talk talk about what had already been said. "We are," despaired Charleston's most cosmopolitan dandy, "the dullest, dreariest ... middle class respectables that ... ever disappointed their stomachs over a French bill of fare."[47]

Middle class! No wonder Carolina's aristocratic pretenses sounded suspect to Carolinians themselves. Nowhere were suspicions more evident than in the Charleston Renaissance's climactic endeavor. *Russell's Magazine,* begun with high hopes in the mid-'50s, had everything South Carolina society could muster on its side. The sheet was published out of John Russell's emporium, Charleston's finest book store. Its contributors included William Gilmore Simms, Carolina's storyteller, and Paul Hamilton Hayne and Henry Timrod, her poets. *Russell's* editor sought a climax of Carolina creativity.[48]

Russell's became instead an orgy of self-flagellation. Hidden amidst heavy articles and dreary poems are gems of lamentation. Simms and Timrod were at their best on how badly the South received Simms. Timrod proclaimed Carolinians "a provincial and not a highly cultivated people." Carolina's poet despaired "of ever seeing within our borders a literature of such depth and comprehensiveness as will ensure it the respect of other countries." Charleston cultivation, Timrod added, consisted of "amateur critics," dedicated to "truism" gleaned "from the rubbish of seventy years agone, and above all to persuade each other that together they constitute a society not much inferior to that in which figured Burke and Johnson, Goldsmith and Sir Joshua."[49]

We cannot escape cultural inferiority, declared the lowcountry's Frederick Porcher in *Russell's* most stunning essays, not while "the drag of provincialism" is "forever clinging to our wheels."[50] Porcher portrayed a country life given over to idleness and "ennui." Trips to Charleston comprised a search for something positive "to think of on my return to solitude."

Porcher accused "many" compatriots of "mourning in secret over the dismal future which awaits us." He lamented "that many of our people are giving cause to our northern enemies to suspect that we are really afraid": afraid of slave insurrection, afraid of economic collapse, afraid of abolitionist attack. Porcher deplored bad managing planters, who both denounced abolitionists the most and displayed the worst southern weakness. "A bad planter is a common nuisance. His negroes are disorderly, ill-cared for, discontented, and rebellious; his estate is unproductive, his character degenerates; and the lower he finds himself falling, the more loudly does he call on the memory of his illustrious ancestors."

Ineffective owners blamed the mess on overseers. Nonsense. Good generals demand good lieutenants. "Look inwards. If your overseer is a sloth, depend upon it, you are a ninny." With entrepreneurial ninnies abounding in South Carolina, Porcher wondered "what will become of our country" (i.e. his state!). What will transpire after "all the bad planters are broken? . . . We are degenerating. We are becoming daily more and more closely bound to the North" and thus "more a dependent province."

Cultural provincialism, continued Porcher, augments economic provincialism. "Southern thought finds no utterance among us; nay, is suspiciously received." We vacation in the North, educate children in the North, import teachers and books from the North. "Our whole fabric of society is based upon slave institutions, and yet our conventional language is drawn from scenes totally at variance." Thus when Northerners urge that "all of life is an unceasing struggle after more" and that "to stand still is to die," we tend to agree. Judging ourselves by their standards, we regard "with something like humiliation our own shortcomings." A Northerner attributes our lack of progress "to the blighting effects of slavery. We are not sure that he is wrong."

Provincials of an alien metropolis, concluded Porcher, are inevitably distastefully defensive. "Our peculiarities . . . have to be defended, excused, ridiculed, pardoned." The independent gentleman should be patient, considerate, forebearing. We instead sound impatient, inconsiderate, overbearing when "perpetually aiming to square" outsiders' "impracticable philosophy" with our practical institution. We can never have "repose," we will ever be "dependents and inferiors," we will always be unhappy until we can make our own world.

- 7 -

Frederick Porcher's unhappiness, so much like Mary Chesnut's, was not with an economy, not even with a culture, but ultimately with a personality—with whether the South Carolinian was a worthwhile creature. That concern about self-worth was the most depressing cloud hanging over Mrs. Chesnut's drawing rooms. Gentlemen supposed to be unrumpled and unruffled felt themselves to be too much on edge, too much prone to lose tempers against outsiders and, worse, against each other. Carolinians who stood for calm command stamped and shrieked when attacked, stormed and stammered when insulted.

They sounded like the old man despairing that he could never again be all that he was. Our ancestors, William Henry Trescot told the South Carolina Historical Society in 1859, were serene, balanced, courteous. The prototype was William Lowndes—confident, calm, no vanity, no noise, in harmony with himself and with others.

Trescot had "not the heart to say we have lost" those "types of characters." But "I fear we are in great danger of losing" them. The constant necessity of "egotistical vindication . . . has fretted the calm old temper, irritated that once famous courtesy, and unbalanced that generous impartiality." We are becoming notorious for "fierce impatience," for "rude and unnatural arrogance." for "petulant suspicion" and "noisy boastfulness."[51]

Francis Pickens, South Carolina's governor during secession, also deplored the end of "those pure and simple days" when "manners and character," when "honor and elegance," when "whatever was lofty and intellectual commanded the admiration of South Carolina." Where once the gentry was all "joyous laugh" and "noble and disinterested friendship," now "political shuffling and management" and "mean devotion to money" drag us down. "May God in his mercy avert it!!" May South Carolinians, through revolution, regain themselves.[52]

- 8 -

There spoke the side of the South Carolina personality despairing over a fall from a romanticized old grace. That failing side of Carolina character, because more complicated, requires lengthier explanation than the simple soaring side. But South Carolinians would never have been such haughty revolutionaries without their scorn for lessers' failures. They were sick about their weaknesses and desperate about their doubts not least because they believed that their encrusted aristocratic hauteur could alone reconcile slavery and republicanism.

They half-suspected they were partly phony Old Englishmen at the mercy of the nouveau century. They half-believed they were stalwart old republicans providentially destined to force mobocracy backward. They were half-cocky about consolidating the old. They half-despaired about battling the new. Somewhere in the swings between one of the most debilitating inferiority complexes in nineteenth-century America and one of the most soaring superiority complexes any ruling class will ever develop lay that appalling eccentric, the South Carolina would-be revolutionary.

Revolution, revolution, revolution, how the beloved word did delight the tongue. With revolution, the fraction of the oldest South still considering slavery indispensable might control Chesapeake Bay apologists. By leading a revolution, the bit of the Lower South hemorrhaging away folk might channel southwestern migrants' energy. Through revolution, Carolina might halt its decline, ascend to new leadership, bring its slipping synthesis between English and American values to aristocratic stability.

But revolution, revolution, revolution, how these reactionaries were terrified of that word. Revolution stood for disastrous civil war unless all those other Southerners they despised and who despised them came to their rescue. Revolution stood for black "barbarians" "Africanizing" the swamps. Revolution stood for Denmark Vesey and Rola Bennett raping and massacring inside Mrs. Chesnut's drawing rooms. Revolution stood for white nonslaveholders streaming down from the mountains to tear up the Constitution of 1808. Revolution stood for rebels as hopelessly at the mercy of the elements as Washington Allston's helpless Elijah. Unless these would-be revolutionaries carried off William Gilmore Simms's sort of nonrevolutionary revolution, they were finished, whether they revolted or not.

They were the least likely revolutionaries. They were the Southerners most likely to revolt. Their most important peculiarity, the final summing up of everything goading and debilitating them, was the anxiety of the gambler terrified of his obsession. They were proud sagging gentlemen desperate for a wild fling—and desperate never to dare anything wild at all.

CHAPTER 14

The First
Confrontation Crisis, I:
Calhoun versus Jackson

Without unpopular initiators, "popular revolutions" usually do not happen. Extreme spirits must strike first because "the people" seldom spontaneously revolt. Tom, Dick, and Harry characteristically prefer small comforts to defying firepower. Nor do the wealthy and powerful often seek out a war which, if lost, must terminate wealth, power, perhaps life itself.

Widespread revolution usually grows out of a narrow faction's seizure of a building, a town, or whatever. The aggressors issue non-negotiable demands. Such demands, if unmet, can lead to bullets. Non-extremists, who would have compromised much to avoid war, are reduced to uncompromising choice. They must decide whether to join or shoot their own zealots.

"Popular revolution," because the populace must be partially goaded to it, requires a delicate dialect between initiators and stragglers. Ultras must be different enough from moderates to believe that compromise politics will destroy everything worthwhile. Moderates must also be close enough to extremists to believe that shooting down zealots will slay too much of value. When moderates are too alienated from extremists, rebellion will be abortive. But when sluggards support revolutionaries, the revolution may become a historic occasion. Historians may even dub it a "spontaneous popular uprising."

Witness the movement towards southern revolution. Secession might never have occurred—and certainly not in 1860–1— if a majority of white Southerners "spontaneously" had had to revolt. Revolution could thrive only when extremists mustered the right nerve to gamble at the right time on confrontation politics. The search for that time and nerve came down to dialogues within South Carolina and between South Carolinians and other Southerners. These dialogues, ultimately productive of "popular revolution," had a long history. They began with South Carolinians' uneasiness about precipitating and relief at escaping their first confrontation situation: the so-called Nullification Controversy of 1832–3.

– 1 –

Throughout the 1820s, the fury necessary to dare a confrontation had been swelling in South Carolina. The Missouri Controversy and the Panic of 1819 ushered in the decade. These simultaneous crises magnified each other's horror. The North's attack on the Slavepower and the economic depression's blow to southern planters together made Carolinians feel besieged from all sides.

In the 1820s, proof multiplied that the Missouri Controversy foretold a movement of conscience throughout the nation and beyond. The Denmark Vesey Conspiracy of 1822 brought the North's speeches on Missouri home to slaves' cabins. The Ohio Resolutions of 1824 and the American Colonization Society petition of 1827 moved Conditional Termination into national politics. The movement to end slavery in the British West Indies made antislavery a trans-Atlantic phenomenon.

These trends early intersected to provoke South Carolina's first nullification of federal law.[1] Free black sailors, when their ships docked in Charleston, could visit the city's blacks. Apparently, some black foreigners, especially from Santo Domingo, encouraged Vesey conspirators in early 1822. Monday Gell, one of Denmark Vesey's prime lieutenants, confessed trying to contact the Santo Domingo government through black seamen.

In late 1822, the Carolina legislature enacted a cordon sanitaire. Black sailors were ordered jailed while their vessels docked in Charleston. When enforcement of this law lapsed, the South Carolina Association, a voluntary organization of wealthy Carolinians, insisted that foreign seamen be jailed, as the law prescribed.

Resulting imprisonments violated treaties between England and America, which gave sailors of both countries free access to each other's ports. England protested to American Secretary of State John Quincy Adams, who protested to South Carolina Governor John Wilson. Almost simultaneously, United States Supreme Court Justice William Johnson, himself a Carolinian, issued a federal circuit decision, declaring that Carolina's seaman law violated the national Constitution.

South Carolinians defiantly continued to jail black seamen. The "duty to guard against insubordination or insurrection," declared the Carolina Senate, is "paramount to all *laws,* all *treaties,* all *constitutions.*" A nullification crisis would have erupted then and there if national authorities had enforced Judge William Johnson's nullified decision. Instead, federal enforcers declined to make a "federal case" out of such a potentially Union-shattering situation. Extremists thus learned that minority veto could bring external saboteurs and internal "traitors" to heel on slavery-related matters.

Carolina victors felt too threatened to gloat over their successful nullification. Continued control required strength and confidence. The banking Panic of 1819 and the ensuing economic depression made Carolinians feel weak and vulnerable.

South Carolinians suffered more than most Americans from the aftermath of the 1819 fiscal crisis. No debtor, North or South, enjoyed the many post-panic years of contracted currency, scarce new financing, and low prices for staples, especially cotton. But in the Chesapeake, hard times, a renewed story, demanded renewal of old strategies. Lower tobacco prices called for more mixed farming and more exchanges of foodstuffs within self-sufficient neighborhoods. While neighborhood barter raised little cash, little coin was necessary. A half-century of bad times had not inspired speculative mortgages. Retrenchment and living off the land are the farmer's friend, so long as no banker demands pay-off in dollars.[2]

In new southwestern cotton belts, problems with paying newly swollen mortgages created demand for both lower federal taxes and a reformed banking system. Still, frontiersmen's problems were less acute and their political protests less desperate than in Carolina. Virgin land gave hard-pressed Southwesterners more leverage to forestall foreclosure. Higher yields on virgin acres could compensate for lower cotton prices.

Mortgage-ridden South Carolinians, raising cotton on debilitated soil, could less well fight back. As for Carolina rice planters, who received only slightly lower prices for their staples, they could not always withstand even light adverse pressure. The cycle of high living and poor management could spiral towards disaster when anything more went wrong. For the most financially troubled absentees, too much went wrong at the turn of the 1820s when coastal hurricanes wiped out several crops.[3]

As the 1820s progressed, escalating numbers of Carolinians, some in the low-country and many more in the upcountry, lost their land and/or moved to fresher southwestern turf. Some 56,000 whites left in the 1820s, and another 30,000 blacks were sold or taken away. Another 76,000 whites departed in the 1830s, with 57,000 blacks also leaving. A state with a little over 500,000 inhabitants lost over 200,000 slaves and capitalists in a terrible 20-year span.[4]

As Carolina rulers saw it, high federal protective tariffs added the final, fatal blow to their aging world's waning vitality. An alien ruling class, with a very different concern about economic vitality, demanded those tariffs. New England manufacturers feared that in a free international market, more advanced British manufacturers could forever undersell less productive American industrialists. But a high American tariff on imported goods would force importers to charge higher prices for non-American products. Then American manufacturers could undersell the foreign competition. Before long, claimed pro-tariff polemicists, American industry would boom, American jobs would increase, American productivity would soar, and American-made goods would cost less than English products had ever fetched.

Hard-pressed South Carolina planters found this long-run argument irrelevant. In the short run, they claimed, higher tariffs forced agriculturalists to pay ruinous prices for manufactured goods. Worse, argued cotton planters who were going broke in upcountry South Carolina, high tariffs devastated demand for raw cotton.

According to this enticingly simplistic theory, a 40% tariff on cotton finished goods led to a 40% higher price to consumers. With Americans having less money to spend after the Panic of 1819, so the argument went, 40% higher prices meant 40% less American sales. Forty percent less manufactured cotton cloth sold allegedly meant that cotton manufacturers purchased 40% less raw cotton, giving planters 40% less income.

Q.E.D.—supposedly. No matter that American consumers had to buy blankets and clothing, necessities all, whatever the price. No matter that English manufacturers hardly sold only to American consumers. You Carolinians are still "as persuaded as if you saw it," an opponent of radical action against the tariff lamented to constituents, "that the manufacturer actually invades your barns, and plunders you of 40 out of every 100 bales that you produce."[5]

This so-called Forty Bale theory turned high tariffs into vivid scapegoats. Neither excessive production on the Southwest's fresh soil nor inadequate yields on Carolina's exhausted turf caused the state's alarming decline and depopulation. Rather, the progressively higher tariffs of 1816, 1824, and 1828 hammered cotton prices down from a yearly average of 18 cents per pound in 1810–19 to 12 cents in 1820–9 and on down to 9 cents in 1830–2.

George McDuffie, a previously obscure congressman from Carolina's cotton-producing upcountry, turned himself into a folk hero by naming and popularizing the Forty Bale theory. McDuffie personified a world 40% disfigured. The anti-tariff agitator's appearance dated from the time when a bullet exploded against his spine in a duel. His body was left a mass of jangled nerves. Most of the time, he brooded by himself, hood pulled around him like a shroud, his frown forbidding even friends to approach.

But when he rose to denounce Carolina's enemies, his frame came alive with outrage. He shrieked. He kicked. He thumped. He spat. He seemed a revivalist in a death struggle with Satan. It was as if the monster tariff, not some malign bullet, had consigned the wounded congressman and limping constituents to an invalidism beyond enduring.[6]

Only the upcountry's other treasured cripple seemed more fanatical than McDuffie. Thomas Cooper, the hunched-over old man who was president of South Carolina College in Columbia, should have borne the title Professor of Revolution. He was the only Carolina revolutionary not reluctant at all, perhaps because he was the only antebellum Carolina leader not Carolina born and raised. Thomas Cooper had not come of age inside a conservative Atlantic seaboard civilization, in years when planters strove to keep the American Revolution unrevolutionary. Rather, Cooper had grown up in France, in years when zealots sought to escalate the French Revolution. Cooper had spent a stormy career in and out of jails on both sides of the Atlantic. He had come to crusty old Carolina, apparently the wrong place for a reckless hothead, at the right time, when tariff and colonization crises were simultaneously occurring. As head of the college and teacher of the senior class in moral philosophy, the experienced revolutionary could educate cautious young heirs into becoming gambling young rebels.[7]

This émigré from France first announced to the American nation that a revolution was brewing down South which might rival the French. We shall, he told an excited Columbia crowd in 1827, soon have "to calculate the value of the Union, and ask of what use to us is this most unequal alliance." The little old agitator stomped around the podium in the manner of McDuffie, bent over, hump back protruding, stabbing the Forty Bale robber with his bayonet of a cane. His historic "calculate the value" speech announced that crippled victims of Forty Bale robbers would calculate the cost of mobocracy.

By 1827, costs of being slave to King Numbers had come to seem exorbitant. Tariffs supposedly robbed and depopulated Mother Carolina. Congressional antislavery speeches allegedly stole the state's domestic peace. Fanatics disguised as African colonizationists would lull Southerners to sleep and diffuse away slaves. Not southwestern competition or exhausted soil or swollen mortgages caused gentlemen's vulnerability. Rather, a permanent majority was taxing away their capacity to endure.

In 1828, the so-called Tariff of Abominations tightened the majority's grasp. The tax on imported goods, set at around 25% in the Tariff of 1816 and raised to around 33% in the Tariff of 1824, now soared to 50%. This majority tyranny, many Carolinians thought, indicated that more than Justice William Johnson's liberation of black seamen must be nullified. Independent gentlemen needed permanent protection against King Numbers.

– 2 –

In 1828, the South Carolina legislature asked the state's best constitutional theorist, the Vice President of the United States, to explain how and why a state could nullify federal law. John C. Calhoun agreed, on condition that his involvement be kept secret. A year after Thomas Cooper informed the nation that South Carolina was calculating the value of the Union, the Carolina legislature, by endorsing Calhoun's anonymously written *Exposition and Protest,* announced that the state was calculating a nullification of national laws.[8]

Calhoun's argument for state veto stretched normal states' rights constitutional ideology to an abnormal extreme. All states' righters assumed that congressional majorities possessed only powers explicitly named in the Constitution. No constitutional clause specifically gave congressional majorities power to protect industry through taxes on imports or to use taxes to colonize and/or free slaves.

Nationalists found constitutional authority in Congress's power "to promote the general welfare." The Founding Fathers, so this expansive broad construction interpretation of the Constitution went, knew constitution-makers could not explicitly enumerate every object of law. Therefore, law-makers received broad mandate to pass anything in the "general welfare."

States' righters answered that a majority, if able to do anything under the guise of the general welfare, could do everything. Moreover, if the Founding

Fathers meant the general welfare clause to authorize everything, they would have specifically enumerated nothing. States' righters usually depended on the Supreme Court to nullify unconstitutional "general welfare" legislation.

Carolina extremists scoffed at that remedy. The majority's President appointed the Court. The majority's Senate approved the appointment. Some restraint on majority tyranny, a majority-controlled court!

Most states' righters called legal secession the remedy, should courts fail to declare general welfare edicts unlawful. State conventions, as limitless constitution-makers, had preceded and created the merely law-making, law-enforcing, and law-judging national agency, alias the federal government. Constitution-makers could legally, peacefully, and morally withdraw from a limited agency which no longer remained within constitutional limits. The people, in unlimited constitution-making state convention assembled, had the right to transfer their state's consent to be governed to another limited agency.

Calhoun transformed this state's rights argument for legally changing law-makers into a rationale for legally negating the law. The Vice President of the United States ridiculed other Americans' notion that the Supreme Court, highest judicial branch of a mere agency, had unlimited power to interpret the Constitution. A branch of a limited agency would then become unlimited constitution-maker. Calhoun urged instead that all branches of the limited agency, whether law-making or law-enforcing or law-judging, must bow when a state convention, as limitless constitution-maker, declared a law null and void because based on powers never granted.

Only other constitution-makers, continued Calhoun, could overrule one constitution-maker's judgement about what powers had been granted. One judge's restraining order can always be appealed to the full bench. After a state convention, acting as preliminary judge, declared it never had granted a power to the federal agency, three-fourths of the entire court, meaning three-fourths of other constitution-making state conventions, could grant the power by constitutional amendment. The overruled state convention could then refuse to consent to the newly revised Constitution. Legal secession could follow legal nullification.

But nullification, Calhoun claimed, remained the best hope to avert secession. Every major social interest in American society could control at least one state. If every state had to concur, all interests would concur—a *concurrent* majority, as Calhoun called it. A concurrent majority of all was by definition a disinterested government, continually possessing every minority's consent.

But a *numerical* majority preying on a numerical minority was interested tyranny. Numerical mobocracy would lead victimized minorities to withdraw their consent to be governed. Anarchy would ensue. Only nullification would save consent and, in the saving, prevent disaster.

Calhoun's critics answered that nullification would paralyze government and guarantee anarchy. If all states had to agree for the general government to do anything, the central authority could do nothing. Calhoun responded that nullification would paralyze not good government but bad politicians. State veto would kill federal taxes not fair to all, meaning most taxes. With excessive taxation ended, patronage-hungry politicians would lose interest in federal office. All interests, knowing a concurrent majority could pass only disinterested laws, would select disinterested representatives. Disinterested quest for the welfare of all would lead to compromise, beneficence, wisdom. America would retreat from the civic corruption of nineteenth-century spoilsmen to the civic virtue of eighteenth-century patriarchs.

The same old-fashioned assumptions lay behind Calhoun's answer to another criticism of his theory: that by protecting white slaveholders from majority attack, he would consolidate black enslavement. Calhoun rejoiced in that charge. He hoped state nullification would stop the federal government from overturning the social hierarchy. Blacks had no right to a freedom that would Africanize America. Property-less whites had no right to tax away gentlemen's property. The upper class had every right to veto the lower. Good paternalists must provide good government for all races.[9]

Calhoun's theory was a Carolina gem. It sought to stop the American slide towards mobocratic egalitarianism by resurrecting patriarchal direction. It sought to stop new tariffs from gutting an aging fragment of the ruling class by insisting that one state's rulers could negate everyone else. It sought to stop some future northern majority from abolishing slavery by giving the southern minority power to veto Yankee fanaticism. It sought to stop some future southern majority from passing colonization alias emancipation by giving Unconditional Perpetualists a veto over Conditional Terminators. It gave patriarchs drawn towards and scared of revolution a nonrevolutionary way to revitalize American Revolutionaries' version of republicanism. Above all else, by shrewdly reducing confrontation politics to a court issuing a judgement, John C. Calhoun touched the most sensitive nerve of his class so lightly as to become Mr. South Carolina forevermore.

– 3 –

Calhoun's actions were long as soothing as his theory. For three years after devising nullification, Calhoun sought to halt the remedy and hide his complicity in it. Instead of pushing minority veto, he sought to rally a numerical majority, thereby implicitly denying that minority veto was necessary.

Calhoun would spend the rest of his life confusing everyone, not least himself, by playing the majoritarian/anti-majoritarian game both ways. Never did he pursue alien strategies more obviously than in 1828. At the very time he was secretly dispatching his first nullification state paper, denouncing majority rule, he was also vice presidential candidate on an all-southern national ticket, seeking to win majority control.

The national presidential election of 1828 pitted Calhoun's running mate, Tennessee's Andrew Jackson, a large slaveholder who had erratically favored states' rights, against Massachusetts's John Quincy Adams, a closet abolitionist who had consistently favored a nationalistic regime. Jackson's opponent seemed to epitomize whatever antislavery tendency existed in the North. Before becoming President, John Quincy Adams had been the Secretary of State who, in the early 1820s, had called Carolina's Negro seamen law unconstitutional. During his 1824–8 presidency, the New Englander had proposed sending an American delegation to the Panama Congress of 1826. That gathering of American nations would have included, if the President had had his way, the United States and Haiti at the same conference table. That indirect recognition of a slave insurrectionists' nation was aborted only because Adams's diplomats failed to arrive at the conference on time.[10]

Adams's economic nationalism proved less abortive. The President envisioned large national taxes financing large national projects. Heavy taxation, in this pre-income-tax age, meant high tariffs on imports. The Tariff of Abominations of 1828, while bearing much Jacksonian input, carried Adams's signature and seemed symbolic of his policy. The President stood for a national government loaded with funds and looking for projects.

Where Adams rivaled his Secretary of State, Kentucky's Henry Clay, for the honor of most powerful nationalist in American life, Andrew Jackson, slayer of Indians and redcoats too, was the American popular idol after he won the Battle of New Orleans in 1815. Jackson, like Calhoun, was a slaveholder and a sometimes opponent of too much national government. With Calhoun second in command in a hopefully states' rights Jackson movement and Jackson in the lead in the nation's affections, South Carolina might triumph in no more extreme way than leading the numerical majority.

Calhoun here deployed the non-extremist strategy he would come back to and reject, come back to and reject, several times over his erratically extremist career. The case for consistent Carolina extremism was that no national majority, not even the southern-led Jackson coalition, would sufficiently protect slaveholding minorities. Calhoun sometimes thought that. But the South Carolinian also sometimes believed Jacksonians could save the South, especially if Calhoun became the Jacksonians' next President.

At these moments, Calhoun's strategy was no different than that of other Southern Jacksonians. Old Hickory's southern sympathizers believed they would give Jackson more votes than could the more nationalistic North. As a majority of the Jackson party, Southerners could wring concessions from their outnumbered northern allies. As the majority party within the nation, the Jackson coalition could force prosouthern legislation upon the anti-Jackson minority.

The election results of 1828 furthered southern hope of commanding the mainstream. Jackson, if ruled by those who primarily elected him President, would reign for the South. While Andrew Jackson won a slight 52.7% popular plurality north of slavery, John Quincy Adams won the free labor states' nod in the Electoral College, 74–73. The most anti-southern section of the North was the most anti-Jackson. John Quincy Adams swept all but one of New England's 51 electoral votes and 68.2% of its popular ballots.

Jackson negated Adams's northern Electoral College majority by securing all but nine of the South's 114 electoral votes and two-thirds of its popular votes. The deeper into the South, the more lopsided was Jackson's landslide. Jackson swept 86.3% of the Lower South's popular votes, 70.7% of the Middle South's, and 54.5% of the Border South's.

These electoral statistics illuminated how a southern minority might indeed command. The South possessed but 40% of the nation's electoral votes—seemingly a hopelessly minority share. Jackson secured 68% of the nation's electoral votes—obviously a potently effective share. And Southerners supplied 59% of Jackson's electoral votes—apparently enough to use his majority coalition to secure their minority triumph.

– 4 –

Jackson's disproportionately southern power base made the slaveholding Vice President seem the legitimate heir of the slaveholding President, assuming both Southerners held the same vision of southernness. Calhoun's and Jackson's many similarities lent that hope. Both worked slave gangs on early cotton frontiers. Calhoun, son of an upcountry cotton planter and representative of western Carolina, was the first dominant Carolina politician not from the Atlantic Coast. Jackson, son of a western wanderer and hero of the Middle South frontier, was the first non-seaboard politician to win the national presidency. Both leaders were of Scotch Irish descent. No leader of such descent had previously predominated in South Carolina or presided in the White House.[11]

Both Southerners came to dominance as wartime nationalists. While Calhoun gained fame as a pre-War of 1812 War Hawk, Jackson secured popularity by winning the great battle of the war. Both Southerners, distressed by American wartime weakness, favored somewhat stronger national government after the war. Calhoun shored up the national army as Secretary of War, while Jackson used part of that army to go after Florida Indians allegedly conspiring with the English.

Both were disillusioned with nationalistic buildup after foreign dangers dissolved and economic disasters struck. In the 1820s, with hard times afflicting planters in both Tennessee and South Carolina, they coalesced against Adams. Having traveled parallel paths from the frontier slavocracy to leadership in a South-induced national administration, these two members of the southern ruling class might perpetuate their class's world view—if their class shared a world view.

– 5 –

Their class did not. The commonplace conception that Jackson and Calhoun fought over tea party punctilio obscures the planters' showdown that did occur. For Jackson and Calhoun, the shared fact of slaveholding was not enough. Their conceptions of masters' right to rule and their method of ruling were as distant as South Carolina was from Tennessee.

The conflict between their views centered on different reconciliations of slavery and republicanism. Jackson, race-obsessed authoritarian, believed upperclass control must end at the color line. In the style of the new Southwest, he aimed at institutionalizing classic herrenvolk democracy: both the complete equality of white men and the absolute superiority of whites over non-whites. His was the new-style American egalitarian republicanism: all whites are superior, no white is dependent, presumptuous elites spread civic vice.

Calhoun, while no less a racist, still believed the best men must govern all races. In the manner of the aging Southeast, he aimed at consolidating classic elitist republicanism: the rule of independent patriarchs in Washington, on plantations, everywhere humans lived. His was the old-style American republicanism: independent gentlemen must impose civil virtue from above, lest demagogues delude dependents below.

The difference between their versions of republicanism began where they grew up, on different slaveholding frontiers. Calhoun's father was an established planter in the late eighteenth-century South Carolina backcountry. The elder Calhoun, like many patriarchs in the newly-old section, came to share coastal squires' assumptions. Père Calhoun's belief that independent gentlemen must save civic virtue was the republican mentality which would, in 1808, bring western and eastern Carolina gentries to concur on an aristocratic state constitution.

Jackson's father, in contrast, wandered over Virginia frontiers. The elder Jackson's habitat was mountains removed from established elites. Père Jackson's hatred of aristocratic power was the sort which would, in 1829, bring western Virginians to war against elitist republicanism.

John C. Calhoun received an education fit for an imperial ruler. He was taught Federalist verities in old New England, at Connecticut's Yale College and at Litchfield Law School. Andrew Jackson, in contrast, taught himself to conquer egalitarian frontiers. He read law in spare moments in frontier offices.

Their brides were as different as their educations. Jackson came to the characteristic frontier alliance with his unpresuming matron, the undereducated, pipe-smoking Aunt Rachel. Calhoun made the appropriate upcountry marriage with a regal lowcountry heiress, the refined, haughty Floride Calhoun. Mr. and Mrs. Jackson found Mrs. Calhoun's imperiousness towards other whites insufferable.

Andrew Jackson had captured American and especially southern imaginations because he personified racially selective imperiousness. He first came to national and to southern prominence as the racist who controlled Indians. He no more would spare the gun to gain hegemony over reds than he would spare the lash to consolidate control of blacks. Contrary to legend, Andrew Jackson did not believe the best Indian was a dead Indian. This American soldier who deported whole tribes adopted and raised an Indian son. This President who removed Indians from white lands sent missionaries onto reservations to raise red inferiors towards white standards. This slaveholder who made a fortune exploiting black laborers dismissed overly exploitative overseers. Jackson would live up to the white man's paternalistic burden, by teaching lesser races if he could, by brandishing the pistol if he must.[12]

Governing white men involved neither pistols nor paternalism. Jackson's was the typical southwestern inclination to avoid any hint that whites were "niggers." To be recipient of operation uplift, even if the uplifter was a Great White Father, was to be inferior. Jackson would allow no one to patronize *him*. Nor would he govern as if any adult white male needed a father. By personifying the New South's racially selective egalitarianism, Jackson made himself the most important Southerner after Jefferson—and the natural enemy of all Southerners, such as Calhoun, who thought that in the new century no less than in the old, Jefferson's natural aristocracy must command whites as well as blacks.

– 6 –

The difference between the President and Vice President was there for all to see—and remains for visitors still to experience—at their two homes. Calhoun's Fort Hill and Jackson's Hermitage were the two most famous southern estates after Jefferson's Monticello. The three, taken together, sum up wither this class was tending. Monticello's fake windows evoke the eighteenth-century patriarch who would camouflage pretensions from nineteenth-century egalitarians. Nothing, in contrast, seems camouflaged about Jackson's and Calhoun's elaborate Greek-style mansions. Both white façades epitomized white men who forced black men to raise white cotton.

But two contrasting out-buildings gave away the difference between Jackson and Calhoun—and the divergent paths their Souths took from Monticello. Both the Tennessean and the Carolinian maintained lesser structures near sumptuous dwellings. Jackson's ex-log cabin was symbol of the egalitarian ascending. Calhoun's white clapboard office was headquarters for the elitist presiding.

Calhoun loved to come home to the detached office, with its columned portico out front. Here, alone and apart, the isolated patriarch born to wealth and power wrote the famous state papers on why King Numbers was a fright. At Jackson's Hermitage, in contrast, a frontiersman worshipful of King Numbers maintained no special cubicle. Jackson's former house was a record of everyman growing richer.

When first developing his sprawling Hermitage plantation, Jackson had lived in a log cabin. As he became more affluent, the cabin became part of a conglomerate. Breezeways connected the original dwelling to other cabins; and the whole affair was covered with white boards. The hybrid house looked like lower-class huts stitched into an upper-middle-class residence.

As Jackson grew still richer, he started over on a new dwelling. Once again, step by step, the building's growth kept pace with the owner's ascension. Eventually, the classic patriarch's white mansion emerged.

But the Hermitage's proud owner loved to show visitors the connected log cabins where he had lived when he was poorer but the same fine fellow. Andrew Jackson relished a soldier's memories of humble marches over exhausting frontiers. He cherished the image of himself clambering down from Duke, his famed bright bay, to hobble on bleeding feet, shoulder to shoulder with fellow whites.

Two of Jackson's original log cabins, shorn by time of their subsequently added middle-class trappings, as they appeared in a photograph of the 1890s. Courtesy, Ladies' Hermitage Association, Hermitage, Tennessee.

His former house bore homage to the less-than-equal who became more-than-equal but who still retained the persona of the leader no better or worse than other whites.

The impact of Jackson's presence and personality was as different from Calhoun's as the abstracted philosopher's office was from the ex-yeoman's abandoned cabins. Both planters had Scotch Irishmen's long, narrow faces and outdoorsmen's long, vigorous strides. But Jackson's statuesqueness was more earthy, more physically threatening. He gloried in passionate intuitions. His temper tantrums were notorious. He was ever thundering that BY THE ETERNAL he would hang them.

One legendary duel epitomized why he was known as gritty everyman. Jackson decided to dare his opponent to kill him with the one shot allowed. After the bullet had missed or entered Jackson's body, Old Hickory planned to measure his man and gun him down. The opponent's bullet ripped into Jackson's chest. Old Hickory, jamming one hand into the gaping wound, cooly aimed, fired, killed. "I should have hit him if he had shot me through the brain," gasped this creature of mud and blood as he staggered off the field.[13]

When Jackson came to the nation's capital in the early 1820s as United States senator and aspirant for the White House, the Washington establishment expected some mud-splattered warrior. Ladies and gentlemen found instead

Calhoun's columned study building, as seen from the columned porch of his Fort Hill mansion. Courtesy, Clemson University, Clemson, South Carolina.

that Jackson's upper-class manner was impeccable. He had learned to ape wealthy gentlemen without learning to be arrogant. He deployed no seer's superiority. His conversation was no soliloquy. Others would write his state papers. His genius (weakness?) was his faith that his intuitions paralleled the instincts of whites living in log cabins, whether clapboarded over or not.

Calhoun, in contrast, came across as egghead beyond everyman. Calhoun's eyes, as blazing as Jackson's, were ever seeking some new abstraction to deconstruct, not some new insulter to shoot. Calhoun's body, as untouched as Jackson's was scarred, never graced battlefields or dueling grounds. Calhoun was never known to lose his temper. His language, as elevated as Jackson's was earthy, was shorn of epithets, chiseled clean and clear. In an age of romantically exuberant oratory, his speeches had no elaborate sentimentality. His logic threatened no man's life. The terror of Calhoun was his shattering mind. He seized onto careless commonplaces, squeezing them in that vise of a mentality, turning living creeds into arcane absurdities.

The abstractionist so comfortable in the isolated study was no lion of the drawing room. He never was known to tell a joke. No one called him Johnny Calhoun. He never indulged in the gossipy banter Mary Boykin Chesnut would make the stuff of Carolina culture. He had no small talk, only large principle. To be his partner at the feasting table was to experience a sermon against numerical mobocracy which threatened to outlast all six courses and cigars and brandy too.

Calhoun's fellow rulers liked or loathed him on the basis of whether he clarified or collapsed their conceptions. To a Nullifier who sat at his feet in the little office apart, he seemed the best professor. "What a mind he has," marveled James Hammond. He makes "everything as clear as a sunbeam. No one alive is equal to him in powers of analysis and profound philosophical reasonings." On the other hand, to a majoritarian scornful of the elitist's negations, he seemed an inhuman abstractionist. Henry Clay described Calhoun as "careworn, with furrowed brow, haggard and intensely gazing, looking as if he were dissecting the last abstraction which sprung from metaphysician's brain, and muttering to himself, in half-uttered tones, 'This is indeed a real crisis.'"[14]

– 7 –

President-elect Jackson marched on Washington, D.C., determined to solve his notion of real crisis: that governors thought themselves better than the governed. Jackson correctly saw that the republican ideal, as defined by the Founding Fathers, still survived in Washington a quarter-century beyond the eighteenth century. Philosopher statesmen in cabinet assembled still laid down policy for the electorate. Congressional leaders in special caucus still nominated the past leader of the cabinet to be the next President of the Union. James Monroe, Madison's Secretary of State as Madison had been Jefferson's, was the last President to turn the White House over to his Secretary of State, John Quincy Adams. Monroe was also the last President to wear knee britches and powdered wigs.

Although Calhoun donned other costumes, he relished the script. His years in Monroe's cabinet as Secretary of War between 1817 and 1825 spanned his most comfortable time in Washington politics. Secretary of State John Quincy Adams would later scorn Calhoun as a sectional zealot. But the Massachusetts leader praised Calhoun during the Monroe years as "above all sectional and factious prejudices more than any other statesman of this Union."[15] Calhoun could be a-southern because South Carolina's imminent sectional anguish had not yet spoiled the state's patriotic nationalism. Nor had the nation's imminent egalitarian style of republicanism yet clashed with South Carolina's elitist inclinations. Mr. Calhoun, cabinet member, was a philosopher among patriarchs. He set policy for national whites as he set assignments for Carolina blacks.

Andrew Jackson's first challenge to elitist rule centrally involved Calhoun. The Secretary of War felt the typical patrician's discomfort in 1819 when General Jackson, with everyman's typical brashness, barged into Spanish Florida to shoot Indians. Jackson had been instructed to pacify the frontier. The general interpreted pacification to mean deterring red men from spilling white men's blood, even if Indians' blood stained another nation's turf.

In Washington, national law and order seemed dependent on precise treaties separating reds and whites, Europeans and Americans. Civil control over the military seemed dependent on boundary makers in government telling brawlers in the field if and when they could violate international boundaries. As Secretary of War, John C. Calhoun especially believed the refined cabinet, not a raw duelist, should decide when to wage warfare. When Calhoun complained in the secrecy of James Monroe's cabinet about the "lawless" general, he reflected patriarchs' fear that popular heroes would seize control in the name of the mob.

Jackson came to know about Calhoun's secret attack. But for once, the warrior declined to return fire. He instead campaigned for President in 1824.

The results turned Jackson from a seeker after egalitarianism to a zealot bent on revenge. Jackson won a plurality of popular presidential votes but not a popular or Electoral College majority. The House of Representatives had to decide. The people's hero expected the people's congressmen to ratify the popular choice. Instead, Henry Clay, whose Kentucky constituents had voted for Jackson, threw Kentucky's congressional votes, and thus the presidency, to Secretary of State Adams. President-elect Adams named Clay to be Secretary of State. Clay thus assumed the office which for a quarter-century had led to the White House. Jackson, charging Corrupt Bargain, vowed that the next time, the people would triumph.

In his campaign of 1828, Old Hickory was the first successful presidential candidate with a popular nickname. His lieutenants, especially Martin Van Buren of New York, developed new electioneering techniques. Campaigners blasted Adams as the last President who would spend the people's dollars on pool tables and other aristocratic amusements. In the subsequent inaugural address and even more clearly in his first annual message, the new President announced an end to government by experts. Any "plain and simple" man, declared Jackson, could administer any office. Offices would go to popular politicians who would make sure *"that the majority is to govern."* After Jackson's inauguration, the happy masses raucously celebrated in their favorite democrat's new White House.[16]

History does not record what South Carolina's favorite elitist had to say about the people climbing in windows and stepping on couches to glimpse the people's President. But during the very period when Old Hickory's campaigners had deliberately whipped up the majority, Calhoun had been in that private study, secretly composing his first formal lecture on majority malevolence, *The Exposition and Protest of 1828.* Where Jackson publicly proclaimed that lieutenants who rallied the people deserved the spoils, Calhoun privately whispered that demagogues who roused the people destroyed civic virtue. Minority veto must dry up the spoils and bring patriarchs back to power.

Six months into Jackson's presidency, Calhoun privately wrote that "the choice of the chief magistrate will finally be placed at the disposition of the executive power itself, through a corrupt system to be founded on the abuse of the power and patronage of the government." The "morbid moneyed action of the Government," Calhoun declared four years later, has created a "powerful, active, and mercenary corp of expectants," and at their head, the President, "on whose will the disposition of the patronage . . . depends." This "irresponsible and despotic power" will perpetuate itself, first by "controlling the Presidential election, through the patronage of the Government; and finally, as the virtue and patriotism of the people decay, by the introduction and open establishment of the hereditary principle."[17]

Calhoun's focus on party politicians as cause of popular decay perfectly expressed the new form of South Carolina's old republicanism. Carolina elitists made their bow to the new egalitarian age by early awarding all white men the vote. But they guarded against mobocratic consequences by gerrymandering their state legislature against numerical majorities, by preserving property qualifications for the legislature, and by giving legislators power to elect everyone else. Above all else, they would maintain patriarchal decision by keeping permanent parties out of Carolina and by usually avoiding state-wide electioneering campaigns.

Calhoun's rhetoric against national party electioneering said it all: eighteenth-century elitist republicanism could be safe from nineteenth-century universal suffrage only if patricians could prevent spoilsmen from rousing the rabble. Jackson's spoils system language answered perfectly: nineteenth-century egalitarianism could be safe from anti-egalitarian snobs only if the people's favorite politicians could rally the majority. Calhoun would nullify the very meaning of the Revolution of 1828 by establishing patriarchal veto of deluded majorities. Jackson's defiant response, that the majority must nullify deluded patriarchs, placed a ruler from Tennessee and a ruler from South Carolina at war over the essentials of slaveholder republicanism.[18]

– 8 –

The Jackson-Calhoun clash over legislative goals, while less severe than the conflict over egalitarian republicanism, also indicated the gulf between South Carolinian and southwestern ruling classes. Most Southerners west of Carolina did not elect Jackson primarily to pass laws South Carolinians—or posterity— think of as southern. Only later would most Southern Jacksonians make the party primarily an anti-tariff or proslavery instrument. In the beginning, to South Carolina's distress, most Southwesterners considered banks and Indians, not tariffs or abolitionists, *the* southern enemies.

Expanding southwestern entrepreneurs, unlike their contracting Carolina counterparts, worried most that Indians were barring the expansion of slavery. For slaveholding frontiersmen, higher cotton yields could offset lower cotton prices. Virgin lands led to higher yields. But the largest and most powerful Indian tribes resided on virgin southwestern frontiers. Jackson, America's most notorious Indian fighter, seemed the proper leader to remove the Creek, Cherokee, and Choctaw nations. Old Hickory as President did just that, moving southwestern Indians to reservations across the Mississippi.[19]

South Carolinians who deliberately chose Carolina over the frontier had no taste for such adventurism. They had neither fresh acres left to develop nor Indians left to remove. They would stop protective tariffs from ruining them.

During the early years of his presidency, the Southwest's favorite Indian remover rarely thought about tariffs and never thought about them in southern terms. Jackson's perspective on tariffs left him confused and confusing. On the one hand, as a states' righter, he distrusted national interventionism and high taxes.

On the other hand, as America's soldier, he knew American industry must supply the nation's army. As a southwestern planter, he believed Southeasterners exaggerated the tariff's pernicious impact. As a small government man, he believed import taxes usefully provided revenue to retire the national debt. So Jackson went both ways in his presidential messages. In the scarce sentences he devoted to this (to him) tangential subject, he called for protective tariffs *and* lower duties.[20]

The President cared far more about a matter Carolinians considered as trifling as removing Indians beyond the Mississippi.[21] Jackson assaulted the National Bank with the same egalitarian rhetoric Calhoun found insidiously dangerous, and Southwesterners cherished, in his spoils system pronouncements. The President thought that Nicholas Biddle, head of the United States Bank, personified the un-American notion that an unelected expert must govern for the people. The Tennessee egalitarian disliked Biddle's endeavor to use a government-chartered bank to control the people's money. Biddle's control from above made slaves of whites.

Calhoun thought this war on Biddle overdone. The South Carolinian saw nothing southern to be gained in demolition of an aristocratic banker. He wished the anti-elitist in the White House would care more about repealing those Forty Bale taxes ruining the Carolina elite.

Jackson and Calhoun first came to public blows not over Indians or banks or tariffs or nullification but over the sexual purity of a woman. That tiff over a female, however, personified their clashing masculine views. The lady in question, one Peggy Timberlake Eaton, was thought in some quarters no lady. She was widely rumored to be a Washington harlot when married to a naval purser named Timberlake in the 1820s. Her favorite Washingtonian was Jackson's favorite Tennessean, John Eaton. Eaton subsequently made Peggy his wife. Jackson made the bridegroom his Secretary of War. The President demanded that his inner circle make the bride welcome. Peggy, announced the President, was "chaste as a virgin."

The new President was in mourning over his own lady. Charges during the 1828 presidential election that Rachel Jackson had not been lady-like before marrying Jackson had apparently hastened her death. During that election, partisan Adams newspapers had reminded readers that Mrs. Rachel Jackson had lived with the general before securing a divorce from a frontier ne'er-do-well. The Jacksons, who had inadvertently married before Rachel's divorce became final, believed themselves victims of vicious slander. Aunt Rachel, ailing anyway, took to her bed. She did not live to see her hero inaugurated. Now Jackson would not abide smears on another woman's reputation.

Martin Van Buren of New York, crafty bachelor, paid court to Mrs. Eaton. Calhoun of Old Carolina, hapless husband, watched his wife snub Peggy. And that is why, as some historians would have it, the mourning Old Hero scorned his slaveholding Vice President and made the nonslaveholding New Yorker his successor.

That superficial explanation of Martin Van Buren's ascendancy misses even at a superficial level the gulf in sexual morals between Charleston and Nashville. Whatever Andrew Jackson did or did not do while Aunt Rachel was still married to an absconding husband, and whatever John Eaton did or did not do while Peggy Timberlake pranced around Washington, both made things right after the fact, as Southwesterners defined rightness. Both married the lady.

Both considered eastern criticism of their affairs to be contempt for commoners' morals. The contemptuous Floride Bonneau Calhoun epitomized the Old East's cutting outrage. In Charleston, a lady left no appearances to be made right after the fact. Mrs. Calhoun, by noticing the scarlet woman, would sanction boorish immorality. She would prostitute Charleston's wish to nullify the American mob's vulgarity.

Jackson knew Mrs. Calhoun's scorn was part and parcel of Mr. Calhoun's nullifications. Floride's contempt for Peggy Eaton's (and for Aunt Rachel's?) kind of morality paralleled Secretary of War Calhoun's scorn for Jackson's frontier lawlessness. Old Hickory had long since learned of Secretary of War Calhoun's "secret" attack on the invasion of Florida.

More important, Jackson knew all about Calhoun's "secret" support of nullification. The President knew that just as Floride Calhoun considered Peggy Eaton (and Aunt Rachel?) too boorish to notice, so John C. Calhoun considered white commoners too vulnerable to demagoguery. The President also knew that his Vice President scoffed at fervor for removing Indians and for destroying elitist bankers. Jackson, master of the color line, would not have bestowed the presidential succession on an elitist who would nullify a white majority, even if the Nullifier's wife had pronounced Peggy Eaton a virgin.

At a famous Jefferson Day Dinner on April 13, 1830, the President cut through petticoat politics to the heart of the matter. Glaring at Calhoun, he toasted "Our Federal Union: It Must be Preserved." Calhoun answered "The Union, Next to Our Liberties the Most Dear." With these words, war was declared within the slaveholding class between herrenvolk and anti-herrenvolk regimes.

CHAPTER 15

The First
Confrontation Crisis, II:
South Carolina versus the South

After Calhoun's and Jackson's Jefferson Day toasts, egalitarian and elitist conceptions of slaveholder republicanism seemed headed for an instant showdown. Confrontation was, however, long delayed and quickly defused. Throughout the crisis, a nervous Mr. Nullifier showed again and again how that very nervousness helped make him Mr. South Carolina.

– 1 –

Long after Southern Jacksonians' majoritarian strategy seemed to Calhoun to fail in mid-1830, he blamed Jacksonians, not a majoritarian strategy. A revamped states' rights majority, he believed, could still render minority veto unnecessary. His hopes centered on important Southern Jacksonians beyond South Carolina who also thought the President dismayingly slow to assault nationalistic tariffs. Restive Southern Jacksonians included Senators John Tyler and Littleton Walker Tazewell of Virginia, George Poindexter of Mississippi, Gabriel Moore of Alabama, Felix Grundy and Hugh Lawson White of Tennessee, George Bibb of Kentucky, and U.S. Attorney General John M. Berrien of Georgia. By attacking protective duties and hiding minority veto, Calhoun sought to rally these powerful gentlemen into a purified new states' rights party. The new coalition might even support him for the presidency. Jackson would then end up the Southerner without a party.[1]

Calhoun's strategy sounds hallucinatory to a posterity aware that Jackson and anti-Jackson parties were consolidating a two-party system, not splitting into some third alternative. Hindsight here blocks understanding of why such an alternative seemed more creditable then. Calhoun and states' rights fellows had experienced much political reorganization. The Federalist Party had dissolved. The Republican Party had split into Adams and Jackson camps. Calhoun correctly foresaw that Southern Jacksonians' restiveness augured some reorga-

271

nization. He had potential sympathizers to court, if Carolina advocates of minority veto would let him seek a new majority.

His most important Carolinian lieutenants would not. Leaders such as James Hamilton, Jr., and George McDuffie believed that Martin Van Buren's victory over Calhoun demonstrated majoritarianism to be hopeless.[2] The northern majority would never lower the tariff. No states' rights majority would rally behind a true Southerner or pure southern principle, unless forced to it. Even states' righters chary about Jackson would be unreliable unless they were bludgeoned away from Jackson's world view. Democracy for whites, despotism for blacks was an inadequate formula for teaching a slaveholding minority to be on guard against *white* majorities. Masters must possess a veto on a mob mastering them.

In the spring of 1830, so Carolina's more extreme spirits conceived, Jackson's color line was becoming not a fortress but a sieve. Southerners were pushing egalitarian creeds past white men's issues to attack black slavery. The chief culprit was Congressman Charles Fenton Mercer of Loudon County, located in northernmost Piedmont Virginia. With western Maryland on one flank and the Valley of Virginia over the mountains to the west, northerly Loudon County was a classic compromising eastern Virginia area. The county, with 16% of its blacks manumitted, had helped lead efforts to democratize Virginia's constitution in the 1820s. Its representatives would seek state removal of blacks in the Virginia Slavery Debate of 1832.

Loudon's Congressman Charles Mercer, a sometime slaveholder, shared his county's heresies. A founding father of the American Colonization Society, Mercer bragged in 1818 that our "state has taken the lead" in wiping from "our institutions the only 'blot' which stains them." In April of 1830, the month of Jackson's Jefferson Day toast, Charles Mercer introduced the American Colonization Society's bill, asking Congress for $50,000 per year for colonizing blacks.[3]

For a tense fortnight in the spring of 1830, South Carolinians feared that Congress would adopt this diffusion scheme. Yet another time, Carolinians threatened disunion. The Mercer bill was tabled. But the episode re-emphasized that Carolina's vulnerability extended beyond Forty Bale robbers. "The tariff," explained John C. Calhoun to a northern friend in the wake of Mercer's effort, "is the occasion, rather than the real cause of the present unhappy state of things." Slaveholders might "in the end be forced to rebel, or submit" to have slavery exhausted "by Colonization and other schemes." This "more alarms the thinking than all other causes."[4]

These "other causes" were alarming too. Cotton prices were heading towards a seventh straight year of under ten cents a pound. Carolinians were fleeing to the Southwest ever faster. Carolina had to awaken the South not tomorrow but now, lest the tariff rob the only wide-awake southern watchmen of even "the physical ability to act."[5]

As Nullifiers explained their strategy for awakening slaveholders elsewhere, once extremists took their stand and demanded surrender or war, southern moderates would have to choose between making "common cause with South Carolina" or putting "her down in violence." Then moderates "would from necessity if . . . not from feeling take their stations at our side." United States Senator William Preston put it well: "The slavery question will be the real issue. . . . Will Louisiana cling to her sugar and give up her negroes?"[6]

Carolina opponents of nullification, calling themselves Unionists, answered that the planter in the White House would cling to white men's majority rule without dreaming of giving up his blacks. In a confrontation situation, Andrew Jackson, hero of the southern white majority, would rally the South by enforcing majoritarian law. South Carolina would be alone against the universe in crying that the minority must veto the majority.

Nullifiers could not get past Carolina Unionists' scary prophesy of a tiny state exposed and isolated, not in 1830 with the prestigious Calhoun still hiding in his study, not when seeking to rally Carolina squires uneasy about disorder. Nullifiers needed a two-thirds legislative majority, according to South Carolina's constitution, to call a convention. Extremists instead secured only a simple majority of legislative seats, and even that only by equivocating on nullification. For this auspicious first time, South Carolina gentlemen had seen the need to gamble with confrontation tactics, had weighed the danger, and had backed away.[7]

Between 1830 and 1832, events made Carolina's more audacious politicians determined to march forward. In his annual message of December 1831, President Jackson finally declared for a reformed tariff, "to relieve the people from unnecessary taxation." He also continued to call for "equal justice" for "the merchant as well as the manufacturer."

The resulting Tariff of 1832 continued what Carolinians considered unequal protection. True, Congress reduced the average 50% duties of the Tariff of 1828 to an average of 25%, the Tariff of 1816's level. Jackson claimed the reform would "annihilate the Nullifiers as they will be left without any pretext of Complaint." To Carolinians, however, the new tariff annihilated reform by continuing 50% protection of the largest northern industries—woolens, cottons, and iron. While many Jacksonian states' righters elsewhere in the South agreed, more Southerners, like the slaveholder in the White House, either praised the compromise or grumbled mildly.[8]

Slavery debates in 1832, like the Tariff of 1832, exemplified, according to Carolinians' special viewpoint, a section unable to see mild trouble as potentially major. In 1831, William Lloyd Garrison commenced his antislavery newspaper, *The Liberator*. Garrison promised that "I will not equivocate" and "I will be heard." In late 1831, after Nat Turner aroused some unexpected listeners, the Virginia legislature's slavery debate proved that Charles Mercer's brand of colonization talk was omnipresent. Any responsible master class, as Carolinians measured responsibility, would have gagged debate and hunkered down to saving slavery. Instead, the Virginia master class, largest in the South, indecisively speculated about terminating bondage. Meanwhile, western nonslaveholders decisively attacked slavery out of resentment that they had been denied white men's egalitarianism. In the largest slavery state, egalitarian sentiment was passing beyond Jackson's color line, to corrode commitment to racial slavery among patricians and especially plebeians.

James Hamilton, Jr., governor of South Carolina during Nullifiers' 1832 campaign, nicely summed up Old Carolina's dismay. Old Virginia's suicidal folly, wrote Hamilton, showed that the South was "infested" with "Yankee influence." The slavocracy had become such a colony of the North, materially because of the tariff, morally because of democratic doubts about slavery, that the enemy had possession of the southern "press, . . . pulpit, trade and . . . institutions of education." Virginia's slavery debate, concluded Hamilton, "is nothing to what we shall see if we do not stand manfully at the Safety Valve of Nullification."[9]

At the congressional session of 1832, Henry Clay's colonization proposal reemphasized the need for Hamilton's safety valve. In the year of nullification, federal revenues, by outpacing expenditures and debt repayment, were inspiring visions of a debt-free government with an annual surplus. Most southern slaveholders preferred to end surpluses by lowering tariffs. Henry Clay, Kentucky planter, would instead keep protective duties high and distribute the spoils.

Clay's Distribution Plan, proposed in the senator's oration of June 20, 1832, would transfer the federal surplus to state coffers. The size of each state's share would be based largely on federal numbers, meaning that slaves would count three-fifths in swelling southern whites' new cash. While laying down "no compulsions," Clay prayed that Southerners would give "special consideration" to using their specially large share for colonization/emancipation.[10]

That was not Unconditional Perpetualists' favorite use of their prized three-fifths clause. Nor were Carolinians happy about Clay's use of southern states' righters' best arguments to sustain his colonization heresy. Virginia conservatives in the late Virginia Slavery Debate had called legislative deportation of blacks beyond the state's resources. Clay would supply federal resources. Virginia states' righters had declared each state must decide on colonization/emancipation. Agreed, said the Kentucky nationalist; here's hoping you decide to use your new funds to fulfill your colonization wishes. As for South Carolina's warning that Upper South states had better not—well, isn't each state supposed to decide for itself?

With Clay's Distribution Plan the latest attempt to rally an American and southern majority for a lily-white nation, Hamilton was the more determined to rally a Carolina majority for patriarchal veto. The popular little governor orchestrated an unprecedented state-wide campaign for mass support. Carolina's citizens, heretofore expected to defer to their betters' decisions, were now begged to decide for nullification. Hamilton wanted no repeat of the electorate's shudder of 1830. In 1832, he meant to win a two-thirds' state majority for nullifying national majorities.

Hamilton aimed at blessed relief from Forty Bale robbers and more blessing still. Protectionists called a protective tariff constitutional because Congress had authority to further the "general welfare." Colonizationists claimed that "general welfare" also authorized national removal of blacks. A South Carolina state convention, assuming its Calhoun-prescribed role as limitless constitution-maker judging limited law-makers, could declare that Congress had never been given unlimited power to pursue the "general welfare." The convention would therefore declare protective tariffs null and void in the state.

Everything Carolinians loathed about nineteenth-century America would then be negated. "The same doctrines *'of the general welfare'* which enable the general government to tax our industry," explained Hamilton, would enable the federal government to establish "colonization offices in our State, to give the bounties for emancipation here, and transportation to Liberia afterwards. The last question follows our giving up" nullification of the tariff "as inevitably as light flows from the sun." But termination of federal hands on blacks would follow successful nullification of the tariff as inevitably as day follows night. Once South Carolina won the principle that one state dominated by one elite could veto any national law, the Forty Bale robber would be routed, a potential northern-Upper South majority for federal colonizing of blacks aborted, patriarchal republicanism resurrected, King Numbers dethroned, elitist domination consolidated over masses white and black.[11]

Slavery's consolidation would here shrewdly be achieved by avoiding the slavery issue, a matter which southern apologists considered no issue yet at all or else a problem to be solved by diffusing blacks away. Instead, the ostensible issue would be a tariff which most Southerners considered too high. Nullification of high federal revenues would also lessen federal resources and power, an objective in line with the South's limited government, strict constitutional construction Jacksonianism. Above all else, most states' rights Southerners, while finding nullification reprehensible, believed that withdrawal of consent to be governed was states' rights stuff. If Jackson coercively enforced a nullified tariff, secession would ensue. Then the South would be forced to see South Carolina brethren as crazy but states' rights brothers.

– 2 –

Hamilton's determined activism endangered Calhoun's continued stalling. The Vice President, still convinced that national parties would imminently be reorganized, still wished to delay minority veto and build his own majority coalition. He had agreed to write a state paper on state veto in 1828 only if his authorship was kept secret. He had stayed invisible during Nullifiers' abortive effort in 1830. As late as mid-1831, he hoped "to occupy a silent & retired position." He "saw many and powerful reasons why as much time should be afforded as was possible before the state & the Union should be called on to take sides finally." He could only "regret to be forced" out of hiding.[12]

Hotheads had had enough of a hidden Nullifier. Campaigners, particularly James Hamilton, Jr., needed Calhoun's help. Newspaper writers, particularly in Thomas Cooper's Columbia, demanded to know "If *Mr. Calhoun* . . . will go . . . with South Carolina." If not, South Carolina would repudiate Mr. South

Carolina.[13] Facing those demands, Calhoun could not longer hide from his own doctrine. In his famous Fort Hill Letter of August 1831, the philosopher of Fort Hill confessed the secret that many politicians long since had guessed. He announced for minority veto of majority law.[14]

The Calhoun who found it "impossible" to keep Carolina "quiet" in 1831 was again in character when raising his voice to stop rather than create revolution. A Carolina radicalism "too deep to be controlled" could, he hoped, at least be "in some degree directed." He would direct the movement towards saving Constitution and Union. He would make a revolutionary remedy designed to avoid revolution the hallmark of Carolina's first confrontation crisis.[15]

– 3 –

Once out of the study, Calhoun became James Hamilton's key agitator. Vice President Calhoun in 1832 lent legitimacy to a remedy too many Carolinians had considered too risky in 1830. Neither Thomas Cooper with his "calculate the value of the Union" utterance nor George McDuffie with his diatribes at Forty Bale robbers was the man for this hour. Rather, the Vice President of the United States, with his abstract assurances that state veto was constitutional and peaceful, could best bring nervous squires to the barricades.

In early October 1832, Nullifiers won the necessary two-thirds' legislative majority to call a convention. The tally showed that black belts overwhelmingly dominated South Carolina and that Nullifiers, somewhat less overwhelmingly, prevailed in black belts. Nullifiers won 18 of the 21 Carolina counties with over 40% slaves, including all five counties 65% or more enslaved. On the other hand, Unionists secured an even split of the eight counties under 40% enslaved and won whopping majorities in three of the four counties under 33% enslaved. Nullification tended to be weakest in the least enslaved, most hilly section of the upper upcountry, the same area where secessionists would lose most decisively in 1851.

The generalization that Nullifiers won by usually carrying the state's black-belt areas obscures the equally significant truth that Nullifiers lost a good third of the state's most enslaved neighborhoods. Black-belt neighborhoods lost were no different than enslaved neighborhoods won in terms of black concentrations or mortgages foreclosed or population departed. Often Nullifier and Unionist neighborhoods were not only exactly the same but right next to each other.

The critical variable in each neighborhood was the opinion of local magnates. Black-belt South Carolina, at this moment when commoners were for the first time asked to decide a vital issue at the polls, remained a highly deferential society. Planters being deferred to correctly saw nullification as a highly debatable solution to upper-class problems. On the one hand, nullification's many wealthy opponents considered defiance of Jackson's majoritarianism a disastrous way to leave Carolina elitist republicans isolated and powerless in the egalitarian republican South. On the other hand, nullification's many wealthy proponents considered a planter veto on mass rule the salutary way to make Carolina's aristocracy the leader of a safe master class. State veto won because more squires thought the remedy promising than thought it counterproductive and because Carolina's nonslaveholder-dominated areas were too slim to exploit a fracture in the ruling class.

In Virginia in 1829 and 1832, in contrast, nonslaveholder-controlled regions were so huge that a split in the slaveholder class paralyzed the regime. The contrast re-emphasized a key reason why the Carolina establishment was always in the vanguard of southern extremist action: nowhere else were slaveholders so numerous in so many of a state's neighborhoods. Still, the dangerous quantity of Nullifiers' upper-class opponents and the excessive popularity of Calhoun's nonrevolutionary case for a revolutionary remedy showed the edginess of these gentlemen as they voted for their first gamble. That apprehensive beginning augured a faltering finale calculated to make Nullifiers more shaky still.[16]

– 4 –

Two weeks after the October state election, a special session of the Carolina legislature called a state convention. Three weeks later, in mid-November 1832, this so-called Nullification Convention declared the Tariffs of 1828 and 1832 unconstitutional. After February 1, 1833, proclaimed the Convention, "it shall not be lawful ... to enforce payment of duties within the state." Federal enforcement of unlawful law would be "inconsistent with the longer continuance of South Carolina in the Union."[17] With those words, the South Carolina ruling class precipitated its first confrontation crisis.

Confrontation crises are of two sorts, depending on whether confrontationists do or do not offer non-negotiable demands. In the first, most potentially revolutionary sort of confrontation, extremists insist that no concessions will solve the crisis. The establishment must either let rebels depart or coerce them back. The secession crisis of 1860–1 was this intractable sort of showdown. The nullification crisis epitomized the second, potentially more malleable sort of confrontation situation. In 1832–3, Nullifiers promised to reaffirm Union, assuming Congress met the state's non-negotiable demand for a non-protective tariff.

Confrontation situations are chess games between confrontationists and the government, with moderates the ultimate referee. In the second sort of confrontation crisis, the game usually revolves around the non-negotiable demands. If moderates consider confrontationists' demands unfair, the government will prevail. If the government resists demands which moderates consider fair, confrontationists may win. Yet confrontationists must have iron nerves along with fair demands. They must not negotiate away non-negotiable demands prematurely, lest they lose their chance to transform the negotiating system.

A chess game over non-negotiable demands can easily degenerate into maneuvers over who will fire the first shot. When that happens, government and extremists again compete to show moderates that the other side is morally compromised. Checkmate is secured when one side is maneuvered into aggressively commencing armed combat. "My life upon it," James Hamilton, Jr., privately promised in February 1833, "if a conflict does occur," the federal government "strikes the first blow."[18]

Andrew Jackson might seem just the warrior to bluster into a first shot. Jackson's tirades all over Washington during the nullification winter assuredly lent impressions of an impulsive slayer. "I will hang the first man of them I can get my hands on to the first tree I can find," he was reported to be raging in late 1832. Senator Robert Y. Hayne of South Carolina told Jackson's old friend, Senator Thomas Hart Benton of Missouri, that "I don't believe he would really hang anybody." Hayne nervously added, "Do you?" "I tell you, Hayne," answered Benton, "when Jackson begins to talk about hanging, they can look out for the ropes."[19]

But those who saw Jackson as conducting government by temper tantrum missed the secret of his killing force. In his every confrontation, the tempestuous Westerner had been the iciest plotter. For all his image as a hothead, Jackson usually fired the second shot. He allowed the enemy to spend initial fury. He then cut aggressors down. He won the Battle of New Orleans that way, and the Bank War, and his most famous duel. The counterpunching warrior now plotted to turn the brainy Calhoun into the provocative assaulter.

Calhoun called minority veto necessary because the permanent majority would never lower the tariff. Jackson's first strategic impulse was to prove that majoritarian politics would yield a low tariff. The tariff had been eased downward in the spring of 1832. In December 1832, Jackson asked Congress to slice duties further.

Jackson's detractors charged that the President, by picking this moment to cave in on low tariffs, had surrendered to minority blackmail. Jackson-haters were right about the timing of the President's conversion. Jackson would not have urged tariff reform only months after declaring the Tariff of 1832 adequate reform unless South Carolina had precipitated a crisis.

But the larger truth was that Carolina confrontationists pointed Jackson in the proper Jacksonian direction. The Old Hero had never bothered much about tariffs. Other issues—banks, Indians, the Corrupt Bargain of 1824—had seemed more worthy of his attention. But once South Carolinians pushed nationalistic tariffs to the center of states' rights consciousness, Jackson could no longer prevaricate. National governmental intervention to raise prices, create jobs, and foster industrial development were superb policies for an anti-Jackson nationalist coalition, strong in urban areas and strongest in New England, America's most industrialized region. The policy made less sense for a states' rights coalition, strong in agrarian areas and overpowering in the Deep South, America's least industrialized area.

Jackson's majority bloc, his southern agrarian wing, had long been restive about Jackson's indifference to tariffs. These Jacksonians now did not want to shoot fellow Southerners who sought the right reform, even if reformers deployed the wrong remedy. Granted, became the standard southern line, South Carolinians were insane. But instead of shooting lunatics, why not slay the out-

rageous law driving them mad? "No law oppressive in its character," declared
Senator Bedford Brown of North Carolina, "should be executed by interposition
of military power, until every pacific measure" has been tried. The obvious pac-
ifism for a states' rights majority was a new tariff. Jackson, by endorsing the
obvious, made Carolina hotheads the more disreputable if they spewed bullets
before Congress decided on now highly negotiable demands.[20]

Jackson also maneuvered to make Nullifiers' first shot especially dishonorable. At the beginning of the crisis, the President plotted to manipulate Nullifiers into shooting down fellow South Carolinians. Jackson would deputize
Carolina opponents of nullification to enforce federal laws. Only after Carolina
insiders had been killed would Jackson bring in "outsiders."[21]

Carolina Unionists, however, refused to be sacrificial lambs. They rejected
Jackson's suggestion that they should impotently wait to be shot. The General's
army, not civilians' bodies, would have to dare Nullifiers to fire first.

Jackson's more viable strategy was to move law enforcement beyond range
of South Carolina's firepower. He instructed federal customs officials to move
from Charleston, where Nullifiers massed guns, to Fort Moultrie, where federal
installations were consolidated. Moultrie, on a sea island some five miles over
the waters from Charleston's Battery, guarded approaches from the Atlantic
Ocean to Charleston harbor.

Jackson instructed revenue cutters at sea to enforce the tariff before a ship
bearing imported goods passed Fort Moultrie's cannons. Unless duties were
paid, cargo would be locked inside the fort's stone walls. South Carolina, lacking a navy, would be hard-pressed to nullify. Should Nullifiers somehow fit out
a gunboat to sail forth and assault a United States navy vessel, Carolinians
would be outrageous aggressors and laughably inadequate attackers too.

Nullifiers' attempt to escape Jackson's trap bore the look of comic failure.
James Hamilton, Jr., now ex-governor but still extremists' prime strategist, sent
some of his rice to Havana in exchange for sugar. He would not, he announced,
pay duties on the sweets. He would allow his goods to be confiscated. But
should the state decide to enforce nullification, his fellows "would go even to
the death with him for his sugar."

Federal officials intercepted the vessel bearing "Sugar Jimmy"'s sugar. They
tucked the sweet stuff away in Fort Moultrie. The dashing Mr. Hamilton had
nary a ship to transport gentlemen to their death for his sugar.

"Sugar Jimmy"'s lost sugar symbolized how shrewdly the President had
schemed. By moving to lower the already lower Tariff of 1832, and by ensuring
that nullification required provocative, pitiful assault on a navy, Jackson sought
to make his southern supporters think South Carolinians too irresponsible to
support.

– 5 –

One presidential strategy, however, reduced the Nullifiers' isolation. Many
states' righters beyond Carolina, while repudiating Nullifiers' notion of living
under a government and vetoing its laws, affirmed each state's right to secede

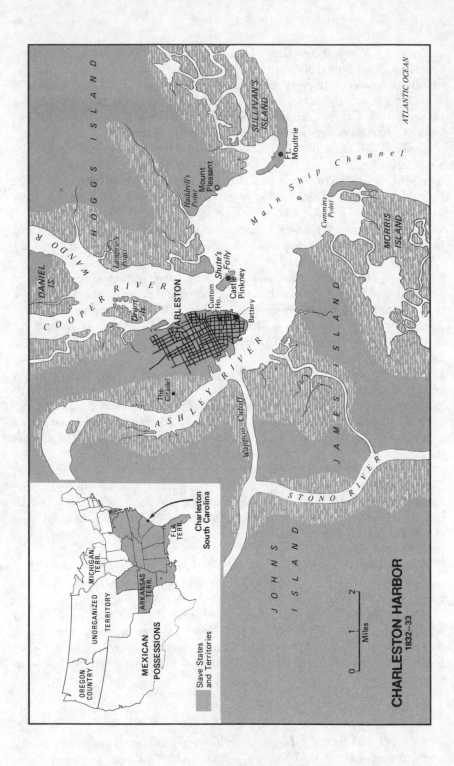

CHARLESTON HARBOR
1832-33

ATLANTIC OCEAN

SULLIVAN'S ISLAND

Ft. Moultrie

Main Ship Channel

Haddrell's Point
Mount Pleasant

Cummins Point

MORRIS ISLAND

HOGGS ISLAND

WANDO R.

DANIEL IS.

Lamprie's Point

COOPER RIVER

Shute's Folly

Castle Pinkney

CHARLESTON

Custom Ho.

Drum Is.

Battery

JAMES ISLAND

The Citadel

ASHLEY RIVER

Wappoo Cutoff

STONO RIVER

JOHNS ISLAND

Miles
0   1   2

Charleston
South Carolina

FLA. TERR.

ARKANSAS TERR.

MICHIGAN TERR.

UNORGANIZED TERRITORY

MEXICAN POSSESSIONS

OREGON COUNTRY

Slave States and Territories

and form another government. Southern states' righters especially believed erring slaveholding brothers must be allowed peacefully to leave the Union.

The southern President went out of his way to attack that southern position. In his Nullification Proclamation of December 10, 1832, Jackson called secession a "revolutionary act," to "be morally justified by the extremity of oppression." A tariff about to be changed was hardly extreme oppression. Nor was a *morally* justified revolution a *legally* justified act. Governors, "by the law of self-defence," could repress "an attempt, by force of arms, to destroy a government." He would save majoritarian Union from traitorous minorities, whether law-breakers called themselves Nullifiers or Disunionists.[22]

New York's Martin Van Buren, Jackson's heir apparent, sought to dissuade the commander-in-chief from chasing a theoretical battle with states' rights constituents. "The present is not a season," urged the ever-practical Van Buren, for "abstract propositions." "Performance of your duty" required only putting down state veto. If that duty alone were performed, Jackson's southern wing would applaud. Southerners "disclaim indignantly the right of a state to resist the execution of the laws, whilst she is in the Union." But broadening the issue to include a state's right to leave the Union "is likely to bring you in collision" with our supporters, especially in "Virginia."[23]

"No, my friend," answered Jackson, "the crisis must now be met." Nullifiers had threatened that secession would follow nullification. Both monstrosities must be destroyed. With the exception of a few "nullifiers and politicians," Jackson considered Virginia "true to the core."[24]

The Virginia legislature pleased Jackson by sending an official commissioner to Carolina, charged with arranging an honorable retreat for the Nullifiers. The commissioner was the most Carolinian of Virginians, Benjamin Watkins Leigh. Leigh limped around Charleston, his club foot reminiscent of the crippled McDuffie and Cooper, his old manners and old-fashioned costumes those of the fading South. This same Leigh had led the Old Order in the Virginia Convention of 1829. He had then insisted that the propertied elite must possess a veto on King Numbers.

Now the old reactionary told South Carolina fossils they had no constitutional right to veto the national mob. Bulwarks against mobocracy, had been, alas, left out of the national Constitution. At the very least, South Carolina should suspend minority veto while Congress considered majority redress. With a Virginian so sympathetic to the Carolina world view calling that view misguided beyond the state, Jackson was right that he had confrontationists potentially cornered.[25]

But Van Buren was right that Jackson's attack on secession could allow Carolina out of the corner. The Virginia legislature, even while sending Leigh to stop South Carolina from nullifying, affirmed that any state could legally secede. Virginia's United States senator, future President John Tyler, was sufficiently outraged at Jackson's anti-secessionism to consider seceding from Jackson's party. Tyler was not alone. Many Southern Jacksonians believed that a party prepared to fire rifles at a seceding state was no states' rights party at all.

Before nullification, Calhoun had been futilely trying to separate these very states' righters from Jackson. Now Jackson, by injecting anti-secessionism into opposition to nullification, was making Calhoun less futile.[26]

Southern restiveness with a not-enough-states'-rights Jackson was illustrated in an early senatorial confrontation on Jackson's so-called Force Bill. That bill, reflecting Jackson's strategy, authorized new ways to enforce the tariff, without force if possible and with more federal troops if necessary. Fifteen of the 24 senators from slaveholding states voted unsuccessfully to table discussion of possible military coercion. The roll call revealed a South split in its usual way. Thirteen of 16 Deep and Middle South senators voted to table the Force Bill. Only two of eight Border South senators concurred.[27]

The vote signaled that in the more southern South, support for Jackson was none too hard. While Southrons applauded Jackson's insistence that states' rights did not justify nullification, they squirmed at Jackson's notion that states' rights did not justify secession. Their selective cheering could land them in Calhoun's camp, if war broke out over secession rather than nullification. Wishing to avoid that debacle, they sought to lower the tariff before state veto led to disunion.

– 6 –

The soft nature of Jackson's southern support gave confrontationists room to maneuver. They had to allow Congress time to meet non-negotiable demands. But if their demands were fair and if other Southerners considered a lesser settlement unfair, slaveholders might oppose a war against secessionists.

Possibilities and dangers in the situation put Carolina's nerves and Calhoun's statecraft to revealing test. Never again in John C. Calhoun's career would the so-called Father of Secession be in the middle of a confrontation situation. Never again would his actions speak so loudly about the true nature of his—and his state's—confrontationism. In January 1833, South Carolina's leader, now resigned from the vice presidency to become Carolina's senator, sent colleagues back home a secret communication, pleading for retreat.

The letter brought back memories of 1831, when Cooper and Hamilton had marched beyond what Calhoun considered prudent extremism. He had then come out of his study, he had told his friends, to steer Carolina towards redress within the Union. Now in early 1833, he told warriors back home that secession, "the most fatal of all steps," should occur only "in the last extremity." The South, he predicted, could prevail in the Union. Enforcement of nullification should be postponed at least a year.[28]

Only briefly in 1831 had Carolina's reluctant revolutionaries moved ahead of their cautious leader. Only too obviously had they needed his soothing legalism to win the uncomfortably close state election of 1832. Only too eagerly in early 1833 were worried leaders ready to concur that minority veto must be postponed. Using as their excuse Benjamin Watkins Leigh's plea that South Carolina give the majoritarian system time to work, Nullifiers suspended nullification. The tariff could be enforced at least until the lame-duck Congress decided whether to lower the duties.

Calhoun, again revealing what kind of confrontationist he was, worked feverishly in Washington to turn temporary reprieve from confrontation into surrender of non-negotiable demands. His concessions to protectionists contrasted revealingly with Jackson's anti-protectionist solution. The Jackson administration threw its support behind the so-called Verplanck Bill, which would have sliced 50% rates to 20% in two years, well within South Carolina's non-negotiable demands.[29]

In early 1833, the Senate Committee of the Whole was considering Verplanck's initiative. Senatorial rules made closure of debate difficult in that committee. The lame-duck session of Congress would end on March 4, 1833. Congress would not come back into session until December 1833. Yankees who wished to save 50% protective tariffs could thus likely talk 20% duties to death until at least the end of the year.

The Jackson administration's stymied Verplanck Bill, together with Southern Jacksonians' dislike for a Jackson who would stymie secession, left Nullifiers with an obviously promising confrontation strategy, a strategy they revealingly lacked the nerve to try. Bolder confrontationists might have offered to mass behind the Verplanck Bill. If our united efforts can produce your moderate President's 20% tariffs, such extremists might have promised Southern Jacksonians, we will drop extremism. But if you allow the protectionist minority to nullify your majority party's wishes, you must allow our minority to withdraw its consent to be robbed.

That never-used strategy, to speculate a little further about this history which did not happen, would likely have produced no quick settlement. The congressional session would probably have ended with Yankee protectionists still talking Verplanck's 20% duties to death. Southern Jacksonians would likely have asked one more chance to pass the Verplanck Bill, at the next Congress nine months hence.

A shrewd confrontationist might have granted this final test. The result might have been a continued protectionist filibuster in the Senate Committee of the Whole in 1833–4 and an increased southern fury at a stalemated establishment. If stalemate had persisted long enough, the distance between southern extremists and moderates might have dramatically shrunk.

In the more likely scenario in 1833–4, an exasperated majority would finally have voted to close the debate and to enact Verplanck's 20% rates. Confrontationists would then have earned respect by delaying long enough so that moderates could secure the non-negotiable demand. Confrontationists, having also enhanced their own self-respect, would then have been prepared for the next confrontation crisis—and the next set of non-negotiable demands moderates might not have been able to secure.

We cannot know if confrontationists could have emerged so triumphantly. We do know that Mr. South Carolina and followers proved unable to test the obvious possibility. Calhoun instead compromised so swiftly and thoroughly, and with such sighs of relief from constituents, that Carolina's memories of nullification became a 30-year shudder.

Calhoun's instrument for aborting nullification was an alliance with the southern hero least like himself. Instead of issuing non-negotiable demands for the Verplanck Bill's 20% tariffs within two years, Calhoun negotiated with the archprotectionist, Kentucky's Henry Clay, towards a Compromise Tariff massively more protectionist than the Jacksonian proposal. Calhoun, Clay, and their lieutenants hammered out the anti-Jackson alternative at secret meetings during early weeks of 1833. At the beginning of talks, Calhoun proposed, with reluctance, that protective tariffs last five years, three more than the Verplanck Bill proposed. Clay demanded nine. Calhoun acquiesced. Calhoun wished ultimate reduction to 15%. Clay demanded 20%. Calhoun surrendered. Calhoun desired a formula for a low valuation of the import to be taxed. Clay's agent demanded a valuation formula calculated to raise tariff proceeds some 10% over the ostensible rates. Calhoun stormed about the bitter pill, then swallowed. At every stage of negotiations, the "Father of Secession" caved in, lest secession ensue.

Final terms of the Calhoun-Clay compromise revealed that Clay had compromised protectionism only in the distant future. The bill left 50% rates unchanged throughout 1833. On the first day of 1834, duties in excess of 20% would be lowered one-tenth of the excess (not, let it be noted, the larger reduction of one-tenth of the whole rate). That new rate of 47% would prevail throughout 1834 and 1835. Similar one-tenth reductions of the excess over 20% would take place biannually, making the rate 44% in 1836 and 1837, 41% in 1838 and 1839, and 38% in 1840 and 1841. Finally and at long last ten years hence, in two big cuts at the beginning and in the middle of 1842, rates would be sliced to 20%—where the Jackson administration's Verplanck Bill would have had them in two years!

Or, to be more accurate, Clay's reductions would descend to Verplanck's level, if protectionists failed to take advantage of their 10-year reprieve. Clay called the final 1842 reductions as sacrosanct as a constitutional provision. But some Congress a decade hence, his protectionist allies hoped, might revise settlements once called holy.[30] That hope would be fulfilled. The July 1, 1842, reduction to 20% would not last out the year. A Whig majority, in the Tariff of 1842, would hoist rates back up to the 35% level. Henry Clay, the Great Compromiser, had compromised protection remarkably little.

Clay compromised not at all on a matter Calhoun considered vital: the constitutionality of protection. Carolina went to the brink to secure not just low tariffs but the principle that any general welfare legislation, whether protection of industries or colonization of blacks, was unconstitutional. But unconstitutional laws cannot be legally enforced for ten years. Clay's "compromise," by enforcing general welfare legislation for a decade, nullified Nullifiers' larger constitutional purposes.

If constitutionally Calhoun had secured nothing, economically he had perpetuated the highest tariffs ever to be charged in antebellum America, throughout the worst cotton depression his constituents would ever suffer. Carolinians had breathed defiance partly because the tariff robbed them, so they thought, of 40 bales per 100. Such thievery, so they believed, would imminently sap their resistance by demolishing their finances. For nine more years, in the settlement bearing Calhoun's stamp of approval, the robbery would continue at or above the Forty Bale rate, while cotton prices would remain debilitatingly low.

Once the Clay-Calhoun settlement reached the Senate floor, the Great Compromiser could do no more for the Compromise Tariff than nudge his supporters out of its way. Clay's fellow protectionists grudgingly agreed not to filibuster but bitterly refused to favor the bill.

Calhoun's fellow Southerners were less bitter about his compromising. If Mr. South Carolina preferred Clay's watery medicine to Verplanck's bracing stuff, how was a moderate to argue? Southern members of the House voted for the settlement, 84-4. Northern Jacksonians split evenly, making northern anti-Jacksonians' unanimous opposition irrelevant. The new tariff passed the House 119-85 and the Senate 29-16. A similar coalition of almost all the Southerners and enough northern states' righters had passed the Missouri Compromise.[31]

Before adjourning, Congress also passed the so-called Force Bill. Majorities of both parties and both sections drew together to bolster Andrew Jackson's authority to collect the duties peaceably if he could, forcibly if South Carolina fired a shot.

– 7 –

On March 1, 1833, Congress finalized passage of the Compromise Tariff and the Force Bill. On March 4, Calhoun commenced a race towards home. The weather was frightful: one of those winter storms, half-rain, half-snow, which makes an Upper South world but half-southern into one long Yankee iceland. Calhoun braved the shivery journey in an open mailcart, his craft skidding through slick mud. Calhoun endured it out of concern that his negotiations might not satisfy hotheads in South Carolina. Once again he remembered the bad times of 1831, when allies had judged him too cautious. Unless he arrived in Columbia before the Nullification Convention reconvened, he feared, Carolinians might yet secede over the non-negotiable.

The shivering traveler arrived in time, only to find that his ordeal in the ice had been needless. A few intractable secessionists such as Thomas Cooper aside, Carolina's zeal had turned as frigid as the northern weather. Few back home had even muttered while their favorite confrontationist compromised and compromised in Washington. Fewer now dared to whisper that his compromising confrontationism had produced much less than Verplanck's uncompromising rates had offered. The fright of standing alone in 1833 had driven confrontationists back to Calhoun's caution of 1831. Throughout the nullification crisis, his every worry had been his world's.

In mid-March 1833, the Nullification Convention, calling the Compromise Tariff "honorable," rescinded its ban on collecting duties. The convention then futilely nullified the now-irrelevant Force Act. Delegates called the settlement "cause for congratulation." An attempt to make that read "congratulation and triumph" was hooted down.[32]

Hooting was in order. Minority veto was finished. The majority would rule as long as Union endured. Jackson's majority, with a nudge from Calhoun's minority, had proved safe on the tariff. But on the subject of whether white apologists should diffuse away black slaves, the minority of Unconditional Perpetualists feared they might not be safe from northern—and Upper South—Conditional Termination majorities.

"Let Gentlemen not be deceived," Robert Barnwell Rhett warned the Nullification Convention as South Carolina dropped nullification forever. "It is not the Tariff—not Internal Improvement—nor yet the Force Bill, which constitutes the great evil." Your "northern brethren," aye, "the whole world are in arms against your institutions." A majority defining its own constitutional limits had every power. "Until this Government is made a limited Government . . . there is no liberty—no security for the South."[33]

"Nullification is dead," rejoiced President Andrew Jackson in 1833, but Nullifiers "intend to blow up a storm on the subject of the slavery question." Despite knowing Northerners have no antislavery views, Calhoun and fellow fanatics "will try to arouse the southern people on this false tale. . . . These men would do any act to destroy the Union."[34]

Calhoun merely a Union-breaker, the early slavery issue merely Calhoun's demagogical fiction: how revealingly the President did misconceive Calhoun and the Carolina gentlemen who momentarily forced their reluctant leader to go ahead with confrontation politics. The President was one of the shrewdest American politicians. His problem was that the gap within the southern ruling class remained so enormous that the great middle possessed not the foggiest notion what drove their own extreme.[35]

That sort of gulf between extremists and moderates makes confrontation politics always a gamble—and always a necessity to committed agitators. South Carolinians learned in nullification times how much daring that gamble takes. Their fortitude proved not up to requirements. Then how could faltering confrontationists scare moderates away from compromise mentalities? With nullification in ruins, the only confrontation strategy still available was secession, a gamble demanding even more gall than nullification. Carolina gentlemen had emerged from their first confrontation crisis drifting as badly as were those they would control, those slaveholding apologists up north in the South.

PART V

THE GAG RULE AND THE
POLITICS OF "MERE" WORDS

After South Carolina extremists retreated from nullification and dared not try secession, they retained only one weapon. They could only bludgeon moderates with argumentative words. No wonder, then, that a Gag Rule Controversy about nothing but "mere" words was a revealing signpost on the road to disunion.

CHAPTER 16

The Reorganization of
Southern Politics

In the early 1830s, Carolina radicals' warnings of a South in danger seemed destined to be ignored, unless some northern menace to slavery surfaced. Immediately after nullification, little about the North seemed menacing. The only root-and-branch abolitionist newspaper, William Lloyd Garrison's *The Liberator,* possessed scant subscribers. The only dangerous Yankee assault had taken a narrowly political form. During the Missouri Controversy, Rufus King and James Tallmadge had denounced the Slavepower sheerly for its undemocratic impact on whites. Even that denunciation had swiftly dissipated.

Then, a couple of years after nullification, emerging Yankee abolitionists made southern extremists more compelling. Calhoun's so-called delusion, the reorganization of political organizations, rapidly materialized. But southern reorganization deviated disastrously from Calhoun's blueprint. The abstractionist and his followers, having been more right than ever about the North, were more isolated than ever from the South—and more dangerously frustrated to be so ignored after being so prescient.

– 1 –

In the mid-1830s, the key new Yankee zealot was a tepid extremist on slavery. Charles Grandison Finney, northern evangelical revivalist extraordinaire, demanded a religious conversion with a political potential more radical than the preacher necessarily intended. Finney's was the gospel that disinterested benevolence should declare holy war on interested selfishness.

Disinterested benevolence. That concept fired Finney's preaching and his reform empire. The revivalist armed with those "mere" words was no wild-eyed screamer. He was a cool ex-lawyer, who presented hell's horror with deathly quiet. He would stand still under the tent, before multitudes from the prairies. He would quietly portray a selfish people defying their selfless Lord. Come to Christ, Finney would almost whisper, and rise up from personal selfishness.

Here a slowly rising finger would break the spellbinder's motionlessness. Ascend to the anxious seat, demanded Finney. Then crusade benevolently for a disinterested world.[1]

Cleansed converts streaming from Finney's tents generally matched the revivalist's unprovoking manner. For every Finneyite who demanded antislavery, thousands worked for less unsettling causes—for starting Sunday schools or for spreading Bibles, for curbing drunkards or for colonizing free blacks, for eating graham crackers or for establishing manual labor schools.[2] Finney himself wished converts who marched against slavery would trod more softly.

But Finney could not control his zealots. Among millions who would cleanse Christ's democracy, a few souls attacked the most apparent sin against republicanism. The leading Finneyite assaulter was Theodore Dwight Weld, who in the mid-1830s briefly vied with William Lloyd Garrison for the title of Mr. Abolitionist.[3]

Garrison's agitations were rooted in old New England in general and Boston in particular. Theodore Dwight Weld, though son of a New England preacher, pushed the movement where Finney was most effective, across midwestern prairies where Yankees were migrating. Weld followed the typical Finneyite migration. After conversion under the master, he joined Finney's so-called Holy Band, worked the western New York frontier's so-called Burned Over District, fought for manual labor schools, and sometimes raised his sweet voice for nothing more controversial than mnemonics (memory improvement).

In 1833, Weld departed from holy conservatism. The new abolitionist's wild hair, sprouting in every direction as if the mane of a porcupine, epitomized the unruly West. Weld consolidated his reputation as wild man by marrying the abolitionizing feminist, South Carolina's Angelina Grimké.

Weld condemned America as democracy's laggart. England, in 1833, had abolished slavery in the British West Indies. Could America do less? Charles Stuart, Weld's friend in the Holy Band and an English reformer come to unreformed prairies, asked the question especially effectively.[4] Weld's answer, his midwestern antislavery lectures, spread antislavery past London, past Boston, towards becoming even more of a trans-Atlantic crusade.

Spiritual conquests need materialistic ammunition. Weld and Garrison, like Kentucky's James Birney, drew on the Tappan fortune. Benjamin and Louis Tappan's previous philanthropies had fostered little more radical than searching streets for prostitutes to reform. Under Weld's influence, the brothers used part of their dry-goods fortune to help form and finance the American Antislavery Society in 1833. By 1835, the swiftly growing society possessed hundreds of local branches and tens of thousands of followers. The question was now, very suddenly, whether a fringe American antislavery movement could convert the American mainstream, North and, yes, South too.[5]

– 2 –

Conversionists aimed first at the South. The newest Finneyite plea took the form not of quiet lawyer touring unsettled provinces. Rather, silent mailings descended on slaveowners. On July 29, 1835, when Charleston Postmaster Alfred Huger opened mail sacks, he uncovered antislavery appeals addressed to South Carolina citizens.

Abolitionists' notion of converting slaveholders was hardly zany in the context of the early 1830s. No intransigent slaveholding class, determined to keep slavery forever, had developed beyond South Carolina. Instead, Maryland and Virginia legislative debates had revealed slaveholders wistfully hopeful about diffusing blacks away. Perhaps peaceable persuasion might fortify the tremulous.

Fearing that result and more, many South Carolinians demanded repression of persuasive, alias incendiary, pamphlets. Postmaster Alfred Huger termed abolitionists' appeal to white consciences a call for black revolution. Delivering such mail, Huger noted, would strew antislavery around Charleston's houses, where blacks could see it. The postmaster locked up the insurrectionary sheets until President Jackson could send instructions.[6]

Charlestonians would not wait. Within 24 hours, "respectable" slaveholders led a mob into the post office. The gang confiscated the letters, then used the mail to fuel a public bonfire. This time, Southerners copied South Carolina. During the long hot summer of 1835, several mobs cleansed post offices.[7]

As for the slaveholding President responsible for delivery of mails, his instructions to Postmaster General Amos Kendall revealed the despot struggling with democracy. Andrew Jackson neither demanded that ideas circulate nor insisted on censorship. The President instead told the Postmaster General to lock up suspicious-looking letters, unless and until recipients demanded delivery. Before dispatching mail, the local postmaster should take demanders' "names down, and have them exposed thru the Publick journals as subscribers to this wicked plan of exciting the negroes to insurrection and to massacre." All "moral and good" Southerners would ostracize the fiends. Few who had asked for their mail would be "so hardened in villainy as to withstand the frowns of all good men."[8]

Jackson here expressed a classic southern mixture of consent and coercion. Just as slaveholders called coercive slavery legitimate in part because Cuffee allegedly consented to be controlled, so Jackson would coercively censor only until some citizen dissented. Then, just as southern communal pressure and community vigilance, not state repression, customarily controlled dissenting citizens and overly harsh slaveholders, so neighbors' ostracism would deter those wishing incendiary mail. Jackson would thus edge public democracy towards coercion while still struggling to retain consent. It was all an unforgettable lesson on how this precariously poised world ideally remained in balance.

Postmaster General Amos Kendall, practical Kentuckian, knew that Southerners were not on ideal behavior. Vicious mobs were the alternative to government censorship. Jackson's instructions to Kendall thus were changed in Kendall's instructions to Huger to read that "circumstances of the case justified detention of the papers." In other words, Huger could censor without Jackson's machinery for ending censorship. Armed with Kendall's instructions, Huger and other southern postmasters cleansed the mail in the fall of 1835, unless mobs seized the task.[9]

Southerners hoped to spread censorship beyond the South. Meetings in southern communities and resolutions in southern legislatures urged Northerners to sanitize the North. Southerners called on northern states to outlaw antislavery appeals and to extradite fanatics to the South for trial.[10]

Slaveholders deployed their usual excuse for such repression. Liberty to speak does not include license to cry fire in crowded theatres. Antislavery agitators would doubly set the social order afire. Slaves would rise in revolt. Slaveholders would erupt from the Union.

Abolitionists answered by denying intention or power to incite slaves. They sent letters to whites, not blacks. They sadly knew black noncitizens could not read. Slaveowners could keep alleged incendiary material away from slaves. Who was master down there?

Slaveowners answered that they meant to master a *Domestic* Institution. Some slaves were literate. Illiterate blacks could see provoking woodcut illustrations enclosed in supposedly peaceful propaganda. Such provocations undermined domesticity and delayed reform. Slavery could be paternalistic only if slaveholders could control servants without frightful repression. Reformers could ease blacks out only if outside agitators ceased frightening southern communities.

Abolitionists here became scapegoats for every southern trouble. Southern apologists moved against slavery too slowly? That was Yankee fanatics' fault. Domestic patriarchs whipped too often? Outsider meddlers were responsible. The upshot of this argument was that Southerners could never end a moral miasma unless Northerners stopped consolidating slavery's most immoral tendencies.

If all that sounded like hypocrisy, the self-serving cant demonstrated something more important: souls needing soothing. The southern response to unconditional abolitionism had the same aspirin-like potentialities as the Conditional Termination argument. To the old notion that a sin could be morally abolished only tomorrow was added the new notion that outside meddlers only further delayed insiders' actions.

A less convoluted defensive postulate would have declared the institution holy and forever to be perpetuated. South Carolinians proclaimed for holy perpetuation in the 1830s and before. That was not the customary southern proclamation elsewhere until the 1850s. Southerners who would exploit slaves while yearning to diffuse them away could only deploy an awkward defensiveness. The awkwardness indicated that more than fear of slave insurrection impelled demands that antislavery attack cease.

Slaveholders admitted they feared white no less than black dissent. The "great and terrible danger" of insurrection, South Carolina's Arthur P. Hayne explained to Andrew Jackson, has little to do with white life and death, much to do with white morale and commitment. Southern whites outnumbered blacks two to one. Life was more in danger on New York and Philadelphia streets. But "a restless feeling" pervaded "the South, and not without just cause, in relation to the Question of Property at the South, and unless this feeling be put at rest, who would desire to live in such a community?"

Southerners would desert a slaveholder community, continued Hayne, because black insurrection would remind white democrats that republican consent was the holy conception of the century. The idea of abstract liberty, once agitated in the North and mailed to the South, would turn some slaves' heads, trouble some slaveholders' consciences, inspire liberty-loving nonslaveholders North and South to turn against liberty's curse. Only "if the Non-Slave-holding States . . . will come forward patriotically, generously, and fairly and unite with the South to prevent Insurrection and to organize a moral power in favour of the South—*then and only then will the South be safe.*"[11]

In early 1836, Professor Henry Nott of Thomas Cooper's South Carolina College explained why northern moral power might overwhelm southern moral power. "Europe is against us, & the North is against us," Nott wrote privately to his representative in Congress, James Hammond. "How do we stand at home? Every town & village is full of northern people, many of whom are feebly with us & many in secret decidedly against us." In "many" of the rural districts too, "the great body of the poor people . . . would on the ground of republicanism as well as religion either be inefficient friends or decided opponents."

"Incendiary publication," continued Henry Nott, would escalate anxiety by encouraging slaves "to escape" and slaveholders to fear "open rebellion and secret poison." In this atomosphere, any slave revolt would be the beginning of the end. "Remember the serious discussions in the Virginia Legislature after the petty affair of Northampton," concluded Professor Nott, and "think what would have been the effect had there been a revolution more extensive, well concerted & bloody at its outset."[12]

Important molders of southern opinion publicly echoed Professor Nott's private opinion that free and open debate would contaminate whites' viewpoints. Duff Green's *United States Telegraph,* published in Washington, D.C., was dedicated to John C. Calhoun's interests. Duff Green's messages in the fall of 1835 reiterated conceptions Calhoun and other Carolinians had advanced since nullification times. The unsteady Upper South, ran the main theme, wished and believed that blacks would someday diffuse elsewhere. Those who speculated about moving blacks out would not stand firm for keeping slaves forever.

Duff Green scoffed at the notion "that the South sleeps on a volcano—that we are afraid to go to bed at night." Green instead feared "the gradual operation of public opinion among ourselves." "Insidious and dangerous invaders" come "in the guise of friendship," seeking "to persuade us that slavery is a sin, a curse, an evil." Green's "greatest cause of apprehension" was that the "morbid sensitivity of our own people" will "make them the voluntary instrument of their own ruin." Green wished to outlaw all talk, North and South, proclaiming slavery an evil.[13]

Northerners, although too democratic to outlaw talk, reassured Southerners that debate could lead nowhere. In the summer of 1835, public meetings in New

York, Philadelphia, Boston, and several smaller cities condemned so-called fanatics as "nigger-lovers" and worse. Freedom for "inferior" blacks, so most Northerners conceived, was not worth a smashed white republic or a deranged national economy.

These sentiments ushered in three decades of northern anti-abolitionism. Northern membership in antislavery societies peaked at around 200,000 in 1840, a figure swollen with females who could not vote, in a year when almost nine times that many Yankee males voted in the presidential election. Abolitionists agitating in the North often received a nonlynching version of a southern reception—rotten tomatoes aimed at the face, red pepper thrust under the nose, violent epithets drowning out the fanatic's voice. Once, in the notorious case of Elijah P. Lovejoy's murder in Illinois in 1837, these distractions escalated into a southern-style lynching.

Precisely this widespread northern opposition to antislavery, deeply rooted in Yankee anxiety about blacks, Union, and commerce, makes explaining the road to disunion difficult.[14] If the North was never committed to abolitionism, why should the South have felt compelled to secede? Troubled by that question, an important group of historians, the so-called Revisionists of the 1930s, revised away slavery as a cause of Civil War. These scholars urged that irresponsible agitators must have used delusive propaganda to whip up a needless combat.[15]

Those 1835 northern meetings, like Yankees' assault on the Slavepower's three-fifths extra power in Missouri Controversy times, supply a better explanation of Northerners' anti-southernism. While most Yankees were not fanatical about liberty for blacks, they demanded egalitarian republicanism for whites. According to prevailing opinions "on the subject of liberty and freedom," explained a Bostonian, and "according to the letter of the Constitution, the States *cannot* prevent by legislation the printing and distribution of pamphlets." Southerners must consider it "enough that the great body of the people in this quarter" condemn "any interference with the internal policy of the slaveholding states." Southerners must not "require of us a course of conduct which would strike at the root of everything we have been taught to consider sacred."[16]

Sacred. That word lay behind Charles Grandison Finney's preaching and Theodore Dwight Weld's crusade. But few Yankees thought blacks' right to liberty so sacred as to chase a holy war with righteous Southerners. Whites' democratic rights, on the other hand, were as precious as the sacrament. The three-fifths clause already provoked northern egalitarian republicans. If Southerners now piled on insistence that Northerners jail dissenters, abolitionists might become more popular.

Fortunately for the Union, South Carolina extremists alone insisted that the North become a closed society. The northern majority, James Henry Hammond of South Carolina wrote the editor of the *New York Evening Star* on August 19, 1835, must not allow abolitionists "an asylum from which to hurl their murderous missiles." Fanatics "can be silenced in but one way—*Terror— death.*" Northern states "must pass laws," dispatching incendiaries "on demand to those whose laws and whose rights they have violated." Unless Northerners extradited incendiaries down South for trial, "we shall dissolve the Union, and *seek by war* the redress denied us."[17]

There echoed Carolina's advanced consciousness. There screeched a zealot out of touch with the southern mainstream. Few Southerners demanded abolitionists' scalps or else. The southern mainstream plea for repressive northern action came down to a request. The irritated northern mainstream was at liberty to reject southern calls to turn the North into a Slavepower jail.

– 3 –

With northern extremists free to agitate, the southern mainstream had to learn to live with a permanent antislavery crusade. The learning was distressing and never complete. Southern edginess about new Yankee extremists swiftly altered the region's political discourse, particularly in Middle and Deep Souths.

The omnipresent new southern issue in 1835 was northern antislavery agitation. The new tone of stridency, omnipresent only in South Carolina previously, yielded periodically ugly debates over which southern politician was most "soft on slavery" and secretly anxious to collaborate with antislavery Northerners. One valued new talent was skill at pinning the label "disloyalty" most firmly on the opponent.

These contests over loyalty became instantly lethal because a critical reorganization of southern politics simultaneously occurred. During the very period when an abolitionist onslaught emerged in the North, a region-wide, highly competitive two-party system appeared in the South. Newly positioned Southern politicians were on the hunt for the tiny margins of victory which assaulting an opponent's loyalty could abundantly provide.

While Andrew Jackson was running for President, southern politics were highly competitive only in Henry Clay's relatively slaveless, highly nationalistic Border South. In 1828, John Quincy Adams secured a respectable 45% of popular votes and 29% of electoral votes in Delaware, Maryland, Missouri, and Kentucky. In 1832, Henry Clay won 68% of these Border South states' popular vote and 77% of their electoral votes.

Deeper in the South, except in Louisiana with its fairly vigorous nationalistic party, Jackson and states' rights were almost unopposed. Politicians love to oppose. Deep and Middle South politicians forfeited by default both chances for appointed patronage from an anti-Jackson presidential administration and chances for elected office should Jacksonian initiatives turn sour.

Southern opportunities widened as Jackson's presidency waned. Old Hickory was the Southwest's man, the perfection of the region's mentality and persona. Southwesterners were stuck instead in 1835–6 behind Martin Van Buren. Jackson told his supporters that the Little Magician was the best successor; and if Old Hickory said so, it must be true. But few slaveholding outdoorsmen would have selected a pudgy, pasty Yankee politician as hero apparent, if their idol had not.

Only intimates found Martin Van Buren heroic. This professional politician possessed great skills at positioning himself on issues, planning campaigns, sensing moods, exploiting advantages. These were insiders' talents, pros' virtuosities, and professionals who worked closely with the so-called Little Magician relished the sly operator. They also believed that Van Buren concocted sleights of hand not just to win the game but also to create a patriotic amalgam of New Yorkers and Virginians, plain republicans north and prestigious planters south, dedicated to saving the Union and spreading white men's egalitarianism. Southern professional politicians who knew Van Buren well and trusted him totally included the Blairs of Maryland and Missouri, who edited the ultra-prestigious and longtime pro-Van Buren *Washington Globe,* and Thomas Ritchie, head of the so-called Richmond Junto of Virginia Democrats and editor of the equally pro-Van Buren *Richmond Enquirer.*

Despite their editorial skills, the Blairs and Ritchies could never sell their image of Van Buren to the southern masses. Southerners who saw the New Yorker only from afar usually visualized a self-serving manipulator. Van Buren's concessions to the South seemed begrudging. His vaunted magic seemed contrived to sink deeper ruts in the middle of the Yankee road. With the trade of an apparent Yankee wirepuller for the Southwest's hero, Jacksonianism lost much of its southern magic before the Little Magician could finesse an issue.

Van Buren's further misfortune was that Jackson's unbeatable southwestern issue was lost. Jackson had accomplished too well what Southwesterners had most elected him to achieve. The old Indian slayer had moved reds out of white frontiersmen's way. Indians, having marched their Trail of Tears to trans-Mississippi reservations, had become the first American Invisible Men. No magic of Van Buren's could make the best initial southwestern reason for Jacksonianism visible again.

With neither Jackson's charisma nor his most charismatic issue capable of being inherited, politicians throughout the South hustled to build an anti-Van Buren party in time for the 1836 presidential election. As is so often true of partisans of the ideologically impure American party, these party builders, seeking different programs, mounted different assaults on the enemy party. Southern anti-Van Buren states' righters called the Yankee too soft on states' rights for slavery's safety. Meanwhile, southern anti-Van Buren nationalists called the New Yorker too committed to states' rights for the South's prosperity.

Anti-Van Buren states' righters had lately seceded from the Democratic Party. Their switch had its origins in the Nullification Controversy. Jackson's choice of the moderate states' righter Van Buren over the extremist Calhoun, the President's relative uninterest in tariff reform, Jackson's anti-secessionist threats in his Nullification Proclamation—all these relatively nationalistic positions made states' righters besides Calhoun wonder whether Jacksonianism was states' rights enough.

The worry increased in 1833–4 when Jackson seized federal monies from the national bank and deposited the lucre in his pet local banks. This transfer of millions, assuredly not enumerated as a presidential power in the Constitution, also arguably defied national law. This latest aggressive national presidential action looked to those states' righters who had half-deserted Jackson over the Nullification Controversy as cause to desert ship entirely.

Deserters usually went straight over to the anti-Jacksonian coalition. That opposing institution would be called the Whig Party by the late 1830s, in honor of its campaign against that alleged monarchical threat to American chaste republicanism, King Andrew. For a short time in the mid-1830s, the party opposing Jackson was instead known as the Opposition Party. Oppositionists who had departed the Jackson coalition resolved to turn Oppositionism into a truer states' rights crusade than Jackson's allegedly phony version.

The more purist of these turncoats hoped that once they demanded states' rights candidates and policies as a condition for their support, nationalistic Oppositionists would surrender. "Our fate is in our own hands," trumpeted Duff Green, Calhoun's favorite editor, to Beverley Tucker, a founder of the Virginia Opposition Party. "We can make the next President, and what is more important, we can make him a thorough-going states' rights republican."[18]

That strategy faced forbidding obstacles, as the more politic party-switchers, such as North Carolina's United States Senator Willie Mangum, well knew. In the North and Border South too, Oppositionists had long been high nationalists. Would the traditional party majority surrender to an upstart states' rights fraction? Worse, states' righters did not always control the new southernmost wing of the Opposition Party. In the blackest black belts, Oppositionists often withered the post-Jackson Southern Democratic Party with nationalistic rather than states' rights attacks.

Nationalists in the Deep and Middle Souths reasoned that the John Adams–Henry Clay American System should attract commercial planters and commercial townsmen. The nationalistic program sought national roads and national banks for those who sold in a national commercial network. Slaveholders selling staples needed sound banks and good transportation, as did townsmen who marketed planters' produce. Southern commercial types, agrarian and urban, arguably hurt themselves when voting against national aids to commerce.

Both the South's States' Rights and Nationalist Oppositionists benefited from the simultaneous emergence of abolitionism, Van Buren's presidential campaign, and outcries about southern disloyalty. States' Rights Oppositionists' problem was that the Jacksonian states' rights coalition might seem more states' rights and thus safer for slavery. These Oppositionists answered that Van Buren, Yankee compromiser, would not be reliable when slavery was on the line. Meanwhile, the South's more nationalistic Oppositionists had to combat southern fears that a nationalistic state used to further the economy could also be used to emancipate slaves. These Oppositionists answered that the phony Van Buren was the real national menace to slavery. Poor Van Buren, already in enough southern trouble because Jackson was such a bear to follow, faced charges that he was disloyal to slavery from every southern direction.

– 4 –

Southern rhetoric about disloyalty was periodically important in struggles between Oppositionists/Whigs and Democrats, from the inception of a true two-party system in 1835 to the system's collapse in the early 1850s. Stridency about disloyalty was especially pivotal in 1835–6, when Oppositionists exploited uneasiness about Van Buren's Yankeeness to help create the first presidential-election-year, two-party system in Middle and Deep Souths. But this style of campaigning was for almost two decades more a periodic distraction than the constant essence of political strife between Southern Democrats and Oppositionists/Whigs.[19] Because antebellum Americans profoundly cared about many things beside slavery, sectional warriors were destined to have an extremely difficult time breaking down either party, as John C. Calhoun would discover time after unhappy time.

Proslavery agitators' greatest problem was that most southern politics were local politics. National presidential campaigns, when slavery issues were most obtrusive and oratory about loyalty most shrill, occurred only every four years. Local elections transpired far more often. Then, local issues were usually exclusively at stake. Oppositionists/Whigs favored using not only national but also state and town governments to boost and to regulate individual entrepreneurial endeavor. Whiggish efforts for government-supported community had a moral as well as an economic purpose. Just as governments on every level must sustain roads and railroads, banks and bounties, so Christian community required state regulation of drinking and fornication, the sabbath and the schools.[20]

Whigs' opponents in the Democratic Party, locally only a little less than nationally, tended to be against government intervention in citizens' moral or economic lives. Democrats championed the untrammeled individual, source they said of the swiftest economic progress and the soundest morality. These party differences led to endless localistic skirmishes over state promotion of market enterprise and of moral behavior, concerns productive of huge voter turnouts in nonpresidential years, matters having nothing to do with slavery or loyalty or anything national at all.

Andrew Jackson became a larger-than-life public figure partly because he personified this main business of the Second American Party System. To Democrats, Jackson was the glorious creature unshackled, the loner against the world, the individual who made history happen. To Whigs, Andrew Jackson, arch-individualist, was the anti-communitarian, the untrammeled egotist, the cowboy contemptuous of rules on the range. Democrats, loving Jackson, championed the individual power of the presidency. Whigs, hating King Andrew, exalted the cooperative judgment of cabinet and Congress. To be a Whig or a Democrat was to believe or disbelieve that the man apart should or must not be corralled, that the cooperative community must or must not boost/control human endeavors—and that Andrew Jackson must—or must never—become the epitome of Romantic America.

These issues were consuming, especially vivid because Jackson dramatized them, particularly riveting because critical to each individual's conception of himself and his relationship to his neighborhood. That is why exclusive focus on outbursts over loyalty to slavery distorts southern day-to-day political life most of the time. Still, loyalty outbursts were periodically important, in part because they eventually became more destructively constant, in part because they were most vital during presidential campaigns, that supreme moment of American political drama.

Each southern party entered presidential contests with slightly under half of the local electorate. The final boost over the top required last-minute conversions or decisions to go to the polls. The politics of slavery and loyalty, irrelevant to southern two-party struggle most of the time, could determine who won the swing fraction in the most famous southern showdowns.

Thus in national presidential years, Oppositionists/Whigs and Democrats did brawl and brawl about who was true-blue to slavery. Zest for these wars was most rampant among Southern Democrats, whose party passed all the national proslavery laws,[21] and among the more states' rights anti-Jacksonians, who needed to prove that the Democracy's triumphs were compromised states' rights victories. The more nationalistic anti-Jacksonians, particularly in the Border South, tended to cringe at such mudslinging.

Still, these nationalists sometimes found their uses for the rhetorical ugliness. By joining their states' rights wing in damning Democrats as soft on slavery, the South's more nationalistic anti-Jacksonians could decontaminate nationalism, dissociate themselves from northern nationalists' anti-Slavepower taint, make state-promoted enterprise as lily-white as egalitarian democracy, and present to commercial planters a program for commercial progress with every boomerang against slavery removed. Protection for slavery, the essence of political activity for the relatively few southern Oppositionist/Whig states' rights purists, was for the relatively larger number of southern Oppositionist/Whig nationalists a periodic precondition for emphasizing truer essences.

Emphasizing those true-blue essences, the old Henry Clay-John Quincy Adams exaltation of nation, commerce, and communal morality, put anti-Jacksonian nationalists in the center of national politicians' Union-saving effort to make everything except slavery the business of national politics. But here as everywhere, slavery made the Southerner an American with a difference. Just as the lyncher was an offstride egalitarian and the patriarch was an offbeat American husband, so the nationalistic Oppositionist who periodically helped strain the Union by emphasizing Democrats' alleged sellout of section was not precisely your normal nationalist. By being somewhat of an abnormality, these nationalists most resistant to shrill loyalty politics especially well revealed that slavery issues could corrode politicians' plans as early as 1835—including schemes of the New Yorker dreaming futilely of becoming the South's new hero.

– 5 –

Martin Van Buren, for all his vulnerabilities as a Yankee seeking the Democratic Party's southern power base, at least presided over a consolidated national party. In 1835–6, Oppositionists were too disunited to call a national convention.[22] Nationalists northward such as John Quincy Adams, Henry Clay, and Daniel Webster shared little except opposition to Van Buren with States' Rights Oppositionists southward. Leaders were not even in enough contact to plot a nation-wide presidential strategy by mail. Rather, each section's politicians informally nominated a regional presidential candidate. Massachusetts opponents of Van Buren nominated their favorite son, the ultra-nationalistic Daniel Webster. Other northern and Border South Oppositionists rallied to a quasi-nationalist, William Henry Harrison of Indiana. Oppositionists in Middle and Lower Souths massed behind that venerable states' righter, Senator Hugh Lawson White of Tennessee.

White, a Tennessee planter and longtime crony of Jackson, had broken with Old Hickory over what he considered Jackson's anti-egalitarian inflation of presidential power. White now urged that Old Hickory, by seeking to dictate Van Buren's succession, was still less a white man's egalitarian. King Andrew was a Caesar who menaced states' rights and egalitarianism both.

Van Buren's black-belt foes furthermore called Hugh White, native-born Southerner, the best protection against abolitionists' agitation and Van Buren's "unsafe" opposition to it. Hugh White's proponents put the final touch on their true-blue southern ticket by nominating for Vice President a tardy but true recent states' rights come-outer from the Democracy, Senator John Tyler of Virginia.

This Opposition Party tactic instantly captured Southern Van Burenites' attention. Anti-Jacksonians had lately swept up governorships in Mississippi and Tennessee, as well as the Tennessee and North Carolina state legislatures. The image of two Southerners from the manor born running against an impure compromiser from abolitionist territory could push the South's ominous new anti-Jackson tide ahead. The notion that only an Opposition administration would uncompromisingly protect slavery had to be disproven, and in a hurry. Southern Democrats thus wrote urgent letters to New York in the fall of 1835, warning Van Buren that the South was slipping away. Van Buren answered with a public letter, condemning abolitionists and insisting that no slaveholder would more resolutely reject fanaticism.[23]

Van Buren's letter sounded defensive. The better defense was an offense. Southern Van Burenites went straight after their southern opponents' Achilles' heel. Southern Oppositionists alleged that Southern Democrats who supported Van Buren, northern trimmer, sold out on states' rights. Well, Southern Oppositionists fought side by side with Northern Oppositionists, those most notorious enemies of states' rights. If Hugh Lawson White stopped Van Buren in the Electoral College, Southern Democrats warned, the House of Representatives would have to decide between Opposition candidates. The huge majority of nationalistic-leaning Oppositionists, so Democrats argued, would never bow to the comparative handful of Hugh Lawson White supporters, unless White surrendered states' rights. Whether White sold out or Webster or Harrison prevailed, the Opposition administration would be outrageously more nationalistic than the Little Magician's. A Southerner must be unsafe on slavery to help further that scenario!

Democrats were traitors to slavery because they supported a New York non-slaveholder over a Tennessee slaveholder! Oppositionists were traitors to slavery because they shared a party with uncompromising Yankee nationalists! Unsound! Untrue! Soft on slavery! These terrible accents dominated political discourse in the lower two-thirds of the South in the season after abolitionists appeared. Only in Henry Clay's Border South were the politics of loyalty usually shunned. Deeper in Dixie, debates about who was loyal would continue to be omnipresent on occasion, especially in presidential election campaigns, for the next quarter-century.[24]

– 6 –

How to explain this strident antebellum rhetoric? The easy way is to dismiss all that inflammatory talk as "mere" words, "mere" politics. Such "meres" will come especially easily to those so-called Revisionist historians who have long thought that "irresponsible agitators" used "mere demogoguery" to cause a "needless " Civil War.

That old explanation contains vital truth. Ambitious political candidates especially exploited fears about disloyalty, for exciting the multitude was the path toward electoral victory. Sometimes no rhetoric worked so well as indicting one's opponent as soft on slaves.

But the "demagoguery" label, while accounting for some demagogues, cannot explain why demagoguery worked. "Demagoguery" reveals nothing about why Southerners eagerly listened to supposedly cynical agitators. Nor does "demagoguery" explain why so-called demagogues often honestly believed in their "propaganda." Any democratic election invites the ambitious to thunder about disloyalty, assuming the label of "traitor" can be made to adhere. No democratic community lacks aspirants who will wax terrible about traitors, assuming enough listeners believe.

Usually, too few voters believe. Charges of "soft on communism" or whatever usually produce an eventual backlash against demagogues. For all the terrible impact of the Republicans' Joe McCarthy on American life in the 1950s, for example, accusations that Democrats were traitors rang true only briefly. That Republican red-baiter, Richard Nixon, shrewdly sizing up the public, shifted from red-baiting to approaching Red China as soon as public sentiment shifted.[25]

Antebellum Deep and Middle Souths never shifted in presidential election campaigns after 1835, when loyalty mudslinging began to be employed. Dispassionate Southerners, particularly in the neutralist Border South, kept calling cries of disloyalty unfair, unreliable, untrue. But charges of treachery rang on and on. Granted, the ambitious exploited southern apprehension. Granted, the exploiting magnified the southern public's inclination to believe that disloyalty abounded. But why the disposition to listen to this "mere" talk?

The talk itself provides clues. Charges of disloyalty customarily revolved around a standard text. The largest theme was usually that southern politicians unreliably counted on northern politicians. That charge struck home because in the provincial and insular southern world, all outsiders were suspect. Southerners universally accepted only one slavery proposition. Southerners must decide the institution's fate.

Instead, southern statesmen in national parties relied on Yankee allies to help decide slavery questions. For a northern President to propose right slavery legislation or for northern congressmen to rally behind properly southern law, Yankees full of talk about friendship to the South must prove as friendly as claimed. The situation invited each party's southern insiders to damn the other party's Yankee outsiders as suspect.

Insiders who trusted suspect outsiders, continued southern loyalty tirades, must themselves be disloyal. That accusation fed on southern disagreement about what loyalty to slavery entailed. Southerners split on what a southern statesman should think and do about the institution, never more so than when loyalty politics began in 1835. Internal southern debate on diffusing slavery away had lately been consuming, especially in Virginia and Maryland. The discussion would never cease. When Southerners sought to define why a man or a principle was traitorously anti-southern, the debate over the identity of *a* South descended toward the gutter.

As is always true when a democratic culture becomes obsessed with loyalty, debate did not just aim at defining the patriotic. The politics of loyalty were also a form of social control, the strongest form of democratic social control short of undemocratic violence. Democrats at moments of crisis tend to escalate charges of disloyalty, seeking to maximize inclinations in the charily disloyal to remain silent. When faced with neighbors' withering hostility, those tempted to dissent often instead demonstrate their soundness. As many American dissenters have unhappily learned, a public opinion armed with "mere" words exerts enormous conformist force.

The southern democratic system, because half-despotic, could deploy more terrible sanctions than verbal violence. Mobs who turned mails into bonfires were a reminder that lynching sometimes deterred dissenters. But in a world semi-democratic and wholly localistic, republican discourse at its most violent, which meant the lethal language of loyalty, was the most terrorizing considered routinely legitimate.

Verbal coerciveness usually sufficed. Not the state's punishment but the neighborhood's condemnation usually countered tyrants' abuse of slaves. Loyalty politics, like Jackson's hope that neighbors would frown down those demanding censored mail, transformed this cultural power into political power. Apologetic softhearts, when facing disloyalty charges, thought twice about advocating antislavery. So too, border neutrals, when facing accusations of traitor, took care about befriending suspect northern politicians.

Politicians were the most suspect of friends. Americans living through the first age of mass parties initiated a permanently schizophrenic attitude towards politicians. On the one hand, politicians were thought to be heroically presiding over the greatest popular drama. On the other hand, pols were thought to be contemptibly hiding behind self-serving masks.

While sometimes scorning their own politicians for wearing masks, Southerners most feared Yankee disguises. Yanks, according to the stock southern image, were ingratiating materialists. Grasping Northerners and ambitious spoilsmen added up to phony politicians, putting on any face for a vote. Such thinking led to that disastrous southern image of Martin Van Buren and those disconcerting attacks on Southerners who championed the New Yorker.

Suspicions of political pretenders also fed on suspicions of domestic pretenders. The image of slaves as deceitful scamps and politicians as delusive schemers fit each other as the hand fit the glove. Cuffee, Professor of Pretense, gave Southerners daily instruction in sham. The slave as teacher molded his pupil towards seeing politics, like all of human life, as one great big suspicious act.

The southern politics of loyalty, then, was not "mere" propaganda, if successful propaganda can ever be "mere." Rather, key cultural anxieties were involved. Those southern charges of sham, disloyalty, unsoundness, played on Southerners' uneasiness about Cuffees, on their suspicions of politicians and Yankees, on their distrust of outsiders and uncertainty about insiders, on the only democratic means of social control available to dictators enmeshed in a republic. Like all successful political tactics, contests over loyalty occurred because the scenario gripped actors and audience alike—and drew forth sounds of amen, amen.

– 7 –

In late 1835, with a two-party battle over loyalty the southern establishment's response to abolitionism, the Deep South's most unpopular actors were more than ever odd men out. Since nullification days, Carolinians had predicted that antislavery was coming. Other Southerners had scoffed. The movement had arrived.

Since 1831, John C. Calhoun had called the Jackson Party insufficient on states' rights. A political reorganization would come, he had foreseen, and states' rights Southerners would start it. Politicians in the two major parties had scoffed. Reorganization had arrived.

But states' rights leaders who had belatedly followed Calhoun out of the Democratic Party had sped right by the South's most famed warrior, into the Opposition Party. These politicians, so Calhoun fumed, had blundered into another compromising situation. An uncompromising states' rights organization required yet another reorganization.

Calhoun here clung to that American will-o'-the-wisp, the ideologically pure party. This genius of a theorist had no use for the practical genius of the American political party: its capacity to mute controversy, effect conciliation, find the middle of the road. Loyalty politics between Southern Democrats and Oppositionists featured a debate about who compromised least with northern allies. Calhoun called any compromising disastrous. Federal compromisers, he charged, deliberately dulled southern apprehensions. National spoilsmen desired a southern region asleep to slavery's dangers and an aristocratic culture infatuated with an egalitarianism mentality. Once demagogic wielders of the new mobocratic politics had dazed the elitists and dazzled the egalitarians, how many days could anti-egalitarian slavery have left?

Calhoun's distrust of mobocratic parties led to his opposition to proposed democratizations of South Carolina. If his state allowed the people to elect the governor and the governor to appoint executive officials, Calhoun declared in the typical Carolina vein, "two violent parties would spring up." No party would dare resist swollen federal power, for the other would stand "*ready to become* the Union Party" and receive "federal aid and patronage." From being the one state sustaining patriarchal republicanism, South Carolina would sink into the egalitarian muck. From being the only state with a "beautiful and well adjusted" aristocratic order, we would become "a wild, factious, and despotick democracy." All that because the people elected the governor![26]

Well, King Numbers elected too many in the Union, worried Calhoun. Too many party politicians anesthetized too many gullible commoners and unwary squires. Now, with antislavery growing and northern penal laws not passed, how were southern spoilsmen counterattacking? Teaching Southerners to insist that Northerners gag abolitionists? No way! Rather, distracting Southerners with arguments about whether Van Buren, the phony, or Harrison, the nationalizer, would be most untrue to the South!

States Rights' Oppositionists wished South Carolina's most famous states' righter would join them in making the Opposition Party uncompromisingly southern. Calhoun toyed with the idea. For all his anti-party rhetoric, he knew the value of capturing a party. For all his distrust of Clay and Webster, he knew he shared much with them. Calhoun and Clay had together passed the Compromise Tariff of 1833, together fought against King Andrews's swelling of presidential power, together winced at the Little Magician's ascension.

An alliance with Clay and Webster, thought Calhoun, did make some philosophic sense. "The wealthy and talented of the North," wrote Calhoun, "have more to fear from their own people" than slaveholders did from slaves. "Needy and corrupt" plebeians, after listening to egalitarian arguments against slavery, might rise up against their own unequal situation. Only an upper class united against all egalitarianisms would save itself North and South. Since the northern upper class predominantly supported the Opposition Party, maybe the southern upper class should join a potential instrument of a-sectional ruling-class salvation.[27]

Calhoun here drove a conservative postulate usually present in the proslavery argument to such a class-obsessed extreme as to seem to deserve the title, the "Marx of the Master Class."[28] But the deeper truth was that Calhoun, like all class-ridden southern thinkers, was too inconsistent to deserve such titles. The South Carolinian wandered between thinking that northern and southern upper classes were the same—and utterly different. Calhoun usually stood aloof from his friends' strategy for capturing the Opposition Party because he believed the northern upper class would always favor national banks, and worse, protective tariffs, and, worse still, African colonization. More friends of states' rights and foes of colonization, Calhoun believed, were in the Democratic Party, including northern laborers battling against northern employers. Despite his abstract wish for a national upper class to keep laborers black and white ground down, this practical ruler more often sought an alliance of lowly northern wage slaves and lordly southern chattel slaveholders.[29]

But if Calhoun sometimes embraced a return to a Jacksonian Party streamlined into a purely states' rights vehicle, he usually urged states' righters to come out of both national parties. The come-outers should unite in a southern convention. The convention should issue ultimatums to the North. Defections to the ideologically pure party would result. Yankees committed to states' rights, and/or northern politicians anxious for patronage from the nation's budding majority party, and/or capitalists anxious to remain in the same Union with southern customers, would ally with the South. National parties would be redrawn the right way, with the South at the head of a states' rights party and John C. Calhoun at the head of the South. Union would be saved, slavery perpetuated, and (this Calhoun did not add), John C. Calhoun, American outsider, would be elected President from within the establishment.[30]

Calhoun's new panacea, an ultimatum-issuing southern convention, resembled his old panacea, an ultimatum-issuing nullification convention. He remained convinced that great interests ruled politics, unless demagogical spoilsmen or religious fanatics clouded class consciousness. He remained persuaded that Yankee capitalists most wished to remain in the same country with southern slaveholders. His southern convention would so raise southern upper-class consciousness as to force truer northern upper-class consciousness. If he was wrong that the Yankee upper crust would cease and desist, a convention of aroused Southerners was just the vehicle to promote secession.

The few non-reluctant revolutionaries in South Carolina, with Professor Thomas Cooper front and center, loathed Calhoun's non-secessionist scenarios. Cooper mightily distrusted Calhoun. The Disunionist especially scorned Calhoun's tendency to consider rejoining the Democratic Party and running for President. Cooper opposed all parties, all Presidents, all Union-saving. The professor saw no hope Yankees would yield to any disunion threat, whether the ultimatum came from a nullifying state or a southern convention. He thought that once free of vulgar mass parties, patriarchs should move straight to revolution. Cooper's insistence on instant secession put Calhoun once again somewhere between Southerners more extreme in South Carolina and Southerners less extreme in the two-party establishment.

– 8 –

By late 1835, the new structure of southern politics was in place. Almost all southern politicians stood behind one of four contestants: Democrats, Oppositionists, Calhounites, Cooperites. Jackson's party remained the favorite to win Deep and Middle South elections, except in South Carolina. But Old Hickory's heir apparent, the Yankee Van Buren, was far more vulnerable in Jackson's area than the Old Hero had ever been. Signs of that vulnerability abounded: in escalating loyalty politics, in some former States' Rights Democrats' desertion to the Opposition, in the willingness of many Southerners who had voted for Jackson to consider state-promoted commerce and morality, so long as antislavery implications had been sanitized out. Oppositionists had already won two Middle South legislatures. They had always won more Border South elections than they lost. A two-party system had assuredly arrived in the South.

The two groups outside this reorganized two-party system, Calhounites and Cooperites, were slim in numbers. Few outside South Carolina stood with John C. Calhoun for a southern convention. Only a couple of Virginians stood with Thomas Cooper for southern disunion.

But the relatively few Calhounites and fewer Cooperites retained ominous leverage. The new southern establishment system had lately revolved around loyalty politics. Extremists could force that political combat to revolve around their disruptive issues. To wrench southern and thereby American two-party politics out of shape, Carolinians on the fringes had to introduce slavery-related demands which no loyal Southerner could ignore. Calhoun, for example, had to respond if Cooperites took a legitimate southern stand, lest Carolinians consider Mr. Nullifier, as in 1831, soft on the necessary extremism. Southern Democrats had to respond to Calhoun's response to Disunionists, lest the Jackson Party be considered, as after Jackson's Nullification Proclamation, soft on states' rights. Southern Oppositionists had to respond to the Democrats' response to Calhoun, lest the Opposition Party be called as dubious friends of slavery as were New England Oppositionists.

Southern national politicians, when competing to be hardest on slavery-related issues, could force northern allies to grant concessions, lest their party lose southern constituents. A Yankee pushed too hard, however, could bridle, lest he lose northern constituents. Either way, party and nation would be under strain. The reorganized southern political system could become a fulcrum, shoving the new abolitionist onslaught onto the establishment's national agenda in divisive ways.

The potential remained hidden in late 1835, when Southerners were journeying to the first congressional session following the antislavery mailings. Carolina extremists despaired of wrenching southern and thus national politics out of the (so they thought) disastrous two-party mold. Without confrontation politics, they could only revolutionize the establishment with the right divisive issue—the most shattering "mere" words.

Shattering words were elusive. No issue could be too extreme, lest moderates feel capable of ignoring it. Demands that the North imprison fanatics, for example, had not and could not inflame the establishment, for most moderates in both sections considered the idea too immoderate. Nor could a slavery issue be too innocuous, lest the mainstream incorporate it without strain. Cleansing southern post offices of incendiary mail, for example, the expected slavery controversy in the Congress of 1835–6, was too nonprovocative to promise national uproar. Mainstream Southerners could censor without Yankee outrage, so long as censorship occurred only in the South.

Nor could extremists' perfect issue be a proposition dividing the South. The most persistent national slavery issue between 1825 and 1835, federally financed colonization, was Carolinians' idea of the monster. In the aftermath of nullification, Calhoun feared colonizers would soon recommence "the work of immediate emancipation," unless "the entire slaveholding states" promptly resisted "at any hazard." But how would all Southerners threaten civil war over colonization, when most Southerners wistfully dreamed of diffusing away blacks?[31]

"I cannot say I have quite given up," South Carolina freshman Congressman James Hammond answered in November 1835, but "I am so much overwhelmed by difficulties surrounding the South that I hate to dwell upon the subject, and never do unless forced to it."[32] There spoke the dominator reduced to changing or destroying a republic only with some still-invisible wisp of a democratic issue. There despaired the extremist imprisoned outside the two-party system, unless a provocative matter could be dreamed up. There fumed a lethal danger to the establishment, if the frustrated bully suddenly found an issue capable of throwing the reorganized southern political structure into a fresh round of loyalty politics.

CHAPTER 17

The Gag Rule, I:
Mr. Hammond's
Mysterious Motion

Civil War buffs who disagree on so much might agree on one proposition: they know less about the Gag Rule Controversy than about any other major slavery crisis. Antebellum specialists who can explain picky details of the Kansas-Nebraska and Fugitive Slave controversies might flunk an exam on such large gag rule questions as why South Carolina's James Henry Hammond initiated the controversy by proposing unprecedently sweeping repression of congressional slavery debate in 1835, on how and why New York's Martin Van Buren and Pennsylvania's James Buchanan obtained different dilutions of Hammond's undiluted silencer in 1836, and on how and why Maryland's William Cost Johnson (who?!) secured Hammond's pure gag in 1840. Civil War experts may also puzzle over why such matters are important.[1]

Contemporaries suffered no such puzzlement. Leaders and followers who failed to silence slavery controversies throughout the 1850s remembered gag contentions as baptisms in failure. Contemporaries understood that contests over gagging congressional slavery debates epitomized why Yankees previously hostile to abolitionists became furious about the Slavepower. Participants also comprehended that this first Jacksonian slavery controversy demonstrated why Jacksonian "Democracy" would become increasingly undemocratic. Contemporaries furthermore understood that the gag rule exposed the impossible plight of the Opposition/Whig Party, should slavery issues ever become paramount. These early scars on the body politic would be opened again and again during the better-known later crises on the road to disunion.

– 1 –

Nothing seizes attention like an unexpected explosion. The Gag Rule Crisis was the Pearl Harbor of the slavery controversy. No one anticipated any such convulsion. Rather, congressmen convening in December of 1835 expected a little spat over abolitionist mail.[2]

No one trembled over that expected disagreement. During the fall, most Northerners had learned they could live with southern censorship of Dixie, so long as censorship stayed South. Most Southerners had meanwhile learned they could live with northern sermons about southern sanitization, so long as Yankees did not interfere with the sanitizers.

President Andrew Jackson, in his annual message to Congress, made contention over antislavery mailings a little more heated than expected by demanding federal rather than southern hands on "fanatics." The South's most popular slaveholder called antislavery "unconstitutional and wicked." America's favorite Democrat would "prohibit, under severe penalties, the circulation in the southern states, through the mail, of incendiary publication."[3] This time, the President would deploy federal officials, not neighbors' frowns, to keep dissenters from receiving abolitionist appeals.

By urging censorship among whites to consolidate despotism over blacks, Andrew Jackson violated the color line which defined Jacksonian Democracy no less than white men's republicanism. Still, Jackson's suggested censorship remained a brief aside, buried in a message emphasizing more democratic proposals. Furthermore, Jackson's momentary tangent was swiftly defeated, with Old Hickory, the leader who usually screamed when crossed, voicing no protest.

President Jackson's proposal remains important as a preliminary sign of what Jacksonian "Democracy" would soon become. That tiny crack in the color line would widen, with Jackson's blessings, because of the mentality Jackson for the first time here exuded in a presidential message. The Tennessee planter, apostle of pure white republicanism, would never allow republican agitation to damage black slavery. Andrew Jackson, majoritarian supreme, would also encourage southern minorities to demand the force of law if control over blacks was threatened. Jackson's proposal was closer to Calhoun's views about northern threats, slavery's weaknesses, and democracy's limits than anything in Van Buren's statecraft. In ensuing years, when this side of Jackson's thought moved from an aside in a presidential message to front and center on Jackson's own agenda, Van Buren's ascendancy over Calhoun within the Jackson Party would be finished, not least because Jackson would undercut his former favorite.

In late 1835 and early 1836, Mr. South Carolina helped delay resurrection of a Jackson-Calhoun alliance by turning on the President's censorship proposal. The nation's most famous southern ultra may seem an improbable opponent of Andrew Jackson's first proposed ultra proslavery law. The southern President, having previously called abolition Calhoun's fantasy, was now giving public lessons on antislavery's "wicked and unconstitutional" nature. The Tennessean was also now urging fellow Southerners to make demands on the North which might further Calhoun's political agenda. If Northern Democrats rejected Jackson-sanctioned censorship, Southern Democrats might secede from the party. Seceders might even attend Calhoun's southern convention. A pure states' rights national organization might result. To a Carolinian desperate for an issue to restructure an establishment, Jackson's suggestion might seem heaven-sent.

Calhoun would not touch the stuff. The Carolinian, enemy of southern moderation and division, risked further dividing the South by urging moderation on the President. A federal government now censoring antislavery mailings, Calhoun warned, might later censor proslavery mailings. Moreover, if Congress could now decide antislavery was incendiary, Congress could later determine repression of abolitionism was immoral. Jackson's pro-southern law "virtually" would "clothe Congress with the power" to destroy Southerners' "lives and property." Calhoun asked instead that Congress authorize each state to censor federal mails within its boundaries.[4]

Southern disagreement over whether to support federal censorship meant that Northerners felt no pressure on the issue. Northerners could go forward to require delivery of the mail. In 1836, the resulting law forbade postmasters from unlawfully detaining mails. The question remained whether federal postal officials, when obeying state laws protecting the public safety from incendiary deliveries, acted unlawfully. Federal postmaster generals answered that local postmasters must obey local law.[5]

For the next quarter-century, a few Northerners sporadically protested when a few Southerners sporadically censored the mails. But so long as neither northern state governments nor the national government acted as censor, most Northerners felt *their* governments remained democratic. Allowing dirty hands to exist in the South was the long-standing price of national Union. The mails controversy showed that most Yankees would pay that price, so long as southern mud stayed in the South. The only losers in the mails controversy, slaves' usual unspeakable loss aside, were southern extremists, who had renounced the one miserable divisive issue they had anticipated when journeying to Congress in the fall of 1835.

– 2 –

Suddenly, in December of 1835, the apparently perfect issue descended into southern extremists' hands. The unexpected bonanza would provide the ideal shock, so it seemed at first, to force Southerners out of compromising national parties. The surprise controversy, as it quickly turned out, instead showed dismayed radicals how thoroughly southern compromisers were stuck in the establishment.

The process began in the fall of 1835, after abolitionists realized that mailings could not convert Southerners. The North's tiny minority of Theodore Dwight Welds hit upon the alternate tactic of sending antislavery petitions to Congress. The gambit was refined so that petitions did not seek the perchance unconstitutional and assuredly radical emancipation of millions of southern slaves. Rather abolitionists prayed for the arguably more constitutional and assuredly more conservative freeing of Washington's several hundred bondsmen. The Constitution gave Congress legislative power over the District. The existence of the nation's most anti-republican institution in the republic's capital seemed particularly unfortunate. After a handful of slaves had been freed in this safe and salutory context, the national govenment might consider spreading abolitionism a mite southward.

That calm train of fiery thought, so congenial to Charles Finney's impassioned style of reasoned revival, brought a blizzard of paper descending on Congress. The new avalanche, looked at closely, hardly seemed menacing. A small percentage of voters signed antislavery petitions. A large percentage of petitioners were not voters, for disenfranchised women and children signed. Petitions sometimes contained no signatures, just lists of citizens, cut out of newspapers and glued to petitions. Even at its most conservative, early abolitionism failed to attract widespread northern support.[6]

Nor did the petition debate start only after many petitions, however signed, descended on Congress. Representatives had traditionally tabled antislavery prayers or buried them in committee. On December 16, 1835, the House reaffirmed traditional procedures by tabling two petitions. Among those voting to table was South Carolina's James Henry Hammond.[7]

On December 18, 1835, a third petition was presented. This time, young Mr. Hammond rose. The freshman congressman urged "a more decided seal of reprobation" for insults to the South. The Carolinian moved that antislavery prayers not be received in the House. Instead of considering and tabling abolitionist appeals, the Carolina reactionary would gag the libertarian subject before it even entered deomcracy's doors.[8]

Southern moderates swiftly realized that James Hammond here wielded an extremist's dream of an issue. Self-respecting Southerners could not ignore their fellow slaveholder's call to defy an attack on their honor. A deliberate decision to allow fanaticism inside congressional chambers would also revive fears awakened during the previous fall's post office crises. Slaves residing in or near Washington would again know about the attack on the Domestic Institution. Slaveholders speculating about easing slavery away would again be instructed that continuing the institution was immoral. An extreme idea catching mainstream attention everywhere in the Western World would again be presented in deceptively moderate form to northern—and southern—moderates.

Congressman Francis Pickens from the South Carolina upcountry, a contemptuous young squire destined to be one of Hammond's rivals to become Calhoun's successor, outdid Hammond in explaining why southern congressmen must gag this abstraction "at the threshhold." Pickens called irrelevant the fact that abolitionists "are, at present, . . . small" in numbers. Fanaticism at first always seems "like a speck in the distant horizon," to be "despised for its weakness." But zealots' "appeal to the passions of the heart" becomes unconquerable as "it spreads and widens." Eventually, fanaticism "sweeps with the fury of the rushing tornado" over "those who at first felt . . . contempt for its impotence."

"The moral power of the world," Pickens warned fellow Southerners, "is against us . . . England has emancipated her West Indies islands. France is also moving in the same direction." Now the United States counterpart knocks on congressional doors. "Sooner or later, we shall have to contend" for "our consecrated hearthstones" or "abandon our country to become a black colony."

Better sooner than later. To conquer fanaticism, we must "meet it and strangle it in its infancy."[9]

South Carolinians' insistence that fanaticism be gagged in its infancy brought a far-off abstraction up close and personal to every southern congressman. James Hammond's procedural motion challenged chummy rules of the clubbiest American political club, the United States Congress. Members' respect for each other's integrity, the source of club *esprit,* underlay Hammond's insistence on change in club governance. Hammond would not allow insult inside the clubhouse. If you are as true to slavery as you claim, the South Carolina radical challenged southern moderates, you will not tolerate a petition calling you a sinner. You will insist that a dishonorable demand for a national hearing on your depravity be halted at the door, even if in the process you snap chummy club ties.

Once again, Francis Pickens outdid James Hammond in pressing the newest Carolina tactic on wary non-Carolinians. If any supposed representative "of the slaveholding race," declared Pickens, "is so bowed down in subservience and servility to party discipline and party organization as to be drawn off this question, for the vile purpose of partisan ascendancy and political triumph in the miserable conflicts of the day, let me say to him, this is no place for him, unless he is prepared to cover himself with prostitution." Nor is Congress any place for a southern gentleman aspiring "to please the dominant interests of this confederacy by sycophancy and flattery, for the purpose of clothing himself in the livery and trappings of office." Any such recreant "is prepared to abandon the inheritance of the fathers, and cover his children with degradation and ruin."[10]

Neither the congressional club nor party politicians who ran the shop could ever be the same after Hammond's and Pickens's challenge. In both sections, mainstream politicians were damned however they responded to the lunatic fringe. Southern congressmen could ignore or water down Hammond's gag. They would thereby please northern political allies at the expense of seeming disloyal back home. Or southern representatives could insist on gagging the constituents of their northern allies. Southrons would thereby become true-blue southern at the expense of making their northern friends less electable in the North.

Yankee congressmen faced an equivalent no-win situation. Northerners could appease southern allies on gags, thereby saving their national political party but risking constituents' displeasure. Or Northerners could defy southern colleagues, thereby appeasing their constituents but risking national political alliances. Hammond's motion endangered every congressman's local seat and national party—and thereby endangered national Union itself.

– 3 –

Nation-smashing, went up the almost immediate accusation, was exactly what James Hammond and Francis Pickens intended. John C. Calhoun, so it was widely charged, secretly conspired to put these young turks up to this assault on Union. Hammond, Pickens, and Calhoun were not the only "disunionist conspirators" suspected. If we could raid Hammond's mailbox, became the northern chorus, we would find an undercover plot to destroy everything national.

Thus was nurtured the northern conception of a Great Slavepower Conspiracy, allegedly conspiring to dominate or destroy democratic Union. Thus ran the first explanation of why James Hammond initiated the Gag Rule Controversy. In discerning whether the first explanation was right, historians can use material that Northerners would have paid a fortune to secure. Hammond's allegedly traitorous correspondence lies open for scrutiny in the Library of Congress, close to the legislative chamber where South Carolina's supposedly treasonous plot reached public fruition. James Hammond was one of those rare leaders, God bless their souls, who saved everything. Hammond's gag rule initiative was one of those rare moments when a culture's way-out ultras captured the mainstream's worried attention. Full sources plus supreme moment add up to rich opportunity. Posterity can discern whether, and if so why, the immoderate Mr. Hammond intended that his motion might push the moderate South down the road to disunion. We can also inquire whether, and if so why, conspirators put this inexperienced provoker up to his historic provocation, and whether, and if so why, John C. Calhoun was the chief Slavepower Conspirator.

Let us ask questions about the conspiracy instead of dismissing it. Throughout the twentieth century, historians have ridiculed the nineteenth-century notion that a Great Slavepower Conspiracy existed. The scoffing correctly emphasizes that the South was too divided and unrevolutionary for a tiny revolutionary crew to plot every step toward revolution. Conspiratorial planning was not even always omnipresent at the most revolutionary moments. Carolina nullifiers had assuredly not secretly plotted strategy with non-Carolinians before moving to the brink of revolution in 1832-3, which is one reason these odd revolutionaries felt so vulnerable on the brink. The only southern conspiracy in the nullification winter involved Calhoun and Clay secretly negotiating on the Nullifiers' non-negotiable demands. The only Great Slavepower Conspiracy in the pre-nullification year involved Virginia Governor John Floyd secretly seeking Deep South governors' collaboration in easing slavery away after the Nat Turner uprising.

The possibility remains that these earlier debacles had taught Carolinians to plot before plunging. In most revolutions, more confident revolutionaries than these once-burned Nullifiers secretly plot first steps before risking revolutionary action. We will see that in 1850-1 and 1860-1 extremists used conspiratorial correspondence to avoid the kind of scary isolation the Carolinians felt during the nullification winter. Did any such secret plot lie behind James Hammond's Union-threatening initiative of 1835-6?

The investigation of whether a Great Slavepower Conspiracy produced Hammond's motion should begin with Hammond himself. Did this freshman congressman intentionally provide the connecting link between revolutionary planning in South Carolina and disruptive agitation in Congress? Were his world views and intentions identical with men from his state who had long plotted separation from the Union? What sort of character was this inexperienced hothead who precipitated one of the great slavery crises?

In a state where an incredible 96% of the population was homegrown, James Henry Hammond was about as close to an outsider as any insider could be. He was not to the manor but to the hut born. His father, Elisha Hammond, was a New England migrant who lived out his days in Carolina as an embittered, impoverished outsider. Elisha at various times was reduced to supplying wormy meat to South Carolina College students and to teaching squires' urchins at the upcountry's Mount Bethel Academy. His frayed self-respect hung on one ambition. He prayed that future generations of Hammonds would be in the Big House conceived.

The resentful father's ambition, internalized by the son, led James Henry Hammond to Thomas Cooper's South Carolina College during the 1820s. Here young Hammond's anguish about being poorer than his fellows eventually drove him to academic achievement they envied. After college, Hammond for months was trapped in a poor lad's profession: tutoring his betters' offspring. The aspiring son seemed to be, even more bitterly, the lowly father reborn.

James Hammond would have none of this destiny. In pushing past Carolinians, he had one legacy of Elisha's Yankee ancestry. Young Hammond possessed a capitalist's force, a materialist's energy, a male ruthlessness too overwhelming to settle for backwoods classrooms. He wanted to be as wealthy, as famous, as much a mover of events as were his rich classmates—and right now.

After his year of tutoring in the backcountry, the aspirant returned to Columbia. He studied law, eked out a small practice, and in early 1830 moved into the political establishment. He became editor of Thomas Cooper's faction's politically fiery newspaper. He now had position. With cash, he could soar.[11]

The quickest way to get rich was to say two words: "I do." James Hammond may have had the most roving, raunchiest eyes in the antebellum South. He also may have toyed illicitly with the most women, black and white. But only one sort of wife would do for this chauvinist. She must be rich. Or rather, she must be fabulously rich.

Around the time he assumed his editorship, Hammond met the proper candidate. Fabulous riches were about all that Catherine Fitzsimons possessed, from a pushy male's perspective. The young Charleston maiden was ugly. She was shy. Her father, an Irishman, was a whiskey importer.

James Hammond would suffer it all for her purse. Catherine's family, including her famous brother-in-law, Wade Hampton II, demanded that she resist the fortune-hunter. Hammond pressed. Miss Fitzsimons, not used to such force focused on her retiring person, yielded.[12]

Hammond's new Big House graced a huge upcountry plantation on the Savannah River, less than a hundred miles from the groom's Columbia haunts. Hammond was disappointed only with the lowish profits "his" plantation yielded. He blamed disappointing yields of cotton on "his" slaves, who he thought had been treated too leniently. The man who would soon pose as paternalist supreme tightened screws on "his" slaves, in the manner of the most ruthless Yankee. As for the would-be gentleman, he was early on seducing "his" female blacks, though he was still years away from sleeping with his favorite black mistress's daughter.[13]

This un-Carolina-like arriviste wished above all else to be Carolina's hero. He captured that reputation as easily as he secured his heiress. He had a brilliant mind. He had learned, probably internalized, Carolina assumptions at South Carolina College. No writer wrote a purer Carolina political gospel than did this self-made saint. No Carolina elitist bragged more exultantly about the state's ancient aristocracy than did this ex-impoverished offspring of a Yankee. No settled gentleman bought such expensive paintings or looked down his nose so triumphantly at plebeians who did not properly appreciate such trappings. No bright young Carolinian more buttered up Carolina's titans than did this aspirant for their approval and position.

The great men of Hammond's upcountry were two, Thomas Cooper and John C. Calhoun. Cooper, ruler of the college, was the only true outsider in South Carolina's ruling class. He thrilled a generation of college boys with tales of their mission, through disunion, to thwart worldwide radicalism. Calhoun was the great politician of Hammond's upper Savannah River section. He enchanted Hammond with talk of Carolina's destiny, through political reorganization, to save slavery and Union too. Both leaders saw their admirer as a talent Carolina needed. James Hammond seemed to possess more drive, more intelligence, more ambition than anyone of his generation. Cooper and Calhoun both praised him as a coming disciple. Hammond cherished both men's compliments. He made both believe he cherished their statecraft.

The upcountry establishment ratified Cooper's and Calhoun's approval, only several years after Hammond captured his heiress, by elevating him, in his first election to anything, into the National House of Representatives for the 1835–6 session. The youthful titan, having climbed so far so fast, had no intention of shrinking into a merely observing freshman congressman. He wanted it all, national notoriety immediately too. He would lead Carolina troops into battle, if he could only find the right issue.

The James Hammond looking for the disruptive issue in late 1835 was thus that weird combination, the ultra-Yankee ultra-Carolinian. He swelled up and postured, as did Carolinians he copied, like the patriarch above American vulgarity. He then seized what he desired, like vulgar capitalists he attacked. His heiress's family rejected him. He still pushed himself upon her, always protesting he was the soul of chivalry. The wife who made him rich desired only a peaceful and respectable home. He still would not give up debauchery with his slavewomen, even while protesting that Yankees-come-South rather than trueblue Southerners bore responsibility for mulattoes. His slaves would not work hard enough. He lashed them into submission, gaining a reputation he confessed to despising above all others, all the time bragging that the southern patriarch was benevolence personified. He was a ruthless young egotist, at once irresistible and useless to resist within the contemptuous world he would personify and perpetuate. Even before he raced off to Congress, the whimpering Carolina gentry, energies depleted after nullification, inclined towards him as to a magnet.

After his gag rule initiative, fellows back home wrote to their suddenly prominent congressman, praising him for radicalizing the establishment. Over a dozen such letters survive in the Hammond papers. Northerners who believed in a Great Slavepower Conspiracy, if they could have read Hammond's mail, would have felt vindicated. "We should have dissolved the union when Charleston was blockaded," wrote Thomas Stark from Carolina. Hammond's motion, prayed Stark, might now disrupt "this corrupt and no longer to be tolerated Union."[14]

Thomas Stark and fellow upcountry elitists shared with Hammond a dismal view of mainstream southern egalitarians. National political parties bribed southern national spoilsmen to care more about party than slavery. Southern demagogues kept southern masses asleep to antislavery danger. Hammond's motion, praised Hammond's pals, might shame southern politicians into acting like Southerners should. Parties might dissolve. The southern rabble might wake up. "It is really necessary to alarm our people," warned E. W. Johnston, editor of Cooper's Columbia newspaper. The slavery question "does not give them half the apprehension it should."[15]

Letters like Johnston's, praying that Hammond's initiative might awaken the South and lead to disunion, came to the congressman almost exclusively from Thomas Cooper's Columbia, South Carolina, crowd. Only one non-Carolinian stands out among Hammond's correspondents. Professor Beverley Tucker of William and Mary College wrote Hammond a spectacular disunion missive. "Now is the time and this is the topic," the Virginia professor instructed Thomas Cooper's student. "Let the decisive step be taken." Yesterday, South Carolina should have stepped from nullification to secession over the tariff.

No matter. Tomorrow, South Carolina could safely secede over slavery. Other Southerners would "see that an attempt to use coercion against" South Carolina "would light the flames of a servile war." Perhaps the non-Carolina South could force the general government to allow South Carolina to secede safely. Other states would then follow. If, on the other hand, non-Carolina slaveholders failed to stop coercion, "they would be constrained to join you, or see their own dwellings consumed by the flames kindled to destroy you." Either way, exulted Tucker, the ensuing southern confederacy "would be the most flourishing and free on earth." The North "would break to pieces."[16]

Hammond used Beverley Tucker's letter the way a believer in a Great Slavepower Conspiracy would have predicted. The Carolina congressman sent the Virginian's letter to others who might be prodded towards disunion—i.e. to pals residing near Thomas Cooper. South Carolina's governor, George McDuffie of Forty Bale fame, exemplified the response. The governor thanked Hammond "for Judge Tucker's letter. . . . I entirely concur with him." We must exorcise the demon, if the magic circle is drawn in blood." Professor Cooper was particularly quick to advise his former student. "I foresee it will end in a dissolution of the Union," counseled Cooper, "for we have no safety in any other measure. But I fear the Southern Van Burenites."[17]

Thomas Cooper sent instructions for the next step toward disunion, should his fears be justified. "Your table will be loaded with insolent petitions," predicted the professor. Eventually, the House northern majority will vote to receive antislavery appeals and refer them to committee. Even a committee report "strongly in favour of the South" must not be tolerated. A House committee which now reported against antislavery could later report against slavery. Southern representatives should accordingly en masse "leave the House." Secession of southern congressmen might lead to secession of southern states.[18]

There it was, the smoking gun, the revolutionary plot, the proof of a conspiracy to break up the Union. None other than South Carolina's Professor of Revolution, the very Thomas Cooper who had first calculated the value of Union back in 1827, was here using secret letters to coach his student, the provoker of the Gag Rule Controversy, towards revolution. But this undeniable proof of revolutionary plotting best shows why revolution was still a quarter-century away. Cooper plotted an initial walk out of the House, not the Union. And what congressman beyond the Carolina delegation would follow Hammond? Southern compromisers were more likely to say good riddance when Nullifiers departed Congress. Thomas Cooper's smoking gun of a letter ultimately displayed not revolutionaries leading the South but conspirators plotting their own exile.

The Cooper crowd's letters reveal another reason why rebellion was far off in 1835. Carolina's secessionists, however desperate about their isolation in the South, were most vicious when cutting up other Carolinians, especially John C. Calhoun. Northerners would have been flabbergasted to learn that revolutionary plotters despised "The Father of Secession" for being so cursedly unrevolutionary. Professor Cooper, not Senator Calhoun, sent James Hammond the disunion advice, and Congressman Hammond shared his teacher's distrust of Calhoun. In 1831, Hammond had helped push Calhoun out of hiding on nullification. In 1833, Thomas Cooper had been one of the few Carolinians who castigated Calhoun for negotiating on non-negotiable demands. In 1836, Hammond privately predicted to E. W. Johnston, Cooper's editorial mouthpiece, that Calhoun would again retreat from radicalism. "Your views about Calhoun," Johnston answered, are "stolen, I think, from myself. I have been, for the last 3 years, steadily cursing Calhoun. . . . We work on here, and make a doctrine popular. Of a sudden, he comes forward, seizes it, . . . and ruins the impression which might have been made on the country, by stitching the whole affair to his own political kite-tail."[19]

While Hammond's mail reveals a Carolina disunion plot not involving Calhoun, did Cooper and fellow conspirators influence James Hammond's gag rule initiative? If the question is posed broadly, in terms of whether Hammond's relations with Cooper and other Columbia ultras helped produce a disruptive attitude, the answer must be, of course. A revolutionary conspiracy, whether or not it causes a revolution, is itself the effect of a revolutionary mentality already successful enough to produce plotting. Hammond's correspondents illuminate Hammond's own isolation from the southern mainstream, his distrust of mobocratic politicians who were allegedly selling out the South, his determination to goad the South out of Union-saving parties. The conspiratorial atmosphere around Thomas Cooper's hothouse college, when combined with Hammond's ambition, yielded a young man in a great big hurry to provoke trouble.

But if the conspiratorial question is posed narrowly, in terms of whether Cooper's coaching directly produced Hammond's provoking motion, the answer must be, no. Cooper conspired. But Hammond acted. The crucial action came *before* the conspiracy. No evidence exists, in a cache of letters full of conspiratorial evidence, that anyone suggested before the event that Hammond help break up the Union by moving that petitions not be received. The evidence proves on the contrary that a major event involving antislavery petitions was unexpected.

Only *after* Hammond moved rejection of the petitions did Cooper and his followers send secret advice to their favorite congressman. We will soon see that in 1836, after Cooper's predicted setback occurred, James Hammond paid no attention to the professor's projected next step. Before and after his historic motion, Hammond followed his own wavering instincts rather than the professor's conspiratorial directives.

Indeed, like most of Cooper's students, Hammond wavered on the big question: whether the professor was right that only revolution would suffice. Cooper and Hammond had come to Carolina radicalism from too different a direction. Cooper had arrived in Carolina after storming the Bastille in Paris. Hammond had taken the Yankee rather than the Jacobinical road to Carolina power. His capitalist's caution about adventurism meshed with other Carolinians' fear of revolutionary disorder. James Hammond was a bit too much like the conservative Calhoun to be Cooper's perfect clone. He was also a bit too much like the precipitous Cooper to be Calhoun's fondest admirer.

Hammond's in-between position was obvious in key sentences written to a congressional colleague right before the Gag Rule Controversy. It is "barely possible," Hammond declared, that "abolitionists may be alarmed. It is equally possible that Northern states may legislate them down."[20]

Calhoun would have rid Hammond's sentence of that "barely." Mr. Nullifier considered it very possible that a creditable disunionist threat would arouse Northerners to censor abolitionists. Cooper would have rid Hammond's sentence of that critical "possible." Carolina's arch-secessionist considered it impossible for the South to defy world-wide antislavery inside the Union.

After Congress passed a gag rule softer than Hammond's, Hammond again wavered between Cooper's and Calhoun's brands of toughness. In June of 1836, Hammond wrote Beverley Tucker that "I have scarcely a hope . . . the dissolution of the Union" can be avoided. In a "purely *Spoils* Government," only a "little hope existed" for a party based on "Principle."[21]

Calhoun would have called those "scarcely a hope"s and "little hope"s too pessimistic. Cooper would have called any hope too optimistic. Thomas Cooper clearly controlled not only too little of the South and too little of South Carolina but also too little of his pupils' mentality to mastermind events. James Hammond, disunion conspirators' closest thing to a point man in Washington, was no puppet.

Rather, Hammond's motion, like the rest of his meteoric rise, came precisely because he clamored ahead without premeditated plot or traditional scruples or inherited positions. Nowhere did old codes inhibit this nouveau pusher. Back home, he seized a wife, slept with "wenches," drove field hands, always with only a thin veneer of gentlemen's scruples. So too in Congress, he seized on a new procedure for destroying petitions, with scarcely a thought of old mechanisms. Since he was a freshman congressman, his mind was not cluttered with memories of how petitions had always been treated. Innocence of precedent gave him the mental flexibility to see an "impromptu" way, suddenly and spontaneously, to condemn antislavery petitions in a new and total way.[22] His attempt to galvanize the South was the instinctive gesture of a radicalized arriviste, in a rush to see if Calhoun or Cooper—or James Hammond—would be the prophet of southern salvation. A world generating such a loose cannon was perchance a worse threat to Union than any tightly controlled conspiracy could have been.

– 4 –

If tired old Carolina radicals rallied with relief behind this fresh new spirit who charged, for a Carolinian, so spontaneously ahead, the nervous gentry found Hammond more attractive still when he displayed the uncertainty hidden behind his boldness. James Hammond, more even than John C. Calhoun, was destined to become the archetypal South Carolina reluctant revolutionary. The reluctance soon to paralyze his actions and already defining his mentality was first obvious in his first full-scale congressional oration, defending his gag rule initiative.

On February 1, 1836, Hammond claimed the House floor for an appeal to authoritarians to conquer King Numbers.[23] Hammond's oratory carried Carolina upper-class consciousness to a color-blind anti-egalitarian extreme. This upper-class position left racist slaveholders, devotees of egalitarian republicanism for whites, too far behind to follow. And then in oratory, as he would in action, Hammond finished the Carolina act. Having charged recklessly ahead to base slavery on universal subordination of all lower classes, he slunk cautiously back to base a Peculiar Institution on racial inequality.

"Domestic slavery," began James Henry Hammond the charger, "produces the highest toned, the purest, best organization of society that has ever existed on the face of the earth." The Slave South, bragged Carolina's nouveau aristocrat, has "a government of the best, combining all the advantages, and possessing but few of the disadvantages, of the aristocracy of the old world." Slaveholders lacked "the exclusiveness, the selfishness, the thirst for sway, the contempt for others, which distinguish the nobility of Europe." Slaveholders had a European gentry's "education, their polish, their minificence, their high honor, their undaunted spirit. Slavery does create an aristocracy—an aristocracy of talents, of virtue, of generosity and courage."

Hammond moved from praise of upper-class Southerners to advocacy of an alliance with upper-class Northerners. He sounded like the Calhoun who briefly considered linking Yankee capitalists and southern planters in a reactionary Opposition/Whig regime. Emancipation, warned Thomas Cooper's prize pupil, is "a mere ramification of the great controversy between hereditary power and ultimate agrarianism." The "sans-*culottes*," proclaiming "equality to all mankind," would soon hunt down northern squires. "On the banks of the Hudson, the Ohio, and the Susquehanna—on the hills, and in the vales of New England—they are mustering their hosts." Gentlemen "of substance" in the North had better look out, for the "bloodhounds they are settling upon us" will "desolate" and "overturn" them.

There spoke a man who considered slaveholding not some peculiar institution on one side of a color line but a typical form of human domination. There was expressed a theory legitimating color-blind, upper-class hegemony over all majorities and all mobs. Hammond here riveted the idea of slavery to a dominator's world view, a conception growing out of slaveholders' rule over their slaves and leading to patriarchal control of all folks poorer. Why was undemocratically gagging belief in abolitionism right in an egalitarian republic? Because the upper class must decide for the masses, lest the masses bring proletarian revolution to America.

Hammond's trouble was that this class-based natural outcome of a slaveholders' world view was unnatural to race-obsessed slaveholders beyond South Carolina. Most North American slaveholders, to say nothing of the nonslaveholder majority North and South, considered an aristocratic outcome most unnatural in an egalitarian republic. Their ruling idea was Andrew Jackson's: domination of blacks must exist alongside of equality for whites. Most Southerners wished a democracy without aristocrats, save for an aristocracy of color.

Hammond swiftly acknowledged the southern majority's hegemony. Perhaps he realized that, after a little indiscreet adventuring, the general had better get back with the troops. Perhaps this elitist general, like so many Carolinians, was partially caught up in the troops' egalitarian ideology. Like the Thomas Dew who first called slavery universally right and then called Virginia too far north for bondage, like the John C. Calhoun who first called for a North-South upper-class alliance and then urged a northern lower class/southern upper class combination, James Hammond could not sustain an elitist's color-blind posture.

James Hammond's praise for upper-class aristocracy thus became, in the next sentence, a hosannah for a classless white democracy. "In a slave culture," he claimed, "every freeman is an aristocrat. Be he rich or poor, if he does not possess a single slave," a white man born with the right skin had "all the natural advantages." So wavered the arriviste who, when a poor freeman, had lusted to be a rich aristocrat and who now, as a newly crowned aristocratic prince, was determined to keep poorer whites outside the Carolina legislature.

At least, defense of racial aristocracy was bringing Hammond back in sight of those he would lead. The Carolina orator continued his retreat by claiming race domination, not class hegemony, was most at stake. "Sir," warned Hammond, emancipation would instantly provoke "civil war between the whites and blacks." Whites would win, but at fearful cost to themselves and zero benefit for disinterested benevolence. "Blacks would be annihilated or once more . . . reduced to slavery."

Let gentlemen not scoff, warned Hammond, that abolitionists were too few to bring off such riot. The New England Anti-Society was ridiculed, but four years ago, because only eleven formed it. National antislavery societies were scoffed at, only two years ago, because scarcely sixty existed.

Now look! Over 300 societies flourished in 1836. They contained over 100,000 members. Some 300 petitions were in Washington. Some 40,000 fanatics signed them. "The deep, pervading uncontrollable excitement," spreading "like wildfire in the prairies," throws "its red glare up to heaven." In the face of that glare, "loyal" Southerners must stand and deliver. "He who shrinks from taking the boldest ground at once is a traitor! A traitor to his native soil!" A traitor to his glorious ancestors. "A traitor to his helpless offspring."

That challenge, coming from a class-ridden zealot who twisted back to emphasize mainstream southern racial fears, had to be met. But did slaveholders, to be true to slavery, have to go as far as a contemptuous squire whose anti-egalitarian attitudes seemed inimical to a slaveholding democrat? And did slaveholders, to be loyal to race control, have to destroy national political parties and menace the Union too? Hammond's motion for an extreme gag on white men's democratic discussion had to be faced—and finessed.

CHAPTER 18

The Gag Rule, II:
Mr. Pinckney's
Controversial Compromise

John C. Calhoun's fellow senators, not James Hammond's fellow House members, first demonstrated how moderates could finesse extremists. On January 7, 1836, Calhoun, repeating Hammond's House initiative three weeks earlier, moved that the Senate refuse to receive antislavery petitions. The prestigious senator, like the unknown congressman, emphasized that antislavery "maliciously" branded slaveholding congressmen as sinners. The Senate must gag insults to "any individual member."[1]

– 1 –

In the House, young Hammond defended his "impromptu" motion with a zig-zag of a speech ending on the brink of disunion. In the Senate, Calhoun defended Hammond's impulsive initiative with remorseless logic on why Carolina's extremism preserved constitutional unionism.

In representative government, Calhoun argued, representatives' dispositions of constituents' petitions properly took two forms. When Congress had constitutional jurisdiction over a prayed-for subject, solons must receive the petition and decide on the prayer. When representatives possessed no constitutional authority to fulfill a request, legislators must refuse to receive a prayer asking them to fracture the Constitution.

Calhoun called congressional seizure of slave property obviously unconstitutional. The Fifth Amendment affirmed that "no person shall be deprived of life, liberty, or property without due process of law." "Are not slaves property?" asked Calhoun. "Can Congress any more take away the property" than it can violate "life and liberty?"[2]

Calhoun here precociously defended a "substantive" rather than "procedural" interpretation of the "due process" clause's protection of property. Most constitutional commentators thought the Fifth Amendment allowed Congress to seize property for the common good, assuming proper *procedures* were followed. Calhoun insisted that no procedure could justify confiscation. The Founding Fathers meant the "due process" clause to keep King Numbers's hands off personal possessions. The federal government could not confiscate slaves or any other property, not even in places, such as national territories and the District, where Congress exclusively governed. With this "substantive due process" argument, Calhoun anticipated Chief Justice Roger B. Taney's provocative reasoning in the Dred Scott decision of 1857.

Calhoun sought to avoid future provocations. By establishing that Congress possessed no constitutional authority to abolish slavery anywhere, he would silence a congressional discussion he feared would inspire abolitionists white and black. The Carolinian at first emphasized black warriors. "A body of men in the northern states," charged Calhoun, stood "ready to second any insurrectionary movement." Congressional discussion could prove more insurrectionary than the fanatics' recent use of southern post offices. Congressmen's talk, Calhoun knew, occurred in a capital containing the weakest slave regime and contiguous to border states containing a small minority of slaves.[3]

Calhoun here again foresaw and would avert a theme destined dangerously to recur. Almost every time Southerners precipitated a national crisis, whether about Texas or fugitive slaves or Kansas, fears began at spots where slave regimes bordered on non-slave societies. Calhoun saw that no iron curtain separated North and South. By imposing silence in the District, Calhoun would plug the ears of nearby slaves.

Calhoun also wanted to plug white ears, North and South. Like Francis Pickens, he conceded that "the real number of abolitionists was small." But "ardent addresses in favor of liberty, so constantly made at the North, must have a deep effect on the young and rising generation." Abolitionists' "bad effect" had lately swept slavery out of the British Empire. The chance of freedom's dogma spreading within the free labor North "was not to be trifled with."[4]

Calhoun also admitted that free discussion might convert southern slaveholders. When first presenting his gag motion, Calhoun dismissed that possibility. He claimed that abolitionists could produce "no . . . change of mind in the southern people." Instead, the more slaveholders "were assailed on this point, the more closely would they cling to their institutions."[5]

Calhoun was more candid in his major gag rule oration, delivered on March 9, 1836. Slaveholders, Calhoun worried, faced "a war of religious and political fanaticism, . . . waged not against our lives, but our character. The object is to humble and debase us in our own estimation, and that of the world." Congressional "assaults on our character and institutions" would compel us "to engage in an endless . . . defence. Such a contest is beyond mortal endurance. We must, in the end, be humbled, degraded, broken down, and worn out."[6]

Free debate must leave us *debased in our own estimation*. There spoke the man worried that his culture would doubt itself. Open discussion "must ultimately" leave us "degraded" in the "eyes of the world." There spoke a statesman frightened that world-wide egalitarianism would turn majorities everywhere against slavery. A slaveholding elite must separate egalitarianism from republicanism, gag antislavery, bar anti-despotic doctrine from entering democratic debates.

As American freedom goes, Calhoun's gag resolution was a serious transgression. But as classic tyranny proceeds, Calhoun proposed thin repression. The Carolinian conceded constituents' right to petition. He admitted that if Congress could constitutionally emancipate Washington slaves, the Senate would have to receive petitions. His twin concessions invited endless debates over his debatable "substantive" due process constitutional interpretation. Constitutional discussions had and would range beyond the Constitution. Dictatorial regimes usually can impose more silence than this. Even at one of his more anti-republican moments, the American slaveholder was too republican to wage all-out war against republican procedure.

Northerners still considered Calhoun's gag resolution almost as intolerable as Carolina's earlier demand that abolitionists be imprisoned. If representatives could not discuss their constituents' wishes, representative government was arguably destroyed. The Calhoun-Hammond extreme position, to most Northerners, meant that the slavocracy's limits on white republican debate at home were being exported beyond the South. White constituents seeing themselves as enslaved, northern senators knew, would fight the Slavepower's repressions. Carolinians were indeed provoking a crisis.

– 2 –

The two northern establishment parties differed in their usual way on how to halt the Hammond-Pickens-Calhoun provocation. Northern anti-Jacksonians sought to save egalitarian republicanism by stonewalling against gag resolutions. Northerner Jacksonians endeavored to salvage Union and party by bending before southern pressure. States' rights Southerners were more powerful in the Jackson than in the Opposition Party, and the Jacksonian power base was located more to the south. Southern Democrats already faced charges that Oppositionists' 1836 presidential candidate in Middle and Deep Souths, the Tennessean Hugh White, would be truer to slavery than the Yankee Van Buren. Southern Democrats who now secured nothing from Martin Van Buren, after James Hammond had challenged their soundness, would be the more vulnerable to Oppositionist onslaughts. Northern Democrats accordingly had to venture far enough south to neutralize pressure on Southern Democrats, while remaining far enough north to appease northern voters.

The first Yankee to solve the gag rule problem would be the last to ride appeasement of the South to the highest national office. James Buchanan of Pennsylvania, in a youthful maneuver which prefigured his mature presidency, urged the Senate to go *almost* all the way with Calhoun. Buchanan's Pennsylvania was an in-between state, north of the Border South, south of more abolitionist-influenced New England. A northern state bordering on the South, like southern states bordering on the North, characteristically found neutrality on slavery wisest for those in the middle. Pennsylvania's senator realized that the new slavery issue menaced Union and that Northern Democrats must appease the party's dominant southern establishment.

James Buchanan wished the Democratic Party to appease the South a tad less than southern extremists desired. No self-respecting Northerner could altogether surrender to southern fanaticism. Nor could any self-respecting republic altogether destroy democratic procedures. Southern Democrats had to give in a smidgeon. Then Northern Democrats could *almost* surrender. The resulting southern-leaning compromise would isolate fanatics North and South, save the Democratic Party and democratic Union, and enhance the position of reasonable men such as James Buchanan.

Buchanan's reasonable idea was to receive, then instantly reject, antislavery petitions. The Pennsylvanian called immediate denial of constituents' prayer "the strongest motion he could make, consistent with the right of petition." The old way, Buchanan pointed out, was to table petitions or to bury them in committee. But tabling a constituent's request allowed a later trip off the table. Dispatching the petition to committee implied its possible later reappearance on the floor. The Senate should instead respond to antislavery with an unmistakable NO, not now, not ever. A received petition could not be more totally rejected.

But republicanism, emphasized Buchanan, required that petitions be received. "The people of the North are justly jealous of their rights and liberties. Among these, they hold the right of petition to be one of the most sacred." If the "right of petition and the cause of the abolitionists must rise or fall together," Buchanan feared "fatal" consequences.

Buchanan scoffed at critics who called his instant rejection and Calhoun's never receiving indistinguishable tyrannies. "What, sir, no difference between refusing to receive a request at all, and actually receiving it and considering it respectfully, and afterwards deciding, without delay" to reject it! No difference between politely rejecting a salesman's pitch and kicking him away from the door before he could speak? Well, he saw the difference. Northern Democrats could, in all conscience, instantly reject abolitionists' prayers, so long as even "fanatics" could dispatch prayers inside democracy's doors.[7]

Calhoun agreed that he and Buchanan proposed critically different gag rules. By voting to receive and instantly reject a petition, argued the Carolinian, "the Senate would claim jurisdiction of the question." Abolitionists whose prayers were received, then not granted, were invited to petition some more, discuss some more, agitate some more, in the belief that a changed public opinion would someday grant more than a respectful reception.

Buchanan's impact on the South was worse, declared Calhoun. Southerners would be taught to accept less than pure southernism in order to save impure parties. Those priorities would yield little compromises every time abolitionists made slight gains.

Instead of allowing abolitionists slightly inside, Calhoun would confront "the enemy on the frontier." The question of "receiving" is "our important pass—it is our Thermopylae." If the vulnerable South let the enemy within the gates, nothing would be "more hapless and degrading than our situation; to sit here year after year, session after session, hearing ourselves and our constituents vilified ... We must ultimately be not only degraded in our own estimation and that of the world, but be exhausted and worn out."[8]

There it was again: abolitionists could influence Southerners to see slavery as degraded. There spoke a senator who knew that the most northern half of the South yearned to diffuse away its "evil." Calhoun urged Southerners to repudiate doubt, to make an absolute commitment to perpetuating slavery before heretical ideas spread. Southern senators must reject Buchanan's partial gag rule. A united South must insist on absolute silence. Then slavery could be saved and Union too. Or as William Preston, the other South Carolina senator, put it, an intransigent South, "the postulate demanded for a southern confederacy," made secession unnecessary.[9]

– 3 –

The trouble with Calhoun's strategy was inherent in Preston's "postulate." Southern divisions that made Thomas Cooper's revolution impossible made Calhoun's non-revolutionary remedy utopian. Almost all of Calhoun's southern senatorial colleagues distrusted uncompromising Southerners and relished compromising national parties. Worse, Calhoun's fear that abolitionist agitation might someday debase slaveholders in their own estimation had seemingly already happened. During the gag rule debates, Henry Clay, hero of the Border South, gave Calhoun an unneeded lesson on why antislavery agitation might infect vulnerable opinion South as well as North.

Instead of instantly rejecting received petitions, as Buchanan proposed, Henry Clay urged that petitioners be heard for longer than an instant. The Kentucky senator would send received petitions to committee, hoping to receive a report back "against granting the prayer." Clay was against granting emancipation without removing blacks. Especially in black belts south of Kentucky, "emancipation must necessarily give the inferior race, in the course of time, a numerical" majority. "If he were a southern man," declared Clay, "he would resist emancipation in every form."

IF he were a southern man! What in the world, one can almost hear Calhoun storming, do you think a slaveholding senator is? Clay was in fact a slaveholder of the Border rather than the Deep South. Like most borderites, he coupled affirmation that present "necessity" now "justified" an "evil" with prayers that diffusions of blacks to Africa and to the Deep South might remove the necessity. He "expressed himself in favor of a gradual emancipation of the black race, if it could be done without ... injurious consequences." He had always believed "that every man, no matter what his color or condition, was entitled to freedom." How different *his* southern utopia would be from James Hammond's "domestic slavery, ... the best organization of society that has ever existed on the face of the globe!"

Clay introduced amendments to Buchanan's instant rejection motion. Clay would turn down antislavery prayers solely on grounds of expediency now, not unconstitutionality forever. Emancipation in the capital was inexpedient for the moment, ran Clay's words, "because the people of the District of Columbia have not themselves petitioned for" emancipation, "because ... Virginia and Maryland would be injuriously affected by such a measure, whilst the institution of slavery continues to subsist within their respective jurisdictions," and because "alarm and apprehension in the States tolerating slavery" disturbed "harmony."[10]

Clay's words opened vistas of someday securing the momentarily forbidden. "Inexpediency" would become expedient if District of Columbia residents petitioned, and if neighboring states emancipated, and if other Southerners "tolerating" (!) slavery no longer were "alarmed." Clay's phrasing hinted that those eventualities might transpire. "Whilst" (!) slavery "continued to subsist"in Maryland and Virginia, the Kentuckian declared—there spoke Upper South slaveholders who expected the Chesapeake's debate on slavery to someday yield, in the spirit of Virginia's Archibald Bryce and Maryland's Henry Brawner, slavery's slow diffusion elsewhere, sometime in the future. Should the Border South prove that removal of blacks could work, then a Lower South only "tolerating" (!) bondage might calm down about the District.

Clay had previously proposed federal laws to achieve these objectives. His Distribution Bill of 1832 had suggested state use of surplus federal funds to colonize emancipated slaves. The man who thought *that* constitutional now urged the constitutionality of emancipating slaves in Washington. And it all came wrapped in a package marked rejecting abolitionists' prayer!

Senate votes on March 9, 1836, showed again that Calhoun's South and Clay's were a world apart. The Senate voted against Calhoun's motion not to receive antislavery, 36-10. Deep South senators voted Calhoun's way, not to receive antislavery petitions, 8-2. The Border South voted Clay's way, to receive emancipationist prayers, 8-0. The Middle South split, 2-2, with 2 abstainers.[11]

The Senate eased Calhoun's disappointment by rejecting Clay's more watery gag resolution. But the Deep South left Calhoun isolated by massing behind Buchanan's almost-total gag motion, without resentment, almost with rejoicing. Even Carolina's other senator, William C. Preston, hailed Buchanan's reception and instant rejection formula as "the next strongest condemnation of abolitionists."

On March 14, Buchanan's gag without Clay's loopholes passed, 34-6. All voting southern senators favored Buchanan's motion. Calhoun abstained. Northern Democrats voted yes. Northern opponents of Jackson, led by Daniel Webster, voted no. Carolina extremists had found the perfect issue to galvanize the South. Their boon had then been stolen, along with a sold-out South, by the Northern Democrats' new would-be prince.[12]

– 4 –

A similar theft transpired in the House of Representatives. But this time a Carolina extremist, not a Pennsylvania politician, pilfered Carolina's idea. And this time the gag rule issue became so locked into establishment controversies between Democrats and Oppositionists that anti-establishment extremists were even more isolated.

The House denouement began with Southern Democratic congressmen's realization that they must respond somewhat positively to James Hammond's initiative. Otherwise, Southern Oppositionists could convict them of softness on slavery during imminent congressional and presidential election campaigns. Political expediency aside, northern extremists' emergence and southern extremists' disunion worried moderate Southern Democrats. The National Democratic Party had to gag antislavery for the sake of slavery, Union, and party—and for the sake of Martin Van Buren's hope of carrying the South.

That message poured in on a wary Little Magician back in New York. Southern allies demanded he prove himself safe to the South by supporting an acceptable gag rule. United States Representative George W. Owens of Savannah, Georgia, for example, urged Van Buren to "put to rest a most delicate and dangerous question." Owens spotted "some *coolness*"on gagging abolitionists among *"the Northern clans."* Van Buren must "use every exertion to bring the weak—the timid and the doubtful *up to scratch*." Should the House hesitate, Owens would consider "the Union as having received its death wound."[13]

The Little Magician saw that no magic would make Hammond's disruption disappear. But Van Buren's strategy to contain the damage was an illusionist's masterpiece. Where James Buchanan would reject antislavery prayers without even committee consideration, Van Buren would secure a committee report against the prayer. By allowing petitions to sink deeper into the House's deliberative processes, Van Buren would forfeit the almost unanimous praise Southerners had showered on the Pennsylvania senator. But as long as most Southern Democrats accepted a committee report against antislavery, their mutterings against committee involvement could be tolerated. Indeed, southern restiveness could show Northerners that Van Buren had hardly caved in to Calhoun. On the other hand, Buchanan's almost total cave-in, without even committee consideration, would be a harder sell in the North.

The gag rule controversy here prefigured these two future Presidents' different roles in subsequent slavery controversies. Van Buren, whose gag rule concessions were more limited and begrudging, would eventually run for President as an anti-Slavepower free-soiler in 1848. Buchanan, who almost went all the way South with his gag rule, would make appeasement of the South the hallmark of his administration in the Lecompton Controversy of 1858. Future Presidents, like most politicians in their generation, were destined to stay on the trail they chose when the Gag Rule Controversy first forced their choice.

Having chosen to impose on the North less of a gag rule than Buchanan desired, Van Buren needed to convince Southern Democrats to accept a more diluted rule than the Senate had passed. Here, the Little Magician truly pulled the rabbit out of the hat. The New Yorker secured a Nullifier to present and sponsor compromise proposals. Henry L. Pinckney, Charleston's representative in the House, was editor of the *Charleston Mercury,* the Nullifiers' showpiece of a newspaper. The youthful Pinckney was considered, like James Hammond and Francis Pickens, a rising young Carolina hotspur. Yet on February 4, 1836, the man hitherto known as fiery Nullifier asked for the House floor to introduce Union-saving retreat.[14]

Southern representatives used parliamentary tactics to deny the "traitor" the floor. Second thoughts did not deter the "recreant." On February 8 Pinckney was back, demanding a hearing. The *Charleston Mercury*'s editor introduced resolutions declaring that petitions on slavery should "be referred to a select committee, with instructions to report that Congress" could not constitutionally interfere with slavery in the states and "ought not" interfere with the institution in Washington, D.C. Pinckney would chair the committee. The National Democratic Party would support his initial resolutions and affirm his final committee report. A Carolinian was in the mainstream's saddle, and no extremist could tear him out.[15]

Why did Henry L. Pinckney compromise on Carolina extremism? Pinckney's Charleston friend Robert Y. Hayne plausibly guessed that a recent religious conversion had made the man unsteady in opinion. Two weeks before the recreant claimed the House floor, Hayne warned Hammond to "keep Pinckney *straight,* and that will not be an easy matter (for *between ourselves* since he has become *a saint* he is strangely self willed and erratic)." Hammond further guessed that the erratic saint was "flattered with the idea of being a second Clay to save the Union."[16]

The scribbler would hazard another guess: that Carolina's latest erratic radical saw himself as a second generation of Pinckneys, sustaining the first generation's record of statesmanship. Only Henry L. Pinckney among leading South Carolina politicans of his era bore the name of a great Carolina Founding Father. Yet this latest Pinckney, for all his respected editorial work with the *Charleston Mercury,* had been less powerful than Calhoun and Cooper and two dozen others. Now, at the moment a religious conversion freed Henry Pinckney to soar, Martin Van Buren invited him to break free of the second rank of Carolina politicians and to strengthen the Union his ancestors had fashioned.

Pinckney himself claimed that he broke with Calhoun because the latter's political position no longer made sense. The novel notion of never receiving antislavery petitions, Pinckney charged, had "united ... the whole North" against a divided South. That debacle insured disastrous defeat. The battle of abolition had to be fought at the North, between "fanatics" and "the great body of the people." By "contending against the right of petition," slaveholders would "change the whole aspect of the question," drive our northern sympathizers "from the field," and "increase abolition." He preferred to "strengthen our friends." He would secure the strongest gag rule possible in Congress and acceptable to the pro-southern northern conscience. And for that he was called traitor to the South!

His treason to South Carolina, Pinckney scoffed, came down to a verbal quibble. He favored gagging petitions after they were received. His former allies favored gagging petitions before reception. Here was "almost a distinction without a difference." What "possible practical importance" existed in all those "mere abstractions" about what form of gag was true-blue southern stuff?[17]

Readers of these pages may cheer Pinckney's question. Why did contemporaries, and why in heaven's name should posterity, take these slight verbal disputes seriously? Why care whether abolition in Washington was inexpedient or unconstitutional, so long as Congress gagged the idea? Why fret whether congressmen refused to receive antislavery petitions, or instantly rejected them, or killed them in committee, so long as abolitionists were automatically silenced?

Because as Henry L. Pinckney knew very well, these "mere" words were loaded weapons in an immensely practical debate. Hammond, Pickens, and Calhoun had stumbled upon, then perfected, a linguistic system forcing Southerners to declare where they *were* on *the* practical question: Did antislavery dangers demand an uncompromising response, and, if necessary, another reorganization of southern politics? "Nonreception" was the most uncompromising condemnation of antislavery, just as "unconstitutional" was the most extreme rejection of abolition in Washington, D.C. These uncompromising words announced that compromising party institutions and compromise sectional settlements, the very stuff of American Union, came second. Hammond's words were an oath of allegiance to purify parties and Union before southern participation could be assured. Should purification fail, Hammond's pledge compelled the South to abandon the political party system and, if necessary, the Union as well.

Hammond's oath of allegiance turned enemies into lepers. The difference between barring lepers at the door and letting them in to state their case was vivid, physical, tangible, something men could see, taste, smell. The difference between calling lepers unconscionable, intolerable, in a word, *unconstitutional*, and calling them unpleasant, inappropriate, in a word, *inexpedient*, was easily felt—and with a shudder.

These "mere" words not only conjured up shuddering images but were wielded as slashing weapons. Extremists possessed only words to force party politicians away from compromising. Ultras could not shoot or gas or imprison softhearts. After the debacle of 1833, Carolinians could not nullify the southern masses either. In this slaveholders' democracy, public opinion was king. Their royal highnesses, party politicians and deluded followers, could only be shamed into intransigence.

Assuming Hammond's "mere" words could shame apologists away from compromising, American political institutions would fundamentally change. Northerners would have to accept the most extreme condemnation of abolitionism, if they meant to keep national political parties together. Southerners would demand the most extreme protection of slavery, if the Union was to survive. Abolitionists would receive the most total condemnation, if they bothered to keep on agitating. Words would compel institutional purification, either in Calhoun's southern convention or in Cooper's southern nation.

Pinckney's words, on the other hand, were like a suit of armor, crafted to protect the political status quo. "Tabling" rather than "receiving" petitions because abolition was "inexpedient" rather than "unconstitutional" were code words declaring that abolition could be stopped without revolutionizing the two-party system. Pinckney's vocabulary gave Southern Democrats a loyally southern way of compromising with Northern Democrats. Pinckney's terminology declared that Little Magicians not to the manor born could be safe on slavery. Pinckney's language sang of a world providentially free from doing or dying for James Hammond's oath of allegiance.

Once Pinckney sprung them from Hammond's linguistic trap, southern moderates could proceed as compromising American politicians. Southerners who apologized for slavery could also continue to pray, with Henry Clay, that slavery would diffuse from the border, that blacks could be dispatched to Africa, that Washington might be delivered some blessed day from the "evil." With the loss of Hammond's "mere" words, other southern wordsmiths, not shamed away from collaboration with outsiders, just might seek legislative removal of an institution called, in Henry Clay's "mere" words, a "temporary curse."

– 5 –

The gag rule tale would have to be finished without its first author. Henry L. Pinckney had blocked James Hammond's terminology and Hammond, in a word, quit. Illness was Hammond's excuse for resigning from Congress and fleeing to Europe three weeks after Pinckney's "treachery." Vicious intestinal pain, Hammond whimpered, paralyzed him. Doctors told Hammond that nerves caused his agony. Hammond nervously agreed.

He had political reason to be nervous. Southern Van Burenites had defused his initiative, just as Professor Cooper had predicted would happen. Cooper had counseled mass southern resignation from Congress, should some Henry L. Pinckney surface. Now Hammond was resigning. Still, with everything on schedule to follow conspiratorial orders from headquarters, Cooper's closest thing to a point man in Washington ignored instructions. A decade and a half later Hammond would advocate the professor's plan, after another South Carolina revolutionary gesture proved impotent. But in 1836, unlike 1851, Hammond did not seek southern exodus from Washington. He did not even write a long public letter, justifying resignation as a protest against southern compromising. One day, he just left. His quiet departure, like his noisy arrival, showed a conspiracy not commanding but despairing of seizing command.

With the political case for resignation not even made, maladies more personal clearly led to Hammond's departure. Hammond himself called a debilitating inferiority complex the cause. "[I] tried," without success, "to lull my own fears—no not my *fears*—my own opinions of myself," Hammond wrote privately soon after leaving Washington.[18]

But why did this striver, having ascended so fast, doubt that he could continue to soar? Analysts who think mental illness is genetic will emphasize the Hammond clan's sometimes emotional instability, before and after James

Henry. Theorists who think compulsively pushy parents characteristically produce compulsively insecure achievers will speculate that Elisha Hammond's
enormous ambitions heaped crushing burdens on his son.

Whatever the source of Hammond's neuroses, his gyrations personified the
Carolina gentry's unsteadiness. Just as Hammond's pattern of charge, then
retreat, was rooted in a desire for glory and a fear of being inglorious which
made his stomach one raging ache whether he charged or retreated, so Carolina's inconclusive outbursts were rooted in a desire for precipitating revolution
and a fear of revolutionary precipitousness which made gentlemen nervous
whether Carolina dared or delayed. South Carolina's cultural hero would never
be Thomas Cooper, remorseless revolutionary. James Hammond, resigning revolutionary, would be the obvious candidate to succeed John C. Calhoun, radical
Union-saver. Carolina would call Hammond back from resignation, again and
again, to strike and then to quit, until the state finally summoned the nerve to
rush past James Hammond's final nervousness about Thomas Cooper's dream.

– 6 –

With Hammond away, treating his stomach, Southern Democrats faced a new
tormentor. As soon as Henry L. Pinckney introduced Martin Van Buren's
diluted gag rule, Henry Wise of Virginia, a youthful House states' righter and
Oppositionist, called the compromiser a "traitor." No southern patriot,
declared Henry Wise, could settle for calling abolition in Washington "inexpedient" rather than "unconstitutional." Nor would a truly southern warrior
settle for merely denying the prayer of a received petition. The Virginia Oppositionist "hissed and spurned" Pinckney "as a deserter." Loyalty politics had
arrived inside the House.

The Speaker of the House, upset that Henry Wise attacked a colleague's
motives, ordered the Virginian to sit. Wise stood. The Speaker appealed to the
House. Wise glared as he lowered his frame. He meant "to characterize the
course of the gentleman as treason to the South," the States' Rights Oppositionist muttered. "God only knows his motives."[19]

Whatever God knew, Southern Democrats realized that Wise's disloyalty
charge was more politically lethal than Hammond's. This time, the accusation
that Southern Democrats were Cuffees, compromisers who only pretended to
secure safety for slavery, came not from Calhounites outside the system but
from the other southern party within the national establishment. If Oppositionists could show that Southern Democrats' compromised gag rule was soft on
slavery, the Tennessee slaveholder, Hugh Lawson White, might crush the New
York nonslaveholder, Van Buren, in an 1836 presidential contest over who was
safest for slavery. By injecting loyalty politics inside the House, Southern Oppositionists escalated pressure on Southern Democrats, who thus had to intensify
pressure on Northern Democrats.

Henry Wise stepped up the pressure on the National Democratic Party
partly because gag rule politics endangered his States' Rights Oppositionist fac-

tion. Uncompromising Oppositionists, when following Calhoun out of a compromising Democratic Party, had promised to make the Opposition Party uncompromisingly for states' rights. Calhoun had declared the party of Clay, Adams, and Webster immune to a states' rights takeover. Now, events seemed to be showing that the great abstractionist was the greater realist. True, Van Buren and the Democratic Party offered only a compromised gag rule. But Northern Oppositionists, led by Daniel Webster, denounced all gag rules. Who would now believe that the Oppositionist Party could best serve slavery? The embarrassing question forced States' Rights Oppositionists to out-Calhoun Calhoun in exposing Democrats' compromises.

But Henry Wise and his ilk were more dangerous than electioneering opportunists. They believed. They considered Martin Van Buren the phoniest protector of slavery. States' Rights Oppositionists damned the Magican too often privately to dismiss their public rhetoric as demagoguery. Not even Van Buren's "non-committal cunning," Abel P. Upshur wrote a fellow Virginia Oppositionist at the time of Van Buren's gag rule maneuvers, can prevent the Little Magician from being forced, by his own party, towards "consolidation" and eventually "emancipation." Upshur believed that, "in five years," Van Buren will free all "slaves in the South," and "all the South will submit." Van Buren had "bought up" Democratic leaders with patronage. Democratic leaders had gulled the people. The situation was "almost hopeless." Only a violent Oppositionist effort to rip off masks and expose compromisers might save slavery from Democrats' proslavery charades.[20]

– 7 –

Southern Oppositionist's gag rule thrust made Southern Democrats squirm. But could Henry Wise's shoving fail to abort his own newborn National Opposition Party? Northern Oppositionists shunned any gag on democratic debate, much less Wise's total silencer. By failing to come out of an alliance with such uncompromising Yankees, States' Rights Oppositionists could mock their claim to be uncompromising Southerners.

Timing provides one key to how Southern Oppositionists could emerge as the most intransigent slaveholders and yet remain in the same party with the most intransigent Northerners. Only in 1836 and 1838 would Southern Oppositionists/Whigs cast more pro-southern congressional votes than Democrats. Later, southern ultras within the Whig establishment would have to forget southern ultimatums or risk expulsion from their national alliance.

But in 1836 the Opposition alliance was not trying to be a unified national party. Each section was running its own presidential candidate on its own platform. The states' righter as Oppositionist, in this temporary situation, served his party best by making the most trouble for Democrats in the Slavepower's homeland.

Even in 1836, Southern Oppositionists could not have made uncompromising demands anathema to their Yankee wing if the gag rule had been the primary issue in Congress or on the hustings. The more important controversy in 1836, as for many years before, involved Andrew Jackson: whether he was a Caesar, whether he could legitimately handpick his successor, whether his mobocratic and demagogical style was preferable to Whiggish chaste republicanism. Oppositionist's main business was opposing King Andrew and his designated Little Magician. Gag rules were a distressing but passing distraction.

Since gag rules did not long remain the focal point of American politics, even in 1836, why focus on origins of the controversy so long and so exclusively? Because this is a history of the road to disunion; and in the Gag Rule Controversy of 1835–6, the slavery issue momentarily showed its potential to wrench everything national out of shape. The moment passed. But the momentary scare prefigured all reasons why slavery contentions were so dangerous.

Nowhere was this more true than with a national anti-Jackson party. Henry Wise, seeking uncompromising gag rules, and Daniel Webster, opposing all gags, could unite politically on nonslavery issues. But if slavery ever became the primary issue and if their party needed to present a united front, Southern Whigs would face an unrelenting double bind. They could ignore or oppose Democrats' campaigns to bolster slavery. Then they would strengthen alliances with anti-Slavepower Yankees at the expense of appearing to be slaveholding wimps, especially in Lower and Middle South presidential elections. Or they could deploy their gag rule gambit of out-Slavepowering the Democracy. Then they would strengthen their southern position at the risk of ruining their national alliance with the North's most anti-Slavepower establishment politicians.

In the perspective of this impossible future, the slavery affair of 1836, for Opposition/Whiggery's more states' rights partisans, bears the look of fleeting mercy. With Henry Wise's gag rule attack, they could put southern heat on the Democracy, without applying any flame to a still barely-national Opposition Party.

– 8 –

In the face of Henry Wise's war on the Van Buren-sanctioned evasive gag rule wording, Henry Pinckney felt driven to seek more uncompromising terminology. A worried Pinckney sought out Wise. The Virginia Oppositionist convinced the Carolina ex-Nullifier that calling abolition only "inexpedient" in Washington, D.C., was unsound. Pinckney agreed to go for the true-blue word "unconstitutional." Pinckney promised Wise, and repeated the promise to South Carolina constituents, that his committee would include that loyal southern phrase in its report to the House.[21]

With Pinckney's promise, southern loyalty tactics had again proved their power to change national slavery politics. Pressure from outsiders, Hammond and South Carolinians, had initially pressed Southern Democrats to press Northern Democrats for some gag rule. Now pressure from insiders, Wise and

Southern Oppositionists, was pressing Southern Democrats to press northern allies for further concessions.

Northern Democrats, again prefiguring the next 25 years of slavery politics, could be pressed only so far. Van Buren had publicly called abolition in D.C. only inexpedient. He could not go for unconstitutionality under pressure now, lest he seem utterly the Slavepower's slave. Pinckney's promise to Wise accordingly became the first casualty of the strain Southern Oppositionists placed on National Democrats.

In May 1836, Pinckney's Select Comiittee recommended to the House that antislavery petitons be tabled "without being printed or referred." Automatic tabling was proper because "Congress possessed no constitutional authority to interfere in any way with with ... slavery in any ... States." Congress also "ought not" interfere "with slavery in the District of Columbia."

Ought not! That code term had scarcely passed Pinckney's lips before Henry Wise screamed he had been betrayed. Pinckney had given Wise an "express pledge" that the committee's resolutions would declare abolition in the capital unconstitutional. The South Carolina traitor, cursed the Virginia Oppositionist, now massed behind "a defense of Southern interest" without "an expression of Southern feeling."[22]

Wise swiftly received further education in compromised southern feeling. Benjamin C. Howard of Maryland, a Democrat, made explicit that border dream of a slaveless future which Henry Clay had left implicit in the Senate. Pinckney was right, said the Marylander, to call District emancipation presently inexpedient. But the constitutional door must be open for future action.

For now Benjamin C. Howard wished Pinckney's gag rule to be imposed on abolitionists. A slaveholder himself, "he left his children surrounded by slaves." His Maryland neighborhood feared that "in the siege which the fanatics of the North were carrying on against the District, some of the bombs" might "burst on the way."

But this Maryland slaveholder was hardly the sort of committed soldier an Unconditional Perpetualist wanted manning bomb shelters. Benjamin Howard bragged to Congress that Maryland had appropriated $200,000 to colonize emancipated slaves. As presiding officer of the Maryland Colonization Society, he could proudly report that this safe form of removal was working so well that "emancipation" was running "ahead" of colonization funds. "An increase of pecuniary means" would "eventuate in the conversion of that State into a non-slaveholding State." This salutary process showed that "humanity as well as policy required" that uplifting Africans "be left to those who best understood their condition."

Slavery in the capital must last as long as slavery in Maryland and Virginia persisted, continued Benjamin Howard. But Congress must retain constitutional power to match the capital's future institutions to its neighbors'. "Suppose," concluded the Marylander, his state would be emancipated "in any given number of years, and the same thing to occur in Virginia." Wise's principles would then consign "the people of the District to a remediless and hopeless condition." Congress must someday extend to the capital the same emancipating laws which hopefully will have "operated upon Maryland and Virginia."[23]

That defense of the Pinckney Resolutions was embarrassing to Pinckney. Pinckney's more agreeable Southern Democratic defender was Representative Jesse A. Bynum of North Carolina. "The senators from Kentucky, as well as from Maryland," warned Bynum, "had dissented from the course which other Southern gentlemen wished to pursue." With the South "divided against itself," slaveholders were "highly impolitic" to insist on ultra measures. Southern Democrats preferred to win everything winnable. Uncompromising Southern Oppositionists evidently preferred total loss.

North Carolina's Bynum called the compromising Pinckney no traitor. Nor were Northern Democrats disloyal allies. They supported a gag rule. Northern Oppositionists opposed all gags. In fact, "four-fifths to five-sixths of the abolition petitions" came from Northern Oppositionists. How could Southern Oppositionists ally with such southern enemies?[24]

John Robertson of Virginia answered for States' Rights Oppositionists. The Pinckney Resolutions, argued Robertson, were made in Albany and decimated southern principle. True southern principle was that Congress could never touch slavery, anywhere. True southern principle was that the subject must never enter these doors, anytime. The Pinckney Resolutions rested southern safety on the shifting ground of political expediency. Even "if I stood alone," climaxed Robertson, "never but with life would I yield up . . . our rights."[25]

Southern Democrats felt Robertson's uncompromising force. Again, Southern Democrats pleaded with Northern Democrats for a more uncompromising gag rule. Again, Van Burenites said no. The Pinckney Gag Rule somewhat protected Southern Democrats against the Wises and Robertsons. Now Northern Democrats had to protect themselves.

On May 26, 1836, the House voted 117-68 to adopt as a standing rule Pinckney's resolution that antislavery petitions be received, then automatically tabled. The minority section won easily because most Northern Democrats voted with the South. Seventy-nine percent of voting Northern Democrats and 87.5% of voting Southerners said aye to Pinckney's rule. Northern Oppositionists voted no, 43-1. A sprinkling of Southern Oppositionists and Carolina extremists abstained or cast a negative protest vote.[26]

Southern abstainers were right that the Democratic Party had hardly secured pure southern principle. But northern states' righters had proved again, as they had in the Missouri Controversy and in the Compromise Tariff of 1833, that they alone would help southern minorities secure congressional majorities. The question remained whether Northern Democrats who had compromised with the Slavepower could long escape undamaged in the North—and whether Southern Democrats who had compromised with Van Buren could survive unscathed in the South.

CHAPTER 19

The Gag Rule, III:
Mr. Johnson's
Ironic Intransigence

While National Democrats felt a victor's elation at the gag rule settlement, South Carolinians again suffered a loser's dismay. Seldom have losers won so much or made winners pay so dearly for a triumph. While South Carolinians had lost Hammond's language, Cooper's objectives, Calhoun's intentions, they had put pressure on their big hate, both national parties. How ironic, then, that South Carolina's first gag rule postmortem centered on what the latest failure meant.

– 1 –

To Thomas Cooper's crowd in Columbia, the moderates' capture of James Hammond's initiative meant that disunion was more necessary and yet more implausible than ever. "The division of opinion" between "slave states paralyzes us," Cooper fumed to William Preston. "We are ready and willing to . . . cut the knot if needful, and quickly too. We think we can depend on being followed by Georgia, Alabama, Mississippi, and Louisiana. If so, I would cut cables and steer away."[1]

That "if" illuminated a plotter far from cutting cables. Cooper's word, "paralyze," captured the only Southerners ready to "cut the knot" of Union. The only nonparalyzed Disunionist, Governor George McDuffie of Forty Bale fame, could find only one outlet for his frustrated energies. The governor built up the army. "I regard a separation from the Union as an event absolutely inevitable," McDuffie wrote privately at the end of 1836. "For two years," he had been "preparing the state for every possible emergency." Fighting words, those, but how could the governor pick a fight for trainees?[2]

John C. Calhoun urged a better way to fight. Calhoun conceded that Yankee fanatics exerted a "baneful influence." He agreed that disunion might "be the consequence." But he stuck with "the supposition that the country and government may be regenerated and the Union saved."

337

Calhoun's supposition still required Southerners to secede from compromising parties. He still wanted an ensuing southern convention to lay down uncompromising ultimatums. He still believed that Northerners, once convinced slaveholders were in earnest, would grant every concession. Otherwise, his convention should go through with Cooper's disunion. "If possible, let us save the liberty of all; but, if not, our own at all events; and by aiming honestly and fairly at the former, we shall the more certainly, if we fail, succeed in the latter." He differed from more disunionist friends not because "I am more certain of success in our political efforts to save the country and its institutions" but because "I am less certain of defeat."[3]

Not more certain the Union could endure but less certain it would fail! That distinction made Calhoun no Father of Secession! If the criterion be results rather than intentions, incredulity is justified. Calhoun's contributions to sectional conflict, especially making nullification and gag rules and attempts to split national parties intellectually respectable, put Union under wicked strain. But Calhoun always expected this strain to save rather than snap national ties. He always conceived that Yankee capitalists and politicians, once forced to choose between plunging into Civil War over despised "niggers" or joining slaveholders in a victorious new national coalition, would act as racist materialists should.

Calhoun's post-gag rule letter to his cherished daughter, Anna Marie, demonstrates how this alleged Father of Secession would have scorned that title. "You say it is better to part peaceably at once," noted the father, "than to live in the state of irritation we do." But that "natural and common conclusion" ignores "how many bleeding pores must be taken up in passing the knife . . . through a body politick." South Carolina must accordingly "resort to every probable means of arresting the evil, and only act, when all has been done, that can be." Then "we shall stand justified before God and man." Anything else will ruin us, for making "two people of one" remains "the most difficult process in the world."[4]

– 2 –

Calhoun's initial difficulty remained passing the knife through national parties. Outside South Carolina after Pinckney's victory over Hammond, slaveholders never debated secession from party much less from the Union. Nor did southern two-party politicians join anti-party Carolinians in concentrating unendingly on gag rule distractions. Much southern campaign rhetoric focused on whether King Andrew should be allowed to hand an imperial presidency to his henchman, the manipulative Little Magician.[5] The question of whether Jackson was a dangerous Caesar, like the oft-discussed issue between Oppositionists/Whigs and Democrats of whether governments local or national should boost a sometimes booming, sometimes panicky market economy, knew no North or South. Such nonsectional issues strengthed the emerging Second American Party System, that competition between two national parties which would dominate

American political discourse between 1836 and 1853. Occasional southern uproars over loyalty and gag rules, on the other hand, weakened everything national.

When southern two-party politicians beyond South Carolina sporadically debated Pinckney's compromise gag rule, the terms of debate dismayed uncompromising extremists. Southern Oppositionists and Democrats differed over which impure party was least compromised on the rule. Southern Democrats bragged that Northern Democrats had helped Southerners pass both Buchanan's Senate and Van Buren's House silencer. In contrast, Northern Oppositionists had voted against all gags. Worse, Daniel Webster, one of Northern Oppositionists' presidential candidates, had been one of those six New England senators who had stonewalled against the Democrats' James Buchanan's almost total gag rule. Which Southerners stood allied with the most unsound northern wing?

Southern Oppositionists answered that Van Buren's phony soundness was more dangerous than explicit unsoundness. The New Yorker's sieve of a gag rule compromised all Southerners who settled for it. Hugh Lawson White and John Tyler, uncompromising slaveholders to the manor born, would be safer for slavery than a Yankee illusionist, who could not camouflage his resentment of the Slavepower.

With that rhetoric, Middle and Deep South Oppositionists sustained their effective 1835 argument that Van Buren, compromising Yankee, was less safe for slavery than Hugh White, uncompromising southern ex-Jacksonian. Partly because of that emphasis on loyalty, partly because White successfully emphasized the Jackson-as-Caesar theme, partly because Caesar dictated to the southern people a squirt of a too-clever magician as successor, Democrats came close to losing a South they had practically monopolized. In the entire South, where Democrats had won 66% of the popular votes in 1828 and 60% in 1832, Van Buren was barely ahead in 1836, with 50% of the ballots. In the Electoral College, where Jackson had won 85% of southern votes in 1828 and 79% in 1832, Van Buren squeaked by with 53% of slaveholding states' support. That margin, while now enough to continue Jacksonian control of the White House, was not remotely enough to guarantee future Jacksonian control of the South.

The shifting southern balance of power masked one constant. The Border South enjoyed politics as usual in 1836, with the Opposition Party once again winning and state aid to a market economy once again popular. In 1836 along the border, little was heard about loyalty to gag rules or whether Hugh Lawson White was to the manor born. Economic boosterism remained the focal point of interest here. Except in Missouri, border Oppositionists shunned the more states' rights Oppositionist candidate, Hugh White, and backed the more nationalistic William Henry Harrison. Harrison carried the same Border South states Clay had won in 1832: Kentucky, Delaware, and Maryland. White in 1836, like Clay four years earlier, lost Missouri.

South of the Border South, nothing was the same. In the Middle South, where Jackson had secured 70% of popular votes in 1828 and 80% in 1832,

Van Buren mustered but 50.4% of the tally. In the Deep South, where Old Hickory had swept 86% of citizens' favor in 1828 and 79% in 1832, the Little Magician received only 51.5% of the count. In 1836, Southern Oppositionists won their first Middle South state ever, Tennessee, and their first Deep South state ever, Georgia. Van Buren's largest Deep South margin was in Alabama, where his whopping 57% of the tally still compared dismally with Jackson's 90% support in 1828 and 100% sweep in 1832. In Louisiana, where Adams and Clay had carried an average of 43% of voters in the two Jackson campaigns, White increased the Oppositionist percentage to 48.6% in 1836. Oppositionists' gains were still more dramatic in Mississippi, where Jackson had secured 81% of the votes in 1828 and 100% in 1832. Van Buren managed to win only 50.7% of Mississippi votes. A shift of only 146 of 19,667 Mississippi voters and 136 of 7,036 Louisiana voters would have given Hugh White three Deep South states. Van Buren then would have retained only Alabama in Deep South areas Jackson had monopolized. The South was indeed a land politically transformed.[6]

– 3 –

These sudden changes, along with less dramatic evolutions in the later 1830s, yielded stability by 1840. In each state and county thereafter, only slight shifts in voting results usually occurred, with victory or defeat usually dependent on tiny changes in voter turnout and/or voter preference. As in 1836, Oppositionists/Whigs would usually have a small lead in the Border South, Democrats would usually attain a small lead in the Lower South, and the Middle South would usually split down the middle.

Total popular votes in national House of Representative elections, 1836–53, supply an excellent illustration.[7] When results of all congressional elections in this period are added up, Oppositionists/Whigs emerge with a three-percentage-point lead in Border South popular votes. Oppositionists/Whigs won a total of 112 Border South House seats during these years, while Democrats secured 90. In the Lower South, in contrast, the same tally over the same years yields Democrats a three-percentage-point lead in popular votes and 185 House seats to Oppositionists/Whigs' 77. The total popular vote for the two parties' House candidates in the Middle South over the 16 years was almost a dead heat, although Democrats won 217 to the Whigs' 138 seats. Andrew Jackson's initial pattern of relatively greater strength southwards and relatively greater weakness northwards in the South, while remaining visible, had become fainter everywhere and almost invisible towards the center.

The election of 1836 pointed towards stable and close alignments in the North too, making the newly-stable southern structure part of a new national solidity. In the North no less than in the South, Oppositionists/Whigs were usually slightly stronger northward, Democrats usually slightly stronger southward. The tier of northern states farthest south, touching on slaveholding states, will here be called the Lower North. The rest of the free states will be called the Upper North. The Upper North, especially New England, had experienced slavery least, had abolished it easiest, and had the longest historical experience with that Puritan/Federalist ideal of Christian organic community which Oppositionists/Whigs inherited. The Lower North, farthest from New England and closest to the South, had possessed slavery recently, had abolished it after hard battle, and was more into the Jacksonian ideal of free-spirited individualists than worshipful of a Whiggish state-fostered community.

As a result, Oppositionists/Whigs were usually slightly stronger in the Upper North, where they attained an almost four-point percentage lead in total congressional votes cast over the 1836–53 period and won 327 seats compared with Democrats' 307. Democrats were usually a little stronger in the Lower North, with a four-point percentage lead in this area's total votes for congressmen and 338 seats to Whigs' 227. These voting patterns explain much about pre-Civil War political activity: why Lower North Democrats more readily submitted to southern pressure than did Upper North Democrats, why Republicans swept the Upper North but lost key Lower North states in 1856, and why Abraham Lincoln talked more radically in northern than in southern Illinois when debating Stephen A. Douglas in 1858. The slight but critical verbal difference between the Lower North's Buchanan and the Upper North's Van Buren on the gag rule prefigured lasting statistical differences between their slightly different Norths.

Statistics on the Southern and National Second American Party systems also illuminate where instabilities lay. Southern states' righters were stuck in an Opposition/Whig Party which leaned the northern way both North and South. They were more vulnerable than Democrats in southern politics because less likely to make their more northerly strongholds budge. If loyalty pressures or their own ideology led States' Rights Whigs to lay down ultimatums on slavery issues, they might have to bid farewell to the Whig Party. The far more numerous centrist Southern Whigs would be only a little less uncomfortable should slavery issues become obsessive, for Upper North Yankees could not abide appeasing the Slavepower.

The Democratic Party was more likely to bend southward, because of its strength in the Lower South and in James Buchanan's appeasing Lower North. Still, the party in general and Martin Van Buren's Upper North faction in particular preferred to duck slavery agitations and to call Oppositionists/Whigs undemocratic on everything else. Unless Van Buren could keep slavery issues such as the gag rule a sideshow, he would be as uncomfortable inside the Democratic Party as states' righters would be inside the Whig Party.

– 4 –

Yankee Whigs were dedicated to increasing Van Buren's discomfort. Why would a true-blue American freeman gag discussion on the white side of the color line? That was Northern Whigs' lethal question. Obstacles to constituents' right to petition congressmen must be scuttled. That was Northern Oppositionists' ever-present response to Northern Democrats' claim to be more democratic than their opponents.

One Yankee political titan epitomized the way that stance mocked Jacksonian so-called Democracy. In 1828, Jacksonians had pilloried John Quincy Adams as a Harvard-trained elitist, not fit to rule over an increasingly egalitarian age. But as Adams saw his electoral defeat, "the sable genius of the South" had undemocratically destroyed "the great object of my life." The majority North had voted to re-elect him. But the minority South, anxious to "rivet into perpetuity the clanking chain of the Slave," had torn down all his efforts to promote "national means and national Energies."[8]

The minority South had once before torn a Yankee nationalist from the people's presidency, remembered Adams the younger. The three-fifths clause had defeated his father in the presidential election of 1800. Now masters of America's most undemocratic institution had spread the monstrosity that *he* was undemocratic!

In American culture, old Presidents, like old generals, usually fade away or write memoirs. John Quincy Adams was an exception. Adams, once evicted from the White House, could not win vindication while languishing on his delapidated Massachusetts farm. His debts were large. His land was unsalable. His floundering grist and flour mill ate into his waning estate.

Financial uncertainty plus political disaster made the exiled ex-President a household terror. His warmly affectionate wife writhed under his coldly forbidding treatment. His confused and unhealthy sons cracked beneath his overbearing expectations. Within a year of his presidential defeat, his eldest son committed suicide. Within five more years, the son carrying on the name John Adams, haplessly struggling to save the family mill business, died too. Through it all, his one effective offspring, Charles Francis, tried to salvage the family estate by putting father on an allowance. The patriarch thanked the son with a verbal scorching.

If it was tough to live with John Quincy Adams through his afflictions, the rejected politician was toughest on himself. The righteous New Englander scrutinized his soul for sins which had brought him down. At the same time, he excoriated selfish sinners who had crushed his selfless crusades. His small frame was covered with eruptions of boils and pimples. His bold, bald head was crimson with fury.

In 1830, his impossible retirement ended. His neighbors called him to the national House of Representatives. Adams accepted demotion from President to freshman congressman partly out of financial need, more because he relished the political stage, and mostly because he craved revenge. He would appeal Jacksonian "Democracy"'s judgment that nationalists were undemocratic. He would overturn slaveholders' victory over democratic nationalism.

Although not publicly an abolitionist, he had long since privately prophesied how some Abraham Lincoln would decree emancipation. At the time of the Missouri Crisis, he had secretly written that if the South severed the Union over slavery, the nation would sever slavery out of military necessity. As "calamitous and desolating as this course of events in its progress must be," scribbled the puritan, "so glorious would be its final issue, that, as God shall judge me, I dare not say that it is not to be desired."[9]

John Quincy Adams came to Congress a decade later, still unsure how the Lord would judge those who desired the catastrophe. At the very least, the republic must not crack until its stronger half could crush the lesser. At his most responsible, the statesman must endeavor to rescue republicanism peaceably from the Slavepower.

The task demanded the diplomatic cunning which had made the pre-presidential Adams a triumphant administrator of foreign policy. The presidential Adams, who had undiplomatically insisted on unpassable nationalist legislation, died with his presidency. Adams saw that the conqueror of the Slavepower must be carefully diplomatic about abolishing black slavery and endlessly relentless about saving white republicanism.

John Quincy Adams's first congressional act showed that the old diplomat had recovered diplomatic savvy. In December 1831, Massachusetts's fledgling representative presented 15 petitions praying for abolition of both slavery and the slave trade in Washington. After introducing the petitions, Adams opposed most of the prayers. He would rid the District of slave auctions but not of slaves.

No Southerner rose to call this too much antislavery. When a Yankee philanthropist wrote to object that Adams was not antislavery enough, the ex-President answered that he opposed stirring up North against South. He was delighted that events were "tending to universal emancipation." But Southerners, not a Yankee, must do the emancipating.[10]

When more antislavery petitions descended on Washington in 1836, John Quincy Adams continued to scold abolitionists for interfering with emancipation. Fanatics could not rally the North and would counterproductively enrage the South.[11] But he would fight for agitators' right to petition. Representatives must debate the represented's requests, lest the House of Representatives become fatally unrepresentative.

The Pinckney Gag Rule had not even been passed before Adams rose to defend white democracy. After Henry L. Pinckney brought up his committee's recommendations and after several Southerners explained why Pinckney proposed gagging too little, Adams explained why any silencing was too much. Before he could proceed, a Georgian moved that the House immediately vote on the Pinckney Gag Rule. "Am I gagged or not?" asked the Massachusetts congressman. The House voted to gag Adams by calling the question. Representatives then voted to gag Adams's constituents by ordering antislavery petitions automatically tabled.[12]

Old Man Eloquent would not allow white men to remain gagged. He was forever finding ways to dodge around the congressional ban and debate whether debate should be allowed. He remained careful not to discuss whether slavery should be abolished. He candidly declared his personal preference for freedom. He even introduced constitutional amendments for emancipation in the South. He saw, however, no hope at present for such amendments and little prospect for ending slavery in the capital. He continued to ask abolitionists, privately and publicly, to cease petitioning for the politically impossible.

He also continued to emphasize the democratic impossibility of gagging unfortunate opinion. His strategy was to question day after day, session after session, whether the latest petition he held in his hand came under the gag rule. His most notorious question, raised on February 6, 1837, concerned whether "a petition from 22 persons, declaring themselves to be slaves," could be presented.[13]

The Speaker of the House asked to see Adams's petition from slaves. Before the Speaker could rule, Waddy Thompson of South Carolina declared that Adams ought to be imprisoned. Fomenting insurrection was illegal, warned the South Carolinian. The madman from Massachusetts should not expect legal indemnity because his insanity spilled forth in Congress. When this "sanctuary is used to throw poisoned arrows, it ceases to be sacred." Thompson moved to censure Adams.[14]

South Carolina's Waddy Thompson, like Virginia's Henry Wise, was at the states' rights extreme of the lately called Oppositionist, now called Whig, movement. Thompson's diatribe against Adams, like Wise's earlier diatribe against Henry L. Pinckney, was the natural outcome of the southern faction's unnatural position. John Quincy Adams's intransigent opposition to Slavepower proposals, like the National Democratic Party's ability to pass some of those proposals, mocked States' Rights Whigs' argument that their national party could best fight for slavery. National Whiggery could hardly outdo the Democracy if that notorious anti-Southerner, the infuriating Adams, spoke for Northern Whigs.

In 1837, Adams answered Thompson's censure motion by revealing that the 22 slaves petitioned to remain enslaved! Should he be indicted for helping slaves retain bonds? Titters filled the House chamber. Thompson, furious, asked whether it is "a light thing, for the amusement of others, to irritate, almost to madness, the whole delegation from the slaveholding states."[15]

Adams, having made a comic character of the sputtering fire-eater, soon twisted the knife in the ridiculous creature. He asked Waddy Thompson "to study a little the first principles of civil liberty." A member of Congress should be indicted for presenting a petition? "If that, sir, is the law of South Carolina," climaxed the inexorable Mr. Adams, "I thank God I am not a citizen of South Carolina."[16]

This time not giggles but "great agitation," the clerk recorded, filled the House. Adams, with his usual cunning, had focused agitation on slaveholders' limits on white liberties. Adams's focus caused Northerners to run away from Waddy Thompson. The House rejected Thompson's motion to censure Adams, 105-21.[17]

Hardly a congressional day went by thereafter without Adams mocking the gag rule and making Southerners debate supposedly gagged debates. Ineffective and anti-republican gag rules became increasingly unpopular in the North. Still, during the late 1830s, most Northern Democrats continued to vote with

Southern Democrats to receive, then table, antislavery petitions. In December 1837, and again in December 1838, the House affirmed gags similar to Henry L. Pinckney's by majorities almost identical in makeup and numbers to Pinckney's coalition.[18]

Northern Democrats denied Adams's contention that their repeated votes for gag rules branded them as slaves of the Slavepower. Most Southerners still wished a rule whereby prayers could not be received. Instead, Northerners approved one whereby petitions were received, then tabled. To the retort that this was a distinction without a difference, Northern Democrats could answer that the difference meant much to the Slavepower. Besides, nothing was undemocratic about receiving a constituent's petition and then tabling it, if too few constituents wanted action. Slave of the Slavepower? The reception/tabling distinction showed this was another of Adams's lies.

– 5 –

Then in 1840, a gag rule tailored to James Hammond's specifications obliterated Northern Democrats' saving distinction. The new uncompromising rule of 1840, like Pinckney's old compromising one of 1836, stemmed in part from the usual presidential-year escalation of southern loyalty politics. In 1836, Oppositionists further southward had finessed the "untrue to the South" accusation by supporting that southern ticket, Tennessee's Hugh Lawson White and Virginia's John Tyler, against New York's Magician and his illusionary gag rule. Now in 1840, President Van Buren, having completed the states' rights rout of the national bank, was running for re-election against the more nationalistic Southern Oppositionists' candidate in 1836, Indiana's William Henry Harrison. Harrison was known to favor a nationalistic economic program. Worse, the nationalistic Harrison had earlier proposed national action to colonize slaves.

Harrison's dubiousness, from southern purists' perspective, seemed so obvious to John C. Calhoun that the South Carolinian momentarily suspended his war against Van Buren. He urged supporters to spend this election back in the Democratic Party.[19] Calhoun's return to the Democracy, if perhaps only for one election, left States' Rights Whigs the more vulnerable to charges of disloyalty. In this uneasy atmosphere, only a few weeks after William Henry Harrison's nomination, the House of Representatives reconsidered Henry L. Pinckney's compromise gag rule. As John Quincy Adams remembered the "somewhat strange, not to say edifying scenes which took place in this House under those mutual cries of Abolitionism," gentlemen "were anxious above all things not to be thought Abolitionists, and most especially the members from the South."[20]

Most especially Congressman Waddy Thompson of South Carolina. When John C. Calhoun took snuff, so it was said, South Carolina sneezed. Well, Calhoun had called for Van Buren's election on good states' rights principle, and Thompson still held out for Whiggery and Harrison. Thompson knew how dubious was the case for rejecting Calhoun's lead. Thompson was full of "repugnance" for General Harrison's "supposed latitudinarianism." He well knew "the ultraism of a large portion of the Whig Party." He had tried to censor that worst of Whigs, John Quincy Adams.

But "the first duty of patriotism," claimed Waddy Thompson, was to drive out Martin Van Buren's "reckless, ignorant, unprincipled pack." Subsequently, "in our own good time," Whigs could settle "our family disputes." Thompson would focus on Van Buren's "corruption, incompetency, and misrule" rather than answer "false and insulting accusations" that by cooperating with Northern Whigs in the election, he pledged "to support" Northern Whig measures.[21]

In January of 1840, Waddy Thompson focused on the compromised Van Buren/Pinckney Gag Rule by introducing an uncompromising rule. Thompson's phrasing was turgid and confusing. But the drift of his tortured language was that the House should refuse to receive petitions instead of automatically tabling them.[22] Thompson demanded that Southern Democrats prove their loyalty by supporting his uncompromising rule. Or would Southern Van Burenites, determined to continue their alliance with phony northern friends, prefer instead Van Buren's compromised gag rule?

Southern Democrats, seeking to evade Waddy Thompson's litmus test of southern loyalty, preferred to debate William Henry Harrison's disloyalty. Congressman Sampson H. Butler emphasized that in 1833 Harrison had suggested using surplus federal revenues for colonization-emancipation. "With this declaration staring him in the face, how could any southern man support" the Yankee nationalist?[23]

Congressman Jesse Bynum of North Carolina furthered Butler's question. Bynum admitted that "five or ten" House Democrats were "in the Abolition ranks." But Bynum saw "65 to 75 deeply died Abolitionists" among Northern Whig congressmen. Bynum did not know whether William Henry Harrison "was an abolitionist." But Harrison "would have to depend" on John Quincy Adams's northern faction "for his election." Hence the danger in Harrison's statement that "if my vote would effect it, every surplus dollar would be appropriated" for colonization/emancipation. Southern Whigs, warned Bynum, should "ponder well this language."

Bynum's offensive provoked a Maryland Whig congressman, William Cost Johnson, into the ultimate gag rule counteroffensive.[25] The Marylander introduced the resolution that "no petition . . . praying the abolition of slavery" anywhere "shall be *received* by this House." Waddy Thompson's verbal meandering towards the same non-reception policy, worried Johnson, might allow Southerners to wander from duty. But Johnson's straightforward language permitted no evasion.

Democrats such as Jesse Bynum, scoffed Johnson, considered any Southerner who supported Harrison "either an abolitionist or an accessory to abolitionism." These demagogues, steamed the Marylander, "may call me enemy to the South." But their Pinckney Gag Rule "went the whole length and breadth of abolition." By receiving antislavery petitions, the House "virtually" invites "abolitionists to send their petitions here." The Pinckney sieve of a gag rule attempted "solely to entrap the South into support of the Administration, by pretending that a gentleman of the North . . . had taken the South under his special care."

Johnson would "not be so unjust as to say that every gentleman who differs with me on this question is an abolitionist." But Southerners must now "vote with me on a proposition which will admit of no doubtful construction." Or would Southern Democrats prefer to demonstrate that their southern zeal was counterfeit?

Why would William Cost Johnson, of all people, insist on the James Hammond/Waddy Thompson gag rule language? Johnson was nothing like a Waddy Thompson-style States' Rights Whig, much less a James Hammond-style South Carolina quasi-disunionist. The author of the perfected gag rule was instead a Henry Clay economic nationalist and a Maryland advocate of diffusing away slavery. William Cost Johnson represented North Maryland's Frederick District, just east of the western mountains. Johnson's constituents owned less than 10% slaves, the lowest percentage in increasingly-less-enslaved North Maryland. Johnson and his constituents revered permanent Union more than "temporary" slavery. "Debate upon this question must cease in this Hall," declared Johnson, "or the Union will, sooner or later, be dissolved."

He would also gag national antislavery discussion to hasten state removal of blacks. He refused to discuss "whether slavery is or is not a moral, social, or political evil. That question was properly discussed only in the state legislatures." Still, Johnson bragged that no other legislature, "not even the loudest and noisiest about abolition, has done as much as Maryland towards emancipation. . . . With munificent liberality, she has founded a colony in Africa, at the expense of some $200,000."

Johnson charged abolitionists with delaying "abolition in Maryland at least a century." Without outside agitation, inside reformers might "have gradually and quietly terminated" the temporary evil. He could not say how much longer Africans would now be "held in servitude." But he could say that black savages, arriving in America "little superior to the orangutan," had "become civilized, humanized, and christianized" under the Domestic Institution. "Philanthropists" were sending back to the Dark Continent "a changed being, with a knowledge of law, moral, and religious duty." Someday, returning ex-slaves may "change the nature of their own wild race at home, and make all Africa a land of civil and religious liberty."

When so soaring, William Cost Johnson sounded like William Henry Harrison, proposing national funds to colonize ex-slaves. Then was not this Maryland visionary untrue to the South, in his longings to diffuse slaves away and in his backing of his true brother, Harrison the colonizer? No no no, Johnson screamed at tormentors. My sort is true on *the* southern subject, that the North must impose nothing on the South. Borderites might not be as vehement on many slavery subjects as slaveholders further south. But Marylanders seeking to return blacks to Africa rivaled Lower South slaveholders in loathing outsiders who "would, in dreamy mysticism, indulge a sickly sentimentality for the imaginary benefit of remote communities." Should Yankee fanatics "require and force a dissolution," the South could count on Maryland. If anyone thought a Marylander false, let them prove themselves as true by voting for his ultra anti-abolitionism.

Johnson's test of loyalty was more than an act of crass partisanship, although the Whig enjoyed twisting the knife in the Democratic Party. The Johnson Gag Rule was also more than an expression of Maryland's quasi-emancipationist ultra-Unionism, although the deepest fears about proslavery disunionism were on display. Johnson's resolution was above all a statement that border Southerners were southern too. The North Marylander, who was about to run for governor, was driven to prove his southernness because Southern Democrats' charge of disloyalty might be believed, especially by South Maryland voters. Johnson was assuredly not rock-hard on slavery, if hardness meant determination to resist internal reform. The resulting political vulnerability drove the southern softheart to a vehement stand against antislavery Northerners. And the vehemence of the William Cost Johnsons meant that at least on the subject of overt Yankee abolitionists, there was indeed *a* South.

With a classic border drifter forcing John C. Calhoun's anti-abolitionist language on Congress, were the Jesse Bynums acting responsibly in baiting the William Cost Johnsons for alleged disloyalty? Absolutely, assuming a ruling class is responsible for saving itself. William Cost Johnson in 1840, like Benjamin Howard battling for the Pinckney Gag Rule in 1836, was looking for ways, especially colonization, to diffuse blacks slowly away. Both Marylanders would have fought to the death for slavery only after some self-righteous outsider had committed some forcible overt act, suddenly emancipating blacks.

Slave perpetualists expected no such outrageous act. Yankee assaults would come Cuffee-like, disguised and camouflaged. Underminers, like Cuffee, would take up poses Southerners themselves applauded. Throughout the Upper South, in theory in Virginia and in legislation in Maryland, slaveholders had sought a slow end to slavery through colonization. Henry Clay, like Thomas Jefferson, had urged national funds to make black removal more practicable. William Henry Harrison had toyed with the scheme. William Cost Johnson approved it. Would the Johnsons fight to the death for the Deep South if some northern gentleman, with malice towards none and charity for all, helped actualize the Upper South's own whitening dream? Or to put the question already omnipresent in colonization struggles and someday to be pivotal in the Civil War, was a border world which hoped to diffuse away slavery southern or northern?

Slaveholding perpetualists residing further southwards possessed impoverished means of mastering the answer. An overweening South Carolinian could not lynch a Marylander or, after the nullification debacle, nullify the waverer. Despots without blood and iron could only slap softhearts around with "mere" words.

Loaded words remained a potent way to deter Southerners from drifting. In a relaxed democratic atmosphere, with all ideas discussable without accusations of treason, the many William Johnsons would have been free to seek out the many Northerners sympathetic with the movement towards a lily-white labor force, with national land proceeds paying for diffusing blacks outside whites' republic. That nurturing atmosphere, precisely what Thomas Jefferson had groped towards with Jared Sparks, was exactly what proslavery perpetuators felt compelled to destroy. Loyalty politics was their best weapon of destruction. The disloyalty club turned an ultra-nationalistic Whig into a raving questioner of other people's loyalty. Does success prove that the loyalty club need not have been swung?

– 6 –

After Johnson pressed his gag rule, Southern Democrats could not escape the Marylander's unforgiving test. To vote down Johnson's "mere" words and reaffirm Van Buren's dodging vocabulary was to proclaim that the Democratic Party's proslavery solutions were indeed shot through with Cuffee-like phoniness. Southern Democrats, unwilling to suffer this setback in a presidential election year, felt compelled to go one better than Johnson in Congress. Southern Democrats thus not only swung behind Johnson's language but demanded that Northern Democrats go for the total gag. And could that supposedly ultra-loyal Maryland Whig wrench a single Northern Whig vote for southern orthodoxy?

Johnson, to his discomfort, could not. Meanwhile, Southern Democrats, to their displeasure, barely bludgeoned enough Northern Democrats behind the ultra-southern gag rule. Northern Democrats, already hounded by John Quincy Adams for half-yielding to the Slavepower, faced dismal alternatives. They could consolidate southern party prospects by caving in to the extremist gag resolution. Northern constituents would then consider them all the more slaves of the Slavepower and enemies of free republican discussion. Or they could please Yankee voters by rejecting total gags. Southern allies would then see them as all the more phony friends of slavery.

The natural result was that Northern Democrats split on the Johnson Gag. The House voted not to receive antislavery petitions, 114-108.[26] That compared to a vote of 126-78 for the December 1838 receive-but-table gag. The difference was that where 56 Northern Democrats had supported and 14 opposed the previous compromise gag, only 26 favored and 36 opposed the uncompromising Johnson Resolution.[27]

The farthest North registered the largest revolt against escalated Slavepower pressure. Upper North Democrats voted 22-13 against the Johnson Gag. Lower North Democrats voted against too, but only 14-13. With a 50-50 split of all Northern Democrats, the minority South could comfortably control a congressional majority. With the 50-50 split now restricted to the North closest to the South, John Quincy Adams barely lost to William Cost Johnson.

Adams would have won except for his parallel hate, the three-fifths clause. In a House apportioned on the one-white-man, one-vote basis, Southerners would not have had the 19 fewer representatives received for black noncitizens in 1840. The Slavepower needed most of those 19 boosts in power to pass the latest gag rule by six votes.

In this supreme example of republicanism, southern-style, gutting republicanism, northern-style, the loser was not so much John Quincy Adams as his great foe, Jacksonian "Democracy." Jacksonian passage of William Cost Johnson's air-tight gag rule mocked even the not-so-democratic Jacksonian formula of pure democracy for whites, no democracy for "inferior" races. The Jacksonian Party's latest appeasement of the Slavepower left the movement undemocratic on both sides of the color line.

William Cost Johnson was the winner in this latest escalation of gagging white egalitarianism, if anyone could be called victorious who had lost so much. True, the Maryland Whig had strained the opposing party. He had also unconditionally gagged outside agitators. But in the name of proving that the National Democratic Party's proslavery postures were compromised, he had shown that only the Democratic Party could enact uncompromising proslavery legislation. Worse, in the name of saving the Union, quieting discussion, propelling black removal forward, Johnson had strained the republic, provoked more violent discussion, and made calm reform impossible. Worst of all, by demonstrating that Northern Democrats were barely trustworthy and that Northern Whigs were utterly untrustworthy when slaveholders demanded protection, William Cost Johnson had played into the hands of South Carolina extremists, who had hoped uncompromising gag rules would destroy both compromising parties.

– 7 –

The Age of Jackson's angriest loser now pressed towards his supreme victory. Again and again in the early 1840s, John Quincy Adams almost ungagged the gag. On three different occasions in mid-1841, the House voted to repeal the Johnson Resolutions. But each time, a revote reinstituted the gag.[28]

Southerners, feeling momentum shifting, needed to make Adams seem to be not a responsible crusader for white republicanism but a fanatical opponent of everything American. On January 24, 1842, they thought they had their man. Adams stunned Congress on that long-remembered day by presenting a petition to abolish the nation. The so-called Haverhill Petition, from 46 citizens of Haverhill, Massachusetts, decried loss of democratic right and asked Congress for "measures peaceably to dissolve the Union." Adams moved that the petition be sent to committee, with instructions to explain why the prayer was misguided.[29]

States' Rights Whigs, as usual, were first to jump all over Adams. Shortly after the Massachusetts congressman introduced his latest firebrand into the House, one Southerner urged that the petition physically be burned. Then Henry Wise of Virginia, the Oppositionist who had first taken on Henry L. Pinckney back in 1836, moved that John Quincy Adams be censored.[30]

Adams, in response, asked the clerk to read the Declaration of Independence. The essence of Americanism, the reading reiterated, was a people's right to alter governments destructive of democratic right. The Haverhill Petition, urged Adams, must not become the first document of the Second American

Revolution. If Congress could not rescue the right of petition, Northerners might have to depart the republic.

But it was "not yet time" for the North to secede. Adams would have the petition referred so that a committee could explain to Haverhill residents that the right of petition would be restored and republicanism redeemed. Nothing was censorable, concluded Adams, about presenting a legitimate prayer from sorely excited constituents in order to soothe their eminently American excitement.[31]

Henry Wise proceeded to light into Adams in a famous two-day speech. The Virginian called the Massachusetts congressman the greatest Union-breaker. Adams answered in an equally notorious long assault. We must not sacrifice free republican debate, declared the Massachusetts congressman, to make a despotic regime safe. If he withdrew the Haverhill remonstrance, "I would consider myself as having sacrificed the right of petition; as having sacrificed the right of habeas corpus; as having sacrificed the right of trial by jury"; as having sacrificed free mails, a free press, free speech; as having sacrificed "every principle of liberty . . . that might not be pleasing to members of the 'Peculiar Institution.'"[32]

Northern congressmen rushed to rescue John Quincy Adams from the Slavepower. The motion to censor him was tabled in the middle of his trial. The old man celebrated by defying the gag with more petitions. He was almost mirthful when the House refused to receive them.

He could afford to smile. Northern Democrats could not much longer risk being called undemocratic towards whites so that petitions need not trouble despots over blacks. At the session after the Haverhill Controversy, the gag squeaked through, 106-102.[33] The next session, the margin was sliced to one vote, 88-87.[34]

In December 1844, the House finally and forever repealed all gag rules, 108-80.[35] Northern Whigs cast their usual unanimous vote against the gag. Southerners continued to vote almost unanimously for the gag. This time, however, Northern Democrats voted 54-16 against Southern Democrats. In 1836, they had voted 53-14 for Pinckney's diluted gag rule; in 1840, they had split 36-26 against Johnson's undiluted gag rule. In 1844, Upper North Democrats polished off the last potential gag, 32-5; Lower North Democrats less overwhelmingly but still decisively voted it down, 22-11. When Slavepower demands could corral only one-third the Democrats in the most friendly half of the North, the time to cease pressing northern friends for gags had arrived.

By finally letting Northern Democrats off the hook on republicanism for whites, Southern Democrats implicitly declared a decade of battle futile. Other crusades, offering richer rewards, had become more pressing. Why squander Northern Democrats, who were needed to annex Texas, in a counterproductive struggle that only made John Quincy Adams more eloquent?

Slaveholders had at last learned the obvious lesson: gag rules deployed too little tyranny to silence antislavery Northerners and too much tyranny for anti-abolitionist Yankees to tolerate. Slaveholders had pushed for insufficient despotic sanctions because theirs was an insufficiently despotic mentality—at least when it came to white republicanism. Dictators immersed in the American egalitarian milieu could only stuff a bit of a handkerchief down John Quincy Adams's damnable throat.

That was no way to silence the Yankee egalitarian roar. The gag rule was always vulnerable because the somewhat closed version of white men's democracy in the South looked not open enough to the North. Northerners and Southerners, while both for white men's republicanism, found in the Gag Rule Controversy that they were republicans with a distressing difference.

- 8 -

Distressed was the word for every American who recalled gag rule scenes and pondered whether such scenarios might be repeated. In the North, Yankee Whigs, having at last stopped Northern Democrats from appeasing the Slavepower on the gag, feared future cave-ins to Slavepower ultimatums. Northern Democrats, having risked so much to gag Northerners so little, bristled at memories of Southern Democrats demanding ever more politically risky gag rules.

Southern memories of the long congressional fight were equally bitter and full of forebodings. Southern Democrats, who had finally secured the most extreme slavery legislation, bristled at memories of Northern Democrats who had melted away from the victorious coalition. Southern Whigs, who had led fights for the extremist gag rules and for the harshest condemnations of Adams, winced at recollections of their endless necessity to prove that a patriotic slaveholder could be part of so anti-Slavepower a party. South Carolina extremists, who had helped put both compromising parties under siege, could see only the same slaveholding spoilsmen staying inside the same compromising coalitions.

With every political faction edgier than ever, almost a decade of compromises and appeasements had solved nothing. The Gag Rule Controversy had but sketched in battle lines and hardened contestants for the worse crisis looming over the expansion of America—and of slavery—in the Southwest.

PART VI

THE ANNEXATION OF TEXAS

The largest turning point on the road to disunion is too often considered off that road. The Texas Annexation Controversy came before the so-called Era of Sectional Controversy. Nationalistic ideologies and interests helped make Texas attractive. National diplomacy was centrally involved. The annexation story thus easily slides into nonsectional sagas.

But the Texas epic emerges most clearly in the context of the coming of the Civil War. The same southern impulses making slavery politics sporadically distracting earlier brought the Texas Annexation Controversy front and center on the national agenda. Many slaveholders' prayers that bondage and blacks would diffuse away, Southerners' apprehension about vulnerable hinterlands, their fear that world-wide opinion would imprison them with multiplying blacks—all of this helped focus southern eyes on Texas. Calhounites' search for "mere" words to reorganize politics along ideological lines, Southern Democrats' and Whigs' forays in loyalty politics, southern states' rights politicians' leverage over the Democratic Party and frustration with National Whiggery—all this thrust slaveholders' concerns about Texas into national and especially National Democratic Party politics. Northern resentment that southern protections of slavery would destroy white republicanism, already omnipresent in Missouri and Gag Rule controversies, ballooned when Southerners demanded gigantic Texas. The resulting crisis mocked Jacksonian "Democracy," de-Whigged the most States' Rights Whigs, and scarred democratic Union. An episode so entwined with the slavery controversy, too much of it unknown, too little of it now connected with sectional contention, all of it replete with zany characters and weird happenings, demands a section of its own.

CHAPTER 20

Anti-Annexation as
Manifest Destiny

Political consequences of annexation were manifestly destined to swell to the size of Texas itself. In territorial mass, the annexed enslaved state would rival the six previous Lower South States combined. The annexation agreement of 1845 would allow the Lone Star State to turn itself into five states. Specters of a doubled Slavepower would loom before Northerners already angry about a southern power bloated by counting slaves as three-fifths additional votes.

Worse, annexation would lead to huger territorial acquisitions and nastier sectional resentments. Admission of Texas into the Union in 1845 would make war with Mexico in 1846 difficult to avert. The rout of Mexico would make American hunger for Mexican land hard to curb. The new empire thus acquired would make a mid-century crisis over slavery's expansion impossible to avoid. Before Texas, tendencies towards secession were merely foreshadowed. After annexation, events would come in a rush.

The reasons why the Lone Star State was admitted to the Union, unlike the consequences, may seem to have little to do with slavery politics. Texans who originally migrated from the United States, as the historical legend has it, delightedly reannexed their destiny to the United States. United States citizens espousing a Manifest Destiny to spread American democracy over the hemisphere, as the story continues, happily invited Texas republicans to share democratic Union. Why elaborately explain so natural a marriage?[1]

Because this natural attraction formula ignores natural forces splitting the two republics apart. Immediately before annexation, both major American parties remained frozen in their decade-long position that Texas was not worth foreign war or sectional combat. In 1843, the American establishment's opposition to annexation drove Texas leaders towards an alternate Manifest Destiny: an English-protected independent republic.

This manifest drift away from annexation initially alarmed only one tiny southern faction, composed of a few stymied States' Rights Whigs and fewer disgruntled Democrats. Members of the annexation clique fed each other

355

rumors that English leaders would trade protection of Texas's independence for emancipation of the Lone Star Republic's slaves. These southern alarmists controlled the presidency. They dominated nothing else. An accident of death had pulled President John Tyler of Virginia into the White House. Tyler's accents of extremism had pushed away popular support. His Accidency's latest extremism, his conception of English interference with Texas slavery, seemed at first to most Americans a wild idea, a demagogue's nonsense. Yet this isolated resident of the White House with his far-out nightmare about England precipitated a stream of events which reversed Texas's and the United States' movement away from each other. The resulting national disasters, fully as destructive as national political idols had predicted, illuminate why the American political establishment had desperately sought to block a despised President's notion of Manifest Destiny. Still, Tyler prevailed.

Faced with this bizarre phenomenon, fine historical intelligences have echoed contemporary charges that John Tyler's supporters cynically used irresponsible propaganda to spread an absurdity.[2] This thesis, with its emphasis on a minority's manipulation of majority opinion, at least rejects the notion that some euphoria about Manifest Destiny transfixed the American majority. But the argument that propaganda yielded otherwise needless disaster also represents a last stand of the Revisionist theory that unscrupulous politicans created an unnatural civil war.

No aspect of Revisionism more demands revising. Nothing was unnatural about President Tyler's and his southern advisors' far-from-cynical beliefs about Englishmen's far-from-fictional speculations about securing the far-from-preposterous object of an independent, emancipated Texas Republic. Rather, this apprehension represented a recurrent nightmare among southern extremists, who ever worried that the southern mainstream would neither notice nor combat Anglo-American silent drift towards antislavery. Nor was anything unnatural about these slaveholding extremists' successful pressure on Southern Democrats, and thus on the National Democratic Party, to pass a law shoring up the Peculiar Institution at its exposed fringes. That was outcome as usual in slavery politics, whether the incident involved gag rules or Texas or fugitives or Kansas. The annexation of Texas was indeed one of the most understandable pre-Civil War events, so long as one understands that unpopular initiators were not paranoids or demagogues or provokers of weird happenings. Rather the President and his main diplomatic lieutenants were coherent ideologues who used established patterns of slavery politics to secure the latest dubiously democratic consolidation of the Slavepower.[3]

– 1 –

Few chief executives anywhere in the hemisphere anytime in the nineteenth century were more frustrated than were Presidents John Tyler of the United States and Sam Houston of Texas in the year 1843. The two Presidents' respective attempts to break free from paralysis ultimately fractured the logjam over

Texas Annexation. Let us examine each chieftain's predicament on the eve of breakthrough, starting with Tyler's.[4]

John Tyler's frustration as the first and last States' Rights Whig President was the climactic frustration of a man's and a faction's doomed attempt to make Whig Nationalism a states' rights crusade. The impossible dream, it will be recalled, had begun back in nullification times. Then Senator Tyler had been a States' Rights Democrat who believed that Andrew Jackson's proposed coercion of South Carolina Nullifiers was unsafe for states' rights and for slavery. Three years later, Tyler switched to the Opposition Party. He would make the anti-Jackson coalition uncompromisingly for states' rights.

Only unusually principled politicians characteristically switch parties. John Tyler was long on states' rights principles. But for an abstractionist who played unconventionally loose with party connection, Tyler was also a conventional two-party politician, as his states' rights intimates despairingly knew. Among Tyler's doubting Virginia friends, the most important was Judge Abel P. Upshur, the zealot ultimately most responsible for pushing President Tyler and the nation towards annexation.

Upshur, leading foe of King Numbers in the Virginia Convention of 1829, invidiously compared Tyler to the great seceder from the Jackson coalition, John C. Calhoun. The South Carolinian, Upshur's idol, broke cleanly from the Jackson Party in 1831. Calhoun then warned followers away from compromised national parties. They should create a new, uncompromising states' rights coalition. Some Calhoun admirers, including Judge Upshur, hoped to triumph more swiftly within the already existing Opposition Party. But Calhoun's most loyal partisans tended to be only nominally Oppositionists. Unlike more centrist politicians such as John Tyler, they doubted that the nationalistic Opposition Party could be transformed into a states' rights vehicle.

Calhounites such as Judge Upshur especially suspected John Tyler because the Virginian crept rather than leapt for his principles. The Virginia senator waited, waited, waited, for almost three years after nullification he waited, until departure from the Jackson coalition could no longer be delayed. When the Jacksonian majority in the Virginia legislature instructed Tyler to resign his seat, the senator stalled, stalled, stalled, for several months he stalled, until resignation could no longer be avoided. Having delayed like a politician so long, he then raced, like a politician, straight to the center of the other party's maneuverings.

The Tyler who switched looked the part of the slaveholder distressed about how southern purity and national partisanship could be combined. John Tyler's face was long, his cheeks hollow, his complexion sallow. His nervous eyes darted erratically, as if searching for some way to be ideologue and politico too. This cadaverous partisan with the thin beak nose and the thin bony hands was in manner all severe gentleman of the Virginia-style Old School. But the question his thin frame exuded whenever he pressed the flesh was whether he would only exhaust himself by trying to be John C. Calhoun and Martin Van Buren mixed up in one package—and an Oppositionist/Whig parcel no less.

Tyler's largest problem was that most Oppositionists lived in the North and championed Daniel Webster's brand of high nationalism. Furthermore, most Southern Oppositionists lived in more northern sections of the South and cheered Henry Clay's version of economic nationalism. The more extreme States' Rights Oppositionists who lived in more southern sections of the South seemed imprisoned in the wrong fortress even in their homeland.

John Tyler escaped from prison in 1836 because the torn Opposition Party made no effort to unite. Southern Oppositionists ran their own states' rights ticket in the Middle and Lower South, featuring Hugh Lawson White for President and Tyler for Vice President. After the multiple-candidate campaign of 1836 lost out to Van Buren, John Tyler and all Oppositionists/Whigs realized that the party would have to run one ticket in 1840. A Whig national party convention would have to be called. The John Tylers would have to attend. Virginians would have to wrench Whig Nationalists towards the states' rights path to power.

Only the exile from both parties seemed capable of producing that miracle. John C. Calhoun might have the charisma, if on a national ticket, to induce a Whig gamble on states' rights. But Calhoun saw no ground for compromise with Clay, that adherent of "consolidation and emancipation." Calhoun could see less ground for accepting second place on a William Henry Harrison ticket. Harrison, lamented Calhoun, "has expressed an opinion in favor of appropriating money to emancipate our slaves" through colonization. Of the two old parties, Calhoun preferred the Democratic coalition. He believed more states' righters were there encamped.[5]

As the presidential election of 1840 approached, Calhoun returned temporarily to the Democratic Party. Martin Van Buren, explained the South Carolinian, had fought the good states' rights fight against the United States Bank. Many of Calhoun's followers, having left the Jackson Party with their man and joined the Opposition Party without him, streamed back with him at least temporarily into the Democratic Party. Other states' rights purists, Abel P. Upshur among them, still thought Van Buren worse than Whiggery. But Upshur was more than ever at the Whig fringes after Calhoun went back for a season to the Democracy.

Meanwhile, states' righters such as John Tyler, deeper inside the Whig establishment, were more awkwardly positioned than ever after Calhoun's move. Then, at this moment of feeling hopelessly trapped in a nationalistic institution, the most nationalistic Southern Whig offered States' Rights Whigs another escape. Henry Clay, of all people, made noises the John Tylers were desperate to hear.

Clay's series of speeches and letters in the late 1830s, culminating in his senatorial address of February 7, 1839, hardly renounced nationalistic Whiggery. Rather, Henry Clay promised to delay agitating for his American System. He still wanted national roads built. But states were building them. He still desired a national tariff. But his Compromise Tariff of 1833 had settled the issue for a decade. He still preferred a national bank. But the people preferred Democrats' banking solutions. His states' rights friends ought to stop punishing him for nationalistic ideas he had stopped pushing.

The worst threat facing the nation, Clay now emphasized, was the abolitionist onslaught. The Border South's hero still called slavery a temporary evil. He again hazily envisioned slaves and blacks diffusing from America. He again hinted that bondage would drift out of his Border South.

But this time Henry Clay's soft prayers for black diffusion came embedded in hard attacks on Yankee meddlers. Where an earlier Henry Clay had hoped states would use distributed funds to finance state colonization-abolition and had prayed that in some distant future the federal government might free the District's slaves, the Kentuckian now stressed that slaveholders must decide slavery's fate. Clay urged secession if Yankees imposed emancipation. Abolitionists, he charged, inspired a southern rage endangering the white man's republic. If Congress and Northerners would keep hands off slaves, the white republic would endure. Then the South would solve its own problem.[6]

Henry Clay hoped that these new emphases might forge a middle position for the divided anti-Jackson party. By coupling a call on fellow nationalists to delay commercial aspirations with a call on fellow Southerners to damn outside meddlers, Clay sought to become a Whig for all regions. By lambasting abolitionist agitation and muting agitation about banks, Clay also arguably demonstrated sounder southern priorities than the Calhoun won over by Van Buren's banking policy. John Tyler, advocate of that position, became leader of States'-Rights-Whigs-for-Clay in the late 1830s.

Calhoun's admirers on the Whig fringes, however, found the new Clay scarcely more admirable than the old. Abel P. Uphsur remained faintly hopeful that States' Rights Whigs, by issuing ultimatums on slavery, could force Northern and Border South nationalists in the party around. Those were not Clay's tactics. The Kentuckian, prizing permanent Union more than temporary slavery. opposed all agitation, for or against slavery. A neutral who would prefer to terminate the Peculiar Institution, declared Abel P. Upshur, "has no merit in my eye, except in being able to turn V. Buren out."[7]

Henry Clay's new stance had less merit in Northern Whigs' eyes. Yankee nationalists had suspected the Border South hero ever since Clay compromised the principle of permanent tariff protection by co-authoring the Compromise Tariff of 1833. No matter that the Kentuckian opposed both sections' ferocities. Northern Whigs still preferred a fresh face and a less sectionally sullied symbol of nationalism. The Northern Whig majority at the first National Whig Convention thus dashed Henry Clay's hopes by selecting as its presidential nominee that war hero almost as beloved as Andrew Jackson, General William Henry Harrison of Indiana.

Northern Whigs' rejection of Henry Clay showed how intractable was Southern Whigs' predicament. A Whig national convention could understandably have declared Virginia's Henry Wise, that advocate of total gags and utter condemnation of John Quincy Adams, too anti-Yankee to head a national ticket. But Henry Clay too southern? Or to ask the question pressing on Clay delegates, how could so northern a party mount a viable southern campaign?[8]

- 2 -

William Henry Harrison's partisans of the 1840 convention had one easy answer: make a southern Clay supporter the vice presidential nominee. The ultimate selection, John Tyler, had a superb resume for the part. The eastern Virginian was a prestigious ex-United States senator and vice presidential candidate on Hugh White's 1836 Oppositionist ticket. Tyler was also a strong but apparently nonfanatical states' righter who had stalled on switching parties for states' rights principles and then had leapt to lead Henry Clay's presidential campaign. No American convention ever selected a more viable reconciliation candidate.

Still, the non-accidental nomination of the man imminently to be known as His Accidency had a tantalizing touch of the haphazard about it. Several names were bandied about the Whig Convention before Tyler swept up delegates. A promising boomlet arose for ex-Senator John Clayton of Delaware. We cannot know whether that popular Border South ultra-nationalist could have appeased enough Middle and Lower South states' rights delegates to become the unity-restoring vice presidential candidate. We do know that the nationalistic Clayton, had he become President, would never have helped extreme states' righters provoke the Texas Annexation Crisis. American history just might have been altered when John Clayton, furious that Henry Clay would not be heading the Whig ticket, refused to allow the convention to consider writing his name under William Henry Harrison's.

John Tyler, ever ideologue and partisan too, was eager to be considered. John Tyler's eagerness, when contrasted with several other Clay partisans' reluctance, led the convention to select the Virginian without apparent reluctance. No Whig delegate was recorded as wondering whether the ex-Jacksonian might become President and then, not at all accidentally, urge states' rights on his nationalistic party.[9]

- 3 -

From this first Whig National Convention emerged the first Whig presidential campaign staged like a Martin Van Buren electoral circus. In this Tippecanoe and Tyler Too effort, bands and barbecues, parades and haranguers whipped up the multitude for the Whigs' heroic general born in a log cabin. Whig seizure of Van Buren's own demagogical concoctions, so the historical myth runs, thus turned the electioneering magician out of the White House.

Nothing that simple occurred. Southern Whigs used the same electioneering hoopla in 1844 and were trounced. The new mastery of media meant little unless the message was right. Southern Whigs' Tippecanoe and Tyler Too campaigners of 1840 emphasized the perfect message to rout the Democracy.

That campaign theme helps explain what most demands explaining: why the National Democracy, the only party capable of enacting national proslavery legislation, often lost black-belt neighborhoods. Whiggery was particularly strong among merchants, lawyers, and journalists in town centers dedicated to serving slaveholders' marketing needs. The cause also swept up many planters and poorer neighbors dedicated to selling staples in state, national, and international markets. States' Rights Whigs had a slightly strained slavery message for such black-belt folk: while Democrats secured only compromised victories for slavery, Whigs would be uncompromising. Nationalistic Whigs had a more natural appeal in a period before slavery dominated everything else: Southern Whigs, as dedicated to saving slavery as any Democrat, would secure better markets for slaveholders' products. All Whigs of whatever persuasion also had the ideal follow-up to the Jackson-as-corrupt-Caesar line of 1836: Whig patriarchs, although just as adept at courting voters, exuded a more high-toned, more disinterested version of civic virtue. That faintly haughty Whiggish tone particularly attracted patricians who found Andrew Jackson's mobocratic crudities slightly embarrassing, maybe even a little dangerous.

No way would gentlemen put electing their patriarchs and selling their crops ahead of keeping their slaves. William Henry Harrison's campaigners, like all Whig partisans in preceding and succeeding presidential campaigns, thus had to show their man was as safe or safer on slavery before other messages could work. But in 1840 Southern Whigs did not yet struggle under the crushing burden which would imminently make the loyalty problem unmanageable. Northern Whigs had not yet turned Southerners down on a critical slavery issue. Gag rule debates were full of portents that Northern Whigs would be less accommodating to Slavepower demands than were Northern Democrats. Gag rules, however, remained a background distraction in 1840 as in 1836. When slavery politics dominated the foreground, the debate still largely involved not impersonal issues but that personality question: Which national ticket contained the true-blue Southerners?

Here the 1840 Tippecanoe and Tyler Too campaign was almost as patriotically southern as the 1836 Hugh Lawson White–John Tyler ticket. While William Henry Harrison lived northwards and had supported national colonization, he was a native Virginian. Harrison, after moving to Indiana at the beginning of the century, had urged Congress to lift the Northwest Ordinance's ban on slavery. Congressman Harrison had voted the South's way during the Missouri Controversy and had arguably lost his seat for it. His running mate, John Tyler, another Virginian, had also fought the good congressional fight in Missouri times. This all-southern team, Southern Whigs declared, would be safer for the South than Martin Van Buren, that compromising New Yorker, who had wished James Tallmadge's post-nati emancipation amendment plastered on Missouri. Moreover, Van Buren's Vice President, Richard Johnson of Kentucky, openly flouted the color line with his mulatto lover.

Having made their candidates seem as sound or sounder on slavery, Harrison's southern campaigners moved on to emphasize the theme which Clay had temporarily muted in 1839 but which he and most Southern Whigs usually considered their party's essence: nonpartisan governmental boosting of commerce and community. Whigs derided Van Buren for presiding over a sour national economy since the Panic of 1837 and for allegedly making banking panic and currency shortage worse. The President had routed national bank recharter, swept federal cash out of all banks, and planted the government's funds in the Treasury Department's vaults.

Some cure for currency contraction, cursed Whigs: Take federal currency out of circulation! Some successor to Jackson, that Caesar who had used patronage to delude voters: a scheming Little Magician who kept the people's funds in his Treasury appointees' vaults. The better way, urged William Henry Harrison's campaigners, was to elect a chaste general who would keep demagogues' hands off the nation's cash. With a nonpartisan anti-Caesar as President, a nonpolitical national bank would be chartered. Then disinterested financiers would pump the nation's stabilized currency back into the national market. Depression-ravaged southern agriculturalists needed better than the credit crunch Van Buren had foisted upon them. Harrison, as sound on slavery, was soundly nonpolitical and sounder on banking.

Harrison's talk of a national bank was not his vice presidential candidate's favorite Whiggish rhetoric. John Tyler, states' righter in harness with nationalists, performed his usual prevarications. He wrote long state papers opposed to national banks—and stuffed them in his drawer. He referred friends and foes to his former speeches on the unconstitutionality of national banks—and quoted with approval Harrison's recent evasive statement that the Constitution granted no power to create banks, "save in the event the power granted to Congress could not be carried into effect without resorting to such an institution."[10] Tyler's waffling recalled Calhoun's prediction: states' righters will be compromised in the National Whig Party.

Southern Democrats, with no need to prevaricate, tore into Southern Whigs' more nationalistic pronouncements. Van Buren campaigners urged that allowing a national bank to use the government's hard cash to spew forth paper currency was no cure for banking panic. Democrats argued that a bank president responsible only to United States Bank shareholders would have unwarranted power over the people's monies. They insisted that national banks violated states' rights and that states' rights protected slavery and that Northern Whigs were enemies of every law protective of slaveholders.

These campaign themes were powerful. The election was close. But William Henry Harrison, that chaste nonpolitician to the manor born who had a program for ending a disastrous depression and unseating Caesar's henchman, had the most powerful southern message—and a powerless southern vice presidential candidate too.

The 1840 victory of Tyler and Tippecanoe, of safety on slavery and reversal of political immorality and economic chaos, represented the first Whig sweep of the entire South. Harrison and Tyler piled up 54% of southern popular votes and 68% of the electoral count. They added new majorities in Deep and Middle Souths to the old majority in the Border South. Harrison won the Border South states he had secured in 1836: Delaware, Maryland, and Kentucky. In the Middle South, where the more states' rights White-Tyler ticket had won only Tennessee in 1836, the more nationalistic Harrison-Tyler duo added North Carolina in 1840. In the Deep South, where White and Tyler had won only Georgia, Harrison and Tyler added Mississippi and Louisiana. Harrison had won a southern mandate—not least to ignore the States' Rights Whiggery of his running mate.[11]

– 4 –

John Tyler immediately became irrelevant inside the new administration. Daniel Webster, Secretary of State, directed a foreign policy not likely to serve slaveholders. Henry Clay, senatorial titan, directed a domestic policy not like'y to please states' righters. Harrison's mandate could secure Clay's program. Since the President, in another chaste putdown of King Andrew the politico, renounced a second term in his inaugural address, the senator might give the next inaugural address. After a dozen years of thrashings, Clay might yet transform the Age of Jackson into the Age of Clay.

Vice President Tyler did not long have to suffer his most impossible situation yet. Before a month of the Harrison administration had passed, Harrison died, after catching a cold on Inauguration Day. The previously irrelevant Vice President became a potentially highly relevant commander-in-chief. Tyler, the states' righter nominated because he had helped rally the South for Clay, might now destroy the Kentuckian's opportunity to rally the nation for nationalism.

Henry Clay vowed to do the destroying. A tiny Whig faction, Clay stormed, must not overwhelm a whopping American majority. A campaign manager elevated by an accident of death, Clay urged, must not negate his own candidate, a statesman enshrined by a lifetime of elections. Dubbing Tyler "His Accidency," the Kentucky senator dismissed the Virginia President as a caretaker. Clay drove a United States Bank through Congress. He defied His Accidency to veto it.

Tyler faced a no-win decision. The President could concede he was His Accidency and become again Clay's cheerleader. The states' righter would then welcome into the statute book a highly nationalistic measure—the very measure Clay, when courting states' righters, had declared irrelevant in 1839. Alternatively, Clay's ex-campaign manager could veto the National Bank and become again the states' righter more loyal to principle than party. Tyler would then exemplify what he had denounced Calhoun for representing—a politician outside both national party institutions.

The harried Tyler repeated his stall of 1832–5. Once again, he was desperate to retain partisan allegiances. Once again, he was anxious to reassert ancient axioms. His confidantes offered colliding advice. Calhounites at the Whig fringes, of whom Virginia's Abel P. Upshur remained the most zealous, insisted that States' Rights Whiggery's first national President must not surrender to nationalism. Meanwhile, pragmatic Southern Whig politicians, of whom North Carolina Senator Willie P. Mangum was the most insistent, urged that the states' rights fragment must not declare war on Whiggery's first national mandate.

This was the time of testing for John Tyler, half-theorist, half-politico, in temperament somewhere between Upshur and Mangum. Upshur thought the politico would triumph. But Mangum became the politician disappointed. Tyler vetoed Clay's banking bill.

Clay secured passage of a less nationalistic banking bill. Again the President wavered. Again Tyler ultimately vetoed. This time, the Whigs' congressional caucus almost unanimously excommunicated the President from the party. John Tyler, politician of the two-party establishment, now reigned outside both parties.[12]

The debacle fulfilled Southern Democrats' longtime prediction. Some chance, Whigs' Deep South opponents had always scoffed, that a States' Rights Whig who threw down the gauntlet would force Whig Nationalists to surrender. Well, Tyler had thrown down the gauntlet, however reluctantly, and States' Rights Whigs had been routed. So how could the Whig Party reorganize American politics along ideological lines safe for the South?

Tyler had only one place to turn for soul mates to help answer that question. Excommunicated by the Whig middle, the President could select only Southerners on the fringes. When all Harrison's cabinet members except Secretary of State Daniel Webster resigned in the fall of 1841, Tyler recruited extreme States' Rights Whigs. Abel P. Upshur, the Calhoun purist pleasantly surprised that Tyler had stood firm, was chosen Secretary of the Navy. After Webster resigned in mid-1843 and an interim Secretary of State died a month later, Tyler promoted Upshur to direct American foreign policy. John Tyler, unable to fathom how Calhounite abstraction could reorganize practical parties, now leaned on the most devoted Calhounite visionary in Virginia.

Abel P. Upshur had special influence because even paralyzed Presidents retain diplomatic authority. John Tyler would have to listen if his Secretary of State could suggest a foreign policy fit to reassert executive authority and build a presidential party. As for Secretary of State Upshur, he cared less about saving Tyler than about proving that a states' rights leader with the right slavery-strengthening issue could remake the Whig Party or remold some third party along Calhoun's ideological lines. But what foreign policy could galvanize Southerners into revolutionizing the two-party system?

– 5 –

The answer came from the other chief executive stymied in mid-1843. President Sam Houston and most Texas compatriots resented being scorned by their homeland. Home, for most Texans, was not on the range but inside the American nation. These chauvinistic Americans had trickled into Texas territories over the previous fifteen years. They had come bearing American-style institutions to seize on American-style opportunity. The Mexican government, having taken empty Texas prairies from Spain as part of the Revolution of 1821, considered southwestern entrepreneurs the most likely migrants. Mexican officials accordingly invited Americans to bring along their despotic alternative to Mexican economic peonage, black slavery, and their democratic alternative to Mexican political despotism, white democracy. Mexican central officials allowed these weird dictatorial democrats to govern themselves at the local level. Salutary Neglect, an earlier version of this policy had been called, when Britain ruled America. Americans indeed found salutary Mexico's neglect.[13]

To Mexican authorities by late 1829, as to English authorities by 1765, neglect seemed no longer salutary. Neglected sovereign power was creating a vacuum inside the area of Mexico least Mexican. A Mexican law of September 15, 1829, accordingly emancipated slaves throughout Mexico. Another law of April 6, 1830, forbade immigration of further Americans.[14]

Americans still kept crossing the border and bringing a few slaves. Texans repeatedly petitioned for redress of grievances. In 1835; Mexican authorities responded in a move reminiscent of England's Intolerable Acts of 1774. Most local autonomy was closed down. Most local democratic proceedings were pinched off. In January 1836, Texans answered with the continent's newest Declaration of Independence.[15]

The Texas War of Independence was shorter than the American. The Mexican commander, Santa Anna, moved troops into Texas and sacked the Alamo. Then on April 21, 1836, Texas General Sam Houston ambushed Santa Anna at San Jacinto, an area within what was to become the city of Houston. The Mexican chieftain, trying to sneak away camouflaged as a private, was captured when his privates cheered him. Fearing death, the hero, done in by his admirers, signed a treaty granting Texas its independence.

Mexican authorities repudiated Santa Anna's treaty. An agreement signed under the gun, went the Mexican argument, could not legitimatize an illegal rebellion. The Mexican government, insisting on sovereign rights in Texas, warned that aiding or annexing the "stolen" republic meant war. Occasional border skirmishes made war not empty talk but likely prospect. The world's newest republic faced a second war of independence as surely as had Americans approaching the War of 1812.

Imminent war hung heavily over the Texas Republic's prospects. Few Texans feared that Mexico might win such a war. Texas was so vast and Mexico's army so limited that a conquering brigade could always be drawn from its source of supplies and then ambushed, as Houston had done to Santa Anna at San Jacinto. But an invading army could again brutalize everything in its path. Texans did not have to be told to Remember the Alamo. Nor did prospective American settlers have to be told that life and property were safer within the United States than in Texas. Southwestern capitalists, still the most likely migrants to Texas, considered slave property particularly unsafe across the bor-

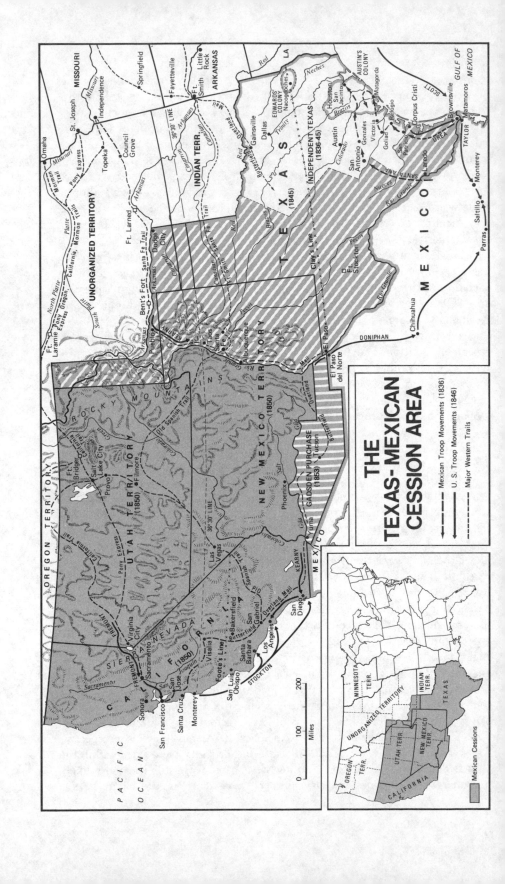

THE
TEXAS-MEXICAN
CESSION AREA

Mexican Troop Movements (1836)
U. S. Troop Movements (1846)
Major Western Trails

Mexican Cessions

der. Worse, if slaves proved badly placed, they could not be legally returned to a United States which had barred slave imports.

The Texas Republic thus had an advanced case of the New World disease: too much land, not enough laborers. The Lone Star Republic possessed insufficient quantities of the Deep South cure: force slaves to develop the tropics. In 1840, something like 15,000 slaves and 60,000 whites dotted Texas's vast plains. A larger population inhabited tiny Delaware. More slaves had lived in slightly enslaved colonial New York. Texas's percentage of slaves, in the area of 20%, matched numbers in the Border South, where slavery was slowly diffusing out. Texas, in its colonial and independent republic phases, was the exception to the rule about North American slavery's geographical locations. This relatively slaveless regime existed not north but south in the South.[16]

Texas, in its colonial and independent republic phases, also lacked the relatively slaveless Border South's alternative solution to the labor problem. No large numbers of white nonslaveholding laborers remotely filled up sprawling Texas. The ratio of land developed to land uninhabited in Texas in the mid-1840s was in the area of one to 40. In comparison, the ratio in the Border South, where free white labor was more plentiful, was around one to two. The ratio in Alabama, Georgia, Mississippi, and Louisiana, where the drain of slaves from older enslaved areas helped solve labor shortages, was around one to three.[17]

Texas's population shortage victimized more than the economy. Slim population made for low tax revenue, a large national debt, and an undermanned army. Such weakness invited another Mexican attack. Potential warfare deterred potential settlers, making war more likely, making vast immigration more unlikely, and thereby spinning Texas leaders dizzy with difficulties.

The American republic, by annexing Texas, could end this vicious circle. The American solution seemed natural to Texans, for Texas seemed to them a little America. American frontiersmen here governed under an American-like constitution after an American-like revolution with the help of American slaveholders. If these two American slaveholding republics were fused, Mexico might be frightened off, and American slaveholders might race west.

So reasoned both Jacksonians who presided over the two republics in 1835–6, when the Texas nation was born. President Sam Houston, an ex-junior officer of Andrew Jackson's in the southwestern army, believed that his old commander would go for the Southwest's Manifest Destiny. President Jackson was indeed a partisan of annexation. But Jackson delayed destiny a bit in 1836, hopeful that he might thus dull Mexico's interest in revenge. On the last day of his administration, Jackson ran out of time. He recognized the independence of Texas. He sipped wine with its agents. He later claimed that his greatest presidential mistake was in failing to celebrate annexation as well as recognition.[18]

Jackson's successor, Martin Van Buren, believed that Old Hickory had already celebrated too much connection with Texas. Van Buren was a far more cautious politician than his former boss. The Little Magician was also far less into western adventurism and not fond of appeasing slaveholders. He considered Texas potentially poisonous to American Union and to his own re-election prospects. John Quincy Adams and fellow Whigs, already making Van Buren squirm over the gag rule, could generate mammoth political capital out of any war with Mexico which was fought to gain a huge slaveholding republic and perhaps still more land for the Slavepower.

Until his first presidential summer, Van Buren would not even allow the Texas representative to present an annexation proposal. The poor fellow, when finally allowed inside the White House, was swiftly turned down. The United States officially informed Texas that peace with Mexico must precede annexation.[19]

After Van Buren's defeat in 1840 and Harrison's death in 1841, Sam Houston dealt with a friendlier administration. John Tyler found Texas intriguing. A thrust for annexation might allow a paralyzed States' Rights Whig President to prove that an uncompromising proslavery issue could make Whiggery or a Tyler-led third party *the* pro-southern movement. In October 1841, the Virginian wrote his Secretary of State, Daniel Webster, of the "possibility of acquiring Texas by treaty.... Could the North be reconciled to it, would anything throw so bright a lustre around us?"[20] Webster let it be known that Yankee Whigs, already enraged with the southern President, would hardly be reconciled to more land for the Slavepower. Tyler responded by lapsing into Tylerism. He stalled.

Sam Houston was not privy to Tyler's exchange of views with Webster. But the Texas president suspected what the American President might enjoy. Houston hit upon a shrewd way of forcing the enjoyable upon an interested but chary politician. He would nourish a southern President's natural worries that England, in hopes of emancipation, might ally with Texas.

In 1842, Houston dispatched two formidable plotters. Ashbel Smith was appointed Minister to England. Isaac Van Zandt was appointed Minister to America. Smith in London soon picked up rumors useful to Van Zandt in Washington. Some Englishmen, Ashbel Smith wrote Isaac Van Zandt on January 25, 1843, had for "some months" speculated about emancipation in Texas. Such souls believed that a republic with few slaves and many problems might trade scarce slaves for large boons. England might entice Texas to emancipate, so Smith claimed to hear in London, by sending many white settlers. Or England might offer cash to bolster Texas's sagging finances. Or Great Britain might intervene in Mexico City, where her diplomats might convince or bribe Mexicans to recognize Texas's independence. Such "equivalents," concluded Smith's report on London rumors, might seem to English abolitionists a fair price for spreading New World abolition beyond the British West Indies. Texans, in turn, might consider emancipating their relatively few slaves a low price for becoming a powerful white man's republic.

Ashbel Smith wrote as if he knew neither what Londonites were speculating nor how much power alleged speculators possessed. His claim to be "certain" that England at least "intended to make an effort" had the ring of a propagandist only "certain" that Washington ears would find London whisperings provocative. Smith seemed to be more straightforward in his assessment of danger. A strong, confident Texas nation, he thought, would shun abolition. But might not a Texas with few slaves, "exhausted, . . . listen in a moment of folly to such overtures?" The diplomat in London urged his Washington counterpart to share that question with Calhoun, Isaac Holmes of South Carolina, Robert Walker of Mississippi, Dixon Lewis of Alabama, and perhaps President Tyler.[21]

The schemer, unable to name a name in London, knew the right annexationist names in America. Isaac Van Zandt flashed Ashbel Smith's letter around as instructed, including at the White House. "I have privately and confidentially presented the situation of our affairs to the President and one of the prominent members of his cabinet" (probably then-Secretary of the Navy Abel Upshur), Van Zandt informed Texas authorities on March 13, 1843. Van Zandt had pointed to England's long-standing antislavery preferences. He had also emphasized the "assertions of those connected with her government" that Texans would be rewarded for renouncing slavery. Texas, as Van Zandt presented the scenario, might trade its few slaves for much cash, many white settlers, and permanent independence, especially if the vulnerable nation was "reduced to the last extremity" against Mexico. The slaveholding President, Van Zandt reported, "listened with much attention."[22]

With attention the cautious Tyler indeed listened. But only one hint of administration action surfaced. In January 1843, *The Madisonian,* the Tyler administration's official newspaper, printed a long pro-annexation letter. A Tyler confidant, ex-Governor Thomas Gilmer of Virginia, wrote the piece. Gilmer called annexation in the North's commercial interest. That notion hung in the air only a moment before John Quincy Adams was booming about the latest plot of the Slavepower.[23] I wish "to annex you," Tyler whined to Van Zandt in April of 1843, *"but you see how I am situated."* Van Zandt passed Tyler's wimper on to President Houston.[24]

An exasperated Houston read the wail as proof that the desperately situated American President lacked nerve to gamble on annexation. Houston understood why annexation would be a gamble. An American presidential election loomed. Henry Clay apparently had a lock on the Whig nomination. Martin Van Buren seemingly had the Democratic Party's nomination secured. Both of these notorious anti-Texas men were determined to keep annexation out of the canvass. With Tyler drifting as usual, America's Manifest Destiny hardly seemed defined by its isolated President's timid gesture towards Texas.

– 6 –

The time had come, Sam Houston believed, to test alternative Manifest Destinies. In mid-1843, the Texas president apparently swerved from seeking apparently unattainable annexation to seeking the apparent next best thing. He would negotiate independence from Mexico. England, Houston hoped, might aid such negotiations. Then independent Texas could attract the migrants to fuel economic take-off.

Houston always considered this alternative vision just that—an alternative. While pursuing English aid for a permanently independent Texas, he always kept in mind possible effects on American willingness to annex. If he could rouse specters of British re-entry into the Western Hemisphere, British-hating Americans might rouse John Tyler from his timidity. A more decisive Tyler effort to annex Texas might alarm Englishmen into protection of an independent Texas. The expanded English push might yield a more committed American pull, then a greater English shove, and so on. Now that circle was not vicious at all for a Texas patriot trying to counter America's failure to act.

The western hero who would play those stronger against each other possessed all necessary duplicity. Sam Houston had studied survival tactics with experts. In his youth, after a mysteriously awful brief marriage on the western frontier, a shattered Houston had mysteriously disappeared from white men's society. He resurfaced three years later, his old self-confidence restored, his new understanding of how to get along set for life. He had saved himself by savouring the forbidden. This white leader had lived with an Indian princess.

He had especially learned how the undermanned survive. Houston's red-skinned hosts endured by ambushing superior white armies, by manipulating powerful white nations, by allowing no white-skin to know what an Indian thought. Sam Houston, the white man who became culturally red and then returned to white civilization, retained the best of Indian tactics.

His appearance signaled the way he operated and the persona he cherished. President Sam Houston marched around Houston City dressed like an Indian chief. Houston's costume was as much his trademark as was the frontier hero Daniel Boone's coon-skin cap. The white chieftain's red man's garb proclaimed that here strides a strategist not predictably of either color, not predictably anything at all. Houston was impossible to pin down, save to the position that a Texas at cutthroats' mercy must trick them all.[25]

The occasion Houston seized in 1843 to play England against America epitomized his duplicitous diplomacy. He accepted a Mexican overture he must have considered unacceptable (but did he?) to talk about a Texas destiny he must have considered disastrous (or did he?). The mystery developed in early 1843, when Santa Anna, once victim of Houston's Indian-like ambush at San Jacinto, now once again Mexico's ruler, indirectly sent Sam Houston a peace proposal. Texans had only to pretend to end their revolution. They should ostensibly re-enter the empire and accept Mexican sovereignty. Then the Mexican government would neglect its duties, allowing Texans to govern themselves.

England endorsed Santa Anna's proposal. English leaders cherished the prospect of Texas stabilized outside the American republic. Santa Anna seemed to be pleading for a face-saving way to achieve that happy result. By offering Santa Anna merely theoretical command, Texans could in practice command their own fate. England offered to ease both sides towards this Manifest Destiny.

Everything about Houston's previous ten years of statecraft shouted No way. Santa Anna's proposal amounted to a return to the Salutary Neglect which had led to Mexican repression, Texas revolution, the Alamo, and San

Jacinto. So how did Sam Houston respond when offered negotiations on the unacceptable?

He agreed to talk. To indicate he was serious about discussions, Houston suspended war with Mexico in June of 1843. In July, he ordered his Washington agents to abort annexation overtures. Shortly thereafter, he sent commissioners down to Mexico City to negotiate with the Santa Anna regime.[26]

Abel P. Upshur became Secretary of State on June 23, 1843, at the time Houston apparently switched strategies. Isaac Van Zandt cheered Upshur as "one of the best for us." Although John Tyler was "fearful to make an important movement," Upshur "has the nerve" to seize "responsibility" and to "act with decision." Upshur had consumed those London rumors Ashbel Smith had fed Van Zandt. Upshur especially remembered Smith's point that Texas, if desperate, might accept otherwise unacceptable conditions.[27]

Now an apparently desperate Houston apparently regarded return to the Mexican empire as negotiable. If Houston would even discuss that massive surrender, he surely would chat about the trifling surrender of a few thousand slaves. English help in ending Mexico's threats and an English promise that English settlers would swarm to the stabilized El Dorado would make comparatively few black freedmen of scant importance, racial or economic. Now if Ashbel Smith could pin down names, dates, places, to confirm London rumors that England would give Texas everything essential if Texas would give up its slaves. Then the zealous Upshur might shove the shaky Tyler towards pursuing the inscrutable Sam Houston, who was making a great show (a sincere show?) of pursuing a Manifest Destiny fit to make American slaveholders shudder.

CHAPTER 21

An Extremist's
Zany Pilgrimage

The first plotter Ashbel Smith inflamed Abel P. Upshur by naming was no famous London schemer. The offender was an obscure lawyer lately driven from Galveston, Texas. The ousted Texan's accomplice was an equally obscure English diplomat lately ostracized from London. Yet these two zanies at their respective culture's fringes momentarily made mainstream antislavery forays seem imminent to the Tyler administration. That saga is worthy of a hallowed place in Texas's outsized legends.

– 1 –

The unlikely protagonist of this tale bore the unlikely name Pearl. Stephen Pearl Andrews was a scarce type in the customarily highly enslaved Deep South— except in not-so-enslaved pre-annexation Texas. Pearl Andrews was a New England "fanatic" agitating on a Lower South frontier.

The first prominent example of the species was Founding Father of Texas. Stephen Austin, native of Connecticut, sporadically opposed slavery during colonial Texas's early years.[1] One question, however, made Austin's effort ever more sporadic. If Texas barred slaveholders, who would come? Migrants from the neighboring Southwest, not voyagers from faraway New England, were most likely to move to the Lone Star Republic. Southwesterners in Louisiana, Mississippi, and Alabama characteristically considered slaves indispensable to develop an empty tropical kingdom. If Texas turned down these pioneers' solution to the labor shortage, the area might have no laborers. Stephen Austin bowed to that argument.

Pearl Andrews, a migrant from Massachusetts via Louisiana a generation later, came with an answer to the question which had stumped Austin. Austin was most powerful in the 1820s, when Southwesterners, the only Westerners likely to move in, were not given to antislavery. Andrews thrived in the 1840s, when millions of western free laborers were choosing between various El Dorados. In these new circumstances, believed Andrews, Texas, by emancipating slaves, could entice enterprising whites.[2]

This speculation about harnessing enterprise to emancipation came naturally to a seeker torn between Christ and capitalism. Andrews's father, a Massachusetts Baptist revivalist, had sought but failed to treat his son to ecstatic conversion. A soul too resistant of the Lord was allied with a body too sickly for extended education. Failing eyesight forced Pearl Andrews to quit Amherst College before graduation.

An older brother out in the Southwest, Thomas Andrews, rescued the troubled teenager. Thomas summoned Pearl to Louisiana. There the elder brother assigned the eastern tenderfoot to help a sister and sister-in-law teach amenities in the Andrews family's female academy.

Before Pearl Andrews was twenty, an infuriated mob forced less tender pursuits. The crowd, excited for obscure reasons, smashed Thomas Andrews's arm. The disfigured brother needed immediate help with his law practice. Young Pearl, still on the shy and effete side, mastered the law, became his brother's partner, and practiced before the Louisiana Supreme Court when still not 21. By the age of 25, now moved to New Orleans, Pearl Andrews was a star of the legal establishment.

The newly-rich lawyer could not forget his father's warnings about Mammon. The Panic of 1837 reinforced the preacher's words. Both Andrews brothers lost fortunes. Thomas Andrews reacted by moving north towards freedom, freeing his wife's slaves and enjoying an emancipator's bliss.

Pearl Andrews instead moved west to Texas, dreaming of the double bliss of an emancipator who would turn materialistic gamble into holy triumph. Andrews's dream of a capitalistic/moral jackpot focused on that greatest western fling, land speculation. In sprawling Texas, even more than in most frontier spots, gamblers could buy uninhabited acres for little on the speculation that inhabitants would come and pay much for the land.[3]

Andrews believed only slavery repelled settlers from Texas. Few slaveholders would risk property in so chancy an area, and not many nonslaveholders would migrate to an even slightly enslaved region. But if slavery was abolished, immigrants would swarm to this lush prairie. Then rising land values would richly compensate slaveholders for lost slaves.

Andrews's economic argument against slavery was pervasively American and more relevant to a laborless frontier than were European theories such as Marxism. Marxists, assuming the typical European condition of too many laborers on too little land, urged that free labor would always outproduce slave labor. That "always," while relevant to entrepreneurs in a Baltimore crowded with many species of laborers, was irrelevant to a Texas without sufficient laborers. The first critical frontier decision involved deciding to come, whether the choice was the laborer's or his owner's.

Andrews honed in on whites' choices. Back in Thomas Jefferson's day, Illinois land speculators, also worried about those choices, had urged repeal of the Northwest Ordinance's bar on slavery. Then slaveholders, supposedly the most likely emigrants, would come and make land speculators rich. Edward Coles and his crowd had countered that free laborers would move faster than slave-holders to an area so far north. In the Maryland Slavery Debate of 1832, Henry Brawner had made Coles's position relevant a step further south. Brawner had argued that if South Maryland sent its too few slaves to Africa, whites would pour in to end the Chesapeake Bay region's population stagnation.

Pearl Andrews, like Edward Coles and Henry Brawner, urged that his under-enslaved area would never fill its empty spaces with Mississippi-like num-bers of slaves. Texans did not have Illinoians' and Marylanders' bar to a flood of incoming slaveholding migrants: a relatively nontropical climate. But pre-annexation Texas possessed an equivalent deterrent to slaveholder migration: a relatively precarious political and military environment. Andrews, like Brawner, believed that only nonslaveholders would extensively people an area relatively unattractive to slaveholders. Slavery, however, had to be eased out before nonslaveholders would rush in.

Elsewhere in the South, arguments such as Andrews's sometimes rallied nonslaveholders against slaveholders. Andrews supposed the two classes pos-sessed the same class interest. Scratch a Texan, believed Andrews, and you will touch a land speculator. Anyone owning raw land, meaning all rich men and many poor men too, prayed that settlers would come and develop the turf.

Further north, in Illinois, Kentucky, and Missouri, frontier land speculators, when seeking to entice whites by deporting blacks, sometimes recklessly gam-bled their necks and enterprises to agitate. Recklessness was neither Pearl Andrews's style nor his conception of how to free an area located much further south. "No country," regretted the new Texan, was "more destitute of moral principle." The "undercurrent of feeling. . . against slavery" was wholly "based upon interest." A successful reformer had to renounce morality, eschew agita-tion, and hint at "the weakness of Texas, particularly as respects money" and "population." Then Texas wheeler-dealers might consider getting rid of a few slaves to bring in much capital and many whites.[4]

During the late 1830s and early 1840s, Andrews became a wealthy Houston lawyer, bought uninhabited land for little, and carefully suggested to slavehold-ing land speculators that slavery cut land values by repelling settlers. This secre-tive mode of persuasion eventually yielded, over four years, a dozen or so wealthy supporters. Then one day, suspicious queries blazed through Houston's streets. Is an abolitionist in our midst? The question provoked demands that Andrews confess any softness on slavery.

Andrews addressed a packed meeting at the Houston Court House on March 13, 1843. In going public, as in private hintings, Andrews remained mas-ter of temperate persuasion. He never breathed the code words, "slavery," "emancipation." He instead emphasized the bonanza for land speculators if almost-empty Texas was packed with people.

Andrews's listeners, at first "moody and silent," greeted his peroration with "an intense and continuous peal of applause." He had sold his drift so cau-tiously that the crowd seemed surprised when the next speaker, a Kentucky slaveholder, told them that they had purchased antislavery. But Andrews's opponent could not blot out the vision of whites pouring into a Texas which few blacks were entering. When this meeting broke up, the establishment in the capital city of a Deep South slaveholding republic was speculating that maybe, just maybe, slavery might be causing the population shortage.[5]

Andrews still feared the consequences of going even carefully public. His cautious recruits, caucusing secretly in his rooms, decided that indirection was no longer prudent. You must publicize your plan, urged Andrews's friends, before others can distort it. You must ride the next steamboat down the Brazos River and up the Gulf to Galveston. There you must quietly indoctrinate before mobs violently intimidate you.

While bowing before the apparent necessity for imprudent pushing, Andrews still chose the prudent Thomas League as his traveling companion. League possessed one sterling credential. He was no "crazy philanthropist." A wealthy slaveholder and lawyer, Thomas League was known to be a "money-getting adventurer," incapable "of any overstrained moral purpose." With this coarse materialist in tow, Andrews would come to Galveston as representative of one money-grubbing establishment come to sell a money-making proposition to another.

The steamboat trip was an incredible Deep South journey. Day and night, excited debate over Andrews's scheme took place on the crowded little vessel. Despite cries of "treason," "disloyalty," "incendiarism," the prevailing notion on board remained that Andrews was no fanatic courting a lynching. Rather, Pearl was a Texas-sized businessman with a Texas-sized idea who just might bring a stampede of settlers to settler-starved Texas.

The riverboat classroom arrived in Galveston Bay, opposite General Moseley Baker's plantation. The ultra-respectable planter pounded at the theme that planters had not brought the population which a slaveless destiny might beckon to Texas. After Baker finished, Andrews counted only some dozen of 300 travelers still opposed. So "malignant and determined" a minority, Andrews still trembled, might accomplish mischief.[6]

Early the next morning, the ship crossed the Bay and arrived in Galveston, there to initiate what Andrews correctly called an "unparalleled" Deep South scene. As Andrews described it, "a whole boat load of excited abolition fanatics," and "a handful of bitter and hostile opponents," were let loose from their detention on board." The "two diverging parties" burst upon a quiet southern town, which had hitherto rested "serene in the belief that no avowed and active abolitionist could live in the republic."

It was all, Andrews exclaimed, like a "burning brand thrust into a cold fluid." Citizens gathered "upon every corner, discussing with agitated and excited voices" this "strange phenomenon" of Deep South "abolitionism." While slaveholders denounced and threatened, the alleged fanatic quietly "engaged in visiting and in actually converting, with the same rapidity" as in Houston City. A day went by. Two. On the third, Andrews planned a meeting of 20 or 30 wealthy converts.

The minority of despots living within a majoritarian republic instead deployed their classic answer to democratic pressure. Before Andrews could agitate in front of his audience of respectables, some 20 armed men led by, who else, a South Carolinian, visited Andrews. They delivered him onto a ship bound back to Houston.[7]

Andrews returned to a town having second thoughts about its conversion. Nightly, groups gathered on Houston's street corners, debating whether to emulate Galveston by pitching the "incendiary" out. Andrews's first week back home was one of "really terrible suspense."

Suspense swiftly gave way to terror. In "the dead of the night," a "wild yell" awakened Andrews and his wife. "At the same instant," a "glare of bright flame penetrated the darkness through the window, and revealed . . . an excited crowd of persons outside." Believing that "a desperate mob . . . had commenced by firing the house," the Andrewses hurriedly dressed. The mob demanded they unbolt the door. They tremulously obeyed. They were swarmed upon by "their neighbors and friends, who had assembled to awaken us, and to assist in extinguishing the flames." Probably a careless servant had started a fire![8]

This nonmobbing mob and the tragic comedy they staged would hardly have stopped a reckless fanatic. Had a pack of friends "mobbed" William Lloyd Garrison, he would have seen the irony as a sign to keep agitating. But Garrison's signs were in the heavens. His zeal for abstract justice was steel against practical consequence.

Pearl Andrews was a different soul. His career as a southwestern businessman had begun when lynchers mutilated his brother's arm. He had no intention of donating two more Andrews arms to mob fury. He decided to pursue Christian entrepreneurship elsewhere, where not "so many obstacles" would be "thrown in the way of my future career." His compatriot in the failed Galveston venture, the slaveholding materialist Thomas League, was still fuller of prudence. League told Galveston vigilantes that his antislavery consisted of plans "to get $1000 apiece for his own slaves from the British Government." He would "then pass them across the Sabine to the States," to "sell them again." With League's un-Christian grossness, Andrews's Christian capitalism came to a denouement the holy capitalist did not find appropriate.[9]

– 2 –

Pearl Andrews's ephemeral Texas campaign gains more lasting importance in the longer perspective of southern dissent. Andrews's attempt to end slavery bore no relationship to the most famous southern slavery debate, the Virginia affair of 1832, with its origins in nonslaveholders' political resentments and slaveholders' domestic unease. Rather, Andrews, like Edward Coles in Illinois and Henry Brawner in Maryland before him, and like Cassius Clay in Kentucky and Frank Blair in Missouri afterwards, urged that in largely white areas, a few slaves repelled many potential white migrants and thus kept underpopulated land underdeveloped. Pearl Andrews had never heard of those population-boost-ers in other states, nor had they heard of him. All simply responded to the same hunger for attracting migration to their area, *the* economic drive North and South in development-obsessed nineteenth-century America.

But a persuasive answer to a pervasive problem, usually the first necessity for reformers, was in the Slave South the second necessity. Reformers first had to win the right to be heard. Pearl Andrews fleetingly intrigued an audience unthinkable elsewhere in the Deep South. Even the planter class briefly listened, briefly wondered. But mere wonderers would not force a handful of proslavery vigilantes to drop firearms. Continuation of Andrews's attempt came down to who was most committed, the few agitators or the few lynchers.

Andrews blinked first, as had James Birney in Kentucky. Verbal abuse about loyalty and chances of a more physical abuse, while creating no more sealed-shut an atmosphere than in a gagged Congress, demanded uncommon courage and zeal from agitators. Few American politicians were that uncommon. Most, like Birney and Andrews, were entrepreneurs seeking the main chance. They were more likely to depart or move undercover than to stand and defy. Slave-holder republicanism was not very republican when it came to debating slavery.

A quasi-despotic version of democracy, however, could stir up democratic resentment without possessing sanctions to crush what it had provoked. That had happened in the Virginia Convention of 1829 and in the gag rule congresses. The relatively few extraordinary souls who defied lynchers could also point to lynch mobs as yet more reason to rid republics of slavery. That would happen with Cassius Clay in Kentucky.

Still, Cassius Clay would find that even when stressing dangers to white republicanism, even in areas where relatively little slavery existed, the bravest leaders could not rally constant heresy. Too many followers fell silent for fear mobs would maraud or cries of disloyalty would taint. In whiter portions of the Slave South of the nineteenth century, as in the segregated and disenfranchised South of the twentieth century, a "better" South existed, but tremulously under cover.

The best hope of bringing a timid internal challenge out into the open, in both centuries, remained that the external world might intervene, to offer southern dissenters boons and protections. Then campaigns for a reformed South might seem more prudent, more profitable, more patriotic. The creation of unintimidated southern discussion would be Abraham Lincoln's fondest hope and disunionists' gravest fear when the Republican President offered national patronage jobs to latter-day versions of Pearl Andrews.

As Lincoln's strategy for building a Republican Party in the South would assume, outsiders' intervention could be particularly helpful when sustaining insiders' ideology and interests. Pearl Andrews, although easily shoved aside in a purely internal campaign, remained of concern because, under the right conditions, outsiders might fan the undercurrent of uncertainty he had revealed. Suppose those London rumors Ashbel Smith had lately pounced on proved prophetic. Suppose mighty England cajoled feeble Mexico into a tripartite international treaty, protecting vulnerable Texas. Suppose Texas could exchange its relatively few slaves for recognition from Mexico, cash for slaveholders, boat-loads of English settlers come to create a land speculators' dream. Suppose fur-ther that a United States nation long shunning Texas never offered annexation. Then the moneygrubbers who had briefly quizzed Pearl Andrews—and even the few who had swiftly silenced the land speculator—might wish to hear their Manifest Destiny reconsidered. But how could outside pressures and incentives open up a Texas which a departing Pearl Andrews was calling too closed for democratic decisions?

– 3 –

An answer arrived on Andrews's doorstep before the disillusioned reformer could quit Houston City. Captain Charles Elliot of the English Royal Navy, Her Majesty's Chargé d'Affaires to Texas, traveled from Galveston to Houston City to see Pearl Andrews. The Englishman came with a plan to procure English aid for a Texas antislavery movement.[10]

Elliot was a minor bureaucrat who made a historic career of sticking his mitts in places a flunky's hands in no way belonged. Elliot had moved from being an unimportant officer in the Royal Navy to becoming an insignificant bureaucrat in imperial offices. Exciting events were happening in the British Empire during Elliot's years of service. The Captain resided where the historic was transpiring. He had been Protector of Slaves in British Guiana when the British Parliament struck down bondage in the empire. He had then been Senior Superintendent of Trade at Canton when the Opium War commenced. Now he was Chargé d'Affaires to Texas, at the time Sam Houston was testing various Manifest Destinies.

Always Elliot's orders were to observe in the provinces, report back to Lon-don, and follow headquarters' orders. Always he was tempted to direct historic events. His tendency to seize initiatives from superiors ran him into the worst trouble in China. There his unauthorized actions helped precipitate the Opium War. He then secured an unauthorized treaty which London swiftly repudi-ated. After the debacle, Elliot's superiors sought a pasture where the bull in the china shop might be safer from self-inflicted harm. The Texas empty ranges seemed just the spot.[11]

Elliot had not been out at pasture for three months before he was urging London to replicate emancipation in British Guiana. I know you do not want to intervene in another republic's internal affairs, Elliot correctly wrote H. U. Addington, Her Majesty's Undersecretary of State for Foreign Affairs, on November 15, 1842. Elliot promised to "abstain from offering" to any Texan his opinion that slavery rotted "the heart of society." He knew that Texans would respond by talking "violently of holding on to their property." But he had learned in British Guiana that a "needy people" will respond "reasonably for a monied consideration."

Elliot proposed English monies to compensate slaveholders for responding reasonably. Texans should be bribed to liberate free blacks as well as slaves.

Abolish "disability upon free people of Colour" and you "would at once bring into this Republic tens of thousands of most abused and intelligent people from the United States." Where Pearl Andrews would solve the labor shortage with free whites, the English chargé would go for free blacks.[12]

Having solved Texans' labor problem and North Americans' race problem, England's statesman had to wait for metropolitan authorities to hail his provincial statecraft. He waited. No answer from headquarters. He urged his plan again. Still no answer. The bureaucrat on the spot, who *knew* he had figured out how to spread English abolitionism in North America, found the wave of history bottled up in the bureaucracy.

Then, just as Elliot was despairing of anyone ever pushing Texas emancipation, Pearl Andrews sailed into Galveston and was shoved back to Houston. Andrews, Elliot learned, would soon depart the republic. The chargé had promised Undersecretary Addington never to press abolition opinions on Texans. But Addington, who would not even answer Elliot's letters, did not understand England's opportunity. A conscience-bound Englishman must go see this Andrews.

He was "exceedingly unwilling," Elliot told Andrews upon being admitted to Pearl's house, that Andrews's "still feasible" project "should be abandoned." In Galveston, Elliot saw symptoms of a vital reaction in Andrews's "favor." Had Andrews guaranteed slaveholders compensation for slaves, he "would have succeeded" and "would still succeed."

Elliot informed Andrews how compensation could be guaranteed. English abolitionists would buy Texas lands, or loan money with Texas lands as collateral, if cash would free slaves. Andrews thus should visit England and propose "pecuniary aids" to placate slaveholders and diplomatic aid against Mexico to please Sam Houston. Elliot would support Andrews with "the strongest letters of introduction and recommendation," even though that intervention would surpass "appropriate duties of the British Chargé d'Affaires." Andrews must promote Elliot's enterprise and hide Elliot's involvement with "necessary . . . prudence."[13]

Before the discussion of prudent strategy was over, the two freedom-fighters struck a deal for their mutual emancipation. Andrews, enslaved by mobs in Texas, would control Texas's destiny from England. Elliot, enslaved by bureaucrats in London, would command England's conscience from Texas. If Andrews received the response Elliot expected, the marriage of the crass and the holy which Andrews had long sought and which Elliot had seen prevail in British Guiana would be consummated. English investors, morally attracted to emancipation and financially attracted to cheap Texas acres, would trade cash for land. English cash would bribe Texas slaveholders to permit emancipation. Abolition would attract English free laborers. Immigrants would seek virgin land. Escalating land values would enrich English philanthropists. When the sacred circle was completed, lofty preachers and mighty capitalists would join hands with an ignored bureaucrat and a skittish agitator in celebrating an earthly victory which Pearl Andrews's father would have called heavenly.

– 4 –

Once the English chargé in Texas had secured his own messenger to England, he sought to prepare his superiors to welcome his errand boy. Stephen Pearl Andrews's recent expulsion from Galveston, Charles Elliot wrote Undersecretary Addington on March 26, 1843, showed that emancipation sentiment was not "general." But "sound opinions" were "gaining strength." As he had seen in British Guiana, "first comes violence, and then comes reflection and sympathy." This fellow Andrews could yet become important.[14]

On June 8, 1843, less than a week after Andrews sailed for England, Elliot sent Undersecretary Addington's superior the blockbuster information that the highest Texas official shared Andrews's viewpoint. The last time I conversed with Sam Houston, Elliot wrote Lord Aberdeen, Her Majesty's Secretary of State for Foreign Affairs, the Texas president called slavery's existence a "subject of deep regret." I answered, Charles Elliot reassured Foreign Secretary Aberdeen, by telling President Houston that Her Majesty's government never even "mentioned" slavery in their "despatches." But since Sam Houston opened the subject, I felt free to express my country's "deep regret" about slavery. President Houston answered, Chargé Elliot reported, that "unless the propitious Moment of Settlement of the difficulties with Mexico should be taken for devising some mode of getting rid of the Mischief, he foresaw that Texas would sooner or later become the 'impound' of the Black and Coloured population of the United States," to the republic's "incalculable injury."[15]

Sam Houston here both expressed sincere morality and deployed his usual amoral tactics. Houston never had much use for slavery. The Texas president rather hoped the curse might slowly disappear. But Houston, like Southerners in the United States who hoped for proper conditions to terminate slavery, cared more about white men's republicanism. So while Houston leveled with Elliot about far-off hopes for freeing blacks, he hid from the English diplomat his immediate strategy for saving his republic.

The Texas president had carefully built a relationship with Elliot. Houston knew what the chargé most wanted to hear and was most likely to pass on to London. English officials, once informed that Sam Houston might consider emancipation, might help Texas gain permanent recognition from Mexico. English intervention might inflame proslavery Americans, which might reinvigorate antislavery Englishmen, which might infuriate proslavery Americans. Out of all this escalating trans-Atlantic interest in Texas, some solution to Texas's problems might come.

Houston probably did not expect the solution to be an emancipated republic. But a slaveless nation full of capital, immigrants, and power would not have displeased this a-southern Westerner, especially if the slaveholding United States was so unconcerned as to let it happen. On the other hand, if Charles Elliot unwittingly helped produce American annexation and perpetual slavery, Sam Houston would not be in tears. He meant to preserve his white men's republic however he could.

Elliot, unaware he might be furthering the wrong Manifest Destiny, sent Houston's vision of antislavery racing after Pearl Andrews across the Atlantic. Elliot thus completed his unauthorized attempt to breathe new life into an expiring Texas antislavery movement. He had clandestinely dispatched Andrews, now a reborn reformer, to England. He had secretly manipulated English authorities towards thinking that their apparently far-out visitor might unknowingly represent the position of the highest Texas authority. Now if only puppetmasters on the metropolitan stage would be true to the antislavery tradition they shared with their provincial non-puppet. Then the former Protector of Slaves in British Guiana would have set the stage for the spread of English abolitionism to the borders of the United States.

– 5 –

If Texas Minister Ashbel Smith in London had discovered the full dimensions of Charles Elliot's anti-Slavepower Conspiracy, what a juicy tidbit could have been sent to Texas Minister Isaac Van Zandt in Washington. But Elliot covered his tracks well enough and Pearl Andrews kept his pledge of secrecy so completely that the extent of the Elliot-Andrews connection was not then—and has usually not been since—fully appreciated.[16] Still, just before Andrews arrived in London, unconnected bits of information about Elliot and Andrews reached a delighted Ashbel Smith. The chief informer was a Texan named Andrew Yates.

Yates had been Pearl Andrews's host in Galveston. Like Andrews, Yates hailed from New England and prospered as a Texas town lawyer. This Galveston insider considered himself "*No abolitionist*. . . . But I do believe that free labor is ten fold more productive of prosperity." I do hope "to see the introduction to this country of free white industrious families of the laboring Classes, well satisfied that they will eventually supercede the Slave."[17]

News about that hope, Andrew Yates believed, would encourage a Texas friend who was in England, trying to recruit English white migrants. On March 19, 1843, one of the three days Andrews was using Yates's house as Galveston headquarters, Yates wrote the London recruiter that "a few individuals" have been "very cautiously" preparing Texans for emancipation. The emancipationist leader, Stephen Pearl Andrews, had lately gone public in Houston, had triumphed, and had found river-bound planters "willing for the measure" on his way down the Brazos and across the Gulf to Galveston. The emancipator would now "proceed with rapid movement through the whole country."

Andrew Yates also reported that from "several conversations with the British minister here" he had "learned that" abolition "would secure for us the warmest support of the British Government in our present struggle" with Mexico. The minister had also hinted that England might provide "means of paying for our slaves." If "you can get access to the Despatches of Captain Elliot by this packet," Yates concluded, "you will find my statements fully confirmed."

Yates's correspondent passed the letter on to Ashbel Smith. Never was a man happier to see someone else's mail. The Yates letter was the first slightly smoking pistol, perhaps confirming those rumors of the previous December. Maybe England *would* offer Texas "equivalents" for emancipation. Ashbel Smith sent Andrew Yates's letter back across the Atlantic, to Isaac Van Zandt in Washington. Someone—perhaps Smith, perhaps Van Zandt, perhaps their American accomplice, Duff Green, whom we will soon meet—leaked the letter to the *Boston Post*. The *Post* published the letter on June 21, 1843. Two days later, Abel P. Upshur assumed direction of American foreign policy.[18]

On June 19, 1843, Ashbel Smith wrote Upshur's favorite Southerner, John C. Calhoun. The Texas minister in London could not say "what active measures the British Government have taken." But an *"unquestionable authority"* had told him of Charles Elliot's "official communication," looking towards "distinct propositions." England's "ultimate purpose," so Ashbel Smith claimed "sincerely" to believe, was to make Texas a "refuge for runaway slaves from the United States, and eventually a negro nation, a sort of Hayti" under British protection. Southerners must act, Smith warned, before the newest St. Domingue loomed on their southwestern flank.[19]

Posterity cannot tell whether this last sensational charge was Ashbel Smith's sincere opinion. The Texan just may have figured out the largest reality behind swirling London rumors. Charles Elliot, the only British official unconditionally seeking to abolish slavery in Texas, *did* want Texas to become a refuge for free blacks. But Ashbel Smith did not have posterity's access to Elliot's secret despatches. Nor does Smith's expression have the tone of the man who knows he is right. The letter to Calhoun reads like the speculations of an alarmist groping in the dark, guessing about what might be there and trying to upset others with the most scary guess available.

The trouble with this latest scare letter, as Ashbel Smith implicitly conceded, was that new facts about old rumors all involved bit players on the historical stage. Pearl Andrews was hardly Texas. Lynchers had stopped his Galveston campaign. Nor was Charles Elliot necessarily England. Nothing linked the underling's Texas maneuvers with his superiors or with Pearl Andrews. Ashbel Smith needed more worrisome names and a more specific plot to help Isaac Van Zandt inflame Abel P. Upshur, that highly inflammable new American Secretary of State.

- 6 -

Pearl Andrews's visit to London, which was destined to supply Ashbel Smith with wonderfully explosive news, began with a quiet voyage to New York City. Upon arrival in the capital of American enterprise, Andrews benefited from another of those dashes of luck which punctuate the annexation story. A delighted Pearl Andrews discovered in New York that he had unknowingly scheduled his visit to London for a time when a World Antislavery Convention would celebrate the tenth anniversary of abolitionists' first Anglo-American victory: emancipation in the British West Indies in 1833. Andrews's New York hosts, leading American abolitionists, might accompany him across the seas, to rally an historic convention for a fresh trans-Atlantic foray.

The northern antislavery leader most enthralled with Andrews's strategy also sought union of the crass and holy. Lewis Tappan, dry goods entrepreneur, used part of his profits to finance the American Antislavery Society. Tappan's brother meanwhile had helped finance James Birney's Kentucky agitations. Most Yankees considered such financing impractical. Pragmatic Northerners saw no way to compensate slaveholders for a billion dollars' worth of slaves, or to cope with post-emancipation race problems involving millions of free blacks, or to persuade slaveholders to surrender peacefully.

Well, thought Tappan, the $15,000,000 perhaps necessary to persuade Texans to surrender some 15,000 slaves was hardly unmanageable. English entrepreneurs might exchange those liberating dollars for a stake in a promising land speculation. Texas slaveholders might turn over their relatively few slaves for cash, with further hopes that whites would pour in to pay more cash for land. As for 15,000 free blacks, they would create an inconsequential race problem amidst hundreds of thousands of white immigrants. This practical idea to harness philanthropy and capitalism might emancipate a vast Deep South area no less.

Lewis Tappan dropped everything, all business appointments and his every philanthropic meeting, to accompany Andrews. The two travelers journeyed first to Braintree, Massachusetts, home of John Quincy Adams. Adams told the pilgrims that "I believe the freedom of this country and of all mankind depends upon the direct, formal, open, and avowed interference of Great Britain to accomplish the abolition of slavery in Texas."[20]

In England, delegates to the World Antislavery Convention shared Adams's hopes upon hearing Andrews's plan. The convention appointed a committee, including Andrews and Tappan, to interview Foreign Secretary Aberdeen. That crusty old cautious Scottish peer received the Tappan-Andrews Committee on June 19, 1843.[21]

Andrews suggested to Lord Aberdeen that English capitalists might raise a fund, say one million pounds sterling, to pay Texas capitalists for slaves. English saints, aside from properly celebrating the tenth anniversary of British West Indies emancipation, could recover philanthropic donations by purchasing heavily discounted Texas land. Emancipation would bring white settlers, who would drive up the price of emancipators' land. Alternatively, English capitalists might grant a large emancipationist loan to the Texas government, with Texas lands serving as collateral. The English government, Andrews suggested to Aberdeen, might help float the loan by guaranteeing the interest.

Lord Aberdeen listened with ultra-cautious interest.[22] The director of British foreign policy, in common with his countrymen, relished the vision of England safely encouraging world-wide emancipation. Aberdeen also savored the concept of a strong Texas republic allied with England and unannexed to the United States. But Aberdeen cared far more about preventing any new exhaustion of English resources in that bottomless pit, a resisting New World. Overextension of England's military power, inspired by vain overconfidence that the Old World could dictate to the New, had horribly weakened England during the wars of the American Revolution and of 1812. Aberdeen and his nation might offer aid to Texas emancipation IF—*if* the aid was nonmilitary, within England's financial resources, desired by Texas, and not opposed to the point of war by Mexico or the United States.

Lord Aberdeen's potential impact on slavery politics was thus intriguingly like that of the first American who had insisted on proper conditions for terminating the institution, Thomas Jefferson. Like Jefferson, Aberdeen would use a great nation's wealth to destroy slavery, so long as wrecking slavery did not ruin the nation. That insistence on national safety gave slaveholders bent on deterrence total power to deny the reformer his conditions. But proslavery warriors did have to be wide awake enough to deter. And the very reactionary intransigence necessary to render tentative reform impractical had the most practical effects on the future of the Union. Nothing would illuminate this process better than southern hard hearts' insistence on annexation, lest ultra-cautious Aberdeens become a little bolder.

Aberdeen's caution had been omnipresent in the British Foreign Office's careful instructions to that incautious chargé, Charles Elliot, not to intervene in Texas's internal affairs. The same safety-first impulses dictated that Aberdeen answer Pearl Andrews with questions in the interview of June 19, 1843. Could a British agent select the Texas land to be put up as collateral? Might an English pledge to pay interest temporarily, should interest payments be momentarily delayed, suffice? Once questions about "legitimate means" were satisfactorily answered, Aberdeen said, Her Majesty's government might help "attain so great and desirable an object."

Lord Aberdeen concluded by asking Lewis Tappan to bring in southwestern newspapers. The British foreign secretary wanted to investigate whether Texas wished English help and how the United States would react to the aid. Aberdeen especially had to find out if this odd duck Andrews represented Texas or only himself. Aberdeen had no clue, for Charles Elliot's report on Sam Houston's views was still crossing the ocean.

Still, Aberdeen's words in the Andrews interview signaled that England might help, assuming Texas signaled that aid was wanted and assuming the United States signaled that help would be permitted. The chief spokesman of English diplomacy called Texas emancipation "desirable," worth "all legitimate means" to achieve a "great consummation." Those words gave Andrews reason to be slightly hopeful about future success.

Andrews instead came away with soaring conviction that success had already been accomplished. The leap is understandable. The seeker needed success not only for the sake of the slave, not only to make his antislavery activities worthwhile, but also to fulfill that drive to achieve purity which his evangelist father had made the burden of earthly life.

To this need to believe was added a Southwesterner's conception of how agents negotiated. Pearl Andrews, provincial lawyer, was used to arranging settlements out of court on the uncomplicated Texas frontier, where New World tycoons signaled how they would plead in order to arrange plea bargains. The Texan had no experience in subtle Old World diplomacy, where slight signals were only signs that more slight signals should be exchanged.

Out of a frontier operator's misreading of a metropolitan sophisticate and out of a seeker's misplaced hopes of heaven achieved came Andrews's conviction that Aberdeen's government would stand behind antislavery loans. Why else would his Lordship ask those specific questions and climax with that encouraging peroration? A banker, after all, does not haggle over collateral unless he intends to grant the loan. Lord Aberdeen made observations which warranted the claim, Andrews was soon gushing all over London, that the English government would guarantee the interest on an antislavery loan!

– 7 –

Andrews's news appalled Ashbel Smith, Texas's man in London. Smith informed his government of Andrews's apparent incredible breakthrough.[23] Ashbel Smith also informed the American most capable of inflaming John C. Calhoun and Abel P. Upshur. It was another piece of luck, once again sending Texas annexation careening forward, that Duff Green happened to be in London to hear Ashbel Smith tell about Pearl Andrews.

No antebellum American asked "Who's he?" about Duff Green.[24] In an age when the editor of a national political newspaper was almost as notorious as the candidate, Duff Green's support of John C. Calhoun was a legend. Green's *United States Telegraph* spread Calhoun's views during the mid-1830s, when Mr. Nullifier declared war on Mr. Jackson. Marriage alliance strengthened ties between the two ex-Jacksonians. Green's son married Calhoun's daughter.

Duff Green remained John C. Calhoun with a difference. Where Calhoun's inflexible view of the world was sustained in the South Carolina he never thought of leaving, Duff Green fought for Calhounite principle with flexible tactics in many Souths. Duff Green, American pitchman, relished running factories, selling newspapers, speculating in western lands. The native-born Marylander invested some cash in Missouri acres, more in Texas bonds, more in Washington newspapers.

Politics remained his main enterprise. Calhoun's viewpoint was his main commodity. He would sell where action was thickest; and in American politics, spoils went to two-party politicians. Once Calhoun lost the good fight within the Jackson Party, Green begged his man to make the Oppositionist/Whig Party a states' rights vehicle. After Calhoun went the other way in 1840, temporarily back to Van Buren and the Democracy, Green offered his services to the Tyler administration while remaining Calhoun's confidant.

President Tyler made use of Duff Green as an agent, sometimes a paid agent, to negotiate free trade with England. From London, Green reported back his opinion that England's abolition of slavery in the British West Indies in 1833 had poisoned free trade. England's colonial capitalists, Green alleged, found freed blacks would not labor effectively. American slaveholders, still able to coerce a naturally slothful race to work, outproduced ex-masters without slaves. Englishmen supposedly believed they needed trade barriers against slave-grown American staples to bail out colonies supposedly victimized by lazy free blacks.

English statesmen reinforced Green's theory. The talk in and out of Sir Robert Peel's governmental circles in the early 1840s was that tropical colonies were less productive than formerly. English leaders sometimes speculated, in and out of Parliament, that emancipation might be the cause and trade barriers the cure. Where Englishmen toyed with such notions, Green translated the intellectual game into dogma believed.

Green's transformation of an English speculation into an American conviction was ironically like that of the other American loose in London. Just as Pearl Andrews, because of his world view, turned Lord Aberdeen's cautious hints about possible aid into certitude emancipating loans were coming, so Duff Green, because of his world view, converted Sir Robert's play with ideas into conviction that English leaders believed West Indies emancipation had proved disastrous. Everything about a slaveholder's viewpoint drove Green towards his mistaken notion. That lazy blacks needed a master, that emancipation would destroy effective black labor, that emancipators would realize too late that their fanaticism had created a monster—all this was Deep South racist thought at the source. Green had been predicting the English disaster in his *United States Telegraph* ever since angrily reporting parliament's emancipation act of 1833.[25] Now he soared as the prophet vindicated.

When Ashbel Smith told Duff Green that Pearl Andrews had secured emancipation promises from Lord Aberdeen, Andrews's miscalculation meshed perfectly with Green's miscalculation. Why of course England would pay to abolish slavery in Texas. Then Great Britain would wreck at least one more efficient slave-based economy. With free Texas a semi-English colony on the United States' border, the English could strike at the largest superior slave-based labor system. Once blacks were nowhere enslaved, England's free black colonies could compete again.

Duff Green swiftly reported Ashbel Smith's news to Secretary of State Abel P. Upshur.[26] He had "learned from a source entitled to the fullest credit," Green wrote, that "a Mr. Andrews, deputed by the abolitionists of Texas to negotiate with the British Government . . . has seen Aberdeen." Andrews proposed, Green reported his source as reporting, that an English company pay for abolition and receive Texas lands in compensation. "The Texas Minister has authorized me to inform you," Green concluded, "that Lord Aberdeen has agreed that the British Government will guarantee the payment of the interest on the loan, upon condition that the Texas Government will abolish slavery."

Duff Green also passed on to Upshur, and the American Secretary of State permanently internalized, the world view making this incredible news creditable: England's calamity with free blacks demanded that rival producers suffer the same disaster. The entire "value" of England's colonial possessions, claimed Green, required emancipating other nation's slaves. Such fanaticism would never stop in Texas. The English protectorate must "become a depot for smugglers and runaway slaves." The Southwest would be in the same mortal danger long afflicting the Border South.

Duff Green, political pitchman, saw partisan advantages no less than southern imperatives in seeking Texas. Both his most recent patron, the hapless Tyler administration, and his long-term patron, the isolated John C. Calhoun, had long searched for the issue to reorganize national parties. Here it was, the concern sure to make Southerners storm out of both parties. Northern politicans would soon swarm into the remade, ultra-southern party, all to stop a threat to slavery Green honestly saw as dire.

"*Come boldly forward and control events,*" emphasized Duff Green to a Tyler administration despairing of controlling anything. "Meet the crisis; make a treaty" of annexation; save slavery; "advance your own fame. . . . When we look at what the abolitionists have done and ask ourselves what will fanaticism sustained by British gold accomplish, we must face the necessity of meeting the issue at once." With those words crossing the ocean, Pearl Andrews's pilgrimage to London began to make history in North America.

CHAPTER 22

The Administration's
Decision

Would Abel P. Upshur rise to Duff Green's call to arms? No one who knew the
Secretary of State could wonder. Just as Duff Green's racist mentality compelled
instant belief in Ashbel Smith's news about Pearl Andrews, so Upshur's oligarchic viewpoint produced instant concern about Green's information. Contemporaries then and historians since have charged that Upshur cynically exploited
Green's and Andrews's "absurdity." The notion is absurd. Abel P. Upshur
reacted just like the soul he was—a reactionary intellectual unbelievably (not
least to himself) in a position to shove the mainstream backward upon hearing
of a future fright.[1]

– 1 –

The key to Upshur, Duff Green's latest patron, was the Virginian's intellectual
affair with John C. Calhoun, Green's long-term patron. Calhoun's importance,
in the forging of a slaveholder world view, was to drive upper-class social attitudes to one natural political extreme. Calhoun believed that unequal social
power demanded unequal political power, that a slaveholding ruling class must
defy King Numbers on all sides of all color lines. Upshur agreed. The Virginia
intellectual would drive one-white-man, one-vote egalitarianism out of nineteenth-century slaveholders' befuddled skulls.[2]

Both Calhoun and Upshur came naturally by their eighteenth-century synthesis of social advantage and political inequality. Each was raised in an Old
South planter family living near the New South. Calhoun's upcountry South
Carolina, located on the fringes of Carolina's semi-mountains and slightly
enslaved areas, was only a little less in contact with the imminently egalitarian
(for whites) South than was Upshur's Accomac County, that least enslaved Virginia Tidewater area and the one most controlled by nonslaveholding fishermen. Not many miles from the Calhoun plantation, James L. Orr would soon
urge Carolina titans to join the national mobocratic chase. Not many miles

from the Upshur plantation, Henry Wise would soon seek to bolster slaveholders by playing court-the-poor demagogue.

Both Calhoun and Upshur attended High Federalist schools, where they
learned to loathe such mixing of social hierarchy and egalitarian politics. Calhoun was educated at Yale, that center of High Federalist despair about Jeffersonian Jacobinism. He went on to have elitism confirmed in the legal training
of Litchfield, Connecticut's arch Tapping Reeve. Upshur matriculated at Yale
and Princeton. He proceeded to imbibe crusty haughtiness in William Wirt's
Richmond, Virginia, law office.

After the War of 1812, Calhoun had a brief fling with nationalistic economic measures before becoming theorist of minority veto in the late 1820s.
Upshur, almost a decade younger, started out as nay-sayer to King Numbers.
While Calhoun was secretly writing essays on the illegitimacy of numerical
majorities, Upshur was openly defending Virginia reactionaires against reforming nonslaveholders. In the state legislature of 1827, Upshur denounced western
Virginia's attempt to call a state constitutional convention. Upshur condemned
"with pity and dismay" the "wild and demoralizing" notion that "he who possesses no property" should "dictate laws for regulating the property of others."[3]
When Upshur failed to block the 1829 convention, he entered the conclave,
there to become, along with Randolph of Roanoke and Benjamin Watkins
Leigh, the most notorious proponent of extra power for the Slavepower.[4]

As the tide of King Numbers and King Andrew rolled over American politics in the 1830s, the Carolinian and the Virginian occupied opposite vantage
points. Calhoun, at the center of national affairs, was a famous United States
senator. Upshur, at the fringes of state affairs, was an almost unknown planter,
judge, and writer. Only in his bit of outmoded Virginia were his contemptuous
bon mots considered wildly witty.

Upshur's heavy-handed scorn for democratic pols emanated from a heavy-
weight of a body. His huge square head topped a huge round frame. Only side
fringes of hair framed his head. The baldness atop made the reactionary ideologue seem all the more pure skull. It was as if nature had marked him as a
man of mind fit to tower above the multitude.

Upshur conceived that the reign of the masses was both symptom and cause
of mobocracy's imminent slaying of slavery. In the good old Jeffersonian days,
which Upshur aimed to resurrect, a world affirming natural aristocracy had
called the Virginia Dynasty to dispense civic virtue from on high. In the bad
new Jacksonian times, which Upshur sought to destroy, a nation declaring a
poor dependent equal to an independent gentleman invited populistic demagogues to spread civic vice. The gullible rabble, putty in the hands of designing
spoilsmen, especially shrieked approval when told that every rude, crude Tom,
Dick, and Harry was equal to enlightened squires. Soon, Yankee hypocrites
would crusade for office by demanding that all inequality, especially slavery,
must be sliced out of the egalitarian body politic. By then, despaired Upshur,
the South's spoilsmen would have left their region too demoralized to resist.

Abel Upshur feared that Old Virginia might be already "irredeemably" demoralized. The state had "suffered materially" from "the withdrawal of so many of her people of property and intelligence, who have gone further South." The Convention of 1829, by widening the suffrage, had multiplied the damage. Withdrawal of the propertied and enfranchisement of the barely propertied had given "very unworthy and incompetent" demagogues disastrous "success."

Virginians demonstrated their enervation by falling for Martin Van Buren, incompetent national demagogue. Van Buren, warned Upshur, would only temporarily compromise on slavery and scoff at abolitionists. Once slaveholders were sufficiently dazed, the magician would lift the antislavery rabbit out of his egalitarian hat. Van Buren's audience, hating inequality, would reward the leveler with four more years of patronage. The deluded South would follow Virginia's lead and submit.[5]

Abel Upshur's anti-Van Buren Whiggery did not yield John Tyler's high hopes that States' Rights Whigs could command the party. Nor did Upshur share his Whiggish friend Nathaniel Beverley Tucker's zest for disunion.[6] Upshur instead usually favored Calhoun's pet panacea—finding the right issue to educate Southerners out of both parties and into a southern convention. Once slaveholders shed a nonslaveholder's consciousness and realized that an unequal social institution demanded an elitist political agenda, planters would create their own party to crusade for their own prerogative. With one party standing foursquare for Slavepower, northern politicians would flock to the potentially dominant new coalition. No need, then, to seek "a Southern Confederacy!—We can get a *Southern Convention*, and what more do we need?"[7]

Upshur's scenario needed an Upshur to bring it off. Some intellectual must use pure ideas to warn Southerners away from impure demagoguery. Upshur hoped that his legal and proslavery articles in the late 1830s would make him the saving man of mind. His writings emphasized that slaveholders lacked the political ideology to match their social conceptions, that a rejection of mobocracy and belief in prerogative would rally a class that could see politicians' deceptions. Planters with unequal social power, when taught to seek unequal political power, might even elevate their teacher to the United States Senate.

Alas, his publications provoked little elevation. "I do not believe 200 people in Virginia know that such a work exists," Upshur groused after one largely unread tome was published. Politicians showed even less interest in the egghead. Whigs only "condescended to think of me" when "they had work for me to do, but as to offices and honors, they reserve them for others." He had, the thwarted patriarch cursed, "frequently had occasion to remark that for the last half of my life I have been almost something."[8]

Almost something! Here, as so often, Upshur sounded like Calhoun. Calhoun too believed he had spent the last half of his life as almost something. Calhoun too prayed that the detached intellectual could reorganize politics along ideological lines. Calhoun too believed that pure southern issues could arouse a pure states' rights party to purify the Union and thus prevent disunion. Calhoun, with his Washington notoriety, could at least dream of becoming the reigning philosopher statesman. But how could Calhoun's clone in the Virginia provinces, unheralded, unread, unknown, ever exercise power over anyone, save over a tiny group of eastern Virginia Neanderthals as powerless as himself?

In mid-1841 the answer amazingly surfaced. President William Henry Harrison died. Abel Upshur's longtime eastern Virginia friend, Vice President John Tyler, became President. After Tyler reluctantly defied the Whig Party and practically the whole cabinet resigned, the President's range of choices shrunk to his own intimates. Upshur, a hero in Tyler's speck of Virginia, was a natural cabinet choice. The former almost-something, now Secretary of the Navy, could urge his theory on a President.

With "nothing to hope for from the Clay portion," Upshur hammered at Tyler, the President must "form a party of his own, of which the St. Rights Party may form a nucleus. In this way, he will draw ... individuals of *both parties* who profess his principles; and when you add to them the multitudes who are always on the strong side, whatever it may be, you have a decided majority." The oft-ridiculed States' Rights Whig dream of becoming more states' rights than Democrats might become reality yet. Calhoun's scoffed-at-dream of a pure states' rights party might at last prevail.[9]

So wrote Abel P. Upshur during his first heady days as the intellectual with power. A year and a half later, the theorist knew how naïve he had been. Clay in the Senate made the issues. Upshur in the cabinet remade nothing. "*I have no hope for the country,*" Upshur despaired to his Virginia friend Beverley Tucker on March 13, 1843, three months before becoming Secretary of State.[10]

This missive to Tucker, never noticed in the history books, should rank with Thomas Jefferson's "Wolf by the ears" letter and one or two others as the most illuminating single southern document on the coming of the Civil War. The letter, written three months before Pearl Andrews's interview with Lord Aberdeen, explains all by itself why the soon-to-be Secretary of State would find Duff Green's news alarming. The letter also reveals why Old South reactionaries with Abel P. Upshur's mentality would precipitate Texan Annexation imminently and revolution in 1860.

Upshur called governmental reform "impossible" because "the people do not wish it." Property holders with "a real stake in the government ... would be right in their opinions, if they were not deceived." But "for a long time, ... political managers" had controlled the government and deluded even the wealthy.

"The radical defect," explained the imminent Secretary of State, "is in the *constitutional body*. How can a country be governed, except by those who *own* it? The moment the right of suffrage ceased to belong to the soil, the axe was laid at the root of our institution.... When those who have no stake in the country are allowed to govern it," one ends up with "the very riot of the largest liberty" and "the rapid overthrow of all free institutions."

"Particular causes" are "at work," declared Abel P. Upshur, "to expedite the catastrophe." The last Congress witnessed both an escalating campaign to spread universal suffrage and an expanding abolitionist "conspiracy against the South & its institutions." Rising egalitarianism on both sides of the color line showed that slavery "must perish, or else it must be fought for." Yet so long as demagogues "shall retain . . . influence, . . . the South will be deceived, and kept asleep, until her hair will be shorn, & the Samson will wake up, only to find himself powerless."

Upshur moved on to his immediate concern. "As connected with this subject," he warned Tucker, "I anticipate an important movement in regard to Texas." A weak republic exposed to Mexican invasion "must make the best bargain it can. England alone can save" Texas, and "England will drive . . . a Jew's bargain." Texas will trade its few slaves for permanent independence.

Should and would the South allow England to fashion a free labor Texas? Upshur saw difficulties both ways. If Texas was emancipated, he "feared" southwestern slavery could not "exist surrounded on all sides by free States." But if Texas remained enslaved, he feared slavery could not persist in the Old South, for Texans would drain away too many slaves. Upshur preferred that slaves be kept in states where they now lived, for then "the natural increase of the slaves will enable every man to be a slaveholder." Instead of a Virginia population divided between shrinking slaveholders and increasing nonslaveholders, wrote the former conservative leader at the Virginia Convention of 1829, you would "have a homogeneous population, bound together by a common interest." Freeing Texas and halting territorial expansion might actually save the institution in the oldest, most worthwhile South!

Abel P. Upshur here prefigured the best argument Whigs of his persuasion would press against the Tyler administration's eventual annexation treaty: an annexed Texas would draw slaves from old states and thus lessen the Slavepower's sway. Upshur also here gave a foretaste of an imminent irony: the most rabid Old South reactionaries often would oppose southern territorial expansionism, even expansion to slaveholder-friendly areas such as Mexico and the Caribbean. Old East oligarchs with Upshur-like mentalities instinctively feared that moving out and conquering might doom a world which needed to stay home and consolidate. Upshur resembled a hero in a William Gilmore Simms novel, preferring settled parishes to lawless frontiers.

But the Virginian also saw that basing policy on a distaste for the beckoning frontier would disastrously isolate Old South reactionaries from New South energy. Most Southerners, continued Upshur's March 13 letter to Tucker, "will take" the view that abolition in Texas would be a disaster. The consequence of English attempts to emancipate Texas will be either a southern "revolution in support of slavery, or a surrender" of slavery "in despair. The latter, I believe, will be the end of it."

Upshur moved on to prove how sincere were his fears. Beverley Tucker, Upshur knew and worried, owned slaves in Texas. "I wish you would weigh these things," Upshur beseeched his friend, "not only as a politician, but as a question involving your own interest. I greatly fear that your slaves in Texas will be lost to you, if you do not remove them." "Nightmares" such as this, gloomed the President's closest advisor, "weigh upon my mind, . . . for every day's observation confirms" that "they are right. But although, as politicians, we may see & deplore these things, it will never do to fold our arms & submit without an effort."

So wrote the man destined to become in three months the Secretary of State whom historians would accuse of cynically spreading some idiocy about English intervention in Texas. The letter reveals instead a reactionary so sure that the English would intervene in Texas that he was privately warning his pal to remove slave property from the soon-to-be-abolitionized zone. The letter also reveals an ideologue determined not to "submit without an effort" to a New World egalitarian "nightmare" epitomized by the danger to Texas.

Most of all, this special document highlights the special situation about to unfold in American history. An anti-extremist political culture, where mainstream pragmatic politicians almost always dominate and zealots on the left or right almost always fume at the fringes, had managed to bring to power, inevitably partly by accident, one of its most far-out extremists. Moreover, this right-wing ideologue was ascending at the right moment and in the right place to give mainstream history a shove in the most shattering direction. A President's accidental death and a section's non-accidental anxieties had meshed to give that American "impossibility," the ultra in command, capacity to maximize a political explosion.

No matter to Abel P. Upshur that his national political experience was limited to waving a despairing pen at compromising mainstreamers. Like James Henry Hammond at the time of the gag rule, Upshur was no shrinking violet of a political novice, ready to defer while the more experienced governed. The Virginia patriarch came to power armed with both pride in his high-minded appropriateness for high office and determination to oust a generation of dim-witted egalitarians. He would be the latest philosopher statesman in the unfortunately disrupted Virginia Dynasty. And this was the warrior, Tyler's new Secretary of State, who received Duff Green's letter, calling on the Tyler administration to seize the Texas issue, reassert the States' Rights Whig vision, awaken the southern ruling class, and forge a national party dedicated to saving slavery.

– 2 –

The surprise, once one sees the world Secretary of State Upshur's way, is that the Virginian did not leap to annexation upon experiencing Green's letter. Instead, this devotee of abstract theory suspiciously scrutinized Green's facts. But then again, Upshur's deliberative approach to evidence came naturally to an ex-judge. Precisely Upshur's combination of zeal for principle and passion for evidence made him seem to the somewhat theoretical, somewhat practical Tyler the right pragmatic abstractionist to have as head counselor.

Upshur's very vigilance about whether facts fit theoretical preconceptions should warn others against knee-jerk dismissal of evidence he judiciously sifted. Judge Upshur found Duff Green's indictment against Great Britain too loose because of the missing connection between Pearl Andrews's supposed proposal and Lord Aberdeen's supposed promise. Readers of these pages may have joined the ex-judge in spying Duff Green's contradiction. Those not as cautiously discerning as the jurist should respect his judiciousness the more.

Duff Green had reported Pearl Andrews as proposing that English financiers of abolition be repaid with Texas land. Green had also reported Lord Aberdeen as answering that the English government would guarantee interest on the loan. What loan, Upshur puzzled, if British capitalists would be paid in land to finance emancipation? Upshur supposed alternative schemes had been proposed. He wrote to his chargé d'affaires in Texas, asking for a clarification of Andrews's "precise terms."

Whatever the terms, Upshur had "no doubts . . . that the English Government has offered its cooperation." The ex-judge was once again judicious in stressing the limited danger of that cooperation. Under normal circumstances, Texas abolitionists "would scarcely merit grave consideration. Their numbers, it is believed, are very small; and the state of public opinion in that country is by no means favorable." Only the "present situation" of Texas made unpopular fanatics potentially popular. Impoverished, underpopulated Texas would be driven to obtain support against Mexico, if not from the United States then from England, even "upon terms of great hardship and many sacrifices." You must accordingly find out, Upshur urged his man in Texas, what transpired between weakened Texas and determined England.[11]

– 3 –

The answer was soon forthcoming, from London instead of from Texas. On July 12, 1843, Foreign Secretary Aberdeen met again with Lewis Tappan. Aberdeen asserted that the British government "would not guarantee the interest" on an antislavery loan and could not *"in its present situation"* consider "advancing money to Texas" (emphasis mine). Perhaps not catching the hint that English policy might change, the discouraged American philanthropist asked whether cabinet members were "so friendly to emancipation as their predecessors were." Can Americans "doubt it?" Aberdeen answered. He "concurred most heartily" with the Antislavery Convention's "general views" on Texas.[12]

On July 20, Aberdeen bluntly asserted to Texas Minister Ashbel Smith his and his nation's antislavery preferences. Ashbel Smith had requested an interview to disabuse Her Majesty's chief diplomat of any notion that Pearl Andrews represented Texas. Aberdeen was equally determined to assure Texans that England might help abolition, if some future Andrews did represent Texas's preferences. The resulting exchange of views was more important than Aberdeen's meeting with Andrews in leading Upshur and Tyler to push annexation.

Ashbel Smith officially informed Lord Aberdeen that Pearl Andrews's adventuring was "wholly unauthorized, disclaimed, and disapproved of" by Smith's government. Andrews, Smith continued, was equally unrepresentative of Texas public opinion. Abolitionists were scarce in the Lone Star Republic. Yet Pearl

Andrews was babbling all over London that the English government had promised him "means of reimbursing or compensating the slaveowners." Are there grounds "for these assertions?" asked Smith.

Aberdeen answered that England would never "interfere improperly." The Texas government must interfere with its own internal institution first. Then England might consider aid to be proper. Pearl Andrews had accordingly been turned down. But "the well-known policy and wish of the British Government to abolish slavery everywhere," added the foreign secretary, made "abolition in Texas . . . very desirable."

Where Aberdeen had hinted to Lewis Tappan that under future circumstances England might finance the desirable, the Scottish peer treated Ashbel Smith to a stronger expectation. Aberdeen "was not prepared to say whether the British Government would consent hereafter to make such compensation to Texas, as would enable the slaveholders to abolish slavery. The object is deemed so important perhaps they might, though he could not say certainly."

Perhaps they might! Ashbel Smith exploded that English compensation would degrade and disgrace Texas. Aberdeen, as if trying to convert Ashbel Smith to Pearl Andrews's views, soothingly observed that "such things can be done as not to be offensive." With those words, Lord Aberdeen officially and slightly reluctantly brought Andrews's part in the annexation drama to an end.[13]

Elsewhere in London, Pearl Andrews had discovered a new mission. This Christian capitalist unsuited to defying mobs had excitedly picked up in British reform circles a safer way to save America with enterprise. The seeker would soon recross the ocean, his soul again on fire, this time zealous to sell English secretarial shorthand as the key to saving American capitalism![14]

The comic climax illuminated why this restless seeker could count but fleetingly in the tale of Texas. For a few weeks, the erratic reformer had indirectly furthered Upshur's and Tyler's suspicion of England. But by the time suspicions about Aberdeen climaxed in annexation, the President and Secretary of State no longer suspected that the Scottish peer's sins included offering Pearl Andrews a loan. The American authorities knew from Ashbel Smith that Aberdeen might offer some future Andrews-style loan only if some future Andrews represented Texas's public and governmental opinion. That announced possible willingness was the lasting aftertaste in Abel P. Upshur's mouth of Pearl Andrews's wacky pilgrimage, no aspect of which struck the American Secretary of State as in the least amusing.

– 4 –

At the July 20 conference with Ashbel Smith where Lord Aberdeen ended Pearl Andrews's Texas adventures, the Englishman gave the Texas minister, and through him the Tyler administration, something more permanent to worry about. On July 1, Aberdeen had begun a new initiative with a dispatch to his chargé d'affaires in Mexico, Percy Doyle. Aberdeen noted that Mexican and

Texan negotiators would imminently discuss Santa Anna's peace proposal: that Texans could govern themselves if they conceded Mexicans' theoretical sovereignty. By insisting on those terms, Aberdeen pointed out, Mexico could at best save only empty honor. Mexican authorities might instead consider "whether the abolition of slavery in Texas would not be a greater triumph, and more honorable to Mexico, than the retention of any Sovereignty merely nominal." Doyle should suggest that Mexico grant Texas independence if Texas would make blacks independent.[15]

Twenty days later, at his conference with Ashbel Smith, Aberdeen officially told the Texas minister of this hitherto secret overture. I have instructed British chargé to Mexico Percy Doyle, the British foreign secretary stated, "to renew the tender of British mediation based on the abolition of slavery in Texas and declaring that Abolition would be a *great moral triumph for Mexico.*" Smith, stunned, claimed Texas would reject any such overture. Whatever you think, Aberdeen closed the interview by emphasizing, your government should know what I think.[16]

Probably within a week of Ashbel Smith storming out of his office, Lord Aberdeen received Charles Elliot's communique about what Sam Houston thought. Elliot reported Houston as desiring, in the best of worlds, that the Texas predicament could be solved in the way Aberdeen had suggested in his despatch of July 1 to Mexico: with Texas and Texas's slaves both permanently free. The signal from Sam Houston apparently encouraged Aberdeen to send a slightly stronger signal to the Mexican government.

On July 31, the British foreign secretary wrote again to Percy Doyle in Mexico City. I lately informed Texas's man in London, reported Aberdeen, that if "Texas should confer entire emancipation," our government would "press that circumstance upon . . . the Mexican Government as a strong additional reason" for their acknowledgement "of the independence of Texas." Doyle "should press . . . earnestly on the attention of the Mexican Gov't our desire that Mexico waive . . . nominal sovereignty" and substitute for it the condition "of the absolute abolition of . . . slavery." Aberdeen thus completed his signs to Texas and to Mexico that England would "press earnestly" the utopian wish Sam Houston had expressed to Charles Elliot, assuming all concerned sent back favorable signs.[17]

Ashbel Smith despatched news of England's position to Sam Houston, with the usual copy to Isaac Van Zandt in Washington. The Texan in London, having for months tried to manufacture worry, was now worried himself. English moral pressure on Mexico was an announced reality; English economic help to Texas was an announced possibility; might not Smith's beleaguered friends in Houston City now go for some English antislavery scenario? "From the paramount influence of England in Mexico," Smith conceded, "the British Government might without difficulty" prod Mexico into insisting on emancipation in exchange for Texas independence. Nor did Smith doubt that Englishmen "can, and if they promise, doubtless will furnish money" to help Texas free its few thousand slaves.

But Smith begged his government to remember Texas's third crying need.

The republic needed not only peace and cash but also settlers. English free laborers would not migrate to Texas, he had been told, even if the Lone Star Republic became an English protectorate.[18]

Back in Texas, slaveholders doubted what Ashbel Smith had been told. Assuming Texas, under England's protection, freed itself of Mexico, and assuming American slaveholders passively allowed a little England on their borders, why wouldn't Englishmen flock to the anglified El Dorado? Some Texas slaveholders worried that, even without international stabilization, incoming free laborers would soon drown out the few slaves.

Albert T. Burnley, for example, wrote Beverley Tucker in September 1843, of his "great uneasiness lately" about English interference. Burnley, a Kentuckian migrated to Galveston, was Tucker's partner in Texas slave investments. Burnley confirmed Upshur's warning to Tucker that English interference would make investment in Texas slaves precarious. "Slaveowners," wrote Burnley, "will not move to the country, while the stability of slave labor is questioned." Preponderances "of nonslaveholders over slaveholders will daily increase." Texas nonslaveholders with "land to sell" could easily be persuaded that "a tide of immigration" from England "would soon make land in demand at a fair price. Suppose this state of things brought about—& many of our most thinking men believe it will be." Suppose also that England offers cash for slaves and help with Mexico. Then abolition could be "acomplished at the polls." Burnley concluded that "the South ought *now* to insist on interference. I tell you, there is danger, & no time to lose."[19] Beverley Tucker probably shared this letter with friend Upshur.

From Texas and from London, Virginians in the White House were hearing that the enduring difficulty went way beyond the flighty Pearl Andrews. The lasting trouble was Texas's bind, what with Mexico menacing, slaveholders rarely immigrating, slaves not extensively present, and America not annexing. Given these abnormal circumstances, Texans might reject slave labor solutions to the population shortage, assuming England promised free labor solutions and enslaved America promised nothing at all.

Yet Upshur and Tyler, even after hearing from Ashbel Smith what Lord Aberdeen was earnestly pressing on Mexico, still did not press for annexation. President Tyler suspiciously noted that the intelligence "derived unofficially" from the same Texas minister to London who had been trying to frighten the administration toward annexation. American action would be mandatory only if the administration received official confirmation that England had pressed "abolition" as "the basis of interference."[20] Secretary of State Upshur, considering confirmation imminent, asked Texas Minister Van Zandt to seek instructions from Sam Houston in case Tyler offered annexation.[21]

Upshur and Tyler swiftly received confirmation. In a public exchange in the English House of Lords in August 1843, Lord Brougham, leader of Her Majesty's opposition, told Lord Aberdeen he saw "a very great chance" that Texas would abolish slavery, assuming Mexico would then recognize the republic. Could the English government convert Mexico to that strategy?

Aberdeen answered that "every effort on the part of Her Majesty's Government would lead to that result." He would not "produce papers." Betraying diplomatic confidences "would not contribute to the end they had in view." But "the noble and learned Lord" could rest assured that Aberdeen was pursuing Brougham's suggestion. Brougham delightedly sat down.[22]

A month later, in late September 1843, the Tyler administration read about this parliamentary exchange in the newspapers.[23] Ashbel Smith had clearly concocted no tale about English desire to influence Mexico. Rather, the English government had publicly announced its effort to prod Mexico towards prodding Texas to emancipate. The initiative, moreover, had bipartisan English approval.

True, Lord Aberdeen's prod, even in its more insistent July 31 form, was but "earnest pressing." The world's richest nation, however, if encouraged by Texas and Mexico and not scared off by the United States, could easily move from verbal pressing to lucrative offers of settlers, cash, and more-favored-nations trade concessions. Mexicans, unable to govern Texas, and Texans, unable to secure sufficient population, might both eventually accept such honorable and profitable terms, always assuming America would not offer the annexation alternative.

To Upshur and Tyler, the time had arrived to rid the world of that assumption. As in gag rule times, antislavery danger was still slight. But once again, the distant threat, if not early checked, looked capable of escalating. Only annexation would be an obviously effective check. Only a steep uphill fight could secure congressional ratification of any annexation treaty.

Nevertheless, the Secretary and the President decided the fight had to be initiated. On October 16, Upshur met with Texas Minister Van Zandt and urged immediate negotiations towards an annexation treaty.[24] The administration had made its decision. Now decision-making on annexation passed to Texans, and ultimately to the American people.

– 5 –

The Tyler administration's decision to seek an annexation treaty has been called precipitious, premature, taken before all the facts were in. The indictment is usually based on the wrong evidence. According to the ancient accusation, Duff Green's erroneous information about Lord Aberdeen's alleged promise to Pearl Andrews produced the administration's decision. But neither Andrews nor Green caused the administration to act. Abel P. Upshur's critical letter to Beverley Tucker in March 1843, shows an ideologue predisposed to believe in English interference months before Green supplied evidence. Upshur's suspicious response to the Green evidence shows an ex-judge determined to set tangled facts straight before deciding. Tyler and Upshur opted for annexation only after a public parliamentary exchange confirmed Ashbel Smith's private report that England had "earnestly" pressed Mexico to pressure Texas towards abolition.

A better indictment of the administration's decision would stress that no one yet knew how Mexico and Texas would respond to Aberdeen's verbal pressing, or whether England would move beyond this pressure to stimulate better responses. Even from a southern extremist's viewpoint, a prudent diplomat could wait and see where Aberdeen's "mere" words might lead. Witness John C. Calhoun's advice to the Tyler administration.

Calhoun wrote Upshur in late August 1843, that England was "using all her diplomatick arts and influence to abolish slavery" in Texas. Calhoun called the danger "great and menacing, involving in its consequences the safety of the Union, and the very existence of the South." Calhoun advised Upshur to demand explanations from England, Mexico, and Texas. "If Great Britain should not explicitly disavow" Texas emancipation, Upshur must "rouse the South." But "annexation ought not" be "agitated," cautioned Calhoun, "till discussion has prepared the publick mind" and until unsatisfactory answers came from England, Mexico, and Texas. Here was hardly the Calhoun of the textbooks: that Father of Secession, always first to press the South towards disruption. Here instead was the Calhoun of the Nullification Controversy: an extremist cautiously trying to delay hotheads from acting prematurely.[25]

Had Tyler, true to his usual delaying tactics, accepted Calhoun's usual advice to wait and see, the President might have discovered that he had exaggerated the English menace. Tyler was right that England ideally wished Texas to emancipate. The President was wrong to buy the Duff Green thesis that England, supposedly desperate about supposedly lazy West Indian free blacks, was determined to force the issue. Lord Aberdeen never shared Duff Green's racist economics. The foreign secretary's concern about abolition was sheerly ideological and as containable as the cynical Green thought every sheerly moralistic commitment to antislavery would be. Only if Texas and Mexico sent back signals of potential interest and only if the United States continued to run away from annexation might England's "earnest pressing" escalate to financial incentives to both Texas and Mexico. But if Mexico or Texas shouted No Thanks, or if the United States turned tail and annexed, England would press no more.

At the moment of deciding to use annexation to halt English pressing, Tyler and Upshur, as Calhoun warned, knew nothing about whether Mexico and Texas would encourage Lord Aberdeen to press on. England's undiplomatic chargé in Mexico City, Percy Doyle, was tangled in a farcical controversy over a stolen English flag at the times Lord Aberdeen's notes of July 1 and 31 arrived. Doyle, putting second things first, poured energies into demanding that Mexicans surrender the emblem.[26]

Before Aberdeen could ask Doyle for the third time to press England's Texas gambit on Mexico, the English foreign secretary received a warning from America. In a November 1843 interview, American Ambassador to London Edward Everett told Aberdeen of the Tyler-Upshur fury about English "earnest pressing." Aberdeen conceded to Everett that England had suggested a Texas-Mexico emancipation rapprochement. The Scottish peer reassured the American that Mexico had not responded. Aberdeen did not promise to cease pressing for a response. But the Englishman now realized that pressing Mexico might counterproductively press America toward annexation.[27]

This new knowledge may have given Lord Aberdeen pause about insisting that Doyle forget the cursed flag and get on with discerning whether Mexico would surrender an emancipated Texas. Before Aberdeen could probe Mexican pre-annexation attitudes further, the announcement of a Texas-American annexation treaty would demand a post-treaty English—and Mexican—policy. We will see that the new Mexican policy would be acceptance of Texas's independence. We cannot know whether English "earnest pressing" or subsequent English offers of delectable trade concessions might have yielded the same Mexican decision to accept the *fait accompli* of Texas independence, had annexation not occurred.

Texas's likely interest in the Aberdeen initiative, assuming the administration had followed Calhoun's advice to wait and see, is equally uncertain despite more pre-annexation evidence. Had Tyler followed his typical policy of waiting, he would have received back only Sam Houston's typical ambiguity. Aberdeen had sent Houston a signal that, assuming the Texas government wished abolition, England might help. Houston sent back a signal that, assuming England was serious, Her Majesty's government should provide more than vague talk of perhaps helping Texans to emancipate. "To my mind," Houston declared in a speech in Huntsville, Texas, in October 1843, "England does not care about the abolition of slavery." Slaves, Englishmen knew, would develop "a new country in one eighth the time it would take by free labor. . . . England don't want you, in my opinion, Gentlemen."[28]

Sam Houston here threw Duff Green back at the English. Don't you believe, Houston in effect challenged Lord Aberdeen, that your emancipated colonies should have stayed enslaved? If England answered with proof of antislavery commitment, the timid Tyler might awaken American slaveholders. If slaveholders still slumbered while England quietly offered cash, migrants, escalating pressure on Mexico, Sam Houston, indifferent himself to slavery, might take emancipation more seriously. Either way, watchful waiting and incremental signals between nations, the stuff of conventional diplomacy and of John Tyler's usual delaying, would slowly reveal where everyone stood. Then a non-precipitious decision could be made.

Judge Upshur had marched on Washington determined to rout such cautious politics. Southerners who waited for overt antislavery acts, steamed the judge, would still be waiting after slavery's fate was sealed. No overt American act would transpire, for demagogical Van Burens camouflaged their every act. No international explosion would occur, for the ultra-cautious Aberdeen and the ultra-duplicitous Houston would steathfully glide towards each other. No one could say whether England could quietly induce Mexico to accept these drifting policies. But did Mexico matter? That tottering regime could hardly stop English financiers and settlers from silently investing in Texas opportunities. Such quiet English transfusions could make Texas too robust for Mexico to challenge. English free labor migrants could meanwhile make Texas slaveholders too superfluous to matter. And nothing more overt would ever occur than "earnest pressing" in a secret diplomatic note.

Upshur believed only annexation would stop this non-overt process. But Northerners would not annex a slave republic unless Southerners demanded it, and Southerners, dulled by demagogues, snoozed. Hints of English interference, alarming to a trained jurist, would not automatically awaken unsuspicious commoners. Judge Upshur would have to become national prosecuting attorney, arranging camouflaged indications so cogently that a southern jury could see the danger of "mere" words. No jury could be summoned, however, until he secured a treaty.

Upshur here, as in so many ways, anticipated revolutionaries of 1860. Southern Unionists would then argue that President-elect Abraham Lincoln threatened no overt acts against slavery. The difference was that in 1860 immoderate extremists, isolated from established institutions, had to make a revolution to force an understanding that abolition required no overt acts. In 1844, Abel P. Upshur, accidentally and not-so-accidentally influencing a President, might use conventional diplomacy to force an awakening.

"England is determined to abolish slavery throughout the American continent and islands," Upshur privately wrote John C. Calhoun on the eve of the administration's decision. The Lone Star Republic's "present condition" created "an absolute necessity" for Texans to throw themselves "upon the protection of some stronger power. That power must be either England or the U. States." If a supine South allowed crafty England to save desperate Texas from revengeful Mexicans, abolition in the Lone Star Republic would be only the "beginning." Louisiana and Arkansas slaves would "find an asylum" by fleeing across the border. An even more encircled South would have more leaks on its frontiers.

The danger, urged Upshur the consciousness-raiser, must be used to educate slaveholders to see through two-party politicians. Texas must be "a *Southern* question, and not one of Whiggism and Democracy." Slaveholders must be "roused" to demand Texas "as indispensable to their security. In my opinion, we have no alternative."[29]

By demanding annexation when even Calhoun counseled less precipitous options, the hell-bent Upshur fed the hesitant Tyler an issue to save the administration. The secretary thereby helped overcome the President's usual inclination to watch and wait. Abel P. Upshur, one of the most obscure American Secretaries of State, was among the most important. By pressing the President to end his delay, Upshur helped make academic the question of what might have happened to slavery in Texas if the United States had continued to allow Lord Aberdeen to press silent signals. With Lord Aberdeen, as with Thomas Jefferson and Pearl Andrews and eventually Abraham Lincoln, committed reactionaries would not permit cautious softhearts to try tentative gestures on not-so-enslaved areas. The question instead was whether unpopular extremists could sell their provocative policy to dissimulating Texans, doubtful Americans, and a distrustful political establishment in both major parties.

CHAPTER 23

Southern Democrats'
Decision

To move ahead on Texas, the Tyler administration had to induce two historical retreats. First, Texas authorities endeavoring to test the English road away from annexation had to turn back towards America. Then American leaders seeking to evade annexation had to risk the issue.

The twin turnaround looked remote, for each retreat from annexation reinforced the other. Sam Houston's movement away from the United States left the American establishment pleasantly free to avoid the problem. American politicians' avoidance left Sam Houston disinclined to gamble on America. How could the weakest President in American history break this vicious circle—and in an election year no less?

Only in one place. The Tyler administration had to squeeze agreement out of Sam Houston before debate could be compelled in America. An American President with scarce a domestic follower retains one initiative. He can negotiate a treaty. He can force the Senate to consider ratification. He can compel would-be Presidents to take a stand on his actions. John Tyler could pressure an evasive establishment to make a historic decision on Texas—if he could convince the fleeing Sam Houston that the decision might be favorable.

– 1 –

Even Secretary of State Abel P. Upshur had trouble convincing himself that the constitutionally required two-thirds senatorial majority for an annexation treaty could be rallied. In late 1843, Upshur outlined his best hope to John C. Calhoun's friend, Virgil Maxcy.[1] First we must obtain the treaty, wrote Upshur. Subsequently we must convince Southerners that only annexation can prevent English-induced emancipation. Then slaveholding politicians might insist on ratification. Enough Northerners inside an existing party might cave in before the demand. Alternatively, determined Southerners might cajole sympathetic Northerners into a new major party. The resulting annexation party might run

Tyler, or more likely Calhoun, for the presidency. Either titan might rally the first ideologically pure states' rights majority.

Upshur here as usual sounded like Calhoun. The right issue might inspire the right reorganization. The Virginian also here displayed Calhoun-like dissimulation: he too wished to dominate mobocratic scenes he affected to despise. The Virginian would have enjoyed four more years in an uncompromising states' rights administration. His greater pleasure would have been that no compromising President, whether Martin Van Buren or Henry Clay, could keep Southerners drugged while English antislavery seeped into Texas. More widely, Upshur considered the South's apathy about Texas a symptom of a ruling class deadened to egalitarianism's corrosive dangers. Calhoun's or Tyler's pro-annexation candidacy, prayed Upshur, might rouse patriarchs to anti-egalitarian vigilance about far more than annexation.

The selfishness infecting Upshur's elitist dream reflected not his wish to secure the presidency for a friend but instead his desire to secure his reputation for the ages. "I can make" this Texas issue, the Secretary of State wrote Beverley Tucker, "the question of the day.... If I can succeed in this matter, it will be something."[2]

I, I, How that I WILL MATTER does soar from the page and illuminate the zealot who would shove lessers backwards. But first the reactionary had to convince Sam Houston that an annexation treaty would pull Texas ahead. That initial step long kept the would-be hero stuck in the Washington mud.

Upshur's largest trouble was that Mexico had requested and secured negotiations with Texas. The English were asking Mexican negotiators to grant Texas permanent independence. Sam Houston considered the upcoming talks in Mexico City worth pursuing, unless the Tyler administration could guarantee a two-thirds annexation majority.

About the lonely Upshur's ability to rally such a huge majority, Houston had reports from Upshur as well as from Texas's man in Washington, Isaac Van Zandt. The American Secretary of State, when offering negotiations towards annexation on October 16, 1843, wrote Van Zandt that a treaty would present annexation in "the most proper" and "strongest manner." But Upshur could not "offer any positive assurance that the measure would be acceptable."[3] Van Zandt, rushing Upshur's letter to Sam Houston by special messenger, added that he saw "little probability that so propitious a moment will soon, if ever again occur."[4]

This promising assessment failed to deliver the key promise: that the most propitious moment would be propitious enough. So Sam Houston dismissed the messenger bearing Washington letters with a shrug. Throughout the fall of 1843, an increasingly desperate Upshur received back from Houston City only a frenzied letter from William Murphy, American chargé at the Texas capital. Texas authorities had leaked to Chargé Murphy copies of recent correspondence between Mexican President Santa Anna, English chargé in Mexico Percy Doyle, English chargé in Texas Charles Elliot, and Texas President Sam Houston. The correspondence revealed that the two English diplomats had served as go-betweens, helping ease Texas and Mexico towards negotiations. Sam Houston, as usual, had encouraged everyone to help him out, leaving all parties free to think he would help them out.

Houston's game was too deep for the poor American diplomat Murphy, whose brain had for weeks been befuddled by an unrelenting Mexican flu. "This most extraordinary correspondence," Murphy raved to Upshur, proved that Texas, under British direction, was drifting towards Mexican rapprochement and emancipation. Unless Upshur took "some immediate *quick step*," warned Murphy, "the great" and "fatal" blow at slavery would "be struck here."[5]

Upshur's response displayed again the judge carefully examining the evidence. The jurist scrutinized every comma and colon in Houston's smokescreen of a correspondence. The judgment was that the Texas president could out-dissimulate any Cuffee in Accomac County. Houston schemed, thought Upshur, to trick Mexico into ceasing combat or to trick England into rescuing Texas. Still, Upshur thought the Texas trickster showed "a remarkably good understanding with England and an obvious leaning towards that power." With England's "influence" being "strenuously exerted and seriously felt," imminent Mexican-Texas negotiations must cause us "uneasiness and apprehension."[6]

The Texas government escalated Upshur's apprehension with its belated answer to the Secretary's offer of annexation negotiations. The response was penned an eternal, to Upshur, six weeks after the messenger bearing annexation proposals had rushed up to Sam Houston. On December 13, 1843, Texas Secretary of State Anson Jones wrote that his country could not trade "the expectations which now exist of a speedy settlement through the good offices of" England "for the very uncertain prospect of Senate ratification of an annexation treaty, however desirable that might be."[7]

Upshur received these to him deadly tidings on January 13, 1844. Seeking help in the emergency, the chief American diplomat confided in the tiny coterie of Washington annexation supporters. The most helpful zealot, because the only one in the Senate, was Robert J. Walker of Mississippi. Second in helpfulness, because possessing a hitherto secret pro-annexation letter from ex-President Andrew Jackson,[8] was Congressman Aaron Brown of Tennessee. If Robert Walker would assure Andrew Jackson that the Senate would ratify a treaty, and if the American ex-President would assure the Texas president that their old dream of annexation could now become reality, Sam Houston might turn away from England.

Senator Walker accordingly wrote ex-President Jackson on January 16, 1844, "confidentially and in haste," that "the annexation of Texas depends *on you*." An annexation treaty, Robert Walker predicted, "would receive the vote of nearly *every* Democrat in the Senate, and many Whigs, and I think *would succeed*. But delay the measure one or two years, and Texas is lost forever. May I then request you to write by the first mail to President Houston, and urge him to ... make a treaty of annexation."[9]

Andrew Jackson swiftly wrote the prescribed letter to Sam Houston.[10]

Meanwhile, Upshur worked on Van Zandt. The American Secretary of State promised the Texas minister that after a treaty was signed and before senatorial ratification was sought, President Tyler would order the American Navy to the Gulf, to protect Texas against Mexico. Van Zandt reported that auspicious offer to President Houston.

Without Americans' fear of "insidious" English attempts to exert "undue influence," Van Zandt also reported to headquarters, "I should despair" of a treaty's "success." But Van Zandt believed that anti-English sentiment would sweep "the entire vote of the South and West, regardless of party," and the whole Democratic Party, regardless of section. Should distrust of England not quite attract the two-thirds majority necessary to ratify a treaty, Van Zandt added, a simple majority in both houses might admit Texas as a new state. Should even that ploy fail, the pro-treaty faction "will neither permit us to be attacked nor cease its powerful support until annexation shall be effected."[11]

Sam Houston soon received corroborating proof of annexationists' staying power. On the same day that Robert Walker wrote Andrew Jackson, Abel P. Upshur wrote his chargé in Texas, William Murphy, instructing Murphy to pass the letter on to Houston. Upshur's letter personally exposed President Houston for the first time to the intransigent annexationist.[12]

"Texas has, for some time past," analyzed Upshur, needed "the protection of some stronger power." Because America had unfortunately snubbed earlier Texas overtures, Texas leaders had to listen to English overtures. "Probably" by "this time," Texas was "in some degree committed to that government."

In explaining why Southerners would not tolerate that commitment, the Virginian was again the judge reconsidering the evidence. Gone from the letter meant for Houston's eyes were the Secretary's old apprehensions about England influencing Mexico to influence Texas. Upshur now believed that Texas would become independent under English auspices, while still retaining slavery. After that, however, slavery could not last "ten years, and probably not half that time."

American slaveholders, the American Secretary of State explained, would never risk that delicate property in a British dependency. Instead, free labor Englishmen would come to the English-secured republic. After a time, England would "stimulate" English migrants to abolish a non-English institution, and she "will furnish the means of accomplishing it."

The same vision of an emancipating English population movement had earlier inspired Pearl Andrews and had lately appalled Albert Burnley, Beverley Tucker's slaveholding partner in Texas. Upshur, a Tucker intimate, had likely seen Burnley's recent letter on the subject. Burnley's conception of future trouble had far less "ifs" involved than old Tyler administration speculations regarding *if* Texas would respond favorably *if* Mexico responded favorably to England's iffy pressure. The Burnley theory was instead a projection of America's past onto Texas's future. White population movement into relatively lightly enslaved areas of the more southern North and the more northern South had helped make slaves dispensable throughout the American borderland. The resulting sale of bondsmen southwards had encouraged Upshur's Williamsburg friend Thomas R. Dew to believe that Virginia was too far north for permanent slavery. Well, Texas was too far south to be allowed that emancipation by population movement which had freed the southern North and was diluting slavery in the northern South.

Northerners would join Southerners, Upshur warned Houston, in finding a free labor, English-allied neighbor intolerable. Northern manufacturers would particularly rage when Texans smuggled English goods duty-free into America. Southern slaveholders would especially storm when runaway slaves fled to emancipated Texas. War between England and America would result. Texas would then be "ground to powder" amidst a world-wide "conflict of stronger powers."

Let Texas instead, counseled Upshur, annex her power to American might. His investigation of "opinions and views of the Senators" had revealed that "a *clear constitutional majority of two-thirds*" would ratify an annexation treaty. But "if Texas shall reject our overtures, and throw herself into the arms of England," the American government would destroy former brothers, become "bitterest foes."

On February 10, 1844, Chargé Murphy handed this carrot and stick of a letter to Sam Houston.[13] Four days later, in the glare of that missive, in consideration that Robert Walker, Andrew Jackson, and Isaac Van Zandt all concurred in Upshur's prediction of a two-thirds majority for ratification, and perhaps out of fear that the unsteady Murphy or the manipulative Van Zandt might leak these tidings to pro-annexation Texans, Houston yielded to Upshur. The Texas president first squeezed out of Chargé Murphy an agreement that American army units would be added to Upshur's promised naval protection, should Mexico attack. Houston also secured Murphy's pledge that the American military would be deployed during the negotiation period, nor merely, as Upshur had promised, after negotiations yielded a treaty.[14]

The crafty student of Indian tactics here expanded his options at the moment a stronger power had apparently forced one dubious option upon him. Should those Upshur–Van Zandt–Walker senatorial estimates prove chimerical, maybe a foolish Mexican attack would force, or clever Texas diplomacy could induce, proslavery Americans to replace antislavery Englishmen as guarantors of Texas's independence. With instructions to pursue that alternative vision should Mr. Upshur's fantasy prove illusory, Houston dispatched a second Texan to help Van Zandt negotiate an annexation treaty.[15]

– 2 –

I, I, I. How Abel P. Upshur had fulfilled the boast that *I* will make history. By chasing a treaty almost all American leaders were fleeing, then imagining a two-thirds majority where none existed, then demanding that Sam Houston act on the chimera, Upshur had manipulated the Texas manipulator towards gambling on America. Houston's reluctant decision, Upshur correctly foresaw, would awaken enough Southerners to demand that enough Northerners stop shrinking from decision. How many Americans have so successfully set their own historic prophecy in motion?

Upshur never had the pleasure of answering that question. The Secretary of State died six days before news of Sam Houston's agreement reached Washington. The manner of his death heaped strange circumstance atop cruel timing.[16] Upshur was killed in another of those accidents which punctuated the Texas saga so often as to compel thought about the accidental in history. On February 28, 1844, Upshur, the Secretary of State who had been Secretary of the Navy, was enjoying a Potomac River cruise aboard the Navy's new sloop of war. A new gun, named "The Peacemaker," was demonstrated. The weapon backfired. The diplomat not unresponsible for the imminent Mexican War was smashed to the deck and killed. The sloop of war bearing "The Peacemaker" was named the *Princeton.* The deceased reactionary, having lately sought nouveau Texas in order to press American history backwards, had 33 years earlier been thrown out of Princeton University for fighting to preserve students' ancient prerogatives. The commander of the *Princeton* was Robert Stockton. The naval captain would soon fulfill the Upshur promise which had helped nudge Sam Houston towards the bargaining table and would ease two nations' soldiers towards their graves. Stockton would command the naval force sent to the Gulf to protect Texas from Mexico.

Upshur's manner of death highlighted ironies in the triumph he never knew he had scored. He had hoped annexation would make the Whig Party, or some reorganized new party, a pure states' rights vehicle. Instead an impure Democratic Party would save a version of Upshur's annexation proposal, and in the saving would prevent John Tyler from organizing Upshur's vaunted pure party. Upshur had hoped that his issue would save slavery in Union. The treaty he did so much to secure instead would damage Union and, because of disunion, slavery too. More personally, Upshur had prayed annexation would transform an Accomac County judge who was almost somebody into a celebrated heir of the Virginia Dynasty. Instead, his death, coming just before an annexation treaty provoked headline confrontations, killed all chance of his becoming known or cheered by any public beyond his province. He had aimed so high, at a world as elevated as he thought his intellect. He left behind a grubby world not knowing which southern visionary was most responsible for pushing the Slavepower towards temporary victory and final devastation.

– 3 –

Abel P. Usphur would at least have approved of the politician-as-intellectual who outshadowed him in history books. John Tyler appointed John C. Calhoun to finish Upshur's work. The new Secretary of State reached Washington on March 29, 1844. The much-delayed second Texas negotiator arrived a day later. Upshur and Van Zandt had already agreed on so much that final negotiations swiftly transpired, without any discernable Calhoun input. On April

12, President Tyler announced that an annexation treaty had been signed and would be sent to the Senate for its advice and hopefully its consent.[17]

Ten days ensued before the document traveled down Pennsylvania Avenue. The administration knew that senators would demand pre-treaty correspondence. Copies had to be made. Upshur's successor also needed time to write a prosecuting attorney's summary, explaining why evidence in Judge Upshur's correspondence should convict England of seeking emancipation in Texas.[18] On April 22, 1844, the Senate received the pre-treaty correspondence, the treaty, and a covering letter from John C. Calhoun, declaring the national treaty a sectional weapon, designed to protect slavery's blessings from England's documented interference.

This infamous Calhoun document, the so-called Pakenham Letter of April 18, 1844, was ostensibly addressed to Richard Pakenham, England's minister to the United States. Calhoun here belatedly answered Lord Aberdeen's communication of December 26, 1843, also ostensibly addressed to Pakenham but written for American authorities.[19] Lord Aberdeen's letter conceded that England was "constantly exerting herself to procure the general abolition of slavery throughout the world." Aberdeen also admitted that he had urged Mexico to link Texas's independence and emancipation. But England, Aberdeen claimed, had never sought "to compel, or unduly control." If "other States act with equal forebearance," Mexico and Texas will continue to "be fully at liberty to make their own unfettered arrangements with each other, both in relation to the abolition of slavery and to all other points."

Calhoun's response sought to show why Judge Upshur had, and a southern jury should, view England's words as indictable offenses. Aberdeen's letter admitted what Upshur had considered damning facts: that England was "constantly exerting herself" to press world-wide antislavery and that Her Majesty's government had counseled Mexico to press antislavery on Texas. To top off a supposedly conciliatory letter, Aberdeen hinted that soft antislavery counsel might escalate into a harder antislavery effort, should proslavery nations dare to issue ultimatums.

Soft persuasiveness seemed to Calhoun hard enough. Assuming America looked the other way, wouldn't Mexico swap already-lost Texas for English trade concessions? Assuming America failed to offer annexation, wouldn't Texas trade a few thousand slaves for English cash, settlers, and protection from Mexico?

Calhoun's Pakenham Letter aimed at driving Southerners to see England's soft threat in this hard-headed way. The administration, wrote the Secretary of State, "regards with deep concern the avowal" that England was "constantly exerting herself" to procure world-wide antislavery. The administration was also appalled that England was urging emancipation as "one of the conditions on which Mexico should acknowledge" Texas. "It would be difficult for Texas in her actual condition," emphasized Calhoun, "to resist" this pressure, even "supposing the influence and exertion of Great Britain" remained within Lord Aberdeen's "limits."

An emancipated Texas, continued the Carolinian, would give "Great Britain the most efficient means of effecting in the neighboring States of this Union what she avows to be her desire to do in all countries where slavery exists." A free labor Texas "would expose the weakest and most vulnerable portions" of slaveholders' "frontiers" to inroads. But while England's hope is to end what she calls our evil, warned Calhoun, our mission is to perpetuate what we consider our blessing. Under southern Christian slavery, bragged the American Secretary of State, "the negro race" has attained an unprecedented "elevation in morals, intelligence," and "civilization." The United States, concluded Calhoun, "acting in obedience" to racial "obligation," and "as the most effectual if not the only means of guarding against the threatened danger ... has concluded an annexation treaty."

Look what Calhoun here outrageously did, administration opponents instantly exploded. The explosion echoes in historical accounts. Calhoun, runs the charge, took a treaty unratifiable unless Northerners acquiesced and made it an obnoxiously southern document. The Secretary took an acquisition defendable on grounds of national military protection and defended it solely as protection of slavery. Calhoun also weighed down the treaty with fulminations about slavery's blessings which all Southerners allegedly already believed and few Northerners could abide. The Secretary of State thus supposedly transformed a treaty ratifiable as national Manifest Destiny into a doomed document pitting North against South. Why would this abstractionist be so pragmatically stupid as to kill his own treaty?

No pre-Civil War mystery is less mysterious. Calhoun here pursued the policy he had deployed since nullification times. First he would find the issue to teach Southerners that outsiders hid antislavery intent behind camouflaged methods of proceeding. His issue would arouse southern apologists from their preference to diffuse blacks away. An awakened Slavepower would then compel Northerners into a pure states' rights party, which would settle the precipitating issue the South's way.

These rouse-the-South-first tactics were hardly Calhoun's quaint addition to the Tyler administration's Texas policy. Upshur had plotted the strategy before conceiving that Lord Aberdeen might nudge Mexico. Tyler would later claim this South-first gambit was Upshur and Calhoun's counterproductive ploy.[20] But the President, at the time, delayed sending the treaty to the Senate so that Calhoun's proslavery letter could be written and Upshur's proslavery correspondence could be copied. That proslavery correspondence, involving Duff Green, Pearl Andrews, and Lord Aberdeen, would have provoked Northerners into correctly seeing the administration's annexation policy as proslavery, had Calhoun never written to Pakenham.

Indictments of Calhoun's Pakenham Letter as unnecessarily proslavery and counterproductive to annexation also rest on misunderstandings of when the southern mainstream mentality evolved and how an American majority came to admit Texas in 1844–5. Calhoun's lesson on slavery's blessing was indeed a stupid addendum, assuming Southerners had universally hailed bondage ever

since the purported Great Reaction of the mid-1830s. But, as we will see, the
Texas Annexation Controversy demonstrates that most Southerners still
yearned to diffuse the "evil" away, only fifteen years before the Civil War.

Again, Calhoun's emphasis on annexation to save slavery was bad statecraft,
assuming Northerners otherwise would have approved of Tyler's treaty. But
nothing would have made Northern Whigs tolerate the document, and Northern Democrats would have to be forced to swallow their distaste for the accord.
Calhoun's scenario of rallying enough slaveholders to push enough Northern
Democrats to stop evading the issue was exactly the way the election of 1844
and its annexation aftermath transpired.

– 4 –

Those who claim history would have happened another way, with sufficient
Northerners accepting Tyler's treaty without sufficient Southerners shoving,
are ignoring the history of this question. Northern Whigs had for years been
warning that this monstrous Slavepower land-grab was coming. Northern Democrats had for years been evading the taint of a Slavepower expansion that was
likely to produce a war against Mexico and still more annexations of formerly
Mexican territory. Just what massive northern power block was now going to
turn against its traditions because a despised President ordered an about-face—
unless some massive southern power bloc compelled such a turnaround?

Assuredly, neither Northern nor Southern Whigs were going to march
behind John Tyler. For a quarter-century, John Quincy Adams's Yankee faction
had been attacking the Slavepower's three-fifths clause as despots' need and
democracy's shame. For a decade, Northern Whigs had warned that Texas
would be the Slavepower's next outsized demand after the gag rule. For three
years, Whigs northern and southern had loathed Tyler as slayer of their popular
mandate. Almost all Whigs were predictably at Tyler's throat from the minute
he announced the treaty, which was two weeks before Calhoun's Pakenham
Letter was published.[21]

For purposes of clarity, the Gag Rule and Texas controversies have here
been separately analyzed. But the artificial segmentation hinders understanding
of Northern Whigs' integrated perception: both slavery issues triumphed in
Congress because the Slavepower enslaved the Democratic Party and thus the
not-so-democratic republic. Artificially segregating Whigs' response to gag and
Texas crises also hinders awareness that the two issues came to climax at the
same time. The same Congress of 1844–5 which abolished the gag rule admitted
Texas.

Another long-related issue, the three-fifths clause, was simultaneously
inspiring its greatest Northern Whig resistance since the Missouri Controversy.
In March 1843, the Massachusetts legislature proposed amending the United
States Constitution to delete the three-fifths clause. On December 21, 1843, John
Quincy Adams presented the proposed amendment to the national House of
Representatives. Adams became chairman of the committee selected to consider

the proposal. When he could not prevail in the committee's deliberations, Adams joined with Ohio's Joshua Giddings in issuing a dissenting report.[22]

A policy awarding tyrants extra representatives for owning slaves, charged the two Yankees, violated "the first and vital principles of republican popular representations." The South's swollen power led to disproportionate numbers of Southerners in the House, the White House, the Supreme Court. The Slave-power's undemocratic power led to undemocratic gag rules. Now Southerners would annex Texas, a huge slave area. The Slavepower would then use its swollen power to drive the United States into a war with Mexico to secure still more slave states. The Slavepower would emerge too gigantic for mere democrats to control.

"The treaty for the annexation of Texas," Adams soon added in his diary, "was this day sent in to the Senate and with it went the freedom of the human race." This "mad project," warned the editor of the *Boston Atlas,* will be resisted "with pen, with tongue, with every nerve and muscle of our body," aye "with the last drop of our blood."[23]

– 5 –

If Calhoun could not harden Northern Whig's already rock-hard opposition to annexation or increase Southern Whigs' loathing of Tyler, did the Pakenham Letter transform the South's traditional best northern friends, the Democrats, into foes of Tyler's treaty? Not a chance. Northern Democrats' opposition to the treaty, like Whigs', preceded the Pakenham Letter and drew on a decade of pre-treaty history. The chief architect of Northern Democrats' long-standing policy of stalling off Texas was now the section's almost unanimous choice for the presidential nomination. The moment Martin Van Buren heard of Tyler's treaty and before he could know Calhoun was writing anybody, he penned his response to the President's initiative. This so-called Hammet Letter was Public Evidence #1 that Tyler's treaty, not Calhoun's polemics, reinvigorated Northern Democrats' traditional unease about annexation.[24]

To Martin Van Buren, Tyler's surprise presentation of an annexation treaty in April 1844 looked like a rerun of James Hammond's surprise demand for a gag rule in December 1835. Once again, Van Buren was cruising towards the Democratic Party's presidential nomination. Once again, a Carolina extremist threw up a last-minute southern roadblock. Once again, Northern Whigs' fury at the South pointed up the political danger for Van Buren in going all the way with far-out slaveholders. Once again, the New Yorker's solution was to give in a little to the South and stand up a lot to Calhoun. The Magician thereby would keep southern extremists isolated, Southern Democrats mollified, Northern Democrats safe, while all the while keeping his presidential bandwagon rolling.

In early 1836, Van Buren's sleight-of-hand had taken the form of the Pinckney Resolutions: admit antislavery petitions and send them to a committee, thereby appeasing northern constituents, then automatically table abolition requests, thereby appeasing Southern Democrats. In late April 1844, the Magician's dexterity shaped the policy enunciated in the Hammet Letter: reject this annexation treaty, thereby helping to win the 1844 presidential election in the North, but hold out possibilities for future annexation, thereby helping to keep Southern Van Burenites distant from Calhoun.

In the Hammet Letter, Van Buren advised the Senate to forget Tyler's treaty. Ratification was premature. Mexican approval had not been sought. The American people had not been consulted. This treaty, a repudiated President's last gasp for political survival, might cause an unnecessary war for an unpopular policy.

The New Yorker's opposition to this annexation treaty, however, came fused with a pledge to administer annexation, assuming he could negotiate Mexican acquiescence in the deed. Van Buren also promised to move ahead with annexation, even if Mexico balked, assuming the American majority wished to risk war. Once the people had spoken, their President must carry out their wishes, "be the consequences what they may."

Van Buren here challenged Southern Van Burenites to prove that the Jackson majority—any national majority—thought war with Mexico preferable to non-annexation of Texas. The ex-President here also announced that he might be friendlier to Texans than he had been during his last White House tenure. Then again, Mexican and/or Yankee rejection of annexation might make the Magician his old unfriendly self.

Van Burenites would soon be claiming that the Hammet Letter was an annexationist's document. Martin Van Buren, so the argument went, pledged to annex Texas the patriotic, peaceful, politic way. He would win the election, then seek Mexican approval for annexation. Should his diplomacy fail, he would let a national Manifest Destiny groundswell sweep Texas into the Union in a few years. Only the South's counterproductive zealotry, Van Burenites concluded, stopped annexation from transpiring the popular democratic rather than the undemocratic Slavepower's way.

The Van Burenite annexationist scenario rested on the alleged probabilities that Sam Houston would have waited while Van Buren slowly tested American and Mexican sentiment, that Mexico would have succumbed to the Magician's magic, or that some infatuation with Manifest Destiny would have overcome the northern public's distrust of Slavepower land grabs and fear of Mexican War. Each of these scenarios, had Martin Van Buren been elected President, is a guess.

Guesses the other way are as plausible. Houston had long since been fed up with Van Buren's stalling. Mexico had long ago determined to stop annexation. Van Buren had long feared that Manifest Destiny sentiment would never overcome northern repugnance for huge enslaved Texas, especially if annexation meant a war against Mexico likely to yield more tropical land for the Slavepower. Martin Van Buren, political strategist extraordinaire, filled his Hammet letter with conditions because Northern Whigs' anti-annexation fury made unconditional annexation too politically risky.

Above all else, the Van Burenite scenario of inert Southerners passively waiting for Northerners to go tipsy over Manifest Destiny is the proverbial *Hamlet*
with Hamlet left out. As we will see, much more than Calhoun's Pakenham
Letter was driving Southern Jacksonians away from Van Buren, towards conviction that delay must be renounced. Maybe in some fantasy where the South
was transformed into a non-South, the North might have secured Texas Van
Buren's way, sometime down some other road. But since the South was the
South, the history which happened turned on whether Southern Democrats
would demand and secure a presidential candidate pledged to immediate
annexation.

Immediacy especially separated Van Buren's Hammet and Calhoun's Pakenham letters. Van Buren, apostle of sectional adjustment the two-party way,
offered southern supporters a delay tolerable in the North. Calhoun, warrior
against two-party compromising on slaves, demanded that Southern Democrats
force Northern Democrats to stop stalling. Van Buren said approach Mexico
one last time, then *maybe* we will annex. Calhoun said no maybes would suffice,
not a moment could be lost. Van Buren spied no crisis requiring instant decision. Calhoun saw Sam Houston drifting into Lord Aberdeen's orbit, unless
America stopped stalling. Van Buren would be politic. Calhoun cried that pol-
itics-as-usual would leave slavery fatally outflanked in the Southwest. The question, in this climactic battle between Van Buren and Calhoun for the soul of
the Jackson Party, was whether southern moderates would demand that Northern Democrats go to war for the Slavepower.

– 6 –

Southern Democrats were at first annexation's only potential soldiers. Southern
Whigs would never risk this battle. They knew that John Quincy Adams-style
Northern Whigs would never budge and that Henry Clay-style Border Whigs
would never waffle more than an inch on so provocative a Slavepower demand.
With the Upshur-Tyler-Calhoun Texas treaty, as with James Hammond's gag
proposal, the politically critical question was whether southern extremists could
pressure moderate Southern Democrats to pressure Northern Democrats into
lining up behind the Slavepower.

Calhoun's effort to push the Democratic Party toward annexation and away
from Martin Van Buren possessed one immediate advantage: Van Buren himself. Southern Democrats usually liked Van Buren's anti-inflationary banking
and currency policies. That attitude had led Calhoun back to Van Buren in
1840. But most Southerners, emulating Calhoun, had never warmed to Van
Buren, had always suspected the Yankee's alleged friendship for slavery, and
had ever considered him a devious manipulator. In the perspective of the illusionist's long-standing image in the South, the Hammet letter was no annexationist's long-run plan but the Magician's latest package of "ifs" and "maybes"
adding up to not much.

Still, Van Buren was the party leader, he had been conceded the party's presidential nomination, and he was the pet of Northern Democrats necessary to win a national election. Calhounite extremists had to convince Southern Democrats that Van Burenite stalling and evasion would be so disastrous for enslaved Texas that an immediate annexation ultimatum would have to be issued to Northern Democrats. Zeal for annexation would furthermore have to be instilled in Southern Democrats almost overnight. The Democratic National Convention would convene less than two months after Tyler sent the Senate the treaty.

For moderates to turn almost instantly immoderate, some predisposition to believe and to worry had to exist. Among Southern Democrats, Texas in fact already stirred vague dreads. A sense of potential crisis especially informed the inaugural address of Governor Albert Gallatin Brown of Mississippi, delivered on January 10, 1844, almost three months before the Texas treaty was signed.[25]

Annexation, Brown told constituents, obviously would be "desirable." The fertile prairies would enrich some Southerners. Texas congressmen and senators would augment southern political security. The vast land mass would consolidate a peaceful Mississippi Valley.

Despite these desirable gains, Mississippi's governor continued, only one circumstance would make the desirable *"indispensable."* The South must not "stand idly by, whilst Texas," a neighboring slaveholding republic, is "drawn inch by inch into the meshes" of England, "a wiley nation that has never failed to do us injury" and is "the national personification" of "stealthily advancing" abolition. Albert Gallatin Brown did not doubt Texans' friendship for America or for slavery. But Texas, "worn down by . . . a protracted war and constantly menaced by a formidable enemy," was almost out of "money and almost without friends." Desperate Texans might have to accept English offers to provide protection against Mexico and to pay for emancipated slaves. Hints "already" abounded in "diplomatic circles" that England would make these offers. Should something harder than hints appear, Brown concluded, Southerners had better demand the *"indispensable."*

Indispensable. Brown's word indicated Calhoun's opportunity. The Pakenham Letter showed Southern Democrats what England preferred to do in Texas, assuming the United States allowed England her preferences. That proof of possible English antislavery counsel and funding, should a non-annexing United States permit England to become Texas's best friend, disturbed some of the most sensible Southerners.

Witness United States Senator William Rives of Virginia. Rives, a Whig, rightly called himself no southern agitator, for "I deeply lament" slavery's "existence." Rives, former Ambassador to France, also rightly called himself "no agitator or alarmist" about "foreign powers." But "I have not been able to blink the import—the true and naked import—of this communication of Lord Aberdeen." Here is "a bold and formal announcement of a settled policy on the part of one Government to use its influence *and exertions* to *procure* the abolition of certain institutions of another."

Some gentlemen, Virginia's United States senator noted, ridiculed Aberdeen's "extraordinary diplomatic paper" as a "mere *wish*" for abolition. "Aberdeen's naked and unreserved" pronouncement, answered Rives, "sounds to my ear very differently from a mere *wish*." The director of English foreign policy had announced, in "all the 'pomp and circumstances' of an official communication," deployment of "moral and diplomatic propagandism (to say the least)."[26] The sober William Rives here demonstrated that Calhoun's words, emphasizing Aberdeen's confessions, had nudged Southerners towards seeing the Texas episode as at least worrisome.

– 7 –

Still, Senator Rives was not worried enough to favor President Tyler's treaty or to demand that the Whig Party run a pro-Texas presidential candidate. With Southern Democrats, as with William Rives, Calhoun could only begin to provoke a sense of crisis. The South Carolinian remained too distrusted as an enemy of two-party politicians. The Pakenham Letter could rally Southern Democrats against the party's northern establishment only if powerful insiders lent instant credibility to the outsider's alarm.

At this moment of acutest need, Calhoun received the most precious Jacksonian gift. For a decade and more, Andrew Jackson had taught Democrats that the arch-Nullifier concocted alarms about slavery solely to break up the Union. By anointing Van Buren rather than Calhoun as heir, Tennessee's favorite slaveholder had steered his movement away from becoming primarily a sectional racist's crusade and towards becoming primarily a national anti-bank instrument.

Now the old general urged a portentous shift. He demanded that his supporters nominate someone other than Van Buren. His former disciple, explained Jackson, disastrously failed to see the Texas situation as an immediate crisis. Jackson's widely circulated opinion lent enormous credibility to Calhoun and fateful legitimacy to Jacksonianism as a pro-South movement.

In the year 1844, Andrew Jackson looked incapable of anything so significant. Old Hickory now usually resided on what looked very much like his deathbed. His coughs turned catching a breath into exhausting exertion. His headaches transformed lifting his head into debilitating vertigo. His rectal discharges soaked sweaty sheets with a blackened crimson mass of putrid clots. His well-meaning physicians purged his already streaming bowels with calomel powders. His would-be saviors also depleted his waning powers with frequent bleedings. His grieving friends invaded his dimming consciousness only with a pale letter now and then. His trembling hand could barely scratch a response.

His barely readable words sufficed. His letters summoned especially his first army, fellow southwestern racists, to new battle against old enemies. Jackson had risen to national prominence as the warrior who swept Englishmen and Indians out of Southwesterners' path. He had piled up mammoth southwestern majorities partly because he figured to continue as President his good work as general. Old Hickory had not disappointed. His Indian removal policies had cleared the way for Georgians, Alabamians, Mississippians, and Louisianians to exploit blacks, without red skins or red coats interfering.

Another old southwestern hero now reminded Jackson of new obligation. Andrew Jackson had promised Sam Houston that an annexation treaty would be ratified. Houston, upon receiving the treaty, called Jackson on the promise. Should ratification be delayed or rejected, Texas's president wrote the American ex-President, Texas's "mortification would be indescribable." She would be a bride "spurned" at the American altar not once but thrice; "all Christendom would justify her" in seeking "some other friend." If American politicians expected to "postpone" ratification "to a more convenient season," to serve "party purposes and make a President," concluded Houston, " let them beware."[27]

Houston here again displayed his ability to know his man and in the knowing to marshal the stronger to fight for the weaker. Jackson began composing public letters almost as soon as he received Houston's private appeal. Old Hickory warned fellow Democrats that "delays are dangerous. Houston and the people of Texas are now united in favor of annexation. The next president of Texas may not be so. British influence may reach him."[28]

Jackson joined Calhoun and Tyler in seeing Texas's vulnerability as England's opportunity. "Mark this," the ex-general commanded: Texas requires "aid from some nation and that aid must not be permitted to come from Great Britain." Jackson concurred with the administration that if America rejected annexation and thereby drove Texans towards England, the Lone Star Republic "will have to resign her negroes to England at $250 a head."[29]

But where Calhoun the Carolinian saw black freedom as the dire threat, Jackson the Southwesterner feared more that both Englishmen expelled to Canada and Indians removed to trans-Mississippi domains would re-enter former haunts. England, once having gained a base in the Lone Star Republic, would excite "hordes of savages within the limits of Texas and on her borders . . . to make war upon our defenseless borders." "British influence exerted over the Indians and negroes, a Canady on our west as well as the north, servile war, an asylum for all runaway slaves"—what a dismal situation all this for the safety of the South and West.[30]

Soon English soldiers would be swarming over white men's dissolving frontier, continued Jackson. British troops based in Texas could seize "Memphis and Baton Rouge," possess "New Orleans, and reduce all our fortifications." Regaining the Mississippi and the Gulf would cost America "oceans of blood and millions of dollars." Texas was the vital "key to our future safety—take and lock the door against all danger of foreign influence," and "without delay, for delay is dangerous."[31]

Jackson did not here endorse Texas as part of any Manifest Destiny to seize the hemisphere. Rather, Jackson, like Calhoun, would protect what had already been captured. The Tennessean, like the Carolinian, saw his world in claustrophobic terms. Englishmen and Indians were closing in. Texas must not be an enemy fortress. The Democratic Party must sweep the shaky Slavepower outpost inside a fortified Union. Jackson's protegé, Van Buren, must be demoted for evading what could not be delayed.

They stood now together, those old enemies, Calhoun and Jackson, as always from different southern worlds, as always seeing southern dangers from different perspectives, but now shoulder to shoulder as if it was still 1828 and John Quincy Adams still must be defeated. The resurrected alliance, however, did not so much recall 1828 as repudiate 1836. Jackson would now make Calhoun's policy rather than Van Buren's candidacy key to a national Jacksonian campaign.

That historic reversal augured such a redefinition of Jacksonian "Democracy" as to make Jackson's old allies beseech the dying leader to change his mind. The chief pleader, Frank Blair, Sr., a powerful Border South Democrat and a devoted member of Jackson's early Kitchen Cabinet, had helped define Jacksonianism as a coalition of moderate Northerners and Southerners, opposed to high nationalism to the north and traitorous sectionalism to the south. Van Buren, Blair's post-Jackson hero, had been the man to further that centrist vision.

Now Blair, editor of the pro-Van Buren *Washington Globe,* begged his old chief to realize that Calhoun remained the same old fiend. The South Carolinian's outrageous letter to Pakenham, Blair charged, deliberately sought "to drive off every northern man from the support of the measure." The result would be Senate defeat of Calhoun's treaty "by an overwhelming vote." Then the arch-Nullifier would urge "dissolution of the Union, and a Southern Confederacy as the only means of obtaining" Texas. Could you be "against Mr. Van Buren," asked Blair, "whose measures under existing circumstances present the only hope of giving Texas again to the whole Union?"[32]

So many times before, Old Hickory had snapped up such bait. This time, the ex-President was not tempted. I grant you, he wrote Blair, that Calhoun's Pakenham Letter is indiscreet. But Jackson "shed tears of regret" over Van Buren's "fatal letter" to Hammet. Jacksonians "cannot abandon principle," however much "we may be attached to men." Van Buren seemed not to understand that "the best interest of the South as well as the safety of our country, are now in jeopardy by the secret interference of England." The "safety of the republic" required instant "annexation regardless of the consequences." The Democratic Convention, concluded the Democratic Party's hero, must nominate someone who understands the Jacksonian imperative.[33]

With this climactic declaration for Calhoun's precipitancy and against Van Buren's delays, Jackson had not so much replotted his course as emphasized a direction there from the beginning. From its inception, Jacksonianism, to Jackson, had involved white men's freedom to exploit equal opportunities, without Indians or bankers or abolitionists or Englishmen interfering. For a time, Jackson had focused on the National Bank as the monster. But southwestern epics had always excited this Southwesterner's imagination. Englishmen had always been a great enemy, Indians a treacherous hindrance, slaves a labor necessity. In hunkering down now to consolidate a safe Southwest and to fortify an outflanked labor system, Andrew Jackson, to John Quincy Adams's delight, high-lighted the old question about Jacksonian "Democracy." Just how democratic could this pro-mail censorship, anti-Indian, pro-gag rule, anti-abolitionist, pro-Slavepower crusade truly be? Adams for two decades had struggled to make the question stick. Now Jackson would glue the question like tarpaper to the mean-ing of his movement.

– 8 –

While Andrew Jackson stressed English pressure as an immediate southwestern crisis, another southwestern Democrat stressed a southeastern crisis. Robert J. Walker, United States senator from Mississippi, had recruited Old Hickory to reassure Sam Houston that a treaty would be ratified. Once Houston agreed to negotiate with Upshur, Walker authored an enormously influential pro-Texas pamphlet. Walker's polemic is allegedly proof positive that preposterous pro-paganda led to annexation.[34]

Robert Walker's "propaganda" urged that an annexed Texas, instead of helping to perpetuate slavery, would beneficiently diffuse blacks away, first from the oldest South, eventually from an emancipated North America. Failure to annex, in contrast, would lead to British-induced emancipation in Texas, then to Yankee-induced emancipation in the South, then to freed blacks swarm-ing northwards towards their liberators.

Southerners' northern allies understandably relished this argument. The Walker thesis transformed sorely pressed Northern Democrats from traitors who knuckled under to the Slavepower into heroes who would diffuse blacks farther from the North. Equally understandably, except to those who cling to the myth that Virginians united behind perpetual slavery in the mid-1830s, Robert Walker lent renewed life to old Upper South prayers that slavery would be diffused to the Deep South.

But the stunner is that the new prophet of abolition through diffusion was a senator from Lower South, New South Mississippi. The shock dulls upon real-ization that Senator Robert J. Walker, temporarily of Mississippi, was born, bred, and remained a representative type of James Buchanan's Pennsylvania. Ever since gag rule days, Buchanan had been bending almost all the way south on slavery policies, while still hoping that the "evil" would someday drain out of America. Buchanan's Lower North posture, while too southern for Van Bur-en's Upper North New York, was right for Pennsylvania, the largest northern state on the South's border. Senator Buchanan would be an avid consumer of Senator Walker's black-removal reasons for annexing Texas. Less than a decade later, Robert Walker, ex of Mississippi, having lived back north since 1845, would be President Buchanan's selection to be governor of Bleeding Kansas.[35]

The Walker-Buchanan allegiance began as a familial connection of Penn-sylvania's leading political clans. Robert Walker's father was a politically influ-ential Pittsburgh attorney. Young Robert, after earning degrees with high hon-ors from the University of Pennsylvania, married the superbly connected Mary

Bache, whose close relatives included some of James Buchanan's closest cronies and Benjamin Franklin, American prophet of pragmatic enterprise. The Bache-Dallas-Walker clans found Buchanan's appeasement of southern anger to be pragmatic wisdom for an enterprising commonwealth close to the fire-eaters.

Robert Walker, Buchananite, early journeyed towards a fire-eaters' mecca. With his brother Duncan Walker, he moved to Natchez, Mississippi, in 1826. There his uncle had grown very rich very quickly as a land speculator. Duncan Walker so craved the habit as to move in 1834 to that grandest arena for land speculation, Texas. Robert Walker remained in Mississippi to tend to family interests.

Events rewarded Robert's caution. Duncan Walker died in 1836, after languishing in Mexican prisons for his part in the Texas Revolution of 1835. Robert Walker, heir to brother Duncan's Texas lands, was determined to avenge his brother's death. Opportunity to help annex Texas and thus punish Mexico came when the Pennsylvanian-turned-Mississippian was elected to the United States Senate in 1836.

This native Northerner secured southern office in the classic outsider's way: by waxing hotter than slaveholders about those cool towards slavery. Robert Walker kept his Yankee-style dislike of bondage to himself. He was the quickest draw in the Southwest at shooting down opponents as soft on slavery. He also surpassed every Southwesterner, including Andrew Jackson, in articulating his adopted region's desire for Texas.

At the height of annexation, Robert Walker bore an unfortunate resemblance to the annexationist he most admired. Lung disorders had turned Senator Walker, like ex-President Jackson, into a cadaver-like creature gasping for breath. Walker was for months at a time as imprisoned in his bedroom as was the dying Jackson. Mississippi's favorite convalescent was barely five feet tall. He weighed under 100 pounds. His withered skin stretched over protruding bones. His huge head bobbed on a shrunken body. He almost seemed to illustrate his theory that loss of the Texas outlet would seal the doom of imprisoned Southerners.

Back when Presidents Jackson and Van Buren had stalled on annexation, Senator Walker had dissented haplessly. When Van Buren drove for the White House during the Tyler years by steering away from Texas, Robert Walker, establishment Democrat, worked on the anti-establishment administration, trying to encourage President Tyler to go for annexation. When John Tyler, maybe a little because of Walker's urging, allowed Upshur to have his way with Sam Houston, and Houston, perhaps a lot because of Jackson's Walker-induced promises, reluctantly agreed to negotiate with Upshur, Walker celebrated rapprochement by writing his *Letter on Annexation.*

In the popular piece, Walker admitted to constituents for the first time, under cover of a useful political reason for annexing Texas, that he hoped his adopted homeland would be drained as clean of slavery as his native Pennsylvania had been. Annexed Texas's vast and fertile prairies, cheered Walker, would draw slaves from cramped and exhausted old southeastern domains. This whitening process would occur "not by abolition, but against and in spite of all its frenzy, slowly and gradually, by diffusion, as it has already thus nearly receded from several of the more northern of the slaveholding states." Purchase of Louisiana and Florida had already helped drain 500,000 blacks from the Chesapeake. Annexation of Texas would double the rate of diminution. Delaware would be drained in 10 years, Maryland in 20, Kentucky and Virginia in 40. From Texas, transplanted slaves would eventually diffuse southward, into still richer tropics. Slavery will thus "disappear from the limits of the Union" by a "gradual and progressive" process, "without a shock, without a convulsion."

Walker contrasted this salutary migration with the convulsive migrations inevitable if Texas was not annexed. Flow of English population to Texas would free the Lone Star Republic. A South hemmed in by an England-supported Texas to the west and Yankees to the north, once coerced by outsiders into emancipation, would swarm with blacks poised to move northwards. Blacks who migrated would drive northern white men's "wages to the lowest point in the sliding scale of starvation and misery." Northern jails and asylums would "be filled to overflowing; if indeed any asylum could be afforded to the millions of the negro race whom wretchedness and crime would drive to despair and madness." Northerners as well as Southerners, concluded this Pennsylvanian ruling in Mississippi, had a racial stake in securing Texas as "the safety-valve of the whole Union, and the only practical outlet for the American Population."

Walker's safety valve argument was reprinted in most newspapers in the black-belt South, Whig and Democratic, just about every time with ecstatic editorial praise. That almost-unanimity indicates the power of Walker's "propaganda." Southern Whigs in particular might have been expected to condemn Southern Democrats' favorite annexation argument. Yet Robert Walker's safety valve conceptions most often went publicly undebated.

The lack of debate is revealing because the proposition was so debatable. Posterity can hardly credit Robert Walker's vision of a Slave South in imminent danger of being imprisoned on too little land with too many blacks. Huge areas of the Southwest remained untilled in 1844, including large sections of rich river bottomlands. The ratio of undeveloped land to available labor was so large as to invite campaigns within ten years to reopen the African slave trade. Yet no southern opponent of annexation apparently ever told Robert Walker to be sensible about all the wide-open spaces beyond some alleged southern jail.

Again, only one southern leader, and he not even a Whig, called Walker on the fantasy that slavery would eventually diffuse out of America through the Texas way-station. Senator Arthur Bagby, Democrat of Alabama, termed "the idea of slavery going off by a sort of insensible evaporation" into "the great desert between Texas and Mexico" as, "to say the least, a bit preposterous."[36] Neither Bagby nor any other southern opponent of Tyler's treaty, Whig or Democrat, called preposterous another of Walker's debatable visions: that annexed Texas would totally drain slavery from the more northern slave states.

With all southern speakers agreeing that Texas could drain the elderly South of slaves, the question remained whether said diffusion would be beneficial. A handful of Southern Whigs called Walker's safety valve pernicious. Waddy Thompson of South Carolina, for example, wondered how addition of one new slave state would compensate for slavery "very soon" disappearing from "Maryland, Virginia, North Carolina, Tennessee and Kentucky." Even in South Carolina, annexation would make slaves "an incumbrance which we shall be glad to get rid of; and I confess for myself that it will afford me very little consolation in riding over my fields, grown up in broom-sedge and washed into gullies, to be told that . . . slavery still exists and is prosperous" in Texas.[37]

Waddy Thompson's public logic recalled Abel P. Upshur's private handwringing in that pivotal March 1843 letter to Beverley Tucker. The imminent Secretary of State had then speculated that annexing enslaved Texas might depopulate the oldest South. Waddy Thompson's 1844 doubts about diffusion also anticipated imminent South Carolina arguments against further Mexican/ Caribbean annexations. Diffusing slaves *out* of the older South, many Southerners' conception of the ideal future as late as the Texas annexation story, would remain this encrusted minority's pet hate.

The very fact that Waddy Thompson's anti-safety valve argument powerfully resonated with one side of advanced southern thought makes the essential point even sharper: how revealing that so sensible a dissent appeared so relatively infrequently in Texas times. Waddy Thompson's cogent dissent is also revealing because founded on not-so-cogent assent to Robert Walker's master assumption: that Texas *would* remove slavery from the older South. When dubious assumptions suffuse all sides of a cultural mentality, a revelation of a world is at hand. Anyone who claims to understand the Slave South must stand ready to explain why, as late as 1844, Southerners found a safety valve to remove slavery instantly plausible—and usually a cause for persistent rejoicing.

– 9 –

Explanation must start with the fact obvious on the face of Robert Walker's argument: that much of this culture still prayed that slavery, under the right conditions, might be terminated. Ever since Jefferson's day, removing ex-slaves had been considered an indispensable condition for black freedom. Ever since Missouri Controversy times, diffusion of slaves into new territories had been considered a viable step in the right black-diluting direction. John Tyler, in Missouri Controversy times the prime congressional advocate of diffusion as a safe route to emancipation, was now the President who called Walker's safety valve southern orthodoxy. In Tyler's eastern Virginia, the most orthodox theorist had lately been Thomas R. Dew, who had called diffusion of slavery southwards the best safety valve for a state too far north to be permanently enslaved.

Thomas R. Dew's conception of beneficial black diffusion had outlasted the prime competing vision. Colonization had seemed to many apologists a plausible alternative removal scheme in the late 1820s and early 1830s. Diffusion to Africa had been debated in Maryland and Virginia legislatures and in the national Congress. But after those confrontations, African colonization came to seem both beyond state resources and lethal to national Union. To adopt a national colonization policy, even to consider Charles Mercer's petition from the American Colonization Society, was to guarantee South Carolina's secession. Safe colonization of blacks in Africa became so politically unsafe as to provoke cries of disloyalty, including from Waddy Thompson, during William Cost Johnson's late gag rule forays.

No one called Robert Walker "untrue." Walker's safety valve, like Thomas R. Dew's, gave stymied visionaries who had dreamed that blacks might be diffused out of a lily-white republic a non-heretical way to dream on. Both Walker and Dew shunned heretical government interference between master and man, as in post-nati or colonization laws. Each would whiten the South by stimulating private sales, per ongoing geographical redistributions of North America's Slavepower base. Dew would push blacks towards the tropics by building state roads and canals. He believed that state internal improvements would invigorate Virginia's economy, attract white migrants to the Old Dominion, and allow entrepreneurs to cash in on superfluous servile labor down river. Walker would pull blacks down from the nontropics by annexing Texas's lush prairies. He believed that annexation would intensify the Lower South demand for slave labor and quicken the drain of blacks away from Upper South regions. Neither diffusionist would deplete government coffers a penny, in contrast with colonization schemes widely considered very expensive.

Walker's mode of removing blacks, cost-free to government, might also bail out hard-pressed capitalists. *In this economically depressed period,* Old South slaveholders, looking for ways to stimulate a sour slave-based economy, conceived that slave diffusion to fresh New South territory might yield economic salvation. *In this period* must be emphasized because an important historical theory holds that Southerners, *constantly* perceiving slavery to be an economic burden, constantly sought fresh land as a pecuniary safety valve.[38]

That explanation misses changes over time. When cotton prices were high, planters believed their labor system was economically better than the North's. The best southern pecuniary moment and one of the most depressed times in the free labor North, the late 1850s, would lead Southerners to soar with pride over the slave labor system's supposed superiority. With cotton selling at 12 cents a pound and prices for scarce slaves mounting towards $2000 in the presecession decade, Slavepower expansionism would be based on euphoria about prosperity rather than on fears of bankruptcy. In the 1850s, some planters would desire more Africans to diffuse *to* already possessed and underenslaved virgin prairies. Meanwhile, imperial merchants would seek more Caribbean land to escalate a booming slave staple economy.

Robert Walker's moment, the mid-1840s, was economically gloomy, which is why his safety valve speculations sound like an attempt to bail out an outmoded labor system. Amidst a depressed economy which had continued with only brief breaks since nullification times, slaveholders feared they would be stuck with useless slaves on worn-out soil. They could not, like impersonal employers, cut losses by slicing payrolls. They could only sell off personal servants at some cost to their consciences and at insufficient gain to their pocketbooks. Losses might swell unless new planters on new lands developed new need for more slaves. Nowhere was the economic tremor of the 1840s more evident than in the older eastern South, where rotten crop yields compounded rotten prices and intensified the search for a way out.

A glorious escape route, once Robert Walker pointed to it, was through the safety valve. Texas prairies were fabled for fertility. *There,* went the dream, one could make a bonanza even with six-cent cotton. Southwestern demand for slaves might increase slave prices, bailing out the less prosperous Southeast. But close the safety valve, heap redundant slaves back on the decaying older South, and black hands would be increasingly idle.

That prospect inspired racial as much as economic fears. With an attitude running from jealousy to disgust, whites had long considered blacks overly promiscuous. What would be the fate of a stagnating South bottled up between the Atlantic on the East, an anglified Texas on the West, and free labor to the North, containing blacks breeding like rabbits? We will be "smothered and overwhelmed by a festering population that was forbidden to migrate," answered Congressman Isaac Holmes of South Carolina, "pent in and walled around on exhausted soil—in the midst of a people strong in idleness" and incited "to revolt and murder." Holmes called imprisonment without a safety valve the most "awful calamity . . . in the widest stretch of his imagination."[39]

United States Senator Chester Ashley of Arkansas echoed Southeasteners' concerns and indicated why Southwesterners thought they might someday need Walker's safety valve too. "Annex or not," feared Ashley, "the time must come when the number of negroes would be so large that their labor must be unproductive." Trapping "this population within the limits where it now exists" could lead only to race war and "utopian schemes of the abolitionists." Annexing "Texas would at least put off the day. He did not say it would finally prevent it; but it certainly would defer it." It would open an outlet through which Southerners "might eventually get rid of an intolerable burden."[40]

– 10 –

Intolerable burden! Southern congressmen and senators talked that way about slavery constantly during the Texas Controversy. Whether William Rives was defending the Pakenham Letter or Robert Walker was extolling the safety valve or Chester Ashley was cringing at a South bottled up, the southern leader who with Calhoun defended slavery as a permanent positive good was as scarce as hen's teeth. Representatives in Congress who called slavery good during the Texas debates, all four (!) of them, were angered to be exceptional on this subject. For example, Isaac Morse, congressman from Louisiana, "denied the principle which seemed to have been assumed here, as a thing being conceded, viz: that slavery was an evil." He regretted "to hear from the lips of any southern gentlemen the admission that slavery was an evil."[41]

Southern lips did emit that admission. The one word explaining the admission, and explaining all other words tumbling from Southern Democrats about a southern crisis, was claustrophobia. Abel Upshur articulated the claustrophobia of a naysayer trapped in King Numbers's republic. John C. Calhoun expressed the claustrophobia of a slaveholding perpetualist, imprisoned with slaveholding apologists and facing English siege. Andrew Jackson voiced the claustrophobia of a Southwesterner potentially squeezed by Englishmen, Indians, and fugitive slaves. Robert Walker illuminated the claustrophobia of the declining Southeast, pent up with too many increasingly dispensable black "barbarians." As Michael Hoke, Democrats' candidate for governor of North Carolina, summed up all these feelings about being hemmed in, England, after "winding herself about us like the terrible anaconda," but awaited "an opportunity . . . to crush us."[42]

Through the safety valve and past the anaconda, annexationists spied relief everywhere. A racially imprisoned culture could send away blacks. A financially depressed region would acquire an economic El Dorado. A politically outnumbered slavocracy would gain at least one new state and two new senators; and immense Texas might later be hacked into more states with more senators. And why should the South be denied this racial outlet, this economic strength, this political power, this safety valve for southeastern woes, this barrier against southwestern Indians, above all this protection against an abolitionized English protectorate smack on slaveholders' Louisiana-Arkansas border? Because Yankees thought Slavepower was immoral! This was indeed a crisis. The South must demand the territory.

– 11 –

Southern drives for territory, historians have proclaimed too many times, involved impractical attempts to procure lands impossible for slaves to work. Let the Texas affair bury this canard forever. Annexation involved the largest acquisition of a southern land mass; some Englishmen did rather hope to plant free labor on it; the land was politically and economically sublime for slavery; and annexationists demanded the soil to solve practical, political, racial, economic, military, demographic, and moral problems at the heart of southern concern for half a century. Texas exploded on Southern Democrats' political agenda—literally exploded faster than even Calhoun had hoped—precisely because so many Southern Democrats for so many reasons suddenly found the Lone Star Republic a merciful practical release.

Not all Southern Democrats jumped to that conclusion. Even if they happened to be Democrats, Southerners agreed on very little. Border South Democrats remained especially antagonistic to a Union-threatening, Mexican War-inviting land grab down South. Frank Blair, Thomas Hart Benton, and other Missouri Jacksonians positively froze at the ascendancy of Calhoun's Slavepower imperialism over Van Buren's a-southern democracy.

Calhoun had always feared that Southerners such as these borderites, not committed to perpetuating slavery forever, would back off from the actions necessary to preserve the system. Jacksonian apologists for slavery in Middle and Deep Souths, enraptured with diffusing slavery away through Robert Walker's safety valve, proved Calhoun was partly wrong. Border South Democrats, however, already had their safety valve: sale of slaves to states further south.

With no reason to feel the claustrophobia of a black belt trapped without an outlet, the Border South's claustrophobia took a different form. The region's inhabitants felt potentially squeezed between Northerners and Southerners who would make border turf a Civil War battlefield. Caring much more about permanent Union than about what they called temporary slavery, the Border's Southern Democrats required a ton more of the proslavery consciousness-raising Calhoun included in the Pakenham Letter before they would risk Slavepower crusades.

Democrats in the Middle and Deep South received all necessary consciousness-raising in the few weeks between the signing of the Texas treaty and the beginning of the National Democratic Convention. Once Calhoun demonstrated English antislavery and Jackson issued a call to the colors and Walker pleaded for a safety valve, Texas became the hottest Middle and Lower South political property since Andrew Jackson's stock soared in the late 1820s. After Texas captured their imaginations, Middle and Deep South Democrats could not nominate someone who would hedge on annexation, lest John Tyler run for re-election as the Southerner who hedged not at all. Tyler's supporters had called a third party national convention, to meet at the same time as the Democratic National Convention. Should the Democratic Party shrink from Texas and Tyler campaign for re-election and the safety valve, the Southern Democratic Party could suffer a defeat worse than the loss to Harrison four years earlier. With this practicality added to other practical reasons why the Texas issue took off among Middle and Lower South Democrats, Slavepower competition to do most for slavery screwed the most pressure yet on Northern Democrats—and on Martin Van Buren.

CHAPTER 24

The Electorate's Decision

Mr. Border South Whig was Mr. Northern Democrat's best hope that Southern Democrats would ease annexationist pressure. Henry Clay, who had a lock on the 1844 Whig presidential nomination, offered annexationists so little that Martin Van Buren in contrast almost looked like a roaring annexationist. In a battle with Clay over Texas, Van Buren could offer the South much more for slavery.

– 1 –

Neither Henry Clay nor any other viable national Whig candidate could offer the South much on Texas or on any slavery-strengthening proposal, for Northern Whigs stonewalled against every Slavepower argument. The contrast between Democrats and Whigs on this point was enormous and never more pivotal than in 1844. Southern Democrats had long since discovered, particularly in gag rule politics, that enough Northern Democrats would probably cave in, however begrudgingly and resentfully, to southern demands. Southern Democrats could campaign to consolidate slavery in Texas, never believing that the crusade might cost them their party—or worse, their nation.

Only briefly had Southern Whigs believed that sectional sprees might be cost free. Back in 1836–8, when the Opposition/Whig movement divided to conquer, the party's states' righters had been more free than Southern Democrats to be loose cannons on gag rule issues. But after the Whig Party united in the late 1830s, Southern Whigs became the politicians deterred from demanding federal consolidation of slavery. Southern Whigs' intransigent northern wing peculiarly taught, as Southern Democrats' appeasing Yankee allies did not, that Southrons who insisted on proslavery legislation would destroy their national party and perhaps their nation.

Southern Whigs thus had to weigh the possibility that Texas might be abolitionized against the certainty that campaigning for annexation would split

426

their party. As partisans no less than patriots, Southern Whigs treasured their party's role in maximizing commerce, restraining Caesars, upholding communal morality national and local against Jacksonian untrammeled individualism. So Southern Whigs swiftly decided that Texas's charms were less precious than Whiggery. Southern Democrats, if faced with the same choice between losing Texas and forfeiting everything else politically dear, might well have opted for party too. The question remained whether Union could endure with only one southern party facing that sobering choice—and whether the party restrained from battling for slavery could prevail in a section eager for Texas.

– 2 –

Henry Clay expressed Southern Whigs' sense of annexation's relatively low priority in his so-called Raleigh Letter of April 17, 1844.[1] The Whigs' imminent presidential candidate issued this statement on Texas almost simultaneously with Calhoun's Pakenham and Van Buren's Hammet letters. While Clay concurred with Van Buren in opposing the Calhoun-Tyler treaty, the two treaty opponents differed on post-treaty annexation policy. Van Buren announced he would go for Texas, even if he could not persuade Mexico to accept the *fait accompli,* assuming a national majority preferred war and annexation to peace and no Texas. Clay, in contrast, would halt annexation unless Mexico assented. He would also deny Texas entrance into the Union, no matter whether Mexico agreed, should "a considerable and respectable portion of the confederacy" express "decided opposition." Only with no "hazard of foreign war" and "general concurrence" of both sections would he annex Texas.

General concurrence! Henry Clay sounded like John C. Calhoun. The Kentuckian's notion that neither section ought to pass a law unless the other section concurred resembled Carolina gospel. Still, one lesson of 1844 was that Clay merely continued his longtime relationship with the spirit of 1832. Only Calhoun changed—changed portentously from negator to apostle of federal impositions.

On slavery issues, Clay had always opposed impositions on either section. In the late 1830s, he had urged that a northern antislavery majority must halt, if the southern minority differed. He now demanded that national annexation must be aborted, if most Northerners objected. Do Nothingism on slavery, for or against, without general concurrence: that would best keep both sections inside the system.

Until Texas, Calhoun too had stood for barring sectional blocs from actions, gagging northern abolitionists from petitioning, stopping federal authorities from censoring southern mails. But with annexation, Calhoun's dogma that only general concurrence justified federal intervention dissolved into the demand that the federal government must intervene to shore up slavery, however many Northerners objected. Southern extremists now would use federal power to save Texas. They would later demand federal action to run down slaves, to protect slavery in national territories, and to annex enslaved Cuba.

King Cotton sought the power of King Numbers. If you Southerners can rally a majority, shrugged Martin Van Buren, I'll defer to your mandate. If Southerners dare defy "considerable and respectable" northern sentiment, warned Henry Clay, I'll bar their way.

Choose ye between us, a delighted Van Buren chortled to Southern Democrats after both candidates' letters were published. Capture your congressional mandate for Texas, he in effect told annexationists, while I stop Henry Clay from nullifying your victory. Once the people demand annexation, we must obey their instruction. But do not press Texas upon me until our mutual masters, the people, speak.

– 3 –

The Magician's very cockiness about finessing Calhoun produced special fury when Southern Democrats scorned his clever stall. Van Buren erred, most of Van Buren's best southern friends sadly concluded, in thinking that delay was tolerable. An exasperated Sam Houston would not wait, England would negotiate a Texas-Mexico settlement, Englishmen would flow into their new El Dorado.[2] Van Buren also miscalculated, Van Buren's friends lamented, in thinking that Southern Democrats' most dangerous opponent was necessarily Clay, who admittedly promised less on annexation. The more threatening foe might be President Tyler, who promised far more. Given the perceived peril, both to slavery in Texas and to Southern Democrats who compromised on immediate annexation, no staller could have many southern votes in the Democratic Convention.

Van Buren's best southern friends sent him that word. Their sorrowing letters read as if a death in the family had occurred. Van Buren's southern cronies had cherished the political wizard, helped bring him to national power, rejoiced in his victories, suffered through his defeats. Now they had to tell him that he was finished in their section.

Thomas Ritchie found the task particularly sad. For two decades, Ritchie, editor of the *Richmond Enquirer,* had been Van Buren's man in Virginia. Now, Ritchie felt compelled to fracture the Albany-Richmond alliance. "I had set my heart upon nothing more sincerely than to see you reelected," wrote Ritchie. "But we cannot carry Virginia for you." Why? I enclose my letters about your Hammet Letter. "Read them and judge for yourself."[3]

Ritchie's mail testified to the Jacksonian South's sense of crisis. "The safety of the South," wrote one Virginia Democrat, demands annexation. "No delay should be indulged." "Yankees must realize," declared another, that Texas "is a speculative question with them; a practical & operating question with us of the utmost magnitude." Northern allies must "give us a Texas candidate, or we must split."[4]

Northern Van Burenites found this latest southern blackmail insufferable. We have eternally caved in on tariffs and gag rules, wrote United States Senator Silas Wright of New York. Now, after "ungrateful" Southerners had refused to delay annexation at least until we could win an election and negotiate with Mexico, "I cannot advise to throw away the North." Wright was "for looking at home some and not South [at] all."[5]

Northern Whigs had for years charged that Van Buren, by looking South, turned the southern minority into a national majority. Van Buren now urged that the northern majority must rule, first in the party, then in the nation. He would begin the Democratic National Convention with a majority of delegates. His followers would demand his nomination. This time, southern bullies must yield to democracy's master, the majority.

– 4 –

Unfortunately for Van Buren, the decisive issue at the late May 1844 Democratic Convention became the size of a legitimate majority.[6] Van Burenites, who would possess a simple majority for their man on the first presidential ballot, demanded nomination by a majority as small as one. The Democratic Convention of 1840 had been newly run on that principle. But anti-Van Burenites, led by Robert Walker, sought a return to the more traditional convention rules of 1832 and 1836: a two-thirds majority necessary for nomination.

Van Buren lost this vote on the rules because his majority was not hard enough. Van Buren's support was particularly soft in areas where a rival chieftain aspired to be the party's nominee, should the New Yorker falter. The best example, James Buchanan's Pennsylvania, was unanimously pledged to Van Buren on the first presidential roll call. But Pennsylvania's "Van Buren" delegates split their votes on the pivotal rules question, 12 for nomination by two-thirds, 13 for simple majorities. In all, northern delegates voted 102–58 for majorities of one, while southern delegates voted 90–14 for nomination only by a two-thirds majority. That split gave anti-Van Burenites their victory on the rules, 148–116. It was the same old story: a healthy fraction of Northerners plus most Southerners gave the minority section majority control over the nation's majority party.[7]

On the first ballot for presidential nomination, the majority section still sought to impose its candidate. Martin Van Buren received 146 votes, 55% of the convention and but 31 votes short of the now-needed two-thirds majority. Only 27 of 161 northern delegates voted against him. Only 12 of 105 southern delegates voted for him. As usual, the most northern areas of the South were least southern. Van Buren won nine of the 30 Border South delegates, and only three of the 75 Middle and Deep South delegates. The numbers posed the issue. Could the black-belt South nullify Van Buren's national majority in the party?[8]

The answer, during the rest of the bitter day, was You bet. Through seven ballots Van Buren's support slowly shrunk. Van Buren loyalists angrily determined to nullify everyone else. On the day's last tally, Van Buren's original 146 delegates had sunk to 99, sufficient to prevent any other candidate's two-thirds majority. The party, in peril of dissolution, adjourned till the morrow.

The respite, for tired delegates, meant more exhausting politicking. Hours of conversing, caucusing, and conniving yielded one conviction. The party needed a new candidate acceptable to all factions. The search for such a soul went in several false directions.

Then an ideal figure emerged. James K. Polk of Tennessee, former speaker of the national House of Representatives, while a fervent annexationist, had stuck with Van Buren after the Texas issue intruded. Young Hickory, as Polk was called, had thus stood positioned as the southern annexationist best suited to heal party wounds by becoming Van Buren's vice presidential nominee. When Van Buren's presidential nomination stalled, Van Burenites grumpily agreed that so acceptable a vice presidential nominee could move up on the ticket. Anti-Van Buren annexationists were not grumpy at all about this slaveholder fervent for Texas.

The party's deliverance was finalized on May 29, 1844, with James K. Polk's unanimous nomination. When the Polk bandwagon rolled through the hall, South Carolinians, with their usual disgust for mere party, observed only as spectators above in the gallery. Someone asked for the Carolinians' approval. "South Carolina *seconds* the nation," came down the answer from on high. John C. Calhoun's treaty had found its home in the Jackson Party, with his state almost back in the fold and Van Buren's supporters restive inside the movement.[9]

The way Southern Democrats had to force even James K. Polk, that loyal Van Burenite, upon Van Buren partisans indicates one last time that unconditional annexation, at least in the campaign of 1844, required an intransigent slavocracy. Still, once Northern Democrats had been bullied into the southern policy, Polk's was a version of annexationism less obnoxious in the North. Young Hickory, although a slaveholder, was primarily a political operator. The Tennessean never understood why others waxed hot on slavery. He never linked bondage and annexation. He saw Texas as military shield of the Southwest and vital to his own goal, an American opening on the Pacific. James K. Polk lusted not as much for Texas, the former Mexican possession, as for that still-retained Mexican prize, California. Polk saw California harbors, particularly San Francisco, as the key to trade routes to the Orient. His was not the southern mentality of the depressed 1840s—claustrophobic, cramped, craving a safety valve, but the southern mentality of the prosperous 1850s—expansive, thrusting out, seeking more land and markets.[10]

Or rather, Young Hickory's was the Young American mentality of the post-Tyler age. Polk was the first Southerner important in the Texas story to fit the Manifest Destiny label. His persona was of an American operator equally interested in the far North and the far South. He would propel democracy and enterprise forward by annexing both Texas and Oregon. The South's drive for Texas had passed from the men needed to secure a party nomination, worried sectionalists who could inflame Southern Democrats, to the man needed to win a national election, the national imperialist who might defuse the North's resentment of the Slavepower.

– 5 –

A week after the Democratic Convention came together on Polk's imperialism, the Senate split apart on Tyler's treaty. A two-thirds majority was required for ratification. Instead the Senate rejected the treaty by over two-thirds, 35–16, on June 8, 1844.[11] Whigs voted 27–1 against ratification, Democrats 15–8 for approval. Northern Democrats barely managed a majority against the Slave-power, 7–5, with one abstaining; Northern Whigs opposed annexation, 13–0. Southern Democrats affirmed the treaty, 10–1; Southern Whigs said no to Tyler, 14–1.

The five Northern Democrats who massed behind the South included James Buchanan of Pennsylvania. On Texas, as he had been on the gag rule eight years earlier, future President Buchanan was to the southern side of ex-President Van Buren. Texas, said Robert Walker's Pennsylvania friend, "will be the means of gradually drawing the slaves far to the South," where they may "finally pass off into Mexico."[12]

The safety valve theory did not appease Van Buren's northern senatorial supporters. But Polk was their man, and Van Buren had promised to follow public orders on annexation. Should Polk's version of imperialism secure him the White House, pro-Van Buren senators might have to rally with Buchanan behind Southern Democrats. Aided by a couple more Whig turncoats, the Democratic Party might then annex Texas by a majority of one, assuming some way could be found for senatorial majorities short of two-thirds to annex.

Before annexation negotiations had begun, Texas Minister Isaac Van Zandt had told Sam Houston that ways might be found for simple majorities to annex. Van Zandt may have gleaned the idea from Abel T. Upshur, or more likely Robert Walker. At any rate, three days after the treaty was defeated, President Tyler suggested how King Numbers might sneak around the Constitution. While the Senate had to approve a treaty by a two-thirds vote, both houses of Congress could admit a new state by respective majorities of one. So forget about annexation by treaty, Tyler urged Congress following defeat of his treaty. Instead admit Texas by simple majorities.[13]

By now seeking to bypass the two-thirds constitutional requirement for ratification after lately insisting on a two-thirds requirement for the Democratic Party's nomination, southern annexationists appeared to be playing fast and loose with majoritarian rules. That appearance was particularly damning to ideologues such as Calhoun, who had long urged that republics required minority safeguards. These Southrons' disregard for any republican procedure in their way caused Yankees and even some key Southerners to bridle at their bullying.

The resulting bitter senatorial confrontation on Tyler's proposed evasion of the two-thirds roadblock was the first public congressional explosion over Texas, the treaty having been considered in secret session. The angriest protagonists were not a Northerner and a Southerner but two warriors from different Souths. George McDuffie, aging former South Carolina Nullifier, defended John

C. Calhoun's new loyalty to King Numbers. Senator Thomas Hart Benton, fiery Missourian, Van Buren partisan, and the only Southern Democratic senator to oppose Tyler's treaty, attacked the latest Slavepower attempt to overcome lack of constitutionally prescribed numbers. Never had the gulf between the young western Border South and the elderly eastern Deep South seemed so cavernous.

Thomas Hart Benton, Missouri's senator ever since the state entered the Union, was no longer the youngest hero of the freshest West. But the senator, like his state, retained a middle-aged vigor. Benton cherished his own scarcely enslaved city, St. Louis, for being barely a southern and utterly a western metropolis. Benton would bet Missouri's future on attracting more white frontiersmen, not on keeping its relatively few black slaves. If that did not sound very southern, so be it. Benton would boost Missouri's western thrust and allow its southernness to diffuse away.

Benton told the Senate that he had long favored annexation, but only to consolidate the West. This nonsense about a southern crisis over Texas was Calhoun's latest attempt to manufacture secession. Tyler's treaty, "far from securing the annexation of Texas, only provides for the disunion of these states."

Benton the Democrat, like Henry Clay the Whig, was the classic border pacifier. He was "no bigot or fanatic in the cause of slavery." He wished to add Texas in a way which would please North as well as South. He would accordingly reduce Texas to the size of the largest current state. He would then abolish slavery "in one half" of the remaining Texas territory. His proposal, he bragged, would "withdraw slavery from the whole left bank of the Rio Grande." He would thus soothe the North and consolidate the Union.[14]

Where Thomas Hart Benton of the more lightly enslaved new Border West would free half of Texas for vigorous free laborers, George McDuffie of the more thickly enslaved ancient Atlantic South would keep all of Texas enslaved to save fading slaveholders. McDuffie looked the way his message sounded: ever so much older than Benton. The comparison seemed the starker because only a decade previously, when Benton had been the middle-aged zealot of the Border Southwest, McDuffie had been the young hotspur of South Carolina. On the stump campaigning for nullification, McDuffie had slashed at Forty Bale demons who would imprison Carolina. But where Benton had picked up momentum with age, McDuffie had aged prematurely. Almost paralyzed from bullet wounds, almost breathless from tuberculosis, almost penniless from Carolina's sour economy, he felt himself and his world to be squeezed as if in an airless closet. His fellow senators could barely hear his whispered plea for an escape valve.

McDuffie believed that British threats endangered Texas, and Texas was necessary for "our very existence." You cannot "pen . . . up" our "superabundant slave population . . . within their present limits." Texas must "operate as a safety valve" until "the Providence of God shall provide some natural and safe way of getting rid of this description of people." You, sir, McDuffie softly hissed at Benton, are the Brutus who would slay your homeland.[15]

Benton retorted that the traitorous McDuffie would slay the republic. As for my being Brutus, declared the Missourian, he would not, like Brutus, fall upon his sword. He would save his weapon for traitors "who appear in arms against their country." With these words, Benton smashed his fist on George McDuffie's desk. McDuffie, sick and emaciated, just stared back.[16]

No playwright could have penned a better transition scene. McDuffie epitomized Neanderthals who longed for Texas to escape a wretched finale. That longing had helped create a severe enough southern sense of crisis to defeat Van Buren and promote Polk. But theories about diabolical English lords had not sufficiently impressed enterprising Northerners, much less marginal Southerners such as Benton. The Upshurs, Calhouns, and McDuffies had exerted their power. The future of the issue now lay with the swaggering Mr. Benton—and with the virile Mr. Polk's ability to win a national mandate for western energy.

– 6 –

James K. Polk's major opponent was Henry Clay, nominee as expected of the Whig Party. The Tennessean's chances over the Kentuckian in the South were enhanced when another Southerner aborted his third-party challenge. President John Tyler had intended to run on a pro-treaty independent ticket if neither Democrats nor Whigs nominated an immediate annexationist. But Polk's nomination made Tyler's race both counterproductive (because annexationist votes would be split) and unwinnable (because the regular party candidate running on the same issue had too great an advantage). Andrew Jackson, intervening for the last time, wrote public letters, enabling Tyler, that old Jacksonian turncoat, to return to the fold honorably and endorse Polk.[17]

A bandwagon for James K. Polk swiftly developed in Middle and Lower Souths. The more Southerners thought about Texas, the more glorious became racial, economic, political, and military boons of Tyler's treaty. Moreover, fear of English manipulation of Texas increased as the campaign progressed, for a new and more sensible theory became omnipresent about how England would intervene.

Abel P. Upshur had anticipated the shift in southern concern. Upshur's first fear, that England would pressure Mexico into pressing Texas to emancipate, had lost its hold on the Virginian even before he pressed Sam Houston into negotiating. Upshur had then envisioned an upsetting second scenario: England would drop its suggestions to Mexico, hoping that a permanently independent Texas would emancipate slaves. Movements of English population to English-protected Texas would succeed where diplomatic ultimatums would fail.

Bases for Upshur's initial apprehension about England pressuring Mexico evaporated the summer after Upshur died. Lord Aberdeen came to realize that the tactic enraged Americans, inspired annexation, and thus made an independent Texas less likely. Aberdeen also came to see that England could hardly pressure Mexico to make emancipation in Texas a precondition for independence, since England had already unconditionally recognized enslaved Texas.

The better way, Aberdeen realized, was to forget about emancipation until Texas secured independence. Then England might quietly help accomplish abolition. By explicitly repudiating former antislavery gestures, Aberdeen would take the heat out of Calhoun's steaming rhetoric; and by helping Texas achieve independence, England would chill Sam Houston's interest in annexation. Aberdeen even toyed with a so-called Diplomatic Act, whereby France and England would guarantee whatever boundaries Mexico and Texas agreed on.[18]

Aberdeen's June 3, 1844, letter to his American Minister Richard Pakenham both answered Calhoun's famous Pakenham Letter and tested the proposed Diplomatic Act on England's man in Washington. "Her Majesty's Government," declared Aberdeen, "have no intention to *press at this time* the abolition of . . . slavery on . . . Texas." Nor would England "press the Government of Mexico to make the abolition of domestic slavery a *sine qua non* . . . for the recognition" of Texas. "But Her Majesty's Government, although abstaining from such interference, do not the less deplore . . . slavery, . . . and they reserve themselves the right, . . . *wherever they may think it expedient* . . . to offer friendly counsel to Texas to take measures for the ultimate liberation of the country from the stain and calamity of domestic slavery." Aberdeen closed by "again unequivocally" reiterating "that counsel alone, and not dictation, would be employed" (emphasis mine).[19]

Aberdeen's underling in Washington had the good sense not to hand Calhoun this letter. Pakenham also kept to himself Aberdeen's language about forbearing only "at this time" from offering Texas "friendly counsel" about "the ultimate liberation of the country from the stain and calamity of domestic slavery." Pakenham instead officially informed Calhoun that Aberdeen had dropped "friendly counsel" to Mexico. Pakenham also shot back a letter to Aberdeen, warning that the proposed Diplomatic Act would hasten annexation. Aberdeen dropped the plan.[20]

The British foreign secretary was now reduced to one antislavery scenario. After enslaved Texas became permanently independent, English settlers, ideas, and cash might propel Texans towards emancipation. That remnant of a position looked to Southern Democrats to be the worst threat yet. As Thomas Ritchie's *Richmond Enquirer* explained such fears on June 29, 1844, if Texas became permanently independent with England's help, "thousands of voters," Englishmen with antislavery inclinations, would flow to England's new protectorate. The new Texans, "at the ballot box, will as effectually accomplish the object [of emancipation] as if it were made a formal article" of a treaty with England and Mexico. Only annexation, concluded Ritchie, could guarantee slavery's survival on our southwestern flank.[21]

Ritchie's conclusion, confirming Upshur's final judgment, remains cogent in retrospect. With hindsight as at the time, one could endlessly dispute whether England could have induced Mexico to induce non-annexed Texas to emancipate. But slavery could indisputably have become shaky in a permanently non-annexed Lone Star Republic, especially if a Texas-England rapprochement had blossomed. American slaveholders would scarcely have moved many slaves into such a dangerous situation, not with all the uninhabited river valleys still left in the southern United States, not when American law barred the importation of slaves from foreign nations. The unintended consequence of the once-again-critical African slave trade edict was that American slaves brought to the foreign republic of Texas could not be legally dispatched back across the border, if English antislavery did advance. Not "propaganda" but the logic of the situation lay behind fears that only nonslaveholders would migrate to a permanently independent Texas. That population movement would make slaves, never relatively prevalent anyway, even more inconsequential.

I have "never feared the *direct* interference of England with slavery in Texas," claimed Albert T. Burnley, who in 1844–5 twice repeated his earlier warning to his partner in Texas slaveholding pursuits, Virginia's Beverley Tucker. But Burnley had worried before and did currently "fear, in case annexation is rejected," that only nonslaveholders will migrate to Texas. Then "the people of Texas (encouraged by England) will themselves abolish slavery by the Ballot Box."

Burnley urged Tucker to think again about what they "had best do in such a contingency." The Texas entrepreneur knew "it is generally thought that we cannot bring our" slaves back across the United States border. Maybe the partners could break the American law. But our enterprise, concluded Burnley, like the institution of slavery in Texas, is "very uncertain."[22] That all-too-plausible uncertainty about unannexed Texas made Southern Democrats' case for annexation in mid-1844 the more treacherous for Henry Clay to ignore.

– 7 –

In late July 1844, a month after Thomas Ritchie's *Richmond Enquirer* warned of England's possible new departure, Henry Clay issued a new public letter on annexation. In this so-called Alabama Letter, Clay declared "no personal objection to the annexation of Texas." He would "be glad to see it, without dishonor, without war, [and] with the common consent of the Union." Even antislavery Americans should consent to annexation, counseled Clay, for slaveholders' migration towards the Caribbean tropics would eventually doom slavery in Texas, as in the South. The institution "is destined to become extinct, at some distant day, in my opinion by the operation of the inevitable laws of population. It would be unwise to refuse a permanent acquisition ... on account of a temporary institution."[23]

Northern Whigs, enraged by Clay's newly announced personal preference for Texas, accused Clay of waffling from his previous opposition to annexation. A slight waffle had occurred. In his April 1844 Raleigh Letter, Clay had said nothing about Texas's desirability under any circumstances. He had only discussed Texas's undesirability under present circumstances.

But Clay's overriding consistency revealed more about the man and his Border South world than did his slight shift. He retained his previous position that only "general concurrence" made slavery-related laws viable. "The paramount duty of preserving the Union intact," Clay continued to emphasize, demanded opposing any slavery law which either section found undesirable.

Southerners noted all these qualifications on Clay's endorsement of possible future annexation. Northerners noted the endorsement itself. With everyone unhappier, the politician who had inched slightly forward inched slightly back. In September 1844, Clay issued still another public letter. This time, he de-emphasized possible future circumstances and re-emphasized opposition to annexation under present circumstances.[24] Once again, opponents said he flip-flopped. Once again they were slightly right. But once again, Henry Clay's consistent opposition to Texas, should the North object now or in the future, courted political defeat in Deep South areas where Whigs had for a decade been gaining.

Whig campaigners, desperate to avoid disaster in the Lower South, had few options, all poor. Several Southern Whigs repeated Waddy Thompson's argument that the safety valve would depopulate the South and thus weaken the Slavepower. More urged that Clay, once President, would act on his personal desire for Texas. Most avoided the subject and stressed Whig commercial policies.[25]

Poor economic times invited that stress. The debilitating cotton depression, the worst and most prolonged in antebellum southern history, was lifting some-what but still hovering as it had been for seven long years. In 1840, Whigs had rallied hard-pressed agriculturalists to demand more from their national gov-ernment than the passive burial of national funds in federal basement vaults. In 1844, Southern Whigs dared to add that protective tariffs might protect south-ern farmers. Prohibitive taxes on imported manufactured cotton goods might boost demand for the South's glut of cotton, since protected American textile factories might expand. Southerners now "very generally considered" free trade "an 'obsolete idea,'" Robert Toombs, Georgia's favorite young Whig, gloated privately to the faction's senior senator, John Berrien.[26]

Toombs here displayed too much youthful enthusiasm about free trade becoming a relic for slaveholders. Yet southern attitudes about the national state were changing. Calhoun's followers now sought national power to shore up slavery on southern fringes. Then why not shore up markets at the southern core?

The question highlighted the southern lesson of 1844. One essence of Southern Whiggery, its faith in using governments state and national to bolster commercial markets, was never more appropriate, never more stressed—and not remotely enough. The trouble was that traditional Whiggery rallied some 45% of southern voters—and 45% was not 50%. In presidential election years, stress on loyalty to slavery could secure the last 5%. That is why southern cries of disloyalty abounded in weeks and sometimes months before a President was elected—and why those periodic cries are such a poor guide to why the solid

45% of each party's constituency remained true to partisan allegiances, no matter what slavery issue came up.

The swing vote remained crucial. In 1836 and 1840, Southern Whigs' skill at loyalty politics had helped secure those elusive final percentage points separating narrow victory from narrow defeat. But in 1836 and 1840 when the New Yorker Van Buren ran against the Tennessean Hugh White and then the Virginia native William Henry Harrison, loyalty debates had focused on a matter congenial to Southern Whiggery: whose candidates were born furthest southwards? Now in 1844, loyalty politics featured a matter devastating to Southrons in John Quincy Adams's party: Which national alliance could secure proslavery legislation? In 1844, Whigs stood damned as soft on Texas, therefore soft on slavery.

Arguments about commercial markets could not then move enough commercial farmers. Worse, annexation was itself a glorious ruling-class economic issue, offering visions of virgin land for slaveholders and multiple buyers for slaves. Worse still, Texas, a landowner's as well as a slaveholder's mecca, offered sublime vistas to nonslaveholders. The Lone Star Republic was the newest New World epitome of vast, cheap, fertile land for the downtrodden. Precisely that lure of wide-open prairies made nonslaveholding English migrants potentially devastating to slavery's prospects in Texas, should American annexation fail.

American development after *American* annexation made more sense to Southerners of all classes. Poor Henry Clay, when he tried to claim a morsel of that solid southern sense for himself, became apostle of nonsense to Northern Whigs.

– 8 –

No wonder, then, that in November 1844, James K. Polk reversed a decade of growth for the Whig Party in the Lower South. Where Hugh Lawson White had carried Georgia in 1836 and William Henry Harrison had added Mississippi and Louisiana in 1840, Clay lost every state in the Deep South. Where White had picked up 48.5% of Deep South popular votes in 1836 and Harrison had soared to 52.3% in 1840, Clay's share sank to 45.4% in 1844.[27]

In Border and Middle Souths, Clay managed to hang on to the five states Harrison had captured in 1840. But the Whig Upper South margin of victory narrowed ominously. Tennessee, home state of Hickories Old and New but a Whig bastion since 1836, now belonged to the Whigs by only 113 votes of some 120,000 cast. Even in the Border South, the Whig percentage sank from 55.7% in 1840 to 50.5% in 1844, the party's weakest showing since 1828.

Clay did much less well than Harrison in the North too.[28] The shift from John C. Calhoun's mentality to James K. Polk's enabled Democrats to claim, rightly, that their candidate was no Slavepower expansionist. Polk wanted Oregon as much as Texas, and California even more. He would oust England everywhere west of the present United States. A presidential campaign for national imperialism divorced from a southern crusade for slavery, a political impossibility in 1844 until the Tyler administration forced the issue and Southern Democrats forced an expansionist candidate, had now become a promising northern reality.

Promising, at least, in the four midwestern states of Ohio, Michigan, Illinois, and Indiana. In this northwestern corner, Democratic campaigners truly were the Manifest Destiny spokesmen unfortunately painted as everywhere omnipresent in latter-day history textbooks. In the Midwest, Polk partisans called acquisition of Texas and Oregon not a southern but a western concern, replete with free land for frontiersmen and safety for American frontiers. That argument helped turn around the two parties' fortunes in the four midwestern states. In 1840, Van Buren had been overwhelmed in Ohio and had won only Illinois, very narrowly. In 1844, Polk overwhelmed Clay in Illinois and lost only Ohio, very narrowly. Throughout the quartet of midwestern states, Democrats' total popular vote rose 20% between 1840 and 1844, while Whigs' rose only 4%.

East of Ohio, Northern Democrats were more chary of Manifest Destiny. In New York, Silas Wright, second only to Van Buren in Van Burenite hearts, ran for governor. Wright espoused the Little Magician's salutory stall rather than James K. Polk's immediate annexationism. "But a few years will pass," Wright predicted, before Oregon and Texas could be "peacefully and honorably" annexed.[29] While Wright honorably stalled on Texas, Democratic politicians in New York and Pennsylvania hustled to court new foreign voters in New York and Philadelphia slums. Henry Clay would blame his defeat on first-time immigrant voters' surge to the Democracy, a ghetto voting wave utterly unlike midwestern farmers surging towards frontier expansionism.

Still, while nothing so simple as a northern referendum on Texas occurred, the issue hurt Clay more than he admitted. The election was so close that little things meant much. Clay's slight waffles on Texas might well have led a few disgusted Northern Whigs to stay home on Election Day. Only a comparative handful of stay-at-homes could have turned the election around, for Polk won by only 5,106 out of 470,062 votes in New York and by only 3,422 out of 52,096 votes in Michigan. The shift of these states' 41 electoral votes would have transformed a 170-105 Polk Electoral College victory into a 146-129 Clay triumph.

To complicate analysis of why Clay lost this election in the North even further, those Yankee Whigs turned off by Clay's Texas waffling had an alternative to staying home. They could vote for the non-waffling third-party candidate, the Liberty Party's James K. Birney. The ex-Kentucky slaveholder pledged never to annex Texas or any other slave territory. Birney picked up 3,632 votes in Michigan and 15,812 in New York, enough ballots to swing both states and thus the election to Polk, assuming Birneyites otherwise would have voted for Clay.

That assumption, unfortunately, is debatable. Birney, a Democrat, was an attractive protest candidate for Jacksonians who disliked Polk's annexationism.

Then again, those Northern Whigs who thought anti-annexationism more important than old Jackson-Whig issues perhaps seized on Birney's candidacy to make that statement.

Amidst all this haze about whether immigrants' votes or Birney's candidacy or Clay's waffling or annexationism's midwestern appeals deprived Whigs of a northern victory, two conclusions remained clear. First of all, northern voters had nothing like demanded Manifest Destiny. While Polk secured 14,838 more Yankee votes than Clay, the anti-annexation candidates, Clay and Birney, together secured 47,462 more northern votes than Polk. Secondly, Polk's formula of desectionalizing Texas and nationalizing expansionism had certainly not killed off the Northern Democracy.

Van Burenites would more likely kill off the national party if they blocked Democrats' southern electoral mandate. Martin Van Buren had promised to follow the election returns in formulating future annexation policy. His northern crowd might now have to bow to southern decision, assuming James K. Polk could keep Texas annexation divorced from Slavepower domineering.

CHAPTER 25

The Congressional Decision

Unfortunately for Van Burenites, Texas and Slavepower aggression could not be kept separate. When the lame-duck Congress returned to Washington in December 1844, the lame-duck Tyler administration reiterated that Senate and House could and should admit Texas by simple majorities.

Tyler and Calhoun's proposal, branded as proslavery because coming from them, soon bore a worse Slavepower taint. A few Southern Whigs sought to reverse electoral defeats they had suffered from being labeled soft on Texas. They would enable Texas, once admitted to the Union, to balloon into five slave states.

– 1 –

On January 13, 1845, Whig Congressman Milton Brown of Tennessee introduced an amendment to the Tyler-proposed joint House-Senate resolutions admitting Texas by simple majorities. Brown's amendment would allow Texas state legislators to carve out of their now-to-be-admitted state up to four areas, each automatically to be admitted as future states. The surviving segment of Texas could remain a fifth state.

The House eventually made explicit Brown's implicit indication that a chunk lying wholly north of the Missouri Compromise 36°30′ line could only be admitted as a free state. But as in the Missouri Compromise, any chunk south of 36°30′ would be admitted, slave or free, as inhabitants desired. The principles of the nation's most sacred compromise, cheered Milton Brown, would avoid future controversy over division of Texas.[1]

Some compromise, scoffed Northerners. The relatively tiny area of vast Texas north of the 36°30′ line was widely considered both uninhabitable and not legitimately part of Texas. Should that inconsequential segment ever be peopled and established as legitimate Texas turf, the region still could not become a free state unless the Texas legislature agreed to let erring brothers go.

440

Texas solons could meanwhile arrange for four enslaved chunks to be cut off south of 36°30′. The remaining part of Texas, including all area north of 36°30′, could remain a fifth slaveholding state.

Milton Brown's ultra-southern Texas proposal recalled Maryland Whig Congressman William Cost Johnson's ultra-tight gag rule proposition. With Texas, as with the gag, anti-party extremists first pressured Southern Democrats to push Northern Democrats. In both cases, however, pressure reached its climax when Southern Whigs competed with Southern Democrats to see who could do most for slavery.

Behind Milton Brown's climactic imperiousness lay Southern Whigs' frustration at Texas politics. The combination of Northern Whigs unwilling to compromise and Southern Democrats eager to secure uncompromising annexation had lately left Southern Whigs haplessly hiding from an inescapable issue. Only in normally Whig Georgia were resulting losses worse than in Milton Brown's Tennessee, usually a Whig stronghold, now a spot where Clay's 1844 margin over Polk was all of 0.01% of votes cast. The Milton Browns felt compelled to reverse this electoral trend before it overwhelmed them.

Joseph H. Peyton, a Tennessee Whig congressman who supported Milton Brown's plan, explained the partisan strategy privately to a political titan back home. Brown's addendum to Democrats' annexation proposal, Peyton cheered, was "well calculated to trip the heels" of Tennessee Democrats and "to prevent them from making capital out of a question that should never have been made a party question." Under our plan to turn the one slave state of Texas into five, "the South could acquire a wonderful increase in political power." Nothing could better "check the infernal spirit of abolitionism."[2]

When publicly defending their strategy for out-doing the Democracy, Milton Brown's Southern Whig supporters demonstrated that they shared Southern Democrats' claustrophobic mentality. Both Whig Senator Ephraim Foster of Tennessee, who wrote Brown's amendment, and Whig Congressman Alexander Stephens of Georgia, who helped guide the measure through the House, presented illuminating addresses. Both the Tennessean and the Georgian were from customary Whig strongholds lost or almost lost in the 1844 elections. Both were eager to strike back at Democrats' damning charge that they were soft on Texas. Yet neither wished to be seen as devoted to slavery. By agitating for annexation while apologizing for slavery, Foster and Stephens deepened the portrait of a trapped world longing for escape valves.

Democrats, charged both these Southern Whig congressmen, endangered the South and the Union by evading the question of Texas's future division. So enormous a land mass invited separation. That controversy could devastate the South. The majority North, declared Foster, would "wash out the stain of slavery" as a condition of dividing Texas. The South, already trapped on its northern flank "and driven back to the shores of the Gulf of Mexico," would next be "commanded to take the water." Foster "for one, answered—No!" The Southern Whig called "upon every" southern senator to "draw the sword" for multiple slave states from Texas.

From this highpoint of southern righteousness, Foster descended to stagger around the question of slaveholders' rectitude. I am, he said, "no advocate of slavery in the abstract. Undoubtedly slavery was an evil." The curse had been "fastened upon us and could not be got rid of." Still, Foster bragged, when "he went home," his "slaves come to him with words of affection and love." Fanatics would insufferably "destroy all these associations."[3]

Alexander Stephens's torturous path towards southern righteousness reveals even more than Ephraim Foster's, for little Alec would soon become a soaring proslavery orator. In 1845, however, Alexander Stephens declared himself "no defender of slavery in the abstract. Liberty always had charms for me." The Georgia congressman had no wish to see slavery "extended to other countries." But "a stern necessity, bearing the marks and impress of the hand of the Creator himself," kept southern blacks enslaved. By adding representatives of already enslaved Texas to slaveholders' congressional contingent, Stephens would expand not slavery but the South's power over its own predicament.[4]

Ephraim Foster and Alec Stephens, like so many apologetic Southerners at the time of Texas, lived on that nervous borderline between shame and pride. They found slavery a festering danger to southern moral, economic, and racial health. They also found outside agitators who would imprison them with free blacks unconscionable. They were proudly forging safety valves for excess slaves and decent relationships with familial servants. And how were their pains rewarded? With northern cries that they were despicable tyrants and that their safety valves must be sealed off!

To add to the fury of the Alexander Stephenses, Democrats had won an electoral landslide by conflating Southern Whigs with the South's worst tormentors, John Quincy Adams and holier-than-thou New England Whigs. Stephens, Foster, and Brown would set the record straight. They would defy Northern Whigs who sounded and acted as if Southerners were depraved. They would bolster slaveholders' control over slavery's fate five times more than Democrats' mere annexation. With that determination, and the resulting Milton Brown Amendment, yet more Southerners, with yet more pride at handling their shame, proposed yet another safety valve, and in the proposing made Texas a southern salvation still harder for Northerners to stomach.

– 2 –

Southern Democrats, as usual, would not allow Whigs to become more successfully aggressive on slavery-related matters. A few of you may be able to propose better southern defenses, Democrats taunted the Milton Browns and Alexander Stephenses, as they had taunted William Cost Johnson on his extreme gag rule proposal. But your party tilts too far northwards to pass anything leaning southwards. Only the Democratic Party can secure a boon to slaveholders because only Southern Democrats can force northern allies to heel.

Southern Democrats were right. Just about every Northern Whig scorned this latest Slavepower power grab. Their Yankee wing's intransigence led most

Southern Whigs in the House to run away from Milton Brown. Among Border South Whig congressmen, no one voted for the Brown Amendment. Even in Middle and Lower Souths, Milton Brown could manage only an even split of Whig congressmen.

Democrats saved Milton Brown Whiggery. Southern Democrats voted to add Brown's amendment to the joint congressional resolution admitting Texas 59-1. Northern Democrats concurred, 50-30. As usual, Lower North Democrats were the South's best allies, voting 33-5 to allow Texas to carve itself into five states. Meanwhile, Upper North Democrats voted Northern Whigs' way, 25-17. So by a vote of 118-101, Milton Brown's future-division amendment was added to the joint congressional resolution admitting Texas by simple majorities. The House then approved the amended joint resolution, with the National Democracy again powering the Slavepower and only eight of 26 Southern Whigs concurring with Milton Brown.[5]

– 3 –

The amended joint resolution now faced a harder test in the Senate. While the South-leaning Democratic Party controlled the House by almost a two-to-one majority, the North-leaning Whig Party controlled the Senate, 28-24. The previous June, this same Senate had scuttled Tyler's treaty of annexation 35-16, with one Northern Democrat abstaining. Only 15 to 24 Democrats and one of 28 Whigs had voted aye. The Whig Lone Ranger was John Henderson of Mississippi. Even if every Democrat now joined Henderson in approving the far more southern package of Texas plus the Brown Amendment, two more Whig senators would be needed for Whiggery, Milton Brown style, to pass.

Southern Whig senators, usually powerless in their party and on the Senate floor, for once could determine a historic outcome. The faction rose to the occasion. Its few members creatively debated among themselves whether the imprisoned South should risk a break for Texas, and whether Southern Whigs should risk a bolt to the Southern Democrats. The result was the most sophisticated discussion yet of that southern claustrophobia everywhere underlying Texas annexation.

These Whig sophisticates were no ivory tower intellectuals. Like Milton Brown and House compatriots, Southern Whig senators were primarily politicians in a tight squeeze. The few Whig senators who supported annexation gloomed most about allowing Southern Democrats all the glory over Texas. The many Southern Whig senators who held the line against Slavepower expansionism worried most about the party-shattering consequences of defying Northern Whigs. Still, the very way these politicoes publicly rationalized their positions indicates again that Southern Democrats' views about Texas had partially infected their opponents.

Senator William Archer of Virginia was the most conflicted Southern Whig, for he relished Robert Walker's safety valve while deploring John C. Calhoun's majoritarianism. Archer, a sometimes Tyler confidant and chairman of the

Committee on Foreign Relations, had told the Senate back in June 1844 that an Upper South world of "mere grain and vegetable production" required a "drain for slave labor in Texas" to achieve "the highest advantage." His constituents also faced race war à la San Domingo without "the appropriate drain for their redundant slaves."[6]

But in February 1845, William Archer emphasized that he feared King Numbers more than he valued the safety valve. Archer trembled at "the will, however transitory or excited, of a numerical majority." The gullible mob was putty in the hands of that "worst of all earthly mischiefs, demagogues, usurping . . . the will of the numerical majority for their own purposes."

The Founding Fathers, cheered this Virginia Whig, had counterpoised a Senate based on property against a House based on numbers. This aristocratic chamber had sole power to decide whether a treaty adding more numbers to the Union should be ratified. A one-third senatorial minority could halt expansive treaties. The South, still possessing over one-third the senators, could safeguard the Constitution at just the point Northerners could swell King Numbers into an absolute despot.

Now, winced William Archer, John C. Calhoun would demolish this minority protection in the name of rallying a simple majority for a joint resolution admitting a slave state. Archer preferred to remember that simple majorities could destroy permanent minorities. No boon such as the safety valve was worth allowing the North dictatorship over how, when, and where American mobocracy would balloon.[7]

William Archer here summoned Abel P. Upshur's principles against Upshur's successors' attempt to detour around the unachievable two-thirds majority for an annexation treaty. In all those years as an almost somebody back in Accomac County, Judge Upshur had called the Constitution the only states' rights hope against King Numbers and demagogical retainers. After becoming Secretary of State, Upshur had played the long shot that annexation might enable states' rights ideologues to oust demagogues and rally mobs.

Archer shuddered at such a gamble. He would love to have Texas, but only the safe constitutional way, by a two-thirds ratification of a treaty. In the name of salvaging minority principle, he would restrain the encircled minority from securing its vital Texas outlet by an illegitimate simple majority.

A couple of Deep South Whig senators, John Berrien of Georgia and Alexander Barrow of Louisiana, attacked the Tyler administration's maneuver more totally than could the Middle South's William Archer because they distrusted Robert Walker's safety valve.[8] An outlet to Texas enabling the South's slaves to drain away looked to these gentlemen like one of those nineteenth-century bleedings fatal to the patient. Berrien and Barrow admitted the South was ill. Because of overproduction, said Louisiana's Alexander Barrow, cotton prices were low. But could prices "be raised by adding to the Union the finest cotton region in the world?" The slave drain from the aging South, regretted Georgia's John Berrien, made slaveholding states increasingly scarce. But would Southerners who rushed to Texas strengthen an institution thereby "shorn of its strength" in "Maryland, Virginia, North Carolina, Kentucky, and Tennessee?"

A South dumping population and wealth through the safety valve, emphasized Berrien and Barrow, would miss the constitutional protections traded for Texas. Fewer southern states would mean greater northern power and vaster free labor commonwealths, increasingly capable of annexing yet more free areas by simple majorities. Southern states' rights "would be placed at the mercy of that most tyrannical of all tyrannical kings, King Numbers."

King Numbers! Calhoun's words, again and again thrown back at Calhoun, emphasized how much Mr. Nullifier had changed. The Carolinian no longer positioned himself where he had stood in the Post Office Controversy, attacking Andrew Jackson's proposed federal censorship of abolitionist mailings, lest majoritarian power later damage the slavocracy. Calhoun now wanted the federal majority's hands heavily laid on a southern hinterland where he judged slaveholders were fatally weak.

In response to his old dirge that the federal power deployed could come back to haunt the South, Calhoun implicitly answered that slaveholders must gamble. Federally secured Texas was vitally needed to shield the South's vulnerable outposts from enemies beyond the gates—beyond the ocean. Compared with this new Calhoun, William Archer, John Berrien, and Alexander Barrow were like old turtles, receding back into crusty constitutional shells.

Calhoun's advantage was that in the 1844 elections, black-belt voters had voted for annexation. Three Whig senators took the lesson to heart. John Henderson of Mississippi, who alone among Whigs had voted for John Tyler's treaty, was now joined by William Merrick of Maryland and Henry Johnson of Louisiana in voting to admit Texas by a simple majority.

The trio of Whigs believed the South must have the Texas outlet. Confine blacks "within narrow limits" and allow multiplying slaves to become "so much more numerous than the whites," emphasized Maryland's William Merrick, and "I cannot contemplate with composure the scene."[9] A South overcrowded with blacks, added Mississippi's John Henderson, would be the more vulnerable to antislavery agitators encamped just beyond. An "Anglo-American" population in Texas, "alien in interest, policy, and nationality," would be "a nucleous, a place of refuge, to which the discontents of our country will resort." And why must Southerners tolerate this incendiary British encampment on their hinterlands? Because, Henderson scoffed, Yankee moralists wished "the slavery interest . . . pressed a little more to the wall," and slaveholders "rendered a little more uneasy."[10]

John Henderson's two new allies, previously his opponents on Tyler's treaty, had lately suffered Democrats' charges that only southern traitors would back anti-Slavepower Whigs against Texas. With relief and resentment, these Southern Whigs now condemned Northern Whigs who had embarrassed them. "Opposition" to Texas, "proceeding from" the northern "*quarter,* for such" an anti-southern "purpose," declared Louisiana's Henry Johnson, "had operated powerfully" to push him towards annexation.[11]

Henry Johnson, convert to annexationism, and Alexander Barrow, still against admitting Texas, were both slavery's defenders. The two Louisiana Whig senators differed only on the best strategy for slaveholders entrapped.

Alexander Barrow, along with John Berrien of Georgia and William Archer of Virginia, believed that escape via safety valves and majorities of one would lead to more hopeless imprisonment. Henry Johnson, along with John Henderson of Mississippi and William Merrick of Maryland, believed that a healthy civilization must cut past cagers, however dangerous the jail break. Both sides in this debate made their cases cogently. The thwarted slaveholder omnipresent in all debaters' rhetoric seemed endangered whether he charged or retreated.[12]

That intellectual stalemate aside—and Southerners could not put aside anxiety about prisons from which there were no good escapes—Southern Whigs' confrontation with each other yielded a political victor. In a Senate split 28-24 the Whigs' way, the three Whigs who deserted an overwhelmingly anti-annexationist party altered the balance of power. Assuming *every* Democratic senator now massed behind Milton Brown's gift to slaveholders, John C. Calhoun would secure a narrow—and perchance dangerous—conquest of King Numbers.

– 4 –

Missouri's Thomas Hart Benton would not allow such a Slavepower triumph. Benton, George McDuffie's antagonist in the previous session and the only Southern Democrat who had voted no on the annexation treaty, would never vote yes on an annexation still more slavery-oriented. Where Milton Brown wished to allow annexed Texas to turn itself into five slave states, Thomas Hart Benton wanted Texas, if annexed, to be split equally into slave and free areas.[13] As Benton had explained to Missouri constituents the previous summer, he relished annexation, "but for none of the negro reasons—or as it ought to be pronounced on this occasion, *nigger* reasons."[14]

Northern Van Buren Democrats considered only Benton's Negro-free annexationism acceptable. These Yankee partisans remained bitter that Southern Democrats had dumped Van Buren for rejecting immediate annexation. Now Southerners' demands had escalated more insufferably, just as had happened with gag rules. "What have northern men ever gained by yielding to" such demands? asked Senator John Niles of Connecticut. "What did Van Buren get for his strong leaning to southern interests, so as to bring upon him the reproach of Northern man with Southern principles?" John Niles could favor Texas only Thomas Hart Benton's way, "as a great national question." He could not tolerate Milton Brown's "hateful" transformation of annexation into so much "a southern question and a slavery question" as to wreck "the Democratic Party of the North."[15]

Southern Bentonians and Northern Van Burenites came to realize that while Brown's potential future division of Texas into five slave states seemed too southern, Benton's freeing of half a slave republic seemed too Yankee. Thomas Hart Benton's realization was especially acute. In January 1845, the Missouri legislature instructed the state's senators and representatives to secure annexation, Slavepower-style.[16] Benton, who forever tiptoed on the edge of being not southern enough even for not-very-southern Missouri, now struck himself as precariously north of his constituents. On February 5, 1845, he edged southwards. He dropped his proposed division of Texas into slave and free territories. He instead introduced a resolution silent on future divisions and calling for fresh negotiations with Texas as to boundaries and other matters.[17]

Benton's proposed new negotiations would erase the taint of the Tyler administration's old slavery-motivated negotiations. A new treaty would also be shorn of the taunt of Milton Brown's five-part potential division. Bentonian annexation would moreover require that two-thirds of the Senate consent to the revised diplomatic accord. The Missourian's wording thus offered national annexation with judicious delay, without surrender to the South, and with the possibility of rejecting any new treaty.

Southern Democrats, denouncing these latest delays and maybes, continued to insist on immediacy and Brown's possible future dividends. Meanwhile, many Northern Democrats dug in their heels behind Benton's salutory stall and golden silence about future divisions. Texas, which could not be annexed even by a simple majority without unanimous Democratic Party support, seemed to be joining the just-scrapped gag rule as a casualty of more southern pressure than Northern Democrats could bear.

– 5 –

The impasse paralyzed the Polk administration before the President-elect could take office. James K. Polk, concerned, negotiated secretly to unite his party. The not-yet-President's private promises remain obscure. But Polk supported a sleight of hand worthy of the Little Magician. Congress, ran the magic formula first devised by Robert Walker, should authorize the President to administer either Thomas Hart Benton's or Milton Brown's versions of annexation. The chief executive could come to the decision which senatorial Democrats lacked the unanimity to make.

For irreconcilable factions to unite behind this nondecision, each group had to believe the imminent President would decide on their version of annexation. Polk, a skilled political dissimulator, left each side with the impression he would administer their policy. Polk meant what he said to Southerners and meant to appear friendly to the Van Burenite faction. Van Buren partisans came away convinced the President-elect would follow Benton's route to annexation. Southern Democrats trusted the Tennessee slaveholder to administer the policy of his fellow Tennessean, Milton Brown. The last inch towards annexation, Abel P. Upshur's dream, required one of those dissimulating politicos, Cuffee-like all things to all voters, which Upshur had introduced annexation to destroy.[18]

On February 27, six days before Polk's inauguration, the Senate voted 27-25 to admit Texas according to Tyler's formula of simple majorities and to give the President the choice of accomplishing that end Brown's or Benton's way. All Democrats and the three turncoat Whigs, Merrick of Maryland, Johnson of Louisiana, and Henderson of Mississippi, voted aye. All Northern Whigs and 12 Southern Whigs voted nay.[19]

The next day, the Democrat-controlled House concurred in the Senate compromise by almost a strict party vote.[20] The Whig count was especially revealing. Of the eight Southern House Whigs who had previously voted for the Milton Brown Amendment, six, including Brown, now voted against annexation possibly with the Brown Amendment, one, Georgia's Alexander Stephens, abstained, and only one, Alabama's James Dellet, voted for the possibility of Texas becoming five slave states.

The Milton Browns had to retreat because their Whiggish bid for Texas had only consolidated Democrats' claim to the treasure. More clearly than ever, Brown's proposition had demonstrated that Democrats had the votes to swell Slavepower and Whigs did not. Teaching counterproductive political lessons at home and infuriating Southern Whigs' best northern friends was no way to escape political claustrophobia. The Milton Browns preferred to cut their losses, disavow their momentary venting of frustration, get with the emerging Whig principle of no further expansionism, and hope that gigantic Texas would satiate Southerners' expansionist appetites.

– 6 –

After the House-Senate joint resolution gave the President his option on annexation, almost everyone thought the next move was the President-elect's. They forgot that His Accidency still resided in the White House. Pushing the historic process he had begun to completion seemed to John Tyler the soul of statecraft as well as a boost for reputation. Delay might encourage the impatient Sam Houston to turn toward England. Benton's formula, new negotiations and then a new senatorial debate on ratification, at very least meant delay. Why give Polk carte blanche to choose an option which might push Texas towards Lord Aberdeen? So thinking, and under Calhoun's urging, President Tyler, on the eve of departing the White House, dispatched a courier to Houston City, offering Texas admission to the Union under Milton Brown's formula for possible future division.[21]

Outraged Van Burenites attacked Tyler for "stealing" a decision Congress had meant to award to Polk. But a commodity retained has not been stolen. Polk still could recall the courier bearing Tyler's decision. On March 7, the new President in fact ordered the old President's courier to halt, pending further orders.[22] Three days later, Polk, after consulting his cabinet, made his decision, *the* decision. Tyler's courier should proceed.[23]

Polk concurred with Tyler's reasons as well as Tyler's reversible decision. Had negotiations been reopened, per Benton's plan, Polk privately explained, "great delay would necessarily have taken place, giving ample opportunities to *British* and *French* intrigues to have seriously embarrassed, if not defeated annexation."[24] Among important southern annexationists, Polk was the least fanatical about slavery on southwestern fringes, about Aberdeen's antislavery gestures, about sparseness of bondage in Texas, and so on. Yet even he, significantly, thought European intrigues made settling the issue a matter of *immediate* crisis.

The only British intriguer wholeheartedly committed to abolition in Texas now escalated his intrigues. Charles Elliot, it will be remembered, was that English chargé in Texas who had sent Pearl Andrews as his messenger to England. Elliot now appointed himself messenger to Mexico. Elliot sought and secured a 90-day delay in Texas's answer to America, so that he might seek Mexico's offer of permanent independence. Then the Lone Star Republic could choose between a secure republican destiny inside or outside the American republic.

Under cover of an absurdly big white hat, Elliot arrived unrecognized in Mexico City. Under the gun of annexation, Mexican authorities agreed to Elliot's proposition. The Texas people could stand free of Mexico, as long as Texans stood free of America.

Elliot, still hiding under the huge hat, marched back on Houston City. This time the camouflage was spotted and the plotter identified. No matter, thought the underling. History has been shaped my, I mean my Lordships' way.[25]

Their lordships differed. Elliot's superiors blasted their underling for an unauthorized intervention they called sure to anger America and make annexation more likely.[26] Their reasoning, unworthy of educated peers, again showed them to be chary abolitionists. America, having already voted to annex, needed no further shove towards annexation. Nor did Mexico, by offering Sam Houston's favorite alternative to annexation, push Texas towards accepting annexation. Elliot did what any determined abolitionist would. He played his last antislavery card. His skittish superiors showed for the last time that they were more worried about too dangerous an involvement with the New World.

Texans, when rejecting Mexico's offer of independence, illuminated a more important reason for Elliot's haplessness. Whatever their commitment to slavery, Texans had been committed to joining the North American slaveholding republic. Texas slaveholders could only falter if American slaveholders allowed their exposed southwestern flank to spin in the wind of England's cautious maneuvers. The game had accordingly always been the American South's to win, assuming the Upshurs and Calhouns convinced enough Southerners to force Northern Democrats' hand. After Southerners squeezed annexation out of the Democratic Party, Charles Elliot could only delay his defeat. On freedom's birthday, July 4, 1845, the Texas Convention virtually unanimously chose to consolidate enslaved Texas in enslaved America.[27] The question was now whether Mexico would permit American acquisition of Texas—and whether Mr. Polk would tolerate Mexico's continued clinging to California.

– 7 –

The answers, and the crises they provoked, would usher in what historians call the Age of Sectional Controversy. But the whole tale of Texas annexation had been an epic of sectional controversy, just as sectional controversy had sporadically festered within Jacksonian America. We have watched the sectionalizing of the Jackson Party as it unfolded, step by tiny step. It is well, after following each twist of a long journey, to step back and survey the terrain.

Andrew Jackson's Texas stand was an appropriate climax for a movement born disproportionately sectional. Jackson always attracted lopsided support in the far South and heavy opposition in the far North. Consequences were long hidden, for Jacksonian Democracy was born national too. Jackson's emphasis on white men's equality was gospel everywhere in the nation, outside the oldest, crustiest South. Jackson's removal of Indians and enslavement of blacks might seem anti-egalitarian to latter-day democrats. But in his time and especially in his Southwest, where democracy perished at the color line, "superior" whites' unequal power over "inferior" reds and blacks furthered chauvinists' ideal egalitarian republic.

Jackson's party organization institutionalized racially-selective egalitarianism. The party rallied white male commoners to shape decisions. The party also sought compromise between its factions, so that no white man unequally imposed his will on another. Jackson's spoils system, annointing every white Tom, Dick, and Harry as equally fit to rule, and his Bank War, assaulting Nicholas Biddle's unequal power over white folk, captured white egalitarian imaginations. John Quincy Adams and fellow Whigs were tagged with the unpardonable American label: undemocratic about whites.

Jackson's war on the Nullifiers also sustained racially selective egalitarianism. Old Hickory most disliked John C. Calhoun for wishing elitists to rule whites as well as reds and blacks. Where Jackson's New South, was removing malapportionment laws, Calhoun's Old Carolina was preserving extra power for richer whites. Unless wealthy folk could veto King Numbers on the national level too, believed Calhoun, all hierarchical authority, including slaveholders', was doomed.

Jackson, by opposing such anti-egalitarian Nullifiers, won the nation's white egalitarian heart all over again. But Martin Van Buren, the rightful heir for Jackson's King Numbers white republicanism, had trouble keeping Calhoun isolated. Emerging abolitionists, with their emphasis on universal equality, made Southerners nervous. James Hammond, no henchman of Calhoun's but as elitist a republican, introduced the gag rule to block uninhibited egalitarian discussion. For the first time, southern party politicians joined Calhoun supporters in urging more slaveholder control over white debate and decision than the three-fifths clause provided, lest control over blacks be lost.

Van Buren handled the anti-egalitarian demand the egalitarian way. He would isolate Calhounites with a compromise wherein neither Southern nor Northern Democrats dictated to the other. The resulting Pinckney Gag Rule violated white men's egalitarianism by somewhat restraining white republican debate. But precisely because the gag was compromised and no Southern Democrat imposed unconditional surrender on a Northern Democrat, the Democratic Party shakily salvaged its white egalitarian mission.

The mission faltered because Van Buren's compromised gag could not hold. Deep in Dixie, when the party system became truly competitive, rivals disputed how to ease apprehensions about outside meddlers. Van Buren's solution, compromise, invited the initial Southern Oppositionist/Whig response: compromising is disloyal. The result was yet another faction in the South, Whig added to Calhounite and Cooperite, occasionally putting pressure on Southern Democrats to support slavery all the way. The final consequence was William Cost Johnson's uncompromising gag rule and Southern Democrats' insistence that Northern Democrats unconditionally surrender to it. Northern Whigs, with absolutely no sympathy for their states' rights brethren, tore into this minority dictation. Northern Democrats, barely enough of them, reluctantly voted that Southerners who enslaved blacks could altogether gag whites.

Still, if the perfect gag rule weakened the Democracy's monopoly over white egalitarianism, the party's national hegemony and unity were barely damaged. The Gag Rule Controversy was a sideshow throughout the late 1830s and earliest 1840s, just as Jackson's post office censorship proposal was an aside in 1835. Bank controversies held center stage. Van Buren sustained control. Calhoun remained out.

Then came annexation, a crisis as important as the Bank War in defining Jacksonian "Democracy," a controversy as important as the Kansas-Nebraska affair in illuminating causes of the Civil War. Once again, as with congressional debate in the District of Columbia, Southerners worried about outside attack on a spot, this time pre-annexation Texas, where slavery was relatively lightly spread. Once again an Old South reactionary who condemned egalitarian white republicanism, this time Abel P. Upshur, provoked the controversy in order to save slavery the elitist way. Once again, Van Buren tried to compromise the white egalitarian way—with a national and democratic party arranging a settlement where no Southern Democrat dictated to a Northern Democrat.

But Van Buren again proved hapless in the face of southern anxiety about controlling blacks. Once again Calhoun's followers and a few Whigs, this time President Tyler and Congressman Milton Brown, pressured Southern Democrats to wring concessions from northern allies. Just enough Northern Democrats again whispered an ever more resentful You win. Northern Whigs issued an ever more thundering How undemocratic. And this time, on this pivotal Texas issue, Andrew Jackson sided with John C. Calhoun against Martin Van Buren.

What remained alien to Jacksonian "Democracy" was not just the joint annexation resolution ultimately passed, implicating the white egalitarian system in shoring up black slavery. Annexation was also inimical to Jacksonian "Democracy" because blackmailing southern minorities insisted that northern majorities cave in or else. Only Polk's dissembling could accomplish for the Democratic Party what nothing could accomplish for the Whigs: keep a national party united when imperious slaveholders lay down ultimatums.

The new centrality of the slavery issue achieved for Northern Whigs what no economic issue had previously effected: pin that curse word undemocratic all over Democrats. John Quincy Adams had his revenge. Agitation about the Slavepower's three-fifths clauses and gag rules and territorial lust was no longer a side issue. Jacksonian "Democracy" stood centrally for minority dictation to the majority, should the Slavepower find federal law necessary to protect slavery. The only trouble, from exultant Northern Whigs' perspective, was that Southern Whigs were as vulnerable for being part of an increasingly anti-southern party as Northern Democrats were vulnerable for being part of an increasingly pro-southern party.

These national disputes occurred partly because of different regional forms of white men's egalitarianism. Slavery led to an especially anti-egalitarian version of mid-nineteenth-century republicanism in eastern Virginia and in South Carolina. Elitist republicans from these ancient areas precipitated the Nullification, Gag Rule, and Texas crises, as they would provoke the Secession Crisis of 1860.

Here and in newer Souths too, dictatorial control over blacks also led sometimes to quasi-dictatorial ways of controlling whites. Lynching, censorship, and cries about loyalty, although neither constantly present south nor always absent north, were a much more valued means of controlling heresy in the South. Southern slaveholders could also be more imperious than northern leaders amongst white folks in neighborhood gatherings. Ultimatums to Van Buren Democrats and gag rules on white discussion were national manifestations of a southern republican atmosphere which allowed uncensored, uninhibited egalitarian discussion to proceed only so far.

The Age of Sectional Controversy was just beginning? Hardly. Rather, during the Age of Jackson, a pattern of controversy over black slavery and its impact on white republicanism developed, within and between sections and parties. In the Texas Annexation Controversy, the pattern finally mocked Jacksonian "Democracy," undercut prospects that Van Buren Democrats could long remain Democrats or that Southern Whigs could long remain Whigs, and carved inexorable ruts a long way down the road to disunion.

PART VII

CRISIS AT MIDCENTURY

While drives to control non-whites conditioned Jacksonian "Democracy," slavery controversies intensified as the Age of Jackson drew to a close. Jackson's politics had acted like preliminary grades of a hill. With the Compromise of 1850 and the Kansas-Nebraska Act, Southerners started to career down the road to disunion.

So posterity thinks. But Disunionists at the time feared that victories on fugitive slaves and Kansas yielded too little protection at slavery's fringes and too much complacency inside the southern establishment. From that perspective, a perspective destined to produce extraordinary efforts to make *a* South in the mid- and late 1850s, the late 1840s and early 1850s did not look like the beginning of a slide towards secession. Rather, mid-century crises looked like little bumps on a trail wandering heaven knows where.

CHAPTER 26

Loaded Words,
Loathsome Collaborations

Immediately after the Texas Annexation Controversy, a different sort of sectional crisis transpired. Enslaved Texas, once in the Union, offered slaveholders obvious practical benefits, as almost all Democrats affirmed and most Southern Whigs could not deny. But the so-called Mexican Cession of land gained from the Mexican War was not so clearly destined to attract slaveholders.

Southern debates over whether slaves could labor extensively in the largely arid Mexican Cession area never waxed very hot. National debate instead exploded over whether slavery was too morally depraved to enter a republic's virgin turf. Once again, as in gag rule days, mostly words were at stake.

Words were more lethal than ever. In the North, a mainstream majority in the late 1840s, not just the tiny abolitionist minority of the mid-1830s, drove towards a national congressional declaration that slaveholders should be banned from the Mexican Cession. Within the South, a notorious critic made external condemnation seem more threatening. Cassius Clay of Kentucky sought collaboration with Yankee assaulters. That defection from within and those poisonous words without led to wider and deeper southern intransigence than the more obviously practical matter of Texas had inspired.

– 1 –

Annexation probably insured a physical war with Mexico and a resulting verbal confrontation over slavery. But had America annexed less land, its enraged neighbor just might have been mollified.

Mexican officials believed that Texas ended at the Nueces River. Texans claimed instead that their empire sprawled 100 miles further south, to the Rio Grande. With the Rio Grande rather than the Nueces marking its boundary, the Texas accession would also swell thousands of square miles upwards, since the Rio Grande flowed west and north of what would become the state's boundaries.

In June–July of 1845, when Texans were weighing Mexico's offer of independence against America's offer of annexation, Lone Star leaders asked if America would secure all disputed turf. President Polk answered that "we will maintain all your rights of territory."[1] Thus did Sam Houston's diplomacy yield its final, fullest fruit.

Polk's conception of fruitful land extended beyond the Rio Grande. The President also meant to press Mexico for Pacific Ocean outlets, especially San Francisco. The American President first tried symbolic pressure. He ordered Zachary Taylor, American commander of troops on the Lone Star State's border, to camp on the allegedly Mexican side of the Nueces River. That encampment would establish the American trans-Nueces claim. At the same time, by remaining on the Nueces and not marching on the Rio Grande, Taylor might soothe Mexican negotiators. Polk sent diplomats to Mexico City to buy California and to secure the Rio Grande as the United States-Mexico border.

In January of 1846, when negotiations in Mexico City stalled, President Polk ordered Zachary Taylor from the Nueces to the Rio Grande. The general marched down in late March. A month later, Mexicans crossed the Rio Grande to ambush Taylor's force. The gory news reached Washington on May 9, 1846, four hours *after* Polk's cabinet had agreed to war but before the President had sent his war message to Congress. The President immediately asked for a national war to repel an alleged invasion.[2]

– 2 –

Polk's Democratic Party swiftly drove declaration of war through Congress. But several Southern Whigs used scarce minutes of debate to doubt whether Mexican invasion of disputed territory justified American invasion of Mexico. John C. Calhoun, once again senator from South Carolina, also urged delay in declaring war. The Mexican government, speculated Calhoun, might repudiate Taylor's ambushers.[3]

This protest was abortive. Only a handful of Whigs dared vote against punishing Mexicans for killing American boys. Calhoun's bravery extended only to abstaining. Even John Quincy Adams reluctantly voted to supply Polk's army.

While Whigs were thus uncomfortably implicated in the Democracy's war, they felt comfortably patriotic in advocating that conquered territory be returned. Democrats usually urged that Mexican land be kept, to pay costs of repelling Mexican "invasion." Whigs usually answered that whoever had invaded first, American armies were now invading Mexico. Some Whigs were willing to keep San Francisco as partial indemnity. For the rest, Whigs' motto was clear-cut: No Territory.[4]

No Territory was the most promising strategy the National Whig Party ever deployed on a slavery issue. No Territory meant no Union-straining crisis, for no territorial slavery controversy could occur unless territory was acquired. No Territory meant also no resumption of the party-straining Texas issue, where Northern Whigs had unyieldingly opposed territory for the Slavepower and Southern Whigs had accordingly to choose between losing their party or losing the Deep South.

No Territory furthermore enabled the party's two wings to espouse the same policy for opposite reasons. Northern Whigs argued that non-annexation of Mexican territory stopped slave extension, for the Mexican tropics were historically and climatically fit for slave labor. Southern Whigs argued that No Territory stopped free labor extension, for much of Mexico was too arid for slave labor and the South lacked enough slaves to settle the rest. Behold the Whig Party, for once united on a slave policy—because for once agreed on how to say no to territory rather than yes or no to slavery.[5]

No Territory especially benefited that long-suffering South Carolina Whig, Waddy Thompson. Thompson had for years been a rare species: a persistent Whig in John C. Calhoun's state after Calhoun repudiated Whiggery. That awkward position plus John Quincy Adams's needling had turned Waddy Thompson, in gag rule times, into a sputtering fire-eater. Thompson had then become, in Texas times, that even lonelier politician: the Southerner who opposed Robert Walker's Texas safety valve. Thompson had argued that Southerners, by populating Texas, would depopulate the South.

After annexation produced war, Waddy Thompson added that the South could not and would not people a Mexico Cession. During the previous 12 months, Thompson told an upcountry South Carolina audience on October 4, 1847, only 2,000 of 300,000 European immigrants had stepped South. The rest, free laborers with "imported sentiments hostile to our welfare," would march on Mexico. The underpopulated South, unable to compete with a population surge originating abroad, would additionally never live happily with "worthless and troublesome" Mexicans of a mongrelized race. Thompson "would consent to be gibbeted, or, if dead, that his bones be dug up and made manure of, if ever a slaveholding state was formed out of" Mexico. Better No Territory than turf destined for free laborers.[6]

Because Texas was seductive, Thompson's earlier No Territory argument had won over few Carolinians, however much his fear that the West would depopulate Carolina fit the Carolina mentality. But now Mexican halfbreeds rather than American slaveholders controlled the frontier ripe for annexation; and this time Carolinians relished Thompson Whiggery. John C. Calhoun, who with Whigs had found Polk's war message troubling, now found the possible fruits of Polk's war alarming. Southerners were better off staying home, declared Calhoun, than living amongst mongrelized Mexicans.

Calhoun revised No Territory to allow annexation of Mexican territory west of Texas. But he favored no annexation below the Rio Grande. He deplored the further advance of American armies. He would withdraw troops to a string of defensive forts guarding the Rio Grande and points west.[7]

Where Calhoun and most South Carolinians rejected acquisitions south of Texas, growing numbers of Southwestern Democrats increasingly sought all of Mexico. The burgeoning All-Mexico movement, the antithesis of Whigs' No Territory solution, swept up many, although never most, Democrats North and

South as Polk's armies advanced on Mexico City. From Northern Democrats' perspective, Mexico would offer trade routes to the Pacific as well as much land to develop. From Southwestern Democrats' perspective, Mexico offered tropical turf for slaveholders.[8]

That expansionist southwestern stance, so different from the Calhoun-Waddy Thompson fear-of-expansionism stance, left South Carolina reactionaries more than ever isolated from New South imperialists. This confrontation within the Lower South over a Mexico Cession would prove fleeting. The similar imminent clash between Deep Souths, Old and New, over Caribbean Expansion would prove more long-lasting—and more destructive of efforts to make *a* South.

– 3 –

Contention over how much, if any, of Mexico should be annexed swiftly spilled into dispute over whether slaveholders should be barred from annexed territory. This newest slavery question emerged on August 8, 1846, when President Polk asked Congress for a $2,000,000 appropriation to conduct negotiations with Mexico. In response, a Northern Democrat, David Wilmot of Pennsylvania, moved that slavery be banned in any territory negotiated from Mexico. The House passed Polk's appropriation bill with Wilmot's Proviso attached, 85-79. Southerners voted almost unanimously against, Northerners almost unanimously for making lands acquired from Mexico off-limits to slaveholders. Only southern power over the Senate plus one helpful Yankee Whig, John Davis of Massachusetts, prevented a bipartisan Yankee coalition from pronouncing slaveholders too depraved to enter the Mexican Cession.[9]

David Wilmot's Proviso recalled the last time a Northerner had initiated a major congressional slavery controversy. James Tallmadge of New York, whose Tallmadge Amendments had precipitated the Missouri Controversy, bore resemblance to the Wilmot Proviso's author. Both Tallmadge and Wilmot were Jeffersonian/Jacksonian states' righters. Both resented the minority South's dominance over the majority party opposing Federalist/Whig nationalism. Where Tallmadge would declare Republicans such as himself as fit to rule as the Virginia Dynasty, Wilmot would annoint Yankees such as Martin Van Buren as more proper republican statesmen than Slavepower annexationists.

Tallmadge differed in being antislavery as well as anti-Slavepower. The New Yorker helped end slavery in his own state. He then moved to terminate slavery in Missouri. David Wilmot never moved to eliminate the institution anywhere. Behind the Pennsylvania Democrat's famous proviso lay the central distinction in northern slavery politics ever after: the difference between a radical seeking to end slavery in old slave areas and a moderate seeking to contain the Slavepower from entering an unenslaved new area.

Tallmadge would invade an already enslaved domain in part because he regretted blacks' enslavement. Wilmot regretted only Slavepower impositions on whites. He had no "morbid sympathy for the slave." Wilmot sought a white man's mecca, where "my own race and own color can live without the disgrace" of "association with negro slavery." David Wilmot, less antislavery than James Tallmadge, may have been more anti-black than John C. Calhoun.[10]

That reactionary racism furthered Wilmot's mainstream impact. Yankees who disliked blacks relished lily-white liberalism. The Wilmot Proviso also well expressed Northern Democrats' fear that further appeasing Southerners would hand Whigs the North. Martin Van Buren's worst scenario had long been a national war to secure still more land and power for the Slavepower than Texas's potential five slave states might already provide. The Wilmot Proviso placed the North's Van Burens in the lead in declaring that white soldiers were dying to expand republicanism rather than Slavepower.

The relatively few Yankee crusaders against slavery also found Wilmot's mere containment proposal attractive. By supporting the not-so-radical Wilmot Proviso, abolitionists might duck the taint of extremism. Meanwhile, by helping to secure moderates' national proscription of the Slavepower, extremists might raise Yankee consciousness. With color-blind abolitionists joining Northern Democrats and Whigs in declaring David Wilmot's racially motivated Proviso sublime, the North was coming together as never before against the Slavepower.

– 4 –

North/South disagreement over barring slavery from any new Mexican Cession, plus Democratic/Whig disagreement over whether a Mexican Cession should transpire, left President Polk increasingly concerned about establishing a national agreement. The longer war persisted, the more Mexican land American armies controlled, the stronger became the All-Mexico movement, the more determined became David Wilmot's anti-Slavepower forces, and the more resolute became Whigs' No Territory dedications. How could escalating conflict yield a two-thirds consensus for a treaty ending the war? Worse, Mexicans would agree to no treaty. An exasperated Polk, in October of 1847, ordered his chief negotiator in Mexico City, Nicholas P. Trist, home.

The miffed subordinate lingered. Trist was accordingly in Mexico City in late 1847 when the Mexicans asked for new negotiations. The defrocked negotiator emerged with the treaty Polk had originally sent him to Mexico City to negotiate. Mexico agreed to "sell" America the Rio Grande border, California, and all territory between. The "purchase" price: a bargain, $15,000,000.

Polk received these delightful results of his underling's insubordination in February 1848. Trist's terms both approximated Calhoun's limited cession proposals and involved much less annexation than the military situation made possible. The treaty was accordingly a viable compromise between No Territory and All-Mexico. After the Senate gave its consent, 38–14, a relieved President and nation could turn fuller attention to David Wilmot's Proviso.[11]

– 5 –

The Wilmot Proviso did not produce a Texas-like instant southern explosion. A year transpired between Wilmot's 1846 proposal and the South's fully developed fury. But the eventual southern response featured a rarely unanimous intransigence. Whigs, Democrats, and Calhounites, lately at odds over how large a Mexican Cession, if any, would help the South, all now agreed that Congress must not bar Southerners from benefiting from the new empire, even if few benefits were possible.

More benefits might have beckoned if the All-Mexico movement had triumphed. More extensive tropical land might have tempted more Southerners to migrate. But the Mexican Cession had been restricted to the same latitude as Texas. Most land west of the Lone Star State was an arid desert. The only obvious agrarian mecca, California, was 700 miles beyond the nearest South.

A speculative southern debate ensued over whether the Mexican Cession would attract slaveholders, assuming the Wilmot Proviso could be defeated. Whigs, having lately called for No Territory, almost always termed the Mexican Cession worthless and/or counterproductive for the slavocracy. Democrats, having often of late urged an All-Mexico solution, often called the portion of Mexico ceded at least fractionally useful. Whigs were most convincing when arguing that slaves would be, at best, marginally used in New Mexico and Utah. From posterity's objective viewpoint, slaves could have worked in mines or factories. But from most Southerners' subjective perspective, cotton and sugar were the path to wealth; and virgin cotton land in Texas and Arkansas beat experimenting with unfamiliar enterprises underground in New Mexico.

Because of cotton mania, Democrats made most sense when urging that slaves could be, at worst, quite useful in California. In the mid-nineteenth century, the area's agricultural potential was rumored to be rich; and in the twentieth century, riches would in fact flow to California cotton producers. To Democrats who speculated that cotton might become King of California, banning the institution also revived claustrophobic nightmares of Texas times: of a Lower South caged from expansion and the repository of Upper South blacks.[12]

Still, differences abounded between the Mexican Cession and Texas. Preannexation Texas was already enslaved. Its agricultural value was already proven. Its geographical position, bordering Louisiana and Arkansas, already had attracted Deep South migration. If unannexed, it could become a nearby English guard over an American racial prison.

In the Mexican Cession, on the other hand, Mexican law had banned slavery. Agricultural potential ranged between unproven and unlikely. The region was too far from southern black belts, especially with huge areas of uninhabited Texas in between, to excite many slaveholder visions of immediate migration or of imminent racial imprisonment. Every practical racial, economic, and political southern value looked more attainable by peopling empty Texas and hacking it into five slave states than by, for example, trying out slaves in New Mexico mines.

More important still, the Mexican Cession did not conjure up the practical danger Southerners spied in every other antebellum slavery crisis: exposure on the South's flanks, where the slave system was weakest. Close by Texas, Missouri, and Kansas inspired immediate senses of crisis and drives to conquer. Distant New Mexico, Utah, California, and Oregon inspired slower senses of crisis, little attempt to populate, and sullen acquiescence in defeat after strident confrontations. Yet Southerners remained exercised enough about the Mexican Cession to demand that the Wilmot Proviso's verbiage be excised. Why this latest concern with "mere" words?

– 6 –

Most Southerners raged primarily because David Wilmot's holier-than-thou stance was so insulting.[13] Southern Whigs, who always called the Mexican Cession useless to slaveholders, focused on the inequity of being branded as republican outcasts more exclusively than did Southern Democrats, who sometimes stressed that slaves might be useful in California. When the Georgia Whig Alexander Stephens labeled "the Wilmot Proviso a humbug" as a practical matter, with all the pecuniary value of "goat's wool," especially Lower South Democrats thought the metaphor a bit overdone. But Democrats agreed with Stephens that the Proviso was above all "an *insult* to the South," our own government's intolerable "expression to the world" that we "deserve public censure and national odium."[14]

David Wilmot, censurer, called up that odious stream of word associations no Southerner could abide: immoral equals inferior equals slave equals "nigger"—equals necessity to combat such pilloring of southern equality. As Peter Daniel of Virginia, a Democrat and an associate judge of the United States Supreme Court, explained to Martin Van Buren, David Wilmot's moral "pretention" was "fraught with dangers far greater than any that can flow from mere calculation of political influence or of [economic] profit." Wilmot "pretends to an insulting exclusiveness or superiority on the one hand, and denounces a degraded inequality or inferiority on the other." A Wilmot Proviso advocate "says in effect to the Southern man, Avaunt! you are not my equal and hence are to be excluded."[15] The question, reiterated Joseph Mathews, governor of Mississippi, in his January 1848 inaugural address, is "whether citizens of the slave states are to be considered as equals."[16]

Scientific no less than egalitarian assumptions demanded that Southerners deny they were too degraded to expand. The American nation was Darwin's before Darwin. A nation seizing territory from neighboring civilizations defined surrendering the right to grow as forfeiting the right to live. Healthy civilizations expand. Diseased civilizations wither. "You are obliged to go forward," declared Governor Francis Pickens of South Carolina on the eve of secession. "You must increase, and the moment you stand still, it will be the law of your destiny to decay and die."[17]

Southerners often questioned whether the David Wilmots would allow slavery to live after forcing slaveholders to stand still.[18] Once Yankee moralists forbade slaveholders from national territories, the Cuffee-like mask might be thrown off. Former agitators against "only" slave expansion might then agitate against slavery itself and for the same reason: because Yankee republicans could not bear anti-republican Slavepower.

The Slavepower retained precarious power to stymie Wilmot's vocabulary.

The Wilmot Proviso could be blocked in the Senate, so long as every southern senator remained true to the homeland. But one defector to the enemy was enough to plaster that detested label, unequal, and that despised position, enslaved, on every Southerner, in and out of Congress.

Defections looked possible in a land where so many had so recently articulated the premise of external critics: that slavery was wrong. Defections were the more possible where potential turncoats were senators, politicians with patronage and power to be gleaned from collaborating with defamers. While Yankee politicians, being Yankees, had to be viewed with great suspicion, southern politicians, being politicians, had to be suspiciously surveyed too.

As with the extremest gag rule, Calhoun and his followers demanded that Southerners in the two-party establishment repudiate suspect vocabulary. This time, two-party politicians did not need reminders that they would appear vulnerably disloyal if they endorsed Van Burenite words. The resulting cascade of southern curses at Wilmot made the South master of its own fate.

But let just a couple of congressional collaborators voice Yankee oaths and verbal mastery would perish. The Proviso would pass. Then far more than words could be lost. The declaration that slavery was unfit to expand might establish an irrepressible momentum to ban the institution from obviously enticing territory later no less than from possibly forbidding territory now. With slaveholders proscribed from expanding and new northern states alone entering the Union, northern majorities could abolish slavery at their pleasure. With southern citizens submitting to insult and with southern politicians gaining patronage by submitting to the North, self-esteem would evaporate, will to endure would dissipate, and morale would collapse.

The South, concluded Calhoun in his major speech on the Proviso, would then become "a mere handful" of states, imprisoned "forever." The national government would "entirely be in the hands of the nonslaveholding States—overwhelmingly." Could we then be safe "at the entire mercy" of Yankee "justice and regard for our interests?"[19] Seldom had Southerners possessed such a practical stake in defending their theoretical equality—or found the necessity for self-defense so insulting and infuriating.

– 7 –

At this moment of heightened awareness of verbal power, a southern heretic spread the wrong words. Context explains why Cassius Clay of Kentucky was disturbing. Clay's voting support, never more than 10% of the Kentucky electorate, was itself no immediate menace. But Cassius Clay's threat to collaborate with Wilmot Proviso supporters represented a breech in the southern fortress at a moment when unity seemed crucial.

Cassius Clay's Kentucky was even more custom-designed for internal dissent than was Virginia, locale back in 1832 of the most extensive Upper South debate over ending slavery.[20] At mid-century, a third of Virginia's population was enslaved, compared with but a fifth of Kentucky's. Worse, while slavehold-

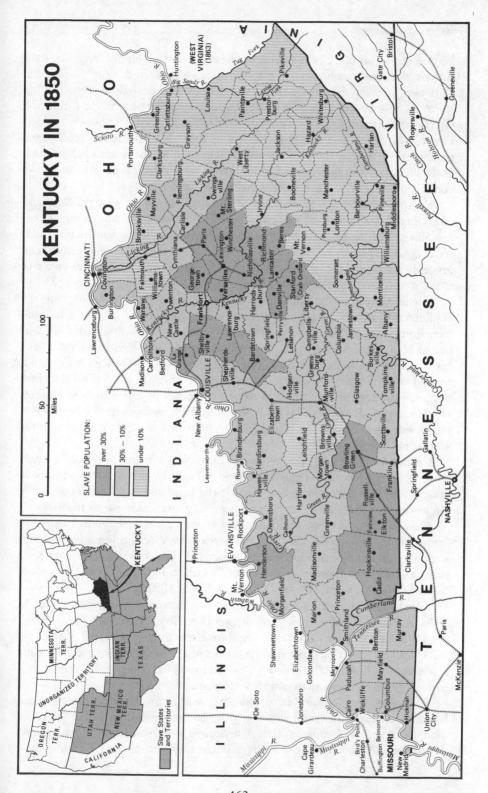

KENTUCKY IN 1850

SLAVE POPULATION:

over 30%

30% — 10%

under 10%

Slave States and Territories

463

ers dominated fat black belts in almost the entire eastern half of Virginia, Kentucky's slavocracy controlled a far narrower, whiter, and more surrounded black belt, running diagonally northeast to southwest through the center of the state. In this fabled Bluegrass area, slanting from Lexington past Bowling Green, percentages of slaves averaged around 25%, a Middle South average. East of the Bluegrass, a semi-mountainous area three times thicker in geographic width averaged under 5% slaves. West and north, an area half as thick as the Bluegrass averaged around 15% slaves. Over a third of the state's counties contained under 10% slaves, over a half under 20%.

Kentucky, while not as southern as Virginia, was more western. Kentuckians suffered from the usual western problem: too much land, not enough laborers. Slavery, prime solution to labor shortages deeper in the Southwest, could never be as widespread in Kentucky's cooler climes. A low percentage of slaves arguably intensified the labor shortage, for potential white settlers preferred free Ohio, immediately to Kentucky's north.

Cassius Clay grew up a rich father's heir on White Hall Plantation, near the confluence of slaveholding and nonslaveholding Kentucky.[21] He came to intellectual maturity at Yale College in thickly populated New England. Clay witnessed New Englanders thriving "luxuriously on a soil which *here* would have been deemed the high road to famine."[22] New England, with its rocky land, teemed with free labor enterprise and dense population. Kentucky, with its lush terrain, was sluggish amidst slave labor and sparse population. Free laborers would rarely rush where slaves trod. Nor would whites work hard where sweating was deemed "nigger." Kentuckians, to flourish in western competition for whites, must push out slaves.

Cassius Clay did not, upon returning from New England, see how to begin pushing. If the Kentucky legislature paid to send blacks to Africa, excessive taxation would deter white emigrants. If the legislature allowed 200,000 free blacks to stay, white emigrants would head to whiter midwestern frontiers.

Cassius Clay's favorite Kentucky law at least prevented the bad situation from growing worse. The Law of 1833 barred slaves from being imported into Kentucky except by emigrants for their own use. That ban, together with Kentucky's drain of bondsmen to the Lower South, helped ease Kentucky's slave percentage down from 24% in 1830 to 21.5% in 1850.

Clay's first campaign involving slavery sought to preserve this first step. In 1840, Robert Wickliffe, Jr., son of the very wealthy slaveholder "Iron Duke" Wickliffe, agitated for Clay's state legislative seat by urging repeal of the Law of '33. When Clay called the edict right because slavery was wrong, Wickliffe branded him "disloyal." Kentucky's real traitors, Clay answered, valued aristocratic property more than majority interests.[23]

Clay won the election. He would never win again. Driven from the legislature as an extremist the following year, he determined to make Kentucky more extreme. His *Lexington True American,* a weekly newspaper inaugurated in June of 1845, brought class warfare implications of the anti-Wickliffe campaign to full consciousness. The Bluegrass newspaper also displayed Clay's cure for Kentucky's labor shortage. The solution did not charm Iron Duke.

Clay's remedy would have been no delight to Iron Duke's slaves either. The Lion of *White* Hall, Clay's appropriate nickname, proposed using the threat of post-nati emancipation to intensify sale of slaves to the Lower South. The Kentucky legislature, Clay urged in 1845, should declare female slaves born after a certain date free when they reached 21. In 1851, Clay would advocate freeing male and female slaves born after 1860 when they reached maturity.

In both campaigns, Clay predicted that Iron Duke and fellow slaveholders would beat the deadline. Some would unload their investments in New Orleans slave auctions. Kinder masters would send their people back to Africa. The legislature, a third of a century hence, could easily compensate patriarchs for those few blacks "of the best quality" who remained.

A population rush to whitened Kentucky, cheered Clay, would ensue. Kentucky's 200,000 slaves had kept out 1,000,000 whites. Kentucky's emancipation would pull in millions of emigrants. Manufacturing would blossom, for enterprising white laborers would buy more for themselves than Iron Duke dribbled out for slaves. Schools would flourish, for a large white population would make for extensive public education. Labor would intensify, for no more "niggers" would be around to make hard work degrading. "Give us *free labor*," concluded Cassius Clay, "and we shall, indeed, become *'the garden of the world.'"*[24]

The Lion of White Hall here pulled old proposals to whiten the least-enslaved South into a fresh synthesis. His view that the state should pass future emancipation, hoping that slaves would be sold down river before emancipating birthdays, recalled dismal results of New Jersey–New York laws early in the century. Clay's proposed legislative encouragement of marketing slaves in Lower South black belts copied Thomas Jefferson Randolph's motion in the Virginia Slavery Debate. His desire to draw in whites by pushing out blacks resembled Henry Brawner's prayers for Maryland.

Cassius Clay joined to those Old Eastern ways of removing slaves the newest western entrepreneurial vision. His notion that ending slavery would entice free farmers, thereby enriching land speculators, paralleled Pearl Andrews's argument several years earlier in Texas. The cautious Andrews, however, had appealed to the wealthy. The bold Clay would appeal over the elite's obstructionary heads to nonslaveholders resentful of the Iron Dukes. Clay's resulting ideological amalgam, while highly racist, conditional, and conservative, was also the most radical form of southern reform yet. It called on the white majority to outvote the propertied elite and to expel the black minority.

That heretical notion made Cassius Clay a Kentucky household name. Everyone, chuckled a fellow emancipator, "wants to see what sort of monster C. M. Clay is. They expect to see a face . . . made of brass & iron."[25]

They assuredly saw a strapping Westerner. The Lion of White Hall was over six feet tall, hard and hulking, with a thick square face and a solid chin. His reformist credentials were equally solid. "Cash" Clay had sacrificed $40,000 to free his slaves before talking about other people's slaves. Bluff, hardy mid-Americans liked that sincerity.

Kentucky frontiersmen also admired a man who risked his life for his principles. Clay shunned the examples of James Birney and Pearl Andrews, who fled north upon intimations of possible lynchings. Cassius Clay, brawling frontiersman, never ran from anything. He seized his bowie knife over such crowning concerns as the genealogies of shorthorn bulls and the origins of Bluegrass seed. He hounded one foe into suicide. He slashed another's skull to the brain. He was such a pro with bowie knives that he filled a pamphlet with his expertise. He was so determined to be heard that he mounted podiums twirling pistols.

In mid-1845, Clay crammed the *Lexington True American's* office with heavier artillery. Iron Duke, to smash the Lion's press, would have to bomb out two four-pound cannon, sundry lances and rifles, and a keg of powder. Clay scorned fear of "treasonable and revolutionary enemies of constitutional liberty. . . . We can die, but cannot be enslaved."[26]

While self-defense, the Kentuckian believed, justified extra-legal brawling, Clay remained otherwise a domesticated reformer. He pointed out to practical Americans that his proposals would free no one for over three decades.[27] "We should not," he counseled a fellow agitator, "needlessly offend any one."[28] Cassius Clay was no fanatic hunting martyrdom. He was a determined politico who fanned nonslaveholders' racist and class hatreds.

Clay's challenge, like Pearl Andrew's Galveston foray, excited slaveholders' uneasiness about democratic processes. Even if 99 out of 100 slaves were Cuffees, should any black be exposed to seditious ideas? Even if most nonslaveholders wished to have all blacks in their neighborhoods enslaved, might they prefer having no blacks around? In 1844 the national Congress had decided that national republicanism required expunging slavery-inspired gag rules. In 1845, citizens in Lexington, Kentucky, had to decide whether slavery was compatible with Cassius Clay's democratic challenge.

In mid-August 1845, his head perhaps turned by typhoid fever, his pen surely driven by venom at the Wickliffes, Clay impelled immediate decision. "Remember," he wrote, "you who dwell in marble palaces, that there are strong arms and fiery hearts and iron pikes in the streets, and panes of glass only between them and the silver plate on the board and the smooth-skinned women on the ottoman." Remember, you Wickliffes, that "the day of retribution is at hand—and the masses will be avenged."[29]

Iron Duke's cronies, not anxious to charge Clay's cannon, secured an injunction against this demand for lower-class revolt. Clay, seeking to abolish slavery by legal process, handed over his armed newspaper office. His press was exiled to Cincinnati. "Thus," lamented Clay, "on the 18th day of August 1845, were the Constitutional liberties of Kentucky overthrown; and an irresponsible despotism of slaveholding aristocracy established on their ruins."[30]

Slaveholders who had expelled the "seditious" press offered their usual rationalization for undemocratic control: Clay's newspaper supposedly fomented slave insurrection. Clay ridiculed the excuse. Fantasies about "insurrection in

Kentucky, where there are about six whites to one black," were absurd. The oligarchy, charged Clay, really feared majoritarian reform in a state where non-slaveholding outnumbered slaveholding families three to one. Slave insurrection was the "Bug-a-boo" used to legitimize "Austrian vigilance." As much as he hated slavery because of its "wrongs to the blacks" and its impoverishing of nonslaveholders, he hated it more "because it will not allow law . . . allow constitutions . . . allow Republicanism."[31]

Clay proceeded to detour around localistic repression. The Louisville neighborhood further north, unlike the Lexington neighborhood further south, relished a free press. Clay re-established his newspaper up in the Ohio River city. Frustrated Bluegrass vigilantes could not lynch him inside that alien locality.

Cassius Clay's opponents were driven back to enchaining his ideas the democratic way, by raising issues and winning elections. In the 1845–9 period, Bluegrass politicians attacked Kentucky reformers' first containment, the Law of 1833, which outlawed most slave importation. In 1848, the Law of 1833 narrowly survived a legislative test. In 1849, modifications tantamount to repeal were passed. A vote for delegates to a convention, charged with writing a new Kentucky constitution, was coincidently imminent. Cassius Clay and his sympathizers hoped to use the new election to regain the old statute. They provoked the most searching southern debate on slavery since that supposedly final discussion, the Virginia Slave Controversy of 1832.

A convention meeting in Frankfort, the state capital situated halfway between Cassius Clay's stronghold of Louisville and his opponents' stronghold of Lexington, initiated confrontation. The eleven reformers, when signing the first call for the provoking convention, declared Kentucky's founding fathers wrong to think that slavery would ease the state's labor shortage. Too few slaves came to Kentucky. Too many whites turned elsewhere. "While the immense stream of [white] immigration has been passing population, wealth, mechanic and manufacturing skill and industry into the States north of us, it seems to have avoided Kentucky as though she had been a land of pestilence." The "withering blight must be ended." Whites proud to labor must replace work-shirking slaves.[32]

On April 25, 159 delegates met in Frankfort to endorse those themes. Henry Clay, Cassius Clay's cousin and Kentucky's most famous statesman, chaired the convention and gave it political respectability. Robert J. Breckinridge, the renowned Presbyterian clergyman, gave the major speech and added religious sanction. Breckinridge would "transmit to our posterity" an implacable "hatred of, and hostility to, this most atrocious of all human institutions." But prudence required reformers to seek no more now than re-enacting the Law of 1833 and empowering a future legislature to emancipate. Breckinridge would rally non-slaveholders, "the only class from whom aid can be expected," by emphasizing that banning black imports would save white jobs.

Some delegates wished a more extreme crusade, seeking termination of slavery now. Others urged a quieter campaign, showing that reformers were not fanatics. Cassius Clay stood in the middle with Breckinridge. "How are we to get at the nonslaveholders," he asked, "but by agitation?" Still, agitation best captured "the ear of the people" when dressed up as moderation. "We *fanatics*," said Clay, "are willing to take your compromise." The Frankfort convention agreed to a Breckinridge-Clay campaign aimed at reinstalling the Law of 1833 and permitting a future legislature to remove slaves.[33]

In the ensuing four-month canvass, a reforming colleague, William M. O. Smith, best summed up Cassius Clay's case. On a June Court Day in Paris, Kentucky, the widely admired Smith began his heretical statement with a southern heretic's necessary disclaimer. He was no outside agitator. He was born and bred a Kentuckian. No "maukish sensibility in favor of the slaves" moved him. "But looking as I do to the interests of the white population, I wish to be clear of them."

Kentucky could get clear of blacks cheaply and easily. Slaves must be barred from entering, and bondsmen born after 1860 must be declared free when they grew up. Most post-nati slaves would be sold south before age 21. The rest could be cheaply sent to Africa. Then Kentucky would no longer have "to play second fiddle to those vile Yankees."

Kentucky, continued William M. O. Smith, was second best because a halfway house, fully benefiting from neither northern nor southern solutions to labor shortage. The northern free labor solution worked best when abundant free laborers labored energetically. Scarce free white labor worked badly in Kentucky, "because slaves have made all labor ... dishonorable." Most Kentucky white free laborers, determined to avoid being considered "white negroes," acted as if hard work was "nigger" work. Most whites elsewhere preferred second-best lands in Ohio to degraded work in Kentucky. Labor shortfall, sloppy wage earners, "and vicious habits of all kinds" abounded.

Kentucky's sloppy form of slavery could not take up the slack. Slavery worked best, Smith maintained, when blacks were abundant and masters were imperious. Kentucky slaves would never be abundant, for labor-starved Lower South planters could use slaves more profitably in more tropical climes. Kentucky masters would never be imperious, for they were too democratic and apologetic. In South Carolina and eastern Virginia, an aristocrat scorned pure democracy and ruled like "a feudal baron." In Kentucky, planters lauded democracy and proclaimed bondage "a great evil."

Slaves latched onto masters' ambivalence. The "faltering hand" of authority encouraged "the governed to become refractory." Governors countered with bribes. The "half free indolent negro" responded with a splendid demonstration of "how to work least for most."

Leniency, admitted Smith, made border slavery milder. But "if slavery *must* exist in a community, let it be slavery and not this halfway sort of slavery." Most Kentucky defenders of slavery conceded that Providence would ultimately drain the "evil" away. As soon as lawmakers gave Providence a nudge, first by banning blacks from coming in, then by encouraging slaveholders to sell out, free laborers would mass to the Bluegrass.[34]

William M. O. Smith was right that most of his opponents believed slavery would fade from Kentucky. True, a few so-called Perpetualists, led by Beverley Clarke, asserted that docile black slaves outworked rowdy white Irishmen. A few others argued that Kentucky often put Ohio's economy to rout. But Cassius Clay's foes, rejecting Beverley Clarke, usually called slavery a curse, doomed in Kentucky.

George W. Johnson's article in *The Frankfort Yeoman* typified the establishment's position. Johnson reminded readers that Cassius Clay, although sometimes narrowing the issue to the Law of 1833, sometimes agitated for emancipation of slaves born hereafter. Clay called compensation to owners unnecessary, for someday-to-be-freed slaves could be sold out of Kentucky.

This cynical non-emancipation, charged George W. Johnson, violated Kentucky benevolence. Kentuckians were bribed to betray family retainers or to desert Kentucky. "If the citizen is conscientiously opposed to selling his slaves, to whom he is attached, and if he loves his native land too well to emigrate, then he is punished for the noblest feelings of our nature."

Nor would the Lower South tolerate "a sudden deluge of blacks." Rather than let faltering Kentuckians push the "dregs of their slave population" upon the tropics, the Cotton Kingdom would ban slave imports. Yet Kentucky's postnati law would still be on the books, freeing blacks. Cassius Clay's statecraft would yield "200,000 slaves breeding *free negroes* in a republic of whites!!!"

A better way, cheered Johnson, was in process. Kentucky's slowly increasing white population depressed slave values at home. The Lower South's steadily advancing western frontier increased slave prices abroad. Kentucky masters would slowly move south or gradually sell bondsmen down river. This whitening of Kentucky, achieved "by the unerring wisdom of the Eternal Legislator," would transpire "without danger, crime, or disturbance of society, by the easy, gradual, and unseen, but imperative action of the law of nature." If Clay would hush, slavery and blacks "will gradually disappear from Kentucky in 70 years."[35]

This typical Kentucky "proslavery" position in the debate of 1849 was as little "proslavery" as was Virginia conservatives' position in the debate of 1832. Once again an Upper South establishment called whitening the state salutary but legislative interference pernicious, for the "curse" was draining away of its own natural accord. A tobacco kingdom near Yankeeland was yet another time considered, in Thomas R. Dew's phrase, too far north to remain permanently southern.

– 8 –

South Carolina planters, if pressed to choose between William M. O. Smith's legislative encouragement of the slave drain and George Johnson's diffusion through private slave sales, would have condemned both. Kentucky voters considered the choice the most important of the half-century. Contestants condemned each other as pirates, fanatics, murderers, oligarchs, rapists, bandits, thieves. Slaves pretended not to hear the charges. Nonslaveholders mulled over appeals for class revolution. Slaveholders muttered about incendiary language.

Ugly accusations soon provoked angry assaults. On June 15 at Foxtown, less than an hour's jaunt from White Hall, Cassius Clay and one Squire Turner, a slaveholder, met in public debate. Turner treated the crowd to a reading of Clay's inflammatory 1845 *True American* issue, calling for lower-class revolt. When Clay denied he was Jacobinical, Cyrus Turner, Squire's son, branded Cassius a liar and smashed him in the face.

Clay grabbed for his knife. He was clubbed to earth. The Turner clan swarmed at him. Tom Turner, Cyrus's brother, pressed a pistol at Clay's temple. The gun sputtered. Tom screamed for another. Cyrus sank a dagger into Clay's side. Cassius heard someone exalt that the Lion was dead.

Clay, fighting unconsciousness, lurched to his feet. Squeezing a bowie knife, he staggered after Cyrus. Turner slipped. Clay leaped atop and slashed out Cyrus's bowels. With one flash of the bowie knife, Cassius Clay captured the stridency of a border confrontation over slavery's fate.[36]

With the same deadly motion, Clay illustrated why he was doomed to lose this election. Clay survived to defend carrying knives and slaying Turner as lamentable but necessary self-defense. He had at least, he wrote, kept himself off "that long list of *tame* victims, who have been murdered in the South, for exercising the liberty of speech." Slavery, he exclaimed, "can no more live without the pistol and bowie knife, than the body without the soul."[37]

But as most Kentuckians saw it, only fanatics created need for bowie knives. If Kentucky's slavery ended Clay's way, it would perish in blood. Most Kentuckians preferred bloodless termination. When election day arrived, Clay's version of how to get rid of slaves attracted only 10% of the voters.

– 9 –

When the Kentucky Constitutional Convention met at the end of the year, more extreme Southwesterners endeavored to use the landslide against Cassius Clay to consolidate permanent slavery. Beverley Clarke, Perpetualists' leader, sought a constitutional guarantee that slaves could be forever imported. If a future legislature banned slave imports with another "infamous Law of 1833," Clarke worried, "the increased demand for laborers" would "be supplied not with blacks but with whites." Ohioans would pour in, "imbued with the spirit of fanaticism and abolitionism." After awhile, Kentucky "will become abolitionized." Beverley Clarke here sounded like Abel P. Upshur, determined that English migrants have no chance to emancipate Texas.

Clarke called emancipation "wretched policy." Slavery, he soared, "elevates the morals . . . and enhances the happiness of both races." He favored "perpetual slavery." He "made that statement with a full knowledge of its length and breadth, height and depth."[38]

John S. Waller spoke for most delegates in marveling at Beverley Clarke's "sublimated abstractions." Clarke's proslavery notions, declared Waller, "are new to me." If slavery is "a blessing in the abstract—a blessing per se," every Southerner should urge "all possible means for the enslavement of the entire black population on earth." No one could maintain "a position so monstrous."[39]

James Guthrie, president of the Convention, was not prepared to join Waller in discussing "the abstract question, whether slavery is an unmitigated curse . . . or an absolute blessing." But President Guthrie proclaimed that someday slavery in Kentucky "will cease." Cheap white laborers would eventually crowd into Kentucky. Depreciated slaves would be forced South. What folly, then, "to provide in this Constitution for the perpetuity of slavery."[40]

Waller and Guthrie commanded the Convention. Delegates voted 55 to 32 against Clarke's motion to ban future Laws of 1833.[41] The legislature of 1850, thrown the problem by the Convention, agreed to a compromise law. Slaves could be imported. But such imports could not be sold for five years. Since half a decade would be an eternity should black imports turn troublesome, Perpetualists would eventually demand repeal of this, as they termed it, virtual Law of 1833.[42]

Kentucky's debate over slavery had stalled, not ended. The stalling place was close to where Virginia controversy had momentarily ceased. Where Virginia legislatures in 1832–3 had exerted some, but not much, governmental pressure to drain blacks out, the Kentucky legislature of 1850 placed some, but not much, governmental inhibition on blacks coming in. Both compromise positions endorsed the *sine qua non* of Conditional Termination: that low percentages of blacks were essential before the institution could be ended. Majorities in both northerly slave states preferred that private slave sales would silently drain blacks southwards.

– 10 –

Cassius Clay would not accept that drifting verdict. Kentuckians' distaste for slavery and dismay about underpopulation, he believed, invited agitators to press on. He knew agitation must seek a slow end to the Peculiar Institution, with the central condition that the emancipated state must be lily-white. His magic formula remained a legislative decree of future emancipation, to accelerate present sale of Kentucky's slaves down south. So urging, Clay ran for governor in 1851. "For the first time in a slave state in the history of nations," he hoped, "a regularly organized" third party will permanently agitate "for the overthrow of oppression."[43]

That strategy required the South no less than the North to permit permanent agitation. In the North, free-soilers campaigned in election after election, slowly educating the mainstream and slightly increasing their votes each time. In Kentucky, Cassius Clay had secured a 10% beginning in 1849; and his argument held promise of gradually rallying more nonslaveholders as it became more familiar.

That was exactly the ongoing debate slaveholders were determined to abort. Republics never are overly tolerant of dissent when their most basic institutions are under foreign or domestic siege; and the Old South's republican slaveholders turned especially proscriptive when faced with continual heresy. The atmosphere combined a little physical violence with much screaming about disloyalty, insurrectionists, enemies of law and order. Peace-loving souls who preferred that slavery and blacks be sent elsewhere might risk a heretical campaign once. But if reformers lost the first time, as heretics normally will, the disposition to brave it all again and again took the abnormal imperviousness of a "Cash" Clay.

Most of Clay's followers were not that willing to be permanently stigmatized as outcasts. They had other missions, other causes, and no desire to live eternally as pariahs among their folk. The Reverend Robert J. Breckinridge, one of Clay's most important allies in 1849, articulated the moderates' submission to the intense pressure for conformity: "Having proved myself faithful to my convictions, I shall now prove myself faithful to the Commonwealth."[44]

Clay wrote to Breckinridge that he could "complain of no one," least of all so brave a cleric, for "you like myself have *suffered* in this." Clay knew "your sphere is the moral, mine the political." The politician saw that the churchman could not forever risk his important religious work, not over a constant reagitation the Kentucky majority thought "premature." Just do what you can, begged the increasingly lonely reagitator. "A word now and then will do much."[45]

The Reverend's word now and then was no match for the establishment's incessant declarations that "Cash" Clay must not convulse Kentucky over and over again. On election day, 1851, Cassius Clay's visible support dropped to 3000 votes, 3% of those voting. A discouraged Cassius Clay now saw need of outside support before inside waverers would step forth. He would form an alliance with northern freesoilers. Then he could emerge as the Southerner waxing most powerful in the newest national establishment.[46]

- 11 -

A Cassius Clay–David Wilmot alliance was an ideological natural. Like Pennsylvania's Wilmot, Kentucky's Clay was more whitener than abolitionist. Both cared most that blacks be contained outside their areas. Both understood each other's usefulness. Clay's bid to form a southern wing of a containment party made Yankee containers seem more national and conservative. No need for outsiders to meddle in the South. Northerners could just hem slavery in. Then southern allies, bolstered by national patronage and prestige, might draw southern dissent out of hiding.

If Cassius Clay became Kentucky's patronage-wielding boss inside a national administration, he could no longer be dismissed as outside the establishment. Kentuckians might then freely debate, with no lynch mobs roaming or bowie knives flashing or crowds demanding loyalty, whether moving blacks beyond

Kentucky was disloyal to Kentucky whites' interests. Then Clay supporters might re-emerge and white migrants might mass to the Bluegrass.

Clay's shift to a northern alliance resembled Pearl Andrews's shift to an English alliance. Neither could prevail unaided, despite persuasive population booster rhetoric, in a semi-closed world where persuasion was not enough. Both prayed that outside aid would crack their worlds wide open. Both relished the prospect of a continual free debate over how to people the frontier. Both would have better chances to win that debate if nonslaveholding migrants, Englishmen in Andrews's case and Ohioans in Clay's, came to an ever-whiter area.

Cassius Clay remained the more persistent threat. Andrews had bailed out when slavery heresies provoked dangerous hostility. Andrews's potential collaborators, those cautious English antislavery lords, had pulled back when America pushed in. But the knife-wielding Cassius Clay was in this war against the Slavepower for the duration. His potential collaborators, Yankee freesoilers, were no less permanently determined to cage the Slavepower. Clay's wish to speak as David Wilmot's southern voice made a united southern stance against the Wilmot Proviso the more vital.

So urged Wilson Lumpkin, the influential Georgia planter, ex-governor, and ex-United States senator. Heretics such as Cassius Clay, Lumpkin privately wrote John C. Calhoun, "are to be found in all the southern states." Such leaders "will be encouraged, at no distant day, to hoist the antislavery banner. . . . Then it will soon be recorded—the slaveholding states, *were*."[47]

Even if Clay's efforts for legislative encouragement of diffusion continued to be routed, slave sales to the Lower South could make Kentucky slowly less southern. The Bluegrass State someday "must be free, we admit," wrote the editor of *Debow's Review* after watching Clay's defeat. The day would come "when the superior southern demand shall draw off by degrees her slaves, and the continued increase of white population shall make the relative proportion of colors but a fraction of what it is now."[48] The tiny fraction of Delaware blacks, added James Hammond, made her "no southern or slave state." As for the rest of the Border South, Hammond wrote John C. Calhoun, "I would infinitely prefer disunion . . . for fear of future Clays."[49]

– 12 –

Hammond here expressed a central reason why southern extremists were developing a crisis mentality. These most worried of Southerners saw David Wilmot's and Cassius Clay's simultaneous emergence as a sign that the clock was ticking against the Deep South. The North appeared to be growing more hostile, the Border South more disposed to debate its southernness. "The settlement of the slavery question ought not to be postponed," a Mississippian wrote John C. Calhoun. Since "we are much stronger now, than we shall be two or five years hence," we must immediately "force Virginia, Maryland, Kentucky, & Missouri to make common ground with us." An important Georgian declared that only "an *early* dissolution of the Union" and a truly "*consolidated*" southern republic could "stop the process by which some states . . . are becoming free, viz, by ridding themselves of their slaves." A South Carolina leader urged that the slavery question must be met imminently, "and the sooner I think the better. . . . How long will Maryland, Western Virginia, Kentucky, Eastern Tennessee and even the western part of N. Carolina feel it their interest to retain slaves?" As James Hammond's brother summed up this extremist position, the Proviso crowd, "disguise it as they may," wished "to abolish slavery in the States." We must therefore "break up" the Union swiftly, before "Ky., Md., Mo. & Tennessee draw off."[50]

– 13 –

Southern centrist politicians called extremist fears exaggerated. Cassius Clay's possible impact, like California's geographic location, seemed to moderates too remote to justify instant disunion. Still, draining of Upper South slaves onto Lower South turf and Cassius Clay's effort to intensify the diffusion made David Wilmot's attempted containment seem a little alarming, even in less alarmist circles.[51] New York and Pennsylvania, Albert Gallatin Brown of Mississippi reminded the United States Senate in 1853, were once slave states. They sent many blacks southwards and ultimately freed the rest. "Virginia, Maryland, and the border states are now undergoing the same process." Within thirty years, the Lower South would contain eight million blacks. "When they become profitless or troublesome, we, too, want a South to which we can send them. We want it, we cannot do without it and we mean to have it."[52] That view of the distant future, and especially southern resentment of David Wilmot's immediate insult, made the question how, not whether, Southerners would resist the Proviso.

CHAPTER 27

Southern Convention,
Without a South

Southern debate about how to oppose the Wilmot Proviso resembled earlier strategic arguments. Once again, Democrats and Whigs differed over the best slaveholder defense. Once again in South Carolina, Calhounites disagreed with secessionists over how to get past the established political parties. But this time, South Carolina secessionists fought each other over how to accomplish disunion. And this time, Calhoun secured a southern convention—and prayed that some South might attend.

– 1 –

David Wilmot proposed his proviso in 1846. By 1848, the North-controlled House and South-controlled Senate were still stymied over the freesoil proposal. The question of whether to ban slavery from the Mexican Cession passed to the people, in a national presidential referendum.[1]

Southern voters had to choose between evasions. Neither major party could stand unqualifiedly for or against the Wilmot Proviso without self-destructing. On the Democratic side, Martin Van Buren and fellow Wilmot admirers would have relished a crusade against Slavepower expansion. But Southern Democrats would then have seceded from the party.

The Democracy's southern wing preferred protection of slave property in the national domain. Alternatively, Southern Democrats would extend the 36°30′ line to the Pacific, submit to the Wilmot Proviso north of the line in the Mexican Cession, and settle for slavery being allowed southward. That compromise would erase Wilmot's insult and might make southern California slave soil.

Most Northern Democrats feared political dangers in the North of inviting the Slavepower to seize half of California. But most of the northern faithful also feared that a party pledged to block slavery's expansion would lose the South. The better way was to fudge. Democrat's favorite fudge, variously labeled Pop-

475

ular or Squatter Sovereignty, sought to defuse nation-shattering controversy by moving contention from Congress to localities most involved. Instead of the House and Senate deciding on the Wilmot Proviso, settlers in the Mexican Cession should decide whether to allow slavery into their territories.

Popular Sovereignty grew out of earlier Jacksonian economic and slavery positions. Distrust for Big Brother/Distant Government had guided Jackson's thrust against national banks, national roads, and other Adams-Clay nationalistic commercial measures. Disdain for congressional talk or action about slavery had inspired gag rules. Applying old Democratic Party solutions to new problems led the party to coalesce behind the presidential candidacy of Michigan's Lewis Cass, an early apostle of Popular Sovereignty.

The decision to let settlers decide masked a strategic nondecision. To Northerners, Popular Sovereignty meant that territorial residents could ban slavery wherever they liked. To Southerners, Popular Sovereignty meant that squatters could abolish slavery only when their area was about to become a state. While a territory was in the national domain, so Southerners argued, the national Constitution dictated that slavery, like all citizens' property, must be protected.

In 1848 and for years thereafter, Democrats ducked this North-South difference. Let-the-people-on-the-spot-decide became a magic formula for not deciding *when* to let local folk decide. Popular Sovereignty as the Democratic Party's solution to the territorial controversy thus became akin to congressional nonsolution of the Texas Controversy. Then Northern and Southern Democrats, unable to agree over whether Texas should be admitted the Thomas Hart Benton northern way or the Milton Brown southern way, had agreed to give the President the option. Now Northern and Southern Democrats, unable to agree on when territorial settlers could vote slavery down, decided that a nondecision on timing would best maintain party unity.[2]

While National Democratic Party traditions yielded a program to evade decision, National Whig traditions yielded no program at all. Whigs had lately possessed an effective answer to Democrats' no-congressional-decision-on-slavery-in-territories: No Territories, period. But No Territories had become irrelevant. Territory had been annexed. Northern Whigs would not allow slavery in annexed turf, just as they previously would not compromise on gag rules or Texas Annexation. And Southern Whigs, having learned from Texas the cost of caving in to their Yankee wing, would not compromise on the Wilmot insult.

With no middle ground on slavery available, Whigs concurred on the perfect candidate: a national hero with no program on slavery, General Zachary Taylor of Louisiana. Southern Whigs relished their resulting favorable position before the southern electorate. The Democracy's ambiguity on Popular Sovereignty removed Southern Democrats' advantage in 1844: that their party alone stood pledged to a clear-cut proslavery program. Meanwhile, Southern Whigs reclaimed their advantage of 1836 and 1840: that their man was to the manor born. Zachary Taylor, large slaveholder from the farthest South, looked safer for slavery than Michigan's Lewis Cass, evasive politico from the farthest North. "Shall it be said," asked Alexander Stephens of Georgia, "that the South can not trust their peculiar interest in the hands of a cotton and sugar planter of Louisiana, but must look for a man in Detroit, who has not a feeling in common with them?"[3]

Stephens's question had a good answer: Whigs' favorite southern general was as ambiguous as Democrats' Popular Sovereignty principle. Zachary Taylor had never defined Whiggery. He hated agitation on slavery. Although served by over 100 bondsmen, his persuasion had always been nationalistic. His profession, the military, furthered interest in building national rather than sectional power. His area, the Louisiana black belt, had nourished the only significant Deep South nationalistic opposition to Jacksonian states' rights principle in 1828. His favorite Whigs were Border South nationalists. Southern Whigs could no more be sure that their Deep South general would lead pro-southern campaigns than Southern Democrats could be sure that Lewis Cass's Popular Sovereignty would be applied only in the post-territorial phase.[4]

Taylor's ambiguity, however, had its Whiggish attractiveness. Southern Whigs' longstanding pleas that their presidential candidates were the more promising sectional partisans had always collided with Whigs' claims to be the more nonpartisan patricians. Taylor was devoutly nonpartisan. He even toyed with running as a No Party rather than the Whig Party candidate.[5] The general's contempt for partisans was a mood for this hour, a moment when two-party politicians were turning off constituents by offering no choices except evasions. Maybe the military hero as anti-politician might bring serenity to the nation—and peace with honor to Taylor's own planting class.

In 1844, when James K. Polk defeated Henry Clay, the Tennessee Democrat had swept all Lower South states and secured 51.4% of southern popular votes. In 1848, the Whigs' Zachary Taylor matched Polk's section-wide popular vote and secured three Lower South states. The President-elect was the first from the Deep South (and the last until Lyndon Baines Johnson in the 1960s). Southern Whigs were hopeful. After the horrors of the Texas issue, Zachary Taylor might yet make Whiggery safest for slaveholders.

– 2 –

Southerners outside the establishment saw no hope in the Election of 1848's campaign or outcome. The contest between an uncertain man and an uncertain principle seemed to anti-party South Carolinians especially disastrous in the face of a growing third party. Martin Van Buren, still fuming that the Democracy had turned him down over Texas in 1844, left the National Democratic Party in 1848, at least temporarily, after the Wilmot Proviso was rejected. The Little Magician, who had long been attacked in the South as Cuffee-like pretender of friendship, accepted the Free Soil Party's nomination. Van Buren ran on the Wilmot Proviso basis. He would not attack slavery in southern states. He would "only" keep it out of new territories.

This containment version of dislike for the bullying Slavepower won Van Buren one out of every seven Yankee popular votes. Because of the Magician's support, in 11 of the 15 northern states the winning presidential candidate received less than 50% of voters' accord. The South's phony old friend apparently possessed leverage over the northern balance of power. In the face of this Free Soil Party, South Carolinians stormed, southern leaders betrayed slavery by debating whether an ambiguous principle or an ambiguous candidate could best save the South.

South Carolinians fell back on their old explanation for treachery at the top: politicos' interest. Not slavery's needs but spoilsmen's appetites and mobocracy's vulnerabilities governed southern politics. Demagogues, desiring national patronage, required national parties and therefore sectional lethargy. Leaders thus lulled the gullible electorate with soothing ambiguities. What might wake up the citizenry?

One answer, campaigns to perpetuate slavery, remained untested. Desire to diffuse slavery through a safety valve remained non-heretical in various Souths located north and west of South Carolina, as the late Texas annexation and Kentucky slavery debates had shown. Only in Carolina were pro-slavery craftsmen such as James Hammond and William Harper routinely polishing perpetual slavery polemics in the 1830s and '40s. "The greater part of" slaveholders outside Carolina, complained Robert Barnwell, Thomas Cooper's respected successor as president of South Carolina College, were "mere negro-drivers, believing themselves wrong and only holding on to their negroes as something to make money out of." Worse, Carolinians themselves had "retrograded . . . and must soon fall into the same category."[6] With Carolina becoming more like the South than the South was becoming like Carolina, politicians would eternally debate ambiguous solutions and voters would understandably snooze.

Most South Carolinians' unambiguous preference remained the same: secede. Most Carolinians' post-nullification deterrent to disunion also remained identical: too scary to secede alone. Only a few Carolinians remained dedicated to their little state forcing revolution on all other Southerners.[7] The more popular secessionist solution in the late 1840s better fit Carolina's reluctant revolutionary mentality. Carolina should secede, but only after waiting to ensure that several other states would cooperate.

James Henry Hammond, a leader of this Cooperative State Secession movement, epitomized the colliding precipitous and cautious impulses that informed the movement. Hammond was that precipitator of the gag rule who had fled to Europe when Southern Democrats compromised his initiative. Hammond's 1836 conspiratorial correspondence with Thomas Cooper's disunion crowd and with Virginia's Beverley Tucker had yielded much provocative rhetoric but little sustained revolutionary planning. In 1842, Carolinians raised their favorite charger/retreater to the governor's chair.

While sitting in that chair, Governor Hammond brought to a grotesque private climax the same passive/aggressive impulses which, when more attractively and publicly deployed, drew Cooperative Secessionists toward him. James Hammond's four nieces, daughters of the powerful Wade Hampton, aged 13 to 18, made themselves available to the governor. These girls came "all of them rushing on every occasion into my arms and covering me with kisses, lolling in my lap, pressing their bodies almost into mine, . . . encountering warmly every part of my frame." No man "of flesh and blood," as the uncle defended his acquiesence in his nieces' pleasure, could "withstand this." He and they let his hands "stray unchecked over every part of" their bodies, including "the most secret and sacred regions—and all this for a period of more than two years continuously." But the uncle with the straying hands would not go too recklessly far. His adventures stopped "short of direct sexual intercourse."[8]

Suddenly, a niece seated atop the governor thought Hammond held back too little. She told her parents. Her father, Wade Hampton, privately declared Hammond beneath contempt. The contemptible uncle responded in his typically aggressive/passive manner. He wandered out-of-doors, making himself available for one of Hampton's bullets. Nothing happened.[9]

After his term as governor was finished, James Hammond passively withdrew to his isolated swamps. He there wrote aggressive tracts in defense of that cause only Carolinians were much defending in the 1840s, perpetual slavery.[10] Meanwhile, this impure author of the purest Carolina gospel awaited Carolinians' next call to lead a charge ahead—but not all the way afield.

Debate between Hammond's more numerous, more cautious Cooperative State Secessionists and Carolina's more scarce, more precipitous Separate State Secessionists left the state's most famous extremist isolated again. Against secessionists of various stripes in South Carolina and against ambiguities of various sorts in the Democratic and Whig parties, John C. Calhoun clung to his favorite post-nullification remedy. A southern convention should issue ultimatums. Then a South united could save itself, in the Union if possible, out of it if necessary.[11]

As usual in affairs southern, a divided society agreed best on what to be against. Democrats, Whigs, Calhoun, Cooperative State Secessionists, and Independent State Secessionists all concurred that Southerners must resist freesoilers. They also agreed that southern divisions undermined resistance. But how could divisions be ended?

– 3 –

Soon after the Election of 1848, Calhoun called a purely southern, nonpartisan congressional caucus to solve that problem.[12] Alas, the South's most committed party politicians were as distrustful as ever of his forays outside party. Georgia's powerful youthful triumvirate—the Whigs' Robert Toombs and Alexander Stephens and the Democrats' Howell Cobb—led the southern congressional establishment's opposition to Calhoun's caucus. Toombs and Stephens urged southern colleagues to rally behind the Whig Party and their own native son, President-elect Zachary Taylor.[13] Cobb urged southern leaders to continue ruling the nation through the Democratic Party.[14]

This southern attachment to national parties, at a moment when neither party served the region's anti-Proviso frenzy, showed the strength of the two-party system in the South.[15] Both national parties, if unsatisfyingly equivocating on new slavery issues, called forth satisfying memories. So many treasured battles had been fought for so many years, at national and especially local levels, for and against individualism and community, a galvanizing presidency and a chaste Congress, entrepreneurial adventures and state-regulated commerce, Old Hickory the hero and King Andrew the Caesar. By saying no to Calhoun, national party leaders, speaking for a million southern voters out in the countryside, declared that party shrines remained too holy to be abandoned over this probably temporary crisis.

Understanding what he was up against, Calhoun wrote a Southern Address long on ambiguous language. Southerners should unite, went the phrasing, "on all necessary measures. Beyond this," Calhoun lamely prayed, "it would not be necessary to go."[16] But most of Dixie's most powerful leaders would go nowhere with John C. Calhoun. After three angry meetings and a final caucus vote, less than 40% of southern congressmen rallied behind Calhoun's vague Southern Address.

Calhoun, perhaps realizing that this fight was his last, determined to appeal over congressmen's heads. The South, he urged in a region-wide correspondence, must at last convoke that southern convention. An ultimatum from a united South might give Northerners pause. That remedy "might yet save the Union, or failing to do that, the South and its institutions."[17]

First, some South had to call a convention. South Carolinians, the only Southerners eager for a new beginning, could not take the lead, lest they thereby brand a southern convention as a prelude to secession. Nor could Carolina extremists openly urge others to step forward, lest that effort too damn the movement. They had to lay low. If they laid too low, no southern convention might be called.

The best non-Carolina hope for a call lay in the Mississippi Slaveholders Convention, meeting in response to Calhoun's Southern Address in October 1849. Calhoun instructed Mississippi correspondents to initiate a southern convention. Mississippi delegates to the Slaveholders Convention kept his instructions under wraps. "We adopted the idea with ardor," Calhoun was told. "But all concurred in opinion, that if we should proceed on a course recommended from South Carolina, we should fail."[18] For the same reason, South Carolina's semi-official secret agent to the Slaveholders Convention declined an invitation to speak. The agent had to work around Mississippians' "dread" of committing "themselves to any mode of action having its origin in South Carolina."[19]

A Carolinian for once did not need to lead. Mississippi's General E. C. Wilkinson, giving the Mississippi conclave's only elaborate address, summed up the need for a southern convention. Wilkinson called California perfect for slave labor. But with no territorial slave code and much "bluster and menace" against slavery, slaveholders felt more comfortable risking fortunes elsewhere.

In California and throughout the Union, lamented Wilkinson, events were moving towards "a speedy annihilation of slavery." Black bondage "is openly talked of everywhere, even among the slaveholders themselves, as a doomed institution." Slaveholders "usually *excused*" bondage as a lamentable necessity and "scarcely ever thought of vindicating it." Once concede slavery is wrong, warned Wilkinson, "and you admit" you must "get rid of it as soon as you safely can."

While slaveholders were becoming more and more demoralized, slavery was becoming "more and more circumscribed." At the time of the American Revolution, eleven of thirteen states were slaveholding. By 1849, five of the eleven had rid themselves of the institution. Delaware would soon join the nonslaveholding majority. Kentucky would not be far behind. Everywhere in more northern climes, agitation, violence, impotent fugitive slave laws, and sale of slaves southwards led masters to abandon the cause. In the Upper South, those who stuck it out were confronted with decreasing slaves, increasing nonslaveholders, and the cry of "down with the privileged few." That cry had resounded with Cassius Clay, and "let no one imagine it is forever dead. It is soon to be revived under a new and more terrible form, and is just as certain ultimately to prevail."

In six to eight years, predicted Wilkinson, what with emancipated states and new states, the North would possess the three-fourths' majority needed for a constitutional amendment. By then, Lower South blacks, augmented by slaves sold from the Upper South, would outnumber whites. Freedmen crowded in black belts would precipitate race war. Only an immediate southern convention could avoid catastrophe.[20]

The Mississippi Slaveholders Convention, accepting Wilkinson's remedy, called all southern states "to counsel together for their common safety." A southern convention, resolved the Mississippians, should meet in Nashville, Tennessee, on the first Monday of June 1850.[21] Calhoun, jubilant that his own brainchild was coming to pass for the first time since nullification, urged Southerners to descend on Nashville. "The course adopted by Mississippi," he wrote Florida's David Yulee, is "the only one that affords any prospect of saving the Union; or if that should fail, of certainly saving ourselves."[22]

James Hammond, distrustful of Calhoun's Union-saving, would use the southern convention to secure Cooperative State Secession. "If the Convention does not open the way to dissolution," he wrote one of Virginia's very few secessionists, Edmund Ruffin, "I hope it shall never meet."[23] At the convention, several states could pre-agree on secession. Then Union could be safely sundered.[24]

Before anything precipitous could be safely accomplished, enough Southerners had to attend the Nashville Convention. Two-party politicians who resolved to stay away formed a Who's Who of southern leaders. The entire Border South, Louisiana, and North Carolina sent nary a delegate. Texas dispatched one, Arkansas scraped up two, Virginia and Florida a bare half-dozen each. Ninety-five percent of Georgia voters stayed home when asked to select representatives. Only South Carolinians marched on Nashville with a full delegation and a fair sampling of state leaders. The southern establishment had expected just such a South Carolina over-representation, which is why the great southern middle remained anchored in Washington.

– 4 –

South Carolina's reactionary revolutionaries should have returned home after their first glimpse of Nashville.[25] Tennessee's capital city, situated in the middle of the Middle South, epitomized why the southern center half-wished South Carolina would drift off to sea. To the north of Tennessee loomed Cassius and Henry Clay's Kentucky. To the south lay William L. Yancey's Alabama and Jefferson Davis's Mississippi. Traveling east in Tennessee from Nashville, one soon came upon mountainous terrain and rednecks fond of Cassius Clay. Traveling west in the state, one edged towards the Mississippi River and planters worshipful of Jefferson Davis. Nashville, hub of so-called Middle Tennessee, was a nondescript, pleasant enough little place, indistinguishable from a dozen other southern—and northern—towns.

Indistinguishable except for the capitol building, pride of Nashvilleans and symbol of their neutralities. The structure, still being finished as the Southern Convention met, towered atop Billy Goat Hill, the highest eminence to be found. To decorate a summit snatched from goats, Nashvilleans imported a Philadelphian, William Strickland. To shape his design, Strickland imported a dab of Greek and a smattering of Scottish. The capitol's exterior was classically Athenian, with a Doric base, Ionic porticoes, and a graceful rectangular shape.

Graceful, if someone had chopped off the top. Strickland crowned his flowing rectangular with a constricted round Greek monument, slapped on a crabbed square base. Inside, the building featured its library, an exact replica of Sir Walter Scott's eighteenth-century study. Strickland's jumbling of other people's styles hinted at a town too much in the middle of other worlds to define its own identity. Strickland's conglomerate also prefigured that equally symptomatic moment, a half-century hence, when Nashvilleans would select, as their Centennial project, a perfect plaster cast model of the imperfect Parthenon.

In the mid-nineteenth century, as in the mid-twentieth, rhythms of the countryside best defined Nashville's native mentality. A few miles down the road lay the Hermitage, long Andrew Jackson's home, now his graveyard. The Big House here was classically Greek too. But lines were simple, without monuments to warriors. One caught few hints of the epic Jackson, massacring the English at New Orleans, slaughtering Indians in Florida, demolishing Nicholas Biddle and aspiring to hang John C. Calhoun.

The Hermitage's atmosphere was surprisingly domestic. Rooms were cramped, windows small, furnishings typified by Jackson's undersized bed. Jackson's original Hermitage dwelling, that lovingly patched and expanded log cabin, remained as relic of ruder, harder, equally pleasant times. Near the house survived Rachel Jackson's garden. Here the old gentleman had spent hours every night, pruning his flowers and mourning his woman. Jackson's basic passions—for his rustic wife, for southwestern opportunity, for American Union and National Democratic Party and the Great White Race—lived on here as naturally as evergreens and cedars lining his driveway. Jackson had left behind a monument, declaring that the southern center stood not for Cassius Clay or John C. Calhoun, not for Athenian democracy or Sir Walter Scott, but for family, party, neighborhood—and against Disunionists who dared to draw near.

To nearby Nashville the handful of Southern Convention delegates straggled, to reconsider the verities Tennessee's hero held most dear.[26] South Carolinians came on tiptoe, as if half-afraid Jackson might be there. "Our policy," James Hammond reported, was "to remain quiet." South Carolinians had to shed their reputation as hotheads and "show that we were reasonable and ready to go as far back to unite with any party of resistance as honor and safety would permit."[27]

By shrinking from initiatives, South Carolina ultras cleared the way for Virginia's Beverley Tucker to become the Convention's notorious extremist. The aging Tucker's new notoriety delighted James Hammond. Of all those unlucky enough to draw breath outside South Carolina, only Edmund Ruffin seemed so delightfully Carolinian.[28]

Beverley Tucker had been writing disruptive missives ever since sending Hammond that disunionist tome of a letter in gag rule times. In *The Partisan Leader,* a prophetic novel about disunion published in 1836, Tucker had made conspiratorial correspondence the key to Cooperative State Secession. "There had been," the novelist fantasized, "a preconcert among the leading men of the several States." Southern statesmen, seeing "that secession must come," had "consulted much together." They had secretly arranged a "nearly simultaneous revolution." Virginia had lagged behind. But the Lower South had "determined to wait for her no longer." The Cotton Kingdom had revolted and kicked Virginia into resistance.[29]

Beverley Tucker's conspiratorial gag rule correspondence with Hammond, advising the congressman to get on with secession, was an early attempt to forge history rather than scribble fantasy. In the early 1840s Tucker, once again playing professor guiding patriots, counseled his Whiggish Virginia friends, President John Tyler and Secretary of State Abel P. Upshur, on Texas. The above-the-battle intellectual feared that mobocratic politics had corrupted Tyler and might infect Upshur. But he saw some hope Upshur would influence Tyler to take on the mob. Tucker also prayed the Secretary could save Texas from England and in the saving salvage Tucker's Texas slaves.

In the late 1840s, having lost his pipeline to the White House, Beverley Tucker resumed his disunionist correspondence with James Hammond. South Carolina, reiterated the Virginian, must secede and thereby force the Upper South to fight. Tucker prayed "to God I were with you in S.C. It is a theatre where a man *can* act." If South Carolinian disunionists failed, "the doom of Sodom is upon us."[30]

This South Carolina view of alternatives was based on a South Carolina-like dismay about egalitarian republicanism. The Virginia aristocracy was more ancient than the Carolinian. Beverley Tucker's forbears had been distinguished in the days when gentlemen ruled Virginia and Virginians ruled the nation. The shift from Jefferson to Jackson seemed to the latest Tucker a plunge from natural aristocrat to demagogic despot. The Jacksonian mass, "uninstructed as the mass always is," and "exposed to the cant of demagogues about the inherent right of a majority to govern," would inevitably plunder the rich and usher in anarchy.[31]

Tucker ridiculed those who relied on the "quaking bog" of popular virtue. "Virtue? O Yes! The *Virtue* of the *people*!!!"[32] Like friend Upshur, he prayed that Virginia would never "relinquish her limitations on the right of suffrage" and "her little harmless aristocracy."[33] But unlike Upshur, Tucker believed that only secession could save national patriarchal republicanism from egalitarian infestation.

Tucker's South Carolina opinions were always tinged with Virginia qualifications. Beverley respected his father, St. George Tucker, Virginia's most thoroughgoing abolitionist in the Age of Jefferson. He also worshipped his half-brother John Randolph of Roanoke, who combined hatred of unchecked majority rule with inclination to manumit his slaves. The tension between hidebound political conservatism and incipient social radicalism, already implicit in Randolph, became a hallmark of Beverley Tucker. The William and Mary law professor told one correspondent that "civilization cannot exist in southern latitudes without slavery." He told another that "I care as little about the property as any man, and if a pledge were demanded would emancipate all I have."[34] Despite his conspiring with Carolinians, Beverley Tucker remained a son of the Middle South on slavery.

When Tucker claimed the podium at Nashville, he was 65 years old, tall and slender, socially as "vain as a peacock," oratorically as savage as Randolph. He exuded both the frost of an upper-crust patriarch and the bitterness of a self-appointed seer long consigned to the sidelines. Here again, he resembled his late friend Upshur, who had long cursed that he was "almost somebody." For over two decades, Tucker had lectured at youngsters, written bad novels, moaned that he would die unheard. Now, as the Southern Convention prepared to listen, his voice was almost a whisper. His lifelong stutter, which had reduced him to waging war with pen alone, made his whisper even harder to fathom.[35]

He was worth straining to hear.[36] Tossing aside discretion, almost choking on his own exaltation, Beverley Tucker displayed the fury of the revolutionary. In Virginia, he said, humane whites elevate black barbarians to Christian civilization. In Ohio, inhuman bosses drag whites into the pigsty. A compromise with Yankee slime, he said, was like a compact with the Devil. The South signed with blood. The North signed with invisible ink—the latest invention emanating from the cesspool.

How different it would be amidst "the magnificent future and glorious destiny of a Southern Confederacy." The new nation would be a natural union based on homogeneous institutions. It would be encircled by a natural boundary, from the Gulf and the Mississippi around to the Ohio, the Potomac, and the Atlantic. It would contain "no compact between power and weakness, simplicity and craft, generosity and selfishness." It would be the greatest nation on the face of the globe.

Southerners shrunk from their destiny, explained Tucker, only because they feared disunion meant war. But Yankees were too crafty to commit suicide. Manufacturers could not support war against their southern suppliers and customers lest economic chaos and lower-class revolt ensue. As for England, if her cotton looms stood "still for one month," not a single "stone" would be "left standing" in her "whole political and social fabric."

South Carolina extremists must have beamed as Tucker anointed cotton as world-wide king. They could not have been quite so happy about the Virginian's addendum. In a southern confederacy, believed Tucker, the South could at last work out the "destiny and destination of the negro race." Slavery was designated by God as "a school of civilization and Christianity." Since Providence demanded that every African be elevated, and since all could not be enslaved in America, uplifted slaves must eventually return as missionaries to their homeland. "The Colonization Society is a feeble, premature, and abortive attempt at this. The Negro has learned but half the lesson."

Graduation required not only catechism in Christianity but also training in freedom. A southern confederacy, within five years, would establish a colony for freedmen on the Gulf. There, isolated from Yankee agitators, "protected, regulated, and controlled by a Southern Confederacy," American blacks would learn their final lessons. "A time would come (and it will come, Sir) which none of us will live to see, when established in complete independence, they will be in condition to go forth from this normal school, and settle colonies of their own on all the coasts of Africa." A southern confederacy would thus enable slavery to "endure until it shall have accomplished that to which it was appointed." Beverley Tucker's revolution would yield St. George Tucker's emancipation.

Tucker's Virginia twist to a South Carolina tirade showed how badly Carolinians were isolated. If so sublime a spirit as Professor Tucker renounced perpetual slavery, who outside of Professor Cooper's graduates was sufficiently Carolinian? That question became more unanswerable as the Southern Convention dragged on. No speaker hit Beverley Tucker's mark. Most delegates aimed at some new national compromise.

By dropping back with the pack, Carolina precipitators ended up provoking nothing. The convention resolved to reconvene after Congress adjourned. Delegates also declared that though slavery should be protected in all territories, they would settle for protection south of the 36°30′ parallel.[37] They would settle, that is to say, for half of California and of other Mexican Cession territories. Nothing was added—and no agreement could have been reached—on what the South should do if the North refused to hand over half an empire.

After traveling home from Nashville and squiring Tucker around Carolina, James Hammond tried to be optimistic. At last, he wrote, the South had resolved. From such a base, Cooperative State Secession could spring.

Hammond knew better. Most Southerners had refused to meet in Nashville.

The rump convention had secured unity by papering over divisions. Resulting resolutions were representative of no one. The southern establishment was working in Washington for compromise and party.

Still, at midcentury, as in gag rule times, mainstream politicians had to pay attention to extreme voices. The Howell Cobbs and Alexander Stephenses knew that the territorial issue, if unresolved, could threaten the southern middle. Northern centrists knew that southern moderates, if left emptyhanded, might be helpless against revolution. Everyone knew that Wilmot's insulting Proviso lent fresh credibility to frayed Carolinians. Should the territorial issue be settled David Wilmot's way, the James Hammonds might yet make a revolution.

But if southern politicos secured honorable compromise, South Carolina would remain isolated. After the Nashville fiasco, Beverley Tucker's *Partisan Leader* continued to read like implausible fiction. James Hammond was again at bay in his swamps, waiting like Cuffee for Massa's Washington decree.

CHAPTER 28

The Armistice of 1850[1]

Two myths dominate histories of the Compromise of 1850. The North-South clash supposedly defined the antagonism. Henry Clay supposedly directed the reconciliation.

The Kentucky Whig instead provoked a controversy as important as the one between warring sections: a bitter clash within the South. Deep South senators demanded and secured critical revisions of Henry Clay's Border South design for sectional adjustment. Especially after slaveholders had made Clay's proposals less northern, the Southern Whig's bills could not have carried the majority section, unless Northern Democrats overcame Northern Whigs' opposition—and perhaps unless President Zachary Taylor, Clay's most threatening Whig rival, died.

Henry Clay's relative powerlessness left entities besides the nation but precariously intact. Southerners more than ever despaired that their section was divided. Southern Whigs more than ever winced that their northern wing was anti-Slavepower. Such longstanding perceptions, much sharpened by mid-century crisis and little dulled by an ambiguous armistice, would swiftly undermine the shaky settlement.

– 1 –

At the end of the 1840s, California's fate took such a northern swerve that only the emergence of other issues made appeasement of the Lower South possible. In 1848–9, discovery of gold in California lured 80,000 fortune hunters westward. Few gold dusters were Southerners. Only an occasional '49er brought a slave. Treasure seekers desired to make California a free labor state immediately. If free laborers' surge towards statehood triumphed, slavery would be barred in 16 states, allowed in 15. Southern control over the Senate, that longstanding counterpoise to the northern-controlled House, might be permanently lost.[2]

Many Southerners reluctantly accepted this unfortunate happening. California territory contained more people than did some states; and few Southerners denied that a state's citizens could abolish slavery. No United States government ban had prevented Southerners from peopling the Golden Hills. In the race to mine nuggets, Northerners had just arguably demonstrated faster feet. With a swifter population surge and not an insulting federal proscription propelling Yankees to victory, why defy a *fait accompli?*

Partly because federal inaction had arguably left another morally officious edict operative. The conventional belief at the time–a viewpoint probably true in retrospect—was that the old Mexican antislavery law remained in force in the Mexican Cession, until a new American law superseded it. In the late 1840s the American Congress, paralyzed over the Wilmot Proviso, had failed to pass a territorial slave law. Doing nothing meant doing something crucial: arguably allowing the emancipating Mexican law to continue. Southern entrepreneurs were reluctant anyway to experiment with valuable slave property in distant, uncertain California. With the Mexican legal ban apparently loading the dice still more in Yankees' favor, as some Southerners analyzed the situation, few slaveholders dared rush to the area.

That judgment led to demands for a fairer race. An American law protecting property of all settlers should replace the Mexican ban on slave property. The resulting fresh legal situation might or might not produce a southern surge towards California. But at least right principles would be secured and an unfair victory nullified.

Believing that Mexican moral proscription might have helped preclude an enslaved California, key slaveholding leaders were determined not to allow David Wilmot or the old Mexican law to bar slavery in other Mexican Cession areas. A countervailing American slave law would rid all New Mexico and Utah territories of the Mexican antislavery ban. Alternatively, congressional confirmation of Texas's extravagant land claim would shield at least some New Mexican territory from past Mexican and/or future Wilmot decrees. Texans claimed their domain, in Mexican times, had sprawled to the Rio Grande, north as well as south. Texas would then have included two-thirds of what became New Mexico and a little of what became Colorado. Less Mexican Cession territory would have been left for Mexican law and/or David Wilmot to declare off-limits to slaveholders.[3]

Most Yankees, and especially capitalists who had invested in Texas bonds, preferred another solution to the New Mexico/Texas boundary. Bondholders' lobbyists swarmed among congressmen, urging the national government to assume obligation to pay off Texas bonds. In exchange for national financial aid, Texas could cede its New Mexican land claim to the national territorial domain. More intransigent Southerners responded that a slave state must not be bribed to shrink its slaveholding borders. But more moderate Southerners saw that a sister state would be financially richer, as would congressmen owning Texas bonds.[4]

Meanwhile, slaveholders might not be land poorer. True, New Mexican turf, when no longer part of enslaved Texas, would be vulnerable to a law against slavery in Mexican Cession territory. But if Congress would defeat the Wilmot Proviso, and if the New Mexican territorial government or United States constitutional law would replace the Mexican ban with protection of the institution, and if enough slaveholders would come, New Mexico might become a slave state. These "ifs" added up to southern territorial prospects so chancy as to make Southerners churlish fellows.

An old irritant resurfaced to make Southerners still edgier. Since gag rule times, some Yankees had wanted to ban slavery in the federal capital. Failing that, reformers wished to bar slave sales in Washington. Federal action to cleanse the republic's capital of an unrepublican institution seemed to most planters symbolically distressing. Abolition in Washington would also be constitutionally distressing. A federal government able to emancipate in the capital could arguably end slavery wherever it had legal jurisdiction, including in new territories and in federal forts within slave states. Moreover, as Calhoun had pointed out long ago, the District as a freesoil enclave might menace neighboring enslaved counties.

Three significantly enslaved counties neighbored on the not-much-enslaved capital city. On the District's Virginia side, slaves comprised 30% of Fairfax County inhabitants in 1850. On the Maryland side, Montgomery and Prince Georges counties contained 32% and 53% slaves respectively at mid-century. Recently, slavery had slowly receded from these areas. Absolute numbers of slaves had dropped over 2,000, or 10% in the three-county region between 1830 and 1850. Washington's hinterlands thus formed both a symbolic and practical example of slavery's greater vulnerability when freer areas were close. If the District became altogether free, a rare black belt north in the South might come under more pressure.

A new federal fugitive slave law could relieve the pressure. In this age of little federal power or police force, Washington officials had to rely on state or local police to capture slave runaways who escaped to the North. Equally important, in this era where a very few Supreme Court and U.S. district judges had to cover all American areas, the federal government needed state and local justices of the peace to provide judicial processes under national fugitive slave edicts.

In its famous decision on *Prigg v. Pennsylvania* in 1842, the United States Supreme Court ruled that state and local officials need not supply police and judicial aid. Since the Constitution gives Congress exclusive power over fugitive slaves, the Court reasoned, state governments could proclaim themselves powerless to chase bondsmen.[5] After the decision, many states passed so-called Personal Liberty laws, barring their officials from performing Washington's fugitive slave chores.

Disappearance of state bureaucratic aid left the federal nonbureaucracy unable to cope with slave runaways, as several post-*Prigg* incidents made clear.[6] Some border slaveholders at mid-century, seeking to shore up the vulnerable law, asked Congress to provide federal posses and legal officials to help chase down human property. That controversial demand, when added to controversies over the District, Texas bonds, New Mexican boundaries, the Mexican Cession, and California, left centrists who would save the nation overwhelmed with their task.

– 2 –

Always before, the National Democratic Party had best played savior. In the Missouri, Nullification, Gag Rule, and Texas controversies, only Northern Democrats had cooperated with southern allies in passing concessions to the South. Southern Whigs could carp that Jacksonian concessions conceded the South too little. Or they could demand further concessions. Thereupon, the National Democratic Party usually delivered more and Northern Whigs always denounced the Slavepower more roundly.

This time, cheered those Southern Whigs who aspired to do most for slavery, everything will change. Never before had a Deep South planter secured the party's presidential nomination. Never before had Southern Whig sectional partisans such as Alexander Stephens and Robert Toombs of Georgia consulted with a President-elect about cabinet nominees. Louisiana's Zachary Taylor, exulted long-frustrated Deep South Whigs, would act as a Southerner should. By seeking national protections of slavery, the President would prove at last that the Whig Party could out-southernize the Democracy.[7]

Deep South Whigs' belief that their one man could turn around their party came partly because Taylor was so friendly to Southerners, partly because the Louisianian seemed too large a slaveholder to turn against his homeland, and mostly from desperation. The Texas issue had proved that slavery measures damaged Deep South Whiggery. The Whigs' No Territory solution had failed to keep measures about slavery out of politics. Emphasis on Taylor, the man to the manor born, had helped raise the candidate to the presidency. To sustain that loyalty theme, the elected Whig President now had to secure pro-southern law, in defiance of his party's northern wing.

But General Zachary Taylor, lover of national military strength, was not the man to stand defiantly for his section.[8] Many months before coming to Washington, Taylor had imbibed the city's longstanding terror of sectionalism.[9] The same impulses propelling Van Buren's Gag Rule and Cass's Popular Sovereignty guided Taylor's proposed way to defuse the crisis of 1850. Once again, a statesman sought to solve congressional slavery controversies by removing the issue from Congress.

Zachary Taylor would let states instead of Congress decide about slavery in the Mexican Cession. Between his inauguration in March of 1849 and his first annual message to Congress at the end of the year, Taylor privately encouraged residents of both California and New Mexico to write a constitution, then request admission as a state, with or without slavery, as each territory's inhabitants wished. Taylor reasoned that skipping the territorial phase, when Congress supervised areas, and rushing to the statehood phase, when Congress had no jurisdiction, would circumvent congressional controversy. Californians already had written their state constitution, Taylor told Congress in his first annual message. New Mexicans would soon follow suit. Congress should admit the two states and thereby escape congressional controversy on slavery in what would otherwise be territories.[10]

Taylor had no wish to complicate this end run around controversy by confronting other disquieting issues, such as fugitive slaves. The Louisianian considered irrelevant what was delightful to Northern Whigs and outrageous to the more sectionally oriented Southern Whigs: that residents of the proposed two new states would choose to be free. Taylor only desired to keep the nation free of slavery controversy. He succeeded in deepening the turmoil in his land and party.

Taylor has accordingly come down in history as a foolish novice, loose from the moorings of party experience and weakening the national institutions he sought to preserve. Much about Taylor furthers the image of a fumbling country bumpkin. He was a poorly educated soldier, short and squat, with a craggy face bordering on the ugly and a down-home way of speaking bordering on the preposterous. ("We are at peace with all of the world," went one of his laughers, "and seek to maintain . . . amity with the rest of mankind.") His most trusted advisers included New York's William H. Seward, that Yankee freesoiler most distrusted in the South.

Still, the image of the stumbler who blundered toward the North misses the point about Zachary Taylor and his style of southernness. His was the orientation of that nationalistic Southern Whiggery long most powerful in Louisiana and especially in the Border South. His program came straight out of his favorite Upper South counselors' late failed efforts. He would restore nonsectional, nonpartisan Whiggery, whole, patriotic, and triumphant.

Zachary Taylor's restoration required removing the side of Southern Whiggery which southern sectional partisans most wanted to emphasize: the native-born Southerner who would be surest to be truest to slavery. That partisan ploy in southern loyalty politics had always mocked the party's self-proclaimed image as rescuer of chaste republicanism from Jacksonian demagogues. Taylor, a Whig partly because a foe of disruptive politics, had been delighted to be nominated for President as a No Party as well as a Whig Party candidate. He would now rule as if No Party had elected him. Hitting Whig politicos where it most hurt, he handed out patronage posts to Democrats and freesoilers as well as to Whigs.[11]

Taylor also defied the very heart of the national spoils system: the newspaper-politician complex. Editors such as Thurlow Weed, Thomas Ritchie, and Duff Green gave their readers, alias voters, partisanly slanted news. Partisan candidates, when elected, repaid partisan editors with plum printing contracts to publish official debates and laws. The plushest and most powerful Whig newspaper had long been *The National Intelligencer,* based in Washington and supporter of Clay and Webster, those famous Whig partisans. Zachary Taylor would offer no printing contract to the likes of the *Intelligencer.* He instead started his own newspaper, with the appropriately classical title, *The Republic.* To edit this anti-insiders' sheet, Taylor imported a Washington outsider, none other than Albert T. Burnley.

Burnley was that Texas slaveholder who had continually warned his partner, Beverley Tucker, and through Tucker the Tyler administration, that only annexation could protect slave investments. This Southwesterner saw no parallel practicality in protecting almost non-existent slavery in New Mexico. Burnley instead latched on to another side of Beverley Tucker Whiggery: that the party must replace spoilsmen with patricians.

On slavery issues especially, Zachary Taylor and his closest advisers aspired to recapture Whiggery's nonpartisan legacy. The President's notion that the slavery issue should be removed from partisan contention recalled the effort back in 1848 of his Secretary of State, John M. Clayton of Delaware. Clayton was the ultra-nationalistic Border Whig who just might have deflected the course of antebellum history when he refused to be considered for William Henry Harrison's running mate in 1840, thus clearing the way for John Tyler, and soon thereafter Abel P. Upshur, and soon thereafter the Texas Controversy so harmful to Whiggery. In 1848, John Clayton, then a United States senator, had tried to muzzle slavery controversy by moving that the supposedly nonpartisan Supreme Court decide all territorial questions. Many Southern Whigs had supported this ultimately defeated Clayton Compromise. Zachary Taylor regretted that Clayton had failed.

Taylor's alternate way of snatching the slavery issue from congressional rabblerousers resembled another failed movement commenced by another Upper South Whig in the President's cabinet, Secretary of the Navy William B. Preston of western Virginia. In 1849, Preston, then in the House of Representatives, had moved to bypass Congress by making the whole of New Mexico and California one huge state. Some Deep South Whigs had at first relished that panacea. The Mexican Cession "cannot be a slave country!" Georgia's Robert M. Toombs had declared. "We have only the point of honor to serve, and this will serve it and rescue the country from all danger of agitation."[12] Taylor's New Mexico/California proposal sought to resurrect that Whig spirit, even if two northern states would result instead of Preston's one.

The President above all else would revitalize that Whig treasure his military blitz through Mexican territory had ironically helped slay: No Territory. By sweeping all Mexican Cession territory into two states, Zachary Taylor would leave no territories left to dispute. No Territory would kill agitation over slavery in territories, restore a Union where sections did not hate each other, allow No Party to make Whig nonpartisanship the saving reality.

Old Rough and Ready was soon thrashing around Washington in a manner reminiscent of Old Hickory. He threatened to veto any congressional plan not as pristine as his. He promised to march on Texas if that slaveholding state refused to honor freesoil New Mexico's boundary claims. Worse, by offering the North two states and showering Northern Whig partisans with the aura of a Deep South planter's nonpartisan administration, Zachary Taylor, general who would be peacemaker, helped lend the party's northern wing a fighting zeal as anathema to most Whigs in the farthest South as was Taylor's program.[13]

Nothing so poisonous had happened to National Whiggery since the only other time Whigs had won a national presidential election and thus had to govern instead of criticizing Democrats' administrations. But this time the poisoner was no Vice President who accidently became President, no states' righter who represented a southern extreme uncomfortable within Whiggery. Zachary Taylor was not John Tyler or Abel P. Upshur. He instead sought to represent all those big slaveholders in all those Whiggish black belts who had long found Jacksonians to be coarse, uncouth, embarrassing, not the way a patrician ought to sound. Such titans wanted peace and quiet, prosperity and union. They asked only that avenues toward silence not be insulting to the South.

Zachary Taylor, seeking a national silence insulting to no one, became instead the butt of insults in his section. That a Southerner so nationalistic, the epitome of the patriarchal Whig spirit, should resurrect No Territory, the most soothing of Whig dogmas, and end up with a program so shattering to National Whiggery illuminates something more than cruel paradox. Zachary Taylor's was the fate of a national party so badly divided that it could not rule on slavery issues, even with its most disinterested statesman pursuing its most nonsectional traditions, without shattering itself on the rock of section.

Taylor, mercifully, did not live to see the shattering. On July 4, 1850, the President sat too long in the torrid sun while helping to celebrate the nation's birth. He then downed too many cherries and too much milk. Within 24 hours, Taylor was in agony. Within five days, he was dead. The new President, Millard Fillmore of New York, was not taken with Taylor's resurrection of past panaceas. Fillmore would approve a new solution, assuming one could be found. Whiggery's fate now hinged on warring Whig congressmen.

The more sectionally combative Southern Whigs had all along been riding for a fall with their Taylor chimera, even assuming the President had been their hoped-for Slavepower warrior. The Whig Party was more than ever too topheavy to the North to become pro-southern. In the Congress of 1850, 64% of southern representatives and senators were Democrats; 58% of northern congressmen were Whigs. Northern Democrats controlled 56% of Lower North seats but only 24% of the Upper North's. Meanwhile, Southern Whigs controlled 52% of Border South seats but only 23% of the Lower South's. No hero, not even an Andrew Jackson, could have molded such predominantly Yankee and border troops into a Slavepower brigade.

– 3 –

Before Zachary Taylor died, another American hero challenged the Whig alias No Party President for control over mid-century issues and the Whig Party. For almost four decades, the Henry Clay who bid to save party, section, and nation from Taylor had been the most powerful slaveholder in Washington, save only for Old Hickory. But no one called the Kentuckian Clay of the South. Henry Clay was Harry of the West. Even more than Thomas Jefferson, whose slavery tradition he carried on, Henry Clay, to the Deep South, epitomized The Problem.

Abraham Lincoln, in contrast, would consider Henry Clay the solution. Lincoln would aspire to be a Henry Clay Whig in the White House partly because of the Kentuckian's nationalistic economics, partly because of Clay's Union-first priorities, and partly because the Illinois Republican and the Kentucky Whig shared the same vision of easing slavery away. Henry Clay, large slaveholder, deployed within the establishment a more politically aware version of the southern apologetics which his cousin, Cassius Clay, hoped might produce a southern wing of a Wilmot Proviso party.

On removing slavery, Henry Clay started out way to the left of cousin Cassius and quickly swerved well to the right. Witness Henry's proposals to the two Kentucky state constitutional conventions, a nice neat half-century apart, which formed bookends around his career. When a young politician just come to Kentucky in 1799, the future Great Compromiser urged an uncompromising end to an "enormous evil." Young Henry would free slaves and give them the "rights of citizens," after "poor orphans" had been properly prepared.[14]

Long before coming to cousin Cassius's aid a half-century later, Henry Clay had retreated to the orthodox notion that the poor orphans should never be let loose in America, much less as citizens. By chairing the 1849 meeting inaugurating the Kentucky slavery controversy and by writing a candid public letter to one Richard Pindell, Clay risked his establishment career in a manner that was not reminiscent of Thomas Jefferson. Clay's Pindell Letter remained a call for Jefferson's panacea: post-nati emancipation of Kentucky slaves born after either 1855 or 1860 at age 25, with three more years of American labor required to pay for mandatory transportation to Africa.[15]

Cassius Clay preferred to let removal from Kentucky pay for itself. He would force slaveholders to dispatch blacks to other states' slave auctions. Henry Clay, too genteel for that coarse remedy, also was no bowie knife-wielding agitator. His public declarations for ending slavery were occasional. Like Thomas Jefferson, he never would have called for class warfare against slaveholders. Again like Jefferson, Henry Clay always urged non-action on slavery, if action endangered Union. Where Cassius Clay, unlike Jefferson, freed all his slaves before attacking slavery, Henry Clay freed only a few of his 60 slaves, sold some, Jefferson-like, to cover debts, and emancipated only the afterborn of the remaining 35, with provision for colonization, in his will. The Kentuckian's final testament, like everything about the Clay/Jefferson version of Conditional Termination, was one great big compromise.

The Great Compromiser had still spent a career troubling slaveholding perpetualists by carrying on Jefferson's apologetic tradition. Clay had urged colonizationists to go for federal aid in 1827. His Distribution Bill of 1832 had called on states to use distributed federal funds to deport freed slaves. His gag rule speech had argued that emancipation in Washington was constitutional and should be essayed after Virginians and Marylanders swept slavery away. He had opposed Tyler's Texas treaty. In 1847, he had denounced further territorial acquisition from Mexico and "emphatically" disclaimed territory "for the purpose of propagating slavery, or introducing slaves from the United States."[16] The Great Compromiser, on the eve of "his" Great Compromise, stood for

David Wilmot's containment, with Abraham Lincoln's eventual addendum that blacks barred from diffusion over liberty's hemisphere might be redelivered to the Dark Continent.

Clay's famous senatorial oration of February 5–6, 1850, brought these lifelong themes to a climax.[17] The myth that the great speech laid down terms of eventual compromise is related to the myth of *a* South. Henry Clay, despite slaveholdings in the top 5% of southern planters, was too thoroughly a Border South man to define a settlement acceptable to Deep South planters.

Amongst Clay's proposals, only the least important secured both affirmation further south and eventual enactment to Clay's specifications. Still, that exception, Clay's suggested reform of Washington's slave trade, rivals Andrew Jackson's initial post office policy as a jewel of a political aside. Clay's gem loses its luster in the conventional generalization that the Kentuckian urged and Congress passed abolition of the slave trade in the District of Columbia.

Rather, the Kentuckian demanded and Congress enacted a law against only the most anti-patriarchal aspects of the slave trade. Henry Clay especially hoped never to see again a slave trader "shock the sensibilities of our nature" by pushing "a long train of slaves" down the avenue connecting the Congress "and the Chief Magistrate of one of the most glorious Republics that ever existed." Clay proposed striking down slave dealers and auctioneers in the republic's capital. The resulting law banned slave depots, auctions, and bondsmen brought into the District "for the purpose of being sold."

But other sorts of "kinder" slave sales could and did continue in the capital. "I do not mean" to abolish, Clay explained, a slave sale "by one neighbor to another." Private sales often put a husband together "with his wife or a wife with her husband." Thus was enacted a southern paternalist's utopia: personal sales of "the people," without impersonal slave traders mocking patriarchy.

Most southern patriarchs found every other Clay proposal intolerable without revision. No revision could have made tolerable Clay's suggested mode, or any mode, of abolition in the District. "It is inexpedient," ran Clay's phrasing, "to abolish slavery in the District of Columbia, whilst that institution continues to exist in the State of Maryland, without the consent of that State, without the consent of the people of the District, and without just compensation."

This sloppy wording, itself indicative of Clay's Border South mentality, could be interpreted as even more fatal to District slavery than Clay perhaps intended. Clay's verbiage invited the conclusion that even "whilst" slavery continued in Maryland, bondage could be abolished in the District, assuming proper consents and compensation. Maryland was already half-emancipated. The most populous and abolitionized half of the state, North Maryland, numerically could and maybe would have turned a state-wide plebiscite on federally compensated District abolition positive anytime after 1850.

Even if Clay meant that the District's abolition must await Maryland's, a critical change in his longstanding position made the liberation of Washington slaves more likely. In gag rule times, the Kentuckian had made Maryland's *and Virginia's* abolition and consent the prerequisite for action against slavery in the District. Clay now dropped the Virginia half of the precondition, he explained, because the District had lately returned all Virginia land originally ceded. Since the capital now stood exclusively on ex-Maryland land, only Maryland need consent. This narrowly legalistic argument ignored slaveholders' true reason for seeking consent of contiguous areas: because slaveholding neighbors cared if free soil was across the border.

Clay's critical revision also made District abolition more likely, for Maryland, unlike Virginia, was slowly evolving towards freedom. Henry Clay hardly here proposed, as the textbook formula has it, abolition of slave sales but not of slavery in the District. Rather, the Kentuckian would preserve private slave sales, abolish public dealers and auctioneers, and abolish slavery itself under forseeable conditions in Washington.

Most slaveholders found too much abolitionism in Clay's proposals for Mexican Cession territories too. His fellow Southerners must understand, instructed Henry Clay, that slavery could not and ought not spread, not into New Mexican territories, not anywhere at all. A New Mexico destined for mining was no place for an institution blessedly destined to diffuse outside the republic. "If nature has pronounced the doom of slavery in these territories—if she has declared, by her immutable laws, that slavery cannot and shall not be introduced there—who can you reproach but nature and nature's God?" Even if God had made slavery profitable, added Cassius Clay's cousin, "I never can, and never will vote, and no earthly power can make me vote, to spread slavery over a territory where it does not exist." He had no wish "to propagate wrongs."

Henry Clay urged Congress to affirm the morally right by admitting California as a free state. As for New Mexico and Utah territories, the Kentuckian considered Mexican abolition in force unless Congress explicitly repealed it. What Mexican law banned, nature's God scorned. Since desert climate would never tempt slaveholders, Congress need not pile the Wilmot prohibition atop Mexican prohibition. Clay instead proposed a preamble to laws organizing the two territories, stating that, "as slavery does not exist by law, and is not likely to be introduced," Congress would establish territorial governments without mention of the institution.

Nor should southern concessions end with language conceding the Mexican Cession now and possibly the District in the future to Northerners. Clay's most damaging proposal, from slaveholders' perspective, involved the boundary between Texas and New Mexico territory. New Mexicans claimed their southern boundary ran due east from El Paso, a third of the way across Texas, before the boundary curved way north. Clay would instead extend New Mexico's southern boundary straight across to the Sabine River.[18]*

Clay thus would reduce Texas to half of its claimed self, just as Thomas Hart Benton had proposed in annexation times. Worse, by lecturing Texans "to be satisfied with" an area "competent to form two or three states," Clay

*See map, p. 366.

would gut Southerners' hard-won authorization to divide Texas into five states.[19] Worse still, the Great Compromiser would excise from enslaved Texas some of the state's lushest river bottom lands, areas where slavery was already well entrenched and would swiftly become massively consolidated.[20] Clay's line would have given to New Mexico the upper reaches of the Brazos, Trinity, and Sabine river valleys and the whole Texas side of the Red River. On the proposed New Mexican side of Clay's boundary line lived in 1850 some 20,000 bondsmen, one-third of Texas's slave population. The area to be sliced from Texas included the county with by far the state's largest slave population (53% enslaved) as well as four of the next six largest (averaging 38% enslaved). All these river valleys naturally conducive to slavery would be swept into a New Mexico Territory where Clay's governing statute would declare that Congress forbear to pass slavery laws since nature's God and Mexican law already banned the institution!

Clay's proposed Texas boundary would likely not have freed those 20,000 slaves, any more than the Northwest Ordinance had freed slaves already in Illinois. Panicky slaveholders might have seized control of the New Mexican legislature or moved their some $15,000,000 investment in forced labor out of the imminently to be freed zone. But Henry Clay's line on the map would have effected one of the largest mutilations of an enslaved state ever to be proposed in an antebellum Congress. This was a compromise?

The Great Compromiser answered that Yankees must make concessions too. The federal government, by assuming the Texas debt, should pay Texans to surrender half their claimed territory. Congress should also hand Southerners an enforceable fugitive slave law. That law, said Clay in yet another defiance of southern orthodoxy, should include jury trials in the South for fugitives extradited from the North.[21] With mutual concessions, concluded Clay while waving a fragment of George Washington's coffin, the Union would be preserved. Without any concessions, he added while glaring at southern hotheads, he would "defy all power upon earth to expel me or drive me" from my country.

Henry Clay's peroration recalled Zachary Taylor's language. The two nationalistic Southern Whigs would both concede the entire Mexican Cession, one way or another, to the North. But colliding ways of conceding showed again that the Deep and the Border South remained different worlds. Taylor, large slaveholder of the southernmost South, sought solutions shorn of David Wilmot's insult to his class. Clay, big slaveowner in the northernmost South, endorsed the insult. Slavery was wrong. It must not expand. It should ideally be expelled from the District. It ought to be removed from half of Texas. So ran this Southerner's idea of a national party's mission.

Not since Thomas Jefferson reached out for a colonization alliance with Jared Sparks had a southern insider stood so ready to work with helpful outsiders to secure a national program so dubious for slavery. Not since Lord Aberdeen sent out tentative feelers about chipping away at New World slavery had a national statesman sought a Manifest Destiny for Texas—and for North

America—so free of enslavement. Like Jefferson's and Aberdeen's cautious gestures towards terminating slavery, Clay's program was so highly conditional on national concurrence and peace that proslavery warriors could easily deter it. But with Henry Clay's plan now vying with Zachary Taylor's as the foundation of National Whiggery, southern intransigents felt compelled to get on with deterrence.

– 4 –

Henry Clay's prime Southern Democrat antagonist launched the anti-Clay onslaught from a weird angle. Mississippi's Senator Jefferson Davis, who had made a minor name for himself in the Mexican War, emerged as the major Deep South opponent of the Border South hero. The Mississippian fought the Kentuckian in the name of slavery's blessings. But Davis's plantation practices implicitly announced that southern slavery was normally not so blessed.[22]

The locale of the Davis family's effort to bend a normally defective institution into abnormal beneficence was called, for other reasons, Davis Bend. Below Vicksburg, the Mississippi River bends west and then almost immediately east again, forming a lush peninsula. The Davis plantations, uniquely nourished on three sides by the South's greatest river, were uniquely managed on a northern principle. Slaves could not be whipped or ironed on Davis Bend until a jury of peers voted to convict the accused. By insisting on jury trials for noncitizens, the Davises implicitly declared that in republican America, legitimate social control required more consent than was acted out in those Massa-Cuffee charades.

A Davis plantation's spot for legitimate republican rapprochement was called the Hall of Justice. Within these "courthouses," slaves were judge as well as jury. Overseers were prosecuting attorneys. Massa Davis retained power only to *lower* the sentence on allegedly disobedient slaves, should he believe a slave jury authorized too many lashes.

Overseers loathed this institutionalization of slaves' overseeing. The employee's unhappiness necessitated the employer's presence. Without slaveowners resident and powerful, slave jurors and exasperated overseers could irrevocably clash. Then indiscriminate lashing, dismissed overseers, exasperated new managers, worse lashings, and more dismissals would ensue. That defect in the Davis system notoriously plagued Jefferson Davis, who spent many months in Washington as senator and cabinet member.

Jefferson Davis still persisted in the novel management system. Persistence despite adversity yielded proof of the senator's sincere belief in Davis Bend's unusual reconciliation of democracy and slavery. When the future Confederate president arose in the Senate to tell Henry Clay that slavery was a permanent positive good, he meant slavery not as usually deployed but slavery as not yet perfected by the orator himself. In 1850, lashing out at Henry Clay's apologetics, Jefferson Davis was a transition figure. He was somewhere between softhearts of the mid-1840s, with their pride that the shame of slavery could be diffused away through the safety valve, and pro-slavery reformers of the mid-

1850s, with their drive to transform permanent slavery into a more benevolent system.

Henry Clay, Jefferson Davis argued in the Senate in 1850, misunderstood the South's mission.[23] The Kentucky slaveholder came "here representing those southern interests which are at stake," and gave up "the whole claim of the South." Clay, not nature's God, surrendered slavery in California and New Mexico. Slaves were better miners than "any other species of labor." So too, slave gangs could best reduce raw California "to cultivation." But no Southerner would risk slave gangs in Mexican Cession territories while "congressional agitation" continued.

Davis especially loathed Clay's condemnation of slavery. Such submission to insult bolstered northern claims "that the South should be restricted from further growth—that around her should be drawn, as it were, a sanitary cordon to prevent the extension of a moral leprosy." So too, Clay's plan for abolition in Washington would make ours a "Constitution formed for the purpose of Emancipation." Clay would permit federal compensation for slaveholders who consented to abolition. This fatal precedent would enable the federal government to "take charge of the negroes of the United States and provide for their emancipation." Southern minorities would be forced "to fill the Treasury, in order that it may be emptied for the purposes of abolition."

And where were Clay's concessions to the South? In deploying federal funds to pay Texas's debt, thereby bribing Texans to surrender half an enslaved state? In urging a new fugitive slave law for Northerners to disobey? In asking free-soilers to forget Wilmot Provisos, so long as law and climate outlawed slavery anyway? In handling fabulous California to Yankees and thereby upsetting the senatorial balance of free and slave states?

The Union's fate, Davis declared, was in northern, not southern hands. If Yankees desired a compromise, let the 36°30' line be stretched to the Pacific. Slavery should be protected south of the boundary, including in southern California. But if Yankees preferred disunion, let them insist on Clay's surrender both north and south of 36°30'.

– 5 –

With Davis's speech, southern congressional battlelines were drawn. Slaveholders might come to lush agricultural areas such as southern California, hoped Deep South Democrats, if government made slavery secure. Anyway, agreed most southern congressmen, Southerners must not be banned as pariahs by any law, Mexican or American. Clay's plan for abolition in the District was anathema. His despoilment of Texas was unthinkable. His proposed laws were too Yankee to be borne.

In the face of this southern attack, Clay's proposed package was stripped of key words and provisions. The subject of abolition in the District was altogether dropped. An amendment pushed Clay's proposed Texas boundary way northward. The revision would restore to Texans half the land, all the then-inhabited turf, and all the enslavable river valleys Clay had wished to slice away.

While revisions of Clay's proposals scotched possible Texas and District emancipations, slavery's status in Mexican Cession territories was not clearly restored. Amended New Mexico and Utah bills were implicitly shorn of the Clay-endorsed Mexican ban on slavery. American law, both bills explicitly declared, would prevail on all territorial questions. But specifically on slavery, what American government's law and when? When a territory became a state, ran the revised bills' only explicit answer, settlers could decide for or against slavery.

That language settled nothing. Almost everyone agreed that settlers must decide at the statehood stage. Popular Sovereignty was a controversial solution to the pre-statehood, territorial stage. Southern Democrats continued to believe that territorial legislatures, by barring slave property, would violate slaveholders' Fifth Amendment property rights. Northern Democrats continued to counter that the populace on the spot could outlaw slavery anytime. Northern Whigs continued to demand either Wilmot's Proviso or Zach Taylor's two free states instead of Popular Sovereignty, however defined. Those colliding attitudes forced the Great Compromiser to throw up his hands. "We cannot settle the question," declared Henry Clay, "because of the great diversity of opinion which exists."[24]

Congress had to settle for a general grant of legislative authority to territorial legislatures, with nothing specifically said about whether the authority extended to regulating or abolishing slavery. Utah and New Mexico territorial legislatures would eventually use the vague authority granted to pass specific slave codes. Those latter-day territorial innovations, not any congressional words, alone justify textbooks' declaration that the settlement of 1850 institutionalized Popular Sovereignty in Utah and New Mexico territories. On Popular Sovereignty the Congress of 1850, like the Democratic Party of 1848, had to settle for fudge.

Congressional fudging on territorial slavery helps explain why Jefferson Davis and fellow Deep South Democrats rejected even the revised package of laws. These Southrons were glad that Clay's affirmation of Mexican law and nature's God had been dropped, that the District emancipation scheme had been eliminated, and that the Texas boundary had been shoved north and west of where any slave labored. The Wilmot Proviso also remained agreeably absent from the revised legislative package.

But the status of slavery and of Popular Sovereignty during the territorial stage remained a blank. Texas would be bribed to throw a still huge, albeit yet unsettled, land mass into this ambiguous realm. California would come into the Union as a free state, theoretically upsetting the North-South parity in the Senate. Why would this legislative package be acceptable to enough Southerners?

– 6 –

Because of that southern boon and northern hate, James Mason's Fugitive Slave Bill. The Virginia senator's bill, as amended and eventually passed, required alleged fugitives accused in the North to be extradited to the South without a jury trial, without right to a writ of habeas corpus, and with no right to testify in their own behalf. No jury trial was provided for in the South after extradition, as Henry Clay had proposed. A court-appointed commissioner would alone decide whether to extradite an accused runaway. The commissioner could summon any Northerner to serve in a fugitive-hunting posse, with a $1000 fine for noncompliance.

The commissioner's own reward was more trivial in dollars but as controversial in form: $10 if he extradited the black to the South, $5 if he let the alleged fugitive go. Extra paperwork involved in extradition allegedly justified the extra $5. Slaveholders' contempt for Yankee morality aside, few framers of the bill probably believed that $5 extra could seduce a Northerner to consign an innocent black to slavery. Still, the doubled payment (or pernicious bribe, as Yankees called it) for extraditing rather than freeing a black was as provocative a red herring as any American Congress ever included in an already provocative proposal.

Yankees begged Southerners to make the bill non-provoking. Northern senators wanted a jury rather than that non-judge, a commissioner, to decide on extradition. They also would allow real judges to issue writs of habeas corpus. Then northern communities would comply with the "just and reasonable" procedure for returning alleged fugitives. But an "arbitrary, oppressive" process was "much less likely to be faithfully executed." Nor would a slave-loathing citizen tolerate being dragooned into hunting down humans who were fleeing towards freedom.[25]

Southern senators believed Northerners had to be dragooned. Permit Northerners to refuse to be slave catchers, Southerners scoffed, and no successful posses could be formed. Allow Yankee juries to block extradition, and no slave would be returned. Without legislation drawn to southern specifications, declaimed James Mason, "you may as well go down into the sea, and recover from his native element a fish which has escaped you."[26]

This controversy showed again that both Yankees and slaveholders were democrats, but with a difference. While the racist North hardly provided color-blind justice, every accused northern black had a right to a jury trial. Southern trials of alleged slave insurrectionists, in contrast, often featured specially appointed commissioners serving as judge and jury. Forcing this non-jury procedure on the North, Yankees protested, meant condemning the accused and their offspring to life imprisonment, without judgment by their peers.

The South's democratic despots, once again revealing their colliding mentalities, defended this anti-republican procedure in republican terms. Jefferson Davis argued that northern jury trials for southern escapees would violate the logic behind the jury system. Extradition enabled justice to be served on the spot "where the facts can best be established." When an alleged murderer flees over state lines, Jefferson Davis asked, do you hold "a jury trial before you give up the man?" Give us back our accused, and our local neighborhoods will know whether the returned black was the alleged fugitive. A southern judge could correct neighborhood error with a writ of habeas corpus.[27]

Henry Clay's proposal, southern jury trials after fugitives' extraditions, would have made Davis's logic unassailable.[28] A Mississippian who provided juries for his own slaves might be thought amenable to the Kentuckian's proposal. But Davis's distinctions between appropriate and inappropriate juries for slaves, like Clay's discriminations between "good" private slave sales and "bad" public slave auctions, illuminate again paternalistic masters struggling against their system's anti-paternalistic tendencies.

Davis's juries on his own plantations were in part an unusual remedy for a usual slaveholder complaint: that impersonal overseers who lashed family servants, like impersonal slave dealers who smashed slave families, mocked a personalized Domestic Institution. Davis considered juries a necessary check on nonowning overseers. But Davis denied that paternalistic owners needed juries to decide whether an alleged escapee was one of "their people." Should a rare paternalist violate his obligation, a stray judge could issue a writ. The northern answer, that republicanism always demands writs *and* juries, contrasted starkly with the Davis retort, that the slaveholder as fair-minded judge made republican juries irrelevant.

Slaveholders' argument for requiring every Yankee to be a slave-catcher also revealed differences between northern and southern regimes—and another intriguingly strained slaveholder position. Within black-belt neighborhoods, the patrol, that sometimes-preserver of communal control over Massa's slaves, could draft any white. By wielding $1000 fines to turn Yankee posses into southern-style patrols, Southerners would impose in the North their legally sanctioned extra-legal means of adding nonslaveholder power to Slavepower.

But the very act of imposition showed how far the South had moved from federal powerlessness and a local neighborhood's domination over its own coercive sanctions. With fugitives, as with pre-annexation Texas and as with post-annexation territorial government, slaveholders wanted federal hands heavily laid on localities, whenever necessary to sustain the Peculiar Institution.[29] James Mason would deploy federal power deep inside Yankee neighborhoods, with white Northerners legally compelled to perform undemocratic process. That proposition indicated to Northerners that despotism would taint every northern citizen. Mason's Fugitive Slave Law would swiftly surpass gag rules as proof that despotism employed against blacks required anti-republican action against whites, South and North too. The obvious question obtrudes: Why did slaveholders insist on a law so potentially destructive of northern—and southern—viewpoints?

– 7 –

Explaining southern motivation for the Fugitive Slave Law requires precision about which Southerners are being analyzed. The question is not why the South demanded. With pressure for a new fugitive law, as with most everything, no South existed. On this peculiar occasion, the usually most intransigent South was the least demanding. In the Congress of 1850, Deep South senators emphasized that this "useless" bill measured up dismally against proposed northern gains. Only a thousand or so fugitives a year successfully escaped to the North, and those mostly from the Border South. A new law, like the old edict, might not stem the small hemorrage at the fringes. James Mason's bill, declared United States Senator David Yulee of Florida, was unenforceable in the North and worthy of "little interest." We in the Deep South, added Henry Foote of Mississippi, are not so "interested in this matter as are those slave states which border on the free states."[30]

Border senators, normally the least insistent Southerners, were the most aggressive on this subject. Kentucky, Maryland, and Virginia, the Old Dominion's James Mason told the Senate in 1850, "have had their attention turned very closely to the subject . . . within the last few years." Not many slaves had to escape before losses totaled "hundreds of thousands of dollars" annually. Senator Thomas Pratt of Maryland concurred that his state, as well as Virginia, Kentucky, Tennessee, and Missouri, are alone "interested practically in the bill." Yet Marylanders lost an unacceptable $80,000 worth of slaves a year, and "I do not know a single case in which the fugitive has been surrendered." While "very few" Northerners committed "this larceny," added Senator David Atchison of Missouri, "there are enough of them" to create "serious concern . . . in the border states."[31]

As Atchison's phrasing indicated, border senators were not to be appeased because "only" a thousand or so constituents were annually robbed. A few thousand fugitives sufficed, moreover, to raise questions about the Border South's fundamental order. In the most northern sections of the South, freedom was literally around the corner. Blacks who lit out for the Ohio River exemplified slaveholders' exposure. Border states could contain group insurrections. But a slave fleeing alone took the problem of black social control to its apogee. The phenomenon had already produced Frederick Douglass, and during the Civil War, it would produce fugitives by the hundred thousands when Yankee armies invaded the Deep South. Could slavery endure where climate was blustery, masters apologetic, blacks few, and enemies close? Or must bondage, to be altogether safe, slowly drain towards the tropics? As in previous Missouri, District of Columbia, and Texas controversies and as in the imminent Kansas controversy, the overriding problem was whether slavery on the fringes could remain in place or whether the South would gradually shrink to fewer and blacker black belts. Fugitive slaves such as Frederick Douglass had forced critical abstractions upon evasive congressmen.

James Mason, designer of the Fugitive Slave Bill, lived personally with slavery's exposure in northern hinterlands.[32] Jefferson County, Mason's turf, was at the northern extreme of the Virginia Valley. The county contained close to 30% slaves, the largest slave concentration in the Valley. Although absolute numbers of slaves in Jefferson County remained stable in the late antebellum period, relative percentage of slaves declined from 31% in 1830 to 27% in 1860.

West of Mason's Jefferson County lay ten Virginia counties bordering Pennsylvania and Ohio. These counties' absolute number of slaves plunged 28% between 1830 and 1850. The decrease over the next ten years would be greater still. At James Mason's northern fringe, some slaves were being sold south, partly because other slaves were fleeing north.

Since Washington, D.C., lay between North and South, southern congressmen personally experienced northern hinterlands' fugitive problem. Three weeks before the Senate took up James Mason's bill, Robert Toombs's and Alexander Stephens's houseservants departed. Both Georgians declared that their "well treated" people had "little reason to run off." Both learned that gun wounds had to be inflicted before their Cuffees "consented" to come "home." Both embarrassed Massas made scapegoats of Yankees who had allegedly helped the slaves escape. Both concurred with North Carolina's ultra-unionist Congressman David Outlaw that "it is abominable, that at the seat of the common government, a portion of the Representatives cannot have their domestic servants, without losing them."

Northern "stealing of slaves," Outlaw wrote to his wife, "furnishes more material for agitation than anything else, because it is a practical evil which we suffer, and a palpable wrong which the North commits, which comes home to the business and bosoms of men."[33] If fury at Washington's supposed kidnappers made Outlaw's letter a momentary exaggeration, the Fugitive Slave Law came out of the same moment. Both the letter and the law demonstrated that an abstraction presses harder on lawmakers when it explodes in their little circle.

– 8 –

With more northerly Southerners for once intransigent about a slavery problem, more southerly Southerners for once felt compelled to support a Border South demand. Southern union, however, swiftly soured. Southerners lit into each other so angrily on terms of the fugitive bill that Mississippi's exasperated Senator Henry Foote wondered whether slaveholders would "suffer eternally" from "discordant opinion and conflicting actions."[34]

This renewed discordance between Border and Deep Souths broke out over what seems at first glance an innocent enough—indeed a highly statesmanlike—proposal. Senator Thomas Pratt of Maryland moved an amendment to Mason's bill on August 20, 1850. Since the federal government was constitutionally obligated to enforce a fugitive slave law, Pratt reasoned, the federal government should compensate a master when northern hostility blocked return of a fugitive.[35]

While the $5/$10 "bribe" to commissioners was the most unnecessarily provocative aspect of the eventual fugitive law, Pratt's proposal may well have been the ideal cure. Armed with the Pratt Amendment in the 1850s, federal officials might have dampened northern rage, by not pursuing fleeing slaves within resisting Yankee communities. They could then have eased southern anger, by providing compensation for lost slaves. Pratt prayed that all southern senators "would upon this question (although they have upon no other) been found shoulder to shoulder."[36]

No way! Too many senators from the Deep and Middle Souths distrusted the Border South too much. The Pratt Amendment, charged Senator Hopkins L. Turney of Tennessee, was intended "to emancipate the slaves of the Border South, and to have them paid for out of the Treasury of the United States." The Tennessee senator believed that Marylanders and Kentuckians "would gladly emancipate their slaves, especially if they could be compensated for them." Pratt's scheme, according to Turney, invited border state residents to tell slaves to flee. Apologists would thereby free their blacks, whiten their region, and enrich themselves! Worse, exclaimed Andrew Butler of South Carolina, "dishonest masters" might encourage "their slaves to run away, so that they might thus obtain an overrated value for them." Butler gloomed that "some enthusiasts would hail with thanksgiving" this "mode of emancipation."[37]

Senator Joseph Underwood, Henry Clay's colleague from Kentucky, answered by conceding that "many" Kentuckians wish slavery had never "existed among us." Furthermore, "many" Kentuckians "are anxious to get clear of it." But only "a very small minority," bragged Underwood, would accept emancipation without race removal. While blacks stay, the Kentucky white would remain "the most ultra southern man you can find on the face of the globe."[38]

Jefferson Davis answered that Thomas Pratt would give Joseph Underwood all requisite conditions for deserting the South. Kentucky blacks would abscond, and the federal government would pay whites to allow the whitening process. Permit the federal government to "interpose its legislative and financial power" between the slaveholder and his property, and "where shall we find an end to the action which antislavery feeling will suggest?"[39]

When voting time on the Pratt Amendment came, almost half the northern senators abstained on this war within the South. The other half of Yankee senators voted against federal bounties for fugitives' owners. Yankee abstentions gave southern senators ability to pass Pratt's bounty in the Senate, assuming they voted strongly enough together. The Upper South rallied 6-3 for Pratt. The Lower South turned him down 8-4.[40] With fugitive slaves, as with Henry Clay's initial package, Deep South senators stood guard against all hints of Conditional Termination.

– 9 –

Deep South senators' attempt to salvage a piece of California revealed again a South divided against itself. The Nashville Southern Convention had called the opportunity to secure half the Mexican Cession an acceptable alternative to the Wilmot Proviso's bar on slaveholders. Jefferson Davis repeated the equal division formula when taking on Henry Clay.

Davis's Mississippi colleague, the quirky and less intransigent Henry Foote, sought slightly less for the South when the bill admitting California came to the Senate floor. Instead of the Southern Convention's and Davis's 36°30′ dividing line, Foote moved that California be divided at the 35°30′ line, approximately

60 miles further south, about at the level of Bakersfield.* Below the 35°30′ boundary, Foote proposed that a new territory, to be called Colorado, should stretch to the sea. Southern migrants might then implant slavery along the southernmost third of the California coast.[41]

The Foote Amendment, if passed, just might have produced an enslaved coastland. The land was rich enough; in the twentieth century, much cotton would be raised in southern California. Some state judges were sympathetic enough; state courts in free California in the 1850s would stall on freeing the few slaves imported during the territorial phase. Some inhabitants were willing enough; in the late 1850s, Californians in the southern half of the state would urge fracture of the commonwealth, in part so they could have slaves. Northern Californians would agree to let their erring brothers depart and form a slave-holders' state. The division of California would be pending in Congress when the Civil War commenced.[42] In the Golden State, as in Edward Coles's Illinois a quarter-century earlier, entrepreneurs would seek a despotism that law, not climates, deterred—and a despotism that democratic courts, despite the law, sometimes allowed.

In 1850, Deep South senators massed behind Foote with the section's most defiant words: give us our shot at California, or we may quit the Union. The Georgia legislature had proposed a state secession convention, should slavery be banned from Mexican lands. Barring slavery from all of California, declared a Georgia senator, would invite that secessionist conclave—and, worse, an assembly of South Carolina hotheads.[43]

The Deep South's least favorite senator scoffed at this ultimatum. Southerners who threatened secession unless California was divided, warned Henry Clay, did not speak for *his* South. Clay was striving to wring Union-saving concessions out of Yankees in exchange for southern acquiesence in free California. If irresponsible Southerners demanded their golden hills, farewell to union. Then, swore Clay, even "if my own state . . . contrary to her duty, should raise the standard of disunion, . . . I would go against Kentucky."[44]

I would go against Kentucky. No antebellum Southerner ever emitted a more revealing sentence. If the Deep South seceded to secure California, the Border South's hero would go with the North. And Henry Clay's border followers? They stood with Prince Hal against the Mississippi land pirate. One Yankee abstained in the eventual roll call on the Foote Amendment. The Yankee abstention gave a unanimous South the ability to win on California in the Senate. Lower South senators provided the needed unanimity for keeping Henry Foote's California maneuver alive. But the Border South voted against slicing off the southern third of California, 4-3, with one abstention. Another pair of Middle South senators abstained. Southern division had defeated the Southern Convention's pet proposition.[45]

The proposition probably had not long to live anyway. As usual, no southern law could pass the House without Northern Democrats' help. Yankee

*See map, p. 366.

appeasers on California would have seemed especially atrocious slaves of the Slavepower. A unanimous southern ultimatum for golden hills would have likely produced civil war right then and there.

No unanimous South was going to appear, for Henry Clay's South stood with the North. Not since Missouri times, when the Border South had voted for free soil in Louisiana Purchase territory north of 36°30', had a southern minority been so determined to endorse the Yankee majority's gain. Not since 1844–5, when Southern Whigs in the Senate had come close to defeating annexation, had southern division seemed so deadly. Now, in the senatorial vote on Foote's California Amendment, the most northern South for the first time cast the decisive votes against the most southern South, and thereby raised the largest question yet about *a* South.

– 10 –

After the Senate settled details of fugitive slave and California bills in late August, voting time on the revised version of Clay's proposals arrived. Clay had initially favored separate votes on each bill. But Henry Foote had convinced the Kentuckian to unite all proposals concerning the Mexican Cession in a so-called Omnibus Bill, to be voted up or down together. Sufficient Northerners would never vote to drop the Wilmot Proviso from New Mexico and Utah territorial bills, went the reasoning, unless the same vote secured free California. Nor would Southerners vote yes on free California, unless their affirmation also scotched the Proviso in Utah and New Mexico.

In pursuing Foote's Omnibus strategy, Henry Clay became a leader without constituents. Deep South senators had spent the session calling the Great Compromiser the slaveholder who sold out. They would vote no on any Omnibus admitting free California. Meanwhile, almost all Northern Whigs echoed their 1840 opinion that Henry Clay, of all people, was too southern. A proper Omnibus, they insisted, must ensure free soil throughout the Mexican Cession.

With Northern Whigs and Deep South Democrats both denouncing Clay's Omnibus, sectional extremes might overwhelm compromisers in a single vote on the parcel. Fearing that setback, Maryland's Whig Senator James Pearce, a Clay admirer, moved removal of the New Mexican territorial bill from the Omnibus Bill. Pearce prayed that some portion of the Compromise would thereby become acceptable to some majority. A momentum for settlement might then build.

Henry Clay, despite his apologetic slaveholder mentality, could be the dictatorial master when crossed. John Tyler had learned that all too well. The defeated Kentuckian, dreams of driving a last historic compromise through Congress shattered, now could not flexibly switch tactics. No matter that the newest ploy, separate bills, was his strategy before Foote convinced him to go for an Omnibus. Clay still blasted James Pearce. To no one's sorrow, the Great Compromiser then left Washington for a much needed rest. He was not destined to return until others had piloted "his" settlement to senatorial victory.

The leading pilot turned out to be not an old Whig but a newly important Democrat, Senator Stephen A. Douglas of Illinois. In seeking to mass his National Democratic Party behind a national adjustment ever becoming less "Clay's," Douglas expanded on Pearce's strategy. The Illinois Democrat would secure a favorable vote on each segment of the new-unraveled Omnibus. That strategy had saved the Missouri Compromise, ironically with Clay's blessings.[46]

Douglas saw that senatorial majorities existed for each piece of the Omnibus. In a Senate evenly divided between the two sections, the North needed only one southern deserter or abstainer to pass the bill admitting free California. Likewise, the South needed only one abstaining Yankee to secure a juryless fugitive bill and to defeat the Wilmot Proviso in Utah and New Mexico. Douglas secured turncoats in the usual places. Southerners voting the North's way on California included most Border South senators and Sam Houston. Meanwhile, Northerners voting the South's way on juryless fugitive slave extradition and on an ambiguous status for slavery in Utah and New Mexico territories were almost always Northern Democrats. In the Senate, the Democratic Party had again supplied the power for a not-so-democratic Slavepower law and had again left its Popular Sovereignty formula deliberately vague.[47]

– 11 –

National Democratic Party strategists in the House of Representatives faced a more difficult test of Douglas' separate bill ploy. The Democratic Party controlled 55% of the Senate but only 48% of the House. Worse, the South commanded 50% of the Senate but only 40% of the House.

The theoretically hardest House majority to fashion, a plurality for the 40% minority's fugitive slave bill, ultimately swelled to surprisingly large proportions, 109-76. Every voting southern congressman said aye; for once, *a* South existed. But the South triumphed for the more usual reason: Northern Democrats, when needed, swallowed their resentment and aided the slaveholders. The Democracy's Yankee wing voted 27-16 for Mason's juryless fugitive slave bill. As usual, Upper North Democrats were least accommodating to the South, voting 7-6 aye. Lower North Democrats massed behind southern colleagues, 20-10. Only three of 74 Northern Whigs voted for the South's favorite bill. In all, northern representatives voted 70% nay. Northern Democrats, caring more about party and Union than about their section's preferences, again gave the minority section its national majority.

Majorities were hardest to attain on the Texas land-for-debt bargain and on the ambiguous status for slaves in New Mexico and Utah territories. More intransigent Northerners wanted to pay nothing to a Texas stripped of its New Mexico land claim. They also wanted to bar slavery in the resulting maximum-sized New Mexico territorial domain. More intransigent Southerners wanted enslaved Texas to keep its entire land claim. They also wanted slavery guaranteed in the resulting minimally sized New Mexico territory.

The key test of whether the American middle would hold against these sectional extremes came on a so-called Little Omnibus Bill, combining the bribe for Texas shrinkage with nondecision on slavery in New Mexico Territory. Upper South Democrats voted 2:1 and Northern Democrats 3:1 yes on the package. Northern Whigs voted 2:1 and Deep South Democrats 3:1 no. Only Southern Whigs could offset the Deep South Democrat/Northern Whig negation and thus save the Little Omnibus and the ultimate national settlement. Southern Whigs went for the Little Omnibus, 24-1, allowing it to squeak through, 108-97.[48] That vote paved the way for the revised version of Clay's proposals to slide through the House and into the statute books.

The saviors of the Little Omnibus were the largest potential losers from the compromise. Southern Whigs secured a national settlement based on a new fugitive slave law and without the insulting Proviso. Northern Whigs scorned that goal. Northern Democrats helped gain it. Southern Whigs' best allies were in the other party. That was a demoralizing burden to carry into the next southern two-party campaign.

Emphasis on Southern Whigs as saviors (and victims) of compromise misses an equally revealing point: the most northern South salvaged the nation. Eighty percent of saving Southern Whig votes came from the Upper South and almost half from the Border South. Border South Democrats were almost as unanimous for the Little Omnibus as were Border South Whigs. The whole nation outside the Border South voted 96-89 against the Little Omnibus. The Border South saved the Little Omnibus and thus national settlement with its 19-1 affirmation.

The Border South's far greater willingness to bend northward received another statistical illustration in the House vote on the North's greatest gain: free California. In the evenly divided Senate, northern victory on California had required at least one southern abstention. In the northern-dominated House, no Southerner had to endorse the victors' spoils. Still, 64% of border congressmen voted to admit California as a free state. Only 27% of the Middle South's representatives and 2% of the Lower South's concurred.

– 12 –

The House's Little Omnibus and California votes climaxed differences which had pitted Deep South against Border South from the moment Clay introduced his proposals. That internal southern strife, while no longer all-out war after the alteration of Clay's initial package, had never yielded a settlement satisfying to both extremes of the South. On Henry Foote's provocative southern chance for California and on Thomas Pratt's soothing bounty for unreturned fugitives, Border and Deep Souths, distrustful in the extreme about each other, barely agreed to an armistice.

Armistice remains the best word for the entire settlement of 1850. In a true compromise, both sides give in a little, concur on mutual concessions, and coalesce to make their agreement work. In the so-called Compromise of 1850, only moderates lived up to the meaning of compromise. The most accommodating Northern Democrats, especially those from the most southern North, came to agreement with the most accommodating Southerners, especially those from the most northern South.

Outside this compromising middle, zealots dismissed any obligation to make other people's armistice work.[49] Northern Whigs cast only 37 of a possible 261 congressional votes for the Utah, New Mexico, and fugitive slave bills. These anti-Slavepower Whigs felt free to nullify the Slavepower's "immoral" fugitive slave law. Meanwhile, South Carolina cast only one of a possible 34 congressional votes and Mississippi only three of a possible 26 votes for the moderates' settlement, outside of the fugitive slave part. Many of these southern naysayers felt free to secede from other Southerners' "sellout."

"Compromise" or "Armistice" or "Sellout," call this settlement what you will, it everywhere failed to defuse explosive questions. The Democrats' uniting principle, Popular Sovereignty, had passed only after being rendered provokingly vague. Could Southern and Northern Democrats continue to agree to disagree on which territorial populace had sovereignty and when? The National Whig Party's uniting principle, No Territory, had proved beyond Zachary Taylor's power to save. With not even a motto left and with Northern Whigs' intransigence leaving Southern Whigs vulnerable to loyalty politics at home, could any national opposition to the Democratic Party endure? Border Southerners' ideologies and actions had again and again hinted that they paid partial allegiance to David Wilmot's vocabulary. Would the Henry (and Cassius) Clays constantly seek out Wilmot Proviso Northerners, unless continually deterred?

Before any of these long-run questions could be answered, an immediate crisis had to be faced. South Carolina secessionists were surpassing their own world-class standards in ranting about sellout. This time, they swore, they would revolt rather than submit. The Armistice of 1850 might not even temporarily prevent disunion.

CHAPTER 29

The Paralysis of
the Old Order

The secession crisis of 1850–52, like the earlier Nullification Controversy and the later disunion finale, involved classic confrontation politics. On each occasion, far-out Carolinians prayed that if bullets replaced ballots, the southern mainstream would shoot Yankees rather than Southrons.

Those precipitous tactics risked the ire of two majorities. A majority of Southerners could resent being forced to the battlefield. A majority of Americans could resent southern ultras' defiance of majoritarian law. An extremist minority of a minority could thus paint itself into a suicidal corner.

Secessionists grated on southern majoritarian sensibilities more in 1850 than in 1860. In the year of Lincoln's election, a northern majority imposed a President on the South. In the year of congressional armistice, the majority of Southerners voted to compromise with the North. How could a victorious southern majority legitimately help sore losers gut the majoritarian process?

Extremists who drove slavery's assumptions past "mere negro" bondage saw no legitimacy problem. These elitists believed that betters should rule majorities on all sides of all color lines. So affirming, South Carolina extremists favored a patriarchal revolution against egalitarians' so-called Compromise of 1850. Simultaneously, eastern Virginia oligarchs favored resisting King Numbers's latest assault on the Old Dominion.

Both states' elitist republicans lost these confrontations. Defeat came partly because each oligarchy lacked the autocratic nerve to defy the majority. The twin failures, intensifying each other, left the Old Order in demoralized disarray.

– 1 –

The Virginia crisis of 1850–1 was a replay of the Virginia Convention of 1829. The overriding issue was identical: Was black slavery compatible with white egalitarianism? Eastern Virginia's predominant answer was the same: The ideology of slavery must transcend color lines and lead those richer to control those poorer. Western Virginia's predominant response never varied: Unless whites could gain an egalitarian republic, slaveholders could not retain blacks.

The issue was once more fought out in the Hall of the House of Delegates in Richmond. The occasion was again a state convention called especially to determine how seats should be apportioned in future Houses of Delegates. Lower house apportionment remained vital because the House of Delegates initiated tax bills. The recurrent problem was that in a one-white-man, one-vote legislature, a western nonslaveholder majority could emancipate slaves through soak-the-rich taxation.

The 1829 Virginia Convention, emulating Jefferson's trick windows at Monticello, had decreed an illusion of reconciliation. The convention majority had coupled the egalitarian West's concept of what should be counted to determine proper apportionment, white men alone, with the elitist East's concept of when the proper count transpired, in 1820, when the West had less whites. Lower house apportionment frozen on 1820 numbers was already anti-egalitarian by 1829, for western Virginia's white population grew faster than eastern Virginia's. The slide away from one-white-man, one-vote grew steeper. By 1850, western Virginia, with 55% of the state's white population, controlled only 42% of lower house and 41% of upper house seats. This skewed legislature elected governors and judges, à la South Carolina. Furthermore, Virginia, for once more anti-egalitarian than South Carolina, denied poorer white males a vote for legislative representatives.

As a growing western white population made Virginia's government ever less egalitarian, pressure increased for a new constitutional convention. As in the late 1820s, the eastern-dominated legislature eventually compromised on a convention stacked against western reformers. The conclave was apportioned on the basis of both white population and taxes paid. Under this "mixed basis" of wealth and numbers, eastern Virginia, with well under half the numbers of white Virginians but well over half the state's taxable wealth, possessed 56% of convention seats.

For several days in 1850 and many months in 1851, this malapportioned convention debated malapportionment of the tax-initiating lower house.[1] Eastern agreement to white egalitarianism, so Westerners repeated the argument of 1829, would create nonslaveholder loyalty to black slavery. Give us representation based on one-white-man, one-vote, claimed Trans-Allegheny leader Waitman T. Willey, "and you secure our fidelity forever." But continued tyranny of rich white over poor white would "destroy western fidelity." The notion that "we cannot have a republican government in Virginia because of slavery," added George Summers, strikes "the deadliest blow" at bondage.[2]

Nonslaveholder control, answered eastern Virginia squires, augured deadlier blows. Waitman Willey's assurances of "loyalty if" demonstrated loyalty uncomfortably thin. Westerners' assault on slavery in 1832 had mocked their protestations of loyalty in 1829. Would it happen again? Westerners, declared William O. Goode, "have assailed the slaveholders as a class." They have called us "proud, and arrogant, and presumptuous." Their insults highlighted "the point of weakness in slave communities."[3]

The point of weakness, Easterners emphasized, transcended class antagonism. Between slave owners and the nonslaveholding white majority, explained James Barbour, "mountains interpose, and no peculiar tie of business or social intercourse binds them in inseparable identity." A majority living far from a minority, added M. R. H. Garnett, possessed none "of those kindly feelings which personal acquaintance awakens." These Virginia squires quailed not so much before proletariat revolution as before geographic imprisonment and a distant lower class as jailers.[4]

To contain majority despotism, reactionaries would insure that numerically fewer and richer Easterners always had more House of Delegate seats than the more numerous and poorer Westerners. As in 1829, they had the convention seats to impose whatever apportionment they liked. But once again, they lacked the class unity to consolidate rich men's rule.

Their prime opponent in the Virginia Convention of 1850–1 epitomized their problem.[5] For fifteen years, eastern Virginia Congressman Henry Wise had championed Slavepower stonewalling against federal mobocracy. Back in gag rule times, this Southern Whig foe of John Quincy Adams had demanded that Southern Democrats gag free democratic discussion more totally than Carolina's "traitor," Henry L. Pinckney, proposed. Yet this same Henry Wise told the Virginia Convention in 1851 that nothing "on God's Almighty earth" stinks more than "monied aristrocracy; and negro aristocracy stinks worst of all."[6]

To aristocrats accused of befouling an American republic, Wise's rhetoric seemed proof of the irresponsible demagogue. Reactionaries were right that this rabble-rouser could talk and did love to court the commoners. But the Old Order missed Henry Wise's conviction that only the New Order's egalitarian tactics could save slavery. Wise saw that the eighteenth-century titan—cool, balanced, elegant, enlightened, handing down rationality from on high—could not command nineteenth-century yeomen. This up-to-speed romantic valued intuition more than abstraction, instinct more than consistency, Everyman more than philosopher-kings. With his hero, Andrew Jackson, Wise saw himself as no better than any white and much better than all blacks. He would show starch-stiff squires how to win their (white) fellows' allegiance.

The people's man wore homespun cloth, rough and rumpled. His sallow neck seemed shrunken inside his disheveled collar. His eyes were sunken, his cheeks hollow, unless swollen with tobacco. Then brown streams of spit punctuated his invective. In his element, stump speaking to screaming crowds, his emaciated frame became a blur, his slurring words a torrent. He looked and sounded like a hungry climber who could not bear folks fattened and privileged.

Henry Wise's slashes at privilege were rooted in his coastal homeland, Accomac County, haven for fishermen. Amidst the camaraderie of men who went to sea, Wise learned that a slaveholder must at least play the democrat. Still, Wise's courting of the masses was not inevitable in Accomac County. That least-enslaved Virginia Tidewater district had also produced Wise's States' Rights Whig colleague, Abel P. Upshur. The former Secretary of State had looked like all head where Wise seemed much mouth, all frosty logician where Wise was romantically impulsive, above all convinced that Wise's loathed "negro aristocracy" must command whites no less than Negroes. Accomac, rare Virginia Tidewater area where slaveholders were massively outnumbered, spawned two antithetical Slavepower strategies: stonewalling against or pretending to join King Numbers.

Henry Wise remained too mercurial to be Upshur's constant antithesis. On national questions, both Accomac County political titans would gag northern majorities and seize Texas, lest democratic procedures overwhelm slaveholder minorities. Yet where Judge Upshur drove elitist purity wherever it led, Wise tended to be foggy about all-out defiance of northern majorities. Henry Wise was always passionately for slavery but a little for Conditional Termination, earlier an Andrew Jackson admirer but a partisan Whig, later a zealous Democrat but a distruster of party as panacea.

Locally as nationally, this eccentric was on both sides of Slavepower strategies. At the 1851 convention, Wise deserted his own class only when elitists insisted on malapportionment in the House of Delegates. Dictatorship of the rich in the lower house, he urged, would "bring on an agrarian war of the poor against the wealth." It would make slave property "odious." It would usher in abolition.

A better way was to trust white commoners in the House of Delegates. "The people are not plunderers." The aristocratic few, "those who attempt, through property, to seize on to political power, are the plunderers to be feared." It is high time, soared Wise, to "bring the question home—shall money rule men or men rule money?'" It is about time, responded Westerners, that an Easterner made some sense.

Easterners almost defeated Henry Wise's mobocratic sense. On one roll call, anti-egalitarians fell only one vote short of giving wealth as much power as numbers in the tax-initiating lower house. But as in 1829, too many slaveholders from Jefferson's western Piedmont and from the southern Valley, as well as too many Easterners from heavily nonslaveholding Tidewater cities and from Wise's fisherman-dominated Accomac County defected. Splits in the slaveholding class and region gave western nonslaveholders a slight balance of power. So the convention opted for important elements of a (white man's) egalitarian regime: universal white male suffrage, popular election of governors, and a one-white-man, one-vote lower house apportionment.

Yet if Henry Wise had prodded Old Virginia into the nineteenth century, his new populism clung to the expiring order. His minority East, with his blessing, retained 60% of the upper house, which would have to approve any tax bill initiated in the lower house. Moreover Wise's tax-initiating House of Delegates, while a white man's mobocracy in 1851, could not remain mobocratic. The House of Delegates' apportionment was based on 1850 figures and frozen at that level for at least fifteen years.

The new constitution, again with Wise's blessings, also froze taxes on slave property. Slaves over twelve could not be assessed for more than $300. Younger slaves could not be a basis for taxation. These provisions *lowered* slaveholders' taxes in 1851. The constitutional $300 limit also prevented adjustment for slave prices, destined soon to skyrocket way over $1000 per "wench" or "boy." No indirect abolition through soak-the-rich taxation could result.[8]

Under Wise's leadership, to sum up convention results, Westerners won command of the tax-initiating House of Delegates. Then elitist republicans restrained egalitarians from confiscating rich folks' fortunes. By 1860, Westerners were again calling the Virginia constitution a bulwark of reaction. Their angry fulminations—and their revolutionary actions—would demonstrate that in 1851, as in 1829 and 1832, Virginia rulers had only stalled off class and regional showdown.

No one could have convinced imperious Easterners that the compromising Henry Wise could stall off anything. To M. R. H. Garnett, upper-class hegemony demanded rulers determined to lord it over commoners. Garnett lamented that aristocratic domination had not been institutionally consolidated and brought to full upper-class consciousness. "This tendency to Radicalism," he wrote William Henry Trescot of South Carolina, "is not natural in a slaveholding community."[9] To which Henry Wise would have replied that a tendency towards reaction is not natural in an egalitarian republic.

Virginia, as usual, came down somewhere in the middle on those questions of elitist versus egalitarian strategy. Trescot, while rejoicing that one Virginian understand slavery's implications, had to pick a quarrel even with Garnett. "You call yourself a democrat," wrote back the South Carolinian. But "that word democrat . . . has betrayed the South. Southern slaveholders in their strange zeal to be good democrats have been untrue to themselves and their position."[10]

Henry Wise had been frozen to no position. Ever after the Convention of 1851, Virginia's newest hero would jump from extreme to extreme. Trying to sort out his forays, realizing ideological confusions and class-geographic conflicts which beset his class and commonwealth, no one could doubt that Monticello's strained balances were relics. The ancien régime was ancient history. But where was the South's "mother state" now heading?

– 2 –

The South Carolina aristocracy plunged into a simultaneous mid-century crisis grieving the loss of its guiding hand. Compassion tempered grief. When he died in March of 1850, John C. Calhoun was spared the agony of heart and lungs ravaged by bronchitis. He was also saved the futility of an old man who had outlived his time.

After the Civil War, careless commentators would claim that Calhoun's ghost led the South to war. Contemporaries knew better. Few claimed Calhoun's tradition during southern debates of the late 1850s. His last Senate speech and posthumously published masterpieces explain why. They reveal a man trapped in the 1830s.

Calhoun's final senatorial scene almost seemed staged to dramatize man beaten by the clock. On March 4, 1850, he was half-dragged into the Senate chamber by none other than James Hamilton, Jr. Sugar Jimmy, Carolina's brightest young star back in nullification times, had long since degenerated into a middle-aged salesman of Texas bonds.[11] After the frumpy Hamilton released the dying Calhoun into a chair, the old man sank, then gripped the wood. His clenching hands seemed drained of blood. His sweaty hair streamed erratically. His emaciated frame was wrapped in funereal flannels. Since he was too frail for speeches, he had passed his manuscript on to South Carolina colleague Andrew P. Butler. Since Butler's eyesight was too weak, he had passed the speech on to James Mason of Virginia. South Carolina's radicals, so often stymied by Middle South moderation, now needed a Virginia voice to be heard.

Those who closed their eyes and willed away incongruities could have believed they were hearing little Jimmy Hamilton in the golden days of '32. The issue, Calhoun had written, was not California or fugitive slaves. The problem was southern fear of the North's permanent majority. The permanent minority must be given countervailing power. Otherwise, secession would ensue.[12]

A day later, Mississippi's Henry S. Foote charged that Calhoun had issued a disunion ultimatum. The charge provoked a last explanation from the extremist who had ever sought to save South and Union too. Ultimatums about disunion, Calhoun told the Senate, were "not to be deduced from any language I used." He had merely predicted that constitutional protection would alone stop secession.[13]

Before the month was out, Calhoun was no more. James Hammond, commissioned to deliver Charleston's eulogy, caught his subject's last and lifelong point perfectly. In recommending some sort of nullification instead of secession, declared the eulogist, "Mr. Calhoun was mainly influenced by that deep, long cherished, and I might almost say superstitious attachment to the Union, which marked every act of his career."[14]

Since no other congressman of 1850 cared about a remedy lost in 1832–3, no one publicly inquired what constitutional amendments the dying leader desired. Nor did anyone ask Mr. Nullifier to explain away the old difficulty with his outmoded panacea. If the South could veto, how could national government avoid paralysis? The curious remained in suspense until 1854, when Calhoun's mature political theory was posthumously published.

In his *Discourse on the Constitution and Government of the United States,* a long exegesis on American national government, Calhoun urged two Presidents, one northern, one southern, each armed with an absolute veto. In his shorter, more theoretical, more famous *Disquisition on Government,* the Carolinian claimed that nullification would work because the best men would rule.[15]

Numerical mobocracies failed, explained Calhoun, because patronage invited the worst men to delude the rabble. Depraved politicians used "slander, fraud, and gross appeals to the appetites of the lowest." With scum ruling the herd, democracy became a disaster. Minorities, being weakest, were victimized most. But campaigns for spoils "thoroughly debased and corrupted" the whole nation.

Under minority veto, dreamed Calhoun, excess taxes would be nullified. Patronage would dry up. Spoilsmen would seek a more lucrative occupation. Majority and minority, both interested in avoiding anarchy, would call disinterested patricians to fill the vacuum. The enlightened would prevail. Compromise would ensue. Union would endure.

There spoke the Carolina gentleman, disgusted with American parties and politicians, nostalgic for the English House of Lords, proud that his was the only American legislature which consolidated eighteenth-century elitist republicanism. But could South Carolina's anti-spoilsmen "utopia" be transferred to nineteenth-century Washington? Those who read the *Disquisition* closely knew that Calhoun's logic placed national government beyond redemption. Calhoun conceded that demagogues could always control mobocracies. He admitted that spoilsmen would never be wise or disinterested enough to compromise and thus avoid anarchy. Calhoun's utopia depended on emptying the pork barrel so thoroughly that pols would retire and patriarchs would rule. Minority veto, he believed, would slice spoils. But would enough payoffs remain to attract politicos?

Modern national states, Calhoun despairingly answered, needed "large establishments, both civil and military." Such irreducible patronage led irresistibly to "hostile parties and violent party conflict." Such contests for "party triumph and ascendency" always overpowered "all regard for truth, justice, sincerity, and moral obligation."

America's most famous logician here locked himself into a logical trap. Whatever social interests would desire under government by nullification, demagogues after irreducible spoils would retain an interest in deluding the gullible. The worst would again rout the best. Compromise would become impossible. Anarchy, that "greatest of all evils," would ensue. Even in the abstract world he loved to haunt, this most union-loving of Carolina autocrats could not save aristocratic republicanism within the national Union.

While Calhoun's posthumous publication placed national republicanism beyond redemption, his farewell advice mocked his recent redemptive strategies. Back in the nullification era, Calhoun had believed that a do-nothing federal government would leave slaveholders safe. But in the age of Texas Annexation, Pearl Andrews and Lord Aberdeen taught the former advocate of federal hands-off that a southern-dominated federal government must lay protective hands all over vulnerable slaveholding outposts. Subsequently, Calhoun no less than the southern mainstream sought national power to salvage Slavepower. The ex-Nullifier demanded federal power in the North to stop slaves from fleeing border states and federal protection in the territories to entice slaveholders to distant provinces.

The leader's final logic would have nullified his post-nullification triumphs.

With their own President possessing a veto, Northerners could have axed Texas Annexation, stymied juryless fugitive extraditions, stopped territorial slave codes. The South would have been trapped with multiplying blacks, with no safety valve, and with an ever-greater chance of losing internal social control.

Calhoun the theorist never quite understood that as practical politician he had wielded his loathed majoritarian system to sustain his treasured minority's control. The disjunction between the theorist without hope and the politico securing success is striking, especially because this abstracted leader was more pragmatically astute than most allies. Many Calhoun admirers were Disunionists. They could not understand why he believed slavery could be consolidated in the Union. More Calhounites were States' Rights Whigs. They could not understand why he thought the Democratic Party might better protect slavery. Almost alone within his faction, Calhoun called the Jackson Party which Calhounites had left perhaps the best hope of securing protective slavery legislation.

Or to be more accurate, Calhoun *sometimes* saw that the Democratic Party might give the lie to his notion that a permanent national majority enslaved the minority South. An eighteenth-century patrician scornful of nineteenth-century parties could not relentlessly realize that a minority could command the nation's majority party. So Calhoun spent a career storming in and out of the Jackson Party. Inside at the beginning, he moved outside to nullify, inside again to support Van Buren in 1840 and Texas annexation in 1844, outside again to oppose Polk's war, still further outside to seek the Nashville Convention. Through it all, he called for a reorganization of national parties, then a recapture of the Democratic Party, a Southern Convention, then southern opposition within Democratic Party conventions, a saving new majority, then a veto of all majorities.

In the end, despite compromise tariffs and gag rules and Texas Annexation, this aging ideologue could not accept minority salvation within a spoilsmen's party—within any partisan coalition. He would gut parties, handcuff federal power, nullify the century. His nullification would have canceled fifteen years when Slavepower wielded majorities.

John C. Calhoun was the early southern watchman, warning of abolitionists in ambush. By lending his prestige to nullification as a middle way, he gave South Carolina ultra views a saving respectability. By continuing agitation in the Gag Rule and Texas Annexation controversies, he helped edge the Lower South towards South Carolina. The momentum he initiated would someday result in revolution.

Still, those who initiate are not necessarily adept at producing conclusions. Nor do those who commence momentum necessarily like the direction in which that momentum veers. Calhoun exemplified the radical who seeks to save rather than to destroy and who never can adjust when less favored later solutions work better than cherished first remedies. The former Nullifier could only heap logic atop logic in futile efforts to make his most unworkable and most repudiated tactic come out right. To escape from their titan's irrelevant nostalgia and seek a revolution he predicted and dreaded, South Carolina had to bury him with honors—and rush on past his grave.

– 3 –

Revolutions thrive on haste. Second thoughts are often sober thoughts. The revolutionary must strike before confidence falters. Immediately after Congress enacted the Armistice of 1850, South Carolinians were tempted to rush. The sellout, gentlemen told each other, threw down the gauntlet. The Union could no longer be suffered.

Langdon Cheves, another ancient Carolina warrior, displayed a revolutionary's reasoning at the hapless second Nashville Convention in November, 1850.[16] Cheves, delivering the only memorable oration at the irrelevant conclave, termed the national settlement a disaster. Cutting down the slave trade in Washington set a precedent for cutting off slave trading between states. Slicing off a third of enslaved Texas meant abolition within a state. Admitting free California meant David Wilmot had triumphed. Against this freesoil victory, what had the South gained? An unenforceable fugitive slave law and a payoff to surrendering Texans!

Why had southern congressmen helped fashion this disaster? Southern politicians, answered Langdon Cheves, were pols first and Southerners second. They valued party supremacy more than sectional safety. They would do anything for patronage, even sell out their homeland.

Armed with a permanent majority and facing a bribable minority, northern politicians, declared Cheves, could attack slavery wherever they desired. Freesoilers claimed to desire only non-extension of slavery. "If their views really went no farther than to pen it up within restricted limits, do they not thereby render it less profitable, less valuable, and more difficult of management?"

But fanaticism "has no stopping place." Southern communities must "reap the storm." Eventual racial holocausts would resemble "the sufferings, the massacre and the banishment, in poverty and misery, of the white proprietors of Hayti." An abolitionized, scorched South would surrender to "some Emperor, bearing and exulting in the title of, perhaps, Cuffy the First."

Secession alone could stave off Cuffee's victory. Disunion risked war. But Americans welcomed war, Langdon Cheves recalled, in 1776 and 1812. Then as now, "it is a question of life and death, morally, politically, and physically." We can "form one of the most splendid empires on which the sun has ever shown. . . . But submit! Submit! The very sound curdles the blood in my veins."

So spoke the hot-blooded warrior, apparently incapable of submission. But Cheves also showed why Carolinians so often submitted. Single state secession, he fretted, would not work. During nullification times, Cheves had warned against going it alone. He had no wish to become a prophet twice vindicated. Secession by four or more states, he exulted, would succeed. Disunion by less, he lamented, involved too great a risk.

While Langdon Cheves in Nashville was showing that memories of nullification might cool Carolina blood, Governor Whitemarsh Seabrook, a wealthy rice planter and among the earliest Nullifiers, was secretly corresponding with other Deep South governors. His disunionist letters vindicated northern images of a Great Slavepower Conspiracy.

Let us again be clear about the Slavepower Conspiracy phenomenon. Ever since the last documentable disunion conspiracy, the James Hammond–Thomas Cooper–Beverley Tucker gag rule correspondence of 1835–6, Northerners had befogged the nature and significance of Southerners' sporadic plotting. Yankees especially erred by calling the sporadic a constant. Unable to understand how the minority regularly secured majority legislation, Northerners imagined a sustained conspiracy to rule or ruin the majoritarian process.

This image of *a* South, united in abnormal conspiratorial control of democracy, missed everything important about the divided South, about normal democratic process, and about how and why southern conspiracies very occasionally operated. Southerners in the National Democratic Party, as the most powerful pressure group in the most powerful political party, usually obtained a typical democratic outcome: triumph of a minority better organized and more committed than silent majorities. The southern minority's most resented victories, aimed at shoring up vulnerabilities at the South's fringes, revealed a region not united in conspiracy but fearful of its own disunity.

The few southern disunionist conspirators stood especially disunited from mainstream southern notions that minority pressure could control majority legislation. To defy that consensus, Disunionists depended on South Carolina to precipitate a confrontation situation. But uneasy revolutionaries controlled that state. These gentlemen would likely require secret assurances from other states before they would again stand alone.

No secret assurances had preceded Carolina's first solo adventure. Carolinians, having plunged into the Nullification Controversy without pledges of support, had lacked the confidence to push confrontation relentlessly far, despite signs that at least some states' rights Southerners might revolt against coercion of secessionists. Memories of that nervous winter informed every subsequent Carolina strategy. Carolinians would never again strike without privately sounding out zealots in other states.

That psychological necessity led Beverley Tucker, in his mid-1830s novel, *The Partisan Leader,* to imagine conspiratorial planning between secessionists in various states about how and when each state would secede. Tucker helped make fantasy fact by joining the sole documentable pre-1850 southern conspiracy: the attempt to use Congressman James Hammond to secure a disunionist finale to the Gag Rule Controversy. The conspiracy went nowhere. Instead of making resignation from Congress an announced prelude to withdrawing from Union, Hammond merely left, with no public announcement.

In 1850, Governor Whitemarsh Seabrook's attempt to pre-arrange a more successful revolutionary outcome started with secret efforts to encourage another state to play initiator. The governor claimed he feared South Carolina's reputation as a hothead would stigmatize any Carolina-initiated revolution. He did not admit to Carolinians' fear that they might never again dare jump first.

Seabrook began his secret plotting with the Lone Star State. Texans, he privately counseled Governor Peter H. Bell on September 11, 1850, should reject the national offer to assume the state debt, keep their territories, and defy the United States. If war resulted, South Carolina would pledge every aid—including "our full quota of men and money." Seabrook envied Bell's opportunity to "arrest the mad career of usurping rulers. Not only our liberty but our lives are in peril."[17]

Texas, however, preferred to opt for peaceful millions from the United States rather than to start South Carolina's civil war. So Seabrook explored alternative plots. Submission to the late sellout, he secretly wrote several Deep South governors on September 20, 1850, would make Southerners "forever mere dependencies of a great Central Head." Despite the emergency, South Carolina had to move cautiously. But as soon as two or more governors gave evidence of determined resistance, in disregard of consequences, Seabrook would convene his legislature to "arrest the career of an interested and despotic majority."[18]

Governor George W. Towns of Georgia, also eager for action, answered that South Carolina must hold back. Towns had called a Georgia convention to consider resistance. Election for delegates would transpire in early November 1850. Seabrook must not convene Carolina's legislature before that time, warned Towns, for the reaction would "contribute largely" to our overthrow.[19]

South Carolinians were "clamorous" for instant action, Seabrook answered. But Carolina's governor was "fully aware" that old Nullifiers' "precipitate movement" might "ruin, perhaps the cause of the South." He would postpone his legislature's session until late November, after Georgia's election.[20]

Revolutionary plotting with Georgia's governor thus led South Carolina's governor to lose two months before convening his legislature. Simultaneous plotting with Mississippi caused further delay when Carolina's lawmakers finally met. On September 29, 1850, Mississippi Governor John Quitman answered Whitemarsh Seabrook's secret inquiries with secret assurances. Quitman had called his legislature to convene on November 18. He would propose a state convention. "Having no hope of an effectual remedy for existing and prospective evils but in separation from the Northern States, my views of state action will look to secession."[21]

On October 23, 1850, a month before South Carolina's legislature would meet, Seabrook wrote to promise Quitman that should "your gallant commonwealth adopt the decisive course" you urge, we "will be found at her side." South Carolinians were "ready and anxious for an immediate secession." They held back only to avoid sabotaging the great movement. Seabrook prayed "that Mississippi will begin the patriotic work, and allow the Palmetto banner the privilege of a place in the ranks." Seabrook's legislative recommendations would depend "very much . . . on your suggestions"—and still more "on the action of your legislature."[22]

Quitman answered South Carolina's governor with a telegram on Novem-

ber 29, 1850. The Mississippi legislature, Quitman wired Seabrook, had called
a state convention a year hence. Quitman's follow-up letter three days later led
Seabrook to exult that Carolina secessionists could "confidently rely" on the
Mississsippi convention to initiate secession. "Your letter, discreetly used," Seabrook wrote back, "had the salutory effect of checking the course of the impet-
uous." The news that Mississippi would act "has enabled me to suspend the
scheme of many prominent men of publicly avowing that in one year, if
unaided by some other state at the time, South Carolina would withdraw from
the confederacy."[23]

Following guidelines of the Seabrook-Quitman secret understanding, Carolina's legislature confined itself to mechanisms for seconding Mississippi. The
legislature called a southern congress to meet in January 1852, several weeks
after Mississippi's convention. If only Mississippi came, so be it. A South Carolina convention was authorized, although its date for convening was to be set
later. The legislature gave Seabrook a third of a million dollars to arm the state
in the interim. His secret correspondence, Seabrook congratulated himself, had
at last pointed Carolina towards responsible revolutionary strategy.[24]

Within three months, Quitman informed Carolinians that the plot had
backfired. Quitman had overestimated Mississippi's revolutionary zeal. His
state, "alarmed by the imaginary evils of an unknown future, may recoil and
pause." South Carolina must "take the lead and confidently act for herself." In
a showdown between Carolina and the United States, Mississippi would join
her Deep South sister. "Soon all the adjoining states would follow." Then Border South states, who would "never abandon the present Union unless forced,"
would be coerced into choosing between North and South.[25]

Quitman here displayed the way a different plot might have yielded a different scenario. Revolutionaries in less flammable areas, Quitman realized too
late, must encourage more fiery regions to provoke confrontation, for the less
fiery might never dare. In the fall of 1850, advice to shun initiatives had helped
give fiery but reluctant Carolinians a patriotic rationale to break stride. Now
the Carolina legislature would not meet until November 1851. That delay
would give Carolina hotspurs time to remember nullification and watch sluggish neighbors repudiate secession. Momentum, that revolutionary treasure,
had evaporated. The conspiracy of 1850–1 had helped make revolution less
likely.

Still, these Carolina conspirators would not necessarily have dared depart
the Union even if Quitman had earlier encouraged them. Conspiracy is a
weapon rather than a panacea. The weapon's use speaks volumes about conspirators' mentality, and the conspiracy of 1850–1 highlighted Jacobins' prayer
that someone else would leap first. South Carolina gentlemen were nothing if
not edgy revolutionaries; and no one scolded Whitemarsh Seabrook for jamming on brakes to see if someone else would accelerate, any more than many
Carolina radicals had damned Calhoun in 1833 for negotiating on the non-
negotiable. In the fall of 1850, South Carolinians had acted like South Carolin-

ians in displaying revolutionary mania. Governor Seabrook had been equally Carolinian in plotting to place Carolina revolutionaries in a temporary strait-jacket—and in conspiring to slip keys over to saner states.

– 4 –

In 1850–1, Georgia's electorate outraced Mississippi's to the pleasure of pronouncing Whitemarsh Seabrook a madman.[26] Georgia's Unionists came to the fall 1850 campaign for choosing delegates to a state convention armed with the national settlement as a soothing solution. They also possessed a trio of leaders who almost cornered the spectrum of southern heroes.

Howell Cobb had never expected to fight for anything side by side with Alexander Stephens and Robert Toombs. Little Alec and Dashing Bobby, leaders of young Georgia Whigs, had spent many an evening ridiculing Fatty Cobb, leader of the Georgia Democratic Party. But after Northern Whig intransigence over the Fugitive Slave Law, the Lower South world of Democrats versus Whigs was cracking apart. Georgia's young Whigs, in danger of becoming politicians without a party, hoped a new Unionist Party might replace old Democratic or Whig institutions. Cobb's strategy differed. He hoped that a temporary unionist coalition would be Whigs' bridge to the permanent Democratic Party.

Cobb, Stephens, and Toombs epitomized more than the old Whig-Democratic battlefield. The Georgia triumvirate also provided classic versions of southern leadership types. Fatty Cobb, richly married to a Lamar, comfortably an insider in Washington, was the quintessence of the man under attack who seeks clubby union with his tormentors. Like John Slidell of Louisiana and Benjamin Fitzpatrick of Alabama, he disliked breaking up anything to do with power, ease, prominence. He helped make the South count in Washington's inner circle.[27]

Stephens, small and unhealthy, personified the provincial, defensively apart. Like James Hammond of South Carolina and Jefferson Davis of Mississippi, he usually remained too far above the crowd to seize, direct, conquer. He customarily posed as an icy statue of angry integrity.[28]

Toombs was the Southerner as medieval knight. Hale and handsome, fond of wine and fleshpots, he was a hothead somersaulting between extremes. He transformed defensiveness into aggressiveness with blinding parries and thrusts. Like Henry Wise of Virginia and Pierre Soulé of Louisiana, he rarely stood still long enough for followers to line up behind him. He secured admiration for his impulsive and dashing forays.[29]

The outsider as insider, the crippled provincial as isolated ideologue, the flamboyant cavalier as charging defender—a society under attack naturally produced and adored this triumvirate. Only one character was missing to make an all-inclusive quartet. The Georgia triumvirate lacked the revolutionary who remorselessly bores from within.

That commodity was in short supply everywhere in the South—and nowhere to be found in Georgia. The Empire State, as Georgia appropriately called itself, was too busy building its empire. In 1850, the southern cotton economy at last turned the corner, moving from hard times since the Panic of 1837 to a decade of prosperity. Southwestern secessionists had to bring off that difficult revolution, the one amidst a prospering people.

An improving economy, a seductive compromise, a splendid triumvirate— Georgia's radicals took a look and fled. The debate over secession had barely begun before so-called Disunionists were complaining about being misnamed. They favored not smashing the country but resisting the congressional sellout. They could resist through economic non-intercourse, or another southern convention, or further congressional redress. Self-named Unionists, Resisters insisted, should be named Submissionists. Only southern traitors would submit to such anti-southern legislation.[30]

Little Alec and friends were not disposed to become another casualty of southern loyalty politics. Nor were Unionists inclined to let Disunionists change names. Day in and day out, campaigning across much of Georgia, Toombs, Stephens, and Cobb warned against secession. Unionists kept attacking apparently vanished secessionists in part because they knew that Disunionist was a more damning label than Resister.

Unionists also persisted out of sincere belief that Resisters remained at heart Disunionists. Their largely false suspicions indicated again how deeply the role-playing, Cuffee-like image infested southern thought. Every Southerner who spoke from any angle on mid-century slavery issues indirectly testified that slaves had helped mold masters to see duplicity as the essence of human relationships.

Granted, Stephens wrote a fellow spirit, our "more sagacious and cunning" foes pretend to be "for some sort of *resistance* under the Constitution." They deceptively urge that "an act of *Nonintercourse*" would be "peaceful and effectual." They knew better. Their real object "is to get the state to take a step that will lead to disunion."[31]

By making the Disunionist label stick no matter where ultras hid, Stephens and company brought off an electoral landslide. Unionists won a virtual monopoly of December 1850 Georgia convention seats. The convention's famous Georgia Platform declared future disunion desirable if southern rights were violated. But delegates also hailed the congressional settlement of 1850 as no such violation. Only 19 of 256 representatives voted against that sentiment.[32]

Nine months later Howell Cobb ran for governor on the platform that secession was illegal as well as inexpedient. Rebellion, declared Cobb, could never be lawful and could only be justifiable when natural rights were horribly violated. Georgia voters affirmed that notion too by awarding Cobb another sweeping triumph. Toombs, who thought Cobb was taking a good thing a bit far, still participated in victory. Dashing Bobby snatched old man John Berrien's senatorial seat. The South's Empire State, for the umpteenth time in its adolescent history, had snubbed its nose at creaking Carolina.[33]

– 5 –

Mississippi showed more respect for southeastern elders. Mississippi's Resistance Party also had to contend with the so-called compromise and an improving economy. But along the deltas and bayous of the South's most fabled river, ultras possessed an advantage compared with Georgia Resisters. No triumvirate of statesmen here called the Armistice of 1850 honorable. Rather, the great culture heroes, from Governor John Quitman and Senator Jefferson Davis down to lesser lights, almost unanimously called the settlement a sellout.[34]

John Quitman began the Mississippi drive for resistance with a classic fire-eater's oration.[35] The governor told Mississippi's lawmakers on November 18, 1850, that he had called them into special session to combat a "deep political intrigue." Yankee fanatics moved against slavery under camouflage. The so-called Compromise of 1850, a "stupendous plot," secured the Wilmot Proviso "in another form." Such "false, hollow, and deceptive" attacks, unless decoded and resisted, would "seal our doom."

Quitman called Yankee sneak attack ominous because Southerners lacked commitment to see through the disguise. Slavery was "a delicate interest." Vague hostility killed it. After "interferences, agitations, disturbances, and injurious" laws, "a sense of political degradation sets in," followed by "decay of spirit" and "deterioration of public morals, not a little promoted by the demoralizing ... temptations to treachery, held out by the splendid patronage of the Federal Government." Demoralized slaveholders, bribed to submit to camouflaged attack, faced "a shaky, lingering, distempered, and precarious existence."

The Mississippi governor called territorial expansion of slavery spiritually no less than practically vital. California, lamented Quitman, could have enabled Southerners to shuck doubt. Slaves could have made California mines hum, California ports boom, California soil yield cotton. Slaveholders could have emerged "confident in the future."

Instead, Congress had bribed Texans to rejoice in their state's mutilation. Slave auctions had been declared too revolting for the nation's capital. California had been pronounced free. In other Mexican Cession territories, Popular Sovereignty, that ambiguous nonsolution, would create doubt about slavery's future and therefore keep slaveholders away. The so-called compromise thus announced that however "slavery districts may be crowded with population," the region "is to be hedged in by a wall of fire."

Governor Quitman urged a state convention and an ultimatum. The state must demand that Southerners receive half the territories and massive constitutional guarantees. Failure was "probable." Secession should follow.

Most Mississippi ultras could have strangled the governor for declaring disunion probable. Mississippi's Resistance Party sought less a policy than an attitude; and a policy of disunion frightened away an attitude of resistance. If the South grew confident in itself, aware of northern deceptions and united in

resistance, Northerners would cease and desist. If southern submission continued to breed deceit, divisions, disloyalty, Yankees would creep ahead.

Quitman's opponents denied that submission to compromise connoted dis-
loyalty. What was conspiratorial about Texans accepting millions for a disputed boundary? And why couldn't Washingtonians join residents of John
Quitman's home town in securing happy relief from dismal slave auctions?
"More than twenty years ago," noted one of Quitman's prominent neighbors,
Natchez by law drove its slave mart out of the city. "Why not drive it from
Washington city as well? All admit it is not a pleasant sight to see." Quitman,
concluded that Natchez citizen, had better realize that "the true patriot knows
'no South, no North, but my country and my whole country.'" In that spirit,
Mississippi's Unionists enlisted for another round of loyalty politics. They
would pin the term "traitor" on the appropriate tail.[36]

Much to the Resistance Party's embarrassment, no cloth was broad enough
to cover Governor Quitman's derriere. The campaign for convention delegates
ran concurrently with Quitman's campaign for re-election, although the gubernatorial election would transpire two months later. The governor's opponent,
United States Senator Henry S. Foote, let no one forget what the chief Resister
had proclaimed "probable." Quitman, warned Foote, etched a self-portrait
when describing how abolitionists played roles. The governor, Cuffee-like,
moved indirectly and undercover towards a revolution he no longer openly
discussed.[37]

Foote knew his man. At the very time most Mississippi Resisters were sincerely seeking more aggressive southern campaigns in the Union, Governor
Quitman was secretly plotting disunion with South Carolinians.[38] Almost all
other leaders of the Mississippi Resistance Party, aware that Quitman was
indeed the conspirator Foote painted, wished their leader would vanish. At their
June 1851 nominating convention, they sought to secure Quitman's resignation
from the gubernatorial race. When Quitman persisted, the party conclave threw
a disguising platform around the candidate. The nominating convention
declared secession rightful and the so-called compromise a disaster. But Mississippi should not exercise "the right of secession ... under existing
circumstances."

Thereafter, Resistance Party newspapers and orators endlessly denied they
sought disunion. They demanded "disapproval of the Compromise" and affirmation of "the *right* of secession." They had furthered the right resistance tactic
when they called the Nashville Convention. They believed that more southern
conventions might save South *and* Union.[39]

It was to no avail. Mississippi voters, sensing that John Quitman's candidacy
involved more dangerous salvations, gave Henry Foote's Unionist Party a 57%
popular vote majority in the September election for convention delegates. Quitman faced a similar debacle in the November governor's election. The governor,
now aware he was killing resistance, retreated to Natchez and temporary retirement. He resigned with characteristic flourish, first picking a fistfight with

Foote.[40] The staggering Resistance Party asked an ailing, reluctant Jefferson Davis to step in.

The substitute was better cast than the original. Davis had been author of the Resistance Party's June Platform, calling secession inexpedient. But Davis would not allow a Union shared with Yankee enemies and border neutrals to deter the Lower South from resistance. Jefferson Davis's campaign against Henry Foote continued his senatorial onslaught against Henry Clay. "In an evil hour," Davis had written his personal physician two years earlier, "some of the most distinguished of southern statesmen admitted that slavery was an evil. This ... takes from us all ground of defense." Northerners, aware of shaky southern opinions, do not believe that southern citizens "with any approach to unanimity will ... maintain the doctrines which their representatives have contended for in Congress." Past "error" must be corrected "in time" to impress the North, "save the constitutional rights of the South, and preserve our Union."[41]

In September of 1851, Davis believed time yet remained. But the Lower South needed to see through the sellout and seize the offensive. The Mississippi Resistance Party, Davis hoped, might whip up healthier attitudes for the next fight in the Union. Submission, on the other hand, would signal the North that Henry Clay might after all speak for the South.

While Davis was continuing his senatorial campaign against Clay, Mississippi's other senator seemed to swerve from senatorial forays. Henry S. Foote, Davis's opponent for governor, had lately sought to divide California at the 35°30' line. Foote had then derided northern determination to possess every golden hill. So why not join Jefferson Davis in resistance, albeit resistance short of John Quitman's conspiratorial disunionism?

Henry Foote had no trouble making his zig square with his zag: while a southern chance for a piece of California would have made the Compromise of 1850 more desirable, he said, the Fugitive Slave Law made the settlement acceptable. That rationale could not cover Foote's gyrations. The Mississippian had moved in a matter of weeks from leading a provocative assault on southern California to leading a soothing campaign against resisting or resenting the loss.

The impulsive Foote spent a career denying that such statecraft was the soul of inconsistency. He was not alone among southern firebrands in protesting overly much on this point. While consistency was hardly the rule in northern politics, the southern milieu nourished more than its share of dashing, darting, Foote-like characters. Bobby Toombs in Georgia, Henry Wise in Virginia, James Hammond in South Carolina—they were all like Foote in being provocative southern knights one moment, soothing anti-provocationists the next. The prominence of such erratic leaders illuminated a culture unsure of its way.

Foote's latest mercurial effort indicated again that loss of the Golden State did not quite touch southern uneasiness at its source. While southern California could theoretically have been a southern boon economically, politically, and psychologically, the region was too remote to inspire section-wide intransigence. The essential southern safety valves were all up close against slaveholder soil: Missouri, Texas, Kansas, and just across the Gulf, Cuba. Foote's decision to go after some distant golden hills, but then not keep going after them and after them, reflected the dominant southwestern mood: that so-called Compromise of 1850 was not quite a life and death matter.

Jefferson Davis shrewdly sustained that mood by urging Southerners to resist but not go to war over the alleged compromise. Still, the future Confederate president could not quite overturn Foote's September 57% landslide over Quitman. Foote hung on to 51% of the vote in November. A bitter Davis, ironically convinced his career was over, accurately explained his narrow defeat. John Quitman had gone "too fast and too far, the public became alarmed, and the reaction corresponded with the action."[42] Several days after Davis was defeated, the Mississippi state convention completed the reaction by voting 73-17 to concur with Georgia that secession was "utterly unsanctioned by the Federal Constitution." Disunion, being "revolution," demanded more extreme provocation than the settlement of 1850.[43]

Those words finalized South Carolina's isolation. The non-Carolina Lower South had repudiated lawful secession in theory and practice. Victorious Fatty Cobbs were in command. Vanquished Jefferson Davises could not rally resistance even inside the Union. After months of watching Mississippi and Georgia demonstrate that Southwesterners wished to make money rather than a revolution, would South Carolina ultras *now* care to clamber out on a revolutionary limb?

– 6 –

Apparently! In May of 1851, an extra-legal conclave of South Carolina's most important leaders, 450 strong, met in Charleston and announced for secession. "If it be our fate to be left alone in the struggle," publicly resolved these precipitators, "alone we must vindicate our liberty by secession." One of the meeting's more prominent participants, D. F. Jamison, future president of the 1860 South Carolina Secession Convention, privately explained that he preferred to risk "chaos than submit with folded arms" to an "appalling" racial "destiny" akin "to the fate of St. Domingue."[44]

This extra-legal meeting felt to participants like a break out of jail. In the late spring of 1851, Carolina revolutionaries felt released from their hesitant history and their hesitant selves. Their confrontation crisis would make all the South like Carolina—or else seal off Carolina from the corrupting universe.

These squires' mid-century view of the world featured corruption everywhere sneaking towards their mecca. Up in the Border South, slavery was spread too thin. Over in the Southwest, slavery's lesson was heeded to superficially. An egalitarian republic antithetical to an inegalitarian institution fostered mobocracy, thus demagogues, thus spoils, thus party politicians dedicated to deluding the southern masses. Yankees, understanding that stealth could conquer the deluded, now sought only far-off territorial outposts. When Southerners momentarily awakened, freesoilers would momentarily pause. When slaveholders paid no heed, the enemy would draw "closer around us."

Southern leaders failed to sound the alarm about distant encirclement, continued this secessionist diagnosis, because "the price of federal honors is *treason to the South*." With "federal gold and office" turning southern politicians' eyes "on the national crib," "a host of enemies will spring up in the very midst of us, that will more endanger our institutions than all our enemies from abroad." Already, Delaware is "to all intents and purposes" a free labor state, and Maryland and Kentucky are "fast losing their hold upon our institutions."

And what were South Carolinians doing about this incremental weakening? Hemorrhaging masters and slaves towards the corrupted South! Losing confidence in their ability to resist insidious encirclement! We must strike now, demanded Carolina secessionists, lest we sink into the morass forever.[45]

Carolina revolutionaries envisioned two purifying scenarios after they struck alone. Perhaps the United States would wish them good riddance and bar Carolina blacks and whites from crossing the border. Wonderful! South Carolina would then hemorrhage no more cash to Washington and no more slaves to Mississippi. Her citizens would stay home, perfect patriarchal republicanism, and make Carolina another Venice.[46]

Or perhaps the United States would declare war after South Carolina declared itself a nation. Wonderful! As one secessionist privately explained that delicious prospect to another, Yankee coercion would drive Southerners "to rally around So. Carolina." We "will form a nucleus for a glorious Confederacy. Don't you think so?"[47]

The question hung like humidity in the thick tropical air. In the long hot summer of 1851, with Mississippi turning against John Quitman, memories of going it alone in nullification times seemed more daunting than ever. The Carolina elite hardly had time to celebrate the May 1851 jailbreak from doubt before some revolutionaries broadcast renewed qualms. Dissenters resolved to turn an October 1851 Carolina election into a referendum on secession. They plunged oligarchic Carolina into a state-wide mobocratic campaign over an issue for the first time since nullification.[48]

These opponents of Separate State Secession portrayed Robert Barnwell Rhett and fellow precipitators as hosts preparing a party after guests had rejected the invitation. Carolina's intended charge after Georgia and Mississippi had retreated would look like dictation. Self-respecting slaveholders would not slavishly obey Carolina after deciding against secession for themselves.

Opponents of Separate State Secession envisioned another, not-so-wonderful finale to a confrontation crisis. In 1832, Jackson had collected nullified tariffs in offshore federal forts. In 1851, federal naval vessels drifting miles from the city could blockade Charleston. If Carolina desperadoes could somehow outfit a ship and chug out to fight, they would be routed, drowned, disgraced. We would be, warned James Hammond, "like Man in the Cage—the laughing stock of heaven and earth."[49] South Carolina's exports, blockaded from being sold abroad, would pile up, unused, useless. Slaves, barred from being sold across the Carolina border to the foreign nation of the United States, would multiply and become as worthless as unsold exports. Whites, preferring New World bonanza to a worse than Old World Calcutta, would flee southwest faster than ever. Whites remaining in trapped Carolina would face racial holocaust. And secession was supported to stop strangulation by a freesoil noose![50]

The plea that Separate State Secession was madness passed for moderation in South Carolina. Yet Carolina's moderation would have been mania anywhere else in the mid-century South. Opponents of Separate State Secession, calling themselves Cooperative State Secessionists, would leave the Union as soon as other state(s) would cooperate. The Cooperative State Secession name measured the cavern between Carolina and the Southwest. Ultras in Mississippi and Georgia, fleeing the fatal label Secessionists, called themselves Resisters. Carolina opponents of ultraism were glad to be labeled Secessionists, so long as Cooperation be added to the name.

In 1851, the most famous Cooperationist pamphleteer, John Townsend, argued for disunion with a skill equal to any Separate State Secessionist's.[51] Townsend, a lowcountry planter, distinguished between two northern enemies. A few open abolitionists mounted frontal assault. The rest, secret abolitionists, deployed disguised siege. "The soft spoken free soiler," warned Townsend, "is on a par with the most brawling and fanatic abolitionist: only that the former is more to be dreaded; since with his . . . plausible 'compromises,' which he knows are deceitful, he lulls us into security, and then stupifies us into non-resistance!"

Role-playing Northern freesoilers bribed Southerners to play roles. "As the North becomes stronger . . . traitors to the South will become more numerous among *her public men;* and the breed of the Badgers, and the Bentons, the Bells, the Houstons, and the Footes will fearfully multiply. . . . We shall be betrayed and weakened, by desertion from our ranks."

The settlement of 1850, continued John Townsend, was the latest instance of fakers North and South hemming in slavery with imperceptible precision. Every such "compromise" had to be treated as disguised abolition. Otherwise, slaveholders would wake up one morning and find themselves penned up in a demoralizingly small area. Better to see through distant deceits now than "when our strength shall have diminished, our allies deserted us, and the spirit of our people crushed and discouraged.'"

Still, John Townsend opposed Carolina seceding alone. He wanted to lay eyes on "The Mighty Nation of the Southern United States," not on "The Little Nation of South Carolina." Others wished to make Carolina another Venice. They forget "that Venice is, at this very moment, under the iron heel of Austrian soldiery."

While the lowcountry's Townsend was rivaling Robert Barnwell Rhett's Separate State Secessionists in explaining why the settlement of 1850 demanded disunion, the upcountry's James L. Orr, another prominent Cooperationist, was outdoing Rhett as tactician of revolution.[52] Orr called cooperation "the panacea for all our ills." He had "no hope" of cooperating with Upper South "grain or tobacco growing regions." If Carolina waited for Virginia, "all is lost." The Deep South must instead provoke a confrontation and present to Virginia and apologizing border slavocrats "the alternative of rallying under the banner of the Free or Slave States." One seceding state, however, would be blockaded, strangled, ruined. Successful confrontation politics required "two of the Slave States, acting harmoniously and in conjunction."

Separate State Secessionists answered that no other state dared. Cooperationists retorted that revolutions take time. "We ask our people to study the history of the American Revolution," urged C. G. Memminger. Some colonies wished to revolt in 1765. They wisely restrained their ardor for a decade, until the rest caught up. Better triumphant disunion in 1860 than abortive secession ten years too soon.[53]

To appease fire-eaters who could not wait, Cooperationists had at their disposal James Hammond's, or rather Thomas Cooper's, blueprint for nonrevolutionary revolution. Fifteen years after the conspiracy of 1835–6, Hammond at last publicized the revolutionary strategy Professor Cooper had secretly counseled. South Carolina, the Hammond of 1851 recommended, should be "in but not *of* the Union." Carolinians should refuse to go to Congress. They should refuse to participate in presidential elections. They should refuse to accept federal appropriations. Semi-secession by nonviolent nonparticipation should come hand in glove with "avowals that we are ready to go further if any will go with us." In preparation for going further, a Carolina navy should be constructed. The state could thus provide a disinterested moral example, prepare for others to enlist, and avoid the deadly blockade facing those who secede without frigates.[54]

Hammond feared that federal frigates offshore might induce "a complete Revolution here." Mountaineers at Carolina's upper fringes could use abortive disunion and social chaos to "change the Government and I fear the whole character of the State."[55] For evidence of that specter, Hammond had only to point to his Cooperative State Secession alliance. Lowcountry and upcountry slaveholding reactionaries led the opposition to Separate State Secession. But upcountry nonslaveholding reformers also fought Disunionists.

The reformers' kingdom was Carolina's northernmost, quasi-mountainous belt of counties. The leading spirit was Benjamin F. Perry, editor of *The Southern Patriot*. The *Patriot's* incessant line was that patriotism to the South included loyalty to the Union. Union-busters, said Perry, were a Carolina minority. To block Union-breakers, Perry demanded majority rule at home.

Perry's statistical proof of minority rule in Carolina made egalitarians wince. Twenty percent of Carolina's white population, residing near the coast, controlled 40% of the House and 50% of the Senate. Fifty percent of the white population, residing nearer the northerly mountains, elected but 33% of the House and 25% of the Senate. Gerrymandering, claimed Perry, would enable one-third of the white population to break up a Union which two-thirds of white Carolinians supported. That absurdity could "not be tolerated by freemen." Slaveholders who demand "equality from the Federal Government,"

Perry warned, must first "give it to citizens of their own state." Virginia's issue had come to South Carolina.[56]

Benjamin F. Perry's egalitarianism, so much like Henry Wise's, was water and gruel compared with the King Numbers tirade of "Brutus," author of the most anti-elitist pamphlet circulating in the state in 1851. Oligarchy in South Carolina, said "Brutus," exists "to guard and secure the interests of the large rice and cotton planters. The interests of men who have to work with their hands are entirely unprotected." Disunion, blockade, chaos, all disastrous to lower-class interests, must at last arouse class consciousness and class revolution. Poor men must teach "masters of overgrown plantations that we cannot always endure."[57]

Those limits of endurance showed that the lightly enslaved, yeoman-dominated corner of the upper upcountry could not be treated too outrageously. An upper-class split over whether to secede alone dared not ignore calls for lower-class resistance. In South Carolina in 1851, after the whole South had accepted the Compromise, Carolinians for defiance were hopelessly squeezed between angry nonslaveholders and worried reactionaries.

Given such towering obstacles to revolution within and without, secessionist rice and sea island cotton planters demonstrated anew that theirs was the South's wackiest corner by sweeping all but one lowcountry rural parish on election day in October 1851. In Charleston and almost all noncoastal rural areas, however, voters overwhelmed immediate secessionists. Anti-secessionist majorities at the state's upper fringes were especially whopping. In the whole state, Cooperationists captured six of seven congressional districts and almost two-thirds of the vote.[58] William H. Trescot, who had lately bemoaned M. R. H. Garnett's Virginia defeats, now mourned a similar disaster closer to home. The popular verdict, he despaired to Garnett, indicates that in South Carolina no less than in the Old Dominion, "democracy will kill slavery as it has destroyed every other conservative institution."[59]

Carolina's defeated secessionists had one ploy left. The Trescots knew that between James Hammond and Benjamin F. Perry loomed as large a disagreement as divided any two men in America. James Hammond, the Cooperative State Secessionist, and Robert Barnwell Rhett, the Separate State Secessionist, were both elitists and ex-Nullifiers. They had more in common with each other than either had with Perry, egalitarian and Unionist supreme. Accordingly, after the election, the Separate State Secessionists' Maxcy Gregg offered to throw his party's support behind Hammond's plan: South Carolinians should secede not from federal Union but from federal offices. Hammond joyously saluted Gregg's acceptance of Cooper's old way to "calculate the value of the Union."[60]

It was too late for joy. A revolution careening backward, no less than a revolution surging forward, develops a momentum of its own. In 1852, when the South Carolina convention finally met, public opinion had retreated past Hammond's plan and craved no secession at all. Robert Barnwell Rhett, forced to resign from the United States Senate, was reduced to flailing editorials in the

Charleston Mercury. James Hammond, turned down for Rhett's seat, was left to fume in his swamp.

By 1852, Hammond's generation of Carolina ultras, having trained for revolutionary races ever since Professor Cooper pointed out the finish line, looked suspiciously like the nag who had been too often to the post. "The whole world," whimpered William J. Colcock, "is against us, and I fear it will not be very long before we will find numerous abolitionists in our midst, who have kept silent hitherto from fear, but who will now be emboldened openly to advocate their sentiments."[61] The elegant William Henry Trescot, as always, dissolved whine in wit. Our "late election," he wrote, "determines that South Carolina, for better or worse, goes with the South. Previous elections have determined that the South, for better or worse, goes with the Union. And if you know whither that is going, in pity to a somewhat alarmed passenger, do tell me."[62]

– 7 –

For clues, Trescot had only to look upstate from Charleston. Into the leadership void created by Calhoun's death and the oligarchy's debility stepped a new-style American politico. James L. Orr, congressman from Benjamin F. Perry's upland area, was a pragmatic opportunist with a message for every season. In late unpleasant times when revolution had been all the rage, the Cooperationist had offered Rhett lessons in revolutionary tactics. With Rhett's remedy now defeated, Orr advised Carolinians to re-enter the National Democratic Party.[63]

Orr had had enough of revolutionaries too frightened to revolt. He could not abide any more of "the folly and absurdity of this transcendental isolation." A nation had to be governed. An institution had to be saved. His state wished to influence. The National Democratic Party was triumphant. It was time to join the American chase.[64]

Orr wanted Carolina politicians drinking with old southern boys at Democratic Party conventions. He wanted Carolina congressmen puffing cigars in congressional caucuses. He wanted South Carolina citizens voting in presidential elections. Carolina plebeians should enjoy campaign hoopla. Carolina politicians should feast on federal spoils. And James L. Orr should become Speaker of the House—until he could claim residence at the White House.

No one could escape the drift of this new menace. Orr was a South Carolina Fatty Cobb. He would import the whole federalizing, compromising, Union-loving, party-worshipping game into a state affecting to loath the stuff. Orr was also a South Carolina Henry Wise. He would save oligarchy by at least pretending to practice egalitarian republicanism. With Orr at the helm, South Carolina might become compromising Virginia—or worse, some uncompromising mobocracy.

Virginia's Convention of 1851 was too recent a trauma and James L. Orr was too ominously like Wise for the battered Carolina regime, especially in the lowcountry, to acquiesce without a struggle. In 1855, Orr's presidential election notions were defeated in the Carolina senate after passing the house. But Orr's optimistic dynamism mocked Trescot's paralyzing preciousness. The Orr faction commanded a third of the state. The Orr ideology seemed in tune with the time. With lowcountry revolutionaries having shot themselves in the foot and a patronage-hungry upcountry federalizer the healthiest warrior around, how could Cooper's students keep Cooper's cause from dying with a whimper?

– 8 –

No one in demoralized Carolina offered an answer. But a devoted deserter belatedly pointed to a viable strategy. William Lowndes Yancey, scion of an illustrious lowcountry family and named after William Lowndes, that luminous lowcountry saint, had long since moved to Alabama. In 1848, Yancey had acted like a Carolinian. He had marched out of the National Democratic Party Convention. One Southerner had followed.[65]

After the Armistice of 1850, Yancey's Alabama faction suffered the typical fate of extremists who would be Carolinians in the Southwest. Yanceyites retreated from secession to resistance. Unionists warned resistance was a ploy. The electorate bought the warning. Yancey's ultra views were defeated at the polls.[66]

Yancey continued to sound like a Carolinian. Both Democratic and Whig parties, he proclaimed in a public letter on May 10, 1851, have "heretofore preyed upon the vitals" of secession movements. But "Union issues of party policy cannot long attract popular attention." Abolitionism would increase. Southern outrage would escalate. National parties would falter. Southern resistance would become more viable.

Resisters accordingly should shun national parties and perfect a local faction. "Every fresh aggression on the part of the general government, tending to irritate and excite the South, will find an organized party whose ranks will inevitably be swelled." Yancey's nucleus, "fully disciplined and fully prepared," would someday save the South. Thomas Cooper's old plan was alive in Alabama.[67]

Within the year, Yancey had seen Carolina's folly. Yancey's Alabama nucleus sought to nominate a states' rights presidential ticket in 1852. Yancey balked. The Democratic Party's Franklin Pierce, he urged, would protect slavery better than the Whig Party's Winfield Scott. More important, southern warriors were massing in the Democratic Party. A commander must not secede from the troops. Better to rejoin and guide than to stand insultingly aloof from potential followers.[68]

The Yancey who came back bore little relation to rival Democratic Party chieftains. His was not the spirit of Fatty Cobb, eager to be clubby in congressional caucuses. He was no Jefferson Davis, certain a properly aggressive South could control the Union. He scorned the way of James L. Orr, playing whichever cards were dealt.

Yancey would cooperate with Southern Democrats now. Then they might cooperate with him later. He would push, push, push, testing whether the National Democracy could obtain southern demands. If Southern Democrats prevailed, he would remain a Democrat. If Southern Democrats failed, they might follow an extremist who had fought their good fight.

Yancey understood why Charleston squires sniffed at his plunge into an egalitarian institution. Elitists left behind in South Carolina were out of touch with the nouveau South. Only a Carolinian become a Southwesterner could seek a more radicalized South inside the Democracy, the Southwest's favorite alternative to disunion. Playing National Democrat was admittedly playing with fire—or, more accurately, aiding and abetting politicians determined to control fire-eaters. But within this ever-more dominant power structure, dreamed this ex-Carolinian, a southern extremist might still rule or ruin the establishment.

CHAPTER 30

The Kansas-Nebraska Act, I: Confrontation in Missouri

In 1854, the Kansas-Nebraska Act demonstrated William L. Yancey's prescience. Slavery ultras could indeed find action aplenty in the National Democratic Party. For a decade and a half, southern competition between Democrats, Disunionists, Calhounites, and Whigs to press hardest for slavery had pushed the Democracy in pro-southern directions. But usually before opponents could carp about the party's victories.

No southern warrior could complain about the Kansas-Nebraska Act. This time, Southern Democrats' overwhelming success disheartened the competition. After the Democracy's triumph, long-vulnerable Southern Whigs had to repudiate the National Whig Party. Congressional victory also left Disunionists wondering if maybe, just maybe, the Democratic Party could save slavery and Union too.

– 1 –

Southern Democrats' drive for the Kansas-Nebraska Act came after tests of whether the faction's latest triumph, the Fugitive Slave Law of 1850, was an empty victory. The tests yielded southern conviction that the fugitive triumph was as useless as previous gag rule victories. Yankee hostility supposedly nullified the return of runaways.

We now know that 90% of the 332 fugitives tried under Mason's juryless Fugitive Slave Law were despatched southwards.[1] Still, contemporaries' myth may convey a more significant reality than posterity's count. Newspapers publicized the few Yankee defiances of the law. The many undramatic compliances went unnoticed. Thus Northerners appeared determined to rob Southerners.[2]

Appearances counted most. The Fugitive Slave Law could only achieve its founders' objective, consolidation of border slavery, if potential fugitives *thought* the North forbidding. Southern blacks and whites had more reason to think Yankees were helping fugitives, given what they read in the newspapers.

Consider these famous headline stories. Shadrack, a Virginia slave, was arrested in Boston in early 1851. A mob tore the defendant from the courtroom and despatched him to Canada. Eight of Shadrack's liberators were indicted. None was convicted.[3]

In September 1851, Edward Gorsuch of Baltimore County, Maryland, and some relatives went after two slaves in Christiana, Pennsylvania. Blacks and two whites massed to defy Gorsuch. Gunfire crackled. Gorsuch was killed and his son badly wounded. Still another crowd freed Gorsuch's slaves. Forty-five whites were arrested. No one was convicted.[4]

Later in the fall of 1851, a Missouri slave known as Jerry was arrested in Syracuse, New York. A mob rescued Jerry from the police station and sent him to Canada. Twenty-six of Jerry's rescuers were indicted. Thirteen escaped to Canada before being tried. Only one liberator was convicted.[5]

The most notorious fugitive case occurred simultaneously with the passage of the Kansas-Nebraska Act. In May of 1854, Anthony Burns, escapee from Virginia, was arrested in Boston. Important Yankee intellectuals, including Theodore Parker, Thomas Higginson, and Wendell Phillips, designed an attack on the courthouse. Higginson called the ensuing melee "one of the very best plots that ever failed."[6] Burns remained a slave.

Still, one of Burns's guards was killed. None of Burns's would-be rescuers was convicted. It cost an estimated $100,000 for a brigade of Massachusetts militia, a phalanx of policemen, a United States infantry company, and a detachment of artillery to return a solitary slave to Virginia.

The slave did not stay south or enslaved. A few months later, Yankees bought and freed the failed fugitive. Anthony Burns's owner received what he would have under Thomas Pratt's proposed amendment to the Fugitive Slave Law: a few hundred dollars for a slave a Yankee community was loathe to return.[7]

In the light of hindsight and with awareness of some 300 runaways returned to slavery under the Fugitive Slave Law, posterity can deride these nation-straining cases as press sensationalism. But Southerners correctly saw that the message coming back from the North, to slaveholders and slaves alike, was that when a fugitive faced extradition, Yankees just might free the accused. One moral seemed clear. Insofar as federal law could shore up hinterlands, the Slavepower had better secure ironclad edicts. That lesson would not be lost on Southerners who pushed Stephen A. Douglas in the Kansas-Nebraska proceedings.

– 2 –

With southern pressing of Douglas on Kansas, as with previous slavery crises, analysis of that vague entity, southern pressure, should begin by asking what Southerner first pressured, and why? That strategy recognizes that events grow not out of thin air but from a precipitator's action. Emphasis on the initial actor also yields insights lingering after analysis shifts to how and why others reacted to the precipitator. Thus James Hammond's provocation of the gag rule crisis highlights unsteady nerves amongst Carolinians wandering between Calhoun's tactics and Cooper's. William Cost Johnson's insistence on an airtight gag rule shows how southern slavery politics made sometimes-warriors of National Whigs. Abel P. Upshur's desperate moves for a Texas treaty reveals the elitist republican at bay against egalitarian republicanism. James Mason's introduction of the juryless fugitive slave bill illuminates distrust of Yankee neighborhoods on southern fringes. So too the southern senator most responsible for nudging Stephen A. Douglas southwards during the Kansas-Nebraska proceedings was a Missourian with a recurrent border vision. Senator Davy Atchison feared that schemes to replace slaves with whites might gain favor inside his not-so-enslaved, underpopulated Missouri frontier—the locale bordering on projected Kansas-Nebraska territories.

In two dozen lightly enslaved spots over two score years, beginning with Edward Coles's Illinois in Northwest Ordinance times, the underlying problem had always been the same. Slavery could not on every frontier solve—could in some scantily populated places make worse—that New World labor shortage which had led Africans to be imported in the first place. By the nineteenth century, too few blacks had been imported for full exploitation of southern resources. Closure of the African slave trade had rendered the slave labor shortfall permanent. Particularly in bad times in black belts, Southerners obscured the problem with their talk of too many blacks, not enough work, racial claustrophobia. But in whiter belts and in better times, Southerners saw truer realities: that blacks were too scarce to go cheaply around, that slaves were slowly being shifted towards the securest and richest and most tropical natural resources, that less tropical or more exhausted or more exposed places increasingly required alternatives to slave labor.

The seductive alternative sporadically voiced in exposed southern hinterlands, whether the speaker was Henry Brawner in Maryland or Thomas Jefferson Randolph in Virginia or Pearl Andrews in Texas or Cassius Clay in Kentucky, was to stop fighting demography, to go with the historical flow, to speed up sales of slaves out so that whites would more speedily come in.[8] Missouri, where that heresy worried Davy Atchison in the early 1850s, was the most exposed southern hinterland. All border states, by definition, had free labor neighbors to the north, Iowa in Missouri's case. But only Missouri also had a free labor neighbor to the east, Illinois, and an uninhibited area to the west, the Louisiana Purchase territory soon to be known as Kansas. Should Kansas be opened for settlement and peopled exclusively with free white laborers, enslaved Missouri would break its own record for number of hostile neighbors.

The most surrounded southern state contained the most severely outnumbered slaveholders, except for Delaware. Compared with Henry Brawner's Maryland or Cassius Clay's Kentucky, Missouri's slavery system in 1850 was by almost any measure scantier: less slaves, lower percentage of slaves, narrower and less enslaved black belts, wider and whiter white belts. No Missouri soil so extensively invited plantations as did the Bluegrass counties running diagonally down Kentucky.

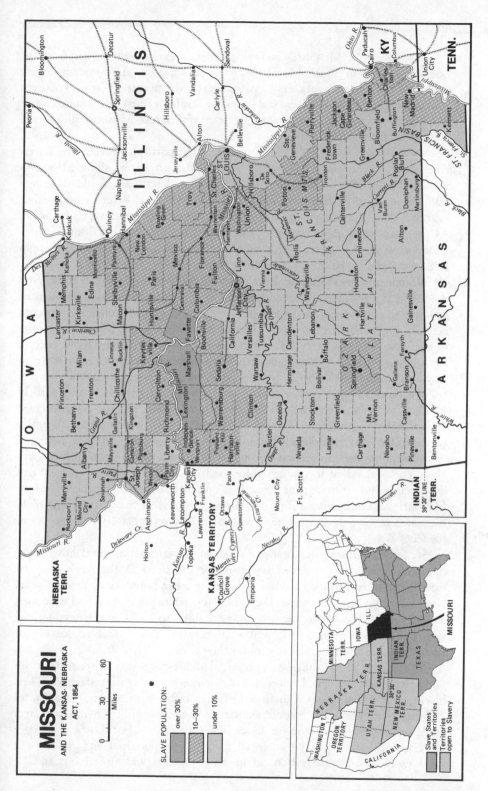

MISSOURI
AND THE KANSAS-NEBRASKA
ACT, 1854

SLAVE POPULATION:
over 30%
10-30%
under 10%

Slave States
and Territories
Territories
open to Slavery

Nor are any of Missouri's bodies of water so extensively enriching as the Chesapeake Bay in South Maryland. Missouri's narrow river system largely delineates the state's edges. The Mississippi River marks Missouri's eastern boundary. The Missouri River establishes the northern third of the state's western edge before turning and streaming southeast across Missouri to join the Mississippi River at St. Louis.

Narrow river deltas in Missouri were usually spottily enslaved. The fewest river-bound slaves worked up north on the Missouri River, along Missouri's western border. Only after the river swerved southeastward could slave percentages in the 20% range be found; and at the Missouri River's eastern edge, near St. Louis, percentages of blacks dropped below that middling figure again. As for Mississippi River counties, no southern state witnessed such paltry enslavement of the stream's lush banks. Missouri's whitish black belts might well be called gray belts.

Whiteness surrounded gray belts. Almost totally white Missouri counties to the north and south sandwiched those most enslaved Missouri River counties running across the state. Mississippi River planters in Missouri were caught between lily-white free Illinois on the east and almost-white Missouri counties to the west. The relatively few planters who worked Missouri River bottom lands along the state's western borders were hemmed between almost slaveless Missouri counties to their east and vacant Kansas territory across the river.[9]

Missouri's slim percentage of slaves in 1850, 13% compared with Kentucky's 21%, was more comparable to colonial New York's. That once-enslaved area, also with percentages of slaves in the middle teens, had had such a spottily concentrated and numerically insignificant black population that potential white migrants had considered slavery no deterrence. Late eighteenth-century New York's flood of incoming whites had driven black relative percentages downwards and sentiment for emancipation upwards. Mid-nineteenth-century Missouri was undergoing a similar whitening process. Between 1830 and 1860, the state's relative slave percentage was cut in half, to under 10% on the eve of the Civil War.

St. Louis, cultural and economic hub of Missouri, illustrated how white immigrants could make slave labor unimportant. In 1830, the city's approximately 2500 slaves formed around 20% of the urban population. Twenty years later, slave numbers were about the same while white population had ballooned almost five times, lowering the percentage of slaves to 3.4%. In the next decade, slave population shrunk a little, and white numbers almost doubled, leaving St. Louis less than 1% an enslaved city on the eve of the Civil War.[10]

The change in St. Louis was a potential archetype, a way of securing white labor's triumph over black serviles without much said against slavery. When blacks were seldom seen or discussed, slavery could seem, as in St. Louis and colonial New York, too inconsequential to deter migrants. Then newcomers could make slaves an ever more dispensable solution to labor shortage.

The trick was to make potential farmers join potential city dwellers in thinking Missouri's relatively small amount of slavery was superfluous. In Cassius Clay's Kentucky, thick black belts made political contention to remove slaves seem a precondition for attracting whites. In Missouri, thin gray belts made debate about blacks perhaps counterproductive. Let the word go out that Missourians considered slavery too unimportant to discuss. Then nonslaveholders might arrive en masse, making slaves and slaveholders ever more superfluous.

– 3 –

Silence on slavery was the gospel of an especially charismatic Southerner. Missouri's leading foe of agitations about slavery was no anti-establishment heretic, no Cassius Clay. In Thomas Hart Benton, pillar of national and state establishments and supreme enemy of Davy Atchison, slaveholders faced a popular hero capable of winning any statewide election.[11]

Thomas Hart Benton believed that his southwestern state was essentially western, with only a trace of southernness. Slavery was not so much wrong (although Benton thought it an evil), not so much a candidate for removal (although he thought its silent evaporation would be salutary) but not worth contending about, especially when contention itself victimized nonslaveholder interests. A statesman must accordingly agitate for free lands, for better railroads, for sounder banks, for anything to promote yeomen's migration. If national politics instead became consumed with slavery, the especially disastrous threat would be to the Union, the last best hope of free citizens. If the Missouri political scene grew rank with Slavepower agitations, the most intolerable consequence would be that yeomen would not come to Missouri.

Benton's life had been a tale of frontier migration. Disgraced after pilfering small sums from roommates at North Carolina College, Benton had moved in the early nineteenth century to Andrew Jackson's Cumberland Valley frontier. There he had become one of the toughest bear hunters, tomahawk throwers, and duelists near Nashville. Andrew Jackson was for a time delighted with this fellow spirit. Then the two tempestuous outdoorsmen were drawn into a barroom brawl between Benton's younger brother and one of Jackson's friends. Thomas Hart Benton told off the great man. Jackson challenged. Benton accepted. Both titans drew, aimed, blazed. Benton's sleeve was torn. Jackson's arm was punctured. Old Hickory soaked two mattresses with blood. Thomas Hart broke Jackson's sword in two before the crowds.

Seldom has a victor been so ripe to be vanquished. Shooting Jackson in Jacksonland was like knifing the Pope in the Vatican. Having been driven west from North Carolina as a consequence of dishonorable disgrace, Benton was now driven west from Tennessee as a consequence of pugnacious pride. In 1815, with $400 in pocket, the migrant arrived at the western outpost of St. Louis.

No Missouri bobcat cut a swath so quickly. Benton's savage aggression and rude sophistication were the perfect combination for a frontier cultural oasis. The duelist strode around town dressed like the groom at a wedding. The dandy was no less a fighter with his pen. Possessed of a superb memory and literary style, Benton wrote newspaper editorials and history books that raised partisan invective to a high art. When Missouri entered the Union in 1820, Benton entered the United States Senate. Missourians kept him there longer than Clay or Webster or Calhoun.

The tiny Senate chamber seemed almost too cramped for Thomas Hart Benton. The western hero often paced back and forth, reminding observers of a caged lion. His frame, the same 5′11″ height as the cadaverous Henry Wise's, carried twice the poundage. Benton's head was large, his shoulders wide, his chest like a barrel. His mouth was usually turned down in fierce frown. His eyes were often naked with hate. He had slain a man in St. Louis for calling him a puppy. His senatorial vendettas earned him the nickname Big Bully Bottom Benton.

Big Bully commenced each day with ice-cold baths, featuring merciless scrubbing with the thick brush. He then donned ruffled shirt, winged collar, and formal cloth. His gold eye-glass perched on his chest, hinting at learning never known to be displayed lightly. "Senator," a man once addressed His Eminence, "this boy walked 200 miles to hear you." "Young man," Benton replied, "you did right."[12]

In the Senate, the Westerner gained the palm he had thrown away in Nashville. He became Jackson's confidante and chief defender. To Benton, Jacksonian mission meant securing a white man's paradise, stretching across the continent and over the seas to encompass Columbus's trade route to India. Only two American sorts would be *personae non gratis*. Benton would tolerate neither paper money banks, with their debilitating panics, nor agitators for slavery, with their allegedly disunionist conspiracies.

Benton never doubted the allegation that Calhounite conspirators provoked every slavery crisis. The Missourian came to conspiratorial certitudes while watching John C. Calhoun during the tariff and gag rule wars of the 1830s. There, as Benton saw it, stood the Union-loving, black-hating North, decorating William Lloyd Garrison with a rope around the neck. There stood the Carolinian, screaming that Yankees were about to strangle slavery. Calhoun could hardly expect to save slavery by infuriating Northerners. The conspirator could only care about breaking up the Union.

The further Jackson receded from center stage, the more Benton carried the war to Calhoun. Southern drives for Texas, denunciations of the Wilmot Proviso, diatribes against free California—they were a Nullifiers' plot against nonslaveholders' beloved Union. Benton was all for Texas, especially if nonslaveholders were guaranteed half ot it. The senator relished President Zachary Taylor's plan for two new free states, not least because agitators for slavery would be banned from the newest West.

Northerners lauded Benton as one Southerner who was an American first. Missouri slaveholders called him a secret freesoiler and abolitionist. At the climax of annexation, the Missouri legislature instructed the senator to drop his mutilation of enslaved Texas. Benton sort of acquiesced. In 1849 the Missouri legislature passed anti-Benton resolutions, applauding Calhoun's Southern

Address and instructing Missouri's congressional delegates to stand by the South. This time Benton renounced his instructions. He would teach southwestern constituents that western mission demanded silencing southern agitators.

The campaign of 1849 was Benton's most notorious. The old battler, belying his 68 years, galloped on horseback over dusty, rutted roads, thousands of miles under the relentless Missouri sun. He would arrive at some remote slaveholders' outpost, mount the podium before hostile eyes, doff his white beaver hat and black silk gloves.

He came, he would say, "to destroy a falsehood . . . and to expose a conspiracy." The "din about northern aggression and encroachment, Wilmot Proviso, abolition of slavery, is only to stir up the people to that deplorable point which precedes all divorces." John C. Calhoun was all "too successful." His "fundamental falsehood . . . pervades this state, and all the slaveholding states." Despite abolitionist temples burned in Philadelphia, anti-abolitionist mobs triumphant in Boston, an abolitionist editor murdered in Illinois, Southerners had been brainwashed into believing Northerners would abolish slavery. Calhoun's henchmen were alive and well in Missouri. They threatened to transform a western paradise of free white labor into a southern inferno of nullification agitation. Well, abolitionists hardly threatened slaveholders. Instead, slaveholders' agitations drove nonslaveholding settlers elsewhere. A champion of western yeomen could not allow nullifying legislators to instruct him to emit Calhoun's disastrous screeches.

Was he loyal to slavery? More loyal than obsessed Nullifiers. His slavery policy was peace and quiet, silence, "no agitation." He understood how easily slaveholders imbibed "groundless apprehensions." He would not "contribute to alarm the country by engaging in discussions which assert or imply danger."

His "personal sentiments," he conceded, are against "slavery, and against" introducing the "evil" where "it does not exist. If there was no slavery in Missouri today, I should be opposed to its coming in." But he saw no remedy, save the healing balm of centuries. He scorned sanctimonious outsiders. He owned slaves. He was "not the least afraid that Congress will pass any law to affect this property." He feared that Nullifiers pretending to be afraid would agitate the Union to death. The West, the Union, slavery itself needed silence. "If that could not be done," he would at least silence himself.[13]

To slaveholding listeners, Benton's silence came too soon, before his future course was clear. At the very least, Benton's demands for quiet on the subject, if successful, would signal to potential emigrants that Missourians would say or do nothing to protect the institution. Slaveholders feared worse. Benton's argument that defense of slavery repelled slaveless migrants from coming to Missouri seemed uncomfortably close to Cassius Clay's argument that slavery itself repelled yeomen from migrating to Kentucky. Slaveholders worried that after incoming whites made all of Missouri like St. Louis, St. Louis's hero would urge silence no longer. Once non-agitation about slavery had rendered slaveholders supine and superfluous, Thomas Hart Benton would agitate to deport blacks and attract still more whites. That was precisely Abel P. Upshur's fear about a stream of non-agitating Englishmen descending on Texas.

The sequel would demonstrate that Missouri slaveholders' suspicions were half-right. After 1854, Benton himself would remain determined never to speak for or against slavery. But some key Benton followers would soon be agitating, Cassius Clay-style, for legislative action that would force Missourians to sell blacks southwards.

Earlier, in the pre-Kansas-Nebraska period, everything about Benton, his supporters, and his slavery posture remained a sphinx. James L. Green, one of Benton's most prominent opponents, caught the mystery perfectly in an 1849 pamphlet.[13] On a prospect so "sickening and heartrending" as abolition, Green declared, "ambiguity" was unacceptable. Benton, complained Green, has never made "himself understood." I *believe* his calls for silence mask a freesoiler. But "many good and worthy citizens" disagree. "To my certain knowledge some of his friends consider him committed to the [Wilmot] Proviso, and others consider him against it."[14]

In 1850, Green and kindred fellows momentarily unseated the sphinx. When Senator Benton came up for re-election, Democrats from the gray belt deserted to the Whigs' candidate, Henry S. Geyer. Benton's ouster was intended as a red flag. Missourians who hoped for a free labor commonwealth, however camouflaged, would not speak for the state.

Benton emulated John Quincy Adams. He would speak from a lowly freshman congressman's post. In 1852, he won election to the national House of Representatives from St. Louis. In 1853, his St. Louis supporters, led by Frank Blair, Jr., sought unsuccessfully to repeal the Missouri legislature's anti-Benton Resolutions of 1849.

Blair Junior was a young political apprentice whose father, Frank Blair, Sr., had warned Jackson to disinherit Calhoun rather than Van Buren over Texas. Blair Junior had come to Missouri to learn the anti-Calhoun Jacksonian trade at Benton's feet. Junior stayed on as Old Bullion's protégé. When Junior's mouth moved, everyone believed, Benton's words came forth.

For a moment in 1853, Blair's lips emitted Cassius Clay's rhetoric. Since Missouri's white laborers outnumber slaveholders "by about five to one," proclaimed the younger Blair, "interests of the vast majority" must "prevail." A bar to slave expansion best served majority interests. Did siding with the people against the rich make him a freesoiler? He would not "take pains to deny it."[15]

Slaveholders cheered Junior's lack of pains. At last, an advocate of present silence on slavery had let future agitation against the institution be seen through the disguise. Alas for the slavocracy's case, young Blair usually remained behind the mask. Benton himself gave off no evidence that he would ever agitate to end slavery. Benton's newspaper, *The St. Louis Democrat,* agitated only against agitations for or against slavery. Any alleged intention to rise up against the institution was here well camouflaged—and in the southern state most vulnerable to hidden subversion.

– 4 –

Benton's followers considered Missouri's other senator the real saboteur. Davy Atchison, charged Thomas Hart Benton, was a poorly disguised Calhounite who agitated to break up the Union. Old Dave, or Bourbon Dave as rednecks called him, was up for re-election in 1855. A showdown with Benton likely loomed. The prospect was daunting. Atchison, champion of the slavocracy in western Missouri River gray belts, understood Benton's power as champion of western nonslaveholders.[16]

Atchison, a quarter-century younger than Benton, had arrived in Missouri not from neutralist Nashville but from Bluegrass plantationland. Bourbon Dave had established himself not in rather cultivated St. Louis but in Missouri's crudest West. Atchison's Missouri River Valley was no place for Bentonian airs— and cussin' Davy had none. A man cherished whiskey to keep warm—and Old Dave was warmer than most. "Niggers" on the bottom lands helped secure profits—and Atchison wished more whites would exploit more blacks. He was tall, florid, coarse. His face was somewhere between imposing and ugly. His personality ranged from swaggering to ferocious.

Damning slavery to his face brought out the ferociously ugly in him. His Missouri River Valley, angry that Benton considered slavery non-essential in the state, believed westernness required southernness. White migrants had not supplied sufficient labor to work river bottom lands. Slaves were needed. Statesmen must protect the vulnerable institution in the border. So believing, Atchison strode into the Senate in 1843.

In Washington, Atchison followed characteristic southwestern trails from Jackson towards Calhoun. A Jacksonian Democrat on economic matters, he got on well with Benton, until Texas matters showed they lived in different Missouris. Atchison would protect Texas hinterlands from alleged English antislavery intent. Benton denied such intent existed. If Slavepower agitators would cease connecting Texas and slavery, declared Benton, Northerners would go for annexation of a not-very-enslaved western area. Then nonslaveholders would stream in. Atchison called that pitch for nonslaveholder support a disguised formula for hemming in slaveholders like lepers. South Carolina Senator George McDuffie called Big Bully the South's worst traitor.

Benton was traitor to southern slaveholders! Atchison was traitor to western nonslaveholders! So raged the argument, whether the issue was Texas or fugitives or Wilmot. In 1853–4, Kansas-Nebraska territories drew the controversy like a magnet. Benton brought great advantages to the Kansas imbroglio. The Missouri Compromise of 1820 had declared future Kansas and Nebraska areas, because north of 36°30′ in the Louisiana Purchase Territory, off-limits for slaveholders, once settlers were allowed to enter. A Congress determined not to talk about slavery had only to establish territorial government, extinguish Indian titles, and invite settlers.

This silence on slavery would place an exclusively nonslaveholding population across the Missouri River from Atchison's slaveholding constituents. Still, political danger loomed in any southern attempt to repeal the Missouri Compromise ban. Northerners, erupting over southern reneging on a sacrosanct compromise, might vote to keep Kansas closed to all settlers rather than allow slaveholders to enter. Atchison supporters might re-emerge as Benton had painted them in the Texas struggle: Calhounites whose proslavery priorities devastated national peace and denied nonslaveholders access to virgin turf.

In trouble on Kansas whether he did or did not agitate against the Missouri Compromise, Atchison long opted for his own form of silence. He led southern congressmen in defeating bills opening Kansas for white settlement, not because slaveholders would be banned but because Indians had not yet been removed. This transparent stall played into Benton's hands. At a time when Missouri nonslaveholders coveted Kansas lands, Atchison said Halt, ostensibly because of Indians but really because the slaveholder minority could not also enter. That was no way to turn the Missouri majority against the very popular Benton. Atchison, champion of Missouri's not-so-numerous slaveholders, was running out of options.[17]

– 5 –

No one monitored Atchison's discomfort more closely than the Chairman of the Senate Committee on the Territories, Stephen A. Douglas of Illinois. Douglas cared little about whether slaves entered this or any territory. He cared passionately about opening the whole West for white settlement. Like Benton, this western Jacksonian wished the continent Americanized from the Atlantic to the Pacific. Indian control over plains between Missouri and the Rockies seemed to him a travesty on white men's Manifest Destiny. "How are we to develop, cherish, and protect our immense interests and possessions on the Pacific," Douglas asked, "with a vast wilderness 1500 miles in breadth, filled with hostile savages, and cutting off all direct communication?" To Douglas, removing the "Indian barrier" and establishing white government were "first steps" towards a "tide of emigration and civilization."[18]

A second step, a centrally located transcontinental railroad, would serve the population surge.[19] Douglas might profit from shares in a central railroad's Illinois branch. That prospect was pleasant but incidental. Douglas's hope of riding the territorial issue to the White House was even more pleasant, but still incidental. Furthering white settlement of territories, like furthering his career as railroad entrepreneur and political aspirant, would providentially sustain white men's democratic and entrepreneurial mission—and would providentially revitalize the Democratic Party.

On Kansas-Nebraska, Douglas could best secure white settlers by avoiding his own doctrine of how migrants should be governed. Like Lewis Cass, this Popular Sovereignty advocate preferred that frontiersmen choose their own institutions. Far-off Washington, D.C., solons, Douglas often emphasized in the classic Jacksonian vein, could not wisely or democratically rule remote prairies.

But in the case of Kansas-Nebraska, the far-off national government had long since intrusively barred slavery north of 36°30′ in the Louisiana Purchase Territory, whatever future settlers might wish. Restoring settlers' right to decide would require repealing the Missouri Compromise. Slaveholders and blacks might then enter a domain reserved since 1820 for Douglas's constituents: black-hating nonslaveholders. Douglas could either repeal a sacred compromise and incense Illinois voters or do nothing about a congressional ban and evade his Popular Sovereignty principles.

Evasion triumphed. For ten years, the Little Giant reported out of his Senate Committee on the Territories bill after bill opening Kansas-Nebraska for white settlement. These bills mentioned neither settlers' rights to decide nor the previous congressional decision, thus leaving the Missouri Compromise proscription silently intact. Southern Democrats stopped these bills in the South-dominated Senate. Kansas-Nebraska remained Indian turf.

In March of 1853, Douglas almost replaced reds with whites. The House of Representatives, despite Deep South grumbling, passed a bill organizing the territory with the Missouri Compromise untouched. Douglas tried to jam the evasive coup through the Senate on the session's last night, in helter-skelter, ill-attended moments before adjournment. He received astounding help. Davy Atchison surrendered.

The Missouri Compromise prohibition of slavery in neighboring Kansas, Atchison told the Senate, ranked with the Northwest Ordinance's outlawing of slavery in neighboring Illinois as the two greatest "errors committed in the political history of this country." But he saw "no hope of a repeal." Slaveholders "might as well agree" to be barred "now as next year, or five or ten years hence." His nonslaveholder constituents demanded territorial access. "You cannot restrain them much longer." Slaveholders must "submit" to the "irredeemable."

Why did Atchison submit to the proscription of slaveholding settlers? Perhaps Atchison expected slaveholding ruffians to invade Kansas, whatever the Missouri Compromise said. Davy's subsequent extra-legalism makes this hypothesis plausible. Or perhaps Atchison wilted before Benton's escalating charges that slavery-obsessed Calhounites were nullifying nonslaveholders' access to virgin Kansas. Political realities in overwhelmingly nonslaveholder Missouri makes that hypothesis more plausible still. Perhaps also Bourbon Dave was drunk. The late hour, Atchison's reputation, and senatorial titters when he confessed mouthing off too much all make the alcoholic hypothesis only dimly outrageous.

Whatever the solution to this mystery, Atchison's turnabout did not turn around national history. All southern senators save those from Missouri balked at Douglas's stampede and Atchison's surrender. Douglas lost 23-17. The South voted against him 19-2.[20]

The defeat augured imminent victory. Southern senators urged delay, not defiance. They spoke not of repealing the Missouri Compromise but of renegotiating Indian treaties as a precondition for acquiescence. With Davy Atchison now an extinct volcano, the proslavery eruption necessary to light up Douglas's evasion of Popular Sovereignty was nowhere to be seen.

– 6 –

Then Atchison returned home and rediscovered what his attitudes entailed. His softening, he found, had hardened Benton's position. Instead of hailing Atchison's surrender as better late than never, Benton followers scoffed that Atchison had forfeited any claim to Missourians' support. Slaveholders, gloated Benton's newspapers, now knew that Old Dave was a southern turncoat. Nonslaveholders, declared Old Bullion, remembered that Bourbon Dave had stymied their entrance into Kansas for a decade. Even a surrendering Atchison, Benton pointed out, had failed to remove southern senators' Kansas blockade. Benton urged Missouri farmers now to negate Atchison's stalling southern friends. Nonslaveholders should spill over the Missouri River and seize Kansas land.

While Benton was trumping Atchison's ace on the pro-western side of the Kansas question, pro-southern Missourians were greeting their senior partner with consternation. Old Dave found his Missouri River Valley loathe to surrender a shot at a Kansas slaveholding regime. Surrender meant conceding that slaveholders were too morally despicable to cross their own river. Surrender meant giving Yankee slave-stealers a base of operations near lightly enslaved Missouri neighborhoods. Surrender meant signaling that Missouri slaveholders lacked the spirit to withstand ambiguous Benton attitudes. Atchison's supporters' pro-southern insistences, when combined with Benton's pro-western blitz, left Old Dave nowhere to go if he wanted someone's support. Nowhere to go, except back to agitation against the Missouri Compromise ban on slaveholders.

He traveled backwards in a hurry. In a tear across the state to rival Benton's, Atchison swore that he would never again give an inch on Kansas. His constituents were not depraved. Slaveholders had as much right as Northerners to take their property to American territories. Missouri River masters could not passively accept an attempt to "jeopardize our slave interest" by bounding us "on three sides by Free States or Territories." Slaveholders must try to avoid living close to "a pious and philanthropic class of men" who "think that they are rendering God's good service in stealing their neighbor's negroes." The Kansas side of the Missouri River must be "open to the slaveholder as well as the nonslaveholder."[21]

Atchison's resurrection as slaveholders' champion served such obvious partisan necessity that some will think explanation need go no further. Cynics about Atchison's partisanship might admit that Benton's partisanship was as much at "fault." Old Bullion surely helped destroy silence on slavery by screaming so triumphantly when his foe for once fell quiet.

But neither titan was playing politics as usual. Each saw himself locked in an epic contest between a West where slavery was vital and a West where slavery was superfluous. Benton thought—with good reason—that the Union was doomed if Atchison insisted on Slavepower entrance into Kansas. Atchison thought—with good reason—that border slavery was doomed if spottily enslaved areas submitted to encirclement.

Lest Atchison again contemplate passiveness, correspondents reminded him why slaveholders demanded action. E. A. Hannegan of Covington, Missouri, wrote that "masterly inactivity" would allow Missourians to relax about Benton's activities. Mastery required unending alarms that Bentonian silence on slavery has done "more for the cause of Abolition than all its open, reckless, and God defying advocates." Atchison must agitate on Kansas to alert the public to the "thousands" of "covert" abolitionists in Missouri, "who now from policy hide their hellish designs."[22]

Claiborne Fox Jackson emphasized the other reason why Atchison's Missouri River domain rejected non-agitation on repealing the Missouri Compromise. "Fox" Jackson, author of the 1849 anti-Benton resolution and future proslavery Civil War governor of the state, preferred letting "Indians have" Kansas *"forever"* to permitting "infernal restrictions" on slavery. Indians, scribbled the Fox, "are better neighbors than the abolitionists, *by a damn sight.* If this is to become 'free nigger' territory, Missouri must become so too, for we can hardly keep our negroes here now."[23] Blatant slave kidnapping from free labor Kansas, western nonslaveholders pouring into not-so-enslaved Missouri, insidious sabotage from Missourians who ostensibly favored silence—this was the claustrophobic noose vivid in Missouri slaveholders' imagination as Atchison descended on Washington, rededicated to safeguarding another exposed southern hinterland.

CHAPTER 31

The Kansas-Nebraska Act, II:
Decision in Congress

Davy Atchison's deployment of minority power would inspire the usual majority cry: an extraordinary Slavepower Conspiracy plotted to rule or ruin America's majoritarian institutions. The diagnosis erred. Atchison exerted influence through Washington's ordinary institutions. Atchison's first success came because of normal living arrangements inside the capital's "homes."

– 1 –

In the 1850s, boarding houses were congressmen's homes away from home. When solons combined to rent boarding houses they called messes, they avoided living with alien fellows. Atchison's mess, located on F Street, was a little piece of Southern Democratic heaven. The slaves, personal servants from back home, were akin to minstrels—Aunt Betty, sucking her beat-up pipe; liveried Isaac, strutting like Massa; sleepy Bill, unable to mobilize until noon. Patriarchs had but to enter the mess to remember why they defended a Domestic Institution.[1]

With the exception of Virginia's Congressman William O. Goode, a conservative leader in the Virginia Slavery Debate of 1831–2 and in the state's Convention of 1850–1, all F Street patriarchs were senatorial powers. Virginia's Senators Robert M. T. Hunter and James Mason were chairmen of the Committees on Finance and Foreign Affairs respectively. South Carolina's Senator Andrew P. Butler was chairman of the Judiciary Committee. Atchison was the Senate's president *pro tempore*. The South's power in the Democracy and the Democracy's power in the nation could make idle chatter over Aunt Betty's yams more telling than White House deliberations.

In the winter of 1853–4, Atchison's chatter was not idle. Missourians, he told messmates, would no longer stay out of Kansas. If the Missouri Compromise continued to bar slavery, slaveholding Missouri would be surrounded, slaves kidnapped, Bentonianism victorious, and gray belts helpless before whites migrating to Missouri. If Kansas was open with slave restrictions removed,

550

slaveholding Missourians would claim it, Big Bully would be defeated, and abolitionizing immigrants would be warned away.

Atchison dismissed rejoinders that climate would keep slavery from Kansas. Missouri slaves worked identical soil across the Missouri River from Kansas. Kansas bottom lands could be as productive of hemp and tobacco. Slavery was just as possible in chilly Kansas as in equally chilly Missouri—and as in the entire non-tropical border area.

Slaveholders, Atchison reassured messmates, had aggressively maintained their institution in Missouri, despite being increasingly outnumbered. They would seize Kansas, however many nonslaveholders opposed them. They wanted Kansas, needed Kansas, had every right to avoid encirclement by capturing Kansas.

Atchison's view of practicalities convinced only some of his messmates. South Carolina's Andrew P. Butler privately wrote that with the Missouri Compromise ban repealed, "Kansas will be filled up soon by slaveholders from the neighboring states." Virginia's William O. Goode publicly declared that "the natural causes which compelled our institutions to Missouri are in full force to carry them to Kansas." Every Missouri slaveholder "who desires to maintain the existing order of things there" sees "an outpost in Kansas as essential to the safety of Missouri." Virginia's Robert M. T. Hunter wavered. "For a moment," he had "permitted" himself the "illusion" of "a slaveholding state in Kansas." He still thought that slavery "might go there for a time." But virgin soil closer to the tropics would eventually draw slaveholders from so chilly a plain.[2]

Yet Hunter supported Atchison as completely as did Goode. Both Virginians pronounced Atchison's moral case against the Missouri Compromise unassailable—unless slavery was immoral. Slaveholders had a right to take their property anywhere—unless slave property was like leprosy. Slaveholders in the hinterlands had a right to seek protection from neighboring thieves—whether or not slaveholders in safer areas thought the protection would work.[3]

The F Street messmates and soon other southern congressmen here replicated recent positions in Wilmot Proviso and Fugitive Slave Law controversies. Just as some Southern Democrats had thought especially southern California would be practical for slavery, so Davy Atchison thought especially the Missouri River area of Kansas fit for the institution. Not all—perhaps not most—southern leaders agreed in either case. But in 1854 as in 1850, few Southrons considered practicality the only issue. With Kansas as with the Wilmot Proviso, slaveholders scorned being proscribed as inferior. With Atchison's attempt to protect Missouri slaveholders, as with James Mason's attempt to extradite fugitive slaves, a self-respecting civilization must support a legitimate warrior, even if his proposed weapon might prove to be ineffective.

– 2 –

Once the F Street messmates lined up behind Davy Atchison, Stephen A. Douglas had to accommodate these chieftains. Douglas had not become the rising star of the southern-dominated national Democracy by conducting head-on collisions with important Southern Democrats. Moreover, the Illinoisan could hardly stonewall against Davy Atchison's insistence on Popular Sovereignty, Douglas's own favorite conception. F Street titans could rally southern senators to pass Douglas's bill and ensure Douglas's dream of peopling the plains. But if Douglas wanted red men to yield before whites, he had to allow settlers to decide for themselves about blacks.

Atchison, Douglas's pal, may have dropped hints about how Northern Democrats might safely appease the F Streeters. In Missouri, Atchison had called for "*virtual* repeal" of the Missouri Compromise.[4] If emphasis could be kept on the virtual, repeal might be non-explosive in the North.

The bill Douglas first reported out of committee, printed in Washington newspapers on January 7, 1854, was so heavy on the virtual as to leave the Missouri Compromise just about unrepealed. The evasive Armistice of 1850 was here perfectly replicated: the people of the territories were explicitly given power to decide on slavery at the *statehood* stage. What about Popular Sovereignty during the *territorial* stage? Douglas's bill, like the laws on Utah and New Mexico territory, remained mute.

On January 10, 1854, newspapers reported a "clerical error" in the bill printed on January 7. The corrected "error" explicitly allowed settlers to decide at statehood *and* territorial stages. The proposed law now affirmed that in the Louisiana Purchase Territory north of 36°30' "all questions pertaining to slavery in Territories, and in the new States to be formed therefrom, are to be left to the people residing therein."

Perhaps Douglas himself here corrected a genuine secretarial mistake. More likely, F Streeters forced a change covered up under the guise of "clerical error." At any rate, the clarified language transcended the settlement of 1850 in a manner crucial to Davy Atchison. Settlers' decision at the moment of statehood, the only Popular Sovereignty explicitly affirmed in Utah and New Mexico laws and in Douglas's original bill, would have loaded the dice against Atchison's small crew of Missouri River Valley slaveholders. After several years of peopling the territory, Yankee settlers would have likely been numerically overwhelming. Neighboring Missourians' best shot at capturing Kansas was to cross the border first, secure slavery in an early territorial decision, and then cling to the *fait accompli* until the statehood vote. The corrected "clerical error" invited that early Atchisonian strike.

To receive that boon, Atchison gave Douglas what the Illinoisan most wanted: no actual repeal of the Missouri Compromise. The Missourian conceded much. Until a territorial legislature passed a slavery statute, the 36°30' line, barring slaveholders, would be operative. If slavery was banned until territorial elections, no slaves would theoretically be there to keep enslaved.

But Bourbon Dave was no man of theory. Not a slave had to be in Kansas, he knew, for slaveholders to triumph. White settlers, not blacks, would decide slavery's fate at the polls; and whites who wished to bring in blacks would likely make their wished-for slave investment legally secure before importing that valuable property. Davy Atchison could aid Northern Democrats by allowing the Missouri Compromise to remain, so long as Missourians would have their chance to spill over the Missouri River, win an early territorial election, supersede the 36°30′ ban, and then bring in slaves.

Douglas compromised too. He would have preferred a replica of the settlement of 1850. Instead, the corrected "clerical error," by explicitly allowing a territorial legislature to counter the Missouri Compromise ban, clarified the 1850 ambiguity about *when* settlers could act in a manner politically dangerous for Northern Democrats.

Still, Douglas's step beyond the Compromise of 1850 at least left the Missouri Compromise both unrepealed and arguably a hindrance to slavery until a territorial legislature acted. "No man was so wild," Douglas privately whispered, "as to think of repealing the Missouri Compromise."[5] His January 10 rapprochement with F Streeters, a classic accommodation between power brokers who needed each other, kept the National Democratic Party a tad short of the northern political wilderness.

– 3 –

Unfortunately for this fleeting accommodation, some of the South's sanest congressmen instantly called the proposed bill too northern. The issue hiding under the bill's phrasing was too familiar to go unnoticed. Leaving the prior Missouri Compromise ban intact in 1854 was like leaving the prior Mexican antislavery bar intact in the late 1840s. Once again, doing nothing was accomplishing something portentous: allowing an insulting theoretical proscription to continue. The insult could again become practical, as perhaps it had been in California, if the ban on slavery discouraged far-off Southerners from coming to Kansas.

In mid-January 1854, that conclusion was spreading around Washington faster than Douglas could work the legislative halls. The Democrats' *Washington Sentinel,* official printer to the Senate, sounded the alarm publicly only a few days after printing Douglas's latest evasion of Missouri Compromise repeal.[6] Simultaneously, Congressman Phillip Phillips of Alabama, a very moderate Democrat on the House Committee on the Territories, lobbied on F Street, telling Atchison and fellows they had to scuttle the 1820 ban.[7]

Then perhaps the most moderate southern senator shredded fading chances to keep the Missouri Compromise proscription. Archibald Dixon, Whig of Kentucky, rose in the Senate on January 16, 1854, two days after the *Washington Sentinel's* editorial, and moved repeal of the Missouri Compromise in Douglas's proposed territory. As with William Cost Johnson daring the Democracy to pass the severest gag and as with Milton Brown challenging the Democratic Party to multiply the potential pro-southern effect of Texas five times, an exasperated Southern Whig had defied the Democracy to go all the way for the South.[8]

Familiar Whig disasters in southern loyalty politics led to Dixon's familiar ploy. The notion that a Whig administration could be as safe for slavery as a Democratic regime, already dubious after Texas, had gone straight downhill ever since the Zachary Taylor debacle. In the Congress of 1850, Northern Whigs' had refused to make any concession to Southern Whigs, even to Henry Clay's initial compromise proposals. Even Border South Whigs had found such so-called political allies newly embarrassing, or rather climactically infuriating. Fury escalated when a few prominent Northern Whigs led rescues of fugitive slaves in the early 1850s.

Southern Whig disaster in the Election of 1852 resulted. That contest pitted the Whigs' latest pet general, Winfield Scott, against the Democrats' latest northern man with southern leanings, New Hampshire's Franklin Pierce. Pierce won 13 of 15 southern states and a 55% popular plurality. Despite Southern Democrats' largest sweep since Andrew Jackson's, Whigs salvaged 48% of the Border South's popular vote and 47% of the Middle South's. The disaster was in the Deep South, where Whigs received under 37% of the popular votes, compared with 50% in 1848. No great switch of Whigs over to Democrats occurred in the four years. Rather, Lower South Whigs sullenly stayed home. Democrats' vote in this region actually dropped 4.3%. Whigs' ballots plummetted 42.7%. The stay-at-home posture caught the dying Southern Whigs' mood: resentful at being de-Whigged, not ready to join gloating Democrats, still looking to oust victorious tormentors.[9]

Instead, Southern Whigs were the ones ousted in the congressional elections of 1853. Their House contingent was reduced to all of 22 seats. The party was now unable to hide, even in an off-year election, from everyone's knowledge that Northern Democrats were the soundest Yankees on slavery.[10]

The Kentucky Whig who in 1854 subjected the Democracy's soundness to climactic test was not so sound himself. Archibald Dixon told Yankee abolitionists that "if anybody has a right to complain of slavery, it is we who are incumbered by it." Someday, cheered Dixon, a "mysterious Providence" will, "in his own good time, break the shackles of the slave."[11] Yet this Henry Clay Whig who occupied the Great Compromiser's senate seat moved to strike Clay's first triumph, the Missouri Compromise, from operating in Douglas's proposed territory.

Dixon portrayed himself not as a troublemaker daring the Democracy but as a conservative healing a nation. The District, he regretted, was rank with sarcasm and hatred. The slavery issue, he proclaimed, must be run forever out of town. The Compromise of 1820, by excluding slavery from Kansas-Nebraska territory, had harmfully institutionalized congressional hands-on. The Compromise of 1850, by letting settlers in New Mexico and Utah make the final decision, had beneficiently institutionalized congressional hands-off. By voiding its youthful error, Congress would reaffirm its mature wisdom and write *finis* to the congressional history of slavery.

Dixon thus joined a long line of national statesmen—Van Buren on the gag rule, Zachary Taylor on No Territory, Douglas on Popular Sovereignty, Benton on non-agitation, Thomas Jefferson on everything—who sought to end controversy by avoiding it and succeeded in making the unavoidable more controversial. In Dixon's hands, the strategy of two generations of national conservatives came to climax—and demonstrated the bankruptcy of avoidance.

New York's Whig Senator William H. Seward claimed that he had put Archibald Dixon up to the motion. Seward, however, hardly sought to avoid controversy. The New Yorker admitted to plotting that Dixon's slavery zealotry might goad Southern Democrats and thus the Slavepower-dominated Democratic Party to demand outrageously much for slavery. Then Whigs could whip up greater anti-southern—and anti-Democratic Party—hatreds in the North.[12]

Seward's bragging about this so-called statecraft helps explain why a generation of historians theorized that irresponsible demagogues precipitated a needless civil war. The New Yorker was even an irresponsible partisan. His plot aimed at a Democracy so pro-southern and a Northern Whig reaction so anti-southern that Southern Whigs could not have stayed in so obnoxiously Yankee a party.

Still, no proof exists beyond Seward's bragging that Dixon followed the New York schemer's instructions. No Southern Whig needed lessons in how to wax more southern than the Democracy.[13] Seward's likely effect, if any, was in failing to discourage a Southern Whig's natural impulses. Back in 1844, when Milton Brown had made his divide-Texas motion, Northern Whigs had demanded that he cease and desist, and Brown had ultimately voted against his own proposal. Such moderating effects of this national party were now over. Whigs could be as southern as they liked in the South, as northern as they liked in the North, as though it were still 1836 and the party was not national at all.

Even had Seward responsibly sought to restrain Archibald Dixon, his chance of saving the Missouri Compromise would have been next to nil. 1854 was not 1844. A decade of Northern Whig anti-Slavepower rhetoric had left Southern Whigs too disenchanted with their Yankee wing and too desperate about their eroding southern position. Moreover, even had Dixon aborted his demand for Missouri Compromise repeal, Southern Democrats such as Phillip Phillips would have likely gone on demanding a revision of the shaky F Street mess— Stephen A. Douglas rapprochement. Still, once Archibald Dixon moved actual rather than virtual repeal, evasion was impossible for the Davy Atchisons. Southern Democrats had never before and would not now allow Southern Whigs to outflank them on slavery questions.

Douglas, who knew the rules of southern politics, looked up Archibald Dixon. He reasoned that if the Kentucky Whig would ease the pressure, Southern Democrats might again settle for virtual repeal of the Missouri Compromise. Douglas and Dixon huddled in a closed carriage, while horses drew them round and round Washington. Their talk, like their frigid journey, was a circle always ending in the same forbidding spot. Before departing the carriage, the Little Giant promised Dixon that he would make the Missouri Compromise inoperative in the new territory.

The next day, Douglas and the other Kentucky senator, the Democrats'

John C. Breckinridge, sought out Phillip Phillips. Breckinridge, another non-fire-eater, epitomized the continued moderation of Southerners who pressed Douglas. Breckinridge and Douglas begged Phillips to find the least inflammatory language to accomplish modification of the Missouri Compromise. Phillips was then to clear the wording with the sovereign phrase-maker.

That sovereign was not Congress or party or even the southern congressional caucus. Douglas charged Atchison's F Street messmates with responsibility for approving Phillips' language. The Illinois senator understood that the tiny group of Southern Democratic titans possessed controlling leverage over Southern Democrats and thus over prospects for passing the bill.

The day after Douglas begged Phillips's help, the sovereigns met down F Street from the mess, in a rear smoked-filled room of the government's Patent Office. Not since the cotton gin had the Patent Office observed a southern invention so fateful as Phillips's phraseology. F Streeters approved Phillips's wording: that the Compromise of 1820, while not repealed, should be declared "inoperative and void" in Kansas-Nebraska. That phrasing left the Missouri Compromise ban still operatively antislavery in Minnesota Territory, another Louisiana Purchase area.

One Democrat could still stymie this carefully selective voiding. President Franklin Pierce might rally Northern Democrats in revolt against making a sacred compromise partially "inoperative." The President, after a cabinet discussion, suggested that Congress couple another nondecision on when Popular Sovereignty could transpire, à la the Armistice of 1850, with a new invitation to the Supreme Court to decide the status of slavery in the Kansas-Nebraska area, per the 1848 Clayton Compromise. Douglas approved. F Streeters declined.

The senator accordingly requested a showdown for all parties at the White House the next day. Pierce protested that tomorrow was Sunday, the holy day. Douglas said this business could not wait. Pierce capitulated.

On the sabbath, Douglas dropped by F Street to pick up Atchison. The gesture conceded the Missourian's stature in pushing the rapprochement between power brokers a little and then a little more southwards. The two key senators, arriving at the White House first, told the President why the Missouri Compromise must become inoperative west of Missouri. The trio was then joined by all F Street messmates, along with John C. Breckinridge and Phillip Phillips. President Pierce, like Douglas, soon agreed to accommodate Davy Atchison, Archibald Dixon, the F Street Mess, and Popular Sovereignty. As in Compromise Tariff and Gag Rule and Texas Annexation and Fugitive Slave Law times, the minority South had seized the leverage of the national majority party.[14]

– 4 –

The next day, exactly a week after Archibald Dixon's motion forced Douglas reluctantly southwards, the Illinois Democrat brought to the Senate floor a bill revised to the Kentucky Whig's specifications. Another key Southern Whig proceeded to inquire how this provocation could help slavery. Making the Missouri Compromise ban on slavery "inoperative and void" in Kansas-Nebraska, John Bell of Tennessee told the Senate, would create in the North "a more decided and deep-rooted hostility to slavery and the whole South." If slaveholders miraculously captured Kansas, then a still "more widely-diffused and more intense anti-slavery sentiment" would "be awakened."

The greater "probability," claimed John Bell, was "that slavery will be prohibited" in Kansas, for odds favoring the more populated North "will deter every prudent slaveholder" from migrating there. Then Missouri, across the river from a neighbor made unnecessarily hostile, would the more quickly "cease to be a slave state." Bell's southern friends had warned him, "in our private and friendly conferences, that a southern man who should" utter such opinions "would be considered a traitor." But a Slavepower minority provoking a northern majority betrayed its own cause.[15]

At every step towards civil war, some Southerner had voiced John Bell's message. Chapman Johnson urging the Virginia Convention of 1829 not to impose a Slavepower regime on an egalitarian majority; Carolina Unionists begging Nullifiers not to defy a national majority; Henry L. Pinckney warning Carolina extremists not to insist on the most provocative gag rules; Henry Clay urging Southerners not to demand Texas; Clay again asking slaveholders not to insist on a fugitive slave bill without a jury provision—these statesmen had argued that a vulnerable minority should cease bullying the majority. Your defensive hysterics are awakening a dangerous giant, the John Bells and Thomas Hart Bentons had for a quarter-century been warning Southerners. You are thereby dooming slavery to the earliest possible death.

That analysis remains haunting. By provoking and losing the Civil War, slaveholders brought on themselves the swiftest way to abolish slavery. Worse, southern provocative defensiveness might have paved the *only* route to emancipation, at least until well into the twentieth century. Did northern abolitionists have the potential appeal or southern apologists the potential bravery to do in the institution, assuming southern hardliners had allowed apologists to work out slavery's fate?

That puzzle will never be solved, for the solution requires writing a history which never happened about an historical path defiantly blocked. Even guesses about where that other road might have wandered are forbidding, for slaveholders' tactics shadowed everything on the path chosen. Southern threats and intimidations powerfully influenced both the North's dislike of abolitionists and the South's wariness about heretics. If another sort of southern ruling class had allowed calm and constructive discussions, without disunion ultimatums or disloyalty cries to deter Jeffersons and Bentons and Clays and Aberdeens and Lincolns—well this master class did not wish to risk *that* fantasy. These slaveholders preferred to go down fighting, if they perished at all, whether or not the John Bells called it death by one's own hand.

– 5 –

The National Democratic Party instantly experienced the hostility which John Bell feared would destroy everything national. The Kansas-Nebraska Bill, if passed, would invite slaveholders onto previously emancipated turf. Worse, republican government, so many Northerners thought, was being annihilated. The majority section was not ruling. A Slavepower Conspiracy was consolidating minority despotism. "A secret conclave," Bluff Ben Wade of Ohio charged in the Senate, "concocted" Douglas's surrender in the dead of "night time."

Douglas's answer was all innocence: I wrote the Kansas-Nebraska bill by myself, with daylight enveloping the study.[16] The southern answer was all injured denial: northern leaders offered us the bill out of their own free will. One Monday morning, both the Northern Democracy's President and its senatorial leader announced that national principles required equal opportunity for slaveholders.

Because so few Southerners participated in the F Street Mess's final arm twisting, some southern congressmen may have believed in this free offering absurdity. More Yankees, however, believed in the North's equally absurd Slavepower Conspiracy thesis. Northerners were right, of course, that a small crew of slaveholders had privately pushed Douglas and Pierce southwards.

Everything else about the Great Slavepower Conspiracy explanation of the Kansas-Nebraska Act erred. Participants at the White House sabbath conference were largely from the Upper South. They were wholly against disunion. Their "conspiracy" consisted of back-room lobbying. Their proof that aggressive minorities can control appeasing or passive majorities was democracy as usual, indeed American democracy as routinely practiced throughout the years of the Democratic Party's pro-southern legislative victories.

Numerical majorities always have an unconquerable remedy: match the minority's aggression. Such an invincible northern majority was beginning to appear in the spring of 1854. Anti-Nebraska zealots, precursors of the imminent Republican Party, attacked Douglas's bill so strongly as to jeopardize passage, particularly in the House of Representatives.

Southerners' big problem at the time of Texas Annexation, the Senate, was no concern this time. Back in 1844–5, when the National Whig Party had been thriving, only three Southern Whig senators had defied Northern Whigs' anti-Texas intransigence. A senatorial majority for annexation had thus required every Northern and Southern Democrat, even Thomas Hart Benton. But in 1854, with the National Whig Party fast going under, most Southern Whigs supported the Southern Democrats' bill. With greater unanimity existing among southern senators, fewer Northern Democratic appeasers were necessary to pass the Slavepower proposal. More than a few Northern Democrats still lined up behind Douglas and the South. The Senate passed the Kansas-Nebraska Bill 37-14 on March 4, 1854. Only four Northern Democrats and two Southern Whigs joined the Northern Whigs in voting no.

Southerners faced larger obstacles in the North-controlled House. Since all northern opponents of the Democracy would vote against the Kansas-Nebraska Bill, passage required that almost half the Northern Democrats vote the South's way. Northern House Democrats faced their usual predicament. They could antagonize either southern allies or northern constituents.

For a time, these hard-pressed Yankees thought they might antagonize no one. They would passively allow Northern Whigs to talk the bill to death. But southern parliamentary maneuvers, particularly Alexander Stephens's ploys, defeated that stall. On May 22, 1854, the clerk called the most important House roll since 1850—arguably the most important since 1787.

The familiar majority then secured the latest and most notorious pro-southern law. Slaveholding states stood 71-11 for the Kansas-Nebraska Bill, and Northern Democrats voted 42-39 with the South. As usual, Lower North Democrats voted strongest the southern way, 28-17. Upper North Democrats voted 22-14 against Kansas-Nebraska, as did Northern Whigs–Freesoilers–Nativists, by a 50-0 count. In all, the free labor states opposed Douglas, 89-42. The Kansas-Nebraska Bill passed, 113-100, even though two-thirds of the majority section voted nay, because seven-eighths of the minority section and half the Northern Democrats voted aye.[17]

The Slavepower's extra representatives aided Northern Democrats in securing the minority's legislation. Because every five slaves counted as three votes in apportioning House representatives, Southerners received 19 more seats than a one-white-man, one-vote egalitarian republic would have provided. The Slavepower needed a third of those extra votes to pass Kansas-Nebraska. Anti-Nebraska forces had yet another reason to denounce the rape of republicanism.

The three-fifths clause had only occasionally been such a crucial factor in national decisions. But on some occasions, like this one, it had a devastating effect. The three-fifths clause had probably made Jefferson rather than John Adams President in 1800. The Slavepower's extra house seats had enabled William Cost Johnson's ultra gag rule to pass. The three-fifths clause had stopped the Tallmadge Amendments in Missouri Controversy times. Now, irony had been piled on irony in the tale of James Tallmadge, Jr. The three-fifths clause, having secured the Missouri Compromise and thus blocked post-nati emancipation in Missouri, had now helped make the Missouri Compromise inoperative and thus perhaps consolidated Missouri's uneasy Slavepower.

– 6 –

The law's final wording offered alternate routes to consolidation. The Missouri Compromise was declared "inoperative and void" in Kansas-Nebraska, and "the people" of either "territory or state" were left "perfectly free to form and regulate their domestic institutions in their own way, subject only to the Constitution of the United States." In other words, Missouri slaveholders were perfectly free to spill over the border immediately and control an early territorial decision. If Yankees instead secured a territorial decree against slavery, Southerners were perfectly free to appeal the edict to the southern-dominated Supreme Court.

That court might strike down a territorial legislature's ban on slavery. Local lawmakers in national territorial domains, having secured their authority from Congress, arguably were no freer than Congress to seize national citizens' (slave) property. According to Calhoun's now old-hat gag rule argument, the Fifth Amendment's due process clause barred seizure of propertied substances, no matter what the procedure. With Northern Democrats giving Southerners every chance to win a race to the territories and a further chance for a favorable Supreme Court decision even if Yankee feet proved swifter, and with Northern Whigs denouncing every appeasing syllable, how could Southern Whigs remain married to the Whig Party?

The unanswerable question highlights the importance of Southern Whigs' reluctance to proceed with the now unavoidable divorce. Thirteen Southern Whigs in the House massed behind the Democrats in the Kansas-Nebraska roll call. If those 13 had remained loyal to the Whig Party, the Kansas-Nebraska Bill would have been defeated. But almost as many Southern Whigs in the House, nine, voted against capitulation to the Democratic Party's legislation. Continued support of the Whig Party by 41% of House Southern Whigs reemphasized how precious was that shrine of party. But the last lonely nine stalwarts knew they could not prevail in southern elections if loaded down with the latest damning evidence of Northern Whigs' intransigence. The National Whig Party could be national no longer.

– 7 –

With the death of national Whiggery, as with the sectionalizing of Jacksonian "Democracy," it is helpful, after following each twist of a journey, to glance back at the whole terrain. From the perspective of the final consolidation of a northern Whiggery hateful to Southern Whigs, the national anti-Jackson movement was from the beginning too sectional. While Jacksonianism began and largely remained strongest in the South and in the southern half of both sections, the Whig Party began and remained disproportionately northern. If the North had had its way in 1828, the anti-Jacksonians' John Quincy Adams would have been the first re-elected northern President. While Whiggery later became highly competitive in the Lower North and Middle South as well as somewhat competitive in the Lower South, Whigs remained most dominant in the Upper North and in the Border South.

As with the Jackson Party, consequences of a disproportionately sectional power base were long hidden. Men became Whigs for largely nonsectional reasons: to further governmental aid to and control of economic growth, to secure Christian moral community, and, especially in the beginning, to make Andrew Jackson, supposed symbol of an age, the archetype of what the age must not become. Against Jackson's untrammeled individualism, Whigs pitted communal action; against the supposed Caesar's imperial presidency, Whigs championed a chaste Congress and cabinet; against the undercapitalized Jacksonian entrepreneur at the mercy of the market's booms and busts, Whigs would use public authority local and national to augment private capital and to smooth economic cycles. This often patriarchal conception of state and community was relevant to dozens of national congressional and presidential elections and to thousands of state and local campaigns. Localistic crusades created among Whigs no less than Democrats a partisan constituency some 45% strong: voters who detested the other party, citizens who considered nonslavery Jacksonian/ Whig issues too important to tolerate slavery's destruction of the Second American Party System. To crack pre-slavery-controversy institutions, slavery issues had to be relentlessly pounded home over a sustained period of time.

Hammering began in national presidential elections. Then national issues best energized provincial constituents and attracted the relatively few local independents. After abolitionists' emergence in 1835, playing on southern fears about slavery proved the easy road to zealotry in national elections.

Southern Oppositionists/Whigs first stepped down that easy road. In their 1835–6 pitch for Tennessee's Hugh Lawson White as a safe Southerner, Southern Whigs for the first time became competitive in national presidential sweepstakes and almost secured a southern dead heat with Martin Van Buren. Similar stress on Whig presidential candidates' southern upbringing helped secure the region for William Henry Harrison in 1840 and for Zachary Taylor in 1848. This sporadic rhetoric safely focused on men, not measures. By emphasizing in the South that presidential candidates were to the manor born, Southern Whigs augmented their own power and did Northern Whigs no harm.

The damage occurred when controversy shifted from who was born southward to who could pass pro-southern law.. Northern Whigs' unending opposition to Slavepower proposals differed substantially from Northern Democrats' compromising maneuvers. The difference stemmed from the anti-Jackson Party's greater northern power base and from Yankee Whigs' conviction, at once fiercely partisan and passionately idealistic, that alleged "Democrats" were wedded to the anti-democratic Slavepower. This anti-Slavepower thrust, critical to John Quincy Adams's forensic duels with Southern Whigs such as Henry Wise and Waddy Thompson, was at first relatively unimportant because nonslavery issues outweighed the gag rule.

Texas was more important. For the first time, the southern election of 1844 focused on which party's measures, not men, were most loyal to slavery. The result was a Southern Whig drubbing. No Territory, the inventive Whig response, sought above all else to eliminate these party-straining, Union-straining slavery measures. But when Polk secured the Mexican Cession, No Territory was irrelevant, and not even Zachary Taylor's ingenious policy could make the panacea relevant again. Despite Southern Whigs' warnings about intolerable insults, Northern Whigs affirmed the Wilmot Proviso, secured free California, said nay to Fugitive Slave Laws and aye to abolition in the District of Columbia. In the Election of 1852 and again in 1853, slavery measures, not men, were most relevant. As always, the Democratic Party better served southern measures.

Demoralized Southern Whigs had only one weapon left. Like William Cost Johnson and Milton Brown earlier, Archibald Dixon would demonstrate that Southern Democrats' victories were compromised triumphs and that Southern Whigs could set the true southern course. But the National Democratic Party, despite Northern Democrats' grumbling, again rose to the challenge. After Democrats' stunning voiding of the Missouri Compromise in Kansas-Nebraska, the national opposition party had to fold in the South.

The Whig Party rather than the Democratic Party succumbed to the slavery issue first because it could never fulfill an American political party's indispensable function: to find the middle of the road. With Northern Whigs unwilling to be accommodating on slavery-related issues, Southern Whigs could only hope that slavery controversy receded back into the safe form of who was born where. Instead, slavery issues kept multiplying. To a slight extent, Southern Whigs victimized themselves, for their periodic stress on the Democrats' allegedly disloyal presidential candidates helped awaken apprehensions in both North and South. To a far larger extent, disruptive proposals escalated for the very reason Southern Whigs first became a viable second party throughout the South in 1836: because Southerners found antislavery insulting and potentially damaging, particularly in lightly enslaved hinterlands. A decade of hammering on Texas, the Wilmot insult, fugitive slaves, Kansas, eventually drowned out pre-slavery issues, even in southern local elections. The Democratic Party, albeit with increasing strain, could compromise on slavery. The Whig Party never could. The resulting crash of a great national institution echoed throughout a profoundly endangered republic.[18]

– 8 –

Southern Democrats' sectional victory endangered their national party too. Never before had appeasing the South so angered the North. Placing Northern Democratic appeasers at risk might prove justified if slaveholders proceeded to use Popular Sovereignty to enslave Kansas and save Missouri. But if the opportunity was dissipated, the F Street messmates who squeezed such a provocative law out of Stephen A. Douglas might have secured the South's emptiest and costliest triumph yet.

Victory, to be worthwhile, had to be scored on both sides of the Missouri River. Thomas Hart Benton, one of only two Southern Democrats in the House who had voted against Kansas-Nebraska, seemed likely to challenge Davy Atchison in the Missouri senatorial election of 1855. The issue figured to be more clear-cut than ever: silence on slavery to make Missouri seem a white utopia versus ferocity on slavery to keep Missouri as an outpost of black servitude.

So sharp a clash, Atchison's advocates hoped, would strip Benton's disguises. Maybe Benton himself, or at least his young turks such as Blair Junior, would agitate honestly for what Atchisonians always thought lay hidden behind Old Bullion's arguments for silence on slavery: a future campaign to dump slaves, slaveholders, and blacks outside a whitened mecca. Then the Missouri election of 1855 might yield a clear-cut determination of slavery's fate in the Border South.

Events across the Missouri River could determine Missouri's decision. Atchison supporters would assuredly try to win an early Popular Sovereignty decision in Kansas. Should border ruffians quickly lose the other side of the Missouri River, Missouri's slavery regime might look hopelessly surrounded. Should border ruffians quickly win by riding roughshod over majority processes in Kansas, Benton's case against despotic polluting of white republicanism might be more compelling than ever.

A politician residing across the Mississippi River would monitor Missouri River happenings with special interest. Illinois's Abraham Lincoln was a leader of the burgeoning anti-Nebraska movement. Like most opponents of the Kansas-Nebraska Act, Lincoln emphasized regaining the old, not gaining anything new. He would restore the Missouri Compromise. He would re-establish the Founding Fathers' anti-slave-expansion policy. Then those inside the South could decide slavery's fate.

Plans such as Lincoln's had always raised specters of collaborations of insiders and outsiders, including Thomas Jefferson and Jared Sparks, and Lord Aberdeen and Pearl Andrews, and Cassius Clay and David Wilmot, who might reinforce each other's exploratory probings. Like many anti-Nebraska compatriots, Abraham Lincoln occasionally dreamed of southern alliances. Lincoln, a former Henry Clay National Whig who did not like being de-Whigged, could conscientiously offer potential southern colleagues Clay's plan of distributing federal revenues to help states colonize slaves. Lincoln was especially watching neighboring Missourians to see whether Benton's followers might seek removal of blacks from the state. A nationally-important local showdown was indeed looming on both sides of the Missouri River.[19]

– 9 –

Missourians could not likely win Kansas alone. Border ruffians could cross the Missouri River first and secure early Popular Sovereignty elections. After Northerners started massing from afar, however, Southerners from afar had better start arriving too.

The congressional Kansas-Nebraska debates created doubt that Southerners would massively come. Davy Atchison's promise to seize neighboring turf gave the issue a bit of the highly practical aspects of a close-by Texas. Some southern congressmen saw Kansas Atchison's way. To others, however, Kansas looked more akin to the distant Mexican Cession. Such southern congressmen massed behind Atchison as sectional patriots, in order to give him a weapon perhaps as illusory as the Fugitive Slave Law—and to scotch an insult akin to the Wilmot Proviso.[20]

But could such an abstract notion bring masses of Southerners to chilly Kansas, when tropical virgin land in Texas and Arkansas beckoned instead? Any such patriotic march on Kansas, in defiance of practical alternatives, would require section-wide cooperation and commitment. In the mid-1850s the southern world remained instead a collection of localized neighborhoods, poorly connected by railroads, poorly integrated by geography, poorly united by ideology. An unending crusade for perpetual servitude had not been remotely achieved. A huge portion of the most populated South still thought that slavery could and should be ended, always assuming that the right conditions existed.

The essence of Conditional Termination had always been distaste—distaste for the Peculiar Institution, distaste for most solutions, distaste for agitators who would crusade for or against the distasteful. Southern crusaders always had more control over such feelings of distaste in Washington than elsewhere. Only in Washington did Southerners from disparate locales crowd into the same hothouse neighborhood. Only in Washington could Southrons stare each other in the face as they demanded demonstration of loyalty. Southern disunity had not yet clearly led to a loss for slavery in Congress, although Southern Whig opposition to Texas had made for a close call, and Upper South repugnance for splitting California had aborted Henry Foote's plans.

Still, uniting to pass statutes in a single Washington neighborhood was one thing. Combining to make use of the statutes after Southerners scattered to different Souths was another. To take the central pre-Kansas example of the phenomenon, southern congressmen had procured the chance to carve Texas into five slave states. The provocative victory had proved worthless because no collective effort had been mounted in the countryside to move population to the Lone Star State and so capture that potential political treasure chest of senators and representatives.

With zest for slavery battles not rampant throughout their culture, the Slavepower in Washington was like the boy sticking his finger in the leaking dyke. Law after law theoretically closed openings in southern outposts. Every law antagonized more Northerners. No law, except the annexation of Texas, made southern frontiers safer. Kansas could repeat the Fugitive Slave Law's counterproductive process.

Recognition of the danger would help stimulate fresh attempts at new polemics, new programs, new postures in the mid-1850s. In the spirit of the Resistance Party of 1850-1, southern crusaders would seek to overcome the almost universal apologetics of the Texas Controversy. A proslavery ideology would have to be perfected. The African slave trade might have to be reopened. More arguably practical areas for slavery, such as Cuba, might have to be annexed. A southern nation might even have to be secured. In the aftermath of the Kansas-Nebraska Act, it would be considered high time—past time— to make *a* South.

Past generations of slaveholders had left behind promising materials to make one world. Elitist Southeasterners, especially those in South Carolina, had gone a long way towards basing a society and viewpoint on a color-blind hierarchy. Egalitarian Southwesterners had made much progress in centering a world and world view on color-infested white chauvinism.

But whichever path toward consistency polemicists chose, their quest for clarity would have to conquer the South's old essence. The region had long *been* its contradictions—been its various people's often colliding, often uneasy reconciliations of antithetical institutions and sensibilities. Proslavery ultras' insistence that the culture live up to one abstraction rather than all others could seem, to scattered and unabstracted southern folk, vaguely—annoyingly—similar to abolitionists' fantasies. With their jarring demand that folks cease enjoying comfortable evasions and at last confront the uncomfortable choices, extremists approached their most potentially productive—and treacherous—stretch of the road to disunion.

Abbreviations
Used in Notes

AHR	*American Historical Review*
ALA	Manuscripts Division, Alabama Department of Archives and History, Montgomery
BC	Berea College Library, Berea, Kentucky
CU	Manuscripts Division, Clemson University Library, Clemson, South Carolina
CWH	*Civil War History*
DU	Manuscipts Division, Duke University Library, Durham, North Carolina
EU	Manuscripts Division, Emory University Library, Decatur, Georgia
FC	Filson Club, Louisville, Kentucky
GA	Manuscripts Division, University of Georgia Library, Athens
GHQ	*Georgia Historical Quarterly*
JAH	*Journal of American History*
JEH	*Journal of Economic History*
JER	*Journal of the Early Republic*
JNH	*Journal of Negro History*
JSH	*Journal of Southern History*
KHS	Kentucky Historical Society, Frankfort
LC	Manuscripts Division, Library of Congress, Washington, D.C.
LSU	Manuscripts Division, Louisiana State University Library, Baton Rouge
MISS	Mississippi Department of Archives and History, Jackson
MO	Manuscripts Division, University of Missouri Library, Columbia
MOHS, C	Missouri State Historical Society, Columbia
MOHS, SL	Missouri Historical Society, St. Louis
MOHR	*Missouri Historical Review*
MVHR	*Mississippi Valley Historical Review*

NC	Southern Historical Collection, University of North Carolina at Chapel Hill Library
PMHB	*Pennsylvania Magazine of History and Biography*
SAQ	*South Atlantic Quarterly*
SC	South Carolina Library, University of South Carolina, Columbia
SCHS	South Carolina Historical Society, Charleston
SCHM	*South Carolina Historical Magazine*
SP	Alexander Stephens Papers, Manhattanville College Library, Purchase, New York
SS	*Southern Studies*
SWHQ	*Southwestern Historical Quarterly*
THQ	*Tennessee Historical Quarterly*
TN	Tennessee Historical Society, Nashville
TU	Manuscripts Division, Tulane University Library, New Orleans, Louisiana
TX	Manuscripts Division, University of Texas Library, Austin
VA	Manuscripts Division, University of Virginia Library, Charlottesville
VHS	Virginia Historical Society, Richmond
VMHB	*Virginia Magazine of History and Biography*
VSL	Virginia State Library, Richmond
WISC	State Historical Society of Wisconsin, Madison
W&M	Manuscripts Division, College of William and Mary Library, Williamsburg, Virginia
W&MQ	*William and Mary Quarterly*
WVU	Manuscripts Division, West Virginia University Library, Morgantown

Notes

Preface

1. This interpretation is hardly my exclusive property. Some superb American historians have worked the southern materials, and I everywhere build on their insights. On general southern antebellum complexity and diversity, I think especially of David Potter, *The South and the Sectional Conflict* (Baton Rouge, 1968), and Carl Degler, *The Other South: Southern Dissenters in the Nineteenth Century* (New York, 1974). The division between the Upper South and Lower South is an important theme in Michael Holt's *The Political Crisis of the 1850s* (New York and London, 1978) and pivotal in Daniel W. Crofts, *Reluctant Confederates: Upper South Unionists in the Secession Crisis* (Chapel Hill, 1989). Finally, my antebellum South bears its relationship to C. Vann Woodward's postbellum South: the same presence of alternative visions, the same power of a wide-awake establishment to stymie sometimes not-so-brave and not-so-liberal southern reformers, and the same threat that external forces may bring overmatched internal alternatives out in the open. See Woodward's seminal *The Burden of Southern History* (Baton Rouge, 1960) and *The Strange Career of Jim Crow* (2nd rev. ed., New York, 1966).

2. Here again, I value those who have earlier stressed somewhat similar viewpoints. On slavery and the Slavepower as a threat to white republicanism, see again Holt, *Political Crisis;* Clement Eaton, *The Freedom-of-Thought Struggle in the Old South* (New York, 1964); Russel B. Nye, *Fettered Freedom: Civil Liberties and the Slavery Controversy, 1830–1860* (East Lansing, 1963); David Brion Davis, *The Slave Power Conspiracy and the Paranoid Style* (Baton Rouge, 1969); Lee Benson, *Toward the Scientific Study of History* (Philadelphia, 1972), 307–26; Larry Gara, "Slavery and the Slave Power: A Crucial Distinction," *CWH,* 15 (1969): 5–18; and most recently William E. Gienapp, "The Republican Party and the Slave Power" in *New Perspectives on Race and Slavery in America,* eds. Robert H. Abzug and Stephen E. Maizlish (Lexington, Ky., 1986), 51–78.

3. While Larry E. Tise, *Proslavery: A History of the Defense of Slavery in America, 1701–1840* (Athens, Ga., and London, Eng., 1987) seems to me to err in denying that proslavery grew irrevocably out of peculiarities of southern society, Tise is correct that the doctrine was not widely established by the mid-1830s and correct that I contributed to the misunderstanding.

Prologue: The Spirit of Montgomery

1. *New Orleans Delta,* February 26, 1861, and *Mobile Advertizer-Register,* June 23, 1861, have excellent physical descriptions of Montgomery at the time of the inaugural. The best source on the mood in the capital is Thomas R. R. Cobb's series of letters to his wife Marion in Cobb Paper, GA. See especially Cobb's letters of February 4 and 15 on fears that divisions in Alabama and the South would lead to reconstruction of the Union.

2. T. R. R. Cobb to Marion Cobb, February 9, 1861, Cobb Papers; Robert W. Barnwell to James L. Orr, February 9, 1861, Orr Papers, NC; Duncan F. Kenner to A. B. Roman, February 9, 1861, Jean U. LaVillebeuvre Papers, LSU.

3. T. R. R. Cobb to Marion Cobb, February 18, 1861, Cobb Papers.

4. Ceremonies and festivities before Davis's inaugural speech are nicely described in *ibid.*

5. Davis's speech is in *A Compilation of the Messages and Papers of the Confederacy, Including Diplomatic Correspondence, 1861–1865,* ed. James D. Richardson, 2 vols. (Nashville, 1905), 1: 32–36.

6. T. R. R. Cobb to Marion Cobb, March 6, 1861, Cobb Papers; Alexander Stephens to Linton Stephens, March 8, 1861, SP.

7. The Rhett clan's distrust of Davis is revealed in Robert Barnwell Rhett, Jr., to George W. Bagby, April 2, 1861, Bagby Papers, VHS.

Chapter 1. St. Louis to New Orleans

1. This chapter and the next rely heavily on travelers' accounts. Pride of place belongs to Frederick Law Olmsted's *A Journey in the Seaboard Slave States . . .* (New York and London, 1856); *A Journey in the Backcountry . . .* (New York, 1860); and *A Journey Through Texas . . .* (New York, 1860). Other important travel accounts include George William Featherstonhaugh, *Excursion through the Slave States . . .,* 2 vols. (London, 1844); Basil Hall, *Travels in North America . . .,* 3 vols. (Edinburgh and London, 1829); Anne Royall, *Mrs. Royall's Southern Tour,* 3 vols. (Washington, 1830–31); Mrs. Frances Trollope, *Domestic Manners of the Americans,* 2 vols. (London, 1832); J. S. Buckingham, *The Slave States of America,* 2 vols. (London, 1842); Charles Lyell, *Travels in North America,* 2 vols. (London, 1845); Lyell, *A Second Visit to the United States,* 2 vols. (London, 1849); Harriet Martineau, *Society in America,* 3 vols. (London, 1837); Alexander Mackay, *The Western World, or Travels in the United States . . .,* 3 vols. (London, 1849); Fredrika Bremer, *The Homes of the New World,* 2 vols. (New York, 1853); Charles Mackay, *Life and Liberty in America . . .,* 2 vols. (London 1859); Amelia M. Murray, *Letters from the United States . . .* (New York, 1856); James Stirling, *Letter from the Slave States* (London, 1857); and William Howard Russell, *My Diary, North and South* (New York and Toronto, 1863).

2. Bremer, *Homes,* 2:234: Gertrude Thomas Diary, entries for May 2, July 12, 1855, October 8, 1858, DU.

3. William Chambers, *Things as They Are in America* (Philadelphia, 1854), 269–86; Joseph Hott Ingraham, *The South-West, by a Yankee,* 2 vols. (New York, 1835), 2:192–97; Samuel R. Latta Journal, entry for December 20, 1850, TU.

4. Olmsted, *Seaboard,* 16–20; C. Mackay, *Life and Liberty,* 2:43ff.

5. Russell, *Diary North and South,* 285.

6. On two brief occasions in this volume, a contemporary dialogue seemed to me the indispensable artistic way to evoke southern moods and emotions. Unfortunately, no one conversation recorded in the sources is complete enough to capture an encounter between northern visitors and southern planters, as conveyed here, or between nonslaveholders and planters, as conveyed in Chapter 3, pp. 46–47. I have therefore in these two instances reconstructed a single dialogue from scattered sources, sometimes changing the

phrasing slightly but never altering the tone or substance of surviving records. I use italics rather than quotation marks to indicate reconstructed dialogues. Footnotes indicate sources for my reconstructions.

The planter here speaking exudes the standard proslavery line of the late 1850s. The best sources on the substance and tone of that mentality include *DeBow's Review*, 1856–60, especially the essays of George Fitzhugh and "Phyron," and *The Pro-Slavery Argument* . . . (Philadelphia, 1853). For superb additional examples of the tone of proslavery dialectics, see Linton Stephens to Alexander Stephens, December 10, 1844, SP, and the Georgia newspaper quoted in Arthur C. Cole, *The Irrespressible Conflict, 1850–1865) (New York, 1934), viii.* On the context of Pompey's speech, see Featherstonhaugh, *Excursion*, 36–38; for his actual words, Kenneth M. Stampp, *The Peculiar Institution: Slavery in the Antebellum South* (New York, 1956), 87.

7. All demographic statistics in this volume derive from *The Statistics of the Population of the United States*, comp. Francis A. Walker (Washington, 1872), 11–74; and from U.S. Bureau of the Census, *A Century of Population Growth; From the First Census of the United States to the Twelfth, 1790–1900* (Washington, 1909).

8. Good descriptions of the St. Louis scene are in James Neal Primm, "Yankee Merchants in a Border City: A Look at St. Louis Business Men in the 1850s," *MOHR*, 78 (1984): 375–86; William Kingsford, *Impressions of the West and South During a Six Weeks Holiday* (Toronto, 1858), 29–37; C. Mackay, *Life and Liberty*, 1:221ff. The files of *The St. Louis Democrat* are the best source on the St. Louis mentality and especially on the Blair viewpoint.

9. Among the better descriptions of steamboat culture are Olmsted, *Seaboard*, 603–8; C. Mackay, *Life and Liberty*, 1:240–41, 294–95; Henry A. Murray, *Lands of the Slave and Free* . . ., 2 vols. (London, 1855), 1:220–34; "Steamboats of the 1850s–1860s: A Pictorial History," comp. Mary K. Dains, *MOHR*, 67 (1973): 265–82.

10. *Natchez Daily Courier*, February 19, March 9, 1860; D. Clayton James, *Antebellum Natchez* (Baton Rouge, 1968).

11. Russell, *Diary North and South*, 270–71; Olmsted, *Seaboard*, 660–62; *New Orleans Delta*, December 7, 1849; Robert Toombs to Julia Toombs, May 3, 1857, Toombs Papers, GA; A. F. Pugh Diary, entries for January 29, February 4, 1859, March 3, 14, 15, 1860, LSU; F. M. Kent to Moody Kent, May 17, 1858, Amos Kent Papers, LSU; John H. Randolph to Moses Liddell, May 15, 1853, Liddell Family Papers, LSU.

12. Good sources on late antebellum New Orleans include the two major papers, *The New Orleans Delta*, especially December 5, 1858, and *The Louisiana Courier*, especially November 28, 1858, and September 26, 1859; Douglas M. Hamilton to William S. Hamilton, March 3, 8, 1853, Hamilton Papers, LSU; A. R. Reed Diary, November–December, 1860, *passim*, LSU; John R. Norris to My Dear Friends, January 13, 1847, Norris Papers, LSU; Gustave A. Breaux Diary, 1859, *passim*, TU; Robert Russell, *North America, Its Agriculture and Climate* . . . (Edinburgh, 1855), 255; Stirling, *Letters*, 153, 179.

Chapter 2. New Orleans to Charleston to Baltimore to St. Louis

1. The following account is drawn from antebellum travelers' incessant complaints about southern railroads and from James A. Ward, "A New Look at Antebellum Southern Railroad Development," *JSH*, 39 (1973): 409–20; Albert Fishlow, *American Railroads and the Transformation of the Antebellum Economy* (Cambridge, Mass., 1965); John F. Stover, *The Iron Road to the West: American Railroads in the 1850s* (New York, 1978); Eugene Alvarez, *Travel on Southern Railroads, 1828–1860* (University, Ala., 1974); Robert C. Black, III, *The Railroads of the Confederacy* (Chapel Hill, 1972); and U. B. Phillips, *A History of Transportation in the Eastern Cotton Belt to 1860* (New York, 1908).

2. A nice feel for the sparseness of southwestern population and the tone of inhabitants is rendered in C. Mackay, *Life and Liberty*, 1: 36ff; Stirling, *Letters*, 177–81; Philip Henry Gosse, *Letters from Alabama* (London, 1859), 153–56; Olmsted, *Backcountry*, 20, 197–204.

3. Benjamin Yancey to Mrs. Yancey, December 8, 1849, Yancey Papers, NC; *Charleston Mercury*, April 9, 1859.

4. C. Mackay, *Live and Liberty*, 2: 34ff.; William E. Baxter, *America and the Americans* (London and New York, 1855), 238.

5. The lowcountry-Charleston mood is nicely illuminated in Jacob Schirmer Diary, SCHS, *passim; Russell's Magazine*, 4 (1859): 471; George A. Gordon to Krilla, June 19, August 12, 1857, Gordon Papers, DU; John Berkeley Grimball Diary, *passim*, NC; C. Mackay, *Life and Liberty*, 1: 307; William Henry Trescot to William Porcher Miles, June 24, 1861, Williams-Chesnut-Manning Papers, SC.

6. Russell, *Diary North and South*, 87ff.

7. Olmsted is particularly helpful on the Virginia Tidewater scene in *Seaboard*, 40–47, 88–92, 134, as is David W. Mitchell, *Ten Years in the United States . . .* (London, 1862), 5–50.

8. Good sources on Richmond include *Richmond South*, January 13, 1858; C. Mackay, *Life and Liberty*, 2: 8–13; Olmsted, *Seaboard*, 19–24; Mitchell, *Ten Years in the United States*, 57–80; and Chambers, *Things in America*, 271–80.

9. See, for example, *Wilmington Republican*, May 17, 1858; *Delaware Gazette*, November 29, 1859.

10. The files of the *Baltimore American* in the 1850s yield the best feel for this increasingly a-southern city. The best secondary account of ongoing changes is Barbara Fields's fine *Slavery and Freedom on the Middle Ground: Maryland During the Nineteenth Century* (New Haven and London, 1985). Claudia Dale Goldin, *Urban Slavery in the American South, 1820–1860: A Quantitative History* (Chicago and London, 1976), and Gary Lawson Browne, *Baltimore in the Nation, 1789–1861* (Chapel Hill, 1980), are also helpful.

11. James R. Killick, "The Cotton Operations of Alexander Brown and Sons in the Deep South, 1820–1860," *JSH*, 43 (1977): 169–94.

12. *DeBow's Review*, 8 (1850): 363.

13. Edward Hungerford, *The Story of the Baltimore and Ohio Railroad*, 2 vols. (New York, 1928).

14. Olmsted, *Backcountry*, 221–65.

Chapter 3. Mastering Consenting White Folk

1. This is written at a moment when a Marxist/non-Marxist squabble over which side of the slaveholder was most "natural" dominates the southern historiographical landscape. May the moment swiftly pass. As Marxists rightly emphasize, sloveholders' class relationship with black dependents generated a world view about dependency which transcended race and led to haughtily hierarchical conceptions of the ideal white society too. As non-Marxists rightly counter, upper-class political relationship with white citizens generated a viewpoint about equality which emphasized race and reserved haughty hierarchy for non-whites. Which predominated? That depends on where in the South, and when. Which was most "natural"? That depends on the ideological prejudices one brings to the evidence, about whether one believes that class or racial-political systems most generate ideologies and institutions. Southern antebellum sources richly illuminate both phenomena. When these two historical camps realize that each has hold of a critical truth, scholars may yet become what their evidence cries for—synthesizers who find both sides of the ruling-class schizophrenia central in explaining the Old South.

The Marxist position is brilliantly elaborated in Eugene Genovese's various books, especially *Roll, Jordan, Roll: The World the Slaves Made* (New York, 1974) and *The World the Slaveholders Made* (New York, 1969). Important replies include James Oakes, *The Ruling Race: A History of American Slaveholders* (New York, 1982); George Frederickson, *The Black Image in the White Mind: The Debate on Afro-American Character and Destiny, 1817–1844* (New York, 1971); Frederickson, *The Arrogance of Race: Historical Perspectives on Slavery, Racism and Social Inequality* (Middletown, Conn., 1988).

2. J. G. A. Pocock, *The Machiavellian Moment: Florentine Political Thought and the Atlantic Republican Tradition* (Princeton, N.J., 1975); Bernard Bailyn, *The Ideological Origins of the American Revolution* (Cambridge, Mass., 1967).

3. Frederickson, *Black Image*, ch. 4.

4. Michael Stephen Hindus, *Prison and Plantation: Crime, Justice, and Authority in Massachusetts and South Carolina, 1767–1878* (Chapel Hill, 1988).

5. Gilberto Freyre, *The Masters and the Slaves* (New York, 1946); Frank Tannenbaum, *Slave and Citizen: The Negro in the Americas* (New York, 1946); Stanley Elkins, *Slavery: A Problem in American Institutional and Intellectual Life* (Chicago, 1959); Carl Degler, *Neither Black Nor White: Slavery and Race Relations in Brazil and the United States* (New York, London, and Toronto, 1971); Charles Boxer, *Race Relations in the Poruguese Colonial Empire, 1415–1825* (London, 1963); John Russell-Wood, *The Black Man in Slavery and Freedom in Colonial Brazil* (London, 1982).

6. An influential book begs to be written on the extent of tenancy in the South and its implications for elitist and egalitarian republicanism. Important steps towards the big book on tenancy are taken in Frederick A. Bode and Donald E. Ginter, *Farm Tenancy and the Census in Antebellum Georgia* (Athens, 1986), and Fredrika Teute, "Land, Liberty, and Labor in the Postrevolutionary Era: Kentucky as the Promised Land," unpubl. Ph.D. diss., Johns Hopkins University, 1988, chs. 6–7. These studies of two southern societies a half-century and half-continent apart both find tenancy rates massively higher than my ultra-conservative 20% estimate. On the other hand, Lacy K. Ford, Jr., *Origins of South Carolina Radicalism: The South Carolina Upcountry, 1800–1860* (New York, 1988), 83–88, thinks 20% is the upper and 12% the lower limit of tenancy rates in South Carolina. Ford seems aware that even 12–20% tenancy proportions pose a problem for his theory that nonslaveholding farmers escaped a dependency lethal to virtuous republicanism, as defined in the eighteenth century. More suggestive on the problem is Harry L. Watson, "Conflict and Collaboration: Yeomen, Slaveholders, and Politics in the Antebellum South," *Social History*, 10 (1985): 273–98.

7. Folk culture as key to southern culture is richly conveyed in Potter, *South and Sectional Conflict*, ch. 1.

8. For examples of cotton ginning as class reconciliation, see James Hammond Plantation Diary, December 13, 1831, February 13, 1845, SC. A particularly insightful discussion of small borrowing and the resentment at dependency it caused is in J. William Harris, *Plain Folk and Gentry in a Slave Society: White Liberty and Black Slavery in Augusta's Hinterlands* (Middletown, Conn., 1985), 95–100. See also Eugene Genovese's "Yeoman Farmers in a Slaveholders' Democracy," *Agricultural History*, 49 (1975): 331–42; and the more subtle rendition of similar ideas in Elizabeth Fox-Genovese and Eugene Genovese, *Fruits of Merchant Capital: Slavery and Bourgeois Property in the Rise and Expansion of Capitalism* (New York, 1983), 249–64.

9. Orville Vernon Burton, *In My Father's House Are Many Mansions: Family and Community in Edgefield, South Carolina* (Chapel Hill, 1985); William G. Shade, "Society and Politics in Antebellum Virginia's Southside," *JSH*, 53 (1987): 163–93; Robert C. Kenzer, *Kinship and Neighborhood in a Southern Community: Orange County, North Carolina, 1849–81* (Knoxville, Tenn., 1987).

10. Pierre van den Berghe, *Race and Racism: A Comparative Perspective* (New York, 1967); Fredrickson, *Black Image;* Kenneth Vickery, "Herrenvolk Democracy and Egali-

tarianism in South Africa and the United States South," *Comparative Studies in Society and History,* 16 (1974): 309–28.

11. Otto H. Olsen, "Historians and the Extent of Slave Ownership in the Southern United States," *CWH,* 18 (1972): 101–16.

12. Alexander Stephens Diary, entry for June 17, 1834, in *GHQ,* 36 (1952): 92.

13. William Thomson, *A Tradesman's Travels in the United States and Canada in the Years 1840, 1841, and 1842* (Edinburgh, 1842), 117; *A Belle of the Fifties, Memoirs of Mrs. [C. C.] Clay . . .,* ed. Ada Sterling (New York, 1905), 217.

14. Michael P. Johnson and James L. Roark, *Black Masters: A Free Family of Color in the Old South* (New York and London, 1984); David O. Whitten, *Andrew Durnford: A Black Sugar Planter in Antebellum Louisiana* (Natchiloches, La., 1981); Larry Koger, *Free Black Slavemasters in South Carolina, 1790–1860* (Jefferson, N.C., and London, 1985).

15. Ira Berlin's *Slaves Without Masters: The Free Negro in the Antebellum South* (New York, 1974) is one of the most illuminating books on the Old South. See also Suzanne Lebsock, *The Free Women of Petersburg: Status and Culture in a Southern Town, 1784–1860* (New York and London, 1984); Marina Wikramanayake, *A World of Shadow: The Free Black in Antebellum South Carolina;* and Gary B. Mills, *The Forgotten People: Cane River's Creoles of Color* (Baton Rouge, 1977).

16. *Mary Chesnut's Civil War,* ed. C. Vann Woodward (London and New Haven, 1981), 205.

17. For a different use of this intriguing document, by a historian who can see no ambiguity in the text, see Ford, *Origins of South Carolina Radicalism,* 372–73.

18. Fred Arthur Bailey, *Class and Tennessee's Confederate Generation* (Chapel Hill, 1987), 20, 41, 69.

19. Olmsted, *Backcountry,* 197–204.

20. Dialogue adapted from Olmsted, *Seaboard,* 572–73.

21. Dialogue adapted from *ibid.,* same pages.

22. A particularly nice description is in Ingraham, *Southwest,* 2: 159ff.

23. For a lovely example, see William M. Cooke to John Rutherfoord, November 26, 1850, Rutherfoord Papers, DU.

24. Gist's Message #1 to the South Carolina legislature, quoted in *Charleston Courier,* November 27, 1860.

25. *Ibid.;* petition from Portsmouth mechanics, December 25, 1851, Legislative Petitions, Portsmouth City, VSL.

26. Points superbly made in Steven Hahn, *The Roots of Southern Populism: Yeoman Farmers and the Transformation of the Georgia Upcountry, 1850–1890* (New York, 1983).

27. Gerda Lerner, *The Grimké Sisters from South Carolina: Rebels Against Slavery* (Boston, 1967); and especially Katherine Du Pre Lumpkin's fascinating *The Emancipation of Angelina Grimké* (Chapel Hill, 1974).

28. Kathryn Kish Sklar, *Catharine Beecher: A Study in American Domesticity* (New Haven, 1973); Nancy F. Cott, *Bonds of Womanhood: "Women's Sphere" in New England, 1780–1835* (New Haven, 1977); Jeanne Boydston, Mary Kelley, and Anne Margolis, *The Limits of Sisterhood: The Beecher Sisters on Women's Rights and Women's Sphere* (Chapel Hill, 1988).

29. The big volume on the subject is Lawrence Stone, *The Family, Sex and Marriage in England, 1500–1800* (New York, 1977).

30. Frederick Marryat, *Second Series of a Diary in America* (Philadelphia, 1840), 255.

31. For illustrations of permissive child-raising spreading South as well as North, see Lyell, *Second Visit,* 2: 168–69; Ray Mathis, *John Horry Dent: South Carolina Aristocrat on the Alabama Frontier* (University, Ala., 1979), 164–65.

32. One of the best recent books on the Old South is especially illuminating on this

subject: Bertram Wyatt-Brown, *Southern Honor: Ethics and Behavior in the Old South* (New York, 1982). Other key volumes on southern white upper-class relationships between the sexes include Jan Lewis, *The Pursuit of Happiness: Families and Values in Jefferson's Virginia* (Cambridge, Eng., and New York, 1983); Steven M. Stowe, *Intimacy and Power in the Old South: Ritual in the Lives of the Planters* (Baltimore, 1987); Daniel Blake Smith, *Inside the Great House: Planter Family Life in Eighteenth-Century Chesapeake Society* (Ithaca, 1980); Jane Turner Censer, *North Carolina Planters and Their Children, 1800–1860* (Baton Rouge, 1984); Jean E. Friedman, *The Enclosed Garden: Women and Community in the Evangelical South, 1830–1900* (Chapel Hill, 1985); Elizabeth Fox-Genovese, *Within the Plantation Household: Black and White Women of the Old South* (Chapel Hill, 1988); and Anne Firor Scott, *The Southern Lady: From Pedestal to Politics, 1830–1930* (Chicago, 1970). I am grateful to Anne Scott for a helpful reading of this chapter.

33. Gertrude Thomas Diary, entries for July 9, 1852, April 11, 1856, DU. This marvelous document will fortunately soon be published, fortunately with Professor Nell Painter as editor. For a suggestive essay on one aspect of its importance, see Mary Elizabeth Massey, "The Making of a Feminist," *JSH*, 39 (1973): 3–22.

34. *The Journal of Thomas B. Chaplin,* Thomas B. Rosengarten, ed., published in Rosengarten, *Tombee: Portrait of a Cotton Planter* (New York, 1986), entry for August 31, 1845.

35. *Ibid.,* entry for May 15, 1851.

36. Allston to Mrs. Allston, March 11, June 2, 1850; same to Benjamin Allston, n.d. [March 1856], Allston Papers, SCHS.

37. *Russell's Magazine,* 4 (1859): 472.

38. *Mary Chesnut's Civil War,* ed. Woodward, 72. The best book on American miscegenation is Joel Williamson's sensitive *New People: Miscegenation and Mulattoes in the United States* (New York, 1980). Degler, *Neither White Nor Black,* and Orlando Patterson, *Slavery and Social Death: A Comparative Study* (Cambridge, Mass., and London, 1982), esp. 261, provide useful comparative perspectives.

39. *Mary Chesnut's Civil War,* 29–31.

40. Russell, *Diary North and South,* 64–65. See also Elizabeth F. Borum to Henry A. Wise, August 29, 1856. Executive Papers, VSL.

41. *Mary Chesnut's Civil War,* 168.

42. Gertrude Thomas Diary, entry for August 18, 1856, DU.

43. *Ibid.,* entry for February 9, 1858.

44. *Ibid.,* entry for February 12, 1858.

45. *Ibid.,* entries for April 2, 1856, January 2, 1859 [misdated 1858].

46. *Mary Chesnut's Civil War,* 169.

Chapter 4. The Domestic Charade, I: Massa's Act

1. Comparative histories are expertly summarized in Peter Kolchin, "Reevaluating the Slave Community: A Comparative Perspective," *JAH,* 70 (1983): 579–601, and in Kolchin's illuminating recent volume *Unfree Labor: American Slavery and Russian Serfdom* (Cambridge, Mass., and London, 1987). Important comparative studies include Elkins, *Slavery;* Tannenbaum, *Slave and Citizen;* Degler, *Neither Black Nor White;* Patterson, *Slavery and Social Death; Slavery in the New World,* eds. Laura Foner and Eugene D. Genovese (Englewood Cliffs, N.J., 1969); and George Frederickson and Christopher Lasch, "Resistance to Slavery," *CWH,* 13 (1967): 315–29.

2. A point nailed down in Philip Curtin, *The Atlantic Slave Trade: A Consensus* (Madison, 1969).

3. Willie Lee Rose, "Masters Without Slaves," in Rose, *Slavery and Freedom,* ed.

William W. Freehling (New York, 1982); James D. Roarke, *Masters Without Slaves* (New York, 1977); Leon Litwack, *Been in the Storm So Long: The Aftermath of Slavery* (New York, 1979); Genovese, *Roll, Jordan, Roll*, 97–112.

4. The somber tone of Kenneth M. Stampp's seminal *The Peculiar Institution*, especially its defining Chapter Four, "To Make Them Stand in Fear," is receding too much from post-Stampp studies. A perusal of James Breeden, ed., *Advice Among Masters: The Ideal in Slave Management in the Old South* (Westport, Conn., 1980), shows that the most ideal regime conceived of automatic coerciveness as mandatory. See also "Agricola" in *DeBow's Review*, 19 (1855): 362; William P. Rives, Jr., to N. B. Layne, February 3, 1857, Rives Papers, LC.

5. Olmsted, *Backcountry*, 85–90.

6. Charles Manigault to Anthony Barclay, April 15, 1847, Manigault Letterbook, SCHM.

7. Rose, *Slavery and Freedom*, ch. 2, nicely describes the change.

8. See Herbert Gutman's persuasive analysis in *Slavery and the Numbers Game* (Urbana, Ill., 1975).

9. Ulrich B. Phillips, *American Negro Slavery . . .* (New York, 1918), emphasized the paternalistic theme, and Genovese, *Roll, Jordan, Roll*, has made the theme more sophisticated and compelling. Genovese emphasizes that paternalism need not connote kindness or permissiveness. But the specific parental permissiveness evolving in romantic America did increasingly involve such soft accents, and southern patriarchs did proudly display some newly softened conceptions of parenting. They also could be harsh, unsentimental, and unyielding, in the old parental style. Here, as everywhere, they wavered between worlds and centuries; and here their wavering helped turn paternalism into an ideal defectively achieved.

10. *Yorkville Enquirer*, September 20, 1860.

11. *Austin State Gazette*, July 22, 1854; Franklin Elmore to Whitemarsh Seabrook, May 30, 1849, Seabrook Papers, LC.

12. Linton to Alexander Stephens, February 20, 1857, SP.

13. Same to same, January 1, February 13, 1861, Stephens Papers, EU.

14. For some good examples, see Gustave A. Breaux Diary, January 1, 4, 1859; TU; Mrs. R. F. W. Allston to Benjamin Allston, July 1, 1857, Allston Papers, SCHS; and especially the largely trouble-free record of an embodiment of genial and generous slave management, the John C. Jenkins Diary, LSU. Masters' use of religion is explored in Janet Cornelius, "God's Schoolmasters: Southern Evangelists to the Slaves, 1830–1860," unpubl. Ph.D. diss., U. of Illinois, 1977. I will discuss this key subject at length in Volume II.

15. *Charleston Mercury*, June 2, 1858.

16. Clement Eaton, *Growth of Southern Civilization* (New York, 1961), 43, 316. Olmsted, *Backcountry*, 286, noticed that house servants joyously welcomed masters home from travels, but huge gangs of impersonal field hands barely noticed the arrival.

17. George Skipworth to John C. Cocke, July 8, 1847, in *Slave Testimony: Two Centuries of Letters, Speeches, Interviews and Autobiographies*, ed. John W. Blassingame (Baton Rouge, 1977), 66–67; Charles and Tess Hoffman, "The Limits of Paternalism: Driver-Master Relations on a Bryan County Plantation," *GHQ*, 67 (1983): 321–35; James Herbert Stone, "Black Leadership in the Old South: The Slave Drivers of the Rice Kingdom," unpubl. Ph.D. diss., Florida State University, 1976; James M. Clifton, "The Rice Driver: His Role in Slave Management," *SCHM*, 82 (1981): 331–53; William L. Van Deburg, *The Slave Drivers: Black Agricultural Labor Supervisers in the Antebellum South* (Westport, Conn., 1979); Olmsted, *Seaboard*, 426–8; Charles Manigault to Anthony Barclay, April 15, 1847, Manigault Letterbook, SCHS.

18. William S. Pettigrew to James J. Johnson, May 11, 1856, Pettigrew Family Papers, NC.

19. Pettigrew to Moses, June 24, July 12, 1856, Pettigrew Papers.

20. Pettigrew to Moses and Henry, December 18, 1857, Pettigrew to Glasgow (Moses's successor), July 4, 1860, Pettigrew Papers.

21. Thomas Affleck, "Duties of an Overseer," in Affleck, *The Cotton Plantation Record and Account Book, No. 3, Suitable for a Force of 120 or Under* (New Orleans, 1859). For another good example, see "Plantation Rules" in William Tait Papers, TX.

22. For some spectacular examples of the overseer's inevitable difficulties with such a precarious role, see Banjamin Roper to Ashbel Smith, June 23, 1852, Smith Papers, TX; A. B Layne (the overseer) to William Rives, July 4, 1856, and Rives back to Layne, July 7, 1856, Rives Papers, LC. The best published collection of overseers' letters is *The Southern Plantation Overseer as Revealed in His Letters*, ed. John Spencer Bassett (Northampton, Mass., 1925). The fullest secondary account is William K. Scarborough, *The Overseer: Plantation Management in the Old South* (Baton Rouge, 1966). Mark S. Schantz has written a superb article on the subject: "'A Very Serious Business': Managerial Relationships on the Ball Plantations, 1800–1835," *SCHM*, 88 (1987): 1–22.

23. For good examples of slaves and drivers exerting impacts on overseer reappointments, see R. F. W. Allston to Benjamin Allston, June 8, 1858, Allston Papers, SCHS; M. Gillis to John R. Liddell, October 22, 1856, Liddell Family Papers, LSU; William Elliott to Mrs. Elliott, February 3, 1859, Elliott-Gonzales Papers, NC; *Southern Plantation Overseer*, ed. Bassett, 55–65, 145, 153–54; William B. Hamilton to Father, November 26, 1858, William S. Hamilton Papes, LSU.

24. "System of Farming in Beaver Bend, Alabama," ed. W. T. Jordan, *JSH*, 7 (1941): 80.

25. James P. Tarry to S. O. Wood, July 1, 1854, Samuel O. Wood Papers, DU.

26. James Hammond to N. B. Tucker, August 31, 1849, Tucker-Coleman Papers, W & M; Linton to Alex Stephens, January 18, 1855, SP.

27. Frederick Bancroft, *Slave-Trading in the Old South* (Baltimore, 1931); Wendell H. Stephenson, *Isaac Franklin: Slave Trade and Planter of the Old South* (University, Ala., 1938).

28. For a good example, see *The Children of Pride: A True Story of Georgia and the Civil War*, ed. Robert Manson Myers (New Haven, 1972), 183–85, 240–58, 267–71, 309–10.

29. James R. Johnston to William S. Pettigrew, November 16, 1855, Pettigrew Family Papers, NC; Charles Manigault to Mr. Haynes, March 1, 1847, Manigault Papers, SCHS.

30. Donald M. Sweig, "Reassessing the Human Dimensions of the Interstate Slave Trade," *Prologue*, 12 (1980): 5–19; Michael Tadman, "Slave Trading in the Antebellum South: An Estimate of the Extent of the Inter-Regional Slave Trade," *JAH*, 13 (1979): 195–220; Judith Kelleher, "New Orleans Slavery in 1850 as Seen in Advertisements," *JSH*, 47 (1981): 32–56; John Withers Clay to C. C. Clay, February 8, 1855, C. C. Clay Papers, DU.

31. *DeBow's Review*, 29 (1860): 368, summarizes and comments on the legal situation. For the best example of a conscientious paternalist wrestling with the problem—and another of the very best documents on this Peculiar Institution—see William S. Pettigrew to John Williams, November 4, 1852, Pettigrew Family Papers, NC. Other revealing examples include Albert T. Burnley to N. B. Tucker, December 22, 1846, Tucker-Coleman Papers, W & M; W. R. Wright to David F. Barrow, December 4, 1856, Barrow Papers, GA; Robert Toombs to Julia Toombs, November 11, 1854, Toombs Papers, GA; Jane L. Morgan to Pa, March 15, 1850, David Campbell Papers, DU; H. McLeod to Stephen Perry, April 23, 1859, James Perry Papers, TX.

32. *Thomas Chaplin Journal*, ed. Rosengarten, entries for May 3 and 5, 1846.

33. T. D. Jones to Eliza, September 7, 1860, Thomas Butler King Papers, LSU. This document, among the half-dozen most important for understanding antebellum slavery, had never been cited when I first saw it; I'll never forget my excitement—and horror—upon "discovering" it. In the hopes of spreading knowledge of the letter widely, I gave

it to my friend Willie Lee Rose to publish in her excellent *A Documentary History of Slavery in North America* (New York, 1976), 448–49. Unfortunately, I still have not seen the letter cited, some 14 years after Mrs. Rose published it. I pray that the emphasis on the letter here, plus the publication of Norrece T. Jones, *Born a Child of Freedom, Yet a Slave: Mechanics of Control and Strategies of Resistance in Antebellum South Carolina* (Middletown, Conn., 1990), an overly-polemical but still penetrating book which shows slave sales as critical to slave control and destructive of "paternalistic compromises," will enrich understanding of the real but tortuous paternalism which masters deployed.

34. *Chaplin Journal,* entry for May 19, 1849.

35. For some excellent examples, see J. E. Taliaferro to Governor John J. Pettus, August 21, 1860, C. C. Martin to Pettus, December 8, 1860, Governors' Records, MISS; A. M. King to Floyd King, August 24, 1858, Thomas King Papers, GA; Samuel R. Latta Journal, entry for April 21–27, 1851, TU.

36. John A. Hamilton to William S. Hamilton, September 21, November 5, 1859, William S. Hamilton Papers, LSU.

37. John A. Hamilton to Father, July 29, 1851, Hamilton Papers.

38. John A. Hamilton to William S. Hamilton, November 5, 1859, Hamilton Papers.

39. As I will urge when discussing proslavery ideology in Volume II, the dogma was as much a call for slaveholders to achieve paternalism as it was a celebration of paternalism achieved. For shrewd comments on the subject, see Bertram Wyatt-Brown, "Modernizing Southern Slavery: The Proslavery Argument Reinterpreted," in *Region, Race, and Reconstruction: Essays in Honor of C. Vann Woodward,* eds. J. Morgan Kousser and James M. McPherson (New York, 1982), 27–50.

40. Russell, *Diary North and South,* entry for August 17, 1861.

41. See, for example, "A Slaveholder," in *Baltimore American,* February 14, 1860.

42. Good secondary accounts of the northern South slavery system include Charles B. Dew, "Sam Williams, Forgeman: The Life of an Industrial Slave in the Old South," in *Region, Race, and Reconstruction,* eds. Kousser and McPherson, 199–240; Loren Schweninger, "The Free-Slave Phenomenon: James P. Thomas and the Black Community in Antebellum Nashville," *CWH,* 22 (1976): 293–307; John Hope Franklin, "Slaves Virtually Free in Ante-Bellum North Carolina," *JNH,* 28 (1943): 284–310; John Hebron Moore, "Simon Gray, Riverman: A Slave Who Was Almost Free," *MVHR,* 49 (1962): 472–84. Excellent examples from the primary sources include Mrs. Isaac B. Hilliard Diary, entry for June 19, 1850, LSU; David Campbell to My Dear Nephew, July 15, 1853, Campbell Papers, DU; John Morrow to John M. Bennett, August 28, 1859, Bennett Papers, WVU; Robert J. Breckinridge, Jr., to Robert J. Breckinridge, Sr., May 8, 1853, Breckinridge Family Papers, LC.

Chapter 5. The Domestic Charade, II: Cuffee's Act

1. Particularly good examples include John Manning to Mrs. Manning, September 21, 1851, Williams-Chesnut-Manning Papers, SC; George Bryan to Stephen Perry, July 13, 1859, James F. Perry Papers, TX.

2. Particularly good examples include *Mary Chesnut's Civil War,* ed. Woodward, 112; *A Confederate Girl's Diary, by Sarah Morgan Dawson,* ed. James I. Richardson (Bloomington, 1960), 45–46, 97; *When the War Ended: The Diary of Emma Le Conte,* ed. Earl Schenck Miers (New York, 1957), 41–49, 53–58.

3. *Thomas Chaplin Journal,* ed. Rosengarten, entry for May 9, 1846; Cecil Harper, Jr., "Slavery Without Cotton: Hunt County, Texas, 1846–1864," *SWHQ,* 88 (1985): 399, has a lovely example of similar camaraderie out hunting.

4. Frances Anne Kemble, *Journal of a Residence on a Georgia Plantation in 1838–1839* (London, 1863), 67–68.

5. Eugene Genovese, *From Rebellion to Revolution: Afro-American Slaves in the Making of the New World* (Baton Rouge, 1979); Kolchin, *Unfree Labor,* 244–52.

6. Historians have rightly emphasized that Herbert Aptheker's *American Negro Slave Revolts* (New York, 1943) is a history not of revolts achieved but of alleged plans gone awry. The book, however, remains a valuable accounting of white fears—and of black potential stirring. Almost every one of Aptheker's reported plots which I have examined turned out to have a degree of white exaggeration *and* a degree of unexaggerated fact. For a superb analysis of white exaggerations, see John Scott Strickland, "The Great Revival and Insurrectionary Fears in North Carolina: An Examination of Antebellum Southern Society and Slave Revolt Panics," in *Class, Conflict, and Consensus: Antebellum Southern Community Studies,* eds. Orville Vernon Burton and Robert C. McMath, Jr. (Westport, Conn., and London, Eng., 1982), 57–95. For an important demonstration that whites had something to fear, see Philip J. Schwarz, *Twice Condemned: Slaves and the Criminal Laws of Virginia, 1705–1865* (Baton Rouge, 1988).

7. I have analyzed the Vesey plot in detail in "Denmark Vesey's Peculiar Reality," in *New Perspectives on Race and Slavery,* eds. Abzug and Maizlish, 25–50. Readers will there find full documentation and, I hope, a convincing answer to Richard Wade's once-influential "The Vesey Plot: A Reconsideration," *Journal of Southern History,* 30 (1964): 144–61. The best book on the subject is John Lofton, *Insurrection in South Carolina: The Turbulent World of Denmark Vesey* (Yellow Springs, Ohio, 1964). For key documents and an excellent introduction, see *Denmark Vesey: The Slave Conspiracy of 1822,* ed. Robert S. Starobin (Englewood, N.J., 1970). Starobin also analyzes the incident well in "Denmark Vesey's Slave Conspiracy of 1822: A Study in Rebellion and Repression," in *American Slavery: The Question of Resistance,* eds. John H. Bracey et al. (Belmont, Calif., 1971). The best primary source is Lionel H. Kennedy and Thomas Parker, *An Official Report of the Trial of Sundry Negroes, Charged with an Attempt to Raise an Insurrection* . . . (Charleston, 1822).

8. Genovese, *Rebellion to Revolution,* 8–10, makes this point particularly well.

9. *Denmark Vesey,* ed. Starobin, 141–42.

10. Johnson Ajibade Adefila, "Slave Religion in the Antebellum South: A Study of the role of Africanism in the Black Response to Christianity," unpubl. Ph.D. diss., Brandeis U., 1975, nicely puts Vesey's dual religious appeal in perspective.

11. Kennedy and Parker, *Official Report,* 75.

12. *Ibid.,* 63.

13. I discuss this point at length in "Denmark Vesey's Peculiar Reality," 39–43.

14. Koger, *Free Black Slavemasters,* 42–43, 176–78.

15. *Congressional Globe,* 36 Cong., 1 sess. (December 8, 1859), 63.

16. *Richmond Enquirer,* February 27, 1860; *Savannah Republican,* February 27, 1860; Robert Barnwell Rhett to William Porcher Miles, January 24, 1860, Miles Papers, NC. For some other choice examples, see *New Orleans Delta,* April 1, 1859; Caroline Pettigrew to Louisa Pettigrew, February 24, 1858, Pettigrew Family Papers, NC.

17. Document B, copy 2, accompanying Gov. Thomas Bennett's Ms., Message #2 to the Senate and House of Representatives, Legislative Papers, South Carolina Archives, June–July Trial, p. 21.

18. Martha Proctor Richardson to My Dear James, August 7, 1822, Arnold-Screven Papers, NC, printed in *Denmark Vesey,* ed. Starobin, 72.

19. The classic essay on the subject is Raymond A. and Alice H. Bauer, "Day to Day Resistance to Slavery," *JNH,* 27 (1942): 318–419. Kenneth Stampp superbly elaborates the theme in ch. 3 of *Peculiar Institution.*

20. For some good examples, see R. F. W. Allston to his son, May 25, 1855, Allston Papers, SCHS; William H. Battle to Mrs. Battle, January 1, 1858, Battle Family Papers, NC; Manigault Plantation Diary, entry for March 22, 1867, NC.

21. Olmsted, *Seaboard,* 480; James Hammond Diary, entry for June 7, 1839, SC;

Florida Plantation Records from the Papers of George Noble Jones, eds. Ulrich B. Phillips and James D. Glunt (St. Louis, 1927), 107–18.

22. *Thomas Chaplin Journal,* ed. Rosengarten, entry for June 2, 1855; David Campbell to My Dear Daughter, October 28, 1851, Campbell Papers, DU; D. G. Conaned to William S Pettigrew, November 6, 1857, Pettigrew's memo of November 11, 1857, Pettigrew Family Papers, NC.

23. Olmsted, *Backcountry,* 77–79; William Hufford to R. J. Brackinridge [sic], June 22, 1853, Breckinridge Family Papers, LC.

24. George W. Neal to David Barrow, December 10, 1851, Barrow Papers, GA; Charles Pettigrew to Mrs. Pettigrew, June 4, 1856, Pettigrew Papers, NC; Mrs. William F. Battle to Mr. Battle, January 21, 1861, Battle Family Papers, NC; *Wilmington Delaware Republican,* April 11, 1859.

25. William K. Ruffin to Thomas Ruffin, January 31, 1850, Thomas Ruffin Papers, NC; S. A. Rees to John [Lamar], December 18, 1854, Cobb Family Papers, GA; *Thomas Chaplin Journal,* ed. Rosengarten, entries for June 18, 20, 1853.

26. *Ibid.,* entries for March 5, 1851, July 10, 1855; Linton Stephens to Alexander Stephens, January 18, 1855, SP.

27. Manigault Plantation Journal, entry for March 22, 1867, NC.

28. E. Coles to John Rutherfoord, September 20, 1853, Rutherfoord Papers, NC; *San Antonio Ledger,* January 16, February 20, August 14, 1858; James A. Spratlin to David Barrow, April 27, 1860, Barrow Papers, GA; *Texas State Gazette,* September 23, 1854.

29. *Wilmington Delaware Gazette,* November 4, 1856.

30. G. M. Wharton to William F. Cooper, April 13, 1850, Cooper Papers, TN.

31. For a nice example, see Mrs. Charles Pettigrew's rememberance of her missing handkerchief after the Panic of 1856 in her letter to Mr. Pettigrew, July 3, 1857, Pettigrew Family Papers, NC.

32. Genovese's *Roll, Jordan, Roll* remains the best synthesis of slave culture. Other key volumes in this historical reconsideration include Sterling Stuckey, *Slave Culture: Nationalist Theory and the Foundations of Black America* (New York, 1987); John Blassingame, *The Slave Community: Plantation Life in the Antebellum South* (New York, 1972); Albert Raboteau, *Slave Religion: The Invisible Institution in the Antebellum South* (New York, 1978); Lawrence W. Levine, *Black Culture and Black Consciousness . . .* (New York, 1977); Thomas L. Webber, *Deep Like the Rivers: Education in the Slave Quarter Community, 1831–1865* (New York, 1978); John B. Boles, *Black Southerners, 1619–1869* (Lexington, 1983); Charles Joyner, *Down by the Riverside: A South Carolina Community* (Urbana, Ill., 1984).

33. Levine, *Black Culture and Consciousness,* is especially fine on this point, as is Sterling Stuckey, "Through the Prism of Folklore: The Black Ethos in Slavery," in *Black and White in American Culture: An Anthology from the Massachusetts Review,* eds. Jules Chametzky and Sidney Kaplan (New York, 1971), 172–191; and Michael Flushe, "Joel Chandler Harris and the Folklore of Slavery," *Journal of American Studies,* 9 (1975): 349–56. The best modern collection of folktales is *American Negro Folktales,* ed. Richard M. Dorson (Greenwich, Conn., 1967).

34. Levine, *Black Culture and Consciousness,* 107.

35. *Ibid.,* 96–97.

36. *Ibid.,* 116.

37. *Ibid.,* 108.

38. Genovese makes the point admirably in *Roll, Jordan, Roll,* 168–83.

39. Peter Kolchin, *First Freedom: The Response of Alabama Blacks to Emancipation and Reconstruction* (Westport, Conn., 1972), 118; Raboteau, *Slave Religion,* 312; Levine *Black Culture and Consciousness,* 51.

40. W. F. Allen, et al., *Slave Songs of the United States* (New York, 1870), 1; C. V. Calverton, *Anthology of American Negro Music* (New York, 1929), 217; Dena J. Epstein, *Sinful Tunes and Spirituals: Black Folk Music to the Civil War* (Urbana, Ill., 1977).

41. Stuckey, *Slave Culture*, expertly takes the point as far as it can go.

42. Dickson D. Bruce, Jr., *And They All Sang Hallelujah: Plain Folk Camp Meeting Religion, 1800–1845* (Knoxville, Tenn., 1974), esp. 53–54.

43. All references to Douglass's *Life and Times . . .* are to the revised edition of 1892, as reprinted by Collier Books, with an introduction by Rayford W. Logan (New York, 1962). Helpful accounts of Douglass include Peter Walker, *Moral Choices: Desire and Imagination in Nineteenth-Century American Abolition* (Baton Rouge, 1978); Waldo E. Martin, Jr., *The Mind of Frederick Douglass* (Chapel Hill and London, 1984); and Dickson J. Preston, *Young Frederick Douglass: The Maryland Years* (Baltimore, 1980).

44. Douglass, *Life and Times*, 44.

45. *Ibid.*, 27, 85–86.

46. *Ibid.*, 31–33.

47. *Ibid.*, 46–47.

48. *Ibid.*, 76–77.

49. *Ibid.*, 96.

50. *Ibid.*, 78–79, 82, 86–87, 98, 101.

51. *Ibid.*, 94.

52. *Ibid.*, 127–33.

53. *Ibid.*, 155–73.

54. *Ibid.*, 183.

55. *Ibid.*, 193–201.

56. *Ibid.*, 150.

57. *Ibid.*, 193.

58. Someday these words may be read as the common sense of the matter. At the moment this book is published, however, I will more likely be called too hard on slave culture, although critics may recognize that I am just as "hard" on slaveholder culture (see Chapter 13).

Ultimately, however, the question is not one of "hardness" or "softness" but of recognition that brutalization damages everyone it touches, both brutalizers and brutalized. Brave and sensitive men and women struggle against the consequences of their involvement in brutalization. Strugglers from below are up against infinitely more; their accomplishments are accordingly more remarkable. But let us remember antebellum slaves could only do so much. They lived under a grinding institution.

In a prescient review-essay a decade ago, Bertram Wyatt-Brown warned against excesses of the new glorification of slave life ("The New Consensus," in *Commentary* 63 (1977): 76–78). Peter Kolchin's important *Unfree Labor* issues a similar warning, as does Wyatt-Brown's latest stimulating essay, "The Mask of Obedience: Male Slave Psychology in the Old South," *AHR*, 93 (1988): 1228–52.

59. Genovese, *Roll, Jordan, Roll*, 120–23, 247.

Chapter 6. Democrats as Lynchers

1. *Charleston Courier*, December 19, 1859; James S. Guignard to James S. Guignard III, December 17, 1859, *Planters and Businessmen: The Guignard Family of South Carolina, 1795–1930*, ed. Arney R. Childs (Columbia, 1957), 81.

2. Levi H. Harris to William T. Walthall, November 29, 1860, Walthall Papers, MISS; *New Orleans Delta*, November 29–30, December 30, 1860.

3. Moncure Daniel Conway, *Autobiography . . .* , 2 vols. (Boston and New York, 1904), 1: 186–91; John d'Entremont, *Southern Emancipator: Moncure Conway, the American Years, 1832–1865* (New York, 1987), ch. 3.

4. Bertram Wyatt-Brown has written a suggestive essay on these matters: "Community, Class, and Snopesian Crime: Local Justice in the Old South," in *Class, Conflict, and Consensus*, eds. Burton and McMath, 173–206.

5. The following account is based on letters in the Pettigrew Family Papers, NC, especially William Pettigrew to David Clayton, December 2, 1852; same to James C. Johnston, December 23 and 24, 1852, January 27, 1853; Johnston to William Pettigrew, December 27, 1852; Johnston to James J. Pettigrew, January 1, 1853; William Pettigrew to James J. Pettigrew, January 1, 1853; T. G. Claughton to William Pettigrew, January 11, 1853; James W. Bell to William Pettigrew, May 2, 1853.

6. Caroline Pettigrew to James J. Pettigrew, September 12, 1860; same to William Pettigrew, September 17, 1860; same to Charles Pettigrew, November 17, 1860, Pettigrew Papers.

7. Charles Pettigrew to Caroline Pettigrew, November 14, 1860, Pettigrew Papers.

8. Malachi J. White to William Pettigrew, October 20, 1860, William Pettigrew to James J. Johnston, October 25, 1860, Pettigrew Papers.

9. *Charleston Mercury,* November 30, December 5, 1859. See also *New Orleans Delta,* December 7, 1860; *Savannah Republican,* April 9, 1960.

10. Thomas T. Gantt to Lisinka Brown, December 10, 26, 1856, Campbell, Brown and Ewell Papers, TN.

11. Linton Stephens to Alexander Stephens, February 3, 1860, SP.

12. Eaton, *Freedom-of-Thought Struggle,* 122–30.

13. *Ibid.,* 130–37.

14. Samuel T. Janney, *Memoirs* (Philadelphia, 1881), 97–98.

15. *Charleston Courier,* January 14–15, 1861.

16. A rich literature is growing on this subject. Some of the most important studies include Daniel J. Flanigan, "Criminal Procedures in Slave Trials in the Antebellum South," *JSH,* 40 (1974): 531–64; J. Thomas Wren, "A 'Two-Fold Character': The Slave as Person and Property in Virginia Court Cases, 1800–1860," *SS,* 24 (1985): 417–31; Judith K. Schafer, "The Long Arm of the Law: Slavery and the Supreme Court in Antebellum Louisiana, 1809–1862," unpubl. Ph.D. diss., Tulane U., 1985; and A. E. Kier Nash, "Fairness and Formalism in the Trials of Blacks in the State Supreme Courts of the Old South," *Virginia Law Review,* 61 (1970): 197–242. These studies tend to concentrate on legal process towards blacks at the appellate level. Arthur Howington, *What Sayeth the Law: The Trial of Free Blacks in the State and Local Courts of Tennessee* (New York, 1986), shows a degree of justice at the trial level too.

17. Genovese, *Roll, Jordan, Roll,* 34.

18. Quoted in Flanigan, "Criminal Procedures," 558–59.

19. The following account is based on Samuel R. Latta Journal, entries for May 24, June 27–8, July 3, October 6, December 6, 1852, October 4–6, 1853, TU.

20. The following account is based on Christopher Morris, "An Event in Community Organization: The Mississippi Slave Insurrection Scare, 1835," *Journal of Social History,* 22 (1988): 93–111; Edwin A. Miles, "The Mississippi Insurrection Scare of 1835," *JNH,* 42 (1957): 48–60; Lawrence Shore, "Making Mississippi Safe for Slavery: The Insurrectionary Panic of 1835," in *Class, Conflict, and Consensus,* eds. Burton and McMath, 96–127; and the most important source, *Proceedings of the Citizens of Madison County, Mississippi at Livingston, in July, 1835 . . .,* ed. Thomas Shackleford (Jackson, 1836). While my emphases differ slightly from his, I am particularly indebted to Mr. Shore, who has taught this professor once again that one's best students can be one's most illuminating teachers.

21. James Lal Penick, Jr., *The Great Mississippi Land Pirate: John A. Murrell in Legend and History* (Columbia, Mo., 1981).

22. The following account is based on Betty Fladeland's excellent *James Gillespie Birney: Slaveholder to Abolitionist* (Ithaca, 1955) and especially on *Letters of James Gillespie Birney, 1831–1857,* ed. Dwight L. Dumond, 2 vols. (New York, 1938).

23. Birney to Ralph R. Gurley, July 12, 1832, April 13, 1833, *ibid.,* 1: 9, 71.

24. Birney to Gurley, April 13, 1833, *ibid.,* 1: 71.

25. Birney to Gurley, December 27, 1832, March 18, 1833, December 3, 1833, *ibid.*, 1: 48–50, 59–63, 96.

26. Birney to Gurley, December 3, 1833, *ibid.*, 1:97.

27. James G. Birney, *Letter on Colonization, Addressed to the Rev. Thornton J. Mills* (New York, 1834), esp. 7, 11, 13.

28. Birney to Gerrit Smith, March 21, 1835, *Letters of Birney*, 1: 190.

29. F. T. Taylor and others to Birney, July 12, 1835, *ibid.*, 1: 197–200.

30. Fladeland, *Birney*, 116.

31. Birney to the Patrons of *The Philanthropist*, August 1835, *Letters of Birney*, 1: 232–34.

Chapter 7. Conditional Termination in the Early Republic

1. Those who have taught us about Jefferson's limitations as "antislavery" man include John Chester Miller, *The Wolf by the Ears: Thomas Jefferson and Slavery* (New York, 1977); Winthrop Jordan, *White Over Black: American Attitudes Towards the Negro, 1550–1812* (Chapel Hill, 1968), 430–36; William Cohen, "Thomas Jefferson and the Problem of Slavery," *JAH*, 66 (1969): 503–26; Donald L. Robinson, *Slavery in the Structure of American Politics, 1765–1820* (New York, 1971), 88–97; Robert McColley, *Slavery and Jeffersonian Virginia* (Urbana, Ill., 1964); and David Brion Davis, *The Problem of Slavery in the Age of Revolution* (Ithaca and London, 1975), 164–84. I am particularly indebted to Professor Davis, not only for his magisterial volume but for his offering warm encouragement to a quarrelsome stranger at an important moment in the evolution of this book.

The latest and one of the most sensitive late twentieth-century exposures of "Jeffersonian antislavery" is Drew R. McCoy's *The Last of the Fathers: James Madison and the Republican Legacy* (New York and Cambridge, Eng., 1989). But even McCoy is in danger of driving the viewpoint too far, especially when he claims that "the dilemma of slavery undid" Madison (252). McCoy's own text shows on the contrary that Madison, far from being undone, retained his belief that his republican legacy could, should, and would eventually lead blacks to be removed from republican America. Only by realizing the persistence of this (to us) noxiously anti-republican side of "Jeffersonian republicanism" can we understand why proslavery perpetualists feared *they* might be undone unless they screamed down such Jefferson-Madison proposals as using the massive proceeds from federal land sales to free and colonize blacks.

2. For an illustration of misunderstandings an author invites by using the word and concept "antislavery" too loosely, see my own first attempt at formulating the thesis in this chapter: William W. Freehling, "The Founding Fathers and Slavery," *AHR*, 77 (1972): 81–93.

3. Davis, *Slavery in the Age of Revolution*, 168, points out that my "Founding Fathers" article falls toward that trap.

4. David Brion Davis, *The Problem of Slavery in Western Culture* (Ithaca, 1966).

5. *The Writings of Thomas Jefferson*, ed. Andrew A. Lipscomb, Library Edition, 20 vols. (Washington, D.C., 1903), 1: 34. Hereafter cited as *Jefferson's Writings*, ed. Lipscomb, and not to be confused with *Jefferson's Writings*, ed. Ford, full citation in note 14 below.

6. *Ibid.*, 2: 226.

7. *Ibid.*, 1: 72, and 9: 418.

8. *Ibid.*, 1: 73.

9. *Ibid.*, 2: 193–94, and 8: 241–42.

10. *Ibid.*, 2: 192.

11. *Ibid.*, 14: 296–97.

12. *Ibid.*, 15: 249.

13. The most balanced treatment of Sally Hemings is in Williamson, *New People*, 42–48. Jordan, *White Over Black*, 429–81, brilliantly analyzes the racial context.

14. *The Writings of Thomas Jefferson*, ed. Paul Leicester Ford, 10 vols. (New York and London, 1892–99), 8: 352. Hereafter cited as *Jefferson's Writings*, ed. Ford, and not to be confused with *Jefferson's Writings*, ed. Lipscomb, full citation in note 5 above.

15. Edward Coles to Thomas Jefferson, July 31, 1814, in "Letters of Governor Edward Coles Bearing on the Struggle of Freedom and Slavery in Illinois," *JNH*, 3 (1918): 158–60.

16. Coles to Jefferson, September 26, 1814, in *ibid.*, 3: 160–62; Jefferson to Coles, August 25, 1814, in *Jefferson's Writings*, ed. Ford, 9: 476–79.

17. *Ibid.*, 9: 477.

18. Edgar J. McManus, *Black Bondage in the North* (Syracuse, 1973), is the best general account of northern slavery, while Arthur Zilversmit's *The First Emancipation: The Abolition of Slavery in the North* (Chicago, 1967) expertly synthesizes the demise of Yankee bondage. Emma L. Thornbrough, "Negro Slavery in the North: Its Legal and Constitutional Aspects," unpubl. Ph.D. diss., U. of Michigan, 1946, contains excellent materials.

19. A point well made in Gary B. Nash, "Slaves and Slaveowners in Colonial Philadelphia," *W&MQ*, 30 (1973): 223–56.

20. Quoted in Zilversmit, *First Emancipation*, 182.

21. Lorenzo J. Green, *The Negro in Colonial New England* (New York, 1942).

22. Thomas E. Drake, *Quakers and Slavery in America* (New Haven, 1950); Sydney V. James, *A People Among Peoples* (Cambridge, Mass., 1963); Edward R. Turner, "The Abolition of Slavery in Pennsylvania," *PMHB*, 36 (1912): 129–42.

23. Simeon Moss, "The Persistence of Slavery and Involuntary Servitude in a Free State (1685–1866)," *JNH*, 35 (1950): 289–314.

24. Edgar J. McManus, *A History of Negro Slavery in New York* (Syracuse, 1966); McManus, "Antislavery Legislation in New York," *JNH*, 46 (1961): 207–16.

25. Claudia Dale Golden, "The Economics of Emancipation," *JEH*, 33 (1973): 70.

26. Zilversmit, *First Emancipation*, 217.

27. *Journal and Essays of John Woolman*, ed. Amelia Mott Gummere (New York, 1922).

28. Virginia is discussed in detail below in Chapter 9. South Carolina in Chapters 12 and 13. Excellent histories of the colonial period in these states include Allan Kulikoff, *Tobacco and Slaves: The Development of Southern Cultures in the Chesapeake, 1680–1800* (Chapel Hill and London, 1986); and Robert M. Weir, *Colonial South Carolina: A History* (New York, 1983).

29. *Jefferson's Writings*, ed. Lipscomb, 1: 28.

30. *The Records of the Federal Convention of 1787*, ed. Max Farrard, 4 vols. (New Haven, 1966), 2: 371–75. Paul Finkelman, generally illuminating "Slavery and the Constitutional Convention: Making a Covenant with Death," in *Beyond Confederation: Origins of the Constitution and American National Identity*, eds. Richard Beeman et al. (Chapel Hill and London, 1987), 188–225, seems to me too cynical when dismissing South Carolina's threats as mere attempts for commercial concessions. I believe that Carolinians meant their ultimatum—and that the majority of convention delegates so believed too. Finkelman's only evidence to the contrary, that the minority against caving in to Carolina dismissed Carolina threats, hardly illuminates why the majority voted to appease those threatening.

31. See Patrick S. Brady's excellent "The Slave Trade and Sectionalism in South Carolina, 1787–1808," *JSH*, 38 (1972): 601–20.

32. In the nineteenth century, the British navy's efforts to suppress the African slave trade drove up the New World price of African imports. But Brazilian and Cuban masters still paid much less for Africans than Lower South slaveholders paid for Upper South

slaves. Compare David Eltis's excellent *Economic Growth and the Ending of the Trana-tlantic Slave Trade* (New York, 1987), esp. 280, with Lewis Gray's classic *History of Agriculture in the Southern United States*, 2 vols. (Washington, 1933), 2: 663–67, and with Robert Evans, Jr.'s sophisticated "The Economics of American Negro Slavery," in Universities National Bureau Committee for Economic Research, *Aspects of Labor Economy* (Princeton, N.J., 1962), 216.

33. Quoted in Merrill Peterson, *Thomas Jefferson and the New Nation: A Biography* (New York, 1970), 283.

34. Paul Finkelman, "Slavery and the Northwest Ordinance: A Study in Ambiguity," *JER*, 6 (1986): 343–70, makes this point especially well. Finkelman's essays and Peter Onuf's fine *Statehood and Union: A History of the Northwest Ordinance* (Indianapolis, 1987) have much influenced this section. While I think Finkelman and Onuf too much discount the role of ideological forces in ridding the Midwest of slavery, they show that my first formulation, "Founding Fathers and Slavery," too much discounted material forces. For a nicely balanced appreciation/critique of the Finkelman position, see David Brion Davis, "The Significance of Excluding Slavery from the Old Northwest in 1787," *Indiana Magazine of History*, 84 (1988): 75–89.

35. William Grayson to James Monroe, August 8, 1787, in *Letters of Members of the Continental Congress,* ed. Edmund C. Burnett, 8 vols. (Washington, D.C., 1921–36), 8: 631–33.

36. The petitions are usefully collected in *Kaskaskia Records, 1778–1790* (Springfield, Ill., 1909), 485–93, and especially in Jacob Piat Dunn, "Slavery Petitions and Papers," *Indiana Historical Society Publications* (Indianapolis, 1894), 2: 443–529. These petitions are extensively discussed in Paul Finkelman's illuminating "Evading the Ordinance: The Persistence of Bondage in Indiana and Illinois," *JER*, 9 (1989): 21–51.

37. The best secondary sources on this critical episode are the Finkelman and Onuf studies cited above and John D. Barnhart, *Valley of Democracy* (Lincoln, Neb., 1970), esp. chs. 9, 11–13; E. B. Washborne, *Sketch of Edward Coles . . .* (Chicago, 1882); and Kurt E. Leichtle, "Edward Coles: An Agrarian on the Frontier," unpubl. Ph.D. diss., U. of Illinois at Chicago Circle, 1982. Useful personal papers of Coles can be found in the Edward Coles Papers, Princeton University Library and the Historical Society of Pennsylvania.

38. *Southern Intelligencer,* May 21 and June 24, 1824.

Chapter 8. The Missouri Controversy

1. *Annals of Congress,* 15 Cong., 2 sess. (February 13, 1819): 1166, 1170.

2. Harold A. Ohline, "Republicanism and Slavery: Origins of the Three-Fifths Clause in the United States Constitution," *W&MQ* (1971): 563–84.

3. These questions are superbly explored in Arthur F. Simpson, "The Political Significance of Slave Representation, 1787–1821," *JSH*, (1941): 315–42.

4. *The Life and Correspondence of Rufus King,* ed. Charles R. King, 6 vols. (New York, 1894–1900), 6:324–25, 690–703; *Annals of Congress,* 15 Cong., 2 sess. (February 16, 1819): 1203–14; Robert Ernst, *Rufus King: American Federalist* (Chapel Hill, 1968).

5. By far the best account of the Missouri Crisis, though one that leaves room for a new monograph, is Glover Moore, *The Missouri Controversy, 1819–1821* (Lexington, Ky. 1953).

6. *Annals of Congress,* 15 Cong., 2 sess. (February 16, 1819): 1214–15.

7. *Ibid.* (February 17, 1819): 273; Moore, *Missouri Controversy,* 54.

8. *Annals of Congress,* 15 Cong., 2 sess. (February 19, 1819): 1273–74; *ibid.* (March 1, 1819): 274; William R. Johnson, "Prelude to the Missouri Compromise: A New York Congressman's Effort to Exclude Slavery from Arkansas Territory," *New-York Historical Society Quarterly,* 48 (1964): 31–50.

9. *Annals of Congress,* 15 Cong., 2 sess. (January 26, 1820): 259–75, esp. 268.

10. *Richmond Enquirer,* February 10, 1820.

11. *Annals of Congress,* 15 Cong., 2 sess. (February 1, 1820), 1025.

12. *Ibid.* (February 17, 1820): 1382–94.

13. *Ibid.* (February 16, 1820): 424–27.

14. Nathaniel Macon to Bolling Hall, Febraury 13, 1820, Hall Papers, AL.

15. *Annals of Congress,* 16 Cong., 1 sess. (February 17, 1820): 428.

16. *Ibid.* (March 2, 1820): 1586–87.

17. Jefferson to Holmes, April 22, 1820, *Jefferson's Writings,* ed. Ford, 10:157–58; Davis, *Slavery in the Age of Revolution,* 184. Davis's broader conclusion, that southern "questioning of slavery" ultimately led to "a resolution . . . which committed the entire society to a moral defense of the slaveholder" (212), seems to me to homogenize a culture which remained subtly divided. This problem, I must add, is but a chink in the armor of the best book on American slavery in the early republic.

18. Jefferson to Gallatin, December 26, 1820, *Jefferson's Writings,* ed. Ford, 10:175–78.

19. *Journal of the House of Delegates of the Commonwealth of Virginia, 1820–21* (Richmond, 1821), 10; William H. Gaines, Jr., *Thomas Mann Randolph, Jefferson's Son-in-Law* (Baton Rouge, 1966).

20. Jefferson to Sparks, February 24, 1824, *Jefferson's Writings,* ed. Ford, 10: 289–92.

21. Phillip J. Staudenraus, *The African Colonization Movement, 1816–1865* (New York, 1961).

22. *Life and Speeches of Henry Clay,* 2 vols. (Philadelphia, 1853), 1: 267–85.

23. *State Documents on Federal Relations . . . ,* ed. Herman V. Ames (Philadelphia, 1906), 203–4.

24. *Ibid.,* 204–8.

25. William W. Freehling, *Prelude to Civil War: The Nullification Controversy in South Carolina, 1816–1836* (New York, 1966), 122–24.

26. *Southern Review,* 1 (1828): 229–30.

27. Brutus [Robert J. Turnbull], *The Crisis . . .* (Charleston, 1827), 64, 128. Turnbull's *Crisis* and Whitemarsh J. Seabrook's *A Concise View of the Critical Situation and Future Prospects of the Southern States . . .* (Charleston, 1825) are the two most important sources on the radical Carolinian vis-à-vis the Colonization Society.

28. *Columbia Telegraph,* August 20, 1833.

Chapter 9. Class Revolt in Virginia, I: Anti-Egalitarianism Attacked

1. The case for the nineteenth-century South as an emerging herrenvolk commonwealth is taken as far as it can go in our best political history of an antebellum southern state: J. Mills Thornton III, *Power and Politics in a Slave State: Alabama, 1800–1860* (Baton Rouge, 1978).

2. Fletcher Green, *Constitutional Development in the South Atlantic States, 1776–1860* (Chapel Hill, 1930); Ralph A. Wooster, *The People in Power: Courthouse and Statehouse in the Lower South, 1850–1860* (Knoxville, Tenn., 1969); Wooster, *Politicians, Planters, and Plain Folk: Courthouse and Statehouse in the Upper South, 1850–1860* (Knoxville, Tenn., 1975).

3. Virginia sectional differences, geographic and demographic, are described in Alison G. Freehling, *Drift Toward Dissolution: The Virginia Slavery Debate of 1831–1832* (Baton Rouge and London, 1982). While my sources and interpretations are not quite the same as my wife's, much of this chapter and the next draws on her findings.

4. I recognize, with Sidney Fiske Kimball, that Jefferson as designer was partly responding to other designs, in this case Palladio's European buildings. I also recognize,

with Silvio A. Bedini, that Jefferson's architectural tricks displayed a mind exuding the eighteenth- and nineteenth-century infatuation with invention and gadgets. But in architectural as in literary criticism, I believe the study of texts sheerly as response to other texts, or of invention sheerly as love of exercising virtuosity, misses the cultural imperatives driving the artist towards creating his own version of inherited forms. As I enjoy Monticello, I most see an aristocrat as democrat shaping European prototypes with a highly revealing personal accent. Fiske, *Thomas Jefferson, Architect* . . . (Cambridge, Mass., 1916); Bedini, *Thomas Jefferson and His Coping Machine* (Charlottesville, 1984). The latest study of Monticello is Jack McLaughlin, *Jefferson and Monticello: The Biography of a Builder* (New York, 1988).

5. Jefferson's version of Enlightenment political theory is most elegantly elucidated in his correspondence with John Adams: *The Adams-Jefferson Letters,* ed. Lester J. Cappon, 2 vols. (Chapel Hill, 1959), esp. 2: 388–89.

6. Leonard Levy, *Jefferson and Civil Liberties: The Darker Side* (Cambridge, Mass., 1963).

7. Jefferson to Samuel Kercheval, July 12, 1816, *Jefferson's Writings,* ed. Ford, 10: 37–49.

8. A. Freehling, *Drift Toward Dissolution,* 43–44.

9. *Ibid.,* 44–48.

10. *Proceedings and Debates of the Virginia State Convention of 1829–1830* (Richmond, 1830), 83–89.

11. *Ibid.,* 257–94.

12. Dickson D. Bruce, Jr., *The Rhetoric of Conservatism: The Virginia Convention of 1829–30 and the and the Conservative Tradition in the South* (San Marino, Calif., 1982); Fred Siegel, "The Paternalist Thesis, Virginia as a Test Case," *CWH,* 25 (1979): 246–61.

13. *1829 Proceedings,* 65–79 (Upshur), 151–74 (Leigh), 312–21 (Randolph).

14. *Ibid.,* 158.

15. *Ibid.,* 321.

16. *Ibid.,* 76.

17. *Ibid.,* 172.

18. *Ibid.,* 319.

19. *Ibid.,* 76.

20. *Ibid.,* 315–16.

21. *Ibid.,* 173.

22. Upshur to Francis W. Gilmer, July 7, 1825, Gilmer Papers, VA; Frank F. Mathias, "John Randolph's Freemen: The Thwarting of a Will," *JSH,* 39 (1973): 263–72.

23. A. Freehling, *Drift Toward Dissolution,* 65.

24. *Ibid.,* 66–69.

25. *1829 Proceedings,* 87.

Chapter 10. Class Revolt in Virginia, II: Slavery Besieged

1. William Styron, *The Confessions of Nat Turner: A Novel* (New York, 1966); *William Styron's Nat Turner: Ten Black Writers Respond,* ed. John Henrik Clarke (Boston, 1968).

2. This account of the Turner revolt is particularly drawn from Nat Turner's own confession, conveniently reprinted in *ibid.,* 102–4. Also helpful in reconstructing the trauma are *The Southampton Slave Revolt of 1831: A Compilation of Source Material,* comp. Henry J. Tragle (Amherst, Mass., 1971); *Richmond Constitutional Whig,* September 3, 1831; *Nat Turner,* comp. Eric Foner (Englewood Cliffs. N.J., 1971). I am indebted to Professor Foner for incisive criticisms of this chapter.

3. The panic is best illustrated in Governor John Floyd's incoming mail, September–

November, 1831, Floyd Executive Papers, VSL. For other choice examples, see Helen Read to Louisa Cocke, September 17, 1831, Mrs. M. F. Robertson to Louisa Cocke, September 24, 1831, Cocke Family Papers, VA.

4. Jane Randolph to Sarah Nichols, undated, Edgehill-Randolph Papers, VA.

5. Thomas Jefferson Randolph to Jane Randolph, January 29, 1832, Edgehill-Randolph Papers.

6. *Ibid.*

7. *The Speech of Thomas J. Randolph, in the House of Delegates . . . on the Abolition of Slavery* (Richmond, 1832).

8. *Richmond Enquirer,* January 12, 19, 1832; *Richmond Constitutional Whig,* January 19, 1832.

9. Floyd to Hamilton, November 19, 1831, Floyd Papers, LC.

10. *The Speech of James McDowell, Jr. (of Rockbridge) in the House of Delegates . . . on the Slavery Question* (Richmond, 1832), esp. 14–15, 19–20, 27–29.

11. *The Speech of William H. Brodnax (of Dinwiddie) in the House of Delegates . . . on the . . . Colored Population* (Richmond, 1832), esp. 25–26.

12. *Speech of McDowell,* 9.

13. *Speech of Brodnax,* 11.

14. *Ibid.,* 13–16.

15. *Ibid.,* 34.

16. See James Gholson in *Richmond Enquirer,* January 21, 24, 1832; *The Speech of John Thompson Brown, in the House of Delegates, . . . on . . . Abolition . . .* (reprinted Richmond, 1860); and William O. Goode in *Richmond Constitutional Whig,* March 28, 1832.

17. *Speech of Brodnax,* 21–22.

18. *Speech of Randolph,* 8.

19. *Richmond Enquirer,* February 14, 1832.

20. *Ibid.*

21. *Ibid.,;; The Speech of Charles Jas. Faulkner (of Berkeley) in the House of Delegates of Virginia, on . . . Her Slave Population* (Richmond, 1832), 21.

22. Faulkner's and Summers's speeches, cited above.

23. A. Freehling, *Drift Toward Dissolution,* 159–63, analyzes these votes.

24. *Richmond Enquirer,* January 17, 1832.

25. A. Freehling, *Drift Toward Dissolution,* 164–65.

26. Thomas Jefferson Randolph to Jane Randolph, January 29, 1832, McDowell to T. J. Randolph, April 18, 1832, Randolph Family Papers, VA.

27. *Speech of Brodnax,* 41–44.

28. *Richmond Constitutional Whig,* January 31, 1832.

29. A. Freehling, *Drift Toward Dissolution,* 182–93.

30. Stephen Scott Mansfield, "Thomas Roderick Dew: Defender of the Southern Faith," unpubl. Ph.D. diss., University of Virginia, 1968.

31. Dew's *Review* was conveniently and accurately reprinted in *The Pro-Slavery Argument,* 287–490.

Recent reinterpretations of Dew, each different but all useful, include Lawrence Shore, *Southern Capitalists: The Ideological Leadership of an Elite, 1832–1885* (Chapel Hill and London, 1986), 24–28, revealing on the Adam Smith theme; Eugene Genovese, *Western Civilization Through Slaveholding Eyes: The Social and Historical Thought of Thomas Roderick Dew* (New Orleans, 1986), and Allen Kaufman, *Capitalism, Slavery, and Republican Values: Antebellum Political Economy, 1819–1849* (Austin, 1982), chs. 5–6, both insightful on the class proslavery theme; and A. Freehling, *Drift Toward Dissolution,* 203–8, penetrating on the too far north theme. These extremely different interpretations, all viably based on Dew's text, reveal the largest importance of the man: this alleged embodiment of the moment when the South became one mind instead exemplified why contradictory tendencies could not this early be molded into a single mentality.

32. *Pro-Slavery Argument*, 319, 459.

33. Quoted in Genovese, *Dew*, 14–15.

34. *Pro-Slavery Argument*, 451–53.

35. *Ibid.*, 482.

36. *Ibid.*, 483–84.

37. *Ibid.*, 482–84.

38. *Ibid.*, 446–47, 478–80.

39. Jesse Burton Harrison, "The Slavery Question in Virginia," in *Aris Sonis Focisque, The Harrisons of Skimino*, ed. Fairfax Harrison (n.p., 1910), esp. 343–48.

40. A. Freehling, *Drift Toward Dissolution*, 216–20.

41. *Ibid.*, 221–28.

Chapter 11. Not-So-Conditional Termination in the Northern Chesapeake

1. The economic transformation is masterfully explicated in Paul G. E. Clemens, *The Atlantic Economy and Colonial Maryland's Eastern Shore: From Tobacco to Grain* (Ithaca, N.Y., and London, 1980).

2. Barbara Fields, *Slavery and Freedom on the Middle Ground*, is the best history of Maryland slavery's decay.

3. [Annapolis] *Maryland Gazette*, November 10, December 1, 1831; *Baltimore American*, March 6, 1832.

4. Manuscript Federal Census of 1830, Charles County, 121, copy in Maryland Hall of Records, Annapolis.

5. This critical document for understanding the Border South establishment was printed in [Annapolis] *Maryland Gazette*, March 22, 1832.

6. *Journal of the Proceedings of the House of Delegates of the State of Maryland, Dec. Sess., 1831* (Annapolis, 1831), 524–26.

7. [Annapolis] *Maryland Gazette*, March 29, 1832.

8. Penelope Campbell, *Maryland in Africa: The Maryland State Colonization Society, 1831–1857* (Urbana, Ill., 1971), 177.

9. The post-1831 story is told in *ibid.* and can be filled out with the superb Maryland State Colonization Society Papers, 1831–1858, Maryland Historical Society.

10. [Annapolis] *Maryland Gazette*, March 29, 1832.

11. Richard Fuller, *Our Duty to the African Race* . . . (Washington, D.C., 1851); Hall in *Maryland Colonization Journal*, 9 (1858): 289–303.

12. *Ibid.*, 10 (1859): 1–13.

13. Berlin, *Slaves Without Masters*, 209; Edmund Ruffin Diary, entry for September 12, 1859, LC.

14. *Delaware Journal*, February 23, 1847; *Delaware Gazette*, February 23, 26, 1847.

15. *Ibid.*, February 23, 1847.

16. *Ibid.*, May 22, November 20, 1857.

17. *Delaware Republican*, October 6, 1859.

18. *Jackson Semi-Weekly Mississippian*, February 21, 1860.

Chapter 12. Origins of South Carolina Eccentricity, I:
Economic and Political Foundations

1. T. S. Eliot, "The Hollow Men," in Eliot, *Collected Poems, 1809–1835* (New York, 1930), esp. 104.

2. Daniel C. Littlefield, *Race and Slaves: Ethnicity and the Slave Trade in Colonial South Carolina* (Baton Rouge, 1981), 74–114; Peter H. Wood, *Black Majority: Negroes in South Carolina from 1670 Through the Stono Rebellion* (New York, 1974), 35–62.

3. The rice plantation is expertly described in David Doar, *Rice and Rice Planting in the South Carolina Lowcountry* (Charleston, 1936), and in Duncan Clinch Heyward, *Seed from Madagascar* (Chapel Hill, 1937). Day-to-day rice activities can be followed in *The South Carolina Rice Plantation, as Revealed in the Papers of Robert F. W. Allston*, ed. J. H. Easterby (Chicago, 1945).

4. Dr. S. H. Dickson, "Essay on Malaria," in *The Proceedings of the Agricultural Convention and the State Agricultural Society of South Carolina* (Columbia, 1846), 169.

5. William H. Trescot to William Porcher Miles, December 4, 1853, Miles Papers, NC.

6. Alice Hanson Jones, *Wealth of a Nation to Be: The American Colonies on the Eve of Revolution* (New York, 1980), 258–341, 343–74.

7. H. Roy Merrens and George D. Tracy, "Dying in Paradise: Malaria, Mortality, and the Perceptual Environment in Colonial South Carolina," *JSH*, 50 (1984): 533–50; Sherman L. Ricards and George M. Blackburn, "A Demographical History of Slavery: Georgetown County, South Carolina, 1850," *SCHM*, 76 (1975): 215–24.

8. Of many contemporary accounts of Charleston, my favorites include *Charleston Courier*, February 13, 1860; C. Mackay, *Life and Liberty*, I: 307; Philo Tower, *Slavery Unmasked . . .* (Rochester, N.Y., 1856), 106–15. Illuminating latter-day interpretations include Kenneth Severns, *Charleston Architecture and Civic Destiny* (Knoxville, Tenn., 1988); Samuel G. Stoney, *This Is Charleston . . .* (Charleston, 1976); William H. and Jane H. Pease, *The Web of Progress: Private Values and Public Styles in Boston and Charleston, 1828–1843* (New York, 1985). But the best source is Charleston itself, a wonderfully preserved museum of olden times.

9. Legaré to Isaac Holmes, October 2, 1832, *Writings of Hugh Swinton Legaré*, ed. Mary Legaré, 2 vols. (Charleston, 1845–46), 1: 207.

10. While the best books on Charleston indoors are Henry F. Cauthen, Jr., *Charleston Interiors* (Charleston, 1979), and E. Milby Burton, *Charleston Furniture 1700–1825* (Columbia, 1955), neither fully explores wider implications of the city's material culture. So too John T. Kirk, *American Furniture and the British Tradition to 1830* (New York, 1982), commences but does not bring to satisfying conclusion the analysis of that rich subject.

11. Featherstonhaugh, *Excursion Through the Slave States*, 157; Hugh Legaré to his sister, August 4, 1833, Legaré Papers, SC; William H. Trescot to William Porcher Miles, June 24, 1861, Williams-Chesnut-Manning papers, SC.

12. Rachel N. Klein, *Unification of a Slave State: The Rise of the Planter Class in the South Carolina Backcountry, 1760–1808,* (Chapel Hill, 1990), tells the story expertly.

13. The transition is obvious in *Family Letters of the Three Wade Hamptons, 1782–1901*, ed. Charles E. Cauthen (Charleston, 1953).

14. *Sacred and Sacred: The Diaries of James Henry Hammond, a Southern Slaveholder*, ed. Carol Bleser (New York, 1988), entry for March 31, 1841.

15. These changes in the Carolina agrarian order are nicely described in Majorie S. Mendenhall, "A History of Agriculture in South Carolina, 1790 to 1860," unpubl. Ph.D. diss., U. of North Carolina, 1940.

16. William A. Schaper, *Sectionalism and Representation in South Carolina*, in *Annual Report of the American Historical Association for the Year 1900*, 2 vols. (Washington, D.C., 1901): 1: 237–463.

17. William Henry Trescot, *Memorial of the Life of J. Johnston Pettigrew . . .* (Charleston, 1870), 29–33.

18. See Kenneth S. Greenberg's superb "Representation and the Isolation of South Carolina, 1776–1860," *JAH*, 64 (1977): 723–43.

19. William Henry Trescot to Miles, September 16, 1855, Miles Papers, NC.

20. Same to same, September 6, 1835, Miles Papers.

21. Trescot to James Hammond, April 15, 28, 1860, Hammond Papers, LC.

22. Hammond to Edmund Ruffin, October 10, 1845, Ruffin Papers, VHS; Hamilton

to Stephen Miller, August 9, 1830, Chesnut-Manning-Miller Papers, SCHS. The haughty tone was so much Carolina leaders' sense of the matter about vulgar mobocracy that illustrations could be multipled endlessly. For some other choice examples, see Alfred Huger to William Porcher Miles, December 12, 1849, Miles Papers, NC; same to Mr. Wickham, June 2, 1858, Huger Papers, DU; David Gavin Diary, NC, *passim;* Russell, *Diary North and South,* 2–3.

23. Lacy Ford's *Origins of South Carolina Radicalism* is the most important book on antebellum Carolina published in some years, a volume which in its fresh information, scope, and prime thesis invites comparison with Miles Thornton's magisterial study of antebellum Alabama. But Ford stretches beyond his evidence in denying that Carolina had an aristocratic political order, in claiming that the upcountry originated South Carolina radicalism, in affirming that upcountrymen were addicted to the ideal of all white men being independent country-republicans and thus needing no civic virtue imposed from above—in short, in confusing South Carolina with Miles Thornton's herrenvolk Alabama.

Ford argues that South Carolina was the first Old South state to approve universal male suffrage, that barbecues to court voters were commonplace in the upcountry, that common voters had to approve big decisions such as secession, and that some upcountry leaders sought both popular election of presidential electors and a one-white-man, one-vote legislative reapportionment. All these good points show that Carolina oligarchs, however addicted to an eighteenth-century tradition of elitist republicanism, did have to live in the new century and did have to rally egalitarian yeomen addicted to nineteenth-century egalitarian republicanism. Those necessities, as we will soon see, confused Carolina's elitist mentality.

But that upper-class world view and its unique sway over this unique state cannot be minimized. Ford's own text shows that in the early 1850s, the *lowcountry* was hotter for secession, that those upcountrymen hottest for democratizing the state in the mid-1850s were coolest on South Carolina's ultimate radicalism, disunionism, that the democratizing campaign lost every time it sought to bring nineteenth-century republican institutions, à la Alabama, to South Carolina, and that efforts for popular presidential elections, a one-white-man, one-vote apportionment, etc., lost not least because upcountrymen did not sufficiently rally behind them and because that upcountry hero, John C. Calhoun, favored the older, anti-egalitarian tradition of patriarchal republicanism. (See Ford, pp. 191, 298–91). Furthermore, the yeoman republican style which Ford emphasizes did not much touch the region he ignores—a lowcountry which did have much—I would say most—to do with originating South Carolina radicalism. Stephanie McCurry's brilliant "The Culture of Inequality: Class, Gender, and the Yeomanry of the South Carolina Lowcountry, 1820–1861," unpublished paper presented to the Organization of American Historians' Convention, April 1988, indicates that whatever might be true in upper reaches of Lacy Ford's upcountry, anti-egalitarian republicanism dominated political practices in the coastal swamps. All fanciers of Carolina history await McCurry's book on the subject, which will be based on her 1988 State University of New York at Binghamton Ph.D. thesis.

For an elucidation closer to McCurry than to Ford on how South Carolina's radical alias reactionary republican tradition originated in the needs and world views of its imperiously old-fashioned master class, see Kenneth S. Greenberg's *Masters and Statesmen: The Political Culture of American Slavery* (Baltimore, 1985). Greenberg confuses matters a bit by sometimes writing as if his elitist political culture was southern rather than South Carolinian. But almost all his examples involve South Carolinians, which is not surprising in a rewrite of a Ph.D. dissertation exclusively on that state. Greenberg's contribution is to highlight why these masters were not the statesmen to allow white men's egalitarianism to master them.

24. Excellent discussions of Carolina's economic decline include George C. Rogers, Jr., *Charleston in the Age of the Pinckneys* (Norman, Okla., 1969); Peter Coclanis, *The*

Shadow of a Dream: Life and Death in the South Carolina Lowcountry, 1670–1920 (New York, 1988); Alfred G. Smith, Jr., *Economic Readjustment of an Old Cotton State: South Carolina, 1820–1860* (Columbia, 1958).

25. *Southern Agriculturalist,* 1 (1828): 255.

26. *Ibid.,* 4 (1831): 505–15, 2 (1829): 1–7.

27. M. J. Manigault to [Gabriel] Henry Manigault, December 6, 1808, Louis Manigault Papers, DU.

28. Robert F. W. Allston to Mrs. Allston, April 24, 1858, Allston Papers, SCHS.

29. Charles Manigault to Alfred Huger, April 1, 1847, Manigault Letterbook, SCHS.

30. *Ibid.*

31. Allston to Mrs. Allston, May 7, 1854, Allston to J. W. Smith, November 25, 1859, Allston Papers, SCHS.

32. W. Freehling, *Prelude to Civil War,* 36–39.

33. Tommy W. Rogers, "The Great Plantation Exodus from South Carolina, 1850–1860," *SCHM,* 68 (1967): 14–21.

Chapter 13. Origins of South Carolina Eccentricity, II: Cultural Foundations

1. James Hammond to [John] Walter, December 26, 1835, Hammond Papers, LC; James Edward Calhoun Diary, entry for January 25–February 1, 1826, SC. I am grateful to John Higham, David Moltke-Hanson, and Kenneth Lynn for their comments on this chapter.

2. Russell, *Diary North and South,* entry for April 27, 1861; William Elliott, *Carolina Sports by Land and Sea* (Charleston, 1846).

3. Ford, *Origins of South Carolina Radicalism,* tells this side of the Carolina story brilliantly well.

4. David Moltke-Hansen, "The Expansion of Intellectual Life: A Prospectus," in *Intellectual Life in Antebellum Charleston,* eds. Michael O'Brien and David Moltke-Hansen (Knoxville, Tenn., 1986), 3–44. While this unusually fine collaborative volume contains a number of excellent essays on the Charleston Renaissance, my favorite is Michael O'Brien's exquisite "Politics, Romanticism, and Hugh Legaré: 'The Fondness of Disappointed Love,'" 123–51, which transcends its subject to supply an acute image of the city's stymied cultural flowering. See also O'Brien's fuller but perchance less affecting *A Character of Hugh Legaré* (Knoxville, 1985).

5. The latest and fullest account of Allston is in William H. Gerdts and Theodore Stebbins, Jr., *"A Man of Genius": The Art of Washington Allston (1779–1843)* (Boston, 1979). John R. Welsh, "Washington Allston: Expatriate South Carolinian," *SCHM,* 67 (1966): 84–98, argues cogently but I think unsuccessfully that not one Allston painting "portrays anything distinctly southern."

6. Theodore E. Stebbins, Jr., Carol Royen, and Trevor J. Fairbrother, *Masterpieces of American Painting, 1760–1910* (Boston, 1983), supplies a sophisticated overview and an excellent bibliography. Fine volumes on paintings of the mid-nineteenth-century American Renaissance include the Metropolitan Museum of Art's *American Paradise: The Work of the Hudson River School* (New York, 1987) and *American Light: The Luminist Movement, 1850–1875,* ed. John Wilmerding (Washington, D.C., 1980).

7. The Allston quote comes from William Dunlap, *History of the Rise and Progress of the Arts of Design in the United States* (first published, 1834; reprinted in 3 vols., New York, 1965), 2:297–98. Allston's ghost-ridden image of boo-hags and boo-dadies haunting a mortal, mournful swampland is akin to the tone replete in Nancy Rhyne, *Tales of the South Carolina Lowcountry* (Winston-Salem, 1982), and Julian S. Bolick, *Ghosts from the Coast: A Collection of Twelve Stories from Georgetown County, South Carolina* (Clinton, S.C., 1966).

Those who would base artistic/literary criticism exclusively on texts as reaction to other texts will see Allston's several darker landscapes as a response to a well-established Gothic artistic tradition rather than as a response to his ancestral milieu. Allston, a highly self-conscious artist, assuredly did know all about Gothic formulas, just as Thomas Jefferson knew all about Palladian architectural formulas. (See above, Chapter 9, note 4.) But here again, I believe that artists are not merely disembodied text-readers, that they are also people responding to social/cultural situations, and that the imperatives of an upbringing help explain why an Allston responded to certain texts rather than others.

8. Quoted in William P. Trent, *William Gilmore Simms* (Boston and New York, 1892), 16–17. Trent's, still helpful volume can usefully be supplemented by the introduction to *The Letters of William Gilmore Simms*, eds. Mary C. Simms Oliphant et al., 5 vols. (Charleston, 1952); by J. V. Ridgely, *William Gilmore Simms* (New York, 1962); by Jon L. Wakelyn, *Politics of a Literary Man* (Westport, Conn., 1973); and most recently by Mary Anne Wimsatt's slightly disappointing *The Major Fiction of William Gilmore Simms* (Baton Rouge, 1989).John McCardell is writing an eagerly awaited new biography; for his preliminary assessment, see "Poetry and the Practical: William Gilmore Simms," in *Intellectual Life in Antebellum Charleston*, 186–210.

9. William Gilmore Simms, *Views and Reviews in American Literature, History, and Fiction*, ed. C. Hugh Holman (Cambridge, Mass., 1962), 34.

10. Simms, *Views and Reviews*, 49. Simms's use of history is well explored in David Moltke-Hansen, "Ordered Progress: The Historical Philosophy of William Gilmore Simms," in *Long Years of Neglect: The Work and Reputation of William Gilmore Simms*, ed. John Caldwell Guilds (Fayetteville, Ark., 1988), 126–47.

11. Simms to James Hammond, December 24, 1847, *Letters of Simms*, 2: 515.

12. Among the best books on the wider American Renaissance are F. O. Matthiessen, *The American Renaissance: Art and Expression in the Age of Emerson and Whitman* (New York, 1941); R. W. B. Lewis, *The American Adam: Innocence, Tragedy, and Tradition in the Nineteenth Century* (Chicago, 1968); Henry Nash Smith, *Virgin Land: The American West as Symbol and Myth* (New York, 1950); and Larzer Ziff, *Literary Democracy: The Declaration of Cultural Independence in America* (New York, 1981).

13. Simms, *Views and Reviews*, 269–73; C. Hugh Holman, "The Influence of Scott on Cooper and Simms," *American Literature*, 29 (1951): 203–18; Louis D. Rubin, Jr., *The Edge of the Swamp: A Study in the Literature and Society of the Old South* (Baton Rouge, 1989), 103–26.

14. Simms's slant on these questions is placed in perspective in Dixon D. Bruce, Jr., *Violence and Culture in the Antebellum South* (Austin, 1979). See also Michael E. Stevens's excellent "The Hanging of Matthew Love," *SCHM*, 88 (1987): 55–61.

15. Simms, *Richard Hurdis* (first published 1838; reprinted New York, 1964), esp. 14–17, 25, 56, 66–67, 137.

16. Simms, *The Partisan* (New York, 1835), esp. 21, 117.

17. Simms, *The Yamassee* (first published 1835; reprinted New York, 1856).

18. Simms, *Guy Rivers* (New York, 1834), esp. 34; Simms, *Mellichampe* (New York, 1836).

19. Simms, *The Yamassee*, 326.

20. *Ibid.*, 437–38.

21. *Ibid.*, 170–77.

22. That Simms was answering Stowe seems clear to me in Simms to Hammond, December 15, 1852, *Letters of Simms*, 3: 222–23. James B. Meriwether has lately denied that contention. He points out that Simms's *book* was published *after* Stowe's *book*. But as Meriwether himself concedes, Stowe's *book* appeared in *serial* form at the very time Simms was writing—and writing, as Meriwether points out, explicit references to *Uncle Tom* into *Woodcraft*. Meriwether finds decisive the negative evidence that nothing about the serial publication of *Uncle Tom* appears in Simms's extant letters. But Simms, a Southerner notoriously aware of the national literary scene, hardly has to demonstrate

to us an awareness of a notorious national literary event. See Meriwether, "The Theme of Freedom in Simms's *Woodcraft*," in *Simms,* ed. Guilds, 20–36.

23. Simms, *Woodcraft* (first published 1852, reprinted New York, 1856), 52.

24. The quotation is from Simms, *Katherine Walton* (Philadelphia, 1851), reprinted in Hugh W. Hetherington, *Cavalier of Old South Carolina: William Gilmore Simms's Captain Porgy* (Chapel Hill, 1966), 155. Hetherington's volume usefully collects and delightfully admires Simms's scattered Porgy scenes.

25. Simms, *Woodcraft,* 449.

26. Charles S. Watson, "Simms's Answer to Uncle Tom's Cabin: Criticism of the South in *Woodcraft*," *Southern Literary Journal* 9 (1976): 78–90; John R. Welsh, "William Gilmore Simms, Critic of the South," *JSH,* 26 (1960): 201–14.

27. Simms, *Woodcraft,* 509.

28. *Ibid.,* 325.

29. *Southern Literary Messenger,* 3 (1837): 641–57.

30. Simms, *Woodcraft,* 513. For a fine appreciation of Eveleigh, see Meriwether, "The Theme of Freedom in Simms's *Woodcraft*," in *Simms,* ed. Guilds, 20–36.

31. Legaré to I. E. Holmes, April 8, 1833, *Writings of Legaré,* 1: 215.

32. In a scintillating but I believe misleading commentary on *Woodcraft,* William R. Taylor argues that Simms's novel ridicules Carolina's Hamlet-like indecision about secession. According to this viewpoint, Porgy's endless stalling for time in the novel, especially the fat man's delaying about choosing between his two ladies, dooms him to failure. Taylor, *Cavalier and Yankee: The Old South and American National Character* (New York, 1957), 268–98.

The interpretation ignores Eveleigh's reason for rejecting Porgy's belated offer: she calls the suitor too imperious, not too vacillating. The *Hamlet* interpretation also ignores the reason for Porgy's successes in the novel: lacking good choices about how to rescue his estate or his slaves, he creatively stalls, waiting for options to improve. Simms, who constantly praised Porgy in the novel for this manipulating "to gain time," wished Carolina leaders to follow the same stalling tactics. "In politics," he wrote Hammond in 1858, "if you cannot gain the victory, you have only to gain time. Time is everything." *Woodcraft,* like everything Simms wrote, votes for order and calm and deliberation and *time,* the very reluctant side of the Carolina reluctant revolutionary which led to Hamlet-like inaction. *Woodcraft,* 384, 454; *Letters of Simms,* 4:19. For a splendid discussion of this particular subject and the most penetrating overall analysis of Simms I have seen, enjoy Simeone Vauthier, "Of Time and the South: The Fiction of William Gilmore Simms," *Southern Literary Journal,* 5 (1972): 3–45.

33. *Mary Chenut's Civil War,* ed. C. Vann Woodward, 366. The best biography of the diarist is Elisabeth Muhlenfeld, *Mary Boykin Chesnut* (Baton Rouge, 1981).

34. *Mary Chesnut's Civil War,* xv–xxix.

35. *Ibid.,* 37, 63, 597.

36. *Ibid.,* 408, 412.

37. *Ibid.,* 794.

38. Compare *ibid.,* 488 and 641.

39. *Ibid.,* 209–11.

40. *Ibid.,* 211–12.

41. *Ibid.,* 29.

42. *Ibid.,* 488.

43. *Ibid.,* 59.

44. *Ibid.,* 690.

45. *Ibid.,* 815.

46. *Ibid.,* 125.

47. William Henry Trescot to William Porcher Miles, August 20, 1853, Miles Papers, NC.

48. Alton Taylor Loftis, "A Study of *Russell's Magazine:* Ante-Bellum Charleston's Last Literary Periodical," unpubl. Ph.D. diss., Duke University, 1973.

49. *Russell's Magazine,* 5 (1859): 385–95.

50. This discussion is drawn from Porcher's essays in *ibid.,* 1 (1857): 97–107, 2 (1858): 193–204, and 6 (1860): 436–45.

51. *Charleston Courier,* May 21, 1859. On Lowndes and the golden age of Carolina republicanism, see Carl J. Vipperman, *William Lowndes and the Transition of Southern Politics, 1782–1822* (Chapel Hill, 1989).

52. Francis Pickens to Beaufort Watts, January 24, 1854, Watts Papes, SC.

Chapter 14. The First Confrontation Crisis, I; Calhoun Versus Jackson

1. This story is more thoroughly told and documented in my *Prelude to Civil War,* 111–16. See also Alan F. January, "The South Carolina Association: An Agency for Race Control in Antebellum Charleston," *SCHM,* 78 (1977): 191–201.

2. John T. Schlotterbeck, "The 'Social Economy' of an Upper South Community: Orange and Greene Counties, Virginia, 1815–1860," in *Class, Conflict, and Consensus,* eds. Burton and McMath, 3–28.

3. My discussion of the lowcountry economy in *Prelude to Civil War* too much minimizes this problem. See Dale E. Swan, *The Structure and Profitability of the American Rice Industry, 1859* (New York, 1975); and Coclanis, *South Carolina Lowcountry.* Vipperman, *Lowndes,* is especially good on the hurricane problem and correct to criticize me for failing to mention that Gray, *History of Southern Agriculture,* 2:1031–32 demonstrates declining rice exports at the turn of the 1820s. But Gray's statistics also show spectacularly rising rice exports in the late 1820s and beyond, the very years when most lowcountry squires seized on nullification. Another look at Gray's statistics thus raises the same old question: Why should lowcountry rice planters whose yields and markets were better than upcountry cotton planters' have moved just as swiftly and angrily to the brink of revolution? One answer is that lowcountry squires faced other economic problems, partly of their own making. Another answer involves the lowcountry's special sensitivity to the first signs of the slavery issue, a sensitivity which made any decline in gentlemen's economic power the more unbearable.

4. Patrick S. Brady, "Political and Civil Life in South Carolina, 1787–1833," unpubl. Ph.D. diss., University of California at Santa Barbara, 1971, pp. 160–66.

5. William Elliott, *Address to the People of St. Helena Parish* (Charleston, 1832), 4.

6. On McDuffie and his Forty Bale theory, see my *Prelude to Civil War,* 145–48, 193–96.

7. On Cooper and his "calculate" speech, see *ibid.,* 128–31; Dumas Malone, *The Public Life of Thomas Cooper, 1783–1839* (New Haven, 1926); Stephen L. Newman, "Thomas Cooper, 1759–1839: The Political Odyssey of a Bourgeois Ideologue," *SS,* 24 (1985): 295–305.

8. Calhoun's draft and the final committee version of the *Exposition and Protest* are usefully reprinted side by side in *The Papers of John C. Calhoun,* eds. Robert L. Meriwether, W. Edwin Hemphill, and Clyde Wilson, 18 volumes to date (Columbia, S.C., 1959–88), 10:442–534. Volume 1 of Calhoun's *Works . . . ,* ed. Richard Crallé, 6 vols. (New York, 1854–57) prints the last version of Calhoun's political theory.

9. William W. Freehling, "Spoilsmen and Interests in the Thought and Career of John C. Calhoun," *JAH* 52 (1965): 25–42; J. William Harris, "Last of the Classical Republicans: An Interpretation of John C. Calhoun,"*CWH,* 30 (1984): 255–67.

10. Samuel Flagg Bemis, *John Quincy Adams and the Union* (New York, 1965), 76–77. Bemis's excellent biography containg the best discussion of Adams's presidency, while Robert V. Remini, *The Election of Andrew Jackson* (Philadelphia, 1963), is the best account of how and why that presidency ended.

11. We are fortunate to have excellent three-volume modern biographies of both these men. Both biographies, like all histories, contain debatable interpretations. But each gives a warmly sympathetic portrait of their protagonist's viewpoint and a richly full

account of the life and times. Charles Wiltse, *John C. Calhoun*, 3 vols. (Indianapolis, 1944–51); Robert V. Remini, *Andrew Jackson and the Course of American Empire 1767–1821* (New York, 1977); Remini, *Andrew Jackson and the Course of American Freedom, 1822–1832* (New York, 1981); Remini, *Andrew Jackson and the Course of American Democracy, 1833–1845* (New York, 1984). Unless otherwise noted, biographical facts in the following account can be found elaborated in these volumes.

12. A point well emphasized, maybe a little over-emphasized, in Michael Paul Rogin's *Fathers and Children: Andrew Jackson and the Subjugation of the American Indian* (New York, 1975).

13. Remini, *Jackson and the Course of American Empire*, 142.

14. Hammond to Isaac Haynes, August 21, 1831, Hammond Papers, SC. The Clay quote comes from Richard Hofstadter, *The American Political Tradition and the Men Who Made It* (Vintage ed.; New York, 1955), 74.

15. *Memoirs of John Quincy Adams . . .* , ed. Charles Francis Adams, 12 vols. (Philadelphia, 1874–77), 5: 361.

16. *A Compilation of Messages and Papers of the Presidents, 1789–1897*, ed. James D. Richardson, 11 vols. (Washington, D.C., 1910), 2: 1001, 1011–12; *The First Forty Years of Washington Society in the Family Letters of Margaret Bayard Smith*, ed. Gaillard Hunt (first printed 1906, reprinted New York, 1965), 290–96.

17. Calhoun to John McLean, September 22, 1829, Calhoun's draft of the South Carolina Nullificaton Convention's "Address to the People of the United States," November 1, 1832, *The Papers of Calhoun*, 11: 75–77, 674–75.

18. Those who have clarified the peculiar strength of anti-partyism in South Carolina and its relationship to older exaltations of independent country patricians include James M. Banner, "The Problem of South Carolina," in *The Hofstadter Aegis: A Memorial*, eds. Stanley Elkins and Eric McKitrick (New York, 1974), 60–93; Robert M. Weir, " 'The Harmony We Are Famous For': An Interpretation of South Carolina Politics," *W&MQ*, 26 (1969): 473–80; Weir, "The South Carolinian as Extremist," *SAQ*, 74 (1975): 86–103; R. Nicholas Olsberg, "A Government of Class and Race: William Henry Trescot and the South Carolina Chivalry, 1860–1865," unpubl. Ph.D. diss., U. of South Carolina, 1972, 74–76, 101–17; George P. Germany, "The South Carolina Governing Elite, 1820–1860," unpubl. Ph.D. diss., U. of California at Berkeley, 1972, 73–88, 222–46; and Mark D. Kaplanoff, "Charles Pinckney and the American Republican Tradition," in *Intellectual Life in Antebellum Charleston*, eds. O'Brien and Moltke-Hansen, 85–122. A long, loving, and one-sided elaboration of relationships between secession and the older republican tradition is provided in Walter K. Wood, "The Union of the States: A Study of Radical Whig-Republican Ideology and Its Influence Upon the Nation and the South, 1776–1861," unpubl. Ph.D. diss., U. of South Carolina, 1978.

19. See here again Rogin, *Fathers and Children*, and also Francis Paul Prucha, "Andrew Jackson's Indian Policy: A Reassessment," *JAH*, 56 (1969): 527–39; William S. Hoffman, "Andrew Jackson, State Rightest: The Case of the Georgia Indians," *THQ*, 11 (1952): 329–45; Ronald N. Satz, *American Indian Policy in the Jackson Era* (Lincoln, Neb., 1975); Arthur H. DeRosier, *The Removal of the Choctaw Indians* (Knoxville, Tenn., 1970).

20. *Messages and Papers of the Presidents*, ed. Richardson, 2: 1000, 1012–13, 1086–88. Professor Michael Holt has suggested to me that Jackson from the beginning positioned himself on the tariff to slam back at Calhoun, a policy in keeping with the President's very early determination to isolate his Vice President. Holt's interpretation, while unprovable, squares with the provable facts that Jackson's hatred for Calhoun preceded presidential tariff pronouncements, transcended Peggy Eaton, and found expression in presidential lines urging against Union-straining agitation on an overwrought subject. Holt's commentary here is typical of his superb critique of my whole manuscript, for which I am very grateful.

21. The Bank and Peggy Eaton stories are told more fully elsewhere, including in my *Prelude to Civil War*, 186–92.

Chapter 15. The First Confrontation Crisis, II: South Carolina Versus the South

1. Calhoun to Samuel D. Ingham, May 4, 25, 1831, *Papers of Calhoun*, 11: 377–80, 390–94; Memorandum by James Hammond dated March 18, 1831, in "Letters on the Nullification Movement in South Carolina, 1830–1834," *AHR*, 6 (1901): 741–44.

2. James Hamilton, Jr., to Hammond, May 3, 1831, *ibid.*, 6 (1901): 745; George McDuffie, *Speech . . . at . . . Charleston, S.C., May 19, 1831* (Charleston, 1831).

3. Charles Fenton Mercer to John Hartwell Cocke, April 19, 1818, Cocke Papers, VA. The Mercer Bill and Carolina's reaction to it are more fully discussed in W. Freehling, *Prelude to Civil War*, 196–99.

4. Calhoun to Virgil Maxcy, September 11, 1830, *Papers of Calhoun*, 11: 229.

5. *Charleston Mercury*, August 4, 1830.

6. William Preston to Waddy Thompson, February 14, 1830, Preston Papers, SC.

7. W. Freehling, *Prelude to Civil War*, 202–13.

8. *Messages and Papers of the Presidents*, ed. Richardson, 2: 1119; Jackson to Van Buren, November 14, December 17, 1831, Jackson to John Coffee, July 17, 1832, *Correspondence of Andrew Jackson*, ed. John Spencer Bassett, 7 vols. (Washington, D.C., 1826–35), 4: 373–74, 383–85, 462–63; Richard E. Ellis, *The Union at Risk: Jacksonian Democracy, States' Rights, and the Nullification Crisis* (New York, 1987), 68–73.

9. James Hamilton, Jr., to James Hammond, January 16, 1832, *AHR*, 6 (1901): 748–49; Hamilton to Edward Harden, August 31, 1832, Harden Papers, DU.

10. *Register of Debates*, 22nd Cong., 1 sess. (June 20, 1832): 1116–17.

11. James Hamilton, Jr., to John Taylor et al., September 14, 1830, in *Charleston Mercury*, September 28, 1832. Every important South Carolina Nullifier echoed such sentiments. W. Freehling, *Prelude to Civil War*, 255–59; Major L. Wilson, "A Preview of Irrepressible Conflict: The Issue of Slavery During the Nullification Controversy," *Mississippi Quarterly*, 19 (1966): 184–93; David F. Houston, *A Critical Study of Nullification in South Carolina* (Cambridge, Mass., 1896), 48–52; Frederick Bancroft, *Calhoun and the South Carolina Nullification Movement* (Baltimore, 1928), 19–20, 115; Charles M. Wiltse, *The New Nation, 1800–1865* (New York, 1961), 115–17, 121.

12. Calhoun to Francis Pickens, August 1, 1831, *Papers of Calhoun*, 11: 445–46.

13. *Columbia Telescope*, June 19, 1831.

14. The Fort Hill Letter is reprinted in *Papers of Calhoun*, 11: 413–39.

15. Calhoun to Samuel Ingham, July 31, 1831, *ibid.*, 4: 441–45.

16. This account of the Carolina election of 1832 has been influenced by excellent criticism of my imperfect formulation in *Prelude to Civil War*, 252–56, 365–69. Jane H. Pease and William H. Pease, "The Economics and Politics of Charleston's Nullification Crisis," *JSH*, 47 (1981): 335–62, offers a far more sophisticated vote analysis of the city than mine. On the rest of the state, I, not surprisingly, prefer Paul H. Bergeron's argument that my voter analysis is somewhat inconsistent, to J. P. Ochenkowski's argument that my analysis is altogether botched. I have nonetheless exploited Ochenkowski's best insights to help straighten out inconsistencies Bergeron accurately describes. Bergeron, "The Nullification Controversy Revisited," *THQ*, 35 (1976): 263–75; Ochenkowski, "The Origins of Nullification in South Carolina," *SCHM*, 83 (1982): 121–53.

While the 1832 voter analysis in *Prelude* is not my favorite part of the book, I am more unhappy with my explanation of what still seems to me right: nullification as, in part, South Carolina's very early response to the slavery issue. I called that response an "overreaction" and explained it as a manifestation of extraordinary fear of slave revolt and guilt about holding slaves. I still think the lowcountry's especially dense black population made emancipation seem especially disastrous and Conditional Termination special folly. I also still think fallout from Denmark Vesey put the coastal gentry on the road to nullification in the Negro Seamen's Controversy. But the Nullification Controversy came almost a decade later; and Carolina's response to the immediately preceding Nat Turner Revolt consisted mostly of concern that fears far-off in the Chesapeake were causing some guilt-ridden Virginia and Maryland gentlemen not to stonewall against nonslaveholder attack.

That Carolina stance was an understandable early response, from the state most hard in its commitment to slavery, to potentially debilitating softness elsewhere. In the wider perspective of continual colonization proposals in national and Upper South state politics in the 1830s, a perspective too much lacking in my narrowly focused localistic study of South Carolina, Carolinians had reason to worry that all the southern world might not be South Carolina. They also had reason to worry about an internal economy more seriously depressed than those in newer southern states, a depopulation foreign to the rest of the Cotton South, and an old republican ideology becoming anachronistic amidst Andrew Jackson's wave of the southern mobocratic future. Crazed overreactors? No way. Rather, desperate old seers, desperate most that their little cockpit of a state might be too divided and debilitated to say NO to the (from their perspective) disastrous trends of American and southern history.

17. *State Papers on Nullification . . .* (Boston, 1834), 28–33.

18. James Hamilton, Jr., to Richard Crallé, February 6, 1833, Crallé Papers, CU.

19. All the quotes in this paragraph are from Ellis, *Union at Risk*, 78.

20. *Register of Debates,* 22 Cong., 2 sess. (Feb. 4, 1833): 338–43. For other examples, see Mississippi's George Poindexter, *ibid.* (January 22, 1833): 179–83; Alabama's Gabriel Moore, *ibid.* (February 13, 1833): 490–91; Virginia's John Tyler, *ibid.* (February 6, 1833): 371–78. That South Carolina was not hopelessly isolated from other Southerners is endlessly demonstrated in Ellis's important *Union at Risk.*

21. Jackson's maneuvers to enforce the laws, together with South Carolina Unionists' and Sugar Jimmy's responses, is discussed and documented more fully in W. Freehling, *Prelude to Civil War,* 278–92.

22. *Messages and Papers of the Presidents,* 2: 1203–19.

23. Van Buren to Jackson, December 27, 1832, February 10, 1833, *Correspondence of Jackson,* 4: 506–8, 5: 19–21.

24. Jackson to Van Buren, January 13, 25, 1833, *ibid.,* 5: 2–4, 12–13.

25. *State Papers on Nullification,* 327–35.

26. The critical tale of southern Jacksonians' partial disenchantment with Jackson and partial sympathy with the Nullifiers is elaborated in Ellis's *Union at Risk,* chs. 3–6.

27. *Register of Debates,* 22 Cong., 2 sess. (January 28, 1833): 246.

28. Calhoun to William Preston [ca. February 3, 1833], *Papers of Calhoun,* 12: 37–38.

29. The tale of the Verplanck Bill and the Calhoun-Clay negotiations is told and documented fully in Merrill D. Peterson's useful *Olive Branch and Sword: The Compromise of 1833* (Baton Rouge, 1982) and in Peterson's still more useful *The Great Triumvirate: Webster, Clay, and Calhoun* (New York, 1987), 212–33.

30. Abbott Lawrence to Henry Clay, March 26, 1833, *Works of Henry Clay,* ed. Calvin Colton, 7 vols. (New York, 1897), 4: 357–58.

31. *Register of Debates,* 22 Cong., 2 sess. (February 25–26, 1833): 1771–1807 (March 1, 1833): 809.

32. *Speeches Delivered in the Convention . . . March, 1833 . . .* (Charleston, 1833); 346.

33. *Ibid.,* 25–26.

34. Jackson to John Crawford, April 9, 1833, *Correspondence of Jackson,* 5: 56.

35. Richard B. Latner, "The Nullification Crisis and Republican Subversion," *JSH,* 43 (1977): 18–38, is good on Jackson's misunderstanding of Calhoun. Jackson's incredulity that Nullifiers sought protection of slavery reflected his Middle South world's

utter inability to see a slavery issue yet. See Paul H. Bergeron, "Tennessee's Response to the Nullification Crisis," *JSH*, 39 (1973): 23–44.

Chapter 16. The Reorganization of Southern Politics

1. Charles Grandison Finney, *Lectures on Revivals of Religion*, ed. William G. McLaughlin (Cambridge, Mass., 1960); Finney, *Memoirs . . .* (New York, 1876); Keith J. Hardman, *Charles Grandison Finney, 1792–1875: Revivalist Reformer* (Syracuse, 1987).

2. Alice Felt Tyler, *Freedom's Ferment . . .* (Minneapolis, 1944).

3. Robert H. Abzug, *Passionate Liberator: Theodore Dwight Weld and the Dilemma of Reform* (New York, 1980); Gilbert H. Barnes, *The Anti-Slavery Impulse* (New York, 1933).

4. Anthony J. Barker, *Captain Charles Stuart: Anglo-American Abolitionist* (Baton Rouge, 1986).

5. Louis Filler, *The Crusade Against Slavery* (New York, 1960); Ronald Walters, *The Antislavery Appeal: American Abolitionism After 1830* (Baltimore, 1976); Bertram Wyatt-Brown, *Lewis Tappan and the Evangelical War Against Slavery* (Cleveland, 1969).

6. "Postmaster Huger and the Incendiary Publications," ed. Frank Otto Gattell, *SCHM*, 64 (1963): 193–201.

7. *Charleston Mercury*, July 30–31, 1835; Charleston *Southern Patriot*, July 30, 1835; Jacob Schirmer Diary, entry for July 29, 1835, *SCHS*; Eaton, *Freedom-of-Thought Struggle*, 196–215.

8. Jackson to Kendall, August 9, 1835, *Correspondence of Jackson*, 5: 360–61.

9. *Congressional Globe*, 24 Cong., 1 sess, 9.

10. The best source for southern meetings' resolutions and northern meetings' answers is *The United States Telegraph*, August through November 1835. This Calhoun-ite newspaper, edited by Duff Green, was obsessed with the subject, reporting its development fully and commenting on its meaning affectingly.

11. Arthur P. Hayne to Andrew Jackson, November 11, 1835, Jackson Papers, LC.

12. Henry J. Nott to James Hammond, March 8, 1836, Hammond Papers, LC.

13. *United States Telegraph*, September 4, 1835.

14. *The United States Telegraph* throughout the fall of 1835 reported on northern anti-abolitionist meetings. For the wider and longer lasting northern distrust of abolitionism, see Leonard L. Richards, *Gentlemen of Property and Standing . . .* (New York, 1970); Merton L. Dillon, *Elijah P. Lovejoy: Abolitionist Editor* (Urbana, Ill., 1961); Leon F. Litwack, *North of Slavery: The Negro in the Free States* (Chicago, 1961).

15. For some good examples, see Avery Craven, *The Coming of the Civil War* (Chicago, 1957); George Fort Milton, *The Eve of Conflict: Stephen A. Douglas and the Needless War* (Boston and New York, 1934).

16. *Boston Mercantile Journal*, reprinted in *United States Telegraph*, September 16, 1835.

17. Hammond to M. M. Noah, August 19, 1835, Hammond Papers, LC.

18. Duff Green to Beverley Tucker, November 9, 1833, in "Correspondence of Judge Tucker," *WMQ*, 12 (1903): 88–89.

19. William J. Cooper's *The South and the Politics of Slavery, 1828–1856* (Baton Rouge and London, 1978) first traced the politics of loyalty and remains an important volume on antebellum southern political history. But Cooper's thesis that slavery was *always the* issue misses the way slavery matters slowly evolved towards overshadowing everything else. To argue that the slavery issue was from its inception continually dominant in southern politics, Cooper has to define the Border South out of the South. The thesis can also only be argued by ignoring local contests over local issues occurring between presidential-election campaigns' eruptions over loyalty. The thesis finally cannot account for the enormous amount—often the greater amount—of rhetoric devoted to

other themes even in presidential years, rhetoric, for example, which makes Southern Whigs' focus on economic nationalism in the mid-1840s hardly the aberration Cooper thinks it.

20. The following account is based on my own reading of Southern Whig sources, on conversations with Michael Holt, who is writing what promises to be *the* book on American Whiggery, and on the burgeoning secondary literature on the subject, including Thomas Brown, *Politics and Statesmanship: Essays on the American Whig Party* (New York, 1985); Daniel Walker Howe, *The Political Culture of the American Whigs* (Chicago and London, 1979); Arthur C. Cole, *The Whig Party in the South* (Washington, D.C., 1913); Harry L. Watson, *Jacksonian Politics and Community Conflict: The Emergence of the Second American Party System in Cumberland County, North Carolina* (Baton Rouge, 1981); Marc W. Kruman, *Party and Politics in North Carolina, 1836–1865* (Baton Rouge, 1983); Paul Murray, *The Whig Party in Georgia* (Chapel Hill, 1948); Herbert J. Doughty, Jr., *The Whigs of Florida, 1845–1854* (Gainesville, 1959); John Mering, *The Whig Party in Missouri* (Columbia, Mo., 1967); William H. Adams, *The Whig Party in Louisiana* (Lafayette, La., 1973); and especially Charles Grier Sellers, Jr.'s seminal "Who Were the Southern Whigs?," *AHR*, 59 (1954): 335–46.

21. Thomas B. Alexander, *Sectional Stress and Party Strength: A Study of Roll-Call Patterns in the United States House* (Nashville, 1967).

22. Points well made in Richard P. McCormick, "Was There a Whig Strategy in 1836?," *JER* 4 (1984): 47–70.

23. *Niles' Weekly Register*, May 2, October 18, 1835; and all the voluminous mail coming to Van Buren from southern supporters in 1835, Van Buren Papers, LC.

24. This warfare can be followed particularly clearly in the *Richmond Whig* and *Richmond Enquirer* throughout 1835–36.

25. Historians, while recognizing the paranoid theme in American politics, have underestimated the American resistance to that mentality. See William W. Freehling, "Conspiracy and Conspiracy Theories," in *Encyclopedia of American Political History: Studies of the Principal Movements and Ideas,* ed. Jack P. Greene, 3 vols. (New York, 1984), 1: 367–74.

26. Calhoun to A. H. Pemberton, November 19, 1838, *Papers of Calhoun*, 14: 472–75.

27. Calhoun to James Edward Calhoun, February 8, 1834, same to Duff Green, August 30, 1835, *ibid.*, 12: 231–32, 547–48.

28. Hofstadter, *American Political Tradition*, ch. 4.

29. Calhoun to Duff Green, July 27, 1837, *Papers of Calhoun*, 13: 525–28.

30. Calhoun to Robert Y. Hayne, November 17, 1838, *ibid.*, 14: 465–68.

31. Calhoun to Francis W. Pickens, January 4, 1834, *ibid.*, 12: 196–98.

32. Hammond to William C. Preston, November 14, 1835, Hammond Papers, LC.

Chapter 17. The Gag Rule, I: Mr. Hammond's Mysterious Motion

1. The best gag rule history is but a slight article: George C. Rable, "Slavery, Politics, and the South: The Gag Rule as a Case Study," *Capital Studies,* 3 (1975) 69–88. One of our best Jacksonian era historians, Lee Benson, is drafting the needed big book on the subject. Some of Benson's intriguing ideas are presented in his *Toward the Scientific Study of History,* 319–23.

2. Any historian who says not a solitary example can be found invites someone to find one. But I have not uncovered any premonition in any congressman's papers which I have examined.

3. *Senate Journal,* 24 Cong., 1 sess., 31.

4. *Papers of Calhoun*, 13: 53–67.

5. Eaton, *Freedom-of-Thought Struggle*, ch. 8.

6. These petitions, an unexplored treasure chest for many sorts of inquiries, are fortunately preserved in the Legislative Papers, 24 Cong., 1 sess., RG 233 (House Petitions), RG 36 (Senate Petitions), National Archives, Washington, D.C.

7. *Register of Debates,* 24 Cong., 1 sess. (December 16, 1835): 1961.

8. *Ibid.* (December 18, 1835): 1966 ff.

9. *Ibid.* (January 21, 1836): 2242–43.

10. *Ibid.*

11. Drew Gilpin Faust, *James Henry Hammond and the Old South: A Design for Mastery* (Baton Rouge and London, 1982), 7–44.

12. *Ibid.,* ch. 4.

13. Hammond to John Walker, December 27, 1836, Hammond Papers, LC; same to Harry Hammond, February 19, 1856, Hammond Plantation Diary, entry for January 8, 1838, Hammond Papers, SC.

14. Thomas Stark to Hammond, April 14, 1836, Hammond Papers, LC.

15. Edward W. Johnston to Hammond, March 9, 1836, Hammond Papers, LC.

16. Beverley Tucker to Hammond, February 17, 1836, Hammond Papers, LC.

17. Hammond to Tucker, March 1, 1836, McDuffie to Hammond, March 11, 1836, Cooper to Hammond, January 8, 1836, Hammond Papers, LC.

18. *Ibid.* See also Cooper's letters to Hammond dated December 15, 17, 1835, February 6, 12, March 2, 20, 27, 31, April 7, 11, 1836, same collection.

19. Johnston to Hammond, February 28, 1836, same collection. See also Johnston's letters of February 20, March 9, 24, 1836, same collection; Cooper to Beverley Tucker, July 27, 1838, Tucker-Coleman Papers, W&M.

20. Hammond to I. W. Hayne, September 1, 1835, same collection.

21. Hammond to Tucker, June 5, 1836, same collection. See also Hammond to Tucker, March 11, 1836, same collection.

22. The "impromptu" word is Hammond's. James Hammond to M. C. M. Hammond, December 25, 1835, Hammond Papers, SC.

23. Register of Debates, 24 Cong., 2 sess. (February 1, 1836): 2448–66. To watch another young Carolina hotspur slipping and sliding around defense of an upper-class-based Slavepower, see Francis W. Pickens in *ibid.* (January 21, 1836): 2249–51.

Chapter 18. The Gag Rule, II: Mr. Pinckney's Controversial Compromise

1. *Papers of Calhoun,* 13: 22. Calhoun's emphasis on honor, omnipresent here as in much of southern rhetoric on gag rules and other slavery questions, raises the question of why arguments which stressed honor were so frequent. I cannot agree with Bertram Wyatt-Brown's otherwise admirable *Southern Honor* that the concept operated independently of southern rage that specifically slavery was being called dishonorable. While Wyatt-Brown is right that concern about honor preceded concern about abolitionists, rhetoric about honor escalated enormously after southern morality came under attack. "Honor," like "loyalty" and "soundness," seems to me a loaded vocabulary for talking about slaveholders' predicament, within and without the South.

2. *Ibid.,* 13: 25.

3. *Ibid.,* 13: 22–23.

4. *Ibid.,* 13: 77.

5. *Ibid.,* 13: 23.

6. *Ibid.,* 13: 104–5.

7. *Register of Debates,* 24 Cong., 1 sess. (February 12, March 2, 1836): 496, 679–89.

8. *Papers of Calhoun,* 13: 104–5, 111–12.

9. William Preston to Beverley Tucker, February 28, 1836, *W&MQ,* 12 (1903): 92–94.

10. *Register of Debates,* 24 Cong., 1 sess. (March 9, 1836): 779.

11. *Ibid.*

12. *Ibid.* (March 14, 1836): 810.

13. George W. Owens to Martin Van Buren, May 16, 1836, Van Buren Papers, LC.

14. *Register of Debates,* 24 Cong., 1 sess. (February 4, 1836): 2482–84.

15. *Ibid.* (February 8, 1836): 2491–2502.

16. Robert Y. Hayne to Hammond, January 18, 1836, Hammond Papers, LC; Hammond to M.C.M. Hammond, February 21, 1836, Hammond Papers, SC. For a stimulating reassessment of Pinckney, see George C. Rogers, Jr., "Henry Laurens Pinckney—Thoughts on His Career," in *South Carolina Journals and Journalists,* ed. James B. Meriwether (Spartanburg, S.C., 1975), 163–75.

17. *Register of Debates,* 24 Cong., 1 sess. (February 8, 1836): 2491; *Pendleton Messenger,* February 26, 1836; Henry L. Pinckney, *Address to the Electors of Charleston District, South Carolina, on the Subject of the Abolition of Slavery* (Washington, D.C., 1836).

18. Quoted in Lawrence T. McDonnell's suggestive "Struggle Against Suicide: James Henry Hammond and the Secession of South Carolina," *SS,* 22 (1983): 109–37, esp. 125. See also *Secret and Sacred Diaries of Hammond,* ed. Bleser, entry for December 16, 1849; Hammond to William Gilmore Simms, October 26, 1858, Hammond Papers, LC; Hammond to M.C.M. Hammond, April 30, 1859, Hammond Papers, LC; Faust, *Hammond,* 181–85.

19. *Register of Debates,* 24 Cong., 1 sess. (February 15, 1836): 2533–35.

20. Abel P. Upshur to Beverley Tucker, March 8, 1836, Tucker-Coleman Papers, W&M.

21. Pinckney, *Address to the Electors of Charleston,* 7–8; *Register of Debates,* 24 Cong., 1 sess. (May 18, 1836): 3756–58.

22. *Ibid.*

23. *Ibid.* (May 18, 1836): 3759–61.

24. *Ibid.* (May 19, 1836): 3772–78.

25. *Ibid.* (May 19–25, 1836): 4010–30.

26. *Ibid.* (May 25, 1836): 4029–31.

Chapter 19. The Gag Rule, III: Mr. Johnson's Ironic Intransigence

1. Thomas Cooper to William Preston, December 31, 1837, Miscellaneous Manuscripts Collection, Huntington Library, San Marino, California.

2. George McDuffie to James Hammond, December 19, 1836, Hammond Papers, LC. See also future Governor Whitemarsh B. Seabrook to Richard Crallé, January 15, 1837, January 10, 1838, Crallé Papers, CU.

3. John C. Calhoun to Francis W. Pickens, August 17, 1836, *Papers of Calhoun,* 13: 278–80.

4. John C. Calhoun to Anna Maria Calhoun, January 25, 1838, *ibid.,* 14: 107–8.

5. This analysis of the presidential campaign of 1836 is based on the following southern newspapers, September and October 1836: *Richmond Enquirer, Richmond Constitutional Whig, Lexington Kentucky Gazette, Louisville Daily Journal, Raleigh Register, Nashville National Banner,* and *Daily Advertizer, Huntsville* (Alabama) *Weekly Democrat, Huntsville Southern Advocate, Savannah Daily Republican, Augusta Chronicle, Milledgeville, Georgia Southern Recorder, Milledgeville Federal Union, New Orleans Bee,* and *Little Rock Arkansas Gazette.* Cooper, *South and the Politics of Slavery,* 94–97, splendidly illustrates but perhaps slightly exaggerates the omnipresence of the slavery issue, while Edwin A. Miles, "The Whig Party and the Menace of Caesar," *THQ* 27 (1968): 361–79, nicely analyzes that intrusive theme.

6. Joel H. Silbey, "Election of 1836," in *History of American Presidential Elections, 1789–1968,* ed. Arthur M. Schlesinger, Jr., 4 vols. (New York, Toronto, London, and Sydney, 1971), 1: 577–640, records the election statistics and expertly analyzes them.

7. This statistical analysis is based on "Candidate and Constituency Statistics of Elections in the United States, 1788–1985," ICPSR Study Number 7757, originally collected and made available by the Inter-University Consortium for Political and Social Research, P. O. Box 1248, Ann Arbor, Michigan, 48106. Of course the Consortium bears no responsibility for my interpretation of their extremely useful statistics. I am grateful to Ms. Robin Kolodny of the Johns Hopkins University for correlating the Consortium's raw data.

8. Quoted in Samuel Flagg Bemis's superb biography of this, I think, greatest of American antebellum statesmen: *John Quincy Adams and the Union*, 150–51.

9. *Memoirs of Adams*, 5: 210 (entry for November 19, 1820).

10. Bemis, *Adams*, 331.

11. *Ibid.*, 331–32. In addition to the Bemis, Leonard L. Richards, *The Life and Times of Congressman John Quincy Adams* (New York, 1986), is fine on its subject.

12. *Register of Debates*, 24 Cong., 1 sess. (May 25, 1836): 4029–31.

13. *Ibid.*, 24 Cong., 2 sess. (February 6, 1837): 1587.

14. *Ibid.*, 1591.

15. *Ibid.*, 1595–98.

16. *Ibid.*, 1679.

17. Bemis, *Adams*, 343–47.

18. *Congressional Globe*, 25 Cong., 1 sess. (December 21, 1837): 44; *ibid.*, 25 Cong., 2 sess. (December 12, 1838): 26.

19. John C. Calhoun to Duff Green, July 17, 1837, Calhoun to William C. Daniels (?), October 26, 1838, *Papers of Calhoun*, 13: 525–28, 14: 444–48.

20. *Congressional Globe*, 27 Cong., 1 sess. (June 1, 1841): 9.

21. Waddy Thompson to Beverley Tucker, November 10, 1841, *WMQ*, 12 (1904): 150–51.

22. *Congressional Globe*, 26 Cong., 1 sess. (January 14, 1840): 121.

23. *Ibid.* (January 27, 1840): 132.

24. *Ibid.* (January 27, 1840): 146–47.

25. William Cost Johnson, *Speech . . . on the Subject of . . . Petitions for the Abolition of Slavery . . . January 25, 27, and 28, 1840* (Washington, D.C., 1840).

26. *Congressional Globe*, 26 Cong., 1 sess. (January 18, 1840): 151.

27. This along with all subsequent analyses of House of Representative roll call votes in this volume are based on "United States Congressional Roll Call Voting Records, 1789–1986 [House of Representatives]," ICPSE Study Number 0004, data collected and made available by the Inter-University Consortium for Political and Social Research. I must once again absolve the Consortium from any errors stemming from my analysis of its data and once again thank Ms. Robin Kolodny for correlating the statistics.

28. *Congressional Globe*, 27 Cong., 1 sess. (June 7, 14, 16, 1841): 27–28, 51, 63.

29. *Ibid.*, 27 Cong., 2 sess. (January 24, 1842): 168.

30. *Ibid.* (January 24, 1842): 168.

31. *Ibid.* (January 25, 1842): 170.

32. *Ibid.* (February 3, 1842): 208.

33. *Ibid.*, 27 Cong., 3 sess. (December 12, 1842): 42.

34. *Ibid.*, 28 Cong., 1 sess. (February 28, 1844): 343.

35. *Ibid.*, 28 Cong., 2 sess. (December 3, 1844): 7.

Chapter 20. Anti-Annexation as Manifest Destiny

1. The classic account of Manifest Destiny remains Albert K. Weinberg, *Manifest Destiny, a Study of Nationalist Expansionism in American History* (Baltimore, 1935). The subject is approached with more irony and sophistication in Frederick Merk, *Manifest Destiny and Mission in American History: A Reinterpretation* (New York, 1963).

Thomas R. Hietala's *Manifest Design: Anxious Aggrandisement in Jacksonian America* (Ithaca, 1983) turns the Manifest Destiny argument around, urging that anxiety and racism, not confidence and democratic mission, fueled not-very-democratic expansionism. Reginald Horseman's *Race and Manifest Destiny: The Origins of American Racial Anglo-Saxonism* (Cambridge, Mass., 1981) strikes a similar note. I feel that Hietala's and Horseman's racist emphasis, like many a useful corrective, goes rather too far; a chauvinistic version of democratic idealism appears to have been important in some quarters, especially among New York City intellectuals and midwestern farmers. See especially Norman A. Tuturow, *Texas Annexation and the Mexican War: A Study of the Old Northwest* (Palo Alto, 1978). I also think the racism label, because conflating racist expansionists North and South, obscures where the greatest pressure for annexation originated: from Southerners specifically anxious about the slaveholding form of racial control. The Hietala racist thesis, like the notion that the Civil War came from southern efforts to preserve a herrenvolk republic of equal whites and unequal blacks, also misses key attempts of color-blind dominators, including the single most important annexationist, Abel P. Upshur, to drive preservation of bondage past "mere negro" slavery to consolidate patriarchal hierarchy for all colors. Still, Merk, Hietala, and Horseman, by making inescapable the limits of the Manifest Destiny explanation, have reopened the field for all who come after.

I am indebted to Professor Bradford Perkins for a discerning critique of my Texas chapters.

2. Federick Merk, *Fruits of Propaganda in the Tyler Administration* (Cambridge, Mass., 1971); Merk, *Slavery and the Annexation of Texas* (New York, 1972).

3. John H. Schroeder, "Annexation or Independence: The Texas Issue in American Politics," *SWHQ*, 90 (1985): 137–64, emphasizes the central importance of the slavery issue. Gerald Douglas Saxan, "The Politics of Expansion: Texas as an Issue in National Politics, 1819–1845," unpubl. Ph.D. diss., North Texas State University, 1979, shows that most politicians' Manifest Destiny was to avoid the issue. While Eugene C. Barker, "The Annexation of Texas," *SWHQ*, 50 (1946): 49–74, remains useful, fuller scholarly accounts are in David M. Pletcher's rather unimaginative *The Diplomacy of Annexation: Texas, Oregon, and the Mexican War* (Columbia, Mo., 1973) and in Charles Sellers's superb *James K. Polk, Continentalist, 1843–1846* (Princeton, 1966). Still, I learned as much from two volumes written early in the twentieth century, not to be missed just because they are older: Justin H. Smith, *The Annexation of Texas* (New York, 1911), and Ephraim Douglass Adams, *British Interests and Activities in Texas, 1838–1846* (Baltimore, 1910).

4. The best biography is Oliver Perry Chitwood, *John Tyler: Champion of the Old South* (New York, 1939). Also useful is Robert Seager II, *and Tyler Too, a Biography of John and Julia Gardiner Tyler* (New York, 1963).

5. Calhoun to Duff Green, July 27, 1837, *Papers of Calhoun*, 13: 525–28.

6. *Congressional Globe*, 25 Cong., 3 sess., (February 7, 1839): Appendix, 354–59.

7. Abel P. Upshur to Nathaniel Beverley Tucker, August 1, 1838, Tucker-Coleman Papers, W&M.

8. The background for and details of Clay's defeat are illuminated in Arthur C. Cole, *The Whig Party in the South* (Washington, 1913), 1–55; Glyndon G. Van Deusen, *The Life of Henry Clay* (Boston, 1937), 320–27; Robert G. Gunderson, *The Log Cabin Campaign* (Lexington, Ky., 1957), 41–77.

9. Accounts of Tyler's nomination include Seager, *and Tyler Too*, 134–35; Lyon G. Tyler, "John Tyler and the Vice-Presidency," *Tyler's Quarterly . . .* , 9 (1927): 89–95.

10. Chitwood, *Tyler*, 190.

11. My account of the presidential campaign of 1840 is based on the newspapers cited above, Chapter 19, note 50. Cooper, *South and the Politics of Slavery*, ch. 4, expertly discusses although I think a tad over-emphasizes slavery themes; while Michael F. Holt, "The Election of 1840, Voter Mobilization, and the Emergence of the Second American

Party System: A Reappraisal of Jacksonian Voting Behavior," in *A Master's Due: Essays in Honor of David Herbert Donald,* ed. William J. Cooper et al. (Baton Rouge, 1985), is excellent on economic issues.

12. Contrast the string of letters from Mangum in 1841, as published in volume 3 of *The Papers of Willie Person Mangum,* ed. Henry Thomas Shanks, 5 vols. (Raleigh, 1950–56), with the letters from Upshur over the same period in Tucker-Coleman Papers, W&M. Accounts of the Tyler-Clay split include George Rawlings Poage, *Henry Clay and the White Party* (Chapel Hills, 1936), chs. 3–7, and Richard Gantz, "Henry Clay and the Harvest of Bitter Fruit: The Struggle with John Tyler, 1841–1842," unpubl. Ph.D. diss., University of Indiana, 1986.

13. Accounts of colonial Texas-Mexican relations include Donald J. Weber, *The Mexican Frontier, 1821–1846: The American Southwest Under Mexico* (Alburquerque, N.M., 1982), and Eugene C. Barker, *Mexico and Texas, 1821–1835* (Dallas, 1928).

14. Alleine Howren, "Causes and Origin of the Decree of April 6, 1830," *SWHQ,* 16 (1913): 378–422; Ohland Morton, *Terán and Texas: A Chapter in Texas-Mexican Relations* (Austin, 1948).

15. William Campbell Binkley, *The Texas Revolution* (Baton Rouge, 1952); Stanley Siegel, *A Political History of the Texas Republic, 1836–1845* (Austin, 1956), 3–37.

16. Good statistics on Texas population during the republic period are impossible to procure; hence the vague language in the text. But I have used Barnes F. Lathrop, *Migration into East Texas, 1835–1860: A Study from the United States Census* (Austin, 1949); *The Handbook of Texas,* eds. Walter P. Webb and H. Bailey Carroll, 2 vols. (Austin, 1952), 1: 321; Albert T. Burnley to Beverley Tucker, June 6, 1841, Tucker-Coleman Papers, W&M. Especially fine, although still uncertain, on elusive black population figures is Randolph B. Campbell, *An Empire for Slavery: The Peculiar Institution in Texas, 1821–1865* (Baton Rouge, 1989), 54–80.

17. Joseph C. G. Kennedy, *Agriculture of the United States . . . Compiled from the . . . Census* (Washington, 1864), 222.

18. Smith, *Annexation of Texas,* 52–62; Remini, *Jackson and the Course of American Democracy,* 362–68.

19. James C. Curtis, *The Fox at Bay: Martin Van Buren and the Presidency, 1837–41* (Lexington, Ky., 1970), 152–56, 166–69; Major L. Wilson, *The Presidency of Martin Van Buren* (Lawrence, Kan., 1984), 149–50.

20. Quoted in Smith, *Annexation of Texas,* 103.

21. Ashbel Smith to Isaac Van Zandt, January 25, 1843, in *Diplomatic Correspondence of the Republic of Texas,* ed. George Pierce Garrison, published as the *Annual Report of the American Historical Association for the Years 1907, 1908,* 3 vols. (Washington, 1908–11), 2: Part 2, 1103–7.

22. Issac Van Zandt to Anson Jones, March 13, 1843, *ibid.,* 2: Part 1, 132–38.

23. Gilmer's letter, originally printed in the Washington *Madisonian,* January 23, 1843, is reprinted in Merk, *Slavery and Annexation,* 200–204. For Adams's rebuttal, see *ibid.,* 205–7.

24. Issac Van Zandt to Anson Jones, April 19, 1843, *Diplomatic Correspondence of Texas,* ed. Garrison, 2: Part 1, 164–67.

25. Interesting studies of Sam Houston include Llerna Friend, *Sam Houston: The Great Designer* (Austin, 1954); M. K. Wisehart, *Sam Houston, American Giant* (Washington, 1962); Marquis James, *The Raven . . .* (Indianapolis, 1929); George Creel, *Sam Houston, Colossus in Buckskin* (New York, 1928); Jack Gregory and Rennard Strickland, *Sam Houston with the Cherokees, 1829–1833* (Austin, 1967); Stan Hoig, "Diana, Taina, or Talihina? The Myth and Mystery of Sam Houston's Cherokee Wife," *Chronicles of Oklahoma,* 64 (1986): 53–59.

26. Smith, *Annexation of Texas,* 43–45; Anson Jones to Issac Van Zandt, July 6, 1843, *Diplomatic Correspondence of Texas,* ed. Garrison, 2: Part 1, 195.

27. Van Zandt to Anson Jones, April 19, 1843, *ibid.,* 2: Part 1, 164–67.

Chapter 21. An Extremist's Zany Pilgrimage

1. Stephen F. Austin to Thomas F. Leaming, July 14, 1830, "The Austin-Leaming Correspondence, 1828–1836," ed. Adreas Reichstein, *SWHG*, 88 (1985): 269.

2. The best biography is Madeleine B. Stern, *The Pantarch: A Biography of Stephen Pearl Andrews* (Austin, 1968). Useful information is also in Charles Shively, "An Option for Freedom in Texas, 1840–1844," *JNH*, 50 (1965): 77–96, and in Harriet Smither, "English Abolitionism and the Annexation of Texas," *SWHQ*, 32 (1929): 193–205.

3. Elgin Williams, *The Animating Pursuit of Speculation: Land Traffic in the Annexation of Texas* (New York, 1949).

4. Quoted in Madeleine B. Stern, "Stephen Pearl Andrews, Abolitionist, and the Annexation of Texas," *SWHQ*, 57 (1964): 499.

5. The courthouse speech is described in Stephen Pearl Andrews, "A Private Chapter of the Origin of the War," Third Paper, 1–3, unpublished ms. in Andrews Papers, W.

6. The steamboat trip is described in Andrews, "Private Chapter," Third Paper, 3–5.

7. The Galveston sojourn is described in Andrews, "Private Chapter," Third Paper, 5–12, and in Joseph Eve to Daniel Webster, March 29, 1843, in *Diplomatic Correspondence of the United States: Inter-American Affairs, 1831–1860*, ed. William R. Manning, 12 vols. (Washington, 1932–39), 12:283–84.

8. Andrews, "Private Chapter," Fourth Paper, 1–5.

9. *Ibid.*, 5; Stern, *Andrews*, 42.

10. Andrews, "Private Chapter," Fourth Paper, 5.

11. Biographical details are from Clagette Blake, *Charles Elliot, R.N., 1801–1875, A Servant of Britain Overseas* (London, 1960).

12. Charles Elliot to H. U. Addington, November 15, 1842, in *British Correspondence Concerning the Republic of Texas, 1836–1846*, ed. Ephraim Douglass Adams (Austin, 1917), 125–30.

13. Andrews, "Private Chapter," Fourth Paper, 5–8.

14. Charles Elliot to H. U. Addington, March 26, 1843, *British Diplomatic Correspondence Concerning Texas*, ed. Adams, 165–69.

15. Elliot to Lord Aberdeen, June 8, 1843, in *SWHQ*, 16 (1912): 200–202.

16. One exception is Justin Smith, who with less information at his disposal than later historians understood this affair rather better. See Smith, *Annexation of Texas*, 112–16.

17. Andrew Yates to Charles Elliot, July 15, 1843, *SWHQ*, 17 (1913): 77–80.

18. The Yates letter, printed first in the *Boston Post*, June 21, 1843, was strategically reprinted again and again in southern newspapers. See *New Orleans Republican*, July 3, 1843; *Galveston Civilian*, August 9, 1843. In his *Reminiscences of the Texas Republic* (Galveston, 1872), 56, Ashbel Smith claimed that he maneuvered Duff Green into leaking the letter to the press. That latter-day claim jibes with Smith's spy-caper explanation to fellow Texan J. P. Henderson on November 14, 1843, Smith Papers, TX: "*Inter nos*, it was I who took care to have our friend Yates' letter published."

19. Ashbel Smith to John C. Calhoun, June 19, 1843, *Papers of Calhoun*, 17: 252–53.

20. Andrews, "Private Chapter," Fourth Paper, 10–11, Andrews Papers, W; Stern, *Andrews*, 45–46; Wyatt-Brown, *Tappan*, 250–52; *Memoirs of John Quincy Adams*, 11: 380.

21. For the Aberdeen-Tappen-Andrews meeting, see Andrews, "Private Chapter," Fifth Paper, Andrews Papers, W; Lewis Tappan Diary, entry for June 19, 1843, LC; Stern, Andrews, 48–49; Smither, "English Abolitionism," 195; Mary Lee Spence, "British Interests and Attitudes Regarding the Republic of Texas and Its Annexation by the United States," unpubl. Ph.D. diss., U. of Minnesota, 1956–57, 44–58; Wyatt-Brown, *Tappan*, 252–53.

22. Wilbur Devereux Jones, *Lord Aberdeen and the Americas* (Athens, Ga., 1958), gives a nice perspective on the Scotsman, as does E. D. Adams, *British Interests, passim.*

23. Ashbel Smith to Anson Jones, July 2, 1843, *Diplomatic Correspondence of Texas,* ed. Garrison, 2: Part 2, 1099–1103.

24. Duff Green, amazingly, still awaits his biographer. A start is made in Fletcher Green, "Duff Green, Militant Journalist of the Old School," *AHR,* 52 (1947): 247–54. Frederick Merk acidly analyzes Green as a diplomatic reporter in *The Monroe Doctrine and American Expansionism, 1843–1849* (New York, 1963), 11–15.

25. Joe Wilkins, "Window on Freedom: South Carolina's Response to British West Indian Slave Emancipation, 1833–1834," *SCHM,* 85 (1984): 135–44.

26. Green to Upshur, July 3, 1843, reprinted in Merk, *Slavery and Annexation,* 221–24.

Chapter 22. The Administration's Decision

1. The best biography, Claude H. Hall's *Abel Parker Upshur: Conservative Virginian, 1790–1844* (Madison, Wis., 1964), is adequate but leaves room for another full-scale foray.

2. My favorite Upshur essay on the connection between proslavery social theory and anti-herrenvolk political theory is "Domestic Slavery, as It Exists in Our Southern States, with Regard to Its Influence upon Free Government," *Southern Literary Messenger,* 5 (1839): 677–87. Upshur's better-known but I think more turgid theoretical formulation is in his pamphlet *A Brief Enquiry into the True Nature and Character of Our Federal Government; Being a Review of Judge Story's Commentaries on the Constitution of the United States* (Petersburg, Va., 1840).

3. *Richmond Enquirer,* February 10, 13, 1827.

4. *Proceedings of the Virginia Convention of 1829–30,* 65–79.

5. Upshur to Tucker, March 8, 1836, Tucker-Coleman Papers, W&M.

6. [Abel P. Upshur], *"The Partisan Leader. A Tale of the Future.* A Review of the Work of that Title," *Southern Literary Messenger,* 3 (1837): 73–89.

7. Abel P. Upshur to Beverley Tucker, January 12, 1840, Tucker-Coleman Papers, W&M.

8. Upshur to Tucker, February 1, 1841, February 14, 1839, December 14, 1840, Tucker-Coleman Papers, W&M. While Upshur was only on the edges of Drew Faust's *A Sacred Circle: The Dilemma of the Intellectual in the Old South, 1840–1860* (Baltimore, 1977), Faust's intellectual history illuminates the psychology of such thwarted men of mind. Still, I feel that Upshur, as well as such Faust insiders as James Hammond, cannot be understood as writing and publishing because of feeling hopelessly thwarted politically. The more accurate formulation is that they wrote in order to cut past infuriating but passable political barriers. A better formulation still is that writing and politicking were both activities aimed at bringing right ideas and therefore right politics before a culture where men of mind usually painfully did not but could—in the case of Upshur, finally did—immensely matter.

9. Upshur to Tucker, October 21, 30, 1841, Tucker-Coleman Papers, W&M.

10. Upshur to Tucker, March 13, 1843, Tucker-Coleman Papers.

11. Upshur to William S. Murphy, August 8, 1843, *Diplomatic Correspondence of the United States,* ed. Manning, 12: 44–49.

12. Lewis Tappan Diary, entry for July 12, 1843, LC.

13. Ashbel Smith to Anson Jones, July 31, 1843, *Diplomatic Correspondence of Texas,* ed. Garrison, 2: Part 2, 1116–19.

14. Stern, *Andrews,* 53–55.

15. Quoted in Smith, Annexation of Texas, 93, and discussed in Adams, *British Interests,* 130–31.

16. Ashbel Smith to Anson Jones, July 31, 1843, full citation above, note 13.

17. Adams, *British Interests,* 138–39.

18. Smith to Anson Jones, July 31, 1843, Smith to William Henry Daingerfield, June 28, July 6, 1843, *Diplomatic Correspondence of Texas,* ed. Garrison, 2: Part 2, 1098–1103, 1109, 1116–19; Elizabeth Silverthorne, *Ashbel Smith of Texas: Pioneer, Patriot, Statesman, 1805–1886* (College Park, Texas, 1982).

19. A. T. Burnley to Nathaniel Beverley Tucker, September 9, 1843, Tucker-Coleman Papers, W&M.

20. John Tyler to Waddy Thompson, August 28, 1843, *W&MQ,* 12 (1904): 140–41.

21. Issac Van Zandt to Anson Jones, September 18, 1843, *Diplomatic Correspondence of Texas,* ed. Garrison, 2: Part 1, 207–10.

22. *London Morning Chronicle,* August 19, 1843.

23. Smith, *Annexation of Texas,* 123.

24. Isaac Van Zandt to Anson Jones, October 16, 1843, *Diplomatic Correspondence of Texas,* ed. Garrison, 2: Part 1, 221–24.

25. John C. Calhoun to Abel P. Upshur, August 27, 1843, *Papers of Calhoun,* 17: 381–83.

26. Smith, *Annexation of Texas,* 94.

27. Edward Everett to Abel P. Upshur, November 3, 16, 1843, *Diplomatic Correspondence of the United States,* ed. Manning, 7: 246–48, 251.

28. Quoted in Herbert Gambrell, *Anson Jones: The Last President of Texas* (New York, 1948), 294.

29. Abel P. Upshur to John C. Calhoun, August 14, 1843, *WMQ,* 16 (1936): 554–57.

Chapter 23. Southern Democrats' Decision

1. Virgil Maxcy to Calhoun, December 10, 1843, *Works of Calhoun,* 17: 599–602.

2. Abel P. Upshur to Beverley Tucker, October 10, 1843, Tucker-Coleman Papers, W&M.

3. Upshur to Isaac Van Zandt, October 16, 1843, *Diplomatic Correspondence of the United States,* ed. Manning, 12: 53–54.

4. Van Zandt to Anson Jones, October 16, 1843, *Diplomatic Correspondence of Texas,* ed. Garrison, 2: 221–24.

5. Murphy's letter of September 23, 1843, to Upshur along with the leaked secret correspondence is printed in *Diplomatic Correspondence of the United States,* ed. Manning, 12: 299–309.

6. Upshur to Murphy, November 21, 1843, *ibid.,* 12: 55–58.

7. Anson Jones to Upshur, December 13, 1843, *Diplomatic Correspondence of Texas,* ed. Garrison, 2: Part 1, 232–35.

8. Andrew Jackson to Aaron V. Brown, February 9, 1843, *Correspondence of Jackson,* ed. Bassett, 6: 201–2.

9. Robert Walker to Andrew Jackson, January 16 [misdated January 10], 1844, *ibid.,* 6: 255–56.

10. See *ibid.,* 6: 264–65, for proof that Jackson did Walker's bidding.

11. Isaac Van Zandt to Anson Jones, January 20, 1844, *Diplomatic Correspondence of Texas,* ed. Garrison, 2: Part 1, 239–43.

12. Upshur to Murphy, January 16, 1844, *Diplomatic Correspondence of the United States,* ed. Manning, 12: 59–65.

13. Murphy to Upshur, February 15, 1844, *ibid.,* 12: 329–31.

14. Murphy to Anson Jones, February 14, 1844, *ibid.,* 12: 327–29.

15. Anson Jones to J. Pinckney Henderson, February 15, 1844, Jones to Van Zandt,

February 15, 1844, Jones to Henderson and Van Zandt, February 25, 1844, *Diplomatic Correspondence of Texas,* ed. Garrison, 2: Part 1, 252–53, 259–60.

16. Hall, *Upshur,* 209–12, describes Upshur's death.

17. Smith, *Annexation of Texas,* 174–76; Van Zandt to Anson Jones, March 5, 20, 25, April 12, 1844, *Diplomatic Correspondence of Texas,* ed. Garrison, 2: Part 1, 261, 263–65, 269–73.

18. John Tyler to Andrew Jackson, April 18, 1844, *Correspondence of Jackson,* ed. Bassett, 6: 279.

19. For the Pakenham exchange, see Lord Aberdeen to Richard Pakenham, December 26, 1843, Richard Pakenham to Abel P. Upshur, February 26, 1844, in *British and Foreign State Papers, 1844–1845,* 33: 232; John C. Calhoun to Richard Pakenham, April 18, 1844, *Senate Documents,* 28 Cong., 1 sess., 50–53. See also Bruno J. Gujer, *Free Trade and Slavery: Calhoun's Defence of Southern Interests Against British Interference, 1811–1848* (Zurich, 1971).

20. Chitwood, *Tyler,* 354.

21. Whigs' long-standing opposition to annexation is discussed many places, perhaps best in Merk, *Manifest Destiny and Mission, passim,* and in Bemis, *John Quincy Adams and the Union,* 449–500.

22. *Massachusetts Acts and Resolves, 1843, 1844, 1845* (Boston 1845), 79; *Congressional Globe,* 28 Cong., 1 sess. (December 21, 1843): 60, 63–67, 73; *House Documents,* 28 Cong., 1 sess., 1–24.

23. Adams quoted in Smith, *Annexation of Texas,* 221; *Boston Atlas,* March 10, 21, 30, 1844.

24. Van Buren's Hammet Letter is conveniently reprinted in *A History of American Presidential Elections,* ed. Schlesinger, 1: 822–28.

25. *Speeches of the Hon. Albert G. Brown . . . ,* ed. M. W. Cluskey (Philadelphia, 1859), 64–65.

26. Rives's speech was widely reprinted, including in *Raleigh Standard,* June 26, 1844.

27. Houston to Jackson, February 16, 1844, *Correspondence of Jackson,* ed. Bassett, 6: 260–64; Remini, *Jackson and the Course of American Democracy,* 353–66.

28. Jackson to William B. Lewis, March 28, 1844, *ibid.,* 6: 275–76.

29. Jackson to Lewis, December 15, 1843, Jackson to Francis P. Blair, May 18, 1844, *ibid.,* 6: 249, 294.

30. Jackson to the editors of the *Nashville Union,* May 13, 1844, Jackson to Francis Blair, May 18, 1844, *ibid.,* 6: 291, 294.

31. Jackson to Lewis, September 18, April 8, 1844, Jackson to Francis P. Blair, May 11, 1844, *ibid.,* 6: 230, 278, 286.

32. Francis P. Blair to Jackson, May 7, 1844, *ibid.,* 6: 283–84.

33. Jackson to Blair, May 7, 11, 18, June 25, 1844, *ibid.,* 6: 283–85, 193–94, 298.

34. Walker's *Letter . . . Relative to the Annexation of Texas . . . ,* first printed in Washington in 1844, is conveniently reprinted in Merk, *Fruits of Propaganda,* 221–52.

35. The standard biography is James Patrick Shenton, *Robert John Walker: A Politician from Jackson to Lincoln* (New York, 1961).

36. *Letter of Arthur P. Bagby, Senator in Congress, to the People of Alabama* (Washington, 1845).

37. *Niles' Weekly Register,* 16 (1844): 316–19.

38. This argument has a long history, dating back to antebellum times, but the fullest modern rendition is in Eugene Genovese, *The Political Economy of Slavery: Studies in the Economy and Society of the Slave South* (New York, 1965).

39. *Congressional Globe,* 28 Cong., 2 sess., Appendix (January 14, 1845): 108.

40. *Ibid.,* 28 Cong., 2 sess., Appendix (February 22, 1845): 283–88.

41. *Ibid.,* 28 Cong., 2 sess., Appendix (January 11, 1845): 93.

42. Hoke's speech of June 3, 1844, was printed in *Raleigh Standard,* June 12, 1844.

Chapter 24. The Electorate's Decision

1. The salient parts of Clay's Raleigh Letter are conveniently reprinted in *History of Presidential Elections,* ed. Schlesinger, 1: 814–17.

2. Southern Democrats' reaction to Van Buren's Hammet Letter is nicely illustrated in "Virginia and Texas," in *John P. Branch Historical Papers of Randolph-Macon College,* 4 (1913): 116–37.

3. Thomas Ritchie to Martin Van Buren, May 4, 1844, *ibid.,* 3 (1911): 250–51.

4. R. Hubbard to Thomas Ritchie, May 18, 1844, John R. Edmunds to Ritchie, May 12, 1844, *ibid.,* 4 (1913): 130–36.

5. Silas Wright to B. F. Butler, May 20, 1844, Wright-Butler Papers, New York Public Library.

6. The best discussion of the Democratic Convention of 1844 is in Sellers, *Polk, Continentalist,* ch. 3. Also useful is James C. M. Paul, *Rift in the Democracy* (Philadelphia, 1951).

7. The vote is accurately recorded in *History of Presidential Elections,* ed. Schlesinger, 1: 829, although the totals of the two columns have been switched.

8. The various presidential roll-call votes can be followed in *ibid.,* 1: 830–36, 840, 849.

9. Quoted in Sellers, *Polk, Continentalist,* 97.

10. Polk's a-southern expansionist thinking is obvious in his April 23, 1844, public letter to S. P. Chase, et al., *Niles' Weekly Register,* 16 (June 8, 1844): 228–29. Polk did not go public with his designs on California until the second year of his presidency. But his private outburst to George Bancroft, about the time of his inauguration, indicates that his continentalism early extended to the soon-to-be Golden State. See Bancroft, "Biographical Sketch of J. K. Polk," p. 25 of typescript, Bancroft Collection, New York Public Library. The background for California fever is conveyed in Norman A. Graebner, *Empire on the Pacific: A Study in American Continental Expansion* (New York, 1955).

11. *Congressional Globe,* 28 Cong., 1 sess. (June 8, 1844): 698.

12. *Ibid.* (June 8, 1844): Appendix, 720–27.

13. *Messages and Papers of the Presidents,* ed. Richardson, 3: 2176–80.

14. *Niles' Weekly Register,* 16 (August 24, 1844): 421–24; *Congressional Globe,* 28 Cong., 1 sess. (June 10, 1844): 699–703.

15. *Ibid.,* Appendix (May 23, 1844): 529–33.

16. The scene is well described in Smith, *Annexation of Texas,* 287.

17. Andrew Jackson to John Y. Mason, August 1, 1844, Jackson to William B. Lewis, August 1, 1844, John Tyler to Jackson, August 18, 1844, *Correspondence of Jackson,* ed. Bassett, 6: 304–8, 315.

18. Aberdeen's new departure is detailed in Pletcher, *Diplomacy of Annexation,* 156–62, and Adams, *British Interests,* 156–80.

19. Aberdeen to Pakenham, June 3, 1844, quoted in *ibid.,* 173.

20. Pakenham to Aberdeen, June 27, 1844, quoted in *ibid.,* 178–80.

21. *Richmond Enquirer,* June 29, 1844.

22. Albert Burnley to Beverley Tucker, October 13, 1844, March 21, 1845, Tucker-Coleman Papers, W&M. See also David Hayden's fascinating report in *Little Rock Banner,* May 1, 1844.

23. The salient parts of this Alabama Letter, July 27, 1844, addressed to Thomas M. Peters, et al., is in *History of Presidential Elections,* ed. Schlesinger, 1: 855–56.

24. *Ibid.,* 1: 857–58.

25. See the Fall 1844 files of the *Little Rock Arkansas Gazette, Milledgeville Southern Recorder, Richmond Whig, Tuscaloosa Independent Monitor, New Orleans Bee, Raleigh Register,* and *Vicksburg Weekly Whig.*

26. Robert Toombs to John M. Berrien, January 28, 1844, Berrien Papers, NC.

27. Election results are conveniently reprinted in *History of American Presidential Elections,* ed. Schlesinger, 1: 861.

28. My analysis of the North in the election of 1844 is based on the most up-to-date secondary sources, especially Sellers, *Polk, Continentalist,* ch. 4.

29. *Washington Madisonian,* September 21, 1844.

Chapter 25. The Congressional Decision

1. *Congressional Globe,* 28 Cong., 2 sess. (January 13, 1845): 129–30. The final wording of the Brown Amendment is conveniently reprinted in Merk, *Slavery and Annexation,* 289–90.

2. Joseph Peyton to William B. Campbell, February 16, 1845, Campbell Family Papers, DU. I managed to miss this wonderful document when going through the Campbell Papers, but fortunately Michael Holt brought it to my attention.

3. *Congressional Globe,* 28 Cong., 2 sess. (January 13, February 27, 1845): 127–28, 359–60.

4. *Ibid.,* 28 Cong., 2 sess. (January 25, 1845): Appendix, 309–14. Five years later, Stephens was still privately confessing that he held "no *very distinct* opinions" about the problems and future destinies of slavery. Alexander Stephens to Linton Stephens, March 25, 1850, SP.

5. *Congressional Globe,* 28 Cong., 2 sess. (January 25, 1845): 193–94.

6. *Ibid.,* 28 Cong., 1 sess. (June 6, 1844): Appendix, 693–96.

7. *Ibid.,* 28 Cong., 2 sess. (February 28, 1845): Appendix, 326–30. For another illuminating speech with a thesis close to Archer's, see Virginia's William C. Rives in *ibid.,* 28 Cong., 2 sess. (February 25, 1844), Appendix, 378–82.

8. For Barrow's speech, see *ibid.,* 28 Cong., 2 sess. (February 19, 1845): Appendix, 390–94. For Berrien's best speech, see *ibid.,* 28 Cong., 1 sess. (June 8, 1844), Appendix, 701–4, reiterated in *ibid.,* 28 Cong., 2 sess. (February 25, 1845): Appendix, 383–87.

9. *Ibid.,* 28 Cong., 2 sess. (February 21, 1845): Appendix, 229–33.

10. *Ibid.,* 28 Cong., 2 sess. (February 20, 1845): Appendix, 406–10.

11. *Ibid.,* 28 Cong., 2 sess. (February 27, 1845): 223–24.

12. For an illuminating example of Southern Whigs' predicament, see John C. Inscoe, "Thomas Clingman, Mountain Whiggery and the Southern Cause," *CWH,* 33 (1987): 42–62.

13. *Congressional Globe,* 28 Cong., 2 sess. (December 11, 1844): 19.

14. *Washington Globe,* August 29, 1844.

15. John M. Niles to Gideon Welles, January 12, 25, 1845, Welles Papers, LC. Niles's many letters to Welles during this congressional session offer the best guide to the Van Burenite mentality.

16. *Local Laws and Private Acts of the State of Missouri Passed at the First Session of the 13th General Assembly, 1844–1845* (Jefferson, Mo., 1845), 403–4.

17. *Congressional Globe,* 28 Cong., 1 sess. (February 5, 1845): 244.

18. Sellers, *Polk, Continentalist,* 205–20, expertly describes these maneuvers and shrewdly analyzes the President-elect's dissimulation.

19. *Congressional Globe,* 28 Cong., 2 sess. (February 27, 1845): 362.

20. *Ibid.,* 28 Cong., 2 sess. (February 28, 1845): 372.

21. Sellers, *Polk, Continentalist,* 215–16; Lyon G. Tyler, *Letters and Times of the Tylers,* 3 vols. (Richmond, 1884–96), 2: 447–48; John C. Calhoun to Andrew J. Donelson, March 3, 1845, *Diplomatic Correspondence of the United States,* ed. Manning, 12: 83–85.

22. James K. Polk to Andrew J. Donelson, March 7, 1845, Donelson Papers, LC.

23. Seller, *Polk, Continentalist,* 217; James Buchanan to Andrew J. Donelson, March 10, 1845, *Diplomatic Correspondence of the United States,* ed. Manning, 12: 85–88.

24. James K. Polk to William H. Haywood, Jr., August 9, 1845, Polk Papers, LC.

25. Merk, *Slavery and Annexation,* 168–70.

26. *Ibid.,* 171.

27. *Ibid.,* 174.

Chapter 26. Loaded Words, Loathsome Collaborations

1. A. J. Donelson to James Buchanan, April 12, 1845, *Diplomatic Correspondence of the United States,* ed. Manning, 12: 400–402; James K. Polk to Sam Houston, June 6, 1845, Polk Papers, LC.

2. Sellers, *Polk, Continentalist,* 227–30, 398–409, expertly traces these matters. See also Glenn W. Price, *Origins of the War with Mexico: The Polk-Stockton Intrigue* (Austin, 1967).

3. *Congressional Globe,* 29 Cong., 2 sess. (May 11, 1846): 792–94, (May 12, 1846): 795–804; *Charleston Mercury,* May 15, 1846.

4. Merk, *Manifest Destiny and Mission,* 149–56, 169–72; John H. Schroeder, *Mr. Polk's War: Opposition and Dissent, 1846–1848* (Madison, 1973).

5. Holt, *Political Crisis of the 1850s,* 57–58.

6. *Greenville Mountaineer,* October 15, 1847.

7. *Congressional Globe,* 29 Cong., 2 sess. (February 9, 1847): Appendix, 323–27, 30 Cong., 1 sess. (January 4, 1848): 96–100; Ernest M. Lander, Jr., *Reluctant Imperialists: Calhoun, the South Carolinians, and the Mexican War* (Baton Rouge, 1980).

8. Merk, *Manifest Destiny and Mission,* 107–43; John D. P. Fuller, *Movement for the Acquisition of All Mexico, 1846–48* (Baltimore, 1936).

9. A sharp short treatment is in Sellers, *Polk, Continentalist,* 476–84. The best full account is Chaplain W. Morrison, *Democratic Politics and Sectionalism: The Wilmot Proviso Controversy* (Chapel Hill, 1967). The best biography is Charles Buxton Going, *David Wilmot, Free-Soiler . . .* (New York, 1924). A valuable essay is Eric Foner, "The Wilmot Proviso Revisited," *JAH* 46 (1969): 262–79. Foner's *Free Soil, Free Labor, Free Men: The Ideology of the Republican Party Before the Civil War* (New York, 1970) and Richard H. Sewell, *Ballots for Freedom: American Antislavery Politics in the United States* (New York, 1976) provide perspectives on northern opposition to Slavepower expansionism.

10. *Congressional Globe* 29 Cong., 2 sess. (February 8, 1847): Appendix, 314–18. For the ferocity of Wilmot's sheerly political hatred of the Slavepower, see Wilmot to Franklin Pierce, July 13, 1852, Pierce Papers, New Hampshire Historical Society.

11. Merk, *Manifest Destiny and Mission,* 180–88.

12. Greater Whig scoffing at slavery's practicality in the Mexican Cession is obvious in important Whig newspapers such as the *Richmond Whig, Milledgeville Southern Recorder, New Orleans Bee,* and *Raleigh Register,* 1847–48, and in the Toombs and Stephens letters expertly collected in *The Correspondence of Robert Toombs, Alexander Stephens and Howell Cobb,* ed. Ulrich B. Phillips (Washington, 1913), 61–104, and in the 1847–48 John M. Clayton and John C. Crittenden Papers, LC. The greater Democratic sense that the Cession might prove helpful, and that the Lower South must not be hemmed in, and that Upper South whites, selling ever more slaves southwards, might adopt ever more insidiously northern opinions is obvious in *The Montgomery Advertizer* and Jackson Semi-Weekly Mississippian. On the whole problem, see Desmond D. Hart, "The Natural Limits of Slave Expansion: The Mexican Territories as a Test Case," *Mid-America,* 52 (1970): 119–31.

13. This interpretation of the South and the Proviso follows, with qualifications, the currently burgeoning republicanism thesis about the causes of the Civil War, an inter-

pretation sweepingly defended in Holt, *Political Crisis of the 1850s,* and more narrowly for Alabama by Thornton, *Power and Politics in Alabama,* and for South Carolina by Ford, *Origins of South Carolina Radicalism.* Like the earlier so-called Revisionist historians, these scholars would revise away notions that moral passion to abolish slavery swept up the North or that attempts to save slavery explain political behavior in the South. But republicanism theorists reject Revisionists' conclusion: that given the alleged emptiness of slavery issues in the antebellum period, irresponsible politicians must have caused needless Civil War. Rather, republicanism theorists explain politicians' stridencies in terms of political world views, particularly the ideology of egalitarian republicanism. Northerners came to believe, runs this theory, that the haughty Slavepower unacceptably threatened a sound republic. Southerners meanwhile came to believe that the North's anti-Slavepower haughtiness unacceptably condemned Southerners as unequal republicans.

Readers of these pages will know that I find this viewpoint extremely helpful in explaining the North, less often the key to understanding the South. On the southern side, elitists scornful of egalitarian republicanism precipitated many crises, including secession. Furthermore, the nature of slavery as a social system led to some not-very-egalitarian-republican means of southern internal control, especially physical violence, verbal proscriptions, and malapportioned legislatures. In the federal sphere, these dubiously egalitarian-republican attitudes spilled over into imperiously demanding southern political styles, censured mails, gag rules, three-fifths clauses, not-so-democratic fugitive slave laws, and draconic sedition laws in bleeding Kansas. These differences between northern and southern styles of republicanism are precisely why anti-Slavepower campaigns in the North, so well explained by republicanism theorists, were so powerful.

Above all else, the egalitarian-republican thesis so useful about the North cannot be as universally applied to the South because the South's highly inegalitarian Peculiar Institution could not be altogether walled off from white men's egalitarian political institutions and attitudes. Republicanism theorists assume that the color line was an impenetrable wall, that black slavery's only impact on white politics was to make white egalitarians more passionately protective of their own equality. The burden of my social history chapters is that the color line could not always hold, that control over blacks often conditioned control over whites and vice versa, that white egalitarianism inevitably acquired some coloration of domineering styles towards blacks. The burden of my political history chapters is that the resulting mongrelized form of social control in the South had its perceived limits, that limits were perceived as most intrusive in the southern hinterlands, and that most antebellum political crises, including Missouri, Gag Rule, Texas, Fugitive Slave, and Kansas controversies began with southern attempts to find practical remedies for these perceived weaknesses at the fringes. That these forays in practicality turned out to be impractical illuminates the comic irony in so much human striving—and the intractable *social* situation which made southern politics transcend the *political.*

This line of analysis has a degree of applicability to the Proviso crisis. Particularly among Lower South Democrats and especially among those early tending towards disunion, Yankees who would cordon Southerners off from expanding and Border South reformers who would push blacks onto the contained Lower South came together in southern visions of imminent catastrophe. Deep South Democrats also often saw particularly California as practical for slavery and one way to win relief from containment. But even these gentlemen talked more often of David Wilmot's insult than about his immediate practical danger; and for the larger number of moderates who thought the diagnosis exaggerated, California was too far off, Border South reform was too distant, and the resulting claustrophobia was too dim to make for an immediate practical crisis. For these centrists, and especially for Whigs, drives to protect *their* equality from Wilmot's insult was pivotal. Michael Holt's *The Political Crisis of the 1850s,* 49–56, splendidly drives that republicanism thesis home.

As will soon be clear, I also think the republicanism thesis helps explain why those Southerners who doubted that Kansas would prove useful to slavery still supported precipitators who called Kansas-Nebraska an indispensable slaveholder practicality. Egalitarian republican explanations sometimes help bypass the "needless war" thesis precisely because the Slave South was deeply implicated in American egalitarian culture. But the democrat as slaveholder was also a quirky American egalitarian. The dialectic between the typicality and the quirkiness reveals ever so much about this slavocracy, and about the national egalitarian and especially Jacksonian strains which this regional variation did centrally imbibe, influence—and violate too.

14. Alexander Stephens to Linton Stephens, January 21, 1850, SP.

15. Quoted in Morrison, *Democratic Politics and Sectionalism*, 65.

16. Quoted in *ibid.*, 66.

17. *Edgefield Advertizer*, November 28, 1860; *Charleston Mercury*, December 4, 1860.

18. See for example Joseph E. Brown in the Georgia state senate in 1850 as quoted in Ulrich B. Phillips, *The Life of Robert Toombs* (New York, 1913), 92; James Hammond to Beverley Tucker, March 25, 1850, Tucker-Coleman Papers, W&M; Jefferson Davis to M. D. Haynes, August 18, 1849, in Supplement to *Jackson Semi-Weekly Mississippian*, October 1849; *Montgomery Advertizer*, November 20–21, 1849.

19. *Congressional Globe*, 29 Cong., 2 sess. (February 19, 1847): 454.

20. The latest full-scale history is Harold D. Tallant, "The Slavery Controversy in Kentucky, 1829–1859," unpubl. Ph.D. diss., Duke University, 1986, but still useful is Asa Martin, *The Anti-Slavery Movement in Kentucky Before 1850* (Louisville, 1918).

21. The best biography is David L. Smiley, *Lion of White Hall: The Life of Cassius M. Clay* (Madison, 1962). A cautionary note is sounded in Stanley Harrold, "Cassius M. Clay and Slavery and Race: A Reinterpretation," *Slavery and Abolition*, 9 (1988): 42–56.

22. *The Writings of Cassius Marcellus Clay . . .* , ed. Horace Greeley (New York, 1848), 174.

23. Smiley, *Lion of White Hall*, 48.

24. *Writings of Cassius Clay*, ed. Greeley, 211–373; *Speech of C. M. Clay at Lexington, Ky., Delivered August 1, 1851* (n.p., n.d.; copy in LC).

25. John M. Fee to Cassius Clay, August 17, 1849, Fee Papers, BC.

26. *Writings of Cassius Clay*, ed. Greeley, 214.

27. *Ibid.*, 337–38.

28. Cassius Clay to John M. Fee, July 8, 1855, Fee Papers, BC.

29. *Writings of Cassius Clay*, ed. Greeley, 285.

30. *Ibid.*, 308.

31. *Ibid.*, 289; *Speech of Clay, August 1, 1851,* 15–18.

32. *Louisville Journal*, January 29, 1849.

33. *Louisville Courier*, May 3–4, 1849.

34. *Ibid.*, July 4, 1849. For other prime examples of this omnipresent line of argument, see the files of the *Louisville Examiner*, 1847–49, and the *Louisville Courier*, 1849.

35. *Frankfort Yeoman*, November 30, 1848. The files of the *Yeoman*, 1848–49, best illustrate the tone of the establishment's campaign. See also George Prentice's illuminating editorials in *Louisville Journal*, January 23, February 23, 1849.

36. *Louisville Courier*, June 25, July 10, September 1, 1849; A. G. Hodges to Orlando Brown, June 18, 1849, Brown Papers, FC.

37. *Louisville Courier*, September 1, 1849.

38. *Frankfort Yeoman*, November 22, 1849.

39. *Ibid.*, December 20, 1849.

40. *Ibid.*, October 18, 1849.

41. *Ibid.*, December 20, 1849.

42. *Ibid.*, February 10, 1860.

43. Cassius Clay to Mrs. G. O. Smith, April 20, 1851, Clay Papers, FC.

44. Quoted in Smiley, *Lion of White Hall,* 142. Clay's most important newspaper backer put the case against constant agitation the same way. *Louisville Courier,* March 3, 1851. For a good example of the intense pressure to conform, see J. G. Davis to Robert C. Breckinridge, June 27, 1851, Breckinridge Family Papers, LC. For a superb analysis of how the same pressures to conform worked in the postbellum South, see C. Vann Woodward, *Thinking Back: The Perils of Writing History* (Baton Rouge, 1986), 14–17.

45. Cassius Clay to Robert M. Breckinridge, February 7, 1851, Breckinridge Family Papers, LC.

46. Cassius Clay to Salmon P. Chase, August 12, 1851, Chase Papers, Historical Society of Pennsylvania.

47. Wilson Lumpkin to John C. Calhoun, January 3, 1849, Calhoun Papers, CU.

48. *DeBow's Review,* 7 (1849): 205.

49. James L. Hammond to John C. Calhoun, March 5, 1850, in *Correspondence of John C. Calhoun,* ed. J. Franklin Jameson (Washington, 1900): 1211.

50. C. R. Clifton to Calhoun, January 30, 1849, Calhoun Papers, CU; Henry L. Benning to Howell Cobb, July 1, 1849, *Correspondence of Toombs, Stephens, and Cobb,* ed. Phillips, 168–72; David Johnson to Calhoun, October 18, 1848, Calhoun Papers, CU; M.C.M. Hammond to James Hammond, December 17, 1849, Hammond Papers, LC. See also Jeremiah Clemens to Calhoun, January 8, 1849, Calhoun Papers, CU.

51. For a good example of this frequent theme in the Democratic establishment press, see *Jackson Semi-Weekly Mississippian,* March 9, 1849.

52. *Speeches of Brown,* ed. Cluskey, 324.

Chapter 27. Southern Convention, Without a South

1. Good accounts of the election of 1848 include Joseph G. Rayback, *Free Soil: The Election of 1848* (Lexington, Ky., 1970); Holman Hamilton, "Election of 1848," in *History of American Presidential Elections,* ed. Schlesinger, 2: 865–96; Norman Graebner, "1848: Southern Politics at the Crossroads," *The Historian,* 25 (1962): 14–35.

2. The ambiguous doctrine is fully discussed in Milo Milton Quiafe, *The Doctrine of Non-Intervention with Slavery in the Territories* (Chicago, 1910), and succinctly defined in David M. Potter, *The Impending Crisis, 1848–1861* (New York, 1976), 58–60.

3. Alexander Stephens to I. W. Harris, February 11, 1848, Stephens Papers, LC. Southern Whigs' loyalty campaign in Taylor's behalf is well explored in Cooper, *South and the Politics of Slavery,* 244–68.

4. Holman Hamilton, *Zachary Taylor, Soldier in the White House* (Indianapolis, 1951), 38–133, is good on the Taylor candidacy.

5. Holt, *Political Crisis of the 1850s,* 62–63, expertly lays out the No Party aspect of the Taylor movement.

6. Robert Barnwell to Robert Barnwell Rhett, November 11, 1844, in "Hamlet to Hotspur: Letters of Robert Woodward Barnwell to Robert Barnwell Rhett," *SCHM,* 77 (1976): 251–52.

7. The battle between these two sorts of secessionists is detailed in Chauncey S. Boucher, "The Secession and Co-operation Movements in South Carolina, 1848–1852," *Washington University Studies,* 5 (1918): 67–129. The fullest version of Carolina's mid-century crisis can be found in John Barnwell, *Love of Order: South Carolina's First Secession Crisis* (Chapel Hill, 1982). The best biography of Rhett is Laura A. White, *Robert Barnwell Rhett: Father of Secession* (New York, 1931). Rhett's spirit suffuses Rhett to Armistead Burt, March 18, 1845, Burt Papers, DU, and Rhett to Robert M. T. Hunter, August 30, 1844, in *Correspondence of Robert M. T. Hunter, 1826–1876,* ed. Charles H. Ambler (Washington, 1918), 70–71.

8. *Sacred and Secret Diaries of Hammond,* ed. Bleser, 173–75.

9. *Ibid.,* 171.

10. James Hammond, *Two Letters on Slavery in the United States, Addressed to Thomas Clarkson, Esq.* (Columbia, 1845). For an extremely revealing Hammond letter on diseased opinion, even in proslavery circles beyond South Carolina, see Hammond to Calhoun, August 18, 1845, *Correspondence of Calhoun,* ed. Jameson, 1045–49.

11. Calhoun to John H. Means, April 13, 1849, *Correspondence of Calhoun,* ed. Jameson, 764–66; Calhoun to Maryland Governor Thomas, January 5, 1850, Calhoun Papers, SC.

12. Wiltse, *Calhoun, Sectionalist,* 377–88.

13. Robert Toombs to John J. Crittenden, January 3, 22, 1849, *Correspondence of Toombs, Stephens, and Cobb,* ed. Phillips, 139, 141; Alexander Stephens to Crittenden, January 17, 1847, Stephens Papers, DU.

14. Howell Cobb to John B. Lamar, January 16, 24, 1849, Cobb Papers, GA; Cobb to his wife, February 8, 1849, Cobb et al. to their constituents, February 26, 1849, both in "Howell Cobb Papers," ed. R. F. Brooks, *GHQ,* 5 (1921): 38–52.

15. See Joel H. Silbey, "John C. Calhoun and the Limits of Southern Congressional Unity, 1841–1850," *The Historian,* 30 (1967): 58–71, and more broadly, Silbey's very important and aptly entitled *The Shrine of Party: Congressional Voting Behavior, 1841–1852* (Pittsburgh, 1967).

16. *The Works of John C. Calhoun,* ed. Richard K. Crallé, 6 vols. (New York, 1854–57), 6: 185–313.

17. John C. Calhoun to Henry W. Conner, February 2, 1849, Calhoun to J. R. Mathews, June 20, 1848, Calhoun Papers, DU.

18. A. Hutchinson to John C. Calhoun, October 5, 1849, Calhoun Papers, CU.

19. D. Wallace to Whitemarsh Seabrook, October 20, November 7, 1849, Seabrook Papers, LC.

20. *Jackson Weekly Mississippian,* November 30, 1849.

21. *Ibid.,* October 5, 1849.

22. Calhoun to David L. Yulee, October 19, 1849, Yulee Papers, University of Florida Library.

23. James Hammond to Edmund Ruffin, February 8, 1850, Ruffin Papers, VHS.

24. Hammond to Beverley Tucker, May 14, 1850, Tucker-Coleman Papers, W&M.

25. Good descriptions of antebellum Nashville include Mary Ellen Gadski, "The Tennessee Capitol: An Architectural History," *THQ,* 47 (1988): 67–120; James H. Atherton to Mary Anne Atherton, November 24, 1831, A. T. Hamilton to John Hamilton, March 10, 1859, both in correspondence by subject file, TN; Olmsted, *Texas,* 35–36. But the best way to visualize the area is to go see it, especially Strickland's capitol building and Jackson's Hermitage.

26. By far the best secondary account is Thelma Jennings, *The Nashville Convention: Southern Movement for Unity, 1848–1851* (Memphis, 1980). By far the fullest and most valuable account by a participant is William F. Cooper to D. R. Arnell, June 18, 1850, in Cooper Letterbook, 1848–61, TN.

27. *Secret and Sacred Diary of Hammond,* ed. Bleser, entry for August 10, 1850. See also D. F. Jamison to Isaac Holmes, September 20, 1850, Holmes Papers, LC.

28. Robert J. Brugger, *Beverley Tucker: Heart Over Head in the Old South* (Baltimore, 1978) is one of the best biographies of a southern fire-eater.

29. Edward William Sidney (pseud. for Beverley Tucker), *The Partisan Leader: A Tale of the Future,* 2 vols. (Washington, 1836), I: 42–43, 65–66.

30. Tucker to Hammond, December 27, 1849, Hammond Papers, LC.

31. Tucker to St. George Tucker, March 10, 1822, Tucker-Coleman Papers, W&M.

32. Tucker to James Hammond, February 17, 1836, Hammond Papers, LC.

33. Tucker to St. George Tucker, March 10, 1822, Tucker-Coleman Papers, W&M.

34. Tucker to Hammond, April 15, 1850, Hammond Papers, LC; Tucker to Thomas Smith, May 15, 1829, Tucker-Coleman Papers, W&M.

35. Good descriptions of the very tense, very haughty Tucker, as he with "great

fear," despite "want of voice," voiced the speech of his life (Tucker to Lucy Ann Tucker, June 8, 1850, Tucker-Coleman Papers, W&M), include Hammond to William Gilmore Simms, June 16, 1850, Hammond Papers, LC; Nashville Convention Ms. in Robert F. W. Allston Papers, SCHS.

36. Nathaniel Beverley Tucker, *Prescience: A Speech Delivered by the Hon. Beverley Tucker of Virginia, in the Southern Convention Held at Nashville, Tennessee, April 13, 1850* (Richmond, 1862).

37. *Jackson Weekly Mississippian,* June 21, 1850.

Chapter 28. The Armistice of 1850

1. I take my chapter title from my favorite chapter in my favorite synthesis of the late antebellum period, David Potter's *The Impending Crisis.* The occasion gives me an opportunity to note the direct impact of an indirect influence which pervades these pages in ways I cannot trace, much less fully acknowledge. When I was first formulating this project, I had several long conversations with Professor Potter. I was then a fledgling and he a titan in our profession. He nevertheless always had the time, patience, and sensitivity to focus unendingly on my notions. His gentle rebukes were always the same. That subtle and complex antebellum world sprawls beyond any simplistic formula. His own book, published posthumously, brilliantly perpetuates that spirit.

2. William Henry Ellison, *A Self Governing Dominion: California, 1849–1860* (Berkeley, 1950); Cardinal Goodwin, *The Establishment of State Government in California, 1846–1850* (New York, 1914).

3. Loomis Morton Ganaway, *New Mexico and the Sectional Controversy, 1846–1861* (Albuquerque, 1944); Kenneth F. Neighbours, "The Taylor-Neighbors Struggle Over the Upper Rio Grande Region of Texas in 1850," *SWHQ,* 61 (1958): 431–63.

4. Holman Hamilton, "Texas Bonds and Northern Profits," *MVHR,* 43 (1957): 579–94.

5. Paul Finkelman, "Prigg v. Pennsylvania and Northern State Courts: Anti-Slavery Use of a Pro-Slavery Decision," *CWH,* 25 (1979): 5–35.

6. Thomas D. Morris, *Free Men All: The Personal Liberty Laws of the North, 1780–1861* (Baltimore, 1974).

7. Robert Toombs to John J. Crittenden, January 3, 1849, *Correspondence of Toombs, Stephens, and Cobb,* ed. Phillips, 139; Alexander Stephens to Crittenden, January 17, 1949, Stephens Papers, DU.

8. Hamilton, *Taylor,* is particularly fine on this point. For a later but not necessarily better biography, see K. Jack Bauer, *Zachary Taylor: Soldier, Planter, Statesman of the Old Southwest* (Baton Rouge, 1980).

9. Zachary Taylor to ?, August 16, 1847, Taylor Papers, LC.

10. *Messages and Papers of the President,* ed. Richardson, 3: 2556–57. See also Taylor's special message of January 23, 1850, *ibid.,* 3: 2564–68.

11. Holt, *Political Crisis of the 1850s,* 72–76, makes this point very well.

12. Quoted in Potter, *Impending Crisis,* 92n.

13. Mark J. Stegmaier, "Zachary Taylor Versus the South," *CWH,* 33 (1987): 219–41.

14. *The Papers of Henry Clay,* eds. James F. Hopkins, et al., 9 volumes published to date (Lexington, Ky., 1959–88), 1: 3–8.

15. Henry Clay to Richard Pindall et al., February 17, 1849, in *Louisville Journal,* March 5, 1849, reprinted in *Works of Clay,* ed. Colton, 3: 346–52.

16. *Ibid.,* 3: 61–69.

17. Unless otherwise noted, this discussion is based on Clay's resolutions and short comments upon introducing them [*Congressional Globe,* 31 Cong., 1 sess. (January 19, 1850): 244–47] and his major speech in their behalf [(*ibid.,* February 5–6, 1850): Appen-

dix, 115–27]. The best book on the congressional deliberations is Holman Hamilton, *Prologue to Conflict: The Crisis and Compromise of 1850* (Lexington, Ky., 1964).

18. The exact language of Clay's resolution on this point: The Texas boundary should run up the Rio Grande River "to the southern line of New Mexico; and thence with that line eastwardly, and so continuing in the same direction to the line as established between the United States and Spain." *Congressional Globe*, 31 Cong., 1 sess., Appendix, 115. The exact language of Clay's explanatory speech of January 29, 1850: The Texas boundary shall follow the Rio Grande "to where it strikes the southern line of New Mexico and then . . . follow on in that direction until it reaches the line as fixed by the United States and Spain in their treaty of 1819." *Ibid.*, text page 245.

19. The Clay quote is from *ibid.*, 245. See the useful comparative maps in Hamilton, *Prologue to Conflict*, 57.

20. William C. Pool, *A Historical Atlas of Texas* (Austin, 1975), and especially William Thorndale and William Dollarhide, *Map Guide to the U.S. Federal Census* (Baltimore, 1987), are useful in locating counties.

21. Clay made this important point in separate comments to the Senate on May 13. *Congressional Globe*, 31 Cong., 1 sess., Appendix, 572.

22. Two books place Jefferson Davis's plantation practices in perspective: James T. Currie, *Enclave: Vicksburg and Her Plantations, 1863–1870* (Jackson, Miss., 1980) and Janet T. Hermann, *The Pursuit of a Dream* (New York, 1981).

23. Davis's speech can be found in *Congressional Globe*, 31 Cong., 1 sess. (February 13–14, 1850): Appendix, 149–57.

24. For Clay's explanation, see *ibid.* (June 7, 1850): 1155. On whether Congress meant to declare Popular Sovereignty operative in the *territorial* phase, I agree with Potter, *Impending Crisis*, 117n, that a law without any declaration on the subject does not declare a policy operative, especially since congressmen declared that a hopelessly divided Congress was in no position to affirm anything more than Popular Sovereignty in the *statehood* phase. The contrast with the Kansas-Nebraska Act is instructive; there Congress explicitly declared Popular Sovereignty could be exercised on slavery in *the territory or the statehood* phases. For a well-argued contrary view, see Robert R. Russel, "What Was the Compromise of 1850," *JSH*, 22 (1956): 292–309.

25. *Congressional Globe*, 31 Cong., 1 sess. (August 19, 1850): Appendix, 1588.

26. *Ibid.* (August 19, 1850): Appendix, 1583.

27. *Ibid.* (August 19, 1850): Appendix, 1588.

28. Some southern congressmen so realized. See Richard Parker to Charles Faulkner, June 20, 1850, Faulkner Papers, WVU.

29. A point wonderfully made in one of the most important essays on antebellum politics: Arthur Bestor, "State Sovereignty and Slavery: A Reinterpretation of Proslavery Constitutional Doctrine, 1840–1860," *Illinois State Historical Society Journal*, 64 (1961): 117–80.

30. *Congressional Globe*, 31 Cong., 1 sess. (August 21, 23, 1850): Appendix, 1601, 1622.

31. *Ibid.* (August 20–21, 1850): Appendix, 1590–1605.

32. For some fine examples of the fugitive slave affair raising basic questions about the Border South, see William S. Beard to R. J. Breckinridge, July 1, 1850, Breckinridge Family Papers, LC; *Charleston Mercury*, July 8, 1857; Charles J. Faulkner in the Virginia House of Delegates, December 15, 1848, quoted in Henry Shanks, *The Secession Movement in Virginia, 1847–1861* (Richmond, 1934), 39–40; E. H. Gouldring to My Dear Friend, August 11, 1848, Gouldring Papers, University of Kentucky Library.

33. David Outlaw to his wife, July 29, August 8, 10, 1850, Outlaw Papers, NC.

34. *Congressional Globe*, 31 Cong., 1 sess. (August 22, 1850): Appendix, 1614.

35. *Ibid.* (August 20, 1850): Appendix, 1591.

36. *Ibid.* (August 21, 1850): Appendix, 1603.

37. *Ibid.* (August 20, 22, 1850): Appendix, part 2, 1598, 1616.

38. *Ibid.* (August 22, 1850): Appendix, 1617.

39. *Ibid.* (August 22, 1850): Appendix, 1614.

40. *Ibid.* (August 22, 1850): Appendix, 1609.

41. *Ibid.* (August 1, 1850): Appendix, 1485.

42. Ward M. McAfee, "California's House Divided," *CWH*, 33 (1987): 115–30; Paul Finkelman, "The Law of Slavery and Freedom in California, 1848–1860," *California Western Law Review*, 17 (1981): 437–64.

43. *Congressional Globe*, 31 Cong., 1 sess. (August 1, 1850): Appendix, 1485–86.

44. *Ibid.* (August 1, 1850): Appendix, 1486–90.

45. *Ibid.* (August 2, 1850): Appendix, 1504.

46. Hamilton, *Prologue to Conflict*, chs. 6, 8, follows the unraveling of the Omnibus and Douglas's rescue job deftly.

47. *Ibid.*, 191–94, prints the Senate roll calls.

48. *Ibid.*, 195–200, prints the House roll calls.

49. Potter, *Impending Crisis*, 113, makes this excellent point.

Chapter 29. The Paralysis of the Old Order

1. The most accessible sources on the convention debates are the 92 convention supplements printed in Richmond newspapers. LC has a good run, and fuller files still are in VSL and W&M. The fullest treatment of the Convention is Francis P. Gaines, Jr., "The Virginia Constitutional Convention of 1850–1: A Study in Sectionalism," unpubl. Ph.D. diss., University of Virginia, 1950. The best short discussion is Craig Simpson, "Political Compromise and the Protection of Slavery: Henry A. Wise and the Virginia Constitutional Convention of 1850–51," *VMBH*, 83 (1975): 387–405. I am indebted to Professor Simpson for his comments on this chapter.

2. Willey's speech of February 24, 1851, and Summers's of June 17, 1851, were printed in supplements 14 and 43 respectively. Revealing runs of letters from western Virginia constituents to Willey and to his convention ally, Gideon Camden, are in the Willey Papers and the Camden Papers, WVU.

3. Goode's speech of April 16, 19, 1851, was printed in supplement 40.

4. Barbour's speech of February 27, 1851, and Garnett's of April 14, 1851, were printed in supplements 15 and 45 respectively. Garnett's speech is a special reactionary republican statement. Even more special is Garnett's pamphlet *The Union Past and Future: How It Works and How to Save It* (Washington, 1850; published under the pseudonym "A Citizen of Virginia"). A fine string of private letters to and from Garnett is in the William Garnett Chisolm Papers, VHS. See also William J. Robertson to M.R.H. Garnett, March 16, 1850, Garnett-Hunter Papers, VA.

5. On Wise, one of the most important southern antebellum politicians, we fortunately have one of the best southern biographies: Craig M. Simpson, *A Good Southerner: The Life of Henry A. Wise of Virginia* (Chapel Hill, 1985). A good physical description of Wise the orator is in John P. Little, *History of Richmond* (Richmond, 1933), 261–66.

6. The quote is from Wise's speech of March 27, 1851, printed in supplement 29.

7. The quotes in these two paragraphs are from *ibid.*, from Wise's speech of May 5, 1851, printed in supplement 38, and from his illuminating exchange with the western Virginia reformer George Summers and the eastern Virginia conservative Robert E. Scott on February 17, 1851, printed in supplement 13. Wise's five-day speech to the convention of April 23–28 was unfortunately never printed, but an incomplete version is in Wise Papers, NC.

8. The convention votes and final wordings are expertly followed in Simpson, *Wise*, 83–85.

9. M.R.H. Garnett to William Henry Trescot, February 16, 1851, William Garnett Chisolm Papers, VHS.

10. Trescot to Garnett, March 14, 1851, Chisolm Papers, VHS.

11. Marilyn McAdams Sibley, "James Hamilton, Jr., Versus Sam Houston, Repercussions of the Nullification Controversy," *SWHQ,* 90 (1985): 164–80; Lawrence S. Rowland, "'Alone on the River': The Rise and Fall of the Savannah River Rice Plantations of St. Peter's Parish, South Carolina," *SCHM,* 88 (1987): 121–50, esp. 142–43.

12. *Works of Calhoun,* ed. Crallé, 4: 542–73.

13. *Ibid.,* 4: 574–78.

14. *Selections from the Letters and Speeches of the Hon. James H. Hammond of South Carolina* (New York, 1866), 233–301, esp. 262.

15. *Works of Calhoun,* ed. Crallé, 1: 1–406. For a more extensive discussion of the interpretation outlined here, see my "Spoilsmen and Interests in the Thought and Career of John C. Calhoun," *JAH,* 52 (1965): 25–42.

16. The best biography is Archie Vernon Huff, Jr., *Langdon Cheves of South Carolina* (Columbia, 1977). For Cheves's oration, see *Speech of Langdon Cheves in the Southern Convention at Nashville, Tennessee, November 14, 1850* (n.p., 1850; copy in LC).

17. Whitemarsh Seabrook to Peter H. Bell, September 11, 1850, Bell Papers, TX.

18. Seabrook to the governors of Alabama, Virginia, and Mississippi, September 20, 1850, Seabrook Papers, LC.

19. G. W. Towns to Seabrook, September 25, 1851, Seabrook Papers, LC.

20. Seabrook to Towns, October 8, 1850, Seabrook Papers, LC. See also Seabrook to John A. Leland, September 18, 21, 1850, same collection.

21. John Quitman to Whitemarsh Seabrook, September 29, 1850, Seabrook Papers, LC. Quitman's 1850–51 correspondence with Seabrook is conveniently available in almost-complete form in J.F.H. Claiborne, *Life and Correspondence of John A. Quitman,* 2 vols. (New York, 1860), 2: 36–40, 123–43. But enough bits and pieces are missing, including some lines here quoted, so that citing the originals seems preferable.

22. Seabrook to Quitman, October 23, 1850, Claiborne Papers, MISS.

23. Quitman to Robert Barnwell Rhett, November 30, 1850, Seabrook Papers, LC: Seabrook to Quitman, December 17, 1850, Claiborne Papers, MISS.

24. Barnwell, *Love of Order,* 138–41, expertly analyzes the legislative proceedings. Seabrook's pleasure with himself is clear in his December 17, 1851, letter to Quitman, Claiborne Papers, MISS.

25. Quitman to John S. Preston, March 29, 1851, Quitman to J. H. Means, May 25, 1851, Claiborne, *Quitman,* 2: 123–27, 135–36.

26. Helpful works on the Georgis crisis of 1850, aside from the biographies cited below, notes 27–29, include Richard H. Shryock, *Georgia and the Union in 1850* (Durham, N.C., 1926); John T. Hubbell, "Three Georgia Unionists and the Compromise of 1850," *GHQ,* 51 (1967): 307–23; Horace Montgomery, "The Crisis of 1850 and Its Effect on Political Parties in Georgia," *GHQ,* 24 (1940): 293–322; Montgomery, *Cracker Parties* (Baton Rouge, 1950); R. P. Brooks, "Howell Cobb and the Crisis of 1850," *MVHR,* 4 (1917): 279–98.

27. The best biography, but one leaving room for yet another, is John Eddins Simpson, *Howell Cobb: The Politics of Ambition* (Chicago, 1973).

28. While William Y. Thompson, *Robert Toombs of Georgia* (Baton Rouge, 1966), has probably superseded Phillips, *Toombs,* a yet finer biography seems possible.

29. Despite the recent appearance of Thomas E. Schott, *Alexander H. Stephens of Georgia: A Biography* (Baton Rouge, 1988), my favorite Stephens biography remains perhaps the best unpublished biography of an antebellum Southerner: James Z. Rabun, "Alexander H. Stephens, 1812–1861," unpubl. Ph.D. diss., U. of Chicago, 1948.

30. The best private letters on the resistance-is-not-secession theme include Alfred Iverson to John M. Berrien, October 23, 1850, Berrien Papers, NC, and John Forsyth to Wilson Lumpkin, October 14, 1851, Keith Read Papers, GA. My favorite Georgia resistance pamphlet is Mirabeau B. Lamar, *Letter to the People of Georgia* (n.p., n.d.; copy in

LC). The best resistance newspapers include the *Macon Journal and Messenger, Milledge-ville Federal Union,* and *Columbus Times.*

31. Alexander Stephens to John J. Crittenden, October 24, 1850, Stephens Papers, DU. See also Stephens to Crittenden, November 11, 1850, same collection; Francis S. Bartow to John M. Berrien, August 14, 1851, Berrien Papers, NC. The best Unionist Georgia sources include the *Milledgeville Southern Recorder* and the *Correspondence of Toombs, Stephens, and Cobb,* ed. Phillips, 163ff.

32. *Debates and Proceedings of the Georgia Convention, 1850* (Milledgeville, 1850).

33. On the intriguing debate within the Unionist Party over whether secession was constitutional, see Stephen to Cobb, June 23, 1851, *Correspondence of Toombs, Stephens, and Cobb,* ed. Phillips, 237–38; Toombs to Cobb, June 9, 1851, *GHQ,* 5 (1921): 45–46.

34. The best monograph is the old but informative Cleo Hearon, "Mississippi and the Convention of 1850," *Mississippi Historical Society Publications,* 14 (1914): 7–229.

35. John A. Quitman, *Message to the Special Session of the Legislature, November 18, 1850* (Jackson, 1850). Quitman's private correspondence shows his total belief in this cause. See Quitman to his wife, September 21, 1850, and to his daughter, October 1, 1850, Quitman Papers, NC. The best biography is Robert E. May, *John Quitman: Old South Crusader* (Baton Rouge, 1985). Also useful is John McCardell, "John A. Quitman and the Compromise of 1850 in Mississippi," *Journal of Mississippi History,* 37 (1975): 239–66.

36. J. P. Walworth to his son, 1850, Samuel Cartwright Papers, in private hands. For an agonized admission that Mississippi must simmer down despite the intolerable so-called compromise, see Jacob Thompson, *Address of Hon. Jacob Thompson of Mississippi, to His Constituents* (Washington, 1851). For a more conventional Unionist statement, see Samuel S. Boyd, *Speech of Hon. Samuel S. Boyd Delivered . . . on the 10th Day of October, 1851* (Natchez, 1851).

37. J. W. McDonald to Quitman, April 3, 1851, Claiborne Papers, MISS.

38. The governor's cynical strategy of making demands in the Union which could not be met and would thus lead to "a new confederacy" is admitted in Quitman to Whitemarsh in Seabrook, June 26, 1851, Seabrook Papers, LC.

39. *Jackson Mississippian,* July 18, 1851; A. Hutchinson to Charles Fontaine, May 20, 1851, Fontaine Papers, MISS.

40. John A. Quitman, "To the People of Mississippi, July 19, 1851," broadside in Quitman Papers, LSU.

41. Jefferson Davis to Samuel Cartwright, June 10, 1849, in *The Papers of Jefferson Davis,* eds. Haskell M. Monroe, Jr., et al. 6 vols. to date (Baton Rouge, 1971–89), 4: 21–23.

42. Davis to James S. Pearce, August 22, 1852, *ibid.,* 4: 300–301.

43. *Journal of the Convention of the State of Mississippi and the Act Calling the Same, 1851* (Jackson, 1851).

44. *Proceedings of the Meeting of Delegates from the Southern Rights Association of South Carolina. Held at Charleston, May, 1851* (Columbia, 1851); D. F. Jamieson to Isaac Holmes, June 16, 1851, James Hammond Papers, LC. See also William Henry Trescot to M.R.H. Garnett, May 15, 1851, William Garnett Chisolm Papers, VHS.

45. *Triweekly South Carolinian,* August 22, 1850; Daniel Wallace, *Letter . . . to His Constituents* (n.p., n.d.; copy in LC); Rutledge (pseudonym for W. D. Porter), *Separate State Secession . . .* (Edgefield, S.C., 1851).

46. Points especially strongly made in the two pamphlets cited above, note 45.

47. W. S. Lyles to James Chesnut, July 1, 1851, Chesnut-Miller-Manning Papers, SCHS.

48. *Cooperation Meeting Held in Charleston, S.C., July 29, 1851* (Charleston, 1851).

49. James Hammond to Beverley Tucker, December 18, 1850, Tucker-Coleman Papers, W&M.

50. The best statements of the Cooperationist case, besides those cited below, notes 51–53, include W. A. Owens, *An Address to the People of Barnwell District* . . . (Charleston, 1851); William J. Grayson, *Letter to . . . Whitemarsh B. Seabrook . . . on the Dissolution of the Union* (Charleston, 1850); files of the *Greenville Southern Patriot* and *Charleston Standard,* July–October, 1851; and the superb Benjamin F. Perry Papers, ALA, 1851–52.

51. John Townsend, *The Southern States, Their Present Peril, and Their Certain Remedy* (Charleston, 1850); *Southern Rights and Cooperation Documents. No. 3* (Charleston, 1851).

52. James L. Orr, *Speech . . . in Charleston, May, 1851* (Charleston, 1851).

53. C. G. Memminger, *Speech . . . in Charleston, Sept. 23, 1851* . . . (Charleston, 1851).

54. James Hammond to Beverley Tucker, April 18, 1851, Tucker-Coleman Papers, W&M. See also the following letters of Hammond to Tucker, same collection: October 1, November 8, 1850, January 24, 1851.

55. *Secret and Sacred Diary of Hammond,* ed. Bleser, 220–21.

56. *Greenville Southern Patriot,* July–December, 1851, esp. June 6, July 25, 1851. The Benjamin F. Perry Papers, 1851–55, ALA, are also full of superb material on this subject. For good perspectives, see Ford, *Origins of South Carolina Radicalism,* and Chauncey S. Boucher, *Sectionalism, Representation and the Electoral Question in Ante-bellum South Carolina* (St. Louis, 1916).

57. Brutus, *An Address to the Citizens of South Carolina* (n.p., n.d.; copy in SC). Brutus was actually no upcountry nonslaveholder, but William Henry Brisbane, formerly a lowcountry slaveholder who had freed his slaves and had been routed from the state when trying to convert others. See Blake McNulty's intriguing "William Henry Brisbane, South Carolina Slaveholder and Abolitionist," in *The Southern Enigma:* Essays on Race, Class, *and Folk Culture,* eds. Walter J. Fraser and Winifred B. Moore, Jr. (Westport, Conn., 1983).

58. Barnwell, *Love of Order,* 198–99, makes detailed election results conveniently available.

59. Trescot to M.R.H. Garnett, May 6, 1852, William Garnett Chisolm Papers, VHS.

60. Maxcy Gregg to Hammond, November 14, 1851, Hammond Papers, LC; *Secret and Sacred Diary of Hammond,* ed. Bleser, 238–50.

61. Charles J. Colcock to William H. Branch, October 29, 1851, Branch Family Papers, NC.

62. William H. Trescot to M.R.H. Garnett, November 16, 1851, William Garnett Chisolm Papers, VHS.

63. William Foran's unpublished "James L. Orr: Pragmatist in Wonderland," typecopy in SC, was the projected kernel of one of the most important books never finished on the Old South. Foran's short piece remains as useful as Roger P. Leemhuis, *James L. Orr and the Sectional Conflict* (Washington, 1979). Ford, *Origins of South Carolina Radicalism,* again provides good perspective.

64. Orr to Benjamin F. Perry, December 9, 1853, Perry Papers, ALA.

65. The best biography is John Witherspoon DuBose, *The Life and Times of William Lowndes Yancey,* 2 vols. (Birmingham, 1892). While Thornton, *Power and Politics in Alabama,* supplies the best account of and perspectives on Alabama mid-century politics, Lewy Dorman, *Party Politics in Alabama from 1850 Through 1960* (Wetumpka, Ala., 1935), and Clarence P. Denman, *The Secession Movement in Alabama* (Montgomery, 1933), are still useful.

66. Indispensable sources on the Yanceyite position include the *Montgomery Advertizer* and *Eufaula Spirit of the South.* Yancey's opponents' case is clear in F.A.P. Barnard, *An Oration Delivered . . . July 4, 1851* (Tuscaloosa, 1851), and in the files of the *Mobile Advertizer.* A good short overview is provided by Henry Mayer, "'A Leaven of Disun-

ion': The Growth of the Secession Faction in Alabama," *Alabama Review*, 22 (1969): 83–116.

67. William Lowndes Yancey to Joel E. Mathews et al., May 10, 1851, Yancey Papers, ALA. See also Yancey to Benjamin Yancey, November 17, 1851, Yancey Papers, NC.

68. Yancey to Benjamin Yancey, September 15, 1852, Yancey Papers, NC: Dorman, *Party Politics in Alabama*, 78ff.

Chapter 30. The Kansas-Nebraska Act, I: Confrontation in Missouri

1. Stanley W. Campbell, *The Slave Catchers: Enforcement of the Fugitive Slave Law, 1850–1860* (Chapel Hill, 1968).

2. Larry Gara, *The Liberty Line: The Legend of the Underground Railroad* (Lexington, 1961), is particularly good on the necessity to separate myth from reality in understanding why this subject was explosive.

3. Campbell, *Slave Catchers*, 148–51.

4. *Ibid.*, 151–52; W. U. Hensel, *The Christiana Riot and the Treason Trials of 1851: An Historical Sketch* (Lancaster, Pa., 1911).

5. Campbell, *Slave Catchers*, 154–57; W. Freeman Galpin, "The Jerry Rescue," *New York History*, 43 (1945): 19–34.

6. Quoted in Campbell, *Slave Catchers*, 126.

7. *Ibid.*, 124–32; Charles Emery Stevens, *Anthony Burns, a History* (Boston, 1856); Samuel Shapiro, "The Rendition of Anthony Burns," *JHN*; 44 (1959): 34–51; Jane H. and William H. Pease, *The Fugitive Slave Law and Anthony Burns* (Philadelphia, 1975).

8. For a wonderful discussion of American Boosterism, see Daniel M. Boorstin, *The Americans: The National Experience* (New York, 1965), 113–68.

9. Harrison A. Trexler, *Slavery in Missouri, 1804–1865* (Baltimore, 1914); Robert William Duffner, "Slavery in Missouri River Counties, 1820–1865," unpubl. Ph.D. diss., U. of Missouri, Columbia, 1974.

10. Lloyd A. Hunter, "Slavery in St. Louis, 1804–1860," *Bulletin of the Missouri Historical Society*, 30 (1974): 233–65. For a broader perspective, see Richard C. Wade, *Slavery in the Cities: The South, 1820–1860* (New York, 1964).

11. Two good complementary modern biographies fortunately exist: William Nisbet Chambers, *Old Bullion Benton, Senator from the New West . . .* (Boston, 1956), and Elbert B. Smith, *Magnificent Missourian: The Life of Thomas Hart Benton* (Philadelphia, 1958).

12. Quoted in Chambers, *Benton*, 338. On Benton's nickname, see *ibid.*, 230; on his senatorial manner, William J. Grayson Autobiography, 215ff, ms. in SC.

13. Thomas Hart Benton, *Speech . . . Delivered . . . at Jefferson City, May 26th, 1849* (n.p., n.d.; copy in LC); Benton, *. . . Speech at Fayette . . . the 1st of September, 1849*) (n.p., n.d.; copy in MOHS, SL). For descriptions of the campaign, see William L. Williams to John C. Calhoun, July 31, 1849, Samuel L. Treet to Calhoun, August 22, 1849, Calhoun Papers, CU.

14. James S. Green, *Letter . . . Dated December 10, 1849 to Messrs. John S. Farish et al. . . .* (n.p., n.d.; copy in MOHS, SL).

15. Frank P. Blair, Jr., *Remarks . . . on the Repeal of the . . . Resolutions* (Jefferson City, Mo., 1853). For perspective, see William Ernest Smith, *The Francis Preston Blair Family in Politics*, 2 vols. (New York, 1933). The Blair faction's open attempt to rid Missouri of slavery after 1855 is obvious in the important Blair Family Papers, LC.

16. A good biography is William E. Parrish, *David Rice Atchison of Missouri, Border Politician* (Columbia, Mo., 1961).

17. P. Orman Ray, *The Repeal of the Missouri Controversy* (Cleveland, 1909), is an older study which, like Justin Smith's *Annexation of Texas*, seems to me more on the

right track than some newer volumes. Useful broader perspectives on origins of Kansas-Nebraska include James Malin, *The Nebraska Question, 1852–1854* (Lawrence, Kansas, 1853), and James A. Rawley, *Race and Politics: "Bleeding Kansas" and the Coming of the Civil War* (Philadelphia and New York, 1969). Useful perspectives on the Atchison-Benton clash include Barbara Layenette Green, "The Slavery Debate in Missouri, 1831–1855," unpubl. Ph.D. diss., U. of Missouri, Columbia, 1980; Donnie D. Bellamy, "Slavery, Emancipation, and Racism in Missouri, 1850–1865," unpubl. Ph.D. diss., U. of Missouri, Columbia, 1971; Benjamin C. Merkel, "The Slavery Issue and the Political Decline of Thomas Hart Benton, 1846–1956," *MOHR*, 38 (1944): 388–407; and Joan E. Lampton, "The Kansas-Nebraska Act Reconsidered: An Analysis of Men, Methods, and Motives," unpubl. Doctor of Arts thesis, Illinois State University, 1979.

18. Quoted in Robert W. Johannsen, *Stephen A. Douglas* (New York, 1973), 399–400. This masterful biography provides by far the best explanation of Douglas's Kansas-Nebraska motives.

19. A factor somewhat over-emphasized in Frank H. Hodder's still useful "The Railroad Background of the Kansas-Nebraska Act," *MOHR*, 12 (1925): 3–22.

20. The Senate's consideration and Atchison's surrender can be followed in *Congressional Globe*, 32 Cong., 2 sess. (March 3, 1853): 1111–17.

21. *Missouri Republican*, August 31, 1853; *Jefferson Inquirer*, July 9, December 17, 1853. For Benton's answer see *ibid.*, August 13, 1853.

22. E. A. Hannegan to Davy Atchison, September 1, 1853, Atchison Papers, MOHS, C.

23. C. F. Jackson to Davy Atchison, January 18, 1854, Atchison Papers, MOHS, C.

Chapter 31. The Kansas-Nebraska Act, II: Decision in Congress

1. For a description of this mess and its inhabitants, see A. P. Butler to Davy Atchison, March 5, 1856, Atchison Papers, MOHS, C. For an indication of the sectionalizing of messes in general, see C. C. Clay, Jr., to C. C. Clay, Sr., December 11, 1858, Clay Papers, DU. The nature and influence of the F Street mess is most fully laid out in Roy F. Nichols's superb "The Kansas-Nebraska Act: A Century of Historiography," *MVHR*, 43 (1956): 187–212.

2. A. P. Butler to William Elliott, February 5, 1854, Elliott-Gonzales Papers, NC: *Congressional Globe*, 33 Cong., 1 sess. (May 19, 1854): 903–8 (Goode), (February 24, 1854): 221–26 (Hunter): *Charleston Courier*, August 3, 1857 (Mason).

3. Hunter's speech, cited above, comes down hard on this point. Butler's senatorial speech, unlike his private letter cited above, stresses the symbolic rather than the practical, even making the old Carolina point that slavery expansion, even when apparently practical, could be impractical if it depopulated the elderly coastal South. *Congressional Globe*, 33 Cong., 1 sess. (February 24, 1854): 232–40. Atchison's position clearly intrigued, influenced, but did not always persuade his messmates.

4. *Jefferson* (Missouri) *Inquirer*, February 17, 1853.

5. Quoted in Johannsen, *Douglas*, 411. Where Roy Nichols, "A Century of Historiography," makes F Streeters the crucial force in the wording of "Douglas's" bill, Johannsen calls that view "exaggerated" and entitles his chapter on Kansas-Nebraska "I Passed the Kansas-Nebraska Act Myself," the transcendent "I" being Douglas, whose own conceptions of strategy, according to Johannsen, controlled the evolving wording of his bill. *Until January 11*, the truth lies between these extremes. Johannsen concedes the critical point: that unless the Illinoisan and the Southern Democrats came to an accommodation, neither could secure a law that both, for different reasons, desperately wished. As to who held the upper hand in that accommodation, the evidence between January 7 and January 10 seems to me inconclusive. While I think Nichols is likely right that Southerners pushed the pre-statehood legislature's right to decide from the accompany-

ing report, where it lay buried on January 7, into the proposed statute's text, where it appeared on January 10, Johannsen may be right that Douglas himself decided that correction of this "clerical error" was the best *strategy* for passing the law. Unfortunately for the Johannsen theory, however, far more than strategy was involved in the far more crucial decision during the following week to declare the Missouri ban "inoperative and void" in Kansas-Nebraska: a southern demand which Johannsen's own text shows that Douglas opposed as long and as hard as he dared.

6. *Washington Sentinel,* January 14, 1854.

7. On Phillip Phillips's activities in January 1854, see his papers, LC, and Henry B. Learned, "The Relation of Phillip Phillips to the Repeal of the Missouri Compromise in 1854," *MVHR,* 8 (1922): 303–17.

8. This Whig motive is particularly obvious in the candid correspondence of Alexander Stephens, floor leader of Kansas-Nebraska forces in the House. See Stephens to Linton Stephens, November 20, 1853, January 25, March 4, May 23, 1854, SP.

9. Good discussions of the 1852 presidential elections include Holt, *Political Crisis of the 1850s,* 119–30, and Cooper, *South and the Politics of Slavery,* 323–40.

10. *Ibid.,* 340–44, nicely analyzes the Whig congressional debacle of 1853.

11. *Congressional Globe,* 33 Cong., 1 sess. (February 4, 1854): Appendix, 140–45. The official Dixon line on why he acted is in Mrs. Archibald Dixon, *The True History of the Missouri Compromise and Its Repeal* (Cincinnati, 1899).

12. William H. Seward to Thurlow Weed, January 7, 8, 1854, Weed Papers, Universtiy of Rochester; Glyndon G. Van Deusen, *William Henry Seward* (New York, 1967), 150.

13. A point well made in Cooper, *South and the Politics of Slavery,* 379.

14. Maneuvers in the crucial last week, although devastating to the Johannsen thesis of Douglas-in-control, are faithfully followed in Johannsen, *Douglas,* 411–16.

15. *Congressional Globe,* 33 Cong., 1 sess. (March 4, 1854): Appendix, 407–15. In the same vein, see Thomas Hart Benton in *ibid.* (April 25, 1854): Appendix, 557–61; Sam Houston in *Austin State Gazette,* November 23, 1855; and John Minor Botts, *Letters . . . on the Nebraska Question* (Washington, misdated as 1853).

16. The Douglas-Wade exchange is in *Congressional Globe,* 33 Cong., 2 sess. (February 23, 1855): Appendix, 216.

17. A useful discussion of House-Senate maneuvers is Gerald W. Wolf, *The Kansas-Nebraska Bill: Party, Section, and the Coming of the Civil War* (New York, 1977). Particularly good on the House side is Roy F. Nichols, *Blueprints for Leviathan: American Style* (New York, 1963), 104–20.

18. The admirable recent effort to show that nonslavery issues such as temperance and nativism helped erode Whiggery in the North *before* the Kansas-Nebraska Act runs the danger of obscuring how profoundly the slavery issue finished off Whiggery in the South. See Williams E. Gienapp's fine *The Origins of the Republican Party, 1852–1856* (New York, 1987), 66, for an example of how such minimizing of slavery's contribution to destroying the Second American Party System can go a little too far.

19. First stages of the anti-Nebraska northern movement are skillfully portrayed in Sewell, *Ballots for Freedom,* 254–65. Lincoln's early role is nicely described in Don E. Fehrenbacher's *Prelude to Greatness: Lincoln in the 1850s* (Stanford, Calif., 1962). The sources of Lincoln's Republicanism in Henry Clay-like southern apologetics is analyzed in perhaps the most important neglected article on the coming of the Civil War, George M. Fredrickson's "A Man But Not a Brother: Abraham Lincoln and Racial Equality," *JSH,* 41 (1975): 39–58.

20. Robert R. Russel, "The Issues in the Congressional Struggle Over the Kansas-Nebraska Bill, 1854," *JSH,* 29 (1963): 187–210, correctly notes that southern speeches went both ways on the question of whether Kansas was practical for slaveholders. For some examples of southern congressmen who thought Atchison would make Kansas practical, in addition to F Streeters cited above, note 2, see South Carolina's W. W. Boyce

in *Charleston Standard,* October 6, 1854, and L. M. Keitt in *ibid.,* October 11, 1854. For some examples of southern congressmen who thought symbolic equality was most at stake, see John Kerr of North Carolina in *Congressional Globe,* 33 Cong., 1 sess. (February 17, 1854): Appendix, 166–68, and Wm. B. W. Dent of Tennessee to Hershel V. Johnson, June 13, 1854, Johnson Papers, DU.

The last word in these professional notes properly belongs to my indispensable fellow professionals. My revisions have been skillfully rendered intelligible by Catherine Grover, Susan Mabie, and especially Joanne Bracken. Joanne and Mike Holt each in their own ways made the final months of revising a time of especially rich fulfillment. Sheldon Meyer then gave the manuscript the sort of rich editorial scrutiny which I had thought perished decades ago. My thanks to these special friends, and to others, cited above, who commented on chapters and sections, and to the many monographers, also noted above, whose collective insights have made this field a triumph of American historical scholarship over the past quarter-century.

Index